ROUTLEDGE LIBRARY EDITIONS:
THE GERMAN ECONOMY

Volume 5

INDUSTRIAL UNEMPLOYMENT IN GERMANY, 1873–1913

INDUSTRIAL UNEMPLOYMENT IN GERMANY, 1873–1913

LINDA ABRAMSON HEILMAN

Routledge
Taylor & Francis Group

LONDON AND NEW YORK

First published in 1991 by Garland Publishers Ltd

This edition first published in 2018
by Routledge
2 Park Square, Milton Park, Abingdon, Oxon OX14 4RN

and by Routledge
711 Third Avenue, New York, NY 10017

Routledge is an imprint of the Taylor & Francis Group, an informa business

British Library Cataloguing in Publication Data
A catalogue record for this book is available from the British Library

ISBN: 978-1-138-29360-1 (Set)
ISBN: 978-1-315-18656-6 (Set) (ebk)
ISBN: 978-1-138-72898-1 (Volume 5) (hbk)
ISBN: 978-1-315-18981-9 (Volume 5) (ebk)

Publisher's Note
The publisher has gone to great lengths to ensure the quality of this reprint but points out that
some imperfections in the original copies may be apparent.

Disclaimer
The publisher has made every effort to trace copyright holders and would welcome
correspondence from those they have been unable to trace.

Industrial Unemployment in Germany, 1873—1913

Linda Abramson Heilman

Garland Publishing, Inc.
New York & London 1991

Library of Congress Cataloging-in-Publication Data

Heilman, Linda Abramson.
Industrial unemployment in Germany, 1873–1913 / Linda Abramson Heilman.
p. cm.——[Modern European history. Germany and Austria]
Originally presented as the author's thesis [Ph. D.]——University of California, Berkeley, 1982.
Includes bibliographical references.
ISBN 0-8153-0419-6 [alk. paper]
1. Unemployment——Germany——History. 2. Germany——Social conditions——1871–1918.
I. Title. II. Series.
HD5779.H394   1991
331.13′7943′09034——dc20   91-13391

Designed by Marisel Tavárez

Printed on acid-free, 250-year-life paper.
Manufactured in the United States of America

This book is for my son,
David Andrew Heilman

ACKNOWLEDGEMENTS

It is a pleasure to recognize the generous assistance of my advisor for the dissertation, Professor Gerald Feldman. His wide-ranging expertise and guidance have made my work easier from the inception of this project to its conclusion. I thank Professor Wolfgang Sauer and Professor Neil Smelser for reading the manuscript. I am also grateful to Professor Sauer for sharing his insights into German history with me in many conversations over the past fourteen years. In addition, I would like to express my gratitude to Professor Hans Rosenberg who consistently offered me the benefits of his vast knowledge and wise counsel from the very beginning of my graduate study.

I am indebted to Ms. Susan Gormley for initially typing the manuscript and to Ms. Gina Oaks for overseeing its final preparation for submission.

At this juncture, I want to thank my family and friends for their continued interest in my progress. Dr. Theodore Bogacz, Dr. Marcella Mazzarelli and Dr. Candy Abramson have been exceptionally helpful at strategic intervals.

TABLE OF CONTENTS

Industrial Unemployment in Germany 1873-1913

PART ONE: METHODOLOGICAL PROBLEMS RELATING TO THE STUDY
OF INDUSTRIAL UNEMPLOYMENT IN GERMANY   2

TERMINOLOGICAL SPECIFICATIONS   2

PERIODIZATION, ECONOMIC FLUCTUATIONS AND HISTORICAL
CHANGE. 13

PREHISTORY, ATTITUDINAL CHANGES AND UNEMPLOYMENT
IN GERMANY AFTER 1913 36

HISTORIOGRAPHICAL ISSUES RELATED TO INDUSTRIAL
UNEMPLOYMENT BETWEEN 1873 AND 1913. 56

PART TWO: QUANTITATIVE DATA, THE SOURCE OF
DISPARITIES BETWEEN THE PERCEPTION AND REALTY
OF INDUSTRIAL UNEMPLOYMENT. 68

PRIMARY SOURCES: ROOT OF DISPARITIES BETWEEN
PERCEPTIONS OF UNEMPLOYMENT AND ECONOMIC REALTY 75

EMPLOYMENT, WAGES, PRICES AND CONSUMPTION
PATTERNS AS ALTERNATE INDICATORS OF UNEMPLOYMENT. . . . 107

        Employment 107

        Wages and Prices 120

        Food and Beverage Consumption. 126

METHODS OF COUNTING THE UNEMPLOYED. 136

        Public Methods of Enumerating the Unemployed . . . 136

        Union Unemployment Funds and the Gathering
        of Statistics. 149

RELIEF INSTITUTIONS AS ALTERNATE INDICATORS OF
UNEMPLOYMENT. 177

        Labor Exchanges. 183

        Labor Colonies and Refuges for the
        Itinerant Unemployed 190

        Begging and Obdachlosigkeit. 198

        Poor Relief. 202

THE UNEMPLOYMENT PROBLEM AS REFLECTED IN THE
1895 CENSUS 217

    The 1895 Census. 218

    Occupation as a Factor in Unemployment 222

    The Duration of Unemployment 236

    Age Distribution of the Unemployed 248

    Sex and Marital Status of the Unemployed 255

    Demography and the Geographical Distribution
    of Unemployment. 263

    Summary. 277

PART THREE: DETERMINANTS OF AGGREGATE
UNEMPLOYMENT LEVELS 286

SEASONAL UNEMPLOYMENT 294

TECHNOLOGICAL CHANGE AS A SOURCE OF UNEMPLOYMENT. . . . 307

THE IMPACT OF POLITICAL POLICY DECISIONS. 316

    Local Unemployment Policies and Programs 327

    The Unemployment Policies of Political
    Parties and Their Leaders. 337

    The Right to Work. 345

    The Role of Women and Children in the Labor
    Market and Its Impact on Employment Policies . . . 351

    The Role of Foreign Competition in Unemployment. . 355

COLLECTIVE PROTECTION AGAINST UNEMPLOYMENT. 365

    The Role of Interest Groups in a Collectivist
    Age. 368

    Labor Unions' Unemployment Policies. 375

A FREE LABOR FORCE: MOBILITY AND UNEMPLOYMENT. 389

    Population Aggregates. 393

    Overseas Migration 396

Internal Migrations, Regional Variations
and Population Distribution. 401

Urbanization 406

INTERNAL CONDITIONS IN THE LABOR MARKET
AND UNEMPLOYMENT. 413

Dissemination of Information in the
Labor Market 413

Structural Change: The Impact of Agriculture
on the Industrial Labor Market 418

Cottage Industries 429

Industrialization as a Factor in Unemployment. . . 436

Secondary Occupations and Alternate Employment . . 451

Economic Crises and the Impact of
Overproduction 463

Wages and Prices 471

Industrial Production, Labor Productivity
and Unemployment 480

MICRO-ECONOMIC VARIABLES IN UNEMPLOYMENT. 487

The Hiring and Dismissal Practices of
Individual Entrepreneurs 487

Short Time as an Alternative to Unemployment . . . 498

Lower Wages as an Alternative to Unemployment. . . 507

Willingness to Work. 514

PART FOUR: MEASURES TO ALLEVIATE INDUSTRIAL
UNEMPLOYMENT. 521

SELF-HELP: INDIVIDUAL VERSUS COLLECTIVE EFFORTS
TO COPE WITH UNEMPLOYMENT 523

THE ROLES OF EMPLOYERS' AND EMPLOYEES'
ORGANIZATIONS 540

THE ROLE OF THE STATE: PUBLIC MEASURES FOR DEALING
WITH UNEMPLOYMENT THROUGH WELFARE AND LEGISLATION . . . 558

PUBLIC INSTITUTIONS FOR THE RELIEF OF UNEMPLOYMENT. . . 573

    Arbeitsnachweise 574

    Public Works Projects. 585

    Labor Houses 599

    Alternatives to Begging: Labor Colonies,
    Verpflegungsstationen, Herbergen zur Heimat,
    Wanderarbeitsstaetten. 606

INSURANCE 629

CONCLUSION. 648

EPILOGUE. 651

APPENDIX: UNEMPLOYMENT IN THE PRINTERS UNION 666

NOTES 673

BIBLIOGRAPHY. 728

PREFACE TO THE RE-ISSUE OF 2017

This edition of <u>Industrial Unemployment in Germany</u> is a reissue of my doctoral dissertation completed at the University of California, Berkeley, in 1982. Thirty-five years later, the book stands on its own as an historical monograph providing a multi-faceted analysis of German unemployment between 1873 and 1913. Today it can also be read as an example of social scientific historiography during the fourth quarter of the twentieth century. Finally, the study has value for the comparative perspective it lends to current economic, social, and political turmoil in Germany, Europe, and the United States.

In 1973-74, the DAAD funded a year of unemployment research, which allowed me to explore thousands of documents, including voluminous handwritten records, scattered across more than a dozen archives. Based in Cologne, I traveled extensively in West Germany and also spent a month gathering material in Potsdam and Merseburg. Many excerpts from primary sources have been included in the text, letting contemporaries discuss unemployment in their own words. Originally, these excerpts added value because so many relevant sources were inaccessible to western historians before the Berlin Wall came down.

The ideas, methodology, and writing style of the book all reflect my thinking as a doctoral candidate in Late Modern European History during the 1970's and early 1980's. When I arrived at Berkeley in 1968, controversy over the Vietnam War was raging. The Civil Rights movement was still reeling from the assassinations of Dr. King and Robert Kennedy. Germany was a divided country, and contemporary historiography clearly reflected the divisions between East and West. Women and minorities did not yet constitute discrete subjects of historical inquiry. The social scientific approach to German history was dominant in Dwinelle Hall and benefitted from the theoretical models of experts in related disciplines across the Berkeley campus and beyond.

Looking back from the perspective of 2016, we again see economic insecurity feeding political extremism. This time, however, the process is being fueled by deindustrialization rather than rapid economic growth. In Europe, we find nationalism in the form of Brexit and right-wing parties resurgent across the continent in response to the largest influx of immigrants since World War II. In recent years, Germany welcomed refugees from Eastern Europe and the Middle East as a corrective to its low birth rate and aging native workforce. Now, however, Angela Merkel's open door policy is under attack by extremists espousing xenophobia, nationalism, populism, protectionism, anti-establishment animus, and resurgent resentment against subsidizing unworthy applicants for unemployment insurance. In this context, it is worth noting that more than 10% of German residents today are foreign-born. The estimated cost to German taxpayers of immigrant inflows in 2017 is expected to top $44 billion. At this writing, legislation is pending to limit unemployment benefits for EU migrants to residents of more than five years unless they qualify based on previous employment. Unemployed immigrants from outside the EU would have to wait even longer to receive even less support.

In the United States, a widespread sense of economic insecurity and disenfranchisement mobilized political movements on the far left and far right during the presidential elections. The center has been challenged by angry voters at the margins who view themselves as the biggest losers from a long list of economic grievances. Widespread frustration stems from stagnant wages, free trade, immigration, affirmative action, Wall Street corruption, dysfunction in Washington, women's entry into the workforce, underemployment, and the slow recovery after the Great Recession. Increased bifurcation of wealth is the order of the day with those at the top gaining smartly. Many others feel like they are barely treading water rather than enjoying a recovery that lifts all boats. While the precise conditions differ today, there are clearly still lessons to be learned on both sides of the Atlantic from the economic, social, and political dislocation, which accompanied industrial unemployment in Germany between 1873 and 1913.

Linda Abramson Heilman
November 1, 2016

INDUSTRIAL UNEMPLOYMENT IN GERMANY 1873-1913

At various intervals between 1873 and 1913, contemporaries advanced the notion that Germany's industrial unemployment constituted the most serious social problem of the day. Significantly, modern interest in work scarcity emerged during a period when the quantitative parameters of the problem remained within manageable limits. Fueled by a crisis mentality derived from the succession of economically grim years after 1873, a persistent gap developed between the perception and reality of unemployment in German industry. As we shall see, this discrepancy was due to ignorance of both the actual dimensions and theoretical causes of job shortages. Popular misconceptions about unemployment were reflected in limited measures to contain its short-term effects and in radical political pronouncements about its long-term consequences.

PART ONE: <u>METHODOLOGICAL PROBLEMS RELATING TO THE STUDY OF</u> <u>INDUSTRIAL UNEMPLOYMENT IN GERMANY</u>

TERMINOLOGICAL SPECIFICATIONS

Germany's unemployed were first recognized as a distinct group within the industrial labor force during the years between 1873 and 1913.[1] There was a tendency during the earlier part of the period to lump jobless workers together with members of the lowest social order who were dependent upon public or private charity for their subsistence. But as the twentieth century unfolded, social critics showed a growing willingness to segregate the unemployed from those who were indigent, vagrant, mendicant, disabled or itinerent. Their differentiation reflected a heightened awareness of the impersonal economic forces at work in industrial society and tended to deflect blame from the unemployed individuals who were increasingly viewed as victims of those forces.

The change in attitude was apparent in the terminology used to describe those without work.[2] During the first years of our period, the word <u>Arbeitslosigkeit</u> was virtually nonexistent in the admittedly scanty literature dealing with conditions in the labor market or among the working classes. By 1876 occasional references to unemployment were scattered through government reports but remained scarce enough to stand out among the far more common discussions of lay-offs and cutbacks. Despite a gradual increase in usage during the 1880's, the term <u>Arbeitslosigkeit</u> did

not appear with great frequency prior to 1890. By the end
of our period, however, it was clearly established in the
working vocabularies of the labor movement, the government
and the public at large.

In addition to language, statistics tended to
reflect the degree of differentiation accorded to the
unemployed as a discrete element in German society. In the
private sector, unions such as the printers kept separate
records on unemployed members receiving compensation well
before 1873. Documents on work shortages in Stuttgart go
back to the 1860's. But these examples were clearly exceptions to a rule which seemed to dictate that when counted at
all, the unemployed were lumped together with criminals,
beggars and recipients of poor relief. Limitations of
primary sources dealing with unemployment during our period
make it imperative that we consider data on begging,
Arbeitsnachweise, sickness, poor relief, occupational
distribution and population shifts. Without these indirect
indicators which camouflaged information by failing to
differentiate clearly between jobless and employed individuals, we would have no way of estimating the extent of
unemployment in the 1870's and 1880's. On a national scale,
the only unemployment count during our period took place as
part of the 1895 census. Other data came from municipalities and occasionally from the individual states. Privately, statistics had more continuity but the unions' data

was not published in any systematic fashion prior to the appearance of the Reichsarbeitsblatt in 1903.

In defining unemployment, there seemed to be a concensus among authors addressing themselves to the subject throughout our period. To be counted as unemployed, an individual had to be financially in need of a job; he had to be willing to work and actively seeking socially sanctioned employment; he also had to be physically capable of work and unable to find a job. In addition, many analysts felt that the laborer had to have a previous post and be unable to find a suitable replacement for economic rather than personal reasons. Here we shall diverge slightly from the contemporary view by including workers entering the labor market for the first time and those returning after a prolonged absence. We shall also include among the unemployed those persons whose loss of work may have been self-induced but not intentional, perhaps caused by poor productivity or occasional, although not chronic, intoxication and absenteeism. The reason why an individual was discharged from a previous position will be of less concern than his inability to procure another, although in both instances our primary interest rests with the underlying economic forces which affected the labor market.

In a useful discussion of concepts related to Unemployment in History[3], John Garraty referred to search and precautionary sources of joblessness. The first term was used to define those occupied in collecting information about potential employment and the latter applied to individuals willing to turn down job offers or abandon an existing position in order to find preferable employment. Both concepts seemed to assume the existence of a buyers' market in which the jobseeker retained the luxury of selecting from among various alternatives to arrive at the best possible situation. Although this might prove unrealistic in a tight labor market, every worker offering to sell his services had certain minimum expectations as he weighed the advantages of retaining his freedom against the disadvantages of lost income.

Related to search and precautionary activities were other sources of joblessness attributable to underemployment plus frictional, cyclical, seasonal and structural varieties of unemployment.[4] All of these concepts assume that there is an ideal condition in the labor market when the economy is in a state of full employment. The latter would seem to occur at least in theory when every individual seeking work is able to find a position which utilizes his skills and when every employer hiring labor is able to find employees capable of performing the desired tasks. In a real market setting, such perfect matching of employer and employee expectations is rarely if ever achieved. And economists, recognizing the utopian nature of the above paradigm, have resorted to labelling full employment as a jobless rate of anything less than a designated small percentage of the labor force. During the period

1873-1913 that percentage, reflecting society's notion of an acceptable level of unemployment, would have been very low in comparison with today's figures.

The difference between 100 percent employment and the currently acceptable estimate of how complete full employment has to be is usually attributed to frictional unemployment. The friction inevitably involved in any labor turnover due to impeded mobility, imperfect dissemination of information and problems affecting those entering the work force, produces time lags which contribute to unemployment. The twentieth-century capitalist concept of frictional unemployment is similar to the nineteenth-century notion popularized by Karl Marx who repeatedly referred to an industrial reserve army.[5] There always had to be a pool of surplus labor--a group of men changing jobs or willing to accept new employment--from which to draw if the economy was to grow rather than stagnate. Thus even for those like Marx who championed the cause of the working classes, a goal of 100 percent employment was deemed to be undesirable, impractical and unattainable.

In addition to the frictional unemployment attendant upon labor turnover, notice must be taken of cyclical unemployment which was a primary source of joblessness during the downswing that characterized the first half of our period. Occasioned by a decline in the demand for goods and services, cyclical unemployment plagued the German, European and American markets at recurring intervals between

1873 and 1913. Compounding the longer cyclical swings depressing the labor market were annual fluctuations in the unemployment rate associated with seasonal changes in general and the arrival of winter in particular. Those engaged in agriculture or the building trades were especially susceptible to periodic climatic variations. Unlike other types of unemployment, onslaught of the seasonal variety was easy to predict. It was the most regularly recurring, had the longest recorded history, and was the most widely documented form of unemployment during the entire nineteenth century.

While seasonal shifts in employment predated the emergence of capitalist economies by hundreds of years, structural unemployment was closely linked to the ongoing process of industrialization. Industrial development entailed changes in the methods of production and in the structure of the labor market. Fluctuations in the supply of and demand for labor were caused by technological advances in sectors such as textiles, by the emergence of whole new industries such as the electrical and chemical conglomerates, by revolutions in transportation such as the introduction of railroads, by migration or an influx of foreign workers, and by discoveries of new sources of precious metals or raw materials. All of these factors had an impact on the German economy and affected the level of structural unemployment during our period.

Of the many forms of joblessness, hidden unemployment and underemployment are perhaps the most difficult to detect. The term hidden unemployment would apply to individuals who gave up looking for jobs and voluntarily withdrew from the labor market. They would no longer be counted among the unemployed because they were not actively seeking positions. Among those most susceptible to hidden unemployment were all women and men at either end of the chronological scale--those of an age to be just entering or leaving the work force. Their number at any given time would be extremely difficult to assess accurately although indirect indicators such as the incidence of migration might provide some clues.

The term underemployment would apply to anyone engaged in unproductive labor perhaps due to a lack of the proper equipment or training. A person trained to do highly skilled work who cannot find a job in his area of expertise and resorts to the performance of unskilled or menial tasks for subsistence is underemployed. Underemployment was a very important, albeit painful, part of the reality of life between 1873 and 1913 when it was relied on as an alternative to more drastic measures affecting the labor force. Rather than laying off some employees, for example, many bosses preferred to decrease the number of hours all workers were engaged. This option spread the hardship of cut-backs equally among many individuals rather than penalizing a few to preserve the status quo for a majority. In addition to those working part time, the underemployed included laborers who divided their efforts between working for others and working for themselves. The woman who did piecework in her home and allocated more time to household responsibilities when an employer's demand for her services was low could be considered underemployed although she was never idle. The same would apply to the small farmer who split his time between tilling his own fields and working the holdings of a large landowner. During the nineteenth century and still today, work done for oneself, despite its utility, would not count as an economic factor in the employment picture.

Related to but distinct from labor done for personal consumption was the saleable output of independent or self-employed individuals. According to Richard Herbst writing at the end of our period,[6] members of all socio-economic classes were to be counted among the unemployed if they were dependent upon jobs for their income and unable to find work. Whether a member of the middle class, the skilled or unskilled work force, anyone obliged to offer his services in the labor market was susceptible to unemployment. Artists, creative and professional people, although occasionally limited by licensing procedures, could work even if the market for their output failed to yield satisfactory compensation. Owners of businesses could not be unemployed although lack of demand for their products could force them to relinquish their independence and seek employment elsewhere.[7] In a free enterprise system such as

Germany's either employers or employees were free to terminate the implied contract of employment. But only the
laborer who was dependent upon a salary and an opportunity
to work which could be withdrawn at the discretion of others
was susceptible to unemployment. Entrepreneurs, artisans
and independent craftsmen could not become unemployed unless
they chose to work for someone other than themselves.[8]

Technically any employee from the highest civil
servant to the lowest factory worker held his post at the
pleasure of an employer and could find himself looking for a
new job. The scope of the following inquiry, however, will
be limited to unemployment among the industrial labor force.
Those involved in the management of industry, although a
group including many titular employees, will not receive
special attention here. When they were counted among the
jobless at all, their susceptibility to unemployment was not
a cause for particular anxiety. Our concern with the middle
and upper middle classes in Germany will be minimal except
as their actions impacted unemployment among the working
classes. Within the workers' ranks, the unionized elite,
which never amounted to more than one third of the industrial labor force during our period, will be singled out for
special consideration because the data on their situation is
so much more complete. The unorganized working proletariat
which was probably most suspectible to vicissitudes of the
labor market will of course be included. But for reasons

which we shall turn to later, it remains far more difficult to obtain an accurate reading on their employment prospects.

The term industrial labor force will be defined rather broadly to include all non-agricultural workers. The changing relationship between agriculture and industry along with its impact on the labor market will be discussed in some detail in the third section of this study. The complex agrarian labor problem which unfolded after the emancipation of the peasantry was aggravated by the simultaneous processes of industrialization and urbanization. Agriculture, as the largest consumer of German manpower during most of our period, played an important part in determining the aggregate level of unemployment. At first it might seem preferable to deal with the entire labor force when speaking of unemployment because there were no hard and fast distinctions between industrial and agricultural workers. At different points in time, the same individual might fall into either or even both job categories. Industrial workers who returned to the countryside during slack periods and farming families who participated in cottage industries were predictably commonplace during an era of rapid economic transition.

While such examples tend to make the distinction between industrial and other workers seem arbitrary or spurious, dealing with the nuances of the agrarian labor situation would make an already unwieldy subject totally unmanageable. Those whose primary source of employment lay

in German industry will be included in our study but those
more dependent upon agrarian pursuits will receive only
cursory treatment here. Factory hands temporarily returning
to rural areas to wait out the slow season will concern us
more than the men or women who supplemented their farm
incomes through secondary employment in weaving or food
processing. Underemployment due to the loss of secondary
occupations will be of less interest than unemployment due
to lay-offs from jobs which provided the bulk of a household's livelihood.

PERIODIZATION, ECONOMIC FLUCTUATIONS AND HISTORICAL CHANGE

To commemorate the fiftieth anniversary of the last Great Depression, the Wall Street Journal ran a front-page article dealing with Kondratiev waves on October 12, 1979. Although the article indicated that there were still severe reservations among academicians about the validity of cyclical theories, it pointed out renewed interest in explanatory models which viewed cycles as the prime movers in producing economic change. Recent interest has been sparked at least in part by the recognition that if Kondratiev was correct, we shall embark upon another long slump sometime within the next decade.

Quite apart from their value as a tool for forecasting the future, long waves and business cycles have been used by historians to shed light on economic developments of the past. Perhaps the most outstanding contribution to German history in this area has been made by Hans Rosenberg whose Grosse Depression und Bismarckszeit appeared in 1967. Despite the multitude of novel and compelling interpretations advanced in Rosenberg's book, a number of historians and economists have questioned his characterization of the trend period between 1873 and 1896 as a great depression.[9] Rosenberg himself acknowledged that the period did not constitute a single uninterrupted cyclical depression as evidenced by continued industrial development and the upward movement of real wages. Although concerned with the period as a whole, he opted for a scheme of internal periodization comprised of three downswings: 1873 to 1879, 1882 to 1886 and 1890 to 1894 with two intervening spans of recovery. The first occurred between 1879 and 1882; the second fell between 1886 and 1889; finally, a third upswing began in 1894 and lasted to the end of the period. During the entire twenty-three years, the only points of economic prosperity came during 1889 and 1896 which contrasted sharply with the ten years of prosperity during both the preceding and subsequent trend periods of 1849 to 1873 and 1897 to 1913. With regard to purely economic criteria, prevailing price movements lent more credence to the notion of depression than statistics on population growth or industrial production.

For our purposes, it is important to emphasize that agriculture constituted the most severely depressed sector of the German economy throughout the downswing between 1873 and 1896. In order to gauge the extent to which German agriculture was affected by the slump which began in 1873, it is worth noting that agrarian price levels did not regain the highs of the early 1870's until 1912. The big East Elbian estates dominated by the Junker elite were hardest hit by competition from large-scale American and Russian grain producers. Cheap foreign labor, economies of scale and developments in transportation threatened their economic base at the same time that rapid modernization linked to industrial development challenged their predominance in the traditional social and political orders. This double-edged sword of agrarian depression coinciding with Germany's industrialization heightened the level of tension[10] and conditioned the response of the old ruling elite to the recurring economic downswings of the late nineteenth century. The crisis mentality which evolved during the so-called depression years was not, however, confined to the upper reaches of Prussian or German society.

Rather than immersing ourselves further in a debate over terminology,[11] we shall limit our characterization of the trend period 1873-1896 to the term great price deflation in order to·reflect the limitations of the corroborative data with respect to German industry. Nevertheless, there is one component of Rosenberg's analysis of the depression which remains crucial to any understanding of the contemporary response to economic change. Rosenberg argued quite correctly that social historians, sociologists and social psychologists are free to accept criteria of depression different from the humanly anonymous standards of economists and economic historians.[12]

Qualitative changes in thought, shifting social relationships and the uneven impact of recurring economic downswings produced ways of thinking about the economy which were not always substantiated by the hard data or the realities of the socio-economic situation. Even if the extant indicators of economic crisis do not measure up to modern expectations about depressions which were formulated primarily with reference to the experience of the 1920's and

1930's, Rosenberg makes a compelling argument about a pervasive depression mentality. That mentality permeated the entire trend period and grew stronger as the number of bad years began to have a cumulative effect on the way contemporaries approached socio-economic problems.

Contrasting sharply with the euphoria which accompanied Germany's unprecedented growth between 1866 and 1873, the ensuing downswing shattered unrealistically high expectations. The pessimism which set in during the severe slump of the Seventies was not alleviated by the brief respite in the economic situation at the end of the decade. The improvements which took place between 1879 and 1882 were barely consolidated before another setback occurred which lasted until 1886. Although not as severe in objective economic terms, the new downswing sharpened the impact of the previous recession. The prosperity which occurred during 1889 soon gave way to yet another slump which per-sisted during the next four years. The pattern of recurrent downturns without sufficient intervals of recovery produced a climate of neurosis and grotesque anxiety about socialism and revolutions, class and religious hatreds--internal enemies ranging from proletarians to Catholics and Jews--suspicion of mobile capital, trade, urbanization and industrialization.

It is an accepted axiom of modern economic theory that the behavior of independent individuals in the market-place will be conditioned at least as much by what they perceive to be true as by truth itself. Over and over again during the last quarter of the nineteenth century, and particularly during the 1890's, Germans responded to unemployment in ways which reflected a mentality based on the expectation of recurrent crisis. The frequently expressed fear that socialists would benefit from unemployment was one of the most common manifestations of this way of thinking.

Despite the fact that unemployment during our period never soared to heights which would alarm us today, it had a major impact on economic analysts and policy-makers under the Second Reich. Even when the economy embarked upon a new wave of prosperity in the mid-1890's, the cumulative effect of the severe crisis of the 1870's aggravated by subsequent reversals left German industry with a fear of relapse which colored the national economic outlook until 1913. With regard to unemployment, its unwieldy distribution and the omnipresent threat of recurrence combined to produce a qualitative fear of its consequences whose intensity far outweighed the real danger reflected in the scant quantitative data that has survived from the first half of our period.

Perhaps one reason why unemployment never reached levels associated with depressions in this century is explained by Alexander Gerschenkron in this excerpt from Continuity in History. Discussing long-term changes in industrial output, Gerschenkron makes the following generalizations:[13]

> In a number of major countries of Europe, industrial
> development did not proceed at an even pace. On the
> contrary, after a lengthy period of fairly low rates of
> growth came a moment of more or less sudden increase in
> the rates, which then remained at the accelerated level
> for a considerable period. That was the period of the
> great spurt in the respective countries' industrial
> development. Its beginning in several cases coincided
> with the lower turning point of the cycle, and it bene-
> fitted in its earlier stages from the forces of cycli-
> cal recovery. But the phenomenon in its entirety was
> altogether different from the cycle. In fact, once the
> spurt in a given country had gathered momentum, it was
> likely to continue through the next international
> depression, unaffected or almost unaffected by it.

As this quotation suggests, the impact of the downswing

which began in 1873 may have been lessened by Germany's

temporal proximity to her "industrial revolution". Here it

is worth noting that Walt Rostow's placement of the "big

spurt" between 1848 and 1873 in Germany seems convincing.

What remains problematic, however, is the failure to view

industrialization as part of an ongoing cyclical process of

economic development rather than a discontinuous kink

inaugurating unprecedented, uninterrupted growth. For

historians interested in changes which occurred in the labor

market over long periods, such a perspective is essential.

For our specific purposes, a model of development fueled by

multiple wavelike cycles goes much farther than a linear

model toward explaining fluctuations in unemployment. As we

shall see, the relative alignment of cycles unfolding at

varying rates over time played a large role in determining

the impact of given economic downswings.

Unemployment, although it has undeniable social

and political causes as well as consequences, is primarily

an economic phenomenon. In developing a scheme of periodization and a paradigm for delineating changes in its incidence over a long interval, we must look to economic theory for assistance. The most useful tool for elucidating developments which occurred in the German labor market between 1873 and 1913 is a model of change triggered by wavelike reverberations that spread through the economy at variable speeds. Among the myriad cyclical movements which have been singled out by economists[14] and economic historians are secular trends which characterized pre-industrial economies, periodically recurring trade cycles of relatively short duration, periodic seasonal swings and irregular exogenous fluctuations which are non-cyclical and non-periodic in nature.[15] All of these types of movement affected the labor market and receive at least passing attention in the analysis which follows. None of them, however, provides a workable model for dealing with unemployment over a forty-year interval which witnessed profound structural as well as cyclical changes in the German economy.

The closest approximation to a working model for our purposes was developed by the economic historian Joseph Schumpeter who attributed change in capitalist economies to cyclical movements generated by exogenous factors, growth and innovations. Political movements, natural disasters, institutional changes, crop failures, chance discoveries of new specie and policy decisions were all factors which

Schumpeter considered external from the vantage point of economic cycles. A special kind of exogenous factor which merited particular consideration is economic growth, a term much-abused by interdisciplinary students of industrialization. Schumpeter defined growth in the following pertinent context.[16]

> By 'growth' we mean changes in economic data which occur continuously in the sense that the increment or decrement per unit of time can be concurrently absorbed by the system without perceptible disturbance. Increase of population, resulting in an increase in the supply of labor of at most a few percent per year...is the outstanding example.

The crucial characteristic of growth such as increases in savings or expansion of the labor supply is that it tends to be distributed over time in a way which facilitates its continuous absorption in the marketplace.

In contrast to growth, another source of economic change is likely to come in bunches which render it incapable of continuous absorption by the capitalist system. This endogenous source of change which Schumpeter termed innovation tends to evoke emulation and produce clusters of reverberations throughout the economy when recently proven methods are introduced into capitalist enterprises for the first time. Internal change in the economic system derives from variations in taste, fluctuations in the quantity and distribution of productive resources and shifts in productive functions. Changing patterns of production and consumption linked to innovations introduced by profit-seeking entrepreneurs are the primary source and only purely internal factor incident to the cyclical movements of industrial economies. In Schumpeter's words:[17]

> If there be a purely economic cycle at all, it can only come from the way in which new things are, in the institutional conditions of capitalist society, inserted into the economic process and absorbed by it! In fact, the cycle seems to be the statistical and historical form in which what is usually referred to as 'economic progress' comes about.

Economic progress in Schumpeter's view was brought about by changes which were cyclical, large-scale, productive of disturbance and linked to particular sectors of the economy.

Because the processes affected by innovation took varying amounts of time to absorb change, it was reasonable to postulate that a multitude of cycles were generated and simultaneously operative. From the theoretically infinite range of superimposed cyclical movements, Schumpeter selected three distinct waves in order to construct an historically verifiable and economically sound model of change in industrial society. The longest of these waves, with a duration ranging anywhere from 54 to 60 years, was named a Kondratiev cycle after the Russian theoretician who did most to document its existence. Although historians initially hesitated to pinpoint the inception of the first long wave with any degree of certainty, there is currently a concensus that it ought to coincide roughly with the period of England's industrial revolution--beginning in the 1780's and ending in 1842.[18] This is important because it emphasizes the point that business cycles of all durations are a unique feature of industrial countries. In addition to the long waves Schumpeter argued that there was sufficient historical data to substantiate the existence of two shorter cycles, named respectively Juglars and Kitchins after their dis-coverers. Each Kondratiev contained six Juglars whose average duration was nine to ten years. Like the longer waves each medium-length fluctuation was linked with a particular industry and a specific cluster of innovations which produced the upswing as well as the process of read-justment. The shortest of the three cycles, the Kitchin, lasted approximately forty months and in every instance there were three Kitchins in each Juglar.

All of the wavelike movements or cycles generated by reactions to clusters of innovation contained four distinct but consecutive phases of prosperity, recession, depression and revival. To assess the impact of the cycli-cal movements on the German economy, it is important to note that the relative alignment of the three waves--Kondratievs, Juglars and Kitchins--conditioned their cumulative effect. If, for example, during the period under consideration the depression phases of all three cycles coincided, the econo-mic repercussions would be more severe than those resulting from the coincidence of a depression phase with one or even two phases of prosperity. As a further guideline in this area, Schumpeter noted that "cycles in most series will tend to be toned down or even ironed out the more a country's economic life is interwoven with international influences and the more its policy approaches Free Trade.[19] Thus,

Bismarck's efforts to shape foreign policy largely in terms of domestic needs and the return to protection in 1879 would be relevant to an assessment of the impact of cyclical fluctuations prior to 1880.

According to Schumpeter, it was essential "for purposes of fundamental analysis"[20] to count cycles from the neighborhood of equilibrium after a revival and before the start of a new period of prosperity. Despite the undisputed theoretical neatness of Schumpeter's model, its application to historical analysis requires a certain amount of flexibility. The periodization employed here begins with the depression phase of one long wave and concludes with a second Kondratiev in the midst of recession. Our primary interest will be with the trend period 1873-1896 when the German economy was engulfed by a long downswing and in the subsequent years of prosperity when changes which first appeared during hard times were institutionalized and absorbed by a more mature industrial society. The year 1873 marked the termination of an unprecedented economic boom in Germany. It also inaugurated the second world economic crisis--after 1857--and the longest, most severe slump of the next forty years. Although the trend period which began in 1897 continued until 1920, by 1913 exogenous factors linked to the approach of war were beginning to impinge heavily on the German economy and push its development in directions which distorted the labor market.[21]

The entire period between 1873 and 1913 coincided roughly with Walt Rostow's "drive to maturity", witnessing the consolidation of gains made during the preceding years of so-called industrial revolution. By the end of our period, railroads were already in the process of giving way to equally revolutionary changes in transportation associated with automobiles and airplanes. The leading roles of steam and steel were supplanted by the electrical and chemical industries and in many areas small businessmen were yielding control over the economy to increasingly large syndicates and cartels. All of these changes made Germany's industrial unemployment problem and the labor market of 1913 quite different from those of 1873.

In order to understand the disturbances which accompanied largescale economic change, a long-range perspective is imperative. Recognizing this fact, Schumpeter attached greatest historical importance to the cycle of longest duration, the Kondratiev. "For no phenomenon of an essentially historic nature can be expected to reveal itself unless it is studied over a long interval."[22] Although Schumpeter would have viewed a mere forty years as inadequate, Hans Rosenberg took an even shorter period of time in his study of the Great Depression. Rosenberg used the trend period 1873-1896 to test the hypothesis that long waves could be employed as a heuristic device to illucidate the interaction among economic forces on the one hand and social and political change on the other. In Rosenberg's schema, long waves provided a model of development and periodization based on the assumption that the economy was in a state of constant flux. Unlike growth theories which viewed industrialization as uninterrupted linear progress, Rosenberg's approach suggested that depressions or panics were cyclically recurring elements in the development of all capitalist economies.

Rosenberg's application of Kondratiev's theories to the trend period 1873-1896 demonstrated that long waves have considerable value as an overall organizing concept for periodization. The contribution of Kondratiev cycles to an understanding of unemployment lies primarily in establishing qualitative relationships between the demand for labor on the one hand and the movement of factors such as wage rates, prices or population on the other. The utility of long waves for our purposes is hinted at by Schumpeter who asserted that "The Kondratieff Cycle is for us but a name for a certain long-time behavior of the price level, the interest rate, employment and so on, none of which is open to doubt."[23] The qualitative advantages of business cycle theory are spelled out in Schumpeter's remarks about the principles underlying his view of economic change.[24]

> These principles do enable us to link up in a general way the behavior of those of our series which are most symptomatic of the pulse of economic life as a whole. These 'systematic' series may be either 'synthetic' as, for instance, series of price levels or of physical volume of production, or 'natural', as, for instance, series of interest rates, clearing-debits, unemployment, pig-iron consumption, at least for the pre-war time, or the sum total of deposits.

Despite the obvious qualitative advantages of applying business cycle theory to our study of unemployment, Schumpeter
points out some limitations of this approach.[25]

> The statement...that in the down-grade of any cycle
> inertia of wages accounts for something in determining
> the amount of unemployment, is too obvious to require
> proof; but not only for practical reasons but also for
> scientific purposes this is entirely irrelevant as long
> as we are unable to say whether this element accounts
> for one per cent or for ninety per cent of the unem-
> ployment figure observed in a given place at a given
> time.

In terms of precisely quantifying the impact which migration
or real wages had on unemployment, business cycles and long
waves in particular are less useful.

While the Kondratiev cycles provide an acceptable
overarching plan of periodization for examining trends in
employment over time, the shorter Juglar cycles come closest
to reflecting the upward and downward movement of demand in
the German labor market. Studies which have been done with
regard to the English, and more recently the Danish, economies during our period indicate that employment in those
countries tended to fluctuate over seven to eleven year
intervals in a cyclical Juglar pattern. While variations
from the norm were reported,[26] as a general rule, the demand
for labor was highest from twelve to twenty-four months
prior to the peak of each trade boom. As expected, unemployment typically peaked when the trade cycle was at its
nadir. But employment tended to decrease more rapidly
during a downswing and increase more slowly during an

upswing than movement of the trade cycle itself would indicate.

Although it would be instructive to incorporate the entirety of Schumpeter's three-cycle scheme of periodization, continuous data which would permit the precise charting of Kitchins is not available for the German labor market during the early years of our period. This may be regrettable from a theoretical viewpoint but in terms of understanding fluctuations in unemployment, a model of internal periodization which relies on Juglar cycles is clearly defensible with respect to actual conditions in the German labor market. Schumpeter himself goes a long way toward acknowledging this point in the following excerpt from his massive study of business cycles.[27]

> All classes or order of classes show differently in
> different series and countries: in some series, such
> as...unemployment, Juglars show best; in others...the
> Kitchins. The latter stand out better, on the whole,
> in America than in England, Juglars better in Germany
> than in England.

Based on the fourth through the sixth Juglars of the second Kondratiev, Schumpeter suggested the useful timetable shown below:[28]

JUGLARS 1870-79, MID 1879-88, AND 1889-97

Prosperity	Recession	Depression	Recovery
1870, 1871, 1st 1/2 1872, 2nd 1/2 1879, 1880, 1881, 1889, 1890, 1891	2nd 1/2 1872, 1873 Mid 1881, 1882, 1883, 2nd 1/2 1891, 1892, 1st 1/2 1893	1873, 1874, 1875, 1876, 1884, 1885, 2nd 1/2 1893, 1894, 1st 1/2 1895	1877, 1878, 1st 1/2 1879, 1886, 1887, 1888, 2nd 1/2 1895, 1896, early 1897

This subdivision provides workable guidelines for the study of unemployment during the deflationary trend period 1873-

1896. Combined with the more complete English and Danish findings on correlations between trade cycles and unemployment, it will aid us in interpreting the scattered clues which have been left behind. For example, since the only national unemployment survey prior to 1913 occurred as part of the 1895 census, it is important to note the economic recovery which took place during June and December of that year. The preceding chart enables us to look at the unemployment census in terms which can be systematically related to the rest of our period. It is also important to know whether there were correlations between migrations or arrests for begging and economic fluctuations if one attempts to assess these phenomena as indirect indicators of unemployment. For this kind of analysis business cycle theory is an indispensible tool of historical inquiry.

We should keep in mind with respect to movement of the Juglars themselves that it is very difficult to specify precise turning points in the curves. As Wolfram Fischer has suggested, perhaps the best we can hope for is a tentative and approximate subdivision of historical time based on the distinction between periods of economic prosperity and points of crisis. In his study of economic fluctuations in the heavily industrialized Ruhr, Fischer drew a picture of upswings punctuated by crises every seven to eleven years, with the most severe interruptions coming during the first two decades of our period.[29]

Prosperity 1868 to 1873	Crisis 1873 to 1879 (with coal 1875 to 1879)
Prosperity 1880 to 1882	1883/86 mild deterior-tion
Prosperity 1887 to 1893	Milder downswing 1893/94
Prosperity 1902 to 1906	Crisis 1907
Prosperity 1908 to 1912	Crisis 1913

In general terms, high unemployment levels corresponded quite closely with the points of crisis outlined in the preceding chart. The value of this two-part analysis of economic change for an understanding of unemployment is indicated in Fischer's assessment of the relationship between crises and the demand for labor.[30]

> Allgemein gilt, dass in einer Wirtschaft mit technis-chen Branchen mit dem hoechsten Zuwachsraten an Arbeitsproduktivitaet--die Arbeiterzahlen nicht im Gleichschritt mit der Produktion wachsen. In Krisen-zeiten werden sie im 19. Jahrhundert schnell abgebaut, zugleich wird, um Kosten zu sparen, die technische Neuerung forciert, so dass die Wiederaufstieg die Arbeiterzahl nur langsam zunimmt.

So the demand for labor was far more responsive to economic crisis than to recovery--in hard times workers were laid off quickly but when prosperity returned the renewed demand for their services lagged behind the prevailing trend.[31]

During recessions there was a tendency to dismiss unproductive or unreliable employees. But where the market for skilled labor was tight during boom periods, management became increasingly reluctant to release the better members of their work force during periodic downswings. In order to

accommodate slack demand without losing potentially irre-
placeable hands, hours were cut, wages declined, men were
transferred and commodities stockpiled.[32]

As a footnote to this pattern of response to
cyclical fluctuation, it is worth indicating that most
strikes and protests came during years when there was a high
demand for labor and the products it manufactured. Economic
booms when overtime was more prevalent than lay-offs tended
to produce a desire for still greater improvements. During
periods of scant demand when workers held their jobs at the
pleasure of employers, organized protest was virtually
non-existent.[33] A parallel pattern existed in politics if
one considered socialist support tantamount to protest. It
is significant that the SDP gained support during periods
when wages and the demand for labor were rising, a pattern
which was particularly evident after 1880.[34] Contrary to
some expectations, prosperity rather than depression consistently made workers active in efforts to improve the
terms of their employment.

Divergent sectors of the economy responded at
variable rates to cyclical fluctuations, and even affiliated
industries occasionally experienced different time lags.
Heavy industries like iron and coal which were directly
linked to railroad construction played a key role in
Germany's industrial expansion during the second half of the
nineteenth century. Although they were closely related,
there was an interesting difference between developments in

the two industries during the 1870's. In response to the crisis of 1873, the iron industry went into an immediate slump but the coal producers were not severely affected until 1875. Differences in employment figures reflect the discrepancy.[35] Ultimately of course neither industry escaped the impact of the protracted downswing which lasted until the end of the decade. The crucial point here is that two allied industries were affected in divergent ways and at varying rates by the same economic events.

It is also important to emphasize in general terms that during periods of structural as well as cyclical change, the role of individual industries varied over time. The degree to which a crisis affected or was caused by one particular concern or group of concerns depended upon the extent to which given industries led the economic curve and on the shifting pattern of two-way linkages between sectors. The relative importance of the iron and electrical industries for example would have been very different in 1873 and 1913. The changing role of agriculture provides another striking illustration of this point. At the beginning of our period, agriculture supplied employment for approximately two-thirds of the German labor force. By 1913 the distribution had changed and industry was the largest consumer of available manpower. Obviously then, an agricultural depression such as the one touched off in 1873 had a much greater impact on the total employment picture during the early years of our period when agrarian production formed a significantly larger part of Germany's total output.

Acutely aware of repeated downswings, contemporaries recognized the inevitability of crises and unemployment as these remarks from the December 14, 1907, edition of Der Beobachter indicated.[36]

> Ploetzlich stehen auf der einen Seite grosse Kapitalsummen in Produkten angelegt. Der Absatz stockt. Die Krisis ist da, und Tausende und Zehntausende von Arbeitern sind arbeitslos. Mann kann diesen Prozess vergleichen mit der Selbstreinigung der Flusse und ihn die Selbstreinigung des Produktionsflusses nennen.

This view was fairly representative of the current understanding of the relationship between periodic downswings and unemployment. Just prior to the beginning of our period-- during the 1860's--two revolutionary treatises on the cyclical nature of change in capitalist economies were published. Both had a profound impact on subsequent attitudes toward cyclical fluctuations. The appearance of Clement Juglar's ideas helped late nineteenth-century thinkers to recognize alternating periods of prosperity and crisis for what they were. The basic contours of his periodization have already been discussed, but we have yet to come to terms with the far more influential opinions of Karl Marx.[37]

Before Das Kapital was published in 1867, the prevailing view of unemployment was that of the classical economists. They considered work scarcity a temporary, self-adjusting phenomenon which affected individuals far more adversely than society as a whole.[38] Recurring idleness was seen as the fault of persons directly involved and it was assumed that all those who really wanted to work would automatically find jobs. While previous theorists viewed unemployment as an aberrant feature of economic development, Marx saw it as a necessary and normal part of industrial capitalism. The system produced unemployment when employers discharged hands because the existing price structure made it more profitable to invest their capital in machines than in wages. This condition would recur whenever expanded production increased the demand for labor and pushed up the level of wages.

According to some non-Marxist theorists,[39] wage rates contained a built-in factor of compensation for probable unemployment which was reflected in the higher earnings of seasonal workers. The suggestion was frequently made that laborers had to be educated to the necessity of saving part of their income for the inevitable periods of slack demand. Those who were discharged in an effort to cut costs were referred to by Marx as industry's disposable reserve army. The skills of this mass of dispensible workers were needed only during peak periods of economic prosperity. Although expendable throughout most of the capitalist business cycle, the labor surplus was seen as an absolute prerequisite for economic booms and the growth which accompanied pronounced upswings.[40]

During much of our period, efforts to cope with unemployment took the form of trying to minimize the severity of its consequences rather than eliminate its causes. For Marx's followers and detractors alike recognized the necessity of a surplus labor supply whose presence was considered essential for progress. Prosperous intervals were generally associated with low levels of unemployment but interludes of price deflation or depression were presumed to produce widespread joblessness. The fact that a certain number of individuals would be unemployed was deemed necessary for the greater good of the economy and the country as a whole. The presence of a permanent industrial reserve army was complacently accepted as an inevitable byproduct of the capitalist market mechanism which required an excess of supply over demand--for labor as for other commodities. In Germany during our period the acceptable range of the necessary labor reserve varied from a high approaching three percent during the winter months to a low of one percent in the summer.[41] It was only when excessive numbers--something well in advance of three percent--were unemployed that contemporaries sought to eliminate rather than merely alleviate the problem.

The overwhelming majority of projects undertaken to deal with unemployment were initiated during times of economic depression when the need was too great to be ignored. Unfortunately, few reformers were willing to adopt a long-range perspective on unemployment; preventive measures were accordingly scarce. When the symptoms of unemployment disappeared, remedies generally evaporated or tapered off gradually, only to be resurrected after the next crisis had begun. The single most important exception to this pattern of stimulus and response was the Arbeitsnachweis which continued to fulfill the function of disseminating information during periods of prosperity as well as depression. Public works projects, various kinds of charity or relief institutions and insurance schemes did nothing to eradicate unemployment. They were needed to mitigate the immediate hardship suffered as a result of lost employment. They were almost invariably introduced in response to crisis and pursued if at all during intervals of economic prosperity with mixed results. Anticyclical policies designed to avert unemployment were virtually nonexistent at all levels of government during our period. Private industry, on the other hand, was ingenious in developing alternate labor practices which made the fight against unemployment most successful on the most basic microeconomic level of the individual firm where decisions about hiring and firing were made on a daily basis.

PREHISTORY, ATTITUDINAL CHANGES AND UNEMPLOYMENT IN GERMANY
AFTER 1913

Although a comprehensive prehistory of the unemployment problem prior to 1873 lies beyond the scope of this
study, it is necessary to understand the climate out of
which conditions in the labor market during our period
evolved. One crucial dimension of the late nineteenth-
century German economy which facilitated fluctuations in
employment was the mobility of the work force. While this
may be taken for granted today, just a few years prior to
national unification, mobility was anything but typical of
German laborers. Laws which emancipated the population from
hereditary restrictions on occupational and residential
choice were enacted as late as the 1860's. The impact of
measures which guaranteed all workers the freedom to seek
any kind of employment in the location of their choice was
compounded by equally revolutionary changes in communication
and transportation.

In addition to introducing minor improvements in
existing roads and waterways, the federal government sponsored the creation of national telegraph and postal services
soon after 1871. These advances naturally had a salutary
effect on the dissemination of information in the labor
market. But none of them had the far-reaching, immediate
and long-term consequences of the advent of railroads which
made movement of the means of production--human and
inanimate--practical on a large scale for the first time.

Between 1849 and 1873 railroads were to Germany what cotton textiles had been to England during the late eighteenth century. Walt Rostow placed the German industrial revolution in the 1850's and 1860's and saw railroads as the leading sector in a rapidly industrializing economy. The crucial point about railroads for our purposes however has less to do with linkages between industries than with linkages between labor markets. The railroads' potential for improving the mobility of the German worker and making it practical for him to move between jobs was as essential to industrialization as the heightened demand for coal and iron which it produced.

Both the railroads and the Freizugigkeitsgesetz of November 1, 1867, played a crucial role in the evolution of the unemployment problem during our period by creating a more nearly perfect freedom of occupational choice. Prior to the advent of that law and a viable system of mass transport, an essential feature of all modern labor markets was missing. It was only after 1870 that unemployment could be understood within the context of a free market situation where either employers or employees had the ability to terminate their relationship and seek alternate arrangements--by hiring new hands or seeking different jobs. During the heyday of guilds, indentured servants, serf-like peasants and class-restricted occupations, labor mobility was virtually non-existent. Previously the mobile population had been confined almost exclusively to illegal vagrants, beggars or highwaymen who preyed on the more stable and respectable elements of society.

The generations which came to maturity before the mid-nineteenth century found the labor market more structured and predictable than those who reached their majority after 1870. Although there had always been mobility among exceptional groups such as artists, many men pursued careers in the same areas as their forebears. With increasing freedom of occupational and geographical choice during our period came uncertainty and unfamiliar responses to vicissitudes in the demand for labor. The advent of economic expansion associated with industrialization opened up a broader panorama which provided those looking for work with a whole array of choices and problems. Whether and where they would find jobs and for how long their employment would last were questions of paramount concern for potentially itinerant laborers who learned to follow and hopefully anticipate the demand for their services.

Presupposing mobility, unemployment in the modern sense has always been associated with urban industrial societies. Poverty linked to lack of a job was not however unique to capitalist economies. In societies where the majority of the labor force was enslaved or working under various degrees of constraint, unemployment was not a pervasive problem. Masters could permit temporary idleness but short of freeing slaves or severing feudal ties they were not in a position to discharge their workers. There were of course individuals in all eras who did not fit neatly into the predominant socio-economic system and, as John Garraty has indicated, unemployment was not unknown in ancient or medieval times. Indeed in historical terms, the poor have always been with us.

In this context there has been a great deal of debate about whether the disadvantaged were better off under industrial society than they had been during the pre-industrial era. Phrased differently, we might ask whether it was worse to be unemployed after 1873 than earlier. The resounding response would be that joblessness was far more severe psychologically, economically and biologically before rapid industrialization began. Both unemployment and under-employment affected larger groups of the population-- estimates for 1846 indicate as many as one third--more harshly during the 1840's than at any time during our period. And according to Wilhelm Abel,[42] need during the mid-nineteenth century was greater in purely agrarian districts than in areas which had already developed inci- pient industries.

During decades when the German states had relied almost exclusively on agriculture, employment tended to be seasonal. Sixteenth-century estimates indicated, for example, that the average man could expect to work 190 days in the summer months and 70 days in the winter.[43] This left him idle for practically one third of the entire year. Even with the many days deliberately set aside for celebrations, such limited employment made it difficult to survive. For those who were unable to find work over even more extended periods of time there was rarely an alternative to sickness, starvation or ultimately death.

Although prior to stagflation economic theories postulated that inflation and unemployment were mutually exclusive, data from the sixteenth through the late eighteenth centuries suggests that years of deflated prices witnessed the greatest demand for labor. Conversely, high prices produced slack demand for day laborers, apprentices and craftsmen at the same time that the cost of items needed for survival was rising. Historically, women and children were the most expendable members of the labor force and this compounded the unemployment problem during pre-industrial times when income was measured in terms of the family's rather than the head of household's earnings.

During the 1840's when Germany was on the eve of her "take-off" to sustained industrial growth, the term pauperism first came into common usage.[44] The prevalence of that term in the extant literature signified the existence of a large and rapidly growing group of individuals who through the most grueling work were barely able to eke out a subsistence wage. Significantly, Wilhelm Abel placed the last hunger crisis of the preindustrial order in 1847 before the crop cycle based on seasonal fluctuations was clearly differentiated from the industrial business cycle discovered by Clement Juglar. Sometime around the 1840's, labor seemed to reach a crisis of declining productivity with output lagging behind population growth. Industrialization, the introduction of machinery and factories, rather than causing or exacerbating the problem, provided a way out for the majority of workers during our period.

Despite well-known losers of industrialization such as the handloom weavers, the economy and the labor force as a whole benefitted immensely from the changes which occurred during the decades immediately prior to the 1870's. The same population increase which had been responsible for sluggish growth in productivity during the preindustrial era provided necessary manpower for implementing technological improvements needed for industrialization. After 1850 small factories which were the predominant unit of production began to appear in far larger numbers in the western German states although the East continued to be almost exclusively engaged in agriculture. Between 1870 and 1913 labor productivity advanced decisively, with output per person employed increasing 1.5 percent per year and output per hour worked rising 2.1 percent.[45] Although regularly recurring downswings were an inherent feature of the new order, unpredictable onslaughts of mass starvation did not plague industrial Germany after the middle of the nineteenth century.

By the 1870's, improvements in transportation, advances in agriculture and increased purchasing power linked to industrialization had greatly diminished the likelihood that widespread hunger would result from economic crises. Furthermore, during the next decade, _laissez faire_ attitudes bequeathed by the Enlightenment began to give way to interventionist tactics and social legislation on the federal as well as local levels. Whereas previous victims of unemployment had been left to fend for themselves, a series of new institutions evolved during our period to help the displaced worker during his time of enforced idleness. Labor exchanges, unemployment insurance programs, _Naturalverpflegungsstationen_ and _Herbergen zur Heimat_ were all products of the long downswing which began in 1873. They reflected a new attitude of social responsibility as well as a growing fear of the latent power of the previously ignored masses.

During the late eighteenth and early nineteenth centuries, the problem of underemployment had become far more pervasive than unemployment. The result was a large number of semi-respectable, marginally productive workers lurking on the fringes of society, supplementing their income from socially sanctioned employment by acting as street scavengers in order to survive.[46] Measures aimed at alleviating the nuisance posed by beggars could be traced back to Charlemagne but a comprehensive history of their evolution will be deferred for now.[47] More germaine to developments which affected the unemployed was the recent history of changing attitudes toward workhouses in German states.

Although a workhouse existed in Bavaria by 1679, it was not until the late eighteenth century that they became common in the states of central Europe. Initially conceived as a palliative to problems of unemployment, workhouses emerged as instruments of those who sought to deter laziness by occupying idle hands. During the first half of the eighteenth century, increasingly repressive measures were adopted. As a corrective to their severity, a number of non-residential workhouses came into being in large German cities just prior to the beginning of the nineteenth century. In weighing the need for these institutions, it is useful to recall Wilhelm Abel's estimate that during the winter of 1800 in Berlin, between thirty and forty thousand people, or approximately one-fifth of the city's entire civilian population, were unable to support themselves by their own efforts.[48] Despite the desparate poverty which these figures reflect, by the early nineteenth century the workhouse was viewed with disfavor. It was not however until our period that alternate methods of coping with the unemployed evolved. Although workhouses fell into disrepute it is important to emphasize that they never disappeared entirely. The Imperial Penal Code which was adopted shortly after 1871 enumerated a number of offenses requiring detention in what had become essentially punitive institutions.

In addition to expanded institutional resources for coping with unemployment, subtle improvements in attitude toward those without work made the plight of the jobless individual easier to bear. During the seventeenth century, the assumption had been that laziness caused the majority of unemployment. The only remedy for the problem was therefore to make it imperative for workers to be on the job as much as possible by lowering wages to a point where the mass of people were forced to work more hours in order to subsist. Excess income was viewed as a deterrent to diligence and since workers were valued exclusively as producers, rather than in their dual capacity as consumers also, the logic of this approach seemed sound. Labor-intensive methods of production and the elimination of foreign competition were believed to foster full employment prior to 1700.

Under the mercantile system, the economic well-being of the individual was subordinated to the common good and policies aimed at full employment were pursued as a means of enhancing the economic power of the state. In its effects, unemployment came to be viewed as a social evil because it deprived the state of output lost through individual idleness. But in terms of causation, a series of political revolutions, crop failures, population increases and industrialization were needed to convince observers that the individuals directly involved were neither personally nor exclusively responsible for their lack of jobs.[49] As we noted earlier, by the late nineteenth century the capitalist system itself was viewed as the ultimate source of the problem and the inevitable residue which it produced became synonymous with unemployment.

Despite many improvements in attitudes toward the unemployed, one especially difficult notion to dispel was that laziness constituted an important source of idleness. According to this view, the unemployed were part of a vicious circle in which their problem was feeding on itself. Not only was unemployment caused by an unwillingness to work. It also tended to make people lazier by undermining their self-confidence and restricting their nourishment until they were no longer psychologically or physically fit to work. The belief that idleness was self-perpetuating had motivated public works projects at Nuremberg and Frankfurt in the fifteenth century[50] and continued to stimulate demands for public employment well beyond the end of our period. Contemporaries observed that it was difficult to inculcate industrious habits in workers who were accustomed to interruptions in their labor occasioned by numerous religious holidays, seasonal slack demand, wars, plagues, inebriation and variable business conditions.[51] In this context, it is significant that the most effective argument advanced by opponents of unemployment insurance pointed up the inability to separate deserving from unworthy recipients, a distinction based on the individual's eagerness to work. The doubts about rewarding work-shy persons abated but never disappeared during our period.

Although the preoccupation with laziness was not abandoned, there was a growing awareness that any monocausal explanation about the sources of unemployment might be too simplistic. The following analysis, written in 1910 by Dr. Otto Most, reflected the sophistication of those who sought to explain what caused unemployment.[52]

> Die Ursachen der Arbeits-, der Stellenlosigkeit sind aber nicht nur koerperliche (Mangel an Arbeitsfaehigkeit), nur in geringerem Masse auch sittliche (Mangel an Arbeitswilligkeit), sondern auch im ganz hervortragendem Masse wirtschaftliche (Mangel an Arbeitsgelegenheit). Und zwar tritt dieses letztgenannte Moment um so mehr in den Vordergrund, je mehr die Volkswirtschaft die stabilen Formen der Vergangenheit verliert und in ihrem Wohler gehen immer enger verknuepft wird mit dem Auf und Nieder der Weltwirtschaft. Die Arbeitslosigkeit aus wirtschaftlichen Gruenden nimmt darum mir der zunehmenden Industrialisierung der deutschen Volkswirtschaft zweitweise einen Umfang an, den man vordem auch nicht einmal geahnt hat, und bringt neben schweren wirtschaftlichen und sittlichen Nachteilen fuer die Betroffenen auch erhebliche Gefahren fuer die oeffentliche Wohlfahrt und Ordnung mit sich.

This tripartite attribution of unemployment to physical incapacity for labor, inadequate desire to work and inability to find a job was typical of the contemporary understanding of the sources of the problem. There was however a growing tendency to recognize only purely economic factors--those leading to an inability to find work--as a cause for general public concern. Assistance to those suffering from physical incapacity was provided on a local level through poor relief and on the federal level through Bismarck's social insurance program. As noted above, semi-invalids and people with chronic health problems who were employable during boom periods frequently advanced claims for disability assistance during recessions. Among those who were unwilling to work, laborers involved in strikes and lockouts accounted for a far higher percentage of lost output than the few who were inherently lazy. Estimates indicated that there were approximately 250,000 convictions for vagabondage in an average year during our period. Add to this another 600,000 who were deflected from the labor market by military service plus an estimated 200,000 persons detained in German prisons and the result would be about one million individuals whose efforts added little if anything to the economic productivity of the country. This was a sizable figure relative to both the labor force and the unemployed during our period.[53]

Before proceeding further, let us return briefly to Dr. Most's analysis of the causes of unemployment in order to complete our consideration of contemporary attitudes toward the problem. He expressed the prevalent belief that unemployment posed certain political dangers for public order. This threat was brought home by memories of revolutionary upheavals in France and by the growth of trade unions and Social Democracy in Germany. Dr. Most also represented a large segment of public opinion in attributing economic dimensions of the unemployment problem to increasing industrialization. The speed with which industrialization occurred and its cumulative impact on the German labor market might be recalled from a few statistics on the growth of the industrial labor force. The number of workers employed in Prussian industries increased from 1.6 million in 1816 to approximately four million in 1867. By 1882 there were 10.7 million industrial workers and by 1895, 12.6 million wage earners were employed in German industry.

According to contemporary perceptions,[54] the expansion of the industrial work force took place at the expense of the agrarian population. The best evidence to substantiate this observation was the mushrooming of major cities; the twin processes of industrialization and urbanization were deemed to be in large measure responsible for unemployment.[55] Adopting a long-range historical perspective, one critic suggested that there was something inherent in the relationship between urban living and unemployment-- the connection could be traced back to antiquity: "Grossstaedtische Arbeitslosigkeit ist an sich keine nur dem modernen Wirtschaftsleben anklebende Erscheinung. Sie war vielmehr bereits in den alten Kulturstaaten Griechenland und Rom in grossem Umfang hervorgetreten."[56] If the problems of unemployment associated with urbanization were not new, observers believed they were aggravated by the pace of industrialization and the concommitant concentration of manpower in Germany's growing cities. When growth was too rapid to be absorbed, unemployment was perceived as its byproduct.

To the extent that contemporaries sought to minimize the amount of industrial unemployment in urban centers, they did so on the employers' part by resorting to reduced hours or wages and on the workers' part by temporarily seeking alternate occupations in non-industrial sectors of the economy. Measures such as the ones suggested by Georg Schanz tended to minimize the number of workers who lost their jobs even during periods of deflated prices. In the following excerpt, note the assumption that unemployment was caused by overproduction and the inference that it could therefore be controlled either by the popular expedient of curtailing output or by the novel alternative of increasing mass consumption. Noteworthy also are the complexities of causation and remedy suggested by Schanz.[57]

> Ich erinnere an die Notstandsarbeiten in den groesseren Staedten, welche freilich mit vielen Schwierigkeiten zu kaempfen haben und oft nur Verschiebungen in der Arbeitslosigkeit bringen; ich erinnere an die Kolonisationen im Innern, um das uebermaessige Zustroemen der Bevolkerung in die Industriecentren abzuschwaechen; ich erinnere an die Bemuehungen der Industriekartelle, der Produktion und Beschaeftigung einen regelmaessigeren Gang zu verleihen: ich erinnere an die Bestrebungen der Arbeiter, durch Verhinderung der Ueberstunden, durch Verkuerzung der Arbeitszeit, Regelung der Stueckarbeit, Einschraenkung der Ueberzahl von Lehrlingen in einzelnen Berufen (Buchdrucker, Kaufleute etc.), die Aufsaugung der ueberschuessigen Arbeitskraefte zu erleichtern, durch Hochhaltung der Loehne die Unterkonsummtion der Massen zu mindern und damit der Ueberproduktion mit ihren Rueckschlaegen vorzubeugen; ich erinnere an den Werth nicht zu kurzer Kundigungszeiten, wodurch der Spielraum zur Erlangung einer neuen Stelle vergroessert wird; ich erinnere an die Versuche der Arbeitgeber, bei schlechtem Geschaeftsgang statt der definitiven Arbeiterentlassungen an einzelnen Tagen die Arbeit ausfallen zu lassen oder die ueberfluessigen Arbeiter in regelmaessigen Wechsel nur zeitweise ausser Arbeit zu setzen und ihnen dabei ein Wartegeld zu zahlen, so dass die ungunstige Konjunktur sich auf alle vertheilt und dadurch leichter ertragen wird. Besonders wendet man neuerdings einer besseren Organisation der Arbeitsvermittelung sein Augenmark zu.

One of the most frequently advanced remedies for unemployment involved projects for the cultivation of wasteland. The argument in its favor went something like this: The urban unemployed who had lost their jobs as a result of seasonal changes or economic crises could be productively occupied reclaiming previously untilled land. This would benefit the workers themselves by keeping them active and fit for future employment; it would eliminate the unproductive expenditure of union, government and private funds to sustain idleness on the part of the unemployed and their families; it would preserve the necessary reserve army for industry and open up new areas of cultivation for agriculture. The last factor was important because there were many observers who maintained that agriculture had nothing to gain from most forms of unemployment relief. Indeed the point was frequently made that the agrarian sector had no unemployment problem, rather the reverse--a scarcity of labor--and agriculture was being forced to subsidize industrial and urban workers on this issue.[58]

Given the fact that urbanization and industrialization were closely associated with unemployment in many minds, it was not surprising that arguments were advanced in favor of reversing or at least retarding both processes. A number of proposals to correct the supposed maldistribution of population were forthcoming along with schemes for bolstering the waning position of artisans, skilled craftsmen and agrarian areas in general. Predominantly lower

middle class losers of industrialization provided an important repository of anti-modern sentiment which manifested
itself with particular vehemence in the heavily industrialized areas of western Germany.[59] This largely negative
bias found expression in opposition to liberals, socialists
and Jews as well as capitalists and the industrial unemployed. Properly manipulated, such sentiments could be
molded into powerful political weapons aimed at retarding or
altering the direction of German economic development.

Those who advocated preservation of the old order
were obviously in favor of arguments which portrayed unemployment as the handmaiden of industrialization and socialist agitation. The much repeated notion that large-scale
unemployment posed a significant threat to Germany's social
peace was typical of this line of thinking. Throughout most
of our period, subscribers could read in local newspapers
that unemployment was the greatest evil of the day. It was
recognized not only as a social problem whose consequences
varied directly with the level of joblessness; it eventually
came to be seen as a personal dilemma for those directly
involved. From 1890 onwards and particularly during the
closing years of our period, there was grudging acknowledgment of the individual suffering occasioned by the loss of
employment. In addition to material deprivation, contemporaries recognized the humiliation of accepting charity, the
trauma of losing property and the demoralization of idleness
which were likely to accompany prolonged unemployment. An

appeal to the Kaiser written in 1890 spoke of suicides motivated by lack of employment and went on to describe idleness as the economic equivalent of death.

Although some observers maintained that purposeless public works projects were as demoralizing as handouts,[60] there was growing sentiment in favor of assuming public responsibility for the unemployed. While the state cared for the aged, sick and infirm after Bismarck introduced social insurance during the 1880's, relief for the unemployed was left to the discretion of private or local authorities during the entirety of our period. An 1884 speech which Bismarck made in the Reichstag inaugurated a discussion of the right to work which was revived in the wake of subsequent cyclical downswings well after 1913. There were frequent demands for expanding the existing social insurance program to include the unemployed, but it was not until the adoption of the Weimar constitution that the federal government explicitly acknowledged its obligation to jobless individuals.

While the years covered by the inquiry which follows ended in 1913, questions raised by the unemployment problem during the Second Reich had far-reaching implications for subsequent developments in German history. Modern solutions to the unemployment problem were demanded and worked out for the first time during the years after 1873. Although later economic crises were more severe and elicited correspondingly extreme resolutions, the patterns of stimu-

lus and response that emerged during our period set precedents which were adapted when similar but not identical
situations arose. Given this assumption, a brief sketch of
the history of unemployment in wartime and Weimar Germany
would perhaps be of use.

The year immediately following the termination of
our study was overshadowed by mobilization for the pending
conflict. The attendant reorganization and dislocation
produced widespread albeit temporary unemployment, particularly among women whose jobs were threatened by the call-up
of their male coworkers. Factories shut down, entire
professions disappeared and thousands of workers were left
to seek alternate employment in war-related industries.
Secretaries, stenographers, authors, tailors, textile
workers, domestic servants, shopkeepers and apartment
managers were among those hardest hit by the transition from
peace to a wartime economy. With the strong controls which
emerged during the course of the First World War,
unemployment subsided and most available hands were put to
work for the duration of the fighting.

With demobilization, a new disruption of the
wartime equilibrium occurred and hundreds of thousands of
laborers were thrown out of work. Their concentration in
politically volatile urban areas has been cited as an
important factor in the Sparticist uprisings which occurred
when more than one quarter of the nation's unemployed
resided in Berlin.[61] Although demobilization never produced

unemployment on the scale which it reached during the 1930's in Germany, it is significant that there were pronounced political repercussions in both instances. Manifesting itself in an erosion of support for middle-of-the-road causes and a preference for extremist groups, during the earlier period the unemployed were a factor in the abortive 1918-19 revolution. Later their presence was reflected in votes for Reichstag candidates from the extreme right as well as the far left of the political spectrum.

During the turbulent period at the end of World War I, the federal government established a series of public works projects entirely similar to enterprises undertaken by municipalities to alleviate unemployment between 1873 and 1913. The network of labor exchanges which evolved during the 1890's was taken over by the federal government in 1919, a move which lessened the subsequent impact of runaway inflation on the labor market. After the hyper-inflation of 1922/23 had been brought under control, the government introduced an unemployment assistance program paid for by joint employer and employee contributions. Such cooperative ventures were suggested during our period but action on a national scale was stubbornly resisted in almost all quarters. Before the Great War industrial entrepreneurs were particularly vocal opponents of mandatory subsidies for the unemployed. It is significant that in the wake of recovering from post-war inflation, Germans shied away from a scheme of real insurance and opted instead for a system based on need. Contrary to the pattern which prevailed before 1913, it was during 1927 when the economy was experiencing a boom and unemployment was at its nadir, that a comprehensive insurance program was finally adopted by the Reichstag. Coverage was extensive in occupational terms with no discrimination against seasonal employees. Despite efforts to distinguish between insurance and relief payments by labeling compensation paid to the unemployed whose benefits had expired as loans, the program was already operating with a big deficit by 1930.[62]

HISTORIOGRAPHICAL ISSUES RELATED TO INDUSTRIAL UNEMPLOYMENT
BETWEEN 1873 AND 1913

There are some methodological questions raised by
recent histories of our period which shed light on alternate
approaches to the study of industrial unemployment. Decided-
ly different interpretations of German development between
1873 and 1913 have emerged and the differences can be
discussed in terms of five basic issues: Continuity vs.
discontinuity, pressures from below vs. influence from
above, domestic vs. foreign policy, theory vs. narration as
an explanatory tool and the role of economic determinism in
historical change. All of these issues merit brief consideration as part of an effort to lend our inquiry about
unemployment a proper historiographical perspective.

The issue of continuity is important for our
purposes because the argument has repeatedly been made that
events in Germany between 1871 and 1914 provided patterns of
behavior which were emulated during the late Weimar years.
The fact that votes for extremist parties fluctuated directly with unemployment levels during the early Thirties raises
questions about the role of work shortages in the downfall
of democracy and the rise of fascism. In addition, recent
suggestions about the continuity of German development
between 1871 and 1945 pose some interesting historiographical problems for the analysis of unemployment during our
period.

The study of industrial unemployment between 1873 and 1913 demands something beyond the use of events during those years as a battleground for rival theories of continuity. The labor market prior to World War I should be analyzed on its own terms. Comparisons between unemployment during our period and the 1930's are instructive but only if the identity of each unique historical epoch is preserved. If we were to take suggestions of continuity at face value and look at unemployment over the entire course of the years between 1871 and 1945, the perspective we would gain on the earlier decades would be quite different and rather distorted. The pre-war labor problems seemed serious in their own right to the men who grappled with them. And it is unlikely that they would have been consoled by the observation that the quantitative dimensions of their dilemma were dwarfed by the scale of unemployment which hit Germany during the 1930's.

Because the levels of unemployment between 1873 and 1913 never approached proportions which were almost commonplace by the end of the Weimar Republic, it would be unfair to compare nineteenth-century methods of treating the problem with what evolved later. Certain modern remedies such as public works projects, insurance and labor exchanges made their initial appearance on a modest scale prior to 1900. Ideologues espousing nationalism, imperialism, and hatred for religious minorities, left-wing politics and industrialization also adopted a distinctly modern flavor during the decades prior to World War I. But from the evidence which exists, it is difficult to establish causal connections between the emergence of these ideologies and discontent stemming directly from unemployment.

Only in the case of socialism is the antipathy easy to document. With regard to industrialization and urbanization the picture is less clear but a plausible case might be made to support the contention that unemployment elicited antimodern feelings in these areas as well. In recent historical analyses of our period, the assumption has been implicit that patterns of thought and action first emerged in response to the so-called Great Depression of the nineteenth century which were applied under similar circumstances during the 1930's. There were certain indisputable similarities but between 1873 and 1913, the anti-modern sentiment attributable to unemployment remained confined to the realm of ideas when it surfaced at all. Between the ideologies of men like Adolf Stoecker and the actions of an Adolf Hitler came the definitive experiences of the Great War and Versailles plus the extreme economic conditions of the Twenties and early Thirties. All of these were indispensible, but by no means inevitable, prerequisites for the political responses to unemployment which emerged during the late Weimar Era.

It would be both pointless and unjust to condemn the German leaders of our period for failures in dealing with industrial unemployment which were never apparent during their lifetimes. No effort will be made to judge the unemployment policies of the Second Reich in terms of ensuing events. Instead, every attempt will be made to look at labor problems between 1873 and 1913 within the limitations dictated by the period itself. Subsequent reactions to unemployment will occasionally be noted but not as a means to chastise individuals who could neither predict nor control the future.

In analyzing unemployment, a scheme of periodization which adheres to the view that developments between 1871 and 1945 constituted a single unit would be misleading. For the reasons alluded to above, it would tend to undervalue labor problems during the years prior to 1913 when aggregate unemployment levels remained low relative to later years. Looking at a longer timespan would focus undue attention on 1933--on the enormous unemployment levels and their political repercussions. There would be an additional temptation to blame precursors rather than those directly responsible for the rise of fascism. This is of course the primary point of contention behind arguments over continuity.

The strongest argument in favor of viewing German history from Bismarck to Hitler as a continuous whole has been made by Hans-Ulrich Wehler. He insists in Das deutsche Kaiserreich[63] that the roots of fascism must be sought not only in the Weimar years but also in the Reichsgrundung era. In Wehler's portrayal of the interval between 1871 and 1918 the German social and political structures remain essentially unchanged despite rapid industrialization. Both the static quality of his analysis and his insistence on the continuity of German history between 1871 and 1945 have come under attack. Wehler is maligned for portraying the 43 years between unification and World War I as a single unit with perhaps one internal subdivision. He is further criticized for disregarding the substantial changes which Germany underwent during those years. By opting for continuity over other criteria in subdividing the German past, Wehler has risked sacrificing the integrity and uniqueness of our historical epoch in an effort to achieve methodological consistency and explanatory neatness.

Much of the problem which critics have had with Wehler's work derives from their conflicting views on the role of theory in history. Whereas most historians are rather reluctant to borrow from other disciplines, Wehler has elevated the use of sociological theory derived from Juergen Habermas and the Frankfurt School to a level of paramount importance in historical analysis. Unfortunately, social theory poses fundamental problems when used as a tool of historical inquiry. Modern concepts do not always produce an accurate reflection of the complexity, singularity and disorder of unpredictable events which occurred before those theories were first espoused. An imperfect fit can result from trying to match historical data with an economic or sociological formula conceived in a vastly different context. There is then an unfortunate tendency for such models to distort the past which is made to conform to rigidly preconceived notions of how things should have been. Rather than using the past as a guideline for theoretical adjustments, aspects of development which do not blend neatly into existing paradigms are often minimized or ignored entirely. The potential for such abuse is abundant both with regard to our period and unemployment. We shall therefore be circumspect in imposing twentieth-century social theory on nineteenth-century men. However, we must acknowledge that the present study grew out of Hans Rosenberg's work on the Great Depression. And in historiographical terms, Rosenberg, like Wehler, has gone a long way toward incorporating social scientific concepts into the analysis of economic problems.

Striking an intermediate note between the problem-oriented approaches of Wehler or Rosenberg and more traditional policy studies, Thomas Nipperdey is representative of German historians who have focused on interest groups and political institutions between 1871 and 1914. Using theory sparingly and relying to a large extent on historical narrative, Nipperdey, Gerhard A.Ritter and Helmuth Boehme have added a great deal of factual information to our understanding of the period. All of their works reject the heavily theoretical orientation of Wehler and are more cautious about tracing a single static line of continuity through Germany's past. They attack the critical orientation of Wehler's methodology and the relationship between structural analysis and narration in recent social history.

Looking at developments in another quarter, we might consider the work of Richard Evans who edited a collection of essays by younger English historians. Unlike Wehler and Rosenberg, the English group is averse to superimposing theoretical models on the past and emerges with a more fluid and disordered reconstruction of events. In this respect, they resemble Nipperdey but on another issue, the Evans group forges ahead of previous interpretations by sidestepping the elitist perspective of many German treatments of political alliances around the turn of the century. A unilateral path of influence percolating downward from the top is rejected by the British historians in favor of a bilateral perspective which also recognizes the upward movement of influence from the broad mass of people. The new approach directs attention to pressures from below and reevaluates the cohesion behind affiliations which produced interest groups. Big business and big agriculture are transformed from a single tightly-knit unit at the center of the historical stage into several potentially opposing factions which had to contend with more diverse middle and lower class interests than previous accounts acknowledged. This recent emphasis on the "grass roots of politics and the everyday life and experience of ordinary people"[64] among historians not shackled by the dialectic of Marxist orthodoxy represents real progress. It bodes well for a fuller understanding of the working class and problems related to unemployment in Germany between 1873 and 1913.

In analyzing industrial unemployment, our primary concern will be with the individuals directly involved. In addition to the unemployed themselves, we shall consider public policy-makers, analysts and shifting alliances of interest groups that came together to affect trade and labor policies. Confrontations between the interests of organized elites and jobless individuals and their impact on unemployment will be a major concern. The approach of the Evans group is germaine to the study of unemployment during our period because so many crucial decisions were made at the grass-roots level. It needs to be emphasized, however, that neither those who see pressure exerted from below nor those who view influence percolating down through society from above have a monopoly on historical truth. What is needed for a successful analysis of unemployment is an understanding of the two-way relationship between so-called masses and elites. As we shall see, influence flowed from both directions.

In a related context we would do well to briefly consider the much-discussed point about the primacy of domestic policy that has been argued at some length by Wehler and others who resurrected the early works of Hans Rosenberg and Eckart Kehr. This approach was necessary to redress the lopsided perspective of German historiography which previously concentrated attention on the paramount role of Bismarck's foreign policy. For a long time diplomatic and political historians who wrote about the Second Reich dealt exclusively with the military, with Bismarck's personality and with the relationship between Prussia and Germany. Policy-oriented studies in which analysis was largely subordinated to narrative are typical of some works produced by Gordon Craig in the United States and Golo Mann in Germany.

In response to this one-dimensional approach, Wehler and a number of other historians have attempted to show how internal considerations affected Bismarck's behavior on the international stage. They have accumulated a mass of data on imperialism, tariffs and more economically oriented aspects of foreign policy which has moved the pendulum in a direction altogether different from prior arguments about the balance of power. In analyzing unemployment, our first concern will be domestic policies which most directly impacted the labor market. But we shall also look at tariff legislation and foreign competition as factors in unemployment. It seems obvious that the time has come to examine the interrelationship between foreign and domestic policy without assigning what appears to be an entirely arbitrary ascendency to either one over the other.

A parallel point suggests itself with regard to interaction among economic, social, and political forces. For some time, historians have tended to elevate events in analytically discrete spheres such as the economy to the role of prime movers in other areas of development emerging with a simple cause and effect response. If one aims for the most accurate recreation of the past, it would seem to be more profitable to examine the two-way interaction between the economy and changes in other areas such as politics or society. The shortcomings of a monocausal economic analysis of historical change are particularly apparent in the writings of the most homogeneous, well-defined and radical school of scholarship--in work produced by the East German Marxist historians. Unfortunately, they have not contributed a great deal more than their western colleagues to our understanding of unemployment. They have of course written endless volumes of economic and working-class history which shed light on problems related to the labor market. But with regard to unemployment per se, disappointing gaps occur in the pages of such standard texts as Hans Mottek's Wirtschaftsgeschichte Deutschlands and Juergen Kuczynski's monumental Geschichte der Lage der Arbeiter unter dem Kapitalismus.[65]

Perhaps the relative disinterest in unemployment which has been exhibited by socialist historians can be traced back to Marx himself. As we have indicated, he saw work shortage as an inevitable byproduct of the capitalist system and one more reason why that system deserved to be dismantled by its victims. As an additional factor in provoking revolution, unemployment was not vigorously opposed because despite individual suffering, its spread would ultimately benefit the masses who would be moved to political protest by economic injustice.

In addition to the socialist histories of Germany between 1873 and 1913, there are a number of purely economic studies of the period which have been produced in the West. David Landes, Ivo Lambi, Geoffrey Barraclough, Karl Hardach and Walther Hoffmann are among those who have written about the German economy without submitting to the ideological confines of dialectical materialism. In this context, it is worth mentioning the recent attempt by Wehler and an international panel of historians to develop the idea of organized capitalism as an alternative to the Marxist notion of state monopoly capitalism. Unfortunately, the utility of this rather general term as an organizing concept for dealing with unemployment is limited.

Although we have focused primarily on shortcomings of recent histories of Germany between 1873 and 1913, our approach to the study of industrial unemployment will borrow from each of them. We shall aim for the theoretical clarity and cohesion which characterize Rosenberg's essay on the Depression years and Wehler's impressive study of imperialism. Without undervaluing the importance of individuals like Bismarck, we shall incorporate the English historians' grass roots approach, showing the two-way interaction between masses and elites, unions and workers, employers and employees, government officials and the unemployed. We shall try to define the interrelationship between economic development and changes in other areas affecting the daily lives of the industrial labor force. We shall attempt to deal with political policy decisions in a balanced manner, attributing adequate influence to both domestic and international considerations affecting the unemployment situation in Germany. We shall rely on social scientific theory more heavily than Nipperday but more selectively and circumspectly than Wehler. Finally, we shall place the years of Germany history, artificially extracted from a continuum for analytical purposes, within the broad mainstream of ongoing development. At the same time, however, every effort will be made to respect the uniqueness of historical events and not distort the past by superimposing preconceived notions or alien ideas on historical figures. In the pages that follow, we shall strive for the direction and intensity of Marxist inquiries without a dogmatic, determinist view of historical change.

PART TWO: QUANTITATIVE DATA, THE SOURCE OF DISPARITIES BE-
TWEEN THE PERCEPTION AND REALITY OF INDUSTRIAL UNEMPLOYMENT

This chapter will analyze the impact which available statistics had on both contemporary and subsequent observations about industrial unemployment in Germany between 1873 and 1913. As we shall see, the spotty and inconsistent nature of hard data in primary sources relating to unemployment was conducive to inaccurate assessments of the problem. During a period of recurrent economic crises without sufficient intervals of recovery, incomplete data was used to fan fears of socialist revolution. Contemporaries who perceived work shortages to be far more pervasive than actual figures indicated established a link between high unemployment and left-wing revolution in the popular imagination. This tendency to introduce a political component into the interpretation of unemployment statistics has had a profound effect on subsequent historical analyses of related issues.

In historiographical terms, the paucity of quantitative evidence has given rise to two competing interpretations of late nineteenth-century unemployment. The first thirteen years of our period have been the subject of the most widely varying estimates because accurate and specific unemployment statistics were virtually nonexistent in Germany before 1886. Since the Marxist polemic requires historical verification of the deterioration of working class circumstances during the industrialization process,

East German historians have used isolated figures on cutbacks in employment to paint the grimmest possible picture of the years after 1873. In discussing unemployment, they have focused on the late 1870's when hard data on conditions in the labor market was especially thin. By multiplying examples of diminished employment plus shorter hours, the Eastern historians have produced estimates of unemployment which approached alarming proportions between 1876 and 1879. The situation during the Eighties would have been worse, according to the Marxists, were it not for the mitigating circumstance of large-scale emigration abroad. In terms of periodization then, the Eastern approach has been to concentrate on a shorter timespan for which the underlying economic indicators are vague or unknown and maximize estimates of unemployment in an effort to demonstrate a marked deterioration in the working class standard of living. The years between 1873 and 1886 have proven more useful for their purposes than later years when the quantitative parameters of the problem are no longer as ill-defined.

In contrast to this approach, Western historians have until very recently maintained that there is no evidence of a severe unemployment problem during our period. Opting to look at longer time frames, they have been content to dismiss the issue by noting the dearth of hard data, minimizing the value of alternate indicators of work shortage such as employment, and estimating that joblessness was contained at something less than three percent under the Second _Reich_. It is no coincidence that this posture tacitly supports the contention that conditions among the working class improved during the course of industrialization.

Eastern historians have approached the problem by isolating individual instances of severe hardship and by accumulating examples of occupations and regions which suffered from diminished aggregate employment and presumably therefore from high unemployment rates as well. From a few extreme cases they deduce that overall conditions were far worse than the bulk of evidence indicates. The western tendency has been to rely almost exclusively on published data of a national and sectoral nature, blurring distinctions among widely divergent regions and industries. The result has been a western interpretation which underestimates the importance of unemployment during our period by dismissing it as something less than three percent and an eastern interpretation which overestimates the extent of underemployment at something approaching 25 percent at least during the 1870's.

To shed light on the different historiographical approaches derived from insufficient data, we might look at the divergent treatment of alternate indicators of unemployment. We shall consider factors such as employment, wages, prices and consumption patterns to show how statistics from the labor market have been manipulated to support contradictory assessments of job scarcity. Once again we shall see that the gap in contemporary knowledge of the underlying situation due to a dearth of quantitative data has given rise to unjustified speculation about the extent of unemployment. In addition to examining that speculation, we shall look at other indices of work shortages in an effort to establish the actual dimensions of the problem between 1873 and 1913.

Throughout our period, the collection of statistics was seen as an essential first step toward resolution of the unemployment problem. It is important to emphasize that enumeration of the unemployed was a novel undertaking without precedent prior to unification. This meant that the methodology of counting jobless individuals had to be worked out in the course of actual surveys. The amount of trial and error plus the substantial literature devoted to methodological considerations reflect the experimental nature of unemployment polls.

Amassing data was perceived as a prerequisite for determining both the extent of unemployment and the economic feasibility of various remedies. In this context we shall consider union unemployment figures and pay particular attention to the exceptionally thorough information gathered by the printing trades. It will become apparent that organizations which collected the most complete statistics were frequently synonymous with those offering the most extensive benefits. The pattern of statistics clearly reflects the grass roots nature of unemployment relief which evolved in Germany during our period.

Quantitative data from relief institutions provides some insights into the success of various remedies. Statistics on poor relief and begging may be taken as an index of the failure of unemployment programs. Data from agencies such as labor yards, refuges and labor exchanges suggests shifting priorities among contemporaries seeking to alleviate work shortages. In using this information, special note should be taken of the extent to which unemployed individuals were differentiated from other relief recipients. The sophistication of efforts to categorize the unemployed tells us a good deal about contemporary attitudes toward those without jobs.

For our purposes, gaps in the unemployment figures are as important as the available evidence. Because quantitative data was collected as a prelude to policy decisions and because contemporaries allowed numbers to define the parameters of the unemployment problem, partial statistics meant piecemeal solutions. As we shall see in the last chapter of this study, the scattered unemployment figures which were gathered both reflected and encouraged a decentralized approach to the entire problem.

The single exception to this rule was the nationwide unemployment count undertaken halfway through our period. In the final section of the present chapter, the statistics amassed as an adjunct to the 1895 census will be used to profile the unemployed. We shall attempt to portray an "ideal type" of jobless industrial laborer by examining census breakdowns on the residence, occupation, skill, age, sex and marital status of unemployed persons. An effort will be made to determine which segments of the German population were most susceptible to the loss of their jobs and least able to secure alternate positions. Having prepared a statistical profile of the "typical" unemployed individual, we shall attempt to place him within a broader macro-economic picture in order to examine the general contours of industrial unemployment in Germany. We shall consider the distribution, degree of risk, frequency and length of unemployment reflected in the nationwide data from 1895 and subsequent statistical publications.

As a prerequisite for analyzing the intensity of contemporary reactions to unemployment in the next two chapters, it is essential to chart the patterns of jobless-ness which emerged during our period. If the overall quantity of unemployment was small in proportion to the qualitative reaction which it produced, we are left to seek an explanation of the disparity by asking who was affected and how their lives were changed. In this context, atti-tudes played an important part. Fear of the revolutionary potential of unemployment on the side of the middle class and anxiety over the uncertainty of economic life among the working class were the primary results of deep-rooted insecurities. In both instances, apprehensions over the prospect of unemployment dovetailed with more general fears of economic instability which had been nurtured by three successive downswings without sufficient intervals of recovery between 1873 and 1895. This atmosphere of anxiety over unemployment was fed by ignorance derived from uncertainty about the extent of the problem. Misinformation stemmed in large measure from the vagueness of the unemployment picture due to incomplete and inaccurate quantitative data.

Given a situation where the absence of nationally comprehensive statistics created ignorance about the overall extent of the problem, every isolated outbreak of unemployment was susceptible to exaggeration. This posed dangers for contemporaries and historians alike. The former were free to draw general unwarranted conclusions from partial evidence whenever it suited their purposes. Likewise, subsequent observers were prone to see large pockets of work shortages such as Berlin experienced between 1876 and 1879 and deduce that overall industrial unemployment in Germany was appallingly high. In neither instance are aggregate figures available to challenge or corroborate overblown claims for the years prior to 1890.

PRIMARY SOURCES: ROOT OF DISPARITIES BETWEEN PERCEPTIONS OF
UNEMPLOYMENT AND ECONOMIC REALITY

In order to lay the groundwork for an assessment
of the quantitative parameters of the problem at hand, it is
necessary to establish the criteria and methods which were
used to measure unemployment. As we shall see, the best
available statistics indicate unemployment rates during our
period which averaged around three percent and rarely
exceeded six percent of Germany's industrial labor force.
These relatively low levels of unemployment elicited a
disproportionately large response from policy makers and
polemicists alike. We know that contemporaries recognized
the inevitability of frictional unemployment which should
have put their minds at ease about the aggregate levels of
joblessness that prevailed during most of the years in
question. How then are we to explain the magnitude of the
qualitative response to a problem whose quantitative
dimensions appear to be so meager?

One plausible explanation for overreactions can be
sought in the inadequacy of the statistical information
itself. The lack of concrete data defining the actual
parameters of unemployment produced a climate of rampant
speculation and overreaction. During the late 1870's and
early 1880's when the unemployment problem was presumably at
its zenith, data with which to determine its precise extent
was not available. The only national unemployment survey
during our period took place after the economy had begun to

recover from its "great depression". During twenty years of economic instability with no hard evidence about the extent of unemployment, cumulative fears about its consequences took on a reality of their own quite apart from actual work shortages. Because no one knew how much unemployment there was, it became easy to prey on ill-defined anxieties about loss of jobs among the working class and loss of property among the middle class. Both the fear of revolution and the haphazard measures to cope with problems related to job scarcity can be attributed to ignorance about the actual extent of unemployment between 1873 and 1913. Had the government taken greater pains to collect, analyze and publicize unemployment statistics, Germans would undoubtedly have realized that a calm, methodical approach was indicated. In order to understand the climate of panic and knee-jerk responses which unemployment elicited, it is necessary to examine the extent of contemporary knowledge about their own situation. Let us begin by considering the accuracy of available unemployment statistics.

One crucial question in determining the accuracy of any quantitative data involves clarification of precisely who was counted as unemployed. Consistency in criteria is one of the most important factors in arriving at figures which are comparable with each other. But over a forty-year period that witnessed a hodgepodge of efforts to poll the unemployed in a myriad of jurisdictions, this problem presented considerable difficulties. Fortunately, however, there were certain shared assumptions which made the dilemma easier to resolve.

First of all, there was widespread recognition of the fact that a small amount of unemployment--usually between two and three percent--was an inevitable byproduct of the operation of the industrial marketplace[1]. This was the standard against which most impartial observers gauged the severity of the unemployment that they hoped to combat. The detachment which that judgment entailed was not always shared by those more intimately acquainted with the unemployment situation. Although society as a whole was prepared to accept a three percent unemployment rate even during good years, for the individual who had to cope directly with the loss of his job, no amount of unemployment could be tolerated. The social injustice occasioned by a work shortage lay precisely in the fact that it was seldom distributed equitably. A few individuals suffered intensely while the vast majority got by totally unscathed. Whether or not one was among the fortunate masses who escaped or the unfortunate few who were engulfed by unemployment greatly affected the degree to which one thought "society" ought to suffer the malaise.

For those facing the prospect of unemployment, the question of culpability frequently arose in conjunction with efforts to obtain relief. The consensus that only "unverschuldet" individuals should qualify for assistance was practically universal and the assumption that those same individuals were the only ones who ought to be counted as unemployed was almost as pervasive. The criteria for differentiating between the culpable and innocent victims of unemployment were outlined quite clearly in this excerpt from the 1895/96 volume of Soziale Praxis[2]:

> Als verschuldet arbeitslos sind diejenigen anzusehen, die infolge freiwilligen Austrittes stellenlos geworden sind, die infolge von Lohnstreitigkeit ihre Stelle aufgegeben, und die ihre Entlassung durch Faulheit, Liederlichkeit, Unvertraeglichkeit, Ungehorsam oder Trunksucht herbeigefuehrt haben. Also der Arbeiter, der aus einer Stelle ausscheidet, weil er eine ihm zugemuthete Verschlechterung der Arbeitsbedingungen (Erhoehung der Arbeitszeit, Herabsetzung des Lohnes) ablehnt, ist durch sein eigenes Verschulden arbeitslos geworden.

Among all victims of unemployment, those unwilling to work because of laziness evoked the most scorn and severest punishments. Designated as "Arbeitsscheu" or work-shy, these individuals frequently resorted to begging and were rewarded for their efforts with incarceration and treatment as criminals. Unlike the work-shy who were universal social outcasts, those involved in labor disputes evoked a mixed response from surveyors of the unemployment situation. Both strikers and men affected by lockouts which originated with management were generally excluded from the ranks of the unemployed. The rationale behind this attitude was that willingness to work constituted a fundamental criteria of unemployment.

One way of differentiating between those who were anxious to work and those who were inactive by preference was to look at the duration of their idleness. Dr. Arthur

Gruenspan in a 1911 article published by <u>Soziale</u> <u>Praxis</u> suggested that recent data showed prolonged unemployment becoming increasingly scarce. Unlike legitimate claimants, individuals who were loathe to work tended to maintain their inactivity as long as possible. The logical conclusion, therefore, was that those unemployed for extended periods of time--in excess of one year for example--were likely to include a high proportion of lazy persons.

To complicate the issue still further we must also consider the case of laborers who were ready and willing to work but concluded that suitable positions were unavailable. Hidden unemployment among women, younger males and older men was prevalent because such marginal workers were the first to be laid off and the last to be hired when economic times were tough[3]. Even for those anxious to avoid unemployment, willingness to work was usually conditional. Variables such as salary, hours, location and type of employment were only a few of the more universal determinants of a person's eagerness to accept a specific job. Not all potential employees were suited to all available positions, and the problem of finding the right person for the right job remained complex. Suitable employment at an acceptable wage required matching individual requirements of employers and employees in each instance. This was precisely the function of the labor exchanges which emerged during the 1890's. Prior to that time, however, chaos reigned in the labor market during periods when the supply of and demand for workers were grossly out of balance with one another.

In addition to a willingness to work, those designated as unemployed had to exhibit a need for paid employment. Individuals with independent means either from personal wealth or pensions were excluded from the ranks of the unemployed. In this context, another criterion is pertinent--the ability to work was a crucial determinant of whether a person counted as unemployed. Invalids, the infirm, disabled, those too young or too old to work, and widows with dependent children were usually excluded from unemployment counts during the early years of our period although some of these persons came to be incorporated into later surveys. As with willingness to work, the question of duration was seen as an important determinant of whether a given disability precluded designation as unemployed. This posed certain problems because it was not always easy to specify the precise cause of idleness at any given point in time. Distinctions between those unemployed for economic reasons and those not working because of illness or disability were difficult in some cases. There was a broad consensus that only persons willing and physically able to work should be counted as unemployed[4].

In addition to being willing and able to work, those designated as unemployed had actually to be without jobs. Although that seems self-evident, categories such as seasonal workers and the amorphous group of "Gelegenheitsarbeiter" posed problems in this context. Independent or self-employed workers also presented difficulties as we noted in the introduction. Those partially unemployed in the sense of working fewer hours, receiving less pay or being forced into unproductive lines of employment were extremely hard to isolate but they required treatment as a discrete group. As the following statement from Soziale Praxis indicates, there was a considerable body of laborers which defied classification as either unemployed or under-employed in the sense of working shorter hours[5].

> Zwischen beiden Klassen steht noch die Klasse der Aushilfsarbeiter, die sich nur gewaltsam unter den einen oder anderen der beiden Begriffe bringen lassen und, streng genommen, eine Sonderbehandlung erheischen. Zu ihnen gehoert jenes Heer von Aushilfkellnern, -friseuren, -koechen, -musikern, die staendig zwischen voelliger Arbeitslosigkeit und Aushilfsbeschaeftigung hin und her pendeln.

While being without a job was a necessary precondition for unemployment, it was not sufficient in and of itself. A Saxon unemployment count undertaken in 1911 listed a number of groups which, although without jobs, did not qualify for enumeration in their survey. These included pensioners, persons of independent means, individuals unfit for work, and casual laborers[6]. It turned out that something in excess of 8000 Saxon residents who lacked paid positions were not designated as unemployed by the first survey of an entire German state since the 1895 census. Given the criteria of unemployment outlined above, let us look more carefully at the primary sources in order to gain a fuller understanding of contemporary knowledge about work shortages.

There are irreparable gaps in the primary sources relating to unemployment during our period which bear careful scrutiny. In this context it is necessary to form a backdrop against which to measure the problems posed by the sources upon which our study is based. The sheer volume of marginally pertinent material combined with the scarcity of directly relevant information makes the inquiry inherently perilous. Much of the difficulty stems from the dispersement of documents. Prior to the 1890's, very few examples of regionally based data are available and with the single exception of the 1895 census no nationally comprehensive figures were collected. Although we attempt to deal with a forty-year period, continuity of quantitative information was unheard of prior to the Reichsarbeitsblatt's publication in 1903. Only after that date can we speak with any semblance of certainty about the numbers affected by unemployment. In addition to the Reichsarbeitsblatt and the Sozialpolitisches Centralblatt (later Soziale Praxis) which began publication in 1892, a number of municipal dailies and weeklies intermittently published scattered data on unemployment.

Handelskammer reports from various industrial centers provide some additional clues as do the archives of the largest private firms such as the Gutehoffnungshutte, Krupp, Siemens and Borsig. It is likely that they would shed considerable light on the unemployment problem from the perspective of management rather than labor. Efforts to divert layoffs by resorting to reduced wages and hours, claims of suspended workers finding almost immediate alternate employment and condescending expressions of paternal interest in employees' well-being dotted the reports which local authorities passed from businessmen to bureaucratic officials in Berlin. The same tone and overall impression would probably be reinforced by inclusion of more information preserved by entrepreneurs and their organizational extensions. Their exclusion here tends to focus our concern more directly on the unemployment problem from the vantage point of those immediately affected--the industrial labor force itself.

The bulk of unpublished data used in this paper is extrapolated from the state archives of East and West Germany. Much of the material consists of handwritten reports on various aspects of labor conditions. Among the myriad details collected under the umbrella heading "Lage der Industrie" were substantial bodies of information on layoffs, cutbacks, strikes, institutional relief measures for jobless individuals, wages and hours, the right to work, changes in the number employed, census results, unions, insurance, labor productivity, business and market conditions. From this potpourri of socio-economic data now scattered across two nations, we shall attempt to reconstruct the specifics of the unemployment situation in Germany.

In addition to archival sources, there were a number of monographs on unemployment which began to appear with growing frequency during the 1890's. The overwhelming majority of these focused on relief through assorted insurance schemes which never materialized during our period. Some raised issues related to methodological problems in general and the dearth of statistics in particular. During the 1870's and 1880's there was also a considerable literature produced on the subjects of poverty, vagabondage and begging. Many of these and subsequent publications were devoted to seeking institutional or collective remedies for socially related problems occasioned by a lack of employment--through labor colonies, labor exchanges, Herbergen zur Heimat or Naturalverpflegungsstationen.

Certain pitfalls present themselves in relying on these findings. The most obvious danger derives from using statistics gathered for other purposes as an index of unemployment. The primary shortcoming of such figures stems from insufficient differentiation of the unemployed as a discrete analytical category. Labor exchange statistics, for example, list all applicants for employment without distinguishing between those already working but anxious to change jobs or those seeking a second occupation to supplement their income and others looking for work as an alternative to idleness. In other words, presently employed, partially unemployed and totally jobless individuals searching for new positions are all lumped together in the exchange figures. As a result, those figures provide a more accurate reading on prospects for labor mobility than on unemployment per se. With regard to statistics on begging, the question of whether individuals chose that lifestyle or resorted to it out of desperation stemming from an inability to find work is central for our purposes. The same applies to numbers dealing with recipients of poor relief--the cause of poverty may have been economically induced unemployment. But relief also could have been necessitated by illness, old age, loss of parents or spouses, insanity and a number of other problems which had nothing to do with unemployment. In very few instances are beneficiaries categorized on the basis of the source of their need.

In the case of sickness insurance, it was a widely recognized and much lamented fact that the number of claims increased significantly during periods of high unemployment. Health insurance was thus deemed to be a periodic albeit involuntary source of unemployment relief. Unfortunately those motivated by economic rather than physical suffering were not anxious to cooperate in efforts to differentiate themselves from the majority of legitimate claimants under the health insurance program. In every branch of social insurance, there was concern about weeding out unworthy applicants. However, their total elimination was an impossible feat which most contemporaries noted with regret and ultimately accepted. As these examples illustrate, diverse statistics from labor exchanges, poor relief, begging and health insurance should not be used interchangeably with unemployment figures. Although they provide essential indirect indications of short-term trends, they cannot be accepted at face value as accurate reflections of industrial unemployment.

The objections outlined above do not take into consideration inaccuracies inherent in these numbers. Statistical errors derived either inadvertently from inadequate methods of counting or more insidiously from the political and economic self-interest of those gathering the data. A particularly unsavory source of error was the political pressure attendant upon unemployment counts such as the one undertaken in Dresden during 1892. The local police there openly tried to interfere with Social Democratic attempts to collect and publicize unemployment statistics. Events in Dresden cannot be viewed as an extreme instance of abuse since the problem recurred in other German cities including Magdeburg during January of 1908. In fact there was widespread apprehension over the political sensitivity of unemployment statistics which led to efforts to suppress their collection and subsequent dissemination especially during recessions.

In an article published in _Soziale Praxis_ during the first economically severe interlude of the present century, Stadtrath Dr. Flesch of Frankfurt indicated that in the past unemployment statistics had been used by workers as a polemical tool which lent credence to their demands for assistance through labor exchanges. According to Dr. Flesch[7]:

> Die Existenz des Uebels der Arbeitslosigkeit braucht nicht mehr bewiesen zu werden; die Erfahrungen der Arbeitsnachweise ergeben klar, dass die industrielle "Reservearmee" vorhanden ist, dass sogar in regelmaessigen Zeiten es nicht immer Muessiggaenger oder untuechtige Arbeiter sind, die keine Arbeit finden. Die Streitfrage, ob die Zahl der Arbeitslosen an sich wesentlich groesser ist als in den Vorjahren, hat relativ untergeordnetes Interesse.

The irony of the last statement must be noted in passing. Precisely when the polemical value of specific unemployment data was deemed to have expired, the Reichsarbeitsblatt began to provide the first continuous figures. It was probably not accidental that the initial appearance of reliable statistics coincided with the view that they had been defused as a political weapon in the arsenal of organized labor. Despite Dr. Flesch's claim, statistical findings were subsequently pressed into service more vehemently than ever by those agitating for unemployment insurance.

With regard to the scattered figures available prior to the twentieth century, their utility for our purposes depends on the groups which were counted and the categories into which surveyed individuals were placed. The tendency to select a portion of any population and generalize from their responses to certain inquiries was commonplace during our period as it is today. Before 1913, however, it was done with far less scientific concern for selecting truly random and representative samples from which to extrapolate information.

The extent to which estimates of unemployment could vary is illustrated by discrepancies between numbers offered by the Berlin Gewerkschaftskommission and Dr. Richard Freund, head of the labor exchanges in the capital as well as the national federation of exchanges. The Commission estimated that there were about 50,000 unemployed workers in Berlin during October of 1901 while Dr. Freund offered 35,000 as his best guess. Comparable discrepancies also occurred during the next economic downturn. In January of 1908 Vorwaerts published unemployment figures for the greater Berlin area of between fifty and sixty thousand while Dr. Freund placed the number at 30,000 and the Gewerkschaftskommission at 25,000 organized unemployed[8]. The difference between estimates derived from trade union data and those dependent upon public labor exchanges was considerable in both instances. In evaluating these numbers, it is important to note that neither the unions nor the exchanges ever had access to more than a third of Germany's industrial labor force during our period. The margin for error was therefore substantial. Such discrepancies compounded by huge gaps in available data go far to explain contemporary confusion about the actual extent of unemployment.

Within the ranks underrepresented in most unemployment counts were dependent family members including women and children, non-union workers, and part-time employees. The extent to which any or all of these groups was included in unemployment surveys affected the outcome to some degree. But the largest single factor in unemployment during our period was seasonally related. Those involved in agriculture, forestry, construction, shipping, mining and so-called Verkehrsgewerbe suffered rates of unemployment during their slack periods which were many times greater than workers in other areas. Unemployment in seasonal trades was caused by weather rather than market conditions and considerable distortion resulted from lumping all workers together. At times--for example during 1905--when lack of jobs in industries not affected by the weather averaged less than three percent, those in seasonal trades were plagued by nearly five times as much unemployment.

Given such disparities, which were by no means unusual, it is far more important to note the differences among occupations than attempt to iron them out by averaging conflicting sets of figures. While a majority of sectors exhibited relatively constant unemployment rates of roughly two to four percent, a number of seasonal trades evinced wide fluctuations, which if incorporated into figures for the labor force as a whole would give a misleading impression of changes in the rate of unemployment. In addition to seasonal differences, periodization, social attitudes, political apathy, variations in definitions and a reluctance to acknowledge existence of the problem all affected unemployment statistics. According to John Garraty, such weaknesses in statistical technique almost invariably resulted in underestimating the number of unemployed individuals at any given time[9].

Keeping this tendency to underrate the problem in mind, let us turn our attention to specific methodological errors in unemployment counts during our period. Since changes in levels of employment have been used with such frequency by East German historians to underpin claims of high unemployment, it is worth noting certain variations in measurements of industrial employment. The two primary methods of counting and the divergent results which they yielded are described below[10]:

> The occupational census (Berufszaehlung) questioned each person as to his occupation. The industrial census (Betriebszaehlung, Gewerbezaehlung) took the firm as the unit of enumeration and asked the number of employees in each. Since individuals were not asked whether they were actually employed and to what extent, the occupational census overstated employment. More serious is the problem of the distribution of employment between industries. A person whose occupation would seem to place him in one industry may actually be employed in another, for instance a woodworker employed in the metal industry. One of Germany's greatest statisticians asserted that the "great mass" of industrial workers were unable to tell correctly in what industry they were employed.

In addition to the maldistribution of individuals stemming from the workers' own confusion about which occupational category they belonged to, note must be taken of the complications derived from secondary employment and labor turnover.

Another serious methodological problem stems from the techniques employed in single counts versus those used in multiple surveys over time. Periodization is a crucial factor in the historical analysis of any problem and unemployment is certainly no exception. If, for example, we select a time frame which can be subdivided into two eras of rapid expansion in employment and one intervening span of much slower growth, the middle interval is likely to look worse than it really was by contrast with what came before and after. This is perhaps one reason why the retarded growth of the years 1873 to 1896 has been labeled a Great Depression. For perspective here, we might consider whether the same designation that was applied to the 1930's suits our period as well. In terms of unemployment, the answer as we shall see must be a resounding negative.

The question of periodization in the usual sense of the term did not apply with great frequency to unemployment counts undertaken in Germany prior to the turn of the century. Most unemployment surveys were isolated tallies which collected data on conditions at a single point in time. They rarely included follow-up studies which would have permitted contemporaries to draw conclusions about the cause, duration or continued probability of unemployment. During an era when labor turnover especially among the unskilled was presumed to be high and when frequent job changes were accompanied by brief intervals of unemployment, such shortcomings were particularly regrettable.[11]

Perhaps the most important prerequisite for using single counts to draw general conclusions about unemployment is sufficient information on the specific point in time at which the survey occurred. One must then be able to relate that historical instant to a larger time frame in order to project what the figures meant in terms of preceding and successive intervals. This is especially important with regard to the 1895 census, conducted in both June and December, because it gives us the most comprehensive picture of unemployment during the period under consideration. The fact that that census was taken in two parts created special problems but it was clearly intended to form a single count with corrections for seasonal fluctuations. Here at least there was some opportunity to properly evaluate those short term unemployed who would subsequently find work and disappear from the statistics if the survey were undertaken a few weeks or months later.

While single surveys without follow-ups presented problems of the sort outlined above, different pitfalls awaited those relying on figures collected over considerable periods. To cite the example of employment statistics again, variations in categories, weather conditions, economic realities and methodological sophistication were among the more irksome discrepancies which made it difficult to compare figures collected at different times. Dangers which plagued both single and periodic surveys ranged from omitting certain individuals entirely to counting others incorrectly or more than once. Residence affected the outcome of unemployment surveys too. People who lived in one geographical area and commuted to work in another were problematic as were non-heads of households whose number was consistently underestimated. Domestic servants residing in their employers' homes posed persistent dilemmas as did all workers whose jobs failed to fit neatly into preconceived categories. Errors in the lists of those to be counted, clerical inaccuracies and false registrations were among the other problems encountered in household surveys of the unemployed.

These potential sources of error were important because they added to contemporary confusion about the extent of unemployment. Unreliable data, insufficient methodological sophistication and inadequate statistics made it easy to exaggerate or underestimate the unemployment problem in accordance with one's needs. The labor situation could thus be exploited by anyone seeking to further or frustrate working-class aspirations. Pathetically little hard evidence was available for those seeking simply to understand the situation by determining how much unemployment there actually was. For that, Germans believed they needed to collect statistics and after 1890 we finally begin to get specific unemployment surveys. Prior to 1890, however, we are left to consider alternate indicators of the extent of work shortages in German industry during years of severe economic hardship. Even with the use of data on employment, wages, prices and consumption which contribute important information, contemporary observers and professional historians have produced a fragmented portrait of unemployment. The decentralized, unsystematic nature of collecting statistics has taken its toll on all assessments of the problem.

CONFLICTING ESTIMATES OF UNEMPLOYMENT IN THE SECONDARY
LITERATURE

In view of gaps in the primary sources, it is not
surprising that unemployment among German industrial workers
between 1873 and 1913 has been treated in a sketchy and
inconsistent manner by historians. Most western scholars--
German, American and British--who have addressed the problem
at all indicate the dearth of underlying quantitative data
which forms a prerequisite for time series analysis. They
refer to the 1895 census, the only national unemployment
survey undertaken during our period, and conclude primarily
from it that aggregate unemployment prior to World War I
remained under three percent. This of course ignores
sizable and largely undisputed variations among regions,
classes and industries over a forty-year period of uneven
social and economic change. It also begs the question of
labor mobility and turnover.

To cite a recent example, the Handbuch der
deutschen Wirtschafts- und Sozialgeschichte[12] acknowledges
that by the end of our period millions of workers changed
jobs annually and in the process experienced short intervals
of unemployment. Unfortunately, however, the Handbuch does
not go on to emphasize the widespread effect those pervasive
but brief interludes had on the working populace. Although
subjected to the uncertainties and vicissitudes of idleness
only for small stretches at any given time, the recurrent
threat of loss of employment had far-flung repercussions on

the mentality and outlook of the labor force. To gloss over this fact and merely refer to a three percent unemployment rate gives a distorted picture of the extent to which conditions in the labor market impinged on the lives of the broad mass of industrial workers.

Perhaps one reason why the unemployment problem hasn't received more satisfactory treatment from western historians stems from the historiographical tradition of analysis from above. Until quite recently[13], very few non-Marxist historians have focused on problems affecting the daily existence of Germany's labor force or changes in its condition over extended periods of time. Neither the elitist perspective nor the static approach of most western historiography has lent itself to fruitful inquiries about unemployment.

In line with Marxist expectations about the deterioration of conditions among the proletariat under industrial capitalism, East German scholarship has advanced some isolated statistics which challenge complacent western assumptions about unemployment. DDR historians explicitly refute the notion that an accurate picture of the situation is conveyed by the statement that unemployment during our period rarely exceeded three percent. Hans Mottek, for example, cites[14] one study of employment in the Berlin iron industry during the 1870's and uses the telling phrase "further increases of unemployment through layoffs". Mottek extrapolates figures from a doctoral dissertation by

Johannes Roessler which focuses on the Berlin labor force. According to Roessler, workers in the capital suffered from an appalling onslaught of underemployment, reaching levels in excess of one quarter of the entire labor force involved in industry and handicrafts. In addition to Roessler, Mottek cites a work by Polish historians[15] who have traced cutbacks in the labor forces of individual industries in less populous regions. To show that unemployment existed outside of large cities, Mottek focuses primarily on Silesia and the textile industry, again offering examples of reduced employment through layoffs. Based on relatively isolated data, he refers in general terms to "Massenentlassungen und Massenarbeitslosigkeit".

Although the east-west dichotomy outlined here holds in general terms, the distinction blurs at certain points. Take for example the following excerpt from a recent work by Martin Kitchen on political economy in Germany which accepts Roessler's figures and Mottek's interpretation of them at face value[16].

> With high unemployment and the outlawing of the socialist unions and party, the working class had little chance but to accept a steady worsening of their position. With falling prices improving the real wages, <u>the main problem for the working class was unemployment</u>. As firms cut back their work force and the population continued to rise, unemployment reached appalling levels. In Berlin in 1879 more than 25 percent of the industrial labourers were unemployed.
>
> Unemployment, cartelization, falling prices and the failure of many firms seemed to be an indication that German industrial capitalism was collapsing from a surfeit of success.

Noteworthy here is the way in which the author unquestioningly translates population increases and cut-backs in the work force of individual firms into unemployment estimates. One problem inherent in equating statistics on layoffs, insurance or employment with unemployment is that it ignores the myriad alternatives to idleness offered by the German economy and society during our period. Those who lost industrial jobs could frequently fall back on a variety of substitute remedies: Agriculture, piece-work at home, domestic service, publicly funded projects or self-employment[17]. In addition there was the crucial remedy of shifts in population through overseas migration and domestic relocation.

Unfortunately for anyone seeking an accurate assessment of work shortage during the 1870's from the Marxist literature, persons laid off from jobs in one locale at a given point in time did not automatically translate into chronic cases of unemployment. During a period of economic transition when movement between predominantly industrial and rural areas was commonplace, fragmentary employment figures distort the sparse statistical picture to an unacceptable degree. Like the western historians, Mottek uses statistics that underrate migration and labor mobility. His approach ignores the sizable number of reported layoffs which were accompanied by indications of subsequent employment. Like his colleague, Juergen Kuczynski, Mottek tends to use the terms layoff and unemployment almost interchangeably and argues that both conditions reached chronic proportions during the late 1870's.

As Kuczynski has emphasized, cut-backs in work were not confined to lay-offs and unemployment. Underemployment and reduced hours were commonly implemented techniques which enabled employers to get through slack periods without relinquishing the services of skilled employees whose output would be in demand once economic conditions improved. Rather than seeing this as an effort to curtail unemployment, the Marxist historians view reduced hours and wages as a selfish move of bourgeois capitalists which further oppressed the labor force by robbing additional workers of needed income. Partial cutbacks admittedly led to a decline in real wages and they are used by East German historians to support the contention that the general lot of the worker deteriorated with industrialization. Because Kuczynski reluctantly acknowledges that the cost of living declined more than the wages of fully employed workers, the high proportion of unemployed and underemployed laborers is essential to his polemic.

Referring to evidence from Handelskammer reports, Mottek maintains that even such biased, management-inspired data fails to support the contention that the workers' lot improved during the 1870's[18]. In his words: "Entscheidend bleibt jedoch, dass die Grunderdepression 1873 bis 1879 mit einer Massenarbeitslosigkeit verbunden war, dass sie zu einer starken Verminderung des Realeinkommens, der

Arbeiterklasse fuhrt."[19] The mass unemployment to which Mottek refers is claimed to have given employers an additional unfair advantage over their men. By preying on an employee's fear of losing his job at a time when work was scarce, management, according to Mottek, was able to impose outrageous conditions on the terms of employment. Extra hours and reduced wages were deemed to be the most common abuses. These in turn elicited a socialist response to unemployment in the form of political appeals to the working classes and subsequent repression by the government.

One of the prime bones of contention between Marxist and western historians involves changes in the workers' standard of living which resulted from industrialization. The absence of continuous hard data facilitating the development of time series for wages, hours and essential determinants of the cost of living have created a stalemate in the controversy over most of the years between 1850 and 1914. Both the early and later parts of the period have been dealt with at length by advocates of the two competing approaches. The lack of hard data for the middle decades of the 1870's and 1880's however make them a cesspool of ideologically motivated claims and counterclaims about changes in German industrial workers' economic and social situation. Nowhere is this more apparent than in discussions of unemployment where speculation in the absence of statistical underpinnings has run rampant.

In explaining the divergence between Eastern and Western estimates of unemployment, one can point an accusing finger at ideological differences. Or one can attribute the dichotomy to the dearth of quantitative data which has survived from the period. The haphazard and uneven nature of the figures lends itself to speculation. There has been a longstanding effort to justify such indulgence by lambasting economic history's overreliance on statistics and quantification as a method of analysis. The following excerpt from the Handbuch der deutschen Wirtschafts- und Sozialgeschichte reflects an apparent willingness to forego statistically sound underpinnings in discussing unemployment. Knut Borchardt casually notes that unusually high levels of unemployment were a characteristic feature of the Grunderkrise which set it apart from other periods: "Zwar haben wir hierfuer keine statistischen Nachweisungen, doch belegen zeitgenoessische Zeugnisse dies ebenso, wie eine Ueberlegung die Annahme einer relativ hohen Arbeitslosigkeit nahelegt."[20] Supposedly as evidence, Borchardt offers the following graph extrapolated from the work of Kuczynski.[21]

Aktienkurse und Arbeitslosenquote 1870—1913

(nach Stat. Bundesamt und J. Kuczynski)

The graph illustrates in pictorial terms what the problem is--a dearth of concrete evidence prior to the late 1880's. It suggests an inverse variance between the two curves which might be used to infer trends for the earlier years. And this is precisely what the East Germans have done with regard to the late 1870's. Given the dearth of hard data at this point, however, speculative hypotheses about vast amounts of unemployment would be difficult to prove.

There are some historians who put scant faith in numbers as reflections of past reality. In a recent article on fluctuations in the Wurttemberg economy during the 1870's, the West German historian Volker Hentschel came out strongly against the tendency to overquantify economic analysis. On the dangers of downplaying qualitative assessment in favor of quantification, he had this to say[22]:

> Das im kern gewiss nicht unberechtigte Bestreben, alles in Mark und Meter, Tonnen und Quoten formulieren zu koennen, bringt zwei Gefahren. Die eine habe ich am Beispiel des Werks von Hoffmann genannt die Rechnung wird mit sovielen Praemissen belastet, dass sie in sich zwar logisch, ihr Ergebnis aber eine Fiktion ist. Die zweite scheint mir nicht weniger unerfreulich zu sein. Die wirtschaftsgechichtliche Forschung wird auf Gebiete eingeengt, die ausreichend Zahlenmaterial zur Verfue-gung halten. Die Rechnung stimmt, die Ergebnisse sind richtig--nur die Relation zwischen Aufwand und histor-ischer Bedeutsamkeit ist auf der Strecke geblieben.

Similar sentiments on the subject of quantification were expressed during our period. One contemporary observer noted that although statistics failed to document unemploy-ment which was either prevalent or critical, workers saw the pinch engendered by a threatened loss of work all around them. So whether or not they were directly affected they lived with the fear of unemployment occasioned by witnessing the destitution and humiliation which came in its wake.

Ultimately, those predisposed to see the suffering caused by an omnipresent threat of impinging economic disaster recognized it with or without statistical verification while those disposed in the opposite direction managed to ignore it. Nevertheless, it is important to emphasize that contemporary students of unemployment had an almost obsessive interest in obtaining an accurate quantitative assessment of the problem. The gathering of numbers was considered an indispensable prerequisite for policy decisions. And it seems reasonable to postulate that the lack of hard data was at least partially responsible for official hesitation to act decisively to eliminate unemployment.

Statistics were used in efforts to convince Germans who remained untouched between 1873 and 1913 that unemployment posed a serious problem. Although well motivated, such attempts were viewed with skepticism by some workers as the following excerpt from an 1892 publication in Hamburg shows[23].

> Dem Arbeiter braucht man keine Vorlesungen darueber zu halten, dass die Arbeitslosigkeit gross ist; er weiss es, sieht es taeglich um sich herum; fuer ihn bedarf es keiner ziffermaessigen Belege dafuer; ohne Kenntniss der Zahl seiner leidenden Kollegen fuehlt er die angeheure Groesse der Noth.

Numbers, in other words, were thought to be less telling than the interpretations attached to them. And by the late nineteenth century observers were wise enough to recognize that statistics lent themselves to manipulation. Actual experience and personal observations were at least as important as printed figures in determining contemporary reactions to unemployment. Given the scarcity of reliable data, subjective readings of the situation took on added significance.

In historiographical terms, it seems evident that neither the Eastern nor Western posture satisfactorily resolves the question of how much employment there was in Germany between 1873 and 1913. Nor do they explain contemporary responses to unemployment or efforts to eliminate the attendant problems. In order to overcome the deficiencies of both methods, we need a more variegated approach to an issue complicated by regional differences, ongoing economic development, demographic shifts and changing policy decisions. An attempt to differentiate among workers in urban and rural areas, heavy as opposed to light industry, union and unorganized trades, seasonal and year-round occupations, skilled and unskilled jobs will be adopted here. In lieu of unsatisfactory attempts to generalize about unemployment in terms which blur or iron out important distinctions, a fresh approach is indicated. The subject requires a treatment which reflects the historical diversity of problems handled by numerous local authorities adopting myriad short-term solutions to meet the immediate needs of the unemployed.

It is our contention that the same statistics which register a three percent unemployment rate overall will, when broken down and analyzed, reveal patterns of distribution that go far to explain the anxieties inconsistent with less specific scrutiny of the historical situation. In other words, it is not necessary to foreshorten one's perspective or distort the level of unemployment by adopting unsound methods as the Marxists have done with respect to the years between 1873 and 1886. Nor is it necessary to underrate available economic indicators and dismiss the unemployment problem with a generalization about three percent levels prior to World War I.

As this chapter is intended to show, a more satisfactory approach to existing quantitative data is to use it in analyzing variegated patterns of unemployment both with respect to the individuals directly affected and the broad contours of a changing economy. It is our intent to demonstrate with statistical analysis that the reaction to unemployment was conditioned by its distribution, duration, timing, predictability, risk and recurrence. A changing matrix of work shortage produced uncertainty and a feeling verging on panic which cannot be explained exclusively in terms of aggregate levels of unemployment.

In analyzing subsequent data, we shall try to work out a methodology for dealing with unemployment statistics in a more comprehensive manner than has yet emerged from the competitive historiographical traditions of East and West Germany. Extant figures, particularly those from the early years of our period, have been used to produce divergent and inherently contradictory estimates of unemployment. Large gaps in the body of directly relevant quantitative data have led historians to rely in varying degrees on indirect indicators of the extent of unemployment. Among the possible alternate indices are figures on wages, population, migration, begging, poor relief, insurance claims, labor exchanges, consumption and employment. The extent to which one weights or validates each of these will determine the emergent patterns of unemployment during periods for which more reliable numbers are lacking.

EMPLOYMENT, WAGES, PRICES AND CONSUMPTION PATTERNS AS
ALTERNATE INDICATORS OF UNEMPLOYMENT

In lieu of hard data on industrial unemployment
during the early years of our period, historians have looked
at other statistics as indirect evidence of conditions in
the labor market. To illustrate the potential contribution
of such information for our purposes, we might consider the
way various analysts have used employment figures to arrive
at estimates of unemployment. In addition, we shall briefly
assess the value of alternate indicators of work scarcity
such as wages, prices and consumption patterns. It is our
contention that the numbers which follow in this section do
no more than give approximate reflections of variable trends
in the marketplace that affected unemployment.

Employment

One of the most obvious and problematic indications of unemployment during much of our period was the body
of statistics on changes in employment. Between 1873 and
1913 a number of attempts were made to count those employed
in various industries. Two methods of estimating employment
levels involved the use of figures from accident insurance
and factory inspection reports. A third method relying on
occupational or industrial census data will receive more
attention here because it has the advantage of providing
clues during the early years of our period when direct
indicators were sorely lacking. It was only after 1895 when
more relevant information was already available that

insurance and factory inspection began to provide indications of employment levels in Germany. While the insurance
statistics overestimated employment in industries such as
construction where a high level of labor mobility was
involved, factory inspectors' numbers corresponded quite
well with those of census takers. It is to the latter form
of employment index that we shall now turn our attention.

Occupational census figures were frequently
collected as an adjunct to more traditional population
surveys. The first national effort to determine the occupational distribution of the German populace during our period
took place on December 1, 1875. Subsequent counts were
conducted during June of 1882, 1895 and 1907. It is significant that the only comprehensive survey dealing with
unemployment per se was broken down into two parts, one
counting jobless individuals during June and the other
during December of 1895. This dual polling technique
reflected a growing awareness of the seasonal nature of
fluctuations in the German labor market. Winter counts
tended to show employment at its nadir in most industries
and the rate of joblessness at its zenith; summer surveys
did the exact opposite.

Although the census figures were fairly comprehensive and accurately recorded, errors occurred in
categorizing both jobs and individuals. As we noted
earlier, those working at more than a single occupation and
those employed in sectors which were difficult to classify

presented special problems. Classifications, despite the aforementioned drawbacks, were reasonably consistent throughout our period which is amazing in view of the tremendous economic changes which impinged on the labor market over those years. To the extent that confusion arose, it could be traced at least in part to different methods of counting.

The Berufszaehlung or occupational census questioned individual workers about their sources of employment while the Betriebs- or Gewerbezaehlung used a microeconomic approach, polling employees in individual firms to determine the numbers working in each industry. As we noted earlier, the former method tended to overestimate the amount of employment. The occupational census failed to specify the extent to which persons who classified themselves as members of a certain profession were actually engaged in that capacity. There was no minimum number of hours per week which a laborer who registered in a given industry had to actually work. The distinction became particularly vague with regard to irregular assistance rendered by family members who pitched in to provide occasional but necessary relief in areas ranging from agriculture to cottage industries or shopkeeping. The occupational census led to a higher proportion of workers assigning themselves to the industrial sector than to other types of employment, thus telling us something about labor's self-image as well as its actual distribution in the economy.

The following graph shows the variable rates of
expansion in industrial employment between 1849 and 1913.
Mining and salt works are classified along with agriculture
as "primary" industries--concerned with the extraction of
natural resources. Here industry and handicrafts are
treated as a single category which includes smelting,
manufacturing, construction and transportation[24]. While
employment in industry had reached one-third of the 1913
level by the mid-nineteenth century and one-half of that
level by 1880, mining employed only one-ninth of its 1913
labor force in 1850 and did not reach the half-way mark
until 1895. At the turn of the century, industry had
attained 80 percent of the 1913 total while mining had
reached two-thirds of its peak figure[25]. The following
chart reflects these movements[26].

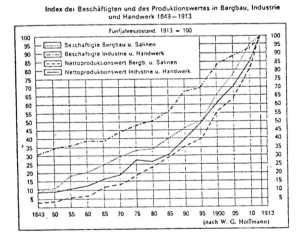

Index der Beschäftigten und des Produktionswertes in Bergbau, Industrie
und Handwerk 1849–1913

The relatively level slope of the curve for industrial
employment during the 1870's and the precipitous rises
during the last halves of both the 1880's and 1890's were

particularly noteworthy. Even more dramatic, however, was the manner in which the number of workers employed in mining took off after 1895.

The preceding estimates are important as indirect indicators of work shortages because the quantity of unemployment at any given time was equal to the number of would-be wage earners minus the quantity of employment. According to the Handbuch der deutschen Wirtschafts- und Sozialgeschichte, the percentage of the total German population which was actively employed during our period averaged about 45 percent. Despite a major population increase, this percentage made modest gains between 1850 and 1913. By 1907 the industrial labor force of approximately 20 million constituted a third of the entire population. With this in mind, we might consider the expansion of employment which occurred in the German economy as a whole between 1873 and 1913.

W.G. Hoffmann estimated that the annual percentage increases in employment during our period were as follows[27]:

1873--1.9	1880--0.4	1890--1.3	1900--1.4	1910--1.2
1874--1.8	1881--0.5	1891--0.5	1901--0.3	1911--0.9
1875--1.8	1883--1.1	1892--0.5	1902--1.0	1912--2.0
1876--1.3	1883--1.2	1893--0.7	1903--1.9	1913--2.5
1877--1.1	1884--1.2	1894--1.5	1904--1.8	
1878--0.9	1885--0.7	1895--1.5	1905--1.4	
1879--1.4	1886--1.9	1896--2.1	1906--1.9	
	1887--1.4	1897--1.7	1907--1.6	
	1888--1.6	1898--1.8	1908--0.7	
	1889--2.2	1899--1.5	1909--1.5	

The sharp drop which set in during 1876 and the unusually low rates of expansion in employment which prevailed for the next 10 years--until 1886--signalled conditions which were conducive to high unemployment. This long interval of diminished growth in employment contrasted sharply with the increases which had occurred during the early seventies. It was followed by briefer but equally intense contractions from 1891 to 1894 and 1901 to 1903. Noteworthy setbacks also occurred in 1908 and 1911. While all of these interludes signalled potential increases in unemployment, none had the kind of deep or lasting impact of the prolonged slump which dominated the labor market during the late 1870's and early 1880's. Significantly, even that period failed to register an absolute decline in employment--during the worst years, the rate of growth diminished distinctly but negative rates were not forthcoming.

What is important from the vantage of unemployment is the annual rate of increase in employment relative to the steady rate of increase in Germany's population. Given the Reich's population growth, it is not unreasonable to postulate that the number of people looking for work expanded more rapidly than employment opportunities resulting in a net increase in unemployment during years when the preceding chart registered anything less than a 1.3 percent figure. To put this relationship into perspective, a brief overview of population growth might be helpful[28]. The German population between 1871 and 1910 increased by more than one-half, with urban areas registering consistently more than 100 percent gains. Berlin's population increased 150 percent,

Hamburg's practically doubled and the other Hanseatic cities underwent expansion which was only slightly less spectacular. While Prussia's population increased 62 percent, that figure camouflaged wide ranging differences. Industrial areas like the Rhineland and Westphalia grew at much faster rates but the agrarian districts of the eastern provinces barely made any gains at all. This fact is not surprising in view of the structural changes which accompained urbanization. The relationships among population, employment, volume of work and hours of work are shown in the following graph extrapolated from Hoffmann's data[29].

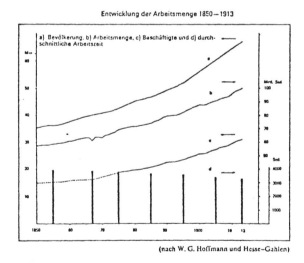

Entwicklung der Arbeitsmenge 1850—1913

(nach W. G. Hoffmann und Hesse–Gahlen)

It is to be noted in the preceding chart that hidden unemployment was disguised by discrepancies and irregularities in counts which failed to differentiate carefully enough between fully and partially productive members of the labor force. However, a tendency to underrate the contributions of women and children to a certain extent cancelled out the distortion which resulted from counting part-time help as full fledged employees.

In a similar manner, conflicting forces simultaneously operative in the labor market tended to produce a relatively stable unemployment picture during much of our period. While the changing structure of employment reflected an increasing number of wage earners moving into jobs which were susceptible to vicissitudes of the labor market, both seasonal unemployment in the sense of dependence on weather and other forms of longterm unemployment resulting from unclear market conditions or higher costs of labor mobility declined sharply in importance. According to Hoffmann, the average rate of increase in employment at 1.2 percent per year between 1850 and 1913 surpassed the annual population growth of one percent. This fact was of crucial importance for unemployment which would tend to decline if all other factors remained constant.

Different readings on the significance attached to employment figures have been a primary source of divergence in estimates of unemployment coming out of East and West Germany. Based largely on changes in employment over time, Marxist historians Juergen Kuczynski and Hans Mottek have ventured boldly into the realm of unemployment projections for periods in which the underlying data is alarmingly sparse. In contrast, more circumspect western economic historians such as the groups around W.G. Hoffmann and those responsible for the _Handbuch der deutschen Wirtschafts- und Sozialgeschichte_ have argued that long-term unemployment was contained at reasonable levels throughout our period. The pattern which emerges from western historiography is one of a relatively high labor turnover with attendant short spans of unemployment. The picture of unemployment which West German economic historians have derived from employment statistics is one of relative stability after 1886 with a three percent rate of joblessness persisting for most years. Around 1910, an estimated five million workers changed jobs annually and in the process experienced unemployment for intervals of two to three weeks[30]. From today's perspective, this sounds like turnover created by the normal operation of the market mechanism or so-called frictional unemployment, a derivative of the inevitable time lag or idleness that accompanies any form of labor mobility.

For the years prior to the mid-1880's, continuous data is scarce almost to the point of non-existence and the reliance on figures detailing changes in employment seems even more perilous. This, nevertheless, is the approach adopted by East German historians like Kuczynski and Mottek who have provided some bold estimates of rampant underemployment during the first part of our period. In the Marxist scheme of things, high unemployment during the 1870's played a major role in the crisis which marked the German economy's transition from free competetion to state monopoly capitalism. It was an important factor in the supposed deterioration of the industrial working class.

Trying to arrive at a set of numbers revealing net real wages in the 1870's, Kuczynski presented the following estimates of unemployment during the first seven years of our period[31].

> Nehmen wir als Neuverluste gegenueber 1872 durch Kurzarbeit bzw. Aufhoeren der Mehrarbeit und Arbeitslosigkeit an:
>
> | | | |
> |---|---|---|
> | 1873 - 1% | 1875 - 12% | 1878 - 5% |
> | 1874 - 10% | 1876 - 7% | 1879 - 2% |
> | | 1877 - 10% | |

For the years between 1879 and 1886 no specific estimates of unemployment were ventured but the implicit abatement was attributed to subsequent overseas migration. In volume three of his massive history of the conditions of German labor under capitalism, Kuczynski offered these assessments of unemployment between 1887 and 1900[32]:

1887 - 1.0%	1891 - 4.5%	1894 - 3.5%	1897 - 1.5%
1888 - 4.5%	1892 - 6.0%	1895 - 3.5%	1898 - 1.0%
1889 - 1.0%	1893 - 3.5%	1896 - 1.0%	1900 - 2.5%

Relying on Kuczynski's figures and scattered statistics on changes in employment during the 1870's, Hans Mottek has argued that underemployment reached epidemic proportions affecting 22 percent of the entire industrial labor force by 1879. In his study of the crisis following unification, he advances the claim in these terms: "insgesamt musste der Zuwachs der Industriearbeiterpotentials der moeglichen Beschaeftigung in der Industrie etwa 14 Prozent und die Unterbescaeftigung in der Industrie unter diesen Voraussetzungen etwa 22,1 Prozent betragen haben."[33] In his more comprehensive economic history of Germany, Mottek makes the additional argument that unemployment during the early 1880's would have been much more severe were it not for a massive exodus to the United States and a decline in the number of hours comprising the normal work week. He maintains that if these two factors had not come into play, unemployment in 1886 would have surpassed the exorbitant levels he believes were reached in 1879[34]. Relying on microeconomic data supplied by individual firms and multiplying examples of lay-offs, reduced hours and cut backs in employment, Mottek paints a remarkably grim and specific picture. His argument however relies on questionable methods.

It is not conclusive evidence to look at employment data in one or more isolated locales or industries and deduce conditions for the economy as a whole. Mottek's approach underestimates the impact of migration and alternate employment in other geographical and occupational areas. It also underrates the growing tendency among employers to stabilize their labor force by distributing the onus of reduced work more equitably through lower wages and hours rather than resorting to lay-offs. To point out that various statistics from Berlin, Silesia and other highly industrialized areas registered diminished employment does not automatically translate into mass unemployment for German industry as a whole. The tacit assumption that it does is untenable and casts severe doubts on the reliability of East German estimates of the situation during the 1870's.

To recapitulate, the picture which emerges from the East German reading of indirect indicators such as employment is one of massive work shortages as the severe economic crisis of the 1870's gains momentum and finally peaks at the end of the decade. When a second downturn occurred after a brief respite, the escalation of unemployment was curbed because pressures in the labor market were mitigated by reduced hours and emigration. By the time a third crisis threatened in the 1890's the economy had regained enough strength to prevent unemployment from rising above six percent. Rather than an era of Great Depression, we are thus left with a shortened period of crisis which had burnt itself out after a particularly intense run of unemployment between 1873 and 1879 and a second more limited episode ending in 1886. Here it is important to emphasize that Kuczynski's figures for the years after 1887 show little variation from western estimates of the problem as we move into an era when hard data is becoming increasingly available. What we are thrown back to is a divergent interpretation of the much more scanty information available for the period between 1873 and 1886. The Marxist historians have used employment statistics to paint the grimmest possible picture of unemployment and general working class misery during those years.

Western historians who have perhaps been overly circumspect in moving from employment statistics to unemployment projections tend to portray the years between 1873 and 1895 as a single whole subsumed under an umbrella term such as Great Depression or Great Price Deflation. Pointing to intervening pockets of economic recovery, they have been content to rue the dearth of specific unemployment figures for the early years of our period and estimate that unemployment was contained at something less than three percent during the later years. The contrast between the two approaches can perhaps best be illustrated in concrete terms by reference to excerpts from Mottek's "Grunderkrise" and Vernon Lidtke's The Outlawed Party, both of which allude to the same data but leave their readers with rather different impressions of the conclusions which can be drawn about unemployment. First Mottek[35]:

> Nach Angaben des Polizeipraesidiums Berlin sei bei 22 bis 28 untersuchten Industriezweigen ein Rueckgang der Beschaeftigung festgestellt worden. Eine weitere Zunahme der Arbeitslosigkeit durch Entlassungen erfolgte in Berlin 1876, wo der Rueckgang der Berschaeftigung in dem von den Fabrikinspektoren erfassen Bereich 14 Prozent betrug. Im Jahre 1877 wurde ein weiterer Rueckgang um etwa 6,3 Prozent gemeldet, waehrend die Arbeitslosigkeit in den Jahren 1878 und 1879 eher ab- als zunahm. Insgesamt kommt Roessler zu der Feststellung "dass bei Inkrafttreten des Sozialistengesetzes rund 25 bis 28 Prozent der Berliner Arbeiter im Bereich der Industrie und des produzierenden Handwerks arbeitslos geworden waren."

Compare the above with Lidtke's more cautious statement following an assertion that "specific data on unemployment is almost entirely lacking for Germany before 1890"[36].

> According to a report of the Berlin Police President, the number of employed persons in Berlin shops and factories had dropped to 29,292 in 1878 from 66,892 in 1875 and then rose again to 73,652 by 1881. These figures give no indication of unemployment percentages since the total labor force available in Berlin is not known for these years, but they definitely suggest a marked rise in the demand for labor in the early Eighties.

Noteworthy here is Lidtke's reluctance to draw conclusions about unemployment rates from employment statistics and his simultaneous willingness to speculate about the implications of job prospects based on the same information.

Despite substantial differences, the picture we get from both western and eastern views of the labor market prior to the 1890's is one of a situation dominated by uncertainty. Based on divergent readings of shaky indirect indicators such as employment, wages and hours or consumption we emerge with a feeling for the unstable nature of labor's hold on its source of livelihood. The prospect of unemployment was a menace which many workers came to take seriously as three successive downturns threatened to eliminate every semblance of stability from already precarious existences.

Wages and Prices

One area where statistical estimates are available for the entirety of our period is wages. Figures on the movement of wage rates in Germany between 1871 and 1913 have been published in a variety of sources over the past fifteen years. Unfortunately for our purposes, only tenuous suggestions about the relationship between wages and unemployment levels have been forthcoming. The following data from a 1968 monograph reflects the superiority of our knowledge about business conditions plus the relative dearth of information about the labor market in general and unemployment in particular[37].

Indicators of Business and Labor Market Conditions in Germany

Year	INDICATORS OF BUSINESS CONDITIONS					INDICATORS OF LABOR MARKET CONDITIONS					
	Industrial Production (1913=100) (1)	Wholesale Prices (1913=100) (2)	Cost of living (1913=100) (3)	Real National Income (1913=100) (4)	Reference Dates, NBER (5)	Employment Rate, Unions (percent) (6)	Employed, Sickness Insurance (millions) (7)	Employed, Workmen's Compensation (millions) (8)	Unemployed, Registered (millions) (9)	Man-days Lost: Strikes (millions) (10)	Lockouts (millions) (11)
1870	18	92	64	36	T						
1871	21	100	69	..							
1872	23	114	72	..	P						
1873	23	120	80	..							
1874	22	112	83	..							
1875	22	100	76	..							
1876	24	95	76	..							
1877	22	91	77	39							
1878	25	83	73	..	T						
1879	26	81	72	..							
1880	25	87	76	..							
1881	27	85	77	..							
1882	28	81	75	..	P			4.081			
1883	30	80	75	47				...			
1884	31	78	72	..				...			
1885	32	75	70	..				...			
1886	33	72	68	..	T			...			
1887	35	73	68	..		99.8		...			
1888	36	75	70	..		96.2		5.191			
1889	39	82	73	..		99.3		5.613			
1890	40	85	75	64	P	97.7		5.933			
1891	41	86	77	64		96.1		6.013			
1892	40	80	76	65		93.7		6.004			
1893	42	77	75	67		97.2		6.097			
1894	45	73	74	69	T	96.9		6.208			
1895	48	72	73	71		97.2		6.434			
1896	53	72	72	74		99.4		6.745			
1897	56	76	74	75		98.8		7.093			
1898	60	79	76	75		99.6		7.379			
1899	64	83	76	78		98.8		7.700		3.3	0.1
1900	65	90	77	80	P	98.0		8.005		3.2	0.5
1901	65	83	78	80		93.3		7.908		2.3	0.1
1902	69	81	78	81	T	97.1		7.955		1.3	0.7
1903	73	82	78	83	P	97.3		8.220		2.8	1.4
1904	78	82	79	85	T	97.9	11.0	8.552		3.6	1.7
1905	79	86	82	85		98.4	11.3	8.808		14.5	4.5
1906	84	92	87	87		98.8	12.0	9.272		8.2	3.4
1907	83	97	88	90	P	98.4	12.2	9.652		6.2	2.8
1908	79	90	88	93	T	97.1	12.0	9.541		2.3	1.4
1909	81	91	90	94		97.2	12.2	9.619		2.8	1.4
1910	89	93	92	95		98.1	12.7	9.979		4.6	13.2
1911	96	94	95	96		98.1	13.3	10.397		7.7	3.8
1912	99	102	100	95		98.0	13.9	10.616		7.7	3.0
1913	100	100	100	100	P	97.1	14.0	10.905		8.8	3.0

Some efforts have been made to formulate an explanation of wage changes in terms of the available labor supply. However, the heterogeneous nature of the labor force and the non-economic determinants of employment practices make this formulation difficult. The problem is further complicated by the fact that "wages do not show a tendency to fall progressively where there is a labour surplus, even when they are above the subsistence level. The rigidity of wages in the presence of unemployment can be accommodated in a theory which postulates a non-linear relation between excess demand or excess supply of labour and the rate of increase of money wages... [At the same time,] the proportion of unemployed labour force has generally shown itself to be a good predictor [of the rate of change of wages] in least-squares regressions"[38].

Relying primarily on emigration and labor exchange statistics, Ashok V.Desai maintains that "throughout the period we are considering, labour for industry was abundant in Germany"[39]. He argues that although specific industries such as sugar and brick manufacturing suffered from labor scarcity and highly skilled workers were frequently in short supply, this reflected limited rather than general short-ages. Most of the empirical studies undertaken to determine the relationship between wages and unemployment show that "the sensitivity of the rate of change of wages to changes in unemployment was low at high levels of unemployment, and that the relation between the two was not close"[40]. Despite the supposed abundance of labor for German industry deduced from an excess of would-be male employees over job vacancies in Arbeitsnachweise statistics after 1896, there is no evidence of "high levels of unemployment" which Desai can cite for most of the period.

In Desai's formulation, the relationship between wages and unemployment boils down to the question of labor supply and demand. The level of wages was affected by the employers' desire to expand their workforce weighed against the availability of labor. The availability of labor was in turn at least partially determined by the prevailing rate of unemployment. Because wages function as a primary incentive to accept employment, the wage rate has to be commensurate with overall conditions in the labor market. Where many workers are free to seek a single job, the wage rate will be less high than where many employers compete for the services of a severely limited labor supply. As a crude but generally applicable indicator we may assume that high wages reflected labor scarcity and low levels of unemployment while the reverse relationship applied within the limitations outlined above. In Desai's terms, the greater the excess of employers' labor requirements over the available pool of workers, the greater the inducements, including higher wages, they were prepared to offer to attract employees[41].

Given these vague theoretical correlations between wages and unemployment, let us look at the underlying empirical evidence. According to available estimates, real wages in German industry rose significantly during the economic boom accompanying the Reichsgrundung. Between

1873 and 1880 they fell, rising rapidly during the following decade and less swiftly during the Nineties. The cost of living figures likewise exhibited a marked increase during the boom which immediately preceded our period and a sharp decrease between 1873 and 1879. They then remained relatively stable until the turn of the century. Roughly parallel movements of real wages, money wages and cost of living indices prevailed during the first half of our period. Desai linked movement of real wages during these years directly to fluctuations in employment[42].

> The increase in real wages in the 1873 boom might be explained partly by the high rates of growth of employment that necessitated rapid wage increases and partly by increases in productivity which made them possible. Conversely, the wage reductions after 1873 were occasioned by declines in productivity and profits and pushed through with the help of reductions in employment.

It should be noted that the number of industries from which the wage rates during the 1870's were computed was very small[43].

Substantial wage increases in capital goods industries and an accompanying rise in employment were attributed to accelerated investment during the 1880's. During the following decades, escalating levels of investment were not accompanied by a corresponding expansion of wages. Wage increases were deemed to be less advisable than reinvestment of profits during an era when an expanding labor supply and better training facilities in the capital goods industries put the work force at the mercy of employers' demand.

Remarkable expansion took place during the 1890's, led in part by the development of new light industries such as electicals and chemicals. During the closing years of the century, for example, AEG's work force in motor production increased more than eightfold[44]. Comparable expansion occurred among its competitors.

Despite the large labor surplus which such rapid growth presupposed, after 1895 the competition for labor became more severe. This was reflected in seasonal trades like brick manufacturing where year-round employment and stockpiling of inventories began to replace short seasonal bursts of feverish activity necessitating difficult hunts for a labor force each spring. Rising wages during the 1890's were precipitated at least in part by increases in employment as rapidly expanding industries offered more money to attract workers. After 1900 heightened demand for consumer goods pushing up the cost of living exerted major pressure on wages. Around the turn of the century, Germany experienced a significant spurt in the rate of growth of employment. This spurt was due to expanded opportunities stemming from increased investment plus an earlier rise in the birth rate which greatly augmented the working-age population. The impact of these factors on the level of real wages is reflected in Desai's estimates of their movement over the course of our period.

Comparison of estimates of real wages

	Our estimates			Kuczynski's estimates			Phelps Brown and Hopkins's estimates		
	Money wages	*Cost of living*	*Real wages*	*Money wages*	*Cost of living*	*Real wages*	*Money wages*	*Cost of living*	*Real wages*
1871	70	106	66	78	95	82	75	103	72
1875	98	113	87	97	104	93	96	107	90
1880	82	104	79	82	104	79	84	109	77
1885	87	99	88	88	96	92	90	97	93
1890	98	102	96	100	103	97	100	105	95
1895	100	100	100	100	100	100	100	100	100
1900	118	106	111	115	105	110	113	105	108
1905	128	112	114	122	113	108	120	115	104
1910	147	124	119	139	126	110	136	128	106
1913	163	130	125	153	137	112	148	136	109

These figures show an upward trend in the movement of real wages throughout the Great Depression and the subsequent years of our period. The single significant reversal occurred during the last half of the 1870's, coinciding with years of peak unemployment.

Food and Beverage Consumption

Shortly after its founding in 1892, Soziale Praxis published an important article on consumption patterns of the Berlin population between 1883 and 1892. As an alternate indicator of unemployment, consumption of basic commodities was telling because it reflected both the income levels and purchasing power of the individuals in a given labor market, factors greatly affected by the prevailing rate of joblessness among the population. Before looking at the data on Berlin in detail, let us consider the situation for Germany as a whole. The following figures reflect the cost of food, fuel, clothing and rent in the country during our period.

In view of deflation, the high cost of animal products such as pork or butter and the surprisingly steep cost of both wheat and rye during economically depressed years were noteworthy. The steady decline in sugar prices contrasted sharply with the stability of beer prices[45].

Price series of commodities entering the cost-of-living index
(1895 = 100)

	Pork	Beef	Veal	Mutton	Lard	Eggs	Butter	Salt	Sugar	Wheat flour	Rye flour	Wheat bread	Rye bread	Potatoes	Coffee	Milk	Beer	Coal	Fuel gas	Lighting gas	Oil	Clothing	Rent
1871	59.0	73.2	..	..	..	..	105.3	..	191.4	..	..	..	..	57.1	97.1	83.5	..	136.8	..	..	..	123.4	..
1872	96.1	83.4	..	..	..	..	101.4	..	135.0	..	..	..	..	98.4	133.3	83.5	..	153.0	..	..	..	132.3	..
1873	106.4	96.3	55.7	94.3	100.6	97.9	113.9	..	184.6	158.3	154.5	..	..	104.3	147.2	83.5	..	210.7	..	..	..	111.0	..
1874	105.6	97.0	83.3	93.5	109.8	94.9	120.6	..	174.5	184.7	159.1	..	..	112.4	151.6	94.1	..	225.1	..	..	..	114.7	..
1875	99.3	88.4	76.7	86.9	112.3	99.5	118.7	..	162.6	172.0	136.4	..	..	87.1	144.1	94.1	..	141.6	..	..	..	126.2	96.5
1876	103.3	85.4	80.0	87.7	115.3	99.5	117.3	..	163.6	153.8	140.9	..	..	85.1	131.3	94.1	..	119.5	..	..	..	103.3	..
1877	101.7	90.0	81.6	88.5	113.5	93.3	112.5	..	133.2	152.7	145.5	..	..	99.1	137.6	94.1	..	103.6	..	..	..	91.5	..
1878	98.9	91.6	82.4	80.4	105.6	91.3	102.9	..	132.4	146.2	127.3	..	..	75.9	113.1	94.1	..	89.1	..	..	..	82.6	..
1879	90.7	90.0	80.0	85.5	101.2	89.5	93.2	..	151.4	142.3	122.7	..	..	85.0	104.6	94.1	..	89.1	..	..	..	86.7	..
1880	96.1	89.2	82.0	85.5	104.3	90.4	105.3	..	154.1	153.3	145.5	..	..	103.3	103.9	94.1	..	94.4	..	..	..	55.2	92.7
1881	100.7	89.2	82.0	89.2	101.8	93.3	108.7	..	160.0	153.8	154.5	132.2	129.4	97.2	90.7	94.1	101.7	94.4	..	..	..	91.4	..
1882	100.7	90.8	82.0	112.0	101.7	109.0	115.0	..	160.0	152.0	140.9	125.7	117.4	83.6	93.1	94.1	101.7	93.3	..	..	..	101.6	..
1883	100.7	94.1	82.5	92.3	113.0	92.5	110.0	..	160.0	142.3	127.3	126.7	111.6	103.9	65.0	94.1	101.7	95.3	..	..	..	92.6	..
1884	94.9	94.1	83.6	93.5	103.3	91.2	103.4	..	143.1	139.7	122.7	126.7	110.0	82.7	75.0	94.1	101.7	92.0	..	..	..	91.1	..
1885	94.9	94.1	82.0	92.6	107.0	91.7	101.5	..	127.7	132.2	118.2	125.7	107.3	36.6	75.0	94.1	97.2	100.9	..	..	..	92.2	93.1
1886	94.2	93.0	83.4	91.0	104.1	90.4	102.3	..	134.5	115.3	113.6	126.7	102.2	39.6	87.3	94.1	97.2	109.9	..	..	..	84.5	..
1887	91.4	89.1	82.5	85.5	105.9	88.5	97.8	..	119.6	115.3	109.1	126.7	100.5	95.1	91.4	94.1	97.2	110.9	..	..	..	55.5	..
1888	92.4	85.3	82.0	87.7	100.8	100.1	..	..	121.7	119.2	113.6	126.7	102.2	100.3	59.2	94.1	97.2	121.9	..	..	..	50.0	..
1889	101.2	91.5	86.9	91.8	120.7	93.5	106.5	..	126.4	127.0	122.7	111.1	111.5	58.3	121.8	94.1	97.2	124.5	..	..	..	84.5	..
1890	100.3	96.5	59.2	112.4	93.3	105.7	100.0	117.7	132.3	131.3	115.6	100.5	82.6	102.2	94.1	97.2	116.9	113.3	100.6	113.2	93.2	99.9	..
1891	103.3	100.9	96.5	102.5	107.1	101.1	126.1	100.0	119.6	146.2	154.5	127.8	135.0	112.2	101.1	94.1	97.2	112.7	117.5	103.5	105.3	92.2	..
1892	103.9	99.3	95.4	100.0	107.0	100.5	108.8	100.0	120.0	133.8	145.4	113.0	129.6	114.1	101.4	94.1	97.2	114.5	117.5	100.6	97.2	92.2	..
1893	104.9	95.1	99.5	90.7	106.8	103.5	110.0	100.0	119.1	111.5	113.6	105.6	106.6	97.6	101.4	94.1	97.2	93.8	117.5	100.6	92.2	94.5	..
1894	104.2	93.4	97.1	97.5	101.2	97.0	105.2	97.5	101.6	100.0	100.0	101.1	101.1	93.1	100.9	94.9	121.1	105.3	100.0	84.2	97.3	..
1895	100.0	100.0	100.0	100.0	100.0	100.0	100.0	100.0	100.0	100.0	100.0	100.0	100.0	100.0	100.0	100.0	100.0	100.0	100.0	100.0	100.0	100.0	100.0
1896	95.1	98.3	97.5	99.2	95.0	96.3	101.3	97.5	105.4	103.8	145.5	101.1	102.1	93.0	93.8	100.0	100.0	99.2	97.4	105.3	101.1	..
1897	101.6	98.1	98.4	99.2	97.1	97.7	103.1	100.0	100.1	115.3	100.1	105.9	111.0	94.3	80.5	95.0	100.0	100.9	95.3	98.9	100.0	101.1	..
1898	107.9	99.7	100.9	101.6	100.7	100.5	103.5	99.0	101.9	130.8	118.2	120.0	119.1	101.5	77.9	94.1	98.9	102.0	100.0	95.9	94.7	103.1	..
1899	104.7	99.7	103.4	102.5	95.8	102.3	105.6	100.0	112.4	115.3	111.6	117.5	117.0	66.9	78.0	94.1	100.0	101.7	100.0	97.2	100.0	101.6	..
1900	102.3	94.5	103.3	103.3	97.1	100.5	107.8	100.0	108.2	115.5	113.3	130.7	119.7	94.2	80.6	94.1	100.0	133.2	100.9	93.3	105.3	105.2	109.3
1901	100.0	99.3	104.7	101.9	101.1	107.3	100.2	102.5	117.3	115.3	118.2	114.4	129.3	94.3	73.6	100.0	100.0	121.6	94.9	105.3	107.3	..
1902	101.6	101.3	108.7	105.2	107.4	101.0	163.3	102.5	117.3	115.3	113.6	113.6	119.3	89.4	76.1	100.0	114.0	100.0	94.7	102.6	105.4	..
1903	109.1	104.0	111.8	111.5	106.4	103.9	103.0	102.5	100.1	115.3	113.9	113.6	121.0	103.3	75.2	105.9	100.9	111.1	94.9	105.3	105.5	..
1904	104.0	105.9	113.6	113.9	120.7	110.1	112.0	100.0	35.0	113.3	113.6	114.4	121.9	112.7	77.3	105.9	100.0	112.3	100.0	94.4	105.3	..
1905	121.8	112.7	121.4	120.5	107.3	117.7	115.1	102.5	95.0	119.2	113.6	116.7	123.6	112.3	75.4	105.9	100.0	116.7	93.5	100.0	114.8	113.3
1906	131.3	119.7	131.1	130.3	113.7	120.0	116.1	101.5	84.1	119.2	122.7	121.1	129.1	94.7	75.4	110.0	101.7	123.3	101.8	95.5	116.6	115.5	..
1907	117.4	129.0	130.8	132.0	107.5	114.9	117.1	90.0	83.7	132.3	136.4	128.0	145.5	75.4	117.7	101.7	127.4	105.3	101.6	116.4	..
1908	117.4	135.1	136.2	131.1	106.7	122.9	101.0	90.0	88.2	142.3	145.5	137.8	140.4	107.2	75.4	117.7	100.9	90.5	109.9	100.0	116.6	..
1909	117.4	120.0	137.0	135.3	113.0	132.1	124.0	91.0	150.0	127.0	138.9	150.0	101.5	64.9	117.7	106.7	127.4	106.1	91.0	107.9	121.6	..
1910	120.3	129.3	144.5	139.4	110.4	126.7	123.9	105.0	91.0	134.3	131.3	130.7	145.0	112.4	80.7	122.3	111.1	127.0	114.4	94.9	105.3	127.0	124.6
1911	119.2	131.5	127.8	143.5	112.0	130.1	131.1	106.5	100.9	142.3	131.8	132.4	136.6	143.5	90.7	132.2	112.8	123.4	110.5	84.3	97.2	126.5	128.1
1912	131.4	141.5	150.7	151.6	119.0	139.0	132.5	102.5	103.0	142.3	132.0	135.0	137.2	130.7	100.1	137.1	112.8	120.1	111.4	57.1	100.0	129.1	135.0
1913	135.9	143.2	103.1	101.5	121.0	140.5	133.3	102.5	91.0	142.3	136.4	135.6	135.1	112.1	33.9	135.6	127.3	112.8	100.6	54.1	113.2	131.0	135.9

Compare the above figures with the following data on food consumption in the capital. The Berlin numbers reveal alternating patterns of demand for expensive items such as meat or fish during prosperous years and a corresponding movement of starch consumption during economically lean years. The figures were given in kilograms per head of

population and indicate the basic outlines of most
Berliners' diets[46].

Year	Bread Grains	Meat	Fish	Potatoes	Fruits, Vegetables and Herbs
1883	171.65	69.49	13.86	59.95	---
1884	174.78	74.77	14.22	60.37	---
1885	171.87	76.24	15.15	67.37	40.64
1886	143.30	79.88	16.56	71.02	36.08
1887	155.78	86.27	14.68	73.54	34.62
1888	152	85.13	14.42	65.55	42.53
1889	129	80.46	17.56	56.98	39.76
1890	126	68.66	17.77	61.94	32.61
1891	132	69.01	16.96	75.12	41.86
1892	149	69.80	13.66	75.08	32.77

The opposite movement of demand for potatoes and vegetables
and the parallel movement of demand for meat and fish consumption are noteworthy. Between 1883 and 1886, substantial
increases in both protein categories plus potatoes and an
accompanying drop in bread and cereal use were registered,
probably reflecting a slight improvement in the nutritional
intake of most Berliners. This trend, established during an
economic slump, experienced a real spurt as people adjusted
to an interlude of prosperity during the late 1880's. When
the third cyclical downswing hit in 1890, the sharp drop in
meat consumption, the gradual decline of fish intake, the
erratic movement of fruits and vegetables plus the marked
increases in the consumption of cheap carbohydrate staples
mirrored conditions in the labor market. This sentiment was
expressed by one contemporary observer in these words: "Das
sich so ergebende Bild zeigt den engen Zusammenhang der
Volksernaehrung mit den Perioden des volkswirtschaftlichen
Gedeihens und Niedergehens die in Berlin ganz analog verlau-
fen sind."[47] In general terms, expensive foodstuffs tended

to sell better during boom periods and measures of economy set in during slumps.

Traditionally, consumption of white as opposed to rye bread has been seen by demographers as an indication of creeping prosperity. The relationship between costs of rye and wheat meals, beef, pork and potatoes during the decade between 1883 and 1892 were as follows[48]:

Year	Cost in Pfennigs of 1 Kilogram of		Cost in Pfennigs of 1 Kilogram of		Cost in Marks of 100 kilograms of Potatoes
	Wheat Meal	Rye Meal	Beef	Pork	
1883	44.6	32.9	118	121	6.45
1884	40.0	30.0	117	120	4.95
1885	37.6	32.1	112	121	6.00
1886	39.3	28.9	115	121	4.40
1887	32.1	26.8	111	120	5.10
1888	35.5	28.8	110	116	5.20
1889	35.6	30.2	114	130	4.77
1890	35.5	32.7	126	144	4.65
1891	37.0	35.0	129	136	7.40
1892	34.8	33.2	128	137	6.52

Comparing these figures with those in the preceding chart indicates the consistent inverse relationship between the price and consumption of meat. Demand was highly elastic for what many people considered essentially luxury food-stuff. The direct and pervasive variance between prices and demand was not duplicated for potatoes or bread--necessities without which people felt literally unable to live regard-less of cost. They could substitute starch in their diets when more expensive protein sources were priced beyond the limitations of their budgets. The relationship between prices of these two food groups tended to dictate the proportions of each substance consumed. A high outlay for potatoes was likely to reflect both expensive meat prices and general hard times, since meat or bread were preferred as dietary mainstays when cost permitted. In other words, elasticity of demand was high for meat, much lower for grain meal and virtually non-existent for potatoes which were used to fill in when other less plentiful or more costly items could not be procured.

Parallel movements of income for the Berlin population help to place the above figures in perspective. Throughout this discussion, it would be well to remember that we are dealing with a period whose overriding economic feature was a significant price deflation. This trend was reflected in the movement of Berlin's average per capita income which increased from 508 Marks in 1870 to 627 Marks in 1875. By the beginning of 1882 that figure had fallen back to 500 Marks. During the following decade it began a gradual but steady recovery as the statistics below indicate[49]:

Year	Total Income per Head of Population	Direct State Taxation per Head in Marks	Urban Taxation per Head in Marks	Average Rent of a Room
1883	534.3	14.07	22.18	597.76
1884	555.2	14.26	22.78	589.00
1885	556.4	14.43	23.30	604.60
1886	561.4	14.50	23.75	608.83
1887	581.8	14.73	24.55	627.44
1888	586.5	14.82	24.89	639.93
1889	603.3	14.98	24.58	649.85
1890	617.5	15.44	25.35	655.70
1891	636.5	15.87	24.66	666.06

The steady increase of average income between 1883 and 1891 was partially absorbed by higher rents and taxes but clothing costs remained largely stationary and enough was left over to permit an expansion of mass consumption.

This tendency and the improved standard of living it entailed were mirrored in the patterns of beverage consumption among the Berlin population[50].

Year	Wine Kg	Coffee, Cocoa, Tea, Surrogate Kg	Beer Liters	Spirits, Alcohol, Brandy, Vinegar Kg
1883	4.98	----	165.07	13.62
1884	6.19	----	173.19	18.83
1885	6.58	2.73	171.78	18.45
1886	6.97	4.00	183.01	18.45
1887	7.51	2.93	192.48	20.94
1888	8.19	2.89	194.24	15.72
1889	8.69	2.79	201.74	8.00
1890	8.43	3.57	199.93	10.88
1891	9.87	4.01	189.96	16.11
1892	7.47	3.20	157.55	14.52

The increased consumption of wine or coffee, and to a lesser extent beer or hard liquor also, reflected the expanding range of mass purchasing power. The tendency to consume beverages once considered luxuries by the population at large persisted in spite of the state's efforts to reap revenues from the sale of these commodities--despite a high tax on whiskey, spirits continued to gain on beer consumption in later years. According to Karl Thiess, beer and whiskey consumption taken together were among the most important material indicators of the overall well-being of the lowest socio-economic classes. Thiess noted the peak which occurred in 1891 and explained the sharp decline during the following year in terms pregnant with meaning for those interested in the correlation between consumption of foodstuffs and unemployment[51].

Das letzte Jahr zeigt fuer alle vier Getraenke ein auffallend starkes Zurueckgehen, und dies laesst in

Verbindung mit der gleich zu konstatirenden Thatsache, dass die Huelfsstoffe der Industrie in ihrem Verbrauch gleichfalls rapide abgenommen haben, mit der weiteren Thatsache, dass die Arbeitslosigkeit im Jahre 1892 notorisch stark gewachsen ist, den ziemlich sicheren Scluss zu, dass in diesem Jahre mit dem Rueckgang der Industrie gleichzeitig auch ein starker Rueckgang in dem Einkommen und der Kaufkraft der ganzen Berliner Bevoelkerung eingetreten ist.

Bad conditions in German industry leading to high unemployment were reflected in the patterns of demand for food and beverages. Comparable indicators such as fuel consumption reinforced the impressions left by trade-offs between necessary and extravagant culinary purchases. Patterns of course differed at various socio-economic levels with those at the lower end of the spectrum more vulnerable to vicissitudes in their position as economic producers and demonstrating this in their capacity as consumers. Those most likely to be laid off or affected by a severe cutback in hours and wages were not necessarily the ones most prone to exercise prudent spending habits, especially with regard to beer and alcohol consumption. While meat and whiskey represented accoutrements of life unthinkingly consumed by those who were better off, such rewards also helped to make existence bearable for the masses seeking solace from the workaday world in access to luxury items.

Consumption patterns such as those outlined above cut two ways in terms of unemployment. On the one hand, they provided an index of mass purchasing power which was affected by the number of persons without jobs. In addition, however, consumption determined the demand for labor in various occupations. If commodities produced were not consumed, cutbacks and unemployment would follow for workers involved in the preparation of those items. In the preceding section, we have dealt with the demand for food, fuel and other basic necessities as an index of unemployment. As we shall see, a majority of the labor force throughout our period worked to produce these essentials of daily life. The manner in which consumers weighed the options and selected alternate combinations of staples therefore had a profound impact on the economy. And it is important to consider the dual role of the working class in their capacity as consumers as well as producers in the German marketplace.

We noted earlier that there was a direct correlation between the consumption of expensive or luxury foodstuffs and economic prosperity. There was also a tendency to substitute cheaper products such as potatoes during economically lean years. While the demand for bread was inelastic, meat consumption fluctuated inversely with price. Like meat, the demand for alcohol and beer appeared to be a good index of prosperity, with consumption peaking during booms and declining during economic recessions. When unemployment increased, income and purchasing power diminished and so did the demand for liquor. Like other optional items, tobacco consumption was sensitive to variations in price and economic well-being. Accordingly, a marked increase in unemployment among tobacco workers was registered in 1909 when a new tax law during a recession boosted the cost for consumers. Both alcohol and tobacco consumption had expanded with disproportionate speed during the prosperous third quarter of the nineteenth century. But with the onset of our period, the growth of demand began to taper off markedly. Consumption patterns show that during recessions luxury goods were among the first items to experience marked declines in demand which would typically peak during prosperity.

In the area of fuel consumption, it is worth noting that the primary users of coal, coke and lignite were industrial and commercial operations rather than private individuals. The argument has therefore been made that the demand for fuel was a better indication of the intensity of production than consumption. Production of coal, coke and lignite expanded steadily between 1883 and 1891 along with industry and the income of the wealthier classes. After 1889 the real income and purchasing power of the poorer classes declined, a pattern echoed by prosperous citizens and big industrial concerns in 1892.

Predictably, downward trends were reflected in diminished consumption as well as cutbacks in production. Looking at sharp declines in production between 1876 and 1879 the East German historian Hans Mottek maintains in "Die Grunderkrise" that there was a distinctive slump in capital goods industries and a lesser but noteworthy contraction in the output of consumer goods. According to

Mottek, western historians have ignored the fact that there was a crisis evidenced by a decline in consumer goods production between 1874 and 1876 and by an even more important contraction in producers' goods as shown by diminished consumption of pig iron. Mottek's work suggests the importance of consumption patterns in identifying the turning points of crises associated with high levels of unemployment.

METHODS OF COUNTING THE UNEMPLOYED

As we have indicated, the gathering of unemployment statistics was considered an essential first step toward determining the extent of need and defining the programs best suited to resolve the attendant problems. Because statistics were viewed as a prerequisite for policy decisions, the ways in which unemployment data was collected tell us a good deal about changing attitudes toward work shortages. The question of who was to assume responsibility for the unemployed was behind debates on issues ranging from the conduct of surveys to the limitation of abuses and assessment of costs. Throughout our period, three primary groups were jockeying for positions, trying to gain power over, or avoid being held accountable for, Germany's industrial unemployed. These groups were: the laborers themselves, individually or collectively; employers, singly or jointly; municipal, state or federal officials. To varying extents, competing interest groups recognized that there was a strong political component in the collection, assembly and dissemination of unemployment statistics. A great deal of attention was therefore paid to the methods of counting the unemployed as contemporaries strove to determine how the jobless should be enumerated and by whom.

Public Methods of Enumerating the Unemployed

The German unemployment statistics which survived from our period have been categorized in a variety of ways based on the methods used in their collection. Richard

Herbst, who did as much as any man to further his contemporaries' knowledge about unemployment, classified surveys under twelve headings. Among the methods he listed were house to house counts and indirect tallies which relied on urban institutions ranging from labor exchanges, public works offices, poor relief administrations, police and tax officials[52].

> 1. Zaehlung von Haus zu Haus 2. Oeffentliche Aufforderung zur <u>Selbstmeldung</u> (Stuttgarter oder sueddeutsche Methode, Melde-system) 3. Oeffentliche Aufforderung zur Einzeichnung in eine oeffentlich aufgelegte Liste 4. Oeffentliche Aufforderung zur Selbstmeldung durch den Oberbuergermeister 5. Indirekt auf Grund der Personenstandsaufnahmen zu <u>Steuerzwecken</u> (saechsische Methode) 6. Ausfuellung einer Zaehlkarte fuer jeden beim <u>Arbeitsnachweis</u> sich meldenden Arbeitssuchenden 7. Feststellung der Arbeitssuchenden, denen durch das staedtische <u>Arbeitsamt</u> keine Stelle vermittelt werden konnte 8. Meldung auf dem Bureau fuer <u>Notstandsarbeiten</u> 9. Stichprobenerhebung in 31 Anwesen, die nach Auskunft des <u>Statistischen Amtes</u> der Stadt Charlottenburg als Arbeitslosenzaehlung eigentlich gar nicht in Betracht gezogen werden kann 10. Kontrollerhebungen der Staedte zu den beiden Reichsarbeitslosenzaehlungen am 14. Juni und 2. Dezember 1895 11. Ermittlung durch die <u>Polizeiorgane</u> 12. Ermittlung durch die Armenpflege.

The communal data referred to by Herbst consisted of unemployment figures compiled by municipal statistical offices. Communal unemployment statistics began to emerge in scattered urban centers during the economically depressed years of the early 1890's. After the turn of the century, local surveys were improved by the incorporation of larger administrative areas and more comprehensive occupational categories. Even by the end of our period, however, the regular annual gathering of unemployment data was an exception rather than the rule in German cities, confined almost exclusively to Cologne, Dresden, Nuremberg and Offenbach according to Dr. Herbst.

The first counts relied on indirect methods and were motivated by a desire to alleviate the effects of joblessness through relief works, labor exchanges or unemployment insurance. In Munich, Koenigsberg and Erfurt enumerations began as part of an effort to determine the numbers dependent upon public work projects. In Hannover the surveys originated with an inquiry into the number of relief applicants who attributed their need to unemployment. Other cities arrived at the process of gathering statistical data on unemployment as an adjunct to their poor relief administration. In Breslau unemployment statistics began to evolve during 1891 when the labor exchange first collected personal information from those looking for work. In all of the above instances, the accumulation of data was directly tied to municipal efforts to alleviate the problems associated with unemployment. Most communal surveys enumerated unemployed laborers rather than employees per se, grouping individuals according to occupation. Although they tell nothing about unemployment beyond a limited geographical radius, municipal statistics reveal a good deal about local efforts to cope with work shortages.

The range of methods used to count the unemployed in various German cities gives some indication of the scope of communal programs by the closing years of our period. In

Cologne, the method of house-to-house counting was used. It produced fairly reliable results with respect to the volume of unemployment among male residents on the day of the survey. Unlike labor exchange officials, the Cologne authorities classified jobless individuals on the basis of family position, age, source and duration of unemployment.

It is significant that in most German cities, statistics were less satisfactory with regard to the female unemployed who were both incompletely polled and less responsive than their male counterparts. Typically, their unemployment was of less concern than that of men who were presumed to be the real backbone of the industrial labor force. The frequent emphasis on unemployment among adult, male heads of households indicates that their lack of work was of primary importance to pollsters and policymakers alike. In Cologne and most other cities, married men were frequently the exclusive beneficiaries of public largesse. Since women were almost always excluded from municipal relief funds, their enumeration was of little interest to municipal census takers or the women themselves. It should be emphasized in this context that many unemployment surveys were motivated by a need to determine the cost of specific relief programs.

Like any house-to-house count, the Cologne system relied heavily on the integrity and goodwill of unemployed respondents in addition to being dependent upon the expertise of census takers with limited training. Surveys modeled on this house-to-house pattern, however, had the distinct advantage of reaching more unemployed workers and questioning them more thoroughly than other methods permitted. Under this system, questionnaires could either be completed by the census taker or the unemployed individual, with the former preferred as the means most likely to achieve an accurate result.

There was so much concern about the accuracy and methods of counting the unemployed between 1873 and 1913 because contemporaries were groping toward solutions to an age-old problem in a new and unfamiliar setting. It was during the late nineteenth century that the methodological questions involved in collecting public as well as private unemployment data were confronted for the first time. It was also during our period that the term unemployment came into common usage and initial efforts were made to define the condition itself. Early statistical undertakings reflect the halting efforts of contemporaries to move toward effective means of coping with job scarcity in an increasingly urban and industrial setting. Due to the novelty of the situation, a considerable interval of trial and error was necessary in order to facilitate the collection of reliable unemployment figures.

Let us briefly consider some of the problems which had to be resolved. With house-to-house counts, for example, the large amount of trained manpower needed to conduct the undertaking formed a major deterrent to its frequent implementation. In many instances, part of the expense involved in relying on this method was defrayed by the volunteer efforts of trade unions and the SDP which provided significant numbers of census takers. The obvious political implications of their contribution created additional headaches which led to lengthy and heated debates. Disagreements arose over whether specific surveys unearthed levels of unemployment that were too high or too low.

Employers and members of government bureaucracies such as the police were among the most obvious repositories for fears about the revolutionary potential of unemployment. Efforts to suppress the gathering of data as part of an anti-Socialist crusade were neither unknown nor infrequent. Unemployment surveys which received support from the unions or SDP elicited much higher levels of response than those ignored or boycotted by labor organizations. It was obvious that workers were much more likely to respond to questions when they believed that answers would alleviate rather than aggravate their condition. If, for example, unemployed respondents were convinced they'd be rewarded for their efforts with public works projects rather than increasingly stiff penalties for begging, they'd be more anxious to fill out a questionnaire. The unemployed needed an incentive to make their existence known but they also required a method of surveying the situation which was conducive to register-ing their answers. This fact elicited a good deal of discussion among advocates of house-to-house counts and voluntary registration systems.

Different methods reflected conflicting attitudes toward unemployed workers and the level of initiative which they could be expected to exercise on their own behalf. If workers were thought to be reluctant to make their existence known, more direct means of counting them were needed. House-to-house surveys counteracted a presumed lack of initiative among the unemployed. Other attempts to make responses to questions easier on those being polled camouflaged assumptions about the laziness and integrity of jobless workers.

German cities adopted various techniques for counting the unemployed. The Cologne system received support in Nuremberg, Augsburg and Fuerth while Elberfeld, Mannheim and Halle attacked the house-to-house method as unworkable. Alternate means of polling the jobless evolved in German cities including Augsburg where a Meldesystem or registration method was adopted. This system depended on the willingness of unemployed workers to make the time and effort to register. In addition to Augsburg, the municipalities of Freiburg im Breisgau, Karlsruhe and Deutsch-Wilmersdorf adopted methods of surveying their unemployed residents through voluntary registration.

The town of Rixdorf, emulating the 1902 Dresden example, adopted an indirect survey technique as an adjunct to the Inland Revenue Enquiry's determination of income tax distribution. The so-called Saxon method relied on occasional enumerations through lists which were used to question each homeowner about the legal status of those residing on his premises. Typically, a good deal of time was required to carry out this form of unemployment survey which was routinely undertaken during the fall months of October or November and thus failed to reflect either a maximum or average level of unemployment.

In Bielefeld a program of notation through the labor exchanges required all those filing for jobs to fill out cards clarifying their employment status. A similar proviso in Braunschweig mandated the identification of job seekers who were unable to be placed by the municipal labor exchange. Random efforts to count the unemployed in Strassburg were marred by the susceptibility of the labor market to weather conditions. This limited the utility of the Strassburg census to shedding light on conditions within very narrowly defined geographical and temporal parameters. Comparability among counts was virtually non-existent.

Many unemployment surveys were undertaken during periods of economic distress and their outcome suffered from the need to locate and question each jobless worker individually. The lack of a permanent center for the regular dissemination of information about changes in the labor market hampered this effort, as did the absence of a uniform method of inquiry. The least satisfactory results seemed to derive from the most impersonal survey methods including the use of ballot boxes where the unemployed were asked to voluntarily insert completed questionnaires. Other forms of voluntary registration through agencies such as census bureaus, labor exchanges or warming halls tended to work well when they received enthusiastic support from organized labor. However, there was no guarantee that unemployed workers would bother to register with such institutions, particularly during hard times when the likelihood of securing work through these avenues was small. Large numbers of polling places, good supervision and precise regulations seemed to insure fairly accurate results for this type of undertaking when the unions and SDP encouraged the participation of their members.[53]

With methods such as house-to-house tallies where census takers were engaged to question the unemployed, it was essential to insure the respondents' confidence in those conducting the surveys. One means of securing such trust in the view of Richard Herbst was to use working-class counters to poll their own kind. Such pollsters were more likely to accurately convey the intent of their inquiries and allay suspicions about the uses to which the data would be put. If the unemployed were convinced that their responses would not be turned to their disadvantage and might even be used to further their own interests, it would be easier for census takers to overcome widespread indifference and apathy. House-to-house counts brought the census directly to the unemployed rather than demanding that they learn and seek out the source of inquiry. This necessitated a lower level of participant initiative and was therefore more likely to produce the desired cooperation than registration systems. In implementing house-to-house surveys, Herbst suggested that pollsters be assigned only one small section in densely populated working-class neighborhoods of large cities. That would facilitate a more thorough, personal and accurate approach to the collection of vital information in crucial areas--advantages which hopefully outweighed the drawbacks of having to engage the services of a large force of skilled census takers.

The results of urban unemployment surveys tended to be dominated by seasonal occupations in general and the building trades in particular. Not surprisingly, they consistently omitted information about conditions among the agricultural labor force. Counts conducted to determine the degree of unemployment on a given day failed to provide information on the duration of joblessness, on its relative extent, cause or the direction in which it was moving. What was lacking from most unemployment surveys conducted during our period was a twofold sense of present economic conditions and historical perspective. The former problem derived from an insufficient awareness of conditions in the labor market at the time when the unemployment counts were undertaken. The lack of historical continuity was due in large measure to the infrequency and irregularity with which the polls were conducted.

In the realm of policy, the timing of unemployment surveys reflected the fact that government at all levels was motivated to amass data when conditions were bad and consider instituting corrective measures after the economy had improved. The seemingly erratic and spotty nature of unemployment statistics was the outgrowth of a flexible policy calculated to contain the consequences of work scarcity rather than search out and eliminate its causes. Short-term measures in limited geographical areas designed to abate the bourgeois fears of revolution and proletarian anxiety born of economic uncertainty were hallmarks of German unemployment policies during our transitional period. Long-term solutions of a nationally comprehensive nature were relegated to the realm of debate rather than policy. The pattern of collecting data on unemployment clearly mirrored and to a certain extent even dictated this piece-meal approach on the policy level.

One proposal for an ideal unemployment survey was advanced by Adolph Braun in Soziale Praxis during 1893. Braun offered a plan for relying on the economic and political institutions of organized labor to inform workers about the particulars of forthcoming surveys. He advocated direct efforts by trained census takers to seek out and question unemployed individuals. The collective resources of unions and working class political machines were to be drafted to awaken labor interest in the project through meetings and publications. Braun's assertion that labor organizations should be used collectively rather than individually to determine the extent of unemployment met with some opposition.[54] Against his proposal, arguments were advanced in favor of relying on statistics compiled by single unions which were thought to be most conversant with the problems and false claims of their own members.

Like Richard Herbst, Braun advocated small areas--preferably between one and three houses--as optimum assignments for a single surveyor. Question cards were preferred to census sheets for the collection of information because cards were considered simpler to use, both for the initial gathering and subsequent organization of information. On a designated weekday, the counters were to poll their residents, returning to question absentees on a Sunday, early morning or late evening visit. It was suggested that the following information be obtained: Residence; Name; Age; Marital Status; Skilled Occupation; Last Employment; Date of Unemployment; Names of Children, their ages, type of employment, present activities; Other Dependent Persons. In addition, these questions were recommended: Is the duration of unemployment caused by illness? Does the wife contribute through her earnings to the support of the family? Does she now have an opportunity to do so?

If the responses to these questions were truthful and accurately reported, Braun believed they would provide invaluable indications as to the circumstances of unemployment, its duration up to a given point in time, its distribution according to age, occupation and residential district. This format would also reveal how many family members were affected by the head of household's loss of work and the extent to which dependents were able to ameliorate the attendant hardship through jobs of their own. These questions suggest that contemporaries viewed unemployment in terms of its impact on families rather than individuals. It is significant that income and expenditure were weighed on a collective rather than personal scale and that the family was still seen as the basic economic unit in the German marketplace. Women and children were regarded as helpmates of adult males. And their earnings were usually considered the first line of defense against the head of household's loss of employment.

Because the collection of data and adoption of policies were integrally related, it is important to note which agencies gathered the information. Those private and public institutions that were in the best position to provide assistance to the jobless were also responsible for amassing the bulk of statistics. The unions and municipalities which offered protection through unemployment insurance were those with a base which included a high proportion of all workers in given geographical areas or occupations, a low proportion of seasonal laborers, and a preponderance of skilled rather than unskilled workmen. The increasingly common tendency to divorce support from physical mobility in the case of unions and the persistent imposition of residence requirements in the case of cities were typical of the German penchant for coping with unemployment on a limited scale.

By the turn of the century both union and municipal statistics reflect an unprecedented, but still grudging, willingness to assume a modicum of financial responsibility for the unemployed. Quantitative data from the last half of our period reveals a growing belief in the necessity of dealing with unemployment at the grass roots level. The spotty nature of the numbers which have survived accurately reflects the fact that solutions to the unemployment problem were built from the bottom up, with individual union and municipal organizations taking the lead. This trend established a pattern which prevailed until after the events of the Great War finally led Germany to adapt local unemployment policies to a national scale.

Union Unemployment Funds and the Gathering of Statistics

All of the previously considered efforts to collect unemployment data came under the auspices of public agencies. In contrast to these public records, the best private statistics which have survived from our period were gathered by the trade unions. Collected as an adjunct to the payment of unemployment benefits for their membership, these figures provide continuous information on the job situation for a powerful segment of German labor. It is important to remember, however, that union unemployment figures reflected conditions for a relatively privileged minority within the industrial work force. Less than one-third of all German workers belonged to trade unions during our period and an even smaller fraction was covered by unemployment funds.

Although generalizations about diverse union memberships are difficult, it must be emphatically noted that estimates of unemployment among organized labor were likely to be well below the rate of joblessness among the working populace as a whole. Union members were typically the most capable and experienced employees, consisting largely of mature males who enjoyed head of household status. During hard times, they were among the last to be laid off and if that eventuality occurred they had access to a variety of institutional support mechanisms which gave them a decided advantage over non-union men in the competition for other jobs. In addition to unemployment benefits, unions frequently afforded their members access to information about employment opportunities before it became available in the general labor market. Although the partial view of the overall unemployment picture provided by union data never approached comprehensive proportions, by the end of our period it had the unique advantage of offering virtually continuous information about an important segment of the industrial labor force.

In trade unions, as in the public sector, most unemployment statistics were gathered as part of programs designed to institute relief measures. For the unions, this almost invariably took the form of insurance funds. While state and municipal authorities argued about whose responsibility unemployment insurance ought to be, a few unions assumed the initiative both in collecting data and providing benefits for their members. Union funds imposed a standard premium on all participants who were thus in a sense self-insured. To cite one example, during the mid-Nineties the Evangelical Trade Unions met in Frankfurt am Main to consider a proposal for unemployment insurance. Insurance would have cost members 10 Pfennigs per week and paid benefits amounting to three Marks per week, probably not enough to be of great help to the average urban family. The problem here was to make the premiums low enough to enable all union members to participate and at the same time make the benefits high enough to afford real relief for unemployed recipients without driving the funds into bankruptcy. Most unions had relatively limited success with their unemployment programs prior to the turn of the century. After twenty years of providing unemployment insurance, the Hirsch-Duncker Associations reported in 1895 that they had expended approximately 48,000 Marks, an average of only 70 Pfennigs for each of their 67,000 members.[55] The Social Democratic unions managed to do somewhat better but even their unemployment insurance programs afforded minimal assistance.

Among the earliest, most vocal and influential advocates of unemployment insurance through trade unions was

Professor Lujo Brentano who taught at Strassburg during the early 1880's. A critique of his views on unemployment appeared in the *Leipziger Zeitung* on September 20, 1882. Brentano maintained that under industrial capitalism the old relationship between employer and employee had been transformed into one where wage earners became sellers of a unique commodity, namely their labor. While other vendors sold tangible products, the laborer in a sense had only himself to sell--his person and the tasks he could perform. Remuneration for a worker's effort was no longer under his own control but subject to the demand of employers. Depressed wages and employment contingent on consumer demand posed overwhelming problems for workers who Brentano felt could only be protected from starvation through unemployment insurance. Insurance alone would give the worker a fair chance to improve his position and stand up for his rights against employers bent on minimizing wage expenditures. Labor parity would begin to emerge with the adoption of unemployment insurance: "der Arbeiter kommt somit durch die Versicherung gegen Arbeitslosigkeit in die Lage jedes anderen Waarenverkaeufers, dass er den Preis seiner Waare selbst bestimmen und somit auch waehrend er beschaeftigt ist, seine wirthschafticliche Lage verbessern kann."[56]

In addition, Brentano argued that workers needed economic protection against illness, old age and death. It was important that premiums on insurance against these potential disasters be paid even when the worker was unemployed and without the ability to cover the costs himself. Unemployment coverage was seen as a prerequisite for the institution and continuation of all other types of labor insurance. According to Brentano, corporations such as trade unions were the logical collective means of inaugurating insurance programs. Unions in his view represented the common interests of all workers in a given trade. They were established at least in part to protect members against the eventuality of unemployment whether it was caused by lack of consumer demand, employers' cost-cutting measures or labor initiated strikes. They worked to control the labor market through manipulations ranging from support for resettlement programs or limitations on the number of apprenticeships to strikes for better wages and hours.

The day after the comments on Brentano's unemployment views appeared in the Leipziger Zeitung, that paper carried another article on trade unions and insurance. According to the article, almost half of Germany's two million organized workers were excluded from union unemployment coverage.[57] A law enacted by the Reich on April 8, 1876, had exempted workers who belonged to other relief funds from compulsory membership in future union ventures. This proviso set up a potential conflict between public-- state or municipal--insurance projects on the one hand and private union undertakings on the other. Four years after the implementation of this law, the total number protected by union assistance funds had declined by more than 100,000 persons--from 829,204 to 716,718 or some 13 percent.

To understand this situation it is important to remember that the natural leaders of labor insurance reform were constrained by politically motivated restrictions. Not surprisingly, the Social Democratic unions' avowed support of unemployment insurance had been hampered by Bismark's anti-Socialist legislation. Many party spokesmen favored state subsidized unemployment benefits but their pleas fell on deaf ears.[57a] Arguing that the workers were unable to save amounts sufficient for their relief in the event of joblessness, the Socialists failed to act decisively and accomplished virtually nothing in terms of securing unemployment support from the government for their constituency.

The Hirsch-Duncker Associations instituted measures that had relatively little effect on their approximately 21,000 members during the 1880's. As the century drew to a close, however, the Hirsch-Duncker organizations began to do more. In 1894, with a membership of 67,000, these Associations paid out 73,000 Marks in unemployment benefits of all kinds (Arbeits-, Reise-, Uebersiedlungs-, Nothstandsunterstuetzung, Beitragsversicherung).[57b] And in 1899, 105,000 Marks were expended. During 1902, trade association members numbered 102,851; their funds collected 800,434 Marks and paid out 749,299 Marks. Of that amount, 246,899 Marks went for unemployment, strikes and lockouts. Relocation and emergencies claimed an additional 62,245

Marks. By 1904, all Hirsch-Duncker Associations offered their members some form of unemployment protection.[58]

Paralleling this progress were gains made in the labor unions. In 1900, from a total of 58 unions, twenty organizations with 226,000 members spent 524,000 Marks on unemployment relief. And during the economic slump which set in the next year--during 1901--more than double that amount was paid out in benefits to unemployed members-- 1,238,197 Marks. More progressive than other branches of organized labor, the printers with about 9000 members and the hat makers with 3000 did the most for their men in terms of unemployment insurance prior to 1890.

In 1882 among all organized workers in Germany, only about 40,000 were formally protected against the eventuality of unemployment. This number amounted to approximately two percent of the German labor force, leaving 49 out of every 50 workers uninsured and dependent on poor relief or public charity in the event of unemployment. Employers' continued opposition to unemployment relief along with plans for labor exchanges reflected widespread middle-class resentment of public subsidies for workers' insurance.

Although there was no typical or representative pattern for unemployment insurance which applied to all unions, we shall briefly consider a few special cases where organized labor did most to protect its membership. In general terms, unions representing men with seasonal occupations such as construction workers were least likely to provide unemployment assistance. Conversely, those involved in trades requiring high levels of skill and those such as the printers which represented a high proportion of all workers active in their profession were most prone to offer unemployment protection. Contemporaries believed that the lower the level of skill and the higher the proportion of physical as opposed to mental labor involved in a job, the easier it would be to find alternate employment.[59]

The Christian trade unions, whose membership on April 1, 1903, was 84,652, did relatively little as a group to further unemployment coverage. By 1904, however, the individual Christian unions of butchers, wood workers, shoemakers and leather workers, metal workers and members of the graphic trades offered some form of unemployment benefits. According to Moritz Wagner, the Socialist unions did most in this area, the breakdown by occupation being as follows:[60]

Union	Height of Total Expenditure in Marks	Annual Average of Expenses
Printers (1880-1900)	1 938 793	92 323
Hatmakers (1886-1900)	251 055	16 737
Sculpters (1891-1900)	221 093	22 109
Porcelain Workers (July 1891-1900)	205 003	21 579
Glovemakers (1895-1900)	158 830	9 927
Coppersmiths (1887-1900)	103 727	7 409
Bookbindeers (1894-1900)	68 291	9 756
Metal Workers (July-end 1900)	50 577	101 100
Brewers (1892-1900)	49 687	5 521
Glass Workers (1892-1899)	42 718	5 339
Lithographers (1899-1900)	24 995	12 497
Cigar Sorters (1892-1899)	22 928	2 866

Union	Height of Total Expenditure in Marks	Annual Average of Expenses
Leather Workers (1897-1899)	18 995	2 374
Commercial Workers (1897-1900)	8 724	2 181
Glaziers (1892-1899)	7 160	895
Confectioners (1899-1900)	2 984	1 482
Moulding Workers	2190	365

Historically, travel subsidies first introduced during the 1840's in the local printers' associations evolved into unemployment payments to laborers not prepared to change their residence in search of jobs. During the economically depressed year of 1879 two important steps in the development of union unemployment benefits occurred. First of all, the Hirsch-Duncker Associations tried unsuccessfully to establish a "Verbandskasse fuer Reisende und Arbeitslose" which despite its failure set a precedent for future action.[61] And the printers' unions voted 26 to 4 in favor of adopting measures to provide unemployment protection for their members.

During the hard times which ensued in the 1880's, little progress was made but by 1886 the glove manufactureres, hat makers, and coppersmiths all adopted unemployment programs through their unions. The sculptors and porcelain workers followed suit in 1891 and two years later there were 11 unions offering unemployment protection: Sculptors, brewers, printers, glass workers, glaziers, glove makers, hat makers, coppersmiths, leather workers, cigar sorters, and harness makers. An increasing number of unions provided coverage by the turn of the century. A 1902

estimate of union expenditure on unemployment relief during
the preceding decade placed the figure in excess of three
million Marks.[62] Broken down by types of organization, the
picture for union labor looked fairly good by 1904.[63]

> Im Jahre 1904 hatten von 62 Zentralverbanden 38 die
> Arbeitslosenunterstuetzung eingefuehrt, alle Hirsch-
> Dunckerschen Gewerkvereine haben diesen Unterstuet-
> zungszweig aufgenommen, und von den christlichen
> Gewerkschaften sind die christlichen Verbaende der
> Fleischer, Holzarbeiter, Schuh- und Lederarbeiter,
> Metallarbeiter, die graphische Gewerbe mit der Ein-
> fuehrung vorgegangen. Die gleiche Entwicklung findet
> sich bei der Unabhaengigen Vereinen und den beruflichen
> Fachabteilungen des Verbandes der katholischen Arbeit-
> ervereine.

An interesting point here is that the unions with the
longest history of unemployment benefits also tended to
incur the largest annual expenditures. The single exception
of the metal workers is explained by the fact that the
available data covered such a brief interval.

An important footnote to figures on expense
occasioned by unemployment relates to the link between
organized labor's record of agitation and strikes on the one
hand and its membership's protection against threatened loss
of work on the other. The following table clearly demonstrates that at least during the 1890's there was some
correlation between the security provided by unemployment
insurance and organized labor's willingness to risk alien-
ating employers by means of strikes.[64]

Year	Unions with Unemployment Protection			Unions without Protection		
	Membership Number	Expenditure for Strikes Marks	Per Head Marks	Membership Number	Strike Expenses Marks	Per Head Marks
1893	46,605	37,066	0.80	174,925	55,611	0.32
1896	61,207	224,104	3.66	267,623	767,613	2.87
1899	103,470	1,228,322	11.87	477,003		4.47

The dual connection between strikes and unemployment was spelled out in these terms:[65]

> Eine Verbindung von Arbeitslosigkeit und Streik findet sich sonst hauptsaechlich in zwei Faellen: der eine Fall ist, wenn jemand ohne selbst zu streiken, aber infolge des Streikes beschaeftigungslos wird (weil z.B. Kohlenmangel eintritt), in diesem Fall wird er als arbeitslos behandelt; der zweite Fall ist, dass nach beendetem Streike jemand, der also nicht mehr streikt und auch keine Streikunterstuetzung mehr erhaelt, keine Beschaeftigung findet. Dieser Fall wird in den meisten Statuten gar nicht beruehrt. Man wird annehmen duerfen dass, wenn er nicht wieder eingestellt wird, er als arbeitslos unterstuetzt wird, eventuell unter dem Gesichtspunkte der Massregelung wegen Eintrittens fuer die Interessen des Verbandes.

Obviously, the security of knowing that members were protected by insurance in the event that strikes led to unemployment tended to increase labor's willingness to use work stoppage as a means for achieving its ends.

Having surveyed the general situation among unions with regard to unemployment coverage, let us briefly turn our attention to the exceptional case of the printers union which offered its members the most complete, long-standing coverage on record. At the outset it is important to note than an 1892 estimate published in Soziale Praxis indicated that approximately 50 percent of all German workers employed in the printing trades belonged to unions. As we maintained earlier, unemployment benefits in the printers unions grew out of older funds for relocation assistance. After 1879, approximately 10 to 15 Pfennigs per member per week were allocated out of union dues for unemployment protection. Compensation initially amounted to 5 or 6 Marks for a period between 10 and 13 weeks or a total ranging from 50 to 78 Marks. Participants in the fund during its first decade-- the 1880's--also received the following coverage: Legal consultation and protection, educational opportunities, investigation of labor disputes, travel subsidies and access to labor exchanges.[66] Two types of unemployment funds, one established in 1875 to aid those traveling in search of work and a second which evolved in 1880 to supply unemployment benefits "am Orte" provided an enviable range of coverage.

Although there were strict rules to eliminate false claims, considerable sums were paid out both in the form of travel and stationary benefits for the unemployed. During the economically depressed years between 1882 and 1885, for example, the printers paid a total of approximately 600,000 Marks in travel and unemployment assistance to 1200 members. At the end of 1892 a new type of arrangement emerged which involved some employers in providing unemployment protection for their labor force. The owners of printing shops with union workers were required to pay between 10 and 20 Pfennigs per employee each week. These contributions went into an unemployment fund to which the men themselves added a weekly stipend of 10 Pfennigs. From this fund, jobless printing assistants were entitled after 26 weeks of contributions to receive one Mark per day for a period of 140 days. As of 1893, the fund was to be administered in conjunction with a nationally based labor exchange through the printers trade union.[67]

Data presented in Appendix A of this study indicates that printers' assistants outnumbered apprentices in the unions by about two to one. Between 1880 and 1901, organized assistants were without jobs for a total of approximately 4.8 million days. With an average weekly wage of 24 Marks, the total cost of unemployment among organized printers amounted to 21.2 million Marks, or just under one million Marks annually for twenty-two years.

Although the printers union had provided unemployment benefits and kept records detailing their members' job status from the beginning of our period, their example in this area was seldom duplicated prior to the 1890's. During that decade both municipal and union authorities began to survey the unemployed sporadically and by the turn of the century, periodic counts were starting to emerge at least for certain segments of the German labor force. Let us begin our analysis of these efforts by looking at the disparate attempts to enumerate the unemployed during the Nineties.

Following on the heels of the grim labor market of 1892, the socialist unions undertook an unemployment count in January of 1893. The survey included 31 cities whose population according to the census of December 1, 1890, was 2,437,214. The estimated population increase between the dates of the 1890 census and the 1893 survey was six percent, meaning that the total number of persons involved was 2,583,447. According to the 1882 census, towns with more than 5000 inhabitants registered 23 percent of their residents as workers or "Arbeitnehmer". Assuming that percentage applied in 1893 also, there would have been 594,193 workers polled by the socialist unions. Of that number, 41,615 or 7 percent were unemployed. The average length of unemployment was 67 days. The geographical distribution was as follows:[68]

Ort	Zahl der Arbeitslosen	Davon verheirathet	Zahl der Angehörigen	durchschnittliche Wochenzahl der Arbeitslosigkeit	Einwohnerzahl am 1.12. 1890
Leipzig	8 608	5 227	9 536	$14^5/_7$	295 025
Möckern ...	160	111	280	$10^5/_7$	4 369
Wurzen ...	190	133	276	—	14 635
Nürnberg ..	1 058	—	—	-	142 590
Stuttgart ...	2 612	1 148	2 357	$6^1/_3$	139 817
Cannstatt ..	203	—	—	—	20 265
Mannheim ..	1 072	512	1 177	7	79 058
Ludwigshafen	400	—	-	—	28 768
Köln mit Vororten	8 851	—	—	$17^1/_7$ ²)	197 081³)
Barmen	1 320	755	1 678	—	116 144
Elberfeld ...	1 889	1 102	2 730	—	125 899
Dortmund ..	427	179	724	—	89 663
Lüneburg ..	302	204	563	$5^1/_3$	20 665
Hamburg ..	4 893	2 658	10 917	—	569 260
Wandsbeck .	511	315	1 161	$7^7/_8$	20 571
Harburg ...	300	—	—	—	35 081

Ort	Zahl der Arbeitslosen	Davon verheirathet	Zahl der Angehörigen	durchschnittliche Wochenzahl der Arbeitslosigkeit	Einwohnerzahl am 1.12. 1890
Lübeck	430	—	1 088	13	63 590
Kassel	965	543	1 393	—	72 477
Gotha	410	—	—	—	29 134
Vororte Gothas	284	167	—	—	—
Zeitz	139	71	166	$7^1/_4$	21 680
Braunschweig	1 403	883	2 038	$13^1/_7$	101 047
Wolfenbüttel	240	149	-.	8	14 484
Wernigerode	120	—	—	—	9 966
Halle	1 002	632	1 710	$11^4/_7$	101 401
Giebichenstein	352	259	746	11	14 454
Schkeuditz ..	117	78	156	$7^3/_7$	5 020
Eilenburg ..	209	156	362	$9^1/_3$	12 447
Stassfurt ...	240	108	290	$9^1/_4$	19 104
Brandenburg	408	312	940	$10^1/_3$	37 817
Rixdorf	2 500	—	-.	—	35 702
Zusammen	41 615	15 702	40 288	—	2 437 214

Although overestimates in cases such as Cologne and underestimates in instances like Hamburg occurred, the preceding figures provide a rough guideline to depressed employment conditions in major urban areas. Other union statistics compiled slightly later however reflect the diversity which was camouflaged by these numbers. Note in particular the wide range of both the incidence and duration of unemployment among organized workers.[69]

Berufsart	Beobachtungs-zeit	Auf Jahr und Tausend beobachter Personen kommen Arbeitslose	Auf den Arbeits-losen kommen pro Jahr Tage der Arbeitslosigkeit
Berg und Grubenarbeiter	1892-93	3.13	15
Steinmetze, Steinhauer, Steinsetzer, Töpfer	1892-94	9.10	29.17
Holzarbeiter	1890-94	55.42	31.89
Lederarbeiter	1891-94	33.21	41.46
Gärtner	1893	-----	42.60
Konfektions- und Textilbranche	1892-94	9.92	45
Bauarbeiter	1891-93	803	49
Nahrungsmittelindustrie und Cigararbeiter	1892-94	36.89	50.27
Dienstboten	1893	-----	52.20
Maschinenbau und Metallarbeiter	1892-94	18.99	56.97
Graphische Gewerbe und Mahler	1880-93	70	60.32
Gewöhnliche Tagearbeiter ohne besondere Branche	1885-94	44.01	61.33
Handlungsgehülfen	1892-94	18.43	62.31
Gehülfen im Gast- und Schankwirthschaft	1893	-----	100.81
DURCHSCHNITT IM ALLGEMEINEN	1880-94	100.19	49.88

The author who compiled these numbers warned his readers against taking any individual statistic at face value since strikes and voluntary unemployment influenced the figures which appeared above. In some instances, the numbers were too high and in others too low--the hope was that excesses would balance underestimates and leave one with an accurate overall view of the relatively large unemployment levels registered during the last downswing of the trend period 1873-96.

Much of the unemployment data which was compiled during the 1890's stemmed from the efforts of organized labor. Nevertheless, of the 56 central labor organizations operating in 1897, only 15 offered their members unemployment insurance. The primary reason for this was the residual fear of confiscation of union funds by the police, another legacy of Bismarck's anti-socialist legislation. The slow growth of membership during economically depressed years retarded the expansion of the German labor movement until the turn of the century. Although clearly representing a minority of the industrial labor force, union expenditure on unemployment relief during 1892 and 1893 was noteworthy. According to Hirschberg: "Die Gewerkschaften gaben...im Deutschen Reich 1892: 357 000, 1893: 305 000 fuer Arbeitslosen Unterstuetzung aus, worunter fuer die Buchdrucker 236 000 bez. 93 000 Mk. (ungerechnet die Reise-Unterstuetzung)".[70] Figures published in Soziale Praxis indicated that between 1892 and 1894, the German unions expended a total of 198,929 Marks on unemployment protection. The same publication's figures for the next triennium registered a pronounced increase. Despite improved economic conditions between 1895 and 1897 trade unions spent 249,793 Marks on unemployment support.[71]

Among the free trade unions, the following expenditures were made for unemployment, with the figures shown in Marks allocated for each member of the organization during the years between 1892 and 1907. (See the chart on the following page.)[72] In those unions which offered unemployment protection, the average expenditure per member amounted to 5.02 Marks per year overall but this figure failed to reflect a range among individual unions which spanned the gamut from a low of 0.16 Marks to a high of

	1892 M.	1895 M.	1898 M.	1901 M.	1904 M.	1905 M.	1907 M.
Buchdrucker	14,72	5,09	5,59	16,59	13,20	9,40	10,40
Glasarbeiter	3,38	1,80	1,13	2,03	2,39	1,19	1,46
Glaser	1,25	0,76	0,39	2,63	3,53	7,22	10,74
Handschuhmacher	9,81	0,67	2,48	20,60	8,98	0,97	17,03
Hutmacher	9,75	7,29	5,29	4,99	6,04	7,21	7,13
Kupferschmiede	3,33	2,40	2,72	7,04	4,55	3,63	4,51
Lederarbeiter	0,32	—	0,31	—	3,67	2,74	8,50
Zigarrensortierer	7,10	2,45	4,59	10,75	4,93	3,20	2,24
Bildhauer	0,10	8,37	9,38	19,72	10,35	11,68	25,64
Brauereiarbeiter	0,18	0,52	0,94	2,02	1,16	0,09	0,75
Porzellanarbeiter	10,14	3,61	3,77	6,83	2,76	2,41	2,34
Buchbinder	—	0,97	2,24	3,79	2,90	3,38	4,56
Graveure	—	—	1,31	3,05	3,37	6,01	4,55
Transportarbeiter	—	—	0,28	0,63	0,53	0,62	0,97
Buchdruckerei-Hilfsarbeiter . .	—	—	—	1,47	1,68	1,01	1,39
Handlungsgehilfen	—	—	—	0,30	0,25	0,43	0,65
Schmiede	—	—	—	2,20	1,42	0,84	1,22
Lithographen	—	—	—	4,01	6,01	5,09	6,16
Metallarbeiter	—	—	—	3,03	2,27	1,89	8,91
Formstecher	—	—	—	1,97	0,96	6,03	10,51
Mühlenarbeiter	—	—	—	—	1,78	1,47	1,32
Bäcker	—	—	—	—	2,94	3,12	3,88
Maschinisten	—	—	—	—	1,74	1,47	5,01
Notenstecher	—	—	—	—	3,90	18,15	27,25
Böttcher	—	—	—	—	2,08	2,56	2,83
Bureauangestellte	—	—	—	—	0,85	0,53	0,75
Schuhmacher	—	—	—	—	0,02	0,92	0,82
Barbiere	—	—	—	—	0,53	1,01	1,45
Holzarbeiter	—	—	—	—	2,20	3,24	5,80
Sattler	—	—	—	—	0,62	3,00	5,58
Tabakarbeiter	—	—	—	—	0,62	1,21	0,80
Bergarbeiter	—	—	—	—	—	0,06	0,05
Gärtner	—	—	—	—	—	0,99	1,44
Tapezierer	—	—	—	—	—	2,92	5,63
Fabrikarbeiter	—	—	—	—	—	2,78	4,16
Portefeuiller	—	—	—	—	—	0,15	0,66
Photograph	—	—	—	—	—	3,93	1,05
Schiffszimmerer	—	—	—	—	—	0,30	0,96
Xylographen	—	—	—	—	—	12,27	6,16
Zimmerer	—	—	—	—	—	1,88	4,18
Gemeindearbeiter	—	—	—	—	—	—	0,16
Steinsetzer	—	—	—	—	—	—	0,18

27.55 Marks. Among the Free Unions, the following had no unemployment protection as late as 1907. Note here the high proportion of occupations affected by seasonal changes in the demand for labor, particularly in the building trades.

Number	Organization	Membership
1	Asphalteure	498
4	Bauhilfsarbeiter	71,268
7	Blumenarbeiter	430
14	Dachdecker	6,403
16	Fleischer	3,035
19	Gastwirtshilfen	6,728
23	Hafenarbeiter	25,168
27	Hoteldiener	3,152
30	Kuerschner	2,193
31	Lagerhalter	1,846
34	Maler	39,009
36	Maurer	193,582
47	Schneider	38,159
--	Waeschearbeiter	2,484
49	Seeleute	7,720
50	Steinarbeiter	19,176
52	Stukkateure	8,293
55	Textilarbeiter	121,265
56	Toepfer	11,914
61	Zivilmusiker	1,188

As a footnote it would be worth mentioning the considerable degree of unmet need which these statistics reflected. During economically depressed years such as 1892, for example, the Gewerkschaft der deutscher Dreschler estimated that approximately 25 percent of its membership was unemployed at some point. In the Vereinigung deutscher Maler, Anstreicher und Lackirer during the same year, an estimated 25 percent of the membership had been unemployed for more than three months.[73] As these figures suggest, seasonal occupations such as the building trades were the most vulnerable to unemployment and least prone to offer collective protection. This failure posed real problems for a major segment of the German labor force.

The growth of the Free Unions' support for the unemployed between 1891 and 1907 is shown in the following table:[74]

Year	Disciplinary Fund	Travel Subsidies	Strike Support	Unemployment Benefits	TOTALS
1891	14737	144338	1037789	64290	1261154
1892	236964	382607	44943	357087	1021601
1893	28331	328748	65356	220926	643361
1894	14630	350455	188980	239750	793815
1895	40307	302603	253589	196912	793411
1896	37346	310000	844372	243201	1434919
1897	30973	289036	881758	260316	1462083
1898	39978	283267	1073290	275404	1671939
1899	55435	313391	2121918	304677	2795421
1900	97092	461028	2625642	501078	3684840
1901	198173	607127	1878792	1238197	3922289
1902	250661	709778	1930329	1593022	4483790
1903	250310	613870	4529672	1270053	6663905
1904	536209	646821	5869519	1599424	8651973
1905	486765	712820	9674094	1991924	12865603
1906	795209	758222	13748412	2653296	17955139
1907	1010045	869148	13196363	6527577	21903133
1891 to 1907	4123165	8083259	59964818	19537134	91708376

The extraordinary expansion of union support in the years after the economic recession of 1901 was particularly dramatic. During the decade between 1898 and 1907, the Free Unions' unemployment payments grew from an annual rate of 275,404 Marks to more than six and a half million--an increase of nearly 2500 percent, or an average annual increase of two and one half times the 1898 figure.

As the preceding chart indicates, by 1907 the German economy had already embarked on the last major downswing before 1913. During 1907, 20 Christian trade unions with a membership of 274,324 workers paid out a total of 3,193,978 Marks. Of that sum, 743,270 Marks went to support strikes and related agitation while only 51,743 Marks were expended on travel and unemployment benefits. Fourteen of the twenty Christian unions offered travel and unemployment subsidies, but 72,617 workers belonged to organizations which supplied no unemployment protection. These included:

Number	Organization	Membership
1	Baecker	650
2	Bauhandwerker und Bauhilfsarbeiter	40135
3	Bayerische Eisenbahner	24112
4	Bayerische Salinen- arbeiter	893
9	Heimarbeiterinnen	4966
19	Telegraphenarbeiter	1861

For those Christian unions offering protection, expenditure per member amounted to 25 Pfennigs.

The record of the Hirsch-Duncker Trade Associations was somewhat better in the area of unemployment support. During 1906, 16 Associations with 118,508 members expended a total of 1,400,131 Marks. The average cost of unemployment benefits per member in all Hirsch- Duncker

Associations was just over one Mark during the relatively good year of 1906. Significantly, the affiliated building trades association was one of the few construction-related organizations to offer any unemployment support. During 1906 its 1222 members received a total of 222 Marks for unemployment relief, an average of 0.18 Mark per member which was well below the figure for the Hirsch-Duncker Associations as a whole. Although it would be dangerous to generalize from this isolated example, the figures here suggest that despite contemporary resistance to the idea, unemployment benefits could be offered in trades which were susceptible to seasonal fluctuations of the labor market.

All of the unions offering unemployment protection tended to impose minimum membership periods as a qualification for eligibility. The term usually amounted to one year but the period ranged from six months to two years. Many unions pegged relief payments to seniority, age and sex. Predictably, recent members, youths and women were compensated at lower rates. Although the progressive printers union failed to impose a specified waiting period for the commencement of relief payments, most unions stipulated a time ranging from three days to two weeks after the loss of one's job for this purpose. After the turn of the century, union payments ranged from 50 Pfennigs to 2 Marks daily and from 4 to 17 Marks weekly. Annually, the maximum payments ran from 16 to 200 Marks and the maximum duration of support from 18 to 140 days, with some unions paying for Sundays as well as weekdays. Relief recipients were required to register periodically with union officials to prevent false claims by men who were still working.

Keeping these criteria for support in mind, it is worth noting that the socialist trade unions conducted an unemployment survey on January 23, 1893, using the house-to-house method with volunteers as counters. Nine professional groups were polled and an estimated 9.3 percent were deemed to be unemployed. 23,583 men, women and children were found to be without work or a visible means of subsistence. The average duration of unemployment was fourteen weeks and five days, but 266 cases were recorded where individuals had been idle more than two years.[75] An article published in Soziale Praxis during 1893 cast doubts on the value of such unemployment figures by noting that they ignored the vast majority of German workers who were not union-affiliated.

To get a fix on the quantity of non-organized unemployed, a number of labor bureaus in the larger cities undertook sporadic surveys after 1890 which relied on varying degrees of union cooperation. Many of the early tallies were of an indirect nature and tended to commence during recessions. A caesura in methods which roughly coincided with the turn of the century was characterized by a more profesional and geographically comprehensive approach. Toward the end of our period, Charlottenburg, Munich, Cologne, Hannover, Magdeburg, Barmen, Dresden and

Stuttgart all instituted unemployment surveys whose success depended on the support of local unions.

Confirming the economically severe circumstances of the early 1890's the Berlin Police Presidium reported an estimated 20,000 unemployed in the capital during the winter of 1891, with the number swelling to triple that amount-- 60,000--the following year.[76] In Magdeburg during 1892 over 1700 persons registered for municipally sponsored employment according to the magistrate in charge. In Krefeld, the mayor's office reported that that year some 63,500 Marks out of a 65,000 Mark fund had been spent to provide jobs for the unemployed, nearly three-quarters of which were weavers. At Cologne during 1892 a daily outlay of 300 to 350 Marks was made to provide bread and soup for the city's unemployed. The municipal authorities in Solingen, Wald and Hohscheid reported during 1892 that the allocation for poor relief had been depleted before the end of the year, leaving the unemployed with fewer public sources of jobs than were needed. There were, in other words, far more applications for work such as street maintenance than could be funded. In Erfurt during 1892, 17,000 Marks were allocated for the employment of jobless heads of households. Some 250 men were paid an hourly wage of 20 Pfennigs or a daily stipend of 1 Mark 80 Pfennigs to do jobs which the city deemed to be in the public interest. To cite one final example, an 1892 survey conducted by the socialist unions in Mannheim indicated that there were about 1500 unemployed in that city.

The preceding data suggests that when unemployment reached significant proportions, the cooperative efforts of municipal and union officials were necessary to keep the situation within manageable bounds. Such cooperation was forthcoming as part of an effort to count the unemployed in the free city of Hamburg during the 1890's. The first major survey was inaugurated during October of 1892. The following questions were to be answered by those who were polled. For future reference, particular note should be taken of questions about reduced wages and hours.[77]

> Vor- und Zuname? Wohnung? Strasse No. Etage? Gewerbe? Arbeiten Sie zu Hause, in der Fabrik oder Werkstatt? Wie alt sind Sie? Jahre. Verheirathet oder ledig? Zahl der zu ernaehrenden Familienangehoerigen? Sind Sie zur Zeit arbeitslos? Seit wann sind Sie arbeitslos? Sind sonst Familienangehoerige, welche mit zum Unterhalt der Familie beitragen, arbeitslos? Waren Sie im Laufe des Jahres, vor der Epidemie, arbeitslos? Wie viele Wochen? Wie viele Stunden pro Tag arbeiten Sie bei regelmaessigem Geschaeftsgang? Wie viele Stunden pro Tag arbeiten Sie jetzt? Wie lange arbeiten Sie schon kuerzere Arbeitszeit? Wie lange betraegt ihr Wochenverdienst? bei regelmaessigem Geschaeftsgang? M.Pf. jetzt? M.Pf.

The statistical commission of the Hamburg Trade Union Cartel prepared 170,000 copies of this questionnaire. The answers to these questions were to be completed and returned to designated registration areas within three days. Here it is worth mentioning that a cholera epidemic had broken out in the city on August 27, 1892, which greatly exacerbated already poor economic conditions. Every effort was made to differentiate between joblessness stemming from health-related problems and unemployment caused by purely economic factors.

At the time of the survey, an estimated 170,000 workers were employed in Hamburg. Approximately nineteen thousand persons responded to the inquiry which thus sampled around eleven percent of the local labor force. The ages of those participating ranged from fifteen to seventy years, with an average age of 34 years. 62 percent or 11,672 respondents were married and had 42,178 family members to support. In contrast, only 55 percent or 2658 of those designated as unemployed were married.

On the 15th of October, 4,893 persons indicated that they had been unemployed an average of 10.4 weeks or a total of 50,375 weeks. The longest recorded period of unemployment, stretching from January 1 to October 15, 1892, was 41 weeks; the shortest was one week. Between January 1 and October 15, 1892, 10,893 persons were unemployed in Hamburg for a total of 135,397 weeks or an average of 12.3 weeks per jobless individual. If one estimated an average daily wage of three Marks, the lost income amounted to 223 Marks per unemployed worker or a sum total of 2,437,146 Marks. This loss was compounded by shortened hours and reduced incomes derived from the cholera outbreak in August. On the 15th of October, 1892, there were more than 20 unemployed persons in Hamburg affiliated with each of the following trades:[78]

Baecker und Konditoren 40, Barbiere und Friseure 24,
Bau- und Erdarbeiter 147, Bleicher, Waescher, Blaetter-
innen 33, Brauer 63, Buchbinder 24, Buchdrucker und
Schriftsetzer 69, Fabrik und gewerbliche Hilfsarbeiter
und Arbeiterinnen 80, Gastwirthsgehilfen 185, Gelegenheitsarbeiter 843, Hafenarbeiter 336, Ewerfuehrer 112,
Kaiarbeiter 27, Schauerleute 42, Speicherarbeiter 90,
Handlungsgehilfen 35, Haendler, Kolporteure, Kraemer
80, Hausknechte und Kontoirboten 85, Heizer und Masch-
inisten 58, Kueper 22, Kutscher 61, Maler und Lackirer
253, Klempner und Mechaniker 48, Schlosser und Masch-
inenbauer 152, Schmiede 99, Musiker 66, Schiffszimmerer
80, Schneiderinnen 141, Schuhmacher und Stepper 52,
Stellmacher und Muehlenbauer 32, Zigarrenmacher 122,
Zigarrensortirer 39, Tischler 267, Toepfer 35, Zimmerleute und Zimmerarbeitsleute 192.

Fortunately, there were several efforts to follow up the
1892 survey with subsequent canvassing of the unemployed in
the city and the surrounding areas.

On February 11, 1894, the unemployed workers of
Hamburg, Ottensen and Altona were enumerated. At the time
of this survey, Vorwaerts estimated that the total number of
workers in Hamburg was well in excess of 120,000 persons.
The survey polled 53,756 workers of whom 34,634 were married
and 19,122 were single. The respondents had 138,851 dependent family members which meant that the statistics reported
on conditions among 192,607 residents, approximately one-
third of the city's population. Of the 53,756 respondents,
18,981 persons were completely unemployed on February 11,
1894. They indicated that they had been unemployed for a
total of 191,013 weeks; 2167 persons had been without work
for more than twenty weeks. Added to these figures, there
were 13,934 persons who classified themselves as partially
unemployed. In addition to ascertaining conditions on

February 11, 1894, the survey questioned workers about their employment status during the preceding calendar year. During 1893, 33,549 of the 53,756 persons polled were unemployed a total of 547,664 weeks or an average of 16.41 weeks per jobless Hamburg resident. 1375 persons had been unemployed for more than ten months, representing an estimated loss of income amounting to almost ten million Marks.

Before concluding this discussion of union unemployment statistics, a final word about their political implications is in order. A great deal of resentment focused on public unemployment subsidies to union members through the Ghent system which will be discussed in subsequent chapters. Fear of anything that conjured up a link between unemployment and socialist revolution tended to evoke an extreme reaction during our period. Efforts to suppress the collection and dissemination of union unemployment statistics must be understood in this context. It did not matter that union data was likely to underestimate the extent of unemployment because their membership constituted an elite within the industrial labor force. Police authorities and powerful pillars of the established order were afraid of the potential incendiary influence of unemployment statistics on anyone sympathetic to the labor movement. Because they were ignorant of the actual parameters of the problem, conservative forces in German society over-reacted to the unemployment situation and deliberately suppressed figures which might have allayed popular anxiety. Finally,

we should reiterate that union support of unemployment
surveys worked as a powerful incentive for labor participation and contributed to the accuracy of select counts in
both the public and private sectors.

RELIEF INSTITUTIONS AS ALTERNATE INDICATORS OF UNEMPLOYMENT

Thus far, we have attempted to illuminate some of the large gaps in our understanding of unemployment among German industrial workers during the years prior to 1890. Many of the lacunae in our knowledge are likely to remain permanent in view of the fact that observers much more closely allied to the problem in temporal terms shared our ignorance. Writing in 1894--approximately half-way through our period--Dr. E. Hirschberg commented pointedly on the state of contemporary knowledge about unemployment:[79]

> Man kennt weder genauer die Industrien noch die Orte, welche betroffen oder verschont sind, weder die Ursachen noch die Wirkungen der Arbeitslosigkeit, weder ihren Umfang noch ihre Natur.

As his remarks indicate, there were serious shortcomings in the nineteenth-century comprehension of both the specific details and general contours of industrial unemployment.

With the turn of the twentieth century, statistical methods gained a certain limited degree of sophistication and at least for the organized labor force the picture became more clearly defined. By 1904 the Reichsarbeitsblatt was voicing optimism about the employment prospects of the nearly one million organized workers in German Fachverbaenden. At that time, the belief was stated that the gathering of accurate unemployment data formed an essential prerequisite for, and a necessary part of, resolving the attendant problems. The statistics which have come down to us should therefore be seen as a measure of simultaneous efforts to combat unemployment itself.

In order to understand contemporary assessments of job scarcity and the responses it evoked, we might take a closer look at information on which they relied. In doing so, we must evaluate gaps in the literature and alternate indicators of unemployment for periods when directly relevant statistics were nonexistent. This is important because it helps to define those areas where speculation in the absence of hard data was likely to occur. It also serves to suggest points of contention among subsequent historical observers approaching our problem from different ideological perspectives.

Despite contemporary recognition of the importance of collecting accurate data on unemployment, the general assessment made by Shulamit Angel-Volkov applies here: "All the figures in the industrial statistics of the nineteenth century are far from being accurate. What they give us is no more than an impression of the scale of some major structural changes".[80] The only continuous figures which have survived as a body were gathered by the trade unions. As we have noted, even union data when looked at in isolation presented a distorted view of unemployment. Because organized labor represented an elite in terms of job opportunities, their unemployment statistics underestimate the extent of the problem among the work force as a whole.

Keeping this reservation in mind, it might be useful at this point to recall the graph which provided pictorial confirmation of gaps in existing knowledge about unemployment.[81]

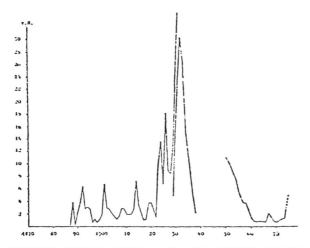

UNEMPLOYMENT QUOTAS IN THE GERMAN EMPIRE
AND FEDERAL REPUBLIC

Given the fact that the graph registers no information whatever prior to the late 1880's, we are forced to consider the possibility of examining alternate or indirect indications of work shortages. While the diagram depicts conditions for the country as whole, it also mirrors the situation in most states where statistics for the 1870's consisted almost exclusively of micro-economic data left behind by individual firms.

Confronted with major gaps in hard data, we shall turn to areas where the statistics, although admittedly imperfect, are superior to the sparse directly relevant numbers. In using these alternate figures as reflections of unemployment, it is essential to remember that most of them were collected by agencies which sought to alleviate the hardship of people unable to find work. The statistics that these agencies left behind were bound to be incomplete for our purposes because not all unemployed workers registered for any given form of relief. Each assistance program had restrictions that disenfranchised certain segments of the jobless population. Residence requirements, secondary employment, sex, age and proof of good standing with previous employers were only a few of the factors used to disqualify potential relief recipients who had no incentive to register for benefits which they could not receive.

In turning to relief institutions as alternate indices of unemployment, it might be well to note once again that observers during the 1890's placed the number of itinerant jobless poor in Germany at 200,000.[82] This figure represented the best contemporary estimate of the problem during the winter months when seasonal unemployment was at its peak. The numbers upon which it was based were gathered at a time when the general business cycle was in the process of recovery. It may therefore be seen as a reasonable reflection of itinerant unemployment during intervals of relatively normal winter economic activity. There were, of course, wide fluctuations in the extent of the problem during our period.

To cater to the needs of the wandering poor, a variety of relief institutions emerged during the nineteenth century. Some of them had explicit geographical restrictions. Local relief measures in the form of work projects to erect or maintain public facilities excluded itinerants by imposing residence requirements. Unfortunately, only sporadic data on the extent of public works projects has survived and most of it comes from the twentieth century-- from years when more extensive directly relevant information is also available. In addition to public works projects which were generally limited to unemployed male residents, a whole series of institutional relief forms emerged in Germany during the decades immediately preceding and following the turn of the century. These included Verpflegungsstationen, Herbergen zur Heimat and Arbeiterkolonien which were developed to meet the needs of the itinerant unemployed for varying periods of time.

Assorted shelters appeared during the 1880's, flourished during the first half of the 1890's and then went into eclipse as the economy took a decisive turn for the better. Available evidence suggests that there were approximately 900 relief facilities in Prussia during 1893 and scarcely a third of those were still in existence twelve years later. Despite all of these efforts, only scattered clues have survived which provide useful bits of evidence about the unemployment situation. Statistics outlining the relative import of relief institutions in terms of Marks expended or numbers served reflect contemporary attitudes toward unemployment and its resolution. If, for example, more money was spent on long range relief through labor yards than on short term aid through _Herbergen zur Heimat_, it was probable that administrators made certain assumptions about the persistence and duration of unemployment. To cite another illustration, the amounts expended on labor exchanges worked to eliminate unemployment while money devoted to refuges did little beyond offering temporary subsistence for the needy. Such expenditures thus provide an accurate indication of priorities as well as expectations about the public's ability to address the causes rather than treat the symptoms of unemployment.

Popular perceptions of the unemployed were reflected in part by the degree to which the jobless were differentiated from other groups of which they formed a statistical part. If, for example, the unemployed were lumped together with beggars, poor relief recipients or health insurance claimants, the measures adopted to eliminate their problems would be quite different. This was true because as we have repeatedly stressed, statistics formed the basis for policy decisions. That fact should be kept in mind as we look at data gathered by labor exchanges, labor colonies, refuges and institutions designed to eliminate begging or administer poor relief. While the former agencies compiled records of limited success in dealing with the unemployed, the latter were a reminder of society's failure to alleviate the hardship of its jobless members.

Labor Exchanges

One primary source of information about the job market came from Arbeitsnachweise or labor exchanges. Although the first of these exchanges appeared during the 1860's, they did not become commonplace for almost three decades. During the early Nineties, their activities were largely the result of local initiative, and the regional nature of their administration persisted even after the establishment of a national organization just prior to the turn of the century.

In looking at statistics compiled by various types of labor exchanges, one ought to remember that they were not counting the unemployed per se. Instead the exchanges recorded the number of persons looking for work through their facilities. Jobless individuals who did not register with the Arbeitsnachweise were never counted and among those seeking positions no consistent effort was made to differentiate between currently employed and unemployed applicants. Establishing precise correlations between the statistics compiled by labor exchanges and the degree of unemployment would be impossible but it is safe to assume that the former provided at least an indirect indication of the latter's extent.

Common sense tells us that when the number of persons looking for work far surpassed the number of open jobs the amount of unemployment was likely to be high. Conversely, when available positions substantially exceeded the number of applicants the unemployment rate tended to be low. It is important to note, however, that during periods of high unemployment the apparent futility of registering with the exchanges may have deterred jobless workers from making their existence known. Another danger lay in the opposite direction with overly zealous workers registering at more than one exchange or on more than one occasion at the same exchange, thus leading to multiple counts of single individuals. Additional errors resulted from persons who found employment in the same or different locations but failed to report their success to exchanges where they had registered.

The perils of drawing precise conclusions from Arbeitsnachweis data were spelled out with regard to the situation in Wurttemberg during the 1870's by Volker Hentschel.[83]

> So unpraezis und inkonsistent die Daten der Arbeits-nachweisbueros stets gewesen sind--Tendenzen lassen doch auch sie erkennen. 1875 wurden in Stuttgart immerhin noch 8.349 Arbeitsangebote registriert, 1877 waren es nur noch 5.040. Die Zahl der Arbeitsgesuche blieb mit rund 9.400 gleich. Dafuer wurden jetzt statt 1.875 Arbeitslosen 9.088 unterstuetzt. 1878 waren es sogar 11.650.

Although there were significant regional variations among the exchanges, the overwhelming majority of the people they served were unskilled laborers--individuals whose lack of specific training made them interchangeable and thus vulner-able to vicissitudes in the labor market. Among skilled workers, those involved in the highly cyclical building

trades such as painters, plumbers or locksmiths were prominently represented among clients of the labor exchanges.
Given this clientele, it is not surprising to find a marked
seasonal fluctuation in data compiled by the exchanges.

This tendency is clearly shown in the following
table which deals with figures from the Centralverein of
labor exchanges in Berlin between 1890 and 1896. For every
100 available positions, the Berlin exchange reported the
following numbers of applicants during various months for a
seven year period.[84]

Year	Jan.	Feb.	Mar.	Apr.	May	June	July	Aug.	Sept.	Oct.	Nov.	Dec.
1890	191.6	179.2	93.3	141.6	146.4	149.5	139.1	104.5	120.2	155.0	186.2	148.2
1891	216.9	180.5	118.3	194.6	201.2	253.8	182.8	130.7	112.4	162.9	192.4	159.2
1892	189.9	237.0	121.5	167.5	166.4	152.9	150.4	96.5	106.2	95.7	198.8	111.7
1893	147.9	157.0	108.0	160.0	189.9	163.6	173.0	129.7	123.5	162.1	183.8	135.1
1894	206.2	144.7	104.5	173.0	190.1	173.1	157.7	136.4	112.0	143.1	184.5	148.8
1895	172.7	115.2	120.0	175.7	154.1	145.0	141.6	106.3	110.5	129.7	140.4	113.9
1896	157.0	117.5	100.0	135.3	135.1	159.5	103.1	125.8	109.8	115.2	132.6	114.5
AVG.	183.2	161.7	109.4	164.0	169.0	171.8	149.7	118.6	113.5	137.7	174.1	133.1

It is interesting to note that the article containing this
chart which appeared in Soziale Praxis was entitled "Berliner Arbeitslosen Kurve 1890-96". This erroneous equation
between jobseeking and unemployment derived from a widespread failure to treat unemployed workers as a distinct and
separate group. Noteworthy also was the perpetually high
level of winter jobseekers, especially during the month of
January, and the abatement of their numbers when warm
weather returned. The consistently steep drop between
February and March with the single exception of 1895 was
significant, as was a second low which recurred in September
and reflected the work available during harvest time. The

remarkable consistency over a seven year period of variable economic conditions was largely attributable to the seasonal nature of Berlin's labor market during the 1890's. The average of the figures cited above, with a few minor exceptions such as the abnormal increase during February of 1892, indicated trends which in direction, if not always in extent, were typical of the entire period. During the later spring months, weather conditions frequently attracted job seekers to urban labor markets like the capital in greater numbers than at the very beginning of the season. The pattern showed a sharp decline in this influx between February and March followed by a steady increase again in April.

The most marked movement in this direction was visible in the largest German cities. Berlin, Breslau and the urban centers from Cologne to Nuremberg evinced particularly strong seasonal increases. In geographical terms, transfers into cities of the southwest were especially pronounced. Those such as Stuttgart residents who already lived in that area formed an exception of sorts, evincing no perceptible change. For Germany as a whole, the following figures from the years 1896 and 1897 show the volume of labor exchange activity during a time of increasing prosperity.[85]

Month	Open Positions		Job Seekers	
	1896	1897	1896	1897
January	13023	15701	23314	23927
February	14668	16619	21639	23149
March	21629	25773	25453	27881
April	21700	23046	25057	25246
May	18643	23003	24246	27693
June	21907	23612	27751	26456
July	20827	26074	27364	29313
August	20473	26659	26153	29605
September	23282	28045	28970	29705
October	20672	24350	28557	29608
November	14901	17856	24445	26620
December	11817	13041	19436	20012
TOTALS	223542	262779	302385	319212

The relatively small number of openings vis-a-vis applicants between November and February of the following year plus the more nearly equal proportions which prevailed during the warmer months from March to October reinforce the notion of a seasonal labor market.

A few statistics on the rate of success of various exchanges may help put their importance into perspective. We know that during the years between its founding in 1883 and January 1, 1905, the central labor exchange in Berlin placed 367,421 men and 34,520 women in a total of 401,941 jobs. For the relatively severe year of 1892 alone, consider the following description of the situation in the capital:[86]

> In Berlin von 45 Nachweisstellen etwa 50,000 Stellen besetzt sind, waehrend sich in ihren 115,000 Bewerber gemeldet hatten. In 39 Vereinen waren 44,000 Vakanzen angemeldet, von denen 32,000 besetzt wurden, in 35 davon waren allein 82,000 Bewerber vorhanden.

The overwhelming majority of persons using the Berlin
exchanges were classified as unskilled workers or members of
the building trades. Of the 535,773 jobseekers who registered in the capital between 1883 and 1904, 376,720 were
unskilled; 86,320 were painters; 28,643 were locksmiths;
12,525 were plumbers and 10,232 were paperhangers. The
proportions of available positions corresponded quite well
with these figures. Of the 411,939 openings, 288,458 were
for unskilled workers, 73,450 for painters, 14,767 for
locksmiths, 9,472 for plumbers and 10,322 for paperhangers.
The respective numbers in each category who found jobs
through the exchanges between 1883 and 1904 were: 258,002
unskilled laborers; 64,095 painters; 16,478 locksmiths;
8,236 plumbers and 6,772 paperhangers. The aggregate
figures by year were:[87]

Year	Registered Job Applicants	Available Positions	Placements
1883	3290	1805	1539
1884	5298	4190	3271
1885	8347	5660	5157
1886	10811	8879	6179
1887	11685	9795	6980
1888	10308	7365	6007
1889	10511	8262	7093
1890	9887	7038	6277
1891	13459	8011	7376
1892	11672	7949	7552
1893	11208	7393	7101
1894	13561	7216	8558
1895	20181	10783	15213
1896	24632	13101	19030
1897	26767	14374	20967
1898	30928	23484	22241
1899	35791	31335	28258
1900	45277	45816	36459
1901	38003	28685	24528
1902	39716	34899	28235
1903	67777	52080	41770
1904	86664	73929	57630
SUMS	535 773	411 939	367 421

One of the first German labor exchanges was
established at Stuttgart in 1865 and during the next thirty

years, it served the following: "der Arbeitsuchenden 246 581 nebst 3357 Lehrlingen, die Zahl der verlangten Arbeitskraefte 188 981 nebst 4329 Lehrlingen; der auswaertigen Stellen wurden 15 481 Personen zugewiesen."[88] During 1894/95 the Stuttgart exchange registered 8570 jobseekers and 6533 jobs; they managed to fill 5690 positions. Over the next few years, the Stuttgart exchange served a growing labor market with varying degrees of success:[89]

Year	Job Openings			Job Seekers			Placements		
	Male	Female	Total	Male	Female	Total	Male	Female	Total
3/4 of 1895	9629	3947	13569	12604	3213	15816	5637	1875	7515
1896	14280	5457	19737	17627	3767	21394	10474	2638	13112
1904	31709	17583	49292	39352	11214	50566	22136	8569	30705

As these figures suggest, the Arbeitsnachweis performed an important function in the German labor market by providing an institutional mechanism for matching job applicants with available positions. We shall see in the fourth part of this paper that it was the only organization which took concrete steps to eliminate unemployment by rooting out its causes. The exchanges, which actually found work for the unemployed and facilitated their return to the economic mainstream, were able to deal with their problem on a more fundamental level than any other institution. Public works projects, refuges and insurance enabled jobless laborers to get through periods of idleness with fewer hardships. But they did nothing to put people back to work in the private sector on a regular basis. The matching of employers, jobs and employees which was the primary function of labor exchanges actually diminished unemployment rather than providing palliatives for its victims.

Statistically, the data that the exchanges accumulated was impressive and the scattered numbers which we have examined here represent only a tiny portion of a voluminous whole. The bulk of that data was published in Soziale Praxis after 1892 and in the Reichsarbeitsblatt after 1903. While it shed light on mobility within the German labor market, the quantitative information from the exchanges had two insurmountable drawbacks which have already been noted and which render its further consideration unnecessary. First, much of the data prior to 1890 was, like all information dealing with the unemployed, spotty and inaccurate when it existed at all. And secondly, it failed to differentiate the unemployed from other job-seekers in any consistent manner.

Labor Colonies and Refuges for the Itinerant Unemployed

Comparing figures from labor colonies with those from institutions geared to short-term relief suggests a change in patterns of unemployment and in assistance rendered to its victims. The economically depressed conditions of the late 1870's and early 1880's formed the background against which labor colonies emerged to serve the needs of those suffering from prolonged work shortages. Their flourishing during the earlier part of our period indicated that unemployment in the wake of economic hard times was thought to involve a few individuals for relatively extended intervals.

The increasing emphasis on short-term relief through refuges and inns after 1890 reflected a different pattern of unemployment, with greater numbers affected for shorter but more frequent interludes.

Predominant during the first years under consideration here, the Arbeiterkolonien or labor colonies were situated primarily in rural areas where inmates went for considerable stays. Their clientele included significant numbers of tramps, seasonal unemployed and strikers as well as a few individuals who were actively looking for jobs. The latter were far more likely to seek assistance in institutions geared to short term--usually overnight--visits. The following figures for the East Prussian colony at Carlshof give some indication of the traffic patterns which emerged during the mid-1880's.[90]

> Die Zahl der eingelieferten maennlichen Corrigenden ist vom Jahre 1884 bis 1887 1321 auf 1175-922-766 gefallen. Von diesen kommen auf erstmalig Eingelieferte in den betr. Jahren: 573-355-252-215, d.h. in 4 Jahren ein Fallen von 62 1/2%; dagegen rueckfaellige Corrigenden 748-820-670-551, d.h. in dem Jahre 1885, das gegen das Eroeffnungsjahr der Kolonie 1884 ein Wachstum von 2634 Gesamtverpflegungstagen aufwies, eine Zunahme nur der Rueckfaelligen von 10%, bei Abnahme der erstmalig Eingelieferten von ca. 30%, von da an ein Fallen auch dieser Rueckfaelligen, aber nur um ca. 22% gegen das Jahr 1884.

As the above excerpt indicates, the numbers of individuals served by each colony at any given time was relatively small. Furthermore, the same individuals tended to reappear in these instututions over time--labor colonies reported recitivism rates ranging from 25 to 60 percent. The following figures show the proportions of those entering the colonies who had been admitted before.[91]

Name of Colony	Percentage of Admissions Which Were Repeat Visitors		
	1887/89	1889/91	1891/93
Wilhelmsdorf	42.6	50.1	52.9
Rickling	39.4	50.6	55.3
Kästorf	55.9	53.8	56.9
Friedrichswille	46.7	54.8	60.8
Seyda	38.5	47.3	48.8
Dornahof	42.0	53.1	49.4
Dauelsberg	32.3	40.4	36.2
Carlshof	44.2	52.4	55.1
Meierei	40.9	54.7	57.4
Wunscha	31.8	39.1	41.2
Ankenbuck	42.3	41.4	47.2
Neu-Ulrichstein	32.4	41.6	43.0
Berlin mit Tegel	27.0	33.1	40.4
Lühlerheim	34.0	48.6	55.5
Schneckengrün	35.0	43.2	45.8
Simonshof	25.2	35.4	41.7
Maria-Veen	54.8	53.7	56.4
Magdeburg	25.9	32.3	41.0
Alt-Latzig	25.0	42.6	58.4
Geilsdorf	----	48.8	52.1
Erlach	----	----	43.5
Friedrich-Wilhelmsdorf	----	39.8	49.5

The fact that such a high percentage of the labor colonies' inmates were repeat entrants was not surprising in view of the large number involved in seasonal professions. Agriculture, mining, construction and commerce accounted for a great many inmates while of the industrially related sectors, only metallurgy contributed a significant quotient.[92] Occupations contributing smaller contingents to the population of labor colonies included woodworking, textiles, clothing, commerce and luxury goods industries. Here it is important to keep in mind that most of those who entered labor colonies--regardless of occupation--were unemployed over extended periods of time. By the turn of the century, colonies provided subsistence primarily for those whose jobs were dependent upon the weather. Towards the end of our period the urban, industrial work force had already developed alternate means of getting through slack periods. With many industrial workers suffering from brief intervals of unemployment the tendency was to devote long-term institutions such as labor colonies to the problems of Germany's rural, non-industrial population.

Dealing with the need stemming from shorter unemployment were the Verpflegungsstationen or refuges for relief in kind. By 1884, there were 595 refuges scattered across Prussia, with the highest concentrations in Saxony, Brandenburg and Westphalia. The following chart shows the development of these refuges between 1884 and 1890.[93]

Die Verpflegungsstationen der Preußischen Provinzen in den Jahren 1884 bis 1890

Provinz	Zahl der Stationen 1884	1885	1887	1890	Mit Arbeitsnachweis waren 1884 verbunden	nicht verbunden	1885 verbunden	nicht verbunden	1887 verbunden	nicht verbunden	1890 verbunden	nicht verbunden	Stationsarbeit forderten 1884 ja	nein	1885 ja	nein	1887 ja	nein	1890 ja	nein
Ostpreußen	81	104	81	82	1	30	19	85	21	41	19	63	1	30	54	50	49	28	50	32
Westpreußen	4	17	22	26	—	4	3	1'	1	21	6	20	3	1	17	—	18	4	25	1
Pommern	4	71	78	78	2	2	50	21	51	17	49	29	—	4	52	19	57	16	67	11
Brandenburg	106	137	145	141	81	25	102	85	88	47	125	16	32	74	77	60	81	55	118	23
Sachsen	114	189	112	115	73	41	111	28	107	5	105	10	40	74	70	69	102	10	110	5
Posen	6	22	19	42	3	3	10	12	10	9	20	22	—	6	8	14	9	9	16	26
Schlesien	32	21	88	112	10	22	14	7	28	59	54	58	5	27	5	16	30	54	57	55
Westfalen	124	115	102	76	45	79	55	60	64	38	59	17	53	71	85	30	93	7	69	7
Rheinprovinz	27	64	72	69	18	9	35	29	34	33	39	50	10	17	34	30	57	14	64	25
Schleswig-Holstein	21	33	29	26	8	13	22	11	23	6	16	10	1	20	8	25	27	1	23	3
Hannover	74	109	95	96	20	54	22	87	54	25	54	42	12	62	83	76	58	35	58	38
Hessen-Nassau	52	83	78	68	16	36	36	47	82	38	41	27	32	20	64	19	70	6	62	6
Berlin	—	—	—	—	—	—	—	—	—	—	—	—	—	—	—	—	—	—	—	—
Summe Preuß. Staat	595	915	917	961	277	318	479	436	514	334	587	364	189	406	507	408	652	239	719	232

Slightly more than half of all German refuges--327--were in urban areas and the vast majority--more than two-thirds-- were financed out of public resources. Between January 1 and May 1 of 1884, the Prussian refuges alone had something in excess of 200,000 visitors.[94] That there was a demand for these institutions during economically severe times was dramatically demonstrated by comparing the above figures with those for the following year. During the months between May 1, 1884, and April 1, 1885, the number of refuges in Prussia increased by more than one-third to 915, with urban centers absorbing much of the growth. East Prussia and Pommerania however experienced the most pronounced expansion, reflecting the depressed condition of German agriculture during this period. Marked increases also occurred in the Rhineland, Hannover and Hesse-Nassau, but the number of refuges in heavily industrialized Silesia and Westphalia actually declined.

The most astonishing growth and also the most important from our perspective was in the number of individuals using these facilities. During eleven months, that number increased fivefold, moving from 200,133 between January 1 and April 30, 1884, to 1,045,045 between January 1 and March 20, 1885.[95] When the economy turned around in 1886, the rate of expansion of the refuges tapered off dramatically, as the following figures for the period show. Data on refuges in Westphalia demonstrate the direct variance between depressed conditions in the economy as a whole and the number of inmates. The marked rise which began in 1889/90 and peaked in 1891/92 was particularly significant as was the steep decline which started in 1895.[96]

1887/88 - 95,347	1891/92 - 174,251	1896/97 - 53,309
1888/89 - 74,295	1892/93 - 126,852	1897/98 - 62,975
1889/90 - 72,214	1893/94 - 130,133	1898/99 - 56,779
1890/91 - 116,428	1894/95 - 107,417	1899/1900 - 64,473
	1895/96 - 69,803	

During the night of January 31-February 1, 1888, the stations served a total of 3712 people, or an average of 384 guests per station, excluding Berlin whose unique situation was thought to distort the figures for Prussia as a whole.[97] According to a publication sponsored by the labor colonies, the refuges performed an invaluable function even during periods when the numbers which they served looked small in comparison with the total unemployment problem. Without these facilities, the impoverished itinerant unemployed who were forced to travel in search of work would have had no place to spend their nights. The result would have been a general public nuisance--unacceptable behavior ranging from begging to theft and more serious crimes.[98]

Although the best and earliest figures which have survived stem from Prussia, the refuges were not confined to Germany's largest state.[99] In Bavaria, for example, the first colony opened its doors on May 1, 1888. Twenty years later there were 295 refuges which fed a total of 576,637 unemployed workers at a cost slightly in excess of 310,000 Marks. By 1890 we have figures for the Empire as a whole and we know that on the night between December 15 and 16 of that year, 1957 Verpflegungsstationen accommodated 9216 impoverished wanderers. The breakdown by individual states showed that German refuges served almost two million indigents who sought food and overnight lodging. The relatively small numbers which used labor colonies as opposed to inns and Verpflegungsstationen was indicative of a different approach to unemployment. The former pattern of catering to the long-term needs of a few chronically jobless individuals gave way during the transitional decade of the 1880's. The new system which emerged served the needs of numerous short-term unemployed, providing temporary assistance during brief but recurrent intervals of idleness.

To a large extent, the 1890's marked a hiatus in the importance of the role which refuges of all kinds played in the German unemployment picture. As institutions like labor exchanges were established and as municipalities adopted public works projects or began to contemplate unemployment insurance, the Verpflegungsstationen went into partial eclipse. Available figures[100] reflect this trend for the years between 1890 and 1898, which witnessed the final segment of the long downswing that had begun in 1873 and finally gave way to prosperity in the mid-1890's.

In conjunction with the refuges which provided shelter and food for itinerant job-seekers, the Herbergen zur Heimat or "inns of the home" offered wayfarers inexpensive lodging and occasionally temporary employment as well. In addition to providing necessary subsistence, these

inns attempted to find more permanent work for their visitors. The next figures show the degree of their success in
the latter respect during years of relative prosperity.
Although slight in terms of numbers actually placed, the
attempt itself represented a significant advance in contemporary efforts to resolve the problems created by unemployment.[101]

Vergleichende Zusammenstellung der Zahl der „Herbergen zur Heimat" sowie
der Stellenvermittlung und Verkehrsvermehrung für die Jahre 1890—1904

Jahr	Zahl der Herbergen ( ) = Betten	In Arbeit gebracht		Verkehr Insgesamt(Herbergs= Stationsgäste,Durch= reisende und Kostgänger)
		absolute Zahlen	In %/o des Ge= samtverkehrs	
1890	362	?		2 746 680
1891	379 (13 870)	43 572	2,09	3 279 647
1893	426	?		3 545 575
1895	439	54 398	2,33	3 681 308
1896	453	98 078	4,32	3 604 693
1897	455	112 920	5,19	3 640 045
1898	457	123 894	5,71	3 688 548
1899	457	132 891	6,58	3 386 972
1900	457 (19 159)	125 789	5,84	3 791 230
1901	462	108 505	4,03	4 261 974
1902	462	109 306	3,72	4 498 815
1903	458	117 154	4,47	4 256 588
1904	461	122 042	5,13	4 089 506

During the twelve years between 1899 and 1910 an
average which ranged from just over two million to just
under three million persons passed through the refuges on an
annual basis.[102] Of those who spent the night, almost all
must have limited their visits to a single evening. The
cost of helping these people never amounted to more than
465,000 Marks per year, an excellent return if one considers
the number of meals, sleeping accommodations and job placement services provided. Less than eight percent of those
needing work were placed during the best of years and only

3.72 percent were placed in the recession year of 1902. However, the approximately 450 inns and refuges were able to find employment for between 108,000 and 160,000 laborers on an annual basis from 1899 to 1910.

Begging and Obdachlosigkeit

If refuges provide statistics which reflect the degree of need met by public unemployment policy, begging affords an indication of the extent to which that need remained unmet. In evaluating the following figures, we would do well to consider the problems which would have existed if relief institutions of the kind considered above had not evolved during our period. If, for example, the inns and refuges had not been available to provide millions of meals and find thousands of jobs annually, the impact of unemployment on Germany between 1876 and 1886 might have produced reactions more extreme than contemporary anxieties.

As we noted in passing, most of the statistics on refuges omitted figures for the capital which were deemed to be grossly atypical of Germany as a whole--so much so that they would distort the remaining numbers. In order to get a sense of what was going on in Berlin, we might consider some of the information on begging which has survived. We know from police records that during 1892 approximately 10,000 individuals--95% adult males--were arrested for begging. According to the statistical yearbook for 1892, an equal number were arrested for Obdachlosigkeit--the overwhelming

majority of which were once again men. In the asylum established to deal with these individuals, average daily occupancy during the administrative year 1891/92 was only 384
persons. However, slightly more than 10,000 inmates spent a
total approaching 140,000 days in the Berlin asylum. This
marked a considerable increase over the previous year when
an average of 177 persons spent a total of 72,942 days
there. The corresponding numbers for 1889-90 were even
lower--a daily average of 165 persons for a total of 67,255
days. An article in Soziale Praxis[103] attributed the
significant increase between 1889 and 1892 to three factors:
1) numerous transfers of Russian immigrants, 2) unemployment
during the winter of 1891/92, and 3) the population increase
compounded by migration of poorer families out of provincial
areas and into the capital. During 1891/92 it became
disturbingly apparent that an increasing number of very old
people and children had been apprehended for the crime of
being destitute and homeless. The extent of the problem in
Berlin around 1890 was reflected in the following
figures:[104]

> Die Abtheilung fuer naechtliche Obdachlose des staed-
> tischen Obdachs wurde waehrand des Jahres 1891/92 von
> 334 670 Personen (gegenueber dem Vorjahre mit 275 777
> Personen und gegenueber dem Jahre 1889/90 mit nur 203
> 039 Personen) besucht. Die Steigerung der Benutzung im
> Berichtsjahre gegen die des Vorjahres betraegt also 58
> 893 Koepfe oder 21,36 pCt. und gegen diejenige des
> Jahres 1889/90 131 631 Koepfe oder 64,83 pCt.

As the next set of statistics indicates, the problem continued to intensify in 1893 and 1894. Particularly during

the winter months, a large number of men spent the night wandering the capital until they were picked up by the police.[105]

	Persons		Absolute Number		Number per Thousand	
	1893	1894	1893	1894	1893	1894
January	67687	87276	793	179	10	2
February	58846	75866	675	524	11	7
March	51478	54240	687	789	13	15
April	28743	27448	626	562	22	20
May	21530	20280	584	462	27	23
June	14585	15420	464	412	32	27
July	12819	11368	315	330	25	29
August	14318	12952	356	367	25	28
September	16697	13741	382	338	23	25
October	20853	18047	427	452	20	25
November	36093	24395	467	606	13	25
December	61746	31733	260	813	4	26

Commitments to the "Asyl fuer Obdachlose" in Berlin during the last quarters of 1893 and 1894 consistently averaged over 10,000 men per month for October, November and December. To put these figures into long-range perspective, consider the following statistics for the Berlin asylum during the years between 1869 and 1893.[106]

Frequency Statistics: Berlin House of Refuge for the Homeless

Year	Women	Girls	Children	Infants	Sums	Men
1869	3759	6659	2370	---	12788	(12/19/70 to 3/3/71
1870	7099	9108	4732	---	20939	12233
1871	7307	7658	3180	---	18145	36974
1872	10294	9557	3173	---	23024	39619
1873	8479	8016	2645	---	19140	57539
1874	6709	5576	1307	---	13592	58350
1875	5962	6184	570	368	13084	73960
1876	5762	6752	602	374	14490	91785
4/1 to 12/31/77	5075	4654	490	174	10393	72274
1878	7005	6391	465	192	14053	106185
1879	8368	6283	525	119	15295	107754
1880	10581	7358	745	340	19024	109935
1881	10798	9206	1025	297	21326	104899
1882	9616	8274	1462	457	19809	104020
1883	11253	7184	1104	376	19917	105241
1884	10118	6573	1015	311	18017	107879
1885	10307	6456	937	333	18033	108241
1886	10935	5815	1678	323	18428	107094
1887	10691	5553	1657	270	17901	107798
1888	10375	5016	1268	237	16659	107218
1889	11115	5243	1032	245	17390	106760
1890	9759	4979	709	141	15447	108072
1891	10870	6132	989	182	17991	109092
1892	10780	6628	878	79	18286	109473
1893	8216	4815	688	99	13720	109206
SUMS	221234	166060	34923	4917	425891	2161591

Particularly noteworthy were the sharp jumps which occurred during the late 1870's and the plateau which was maintained with relatively slight variation thereafter, despite a steady increase in population. The former factor would seem to lend credence to East German contentions about abnormally high unemployment rates in the capital between 1876 and 1879.

By the final decade of our period, the relative importance of homelessness as an indicator of the economy had declined. While its incidence diminished, that of begging continued to remain fairly stable. Figures from the Prussian labor houses during 1907 and 1908 showed that of almost 7000 persons detained, more than two-thirds were committed for begging while a mere ten percent were incarcerated because they were homeless. It should be noted here that only a small proportion of the total number of persons prosecuted for begging were actually assigned to labor houses which remained a secondary punishment during much of our period. This fact was reflected in statistics on the incidence of mendicancy in Berlin.[107]

Year	Commitments to Labor House for Begging	Apprehensions	Prosecutions	Convictions
1889-90	709	---	---	---
1890-91	656	---	---	---
1891-92	916	---	---	---
1892-93	1253	---	---	---
1894	1087	21678	19244	11216
1895	925	19318	16780	9434
1896	824	22048	19064	10858
1897	715	23434	20343	10681
1898	633	20378	16931	8781
1899	735	16556	13672	7043
1900	641	17344	14097	7246
1901	868	20574	17054	9885
1902	984	23582	18962	11545
1903	1053	21576	17524	10706
1904	1008	19019	15562	10059
1905	823	16148	13197	8301

The differences between the numbers in the second and third columns above should be attributed to those who were merely chastised and discharged without further action by the authorities. The fact that the total number of apprehensions declined significantly during a period when the population in the capital expanded continuously was testimony to the marked improvement which the economy underwent between 1894 and the end of our period. During times of economic prosperity, both unemployment and begging were at a minimum while the reverse was true during severe downswings. The latter assertion is attested to by the figures for commitments to workhouses in the empire as a whole for the period between 1877 and 1881. During the three years from 1877 to 1879 alone the number of commitments for begging and vagrancy increased by almost fifty percent. In 1877, commitments totalled 219,514; as the economic situation deteriorated that number climbed to 280,518 in 1878 and reached 316,846 the following year. With the respite that came at the beginning of the new decade, the numbers began to level off at 320,548 during 1880 and 320,259 during 1881.[108]

Poor Relief

One of the most obvious alternate indicators of unemployment with a long-standing record of quantifiable data was the form of public compensation designated by the umbrella term of Armenpflege or poor relief. Recipients of poor relief included such diverse elements as widows, orphans, cripples, deaf and blind persons, the aged, and alcoholics as well as unemployed or underemployed workers. In many instances it was difficult to differentiate those who were unemployed for economic reasons from those who were idle or destitute for reasons which had nothing to do with fluctuations in the labor market. Failure to distinguish the unemployed from other recipients of poor relief became less common as contemporaries began to recognize jobless individuals as a discrete group. Treatment of the unemployed through institutions other than poor relief played a major role in their differentiation. Although overly general categories present drawbacks to reliance on poor relief statistics, the fact that those numbers are available for the early years of the Empire makes them an invaluable source of information.

As with many institutions during our period, statistics on poor relief were frequently better at the state and local levels than on a national scale. Some of the best figures which have survived are from the relatively industrial kingdom of Saxony. We know that during 1880 the Saxon population of 2,972,805 persons provided poor relief for 93,699 individuals--62,269 received prolonged support and 31,430 received temporary assistance. The richest Saxon city, Leipzig, had the highest concentration of poor--at 9.78 percent of its population, Leipzig's average was approximately triple that of the kingdom as a whole.

Estimates showed that Saxony in 1880 had 3.15 recipients of poor relief per 100 residents. During the same year, other German states and European nations reported the following comparable percentages of poor among their populations: Schleswig-Holstein 4.16, Hannover (1879) 3.20, Oldenburg (1875) 4.16, Baden (on October 1, 1881) 2.49, Wurttemberg (1875) 4.84, England and Wales (1881) 3.13, France (1878) 3.16, Sweden (1878) 4.45, Netherlands (1878) 4.47, Switzerland (1870) 4.67. The similarity between German Saxony, France and highly industrialized England is striking as is the relatively small range of variance within western Europe.

Saxon poor relief statistics from 1880, 1885 and 1890 indicated that sickness was the primary source of need, accounting for between one-fourth and one-fifth of the total numbers helped during those years. The second most prevalent cause of need was listed as "grosse Kinderzahl". The third, and for our purposes most important, was "Arbeitslosigkeit und unzugaenglicher Verdienst". The numbers attributable to the latter category steadily diminished during the course of the Eighties if the Saxon statistics were accurate. Unemployed poor relief recipients in Saxony number 19,864 in 1880, or 21.2 percent of all those on relief. In 1885, 15,238 unemployed constituted 17.3 percent of the total and by 1890 a further decline left their number at 12,848 or 15.85 percent of those supported under the poor

law administration.[109] Looked at somewhat differently, for
every 10,000 inhabitants of Saxony, 48.2 in 1885 and 36.7 in
1890 received poor relief payments as a result of unemployment or insufficient wages. Among recipients of long-term
assistance as well as those exhibiting short-term need,
there was a consistent decline in the absolute number of
Saxon beneficiaries between 1885 and 1890. This was due in
part to overall improvements in the economy during the last
half of the 1880's. But it was also attributable to the
emergence of other kinds of assistance for the unemployed
who were increasingly anxious and able to escape the stigma
associated with poor relief.

Whenever any kind of unemployment benefits were
provided during our period, the question of culpability
arose. In cases where fault was assigned to Saxon relief
recipients, work-shy and vagrant individuals accounted for
2516 cases during 1885 and 1927 cases during 1890. In other
words, for every 100 persons who were supported by poor
relief, 2.84 percent in 1885 and 2.38 percent in 1890 were
deemed to be unemployed or insufficiently compensated due to
their own aversion to work. In relation to the total
population of Saxony, during 1885 7.9 per 10,000 residents
received assistance attributable to their unwillingness to
work; during 1890 that number had fallen to 5.5 per 10,000
inhabitants. Of every 100 relief recipients, the category
of unemployment and insufficient income accounted for 17.8

"unverschuldet" and 9.11 "verschuldet" persons during 1885; the same numbers for 1890 were 15.62 "unverschuldet" poor and 16.53 "verschuldet".

The distinction between short-term and long-range dependence attributable to unemployment was spelled out as follows:[110]

> Die Unterstuetzungsfaelle wegen Arbeitslosigkeit, unzulaenglichen Verdienst etc. vertheilen sich ziemlich gleichmaessig auf dauernd und voruebergehend Unterstuetzte. Den dauernd Unterstuetzten dieser Kategorie gehoeren in der Hauptsache diejenigen an, welche wegen geschwaechter Arbeitskraft den Lebensbedarf fuer sich und ihre Angehoerigen nicht mehr zu decken vermoegen, zu den voruebergehend Unterstuetzten dagegen mehr solche, welche zwar noch voellig Arbeitsfaehig sind, aber wegen zeitwillig mangelnder Arbeitsgelegenheit auf Almosen angewiesen sind.

In passing, it is worth noting that for every 1000 inhabitants of Saxony, 16.7 received poor relief in 1885 and 14.3 received assistance in 1890. The corresponding figures for the major Saxon cities were significantly higher, with Dresden reporting 34 in 1885 and 29 in 1890, Leipzig 32.6 and 22.2, Chemnitz 23.8 and 21.4. The more rural administrative districts surrounding these urban cores brought the figures down close to the averages for the kingdom as a whole.

Regarding differences among German states, the distinction between poor relief in predominantly industrial and agrarian areas was considered important by contemporaries. The following comments on conditions in Saxony were typical in this regard:[111]

Die saechs. Armenstatistik zeigt, dass die industriellsten Gegenden, in denen man gewoehnlich das meiste Proletariat vermuthet, keineswegs in der Regel eine hohe Armenziffer ausweisen, sondern dass vielmehr die reichsten Staedte am unguenstigsten stehen. Die Industrie pflegt durch Knappschafts-, Hilfs-, und andere Kassen fuer ihre Armen zu sorgen und giebt auch schwaecheren Kraeften noch Arbeitsgelegenheit. Faullenzer sind da weniger geduldet, ebenso wenig wie auf dem Lande; dagegen pflegt man in reichen Staedten die Almosen oft ueberreichlich und planlos zu Verabreichen und dadurch Beduerftige aus der Naehe und Ferne anzulocken.

For comparative purposes, we might note that statistics on poor relief for the German empire in 1885 indicated that unemployment was the source of need listed by "35 427 Familienvorstaende und Einzelpersonen (sowie 60 041 dazu gehoerige Ehefrauen und Kinder unter 14 Jahren)."[112] In other words, a total of just over 95,000 persons depended upon poor relief due to head of household unemployment which accounted for four percent of the entire number of beneficiaries in Germany during 1885. Compare the first set of figures below[113] for the entire nation with the second set for Saxony alone.

Arbeitslose unter den Armen im deutschen Reiche 1885.

Es betrugen die In Folge	Selbstunterstützten (Familienvorst. u. Einzelne)	%	Mitunterstützten (Ehefrauen, Kinder unt. 14 Jahr.)	Zusammen	%
Arbeitslosigkeit	35 427	4	60 041	95 468	6
Arbeitsscheu	11 315	1,3	11 213	22 528	1,4
Trunk	13 960	1,6	18 464	32 424	2,0
Altersschwäche	196 093	22,1	38 859	234 952	14,8
Krankheit des Unterstützten od. in dessen Familie	242 698	27,4	201 800	444 498	27,9
Körperliche oder geistige Gebrechen	142 800	16,1	54 292	197 092	12,4
Tod des Ernährers	133 023	15,0	140 916	273 939	17,2
Unfall (Verletzung oder Tod des Ernährers, eigene Verletzung)	23 874	2,7	28 678	52 552	3,3
Grosse Kinderzahl	21 360	2,4	93 786	115 146	7,2
Sonstige	66 021	7,4	57 766	123 787	7,8
	886 571	100	705 815	1 592 386	100

Six percent of Germany's poor relief recipients were unemployed in 1885. Double that percentage attributed their need to unemployment in Saxony during the same year--12.6 percent in the cities and 13.3 percent in the kingdom as a whole. Note in the following chart the decline in categories related to unemployment such as drunkenness and work aversion during the late 1880's.[114]

Es wuerden unterstuetzt in den Jahren 1885 und 1890 von 100 Selbstunterstuetzten

infolge von	in den Staedten		im Koenigreich	
	1885	1890	1885	1890
Krankheit	39,05	34,03	27,71	25,58
hohem Alter	13,16	15,75	17,09	20,48
Arbeitslosigkeit etc.	12,63	13,02	13,26	12,53
Gebrechen	8,23	8,79	11,96	12,57
Verwaisung	5,83	7,10	7,36	7,64
grosser Kinderzahl	4,51	5,21	5,04	5,48
Unfall	1,62	0,94	2,15	1,24
Trunksucht	4,01	3,15	4,43	3,41
Arbeitsscheu	3,22	3,09	3,28	2,93
Verlassen seitens des Ernaehrers	2,78	2,78	3,00	2,71
Verwahrlosung	2,73	3,70	2,49	3,07
Strafverbuessung des Ernaehrers	1,25	1,37	1,32	1,36
Selbstmord resp. -versuch	0,18	0,21	0,26	0,34
Schwangerschaft	0,18	0,32	0,20	0,26
Auswanderung	0,05	0,18	0,03	0,12

The figures for Saxony camouflaged significant variations among divergent parts of the kingdom. With regard to unemployment in the various administrative districts, the 12-13 percent figures shown above included on the one hand Loebau with 7.53 percent of its poor relief attributable to unemployment. However, they also incorporated data from Zittau with 16.22 percent, Dresden-Altstadt with 17.69 percent and Floeha with 18.1 percent of those claiming assistance basing their need on unemployment.

Saxon poor relief statistics contained figures on migration which provided another index of conditions in the labor market. Since job availability was a major factor in the selection of one's residence, we might allude briefly to the connection between migration and unemployment. During the 1880's when German overseas migration was at its peak, Saxony lost only eight percent of its population. Over the course of that decade, unemployment declined as a factor in poor relief. For the _Reich_ as a whole, 2.5 million persons emigrated between 1871 and 1895. The exodus subsided when economic conditions improved. Despite substantial overseas migration, the German population increased from 45.3 million in 1880 to 49.5 million in 1890. As we have already indicated, East German historians view migration as a major factor in containing the unemployment problem, particularly during the Eighties.

We have relied on the Saxon poor relief statistics cited above because they form one of the most comprehensive sets of figures from a heavily industrialized area available before 1890. In order to place these numbers in perspective, however, it would be helpful to look at Saxon conditions within the context of other German states. Among the more reliable figures for this purpose were those reflecting expenditure for poor relief during 1880 and 1881. Industrial Saxony emerged as fairly typical of the major states, expending 1.2 Marks per head of population, below Baden's 1.93 Marks and well above Prussia's .86 Marks.[115]

Expenditure for Poor Relief in German States 1880/81

STATE	POPULATION	COST OF RELIEF TO THOSE RECEIV- ING PERMANENT TOTAL SUPPORT	COST OF RELIEF TO THOSE RECEIV- ING PERMANENT PARTIAL SUPPORT	COST OF RELIEF TO THOSE RECEIV- ING TEMPORARY SUPPORT	SUM OF COLUMNS 3, 4 AND 5 MARKS	MARKS PER HEAD OF POPULATION
Prussia						
a. Cities	9707976	5511483	3993266	1923366	11428115	1.18
b. Land	17571135	6436114	4186045	1399711	12021870	0.68
	27279111	11947597	8179311	3323077	23449985	0.86
Bavaria						
a. Cities	1873691	1679620	970887	414914	3065421	1.64
b. Land	3411087	2671685	916748	614147	4202580	1.23
	5284778	4351305	1887635	1029061	7268001	1.38
Saxony						
a. Cities	1222131	573305	1100602	372128	2046035	1.67
b. Land	1750674	295114	1053725	158764	1507603	0.86
	2972805	868419	2154327	530892	3553638	1.20
Wurttemberg						
a. Cities	1026662	916991	327431	140569	1384991	1.35
b. Land	944456	633182	328680	111995	1073857	1.14
	1971118	1550173	656111	252564	2458848	1.25
Baden						
a. Cities	350225	919895	212523	52693	1185111	3.38
b. Land	1220029	1298596	469038	168363	1846797	1.51
	1570254	2128491	682361	221056	3031908	1.93
Hesse						
a. Cities	409187	311676	123170	81729	516575	1.26
b. Land	527153	313495	159860	71818	545173	1.03
	936340	625171	283030	153547	1061748	1.13
Mecklenburg-Schwerin						
a. Cities	238889	305870	245866	64542	616278	2.58
b. Land	338166	491682	299731	32821	824234	2.44
	577055	797552	545597	97363	1440512	2.50
Sachse-Weimar						
a. Cities	127517	48193	50306	17550	116049	0.91
b. Land	182060	19044	16679	5134	40857	0.22
	309577	67232	66985	22684	156906	0.51

In addition to figures for entire states, there were a number of regional and local efforts to preserve information about poor relief. We have, for example, data from the Rhenish district of Gladbach, an industrial area with a population of approximately 125,000 during the early years of our period. The following numbers on the cost of poor relief per head of population indicated a substantial variation from the Prussian figures of which they formed a small part. Note here that the average expenditure for poor relief per resident in Prussia during 1880/81 was less than one Mark while that for the district of Gladbach was in excess of three Marks and for the city of Muenchen-Gladbach itself 4.33 Marks. Substantial differences between urban and rural expenditures within the same district should be stressed. The following table reflects the fact that in every state, cities expended significantly more on poor relief per capita than rural jurisdictions. Finally, it is worth emphasizing the significant, steady increase in the cost of poor relief during the economically troubled years between 1875 and 1881.[116]

Kreis Gladbach: Cost of Poor Relief per Head of Population

City	1873	1875	1877/78	1880/81	1881/82
München-Gladbach	2.92	2.90	3.87	4.33	3.90
Odenkirchen	1.47	1.54	2.18	1.70	1.58
Rheindahlen	1.53	1.78	2.12	2.40	2.32
Rheydt	2.46	2.40	2.67	2.89	2.85
Wiersen	2.43	2.14	3.49	3.61	3.63
Sum of Cities	2.45	2.41	3.27	3.50	3.31
Rural Areas					
Korschenbroich	1.03	1.12	0.91	1.10	1.16
Gladbach Land	2.22	2.35	2.41	2.66	2.98
Hardt	1.61	1.54	2.03	2.22	2.40
Kleinenbroich	1.26	1.07	1.25	1.31	1.43
Lindberg	1.28	1.49	1.26	1.75	1.78
Naarsen	0.90	0.81	1.84	2.96	2.47
Neuwerk	0.97	1.04	1.55	2.05	2.33
Schelsen	1.55	1.70	2.05	2.11	2.25
Schielban	0.52	0.67	1.20	1.26	1.57
Sum of Rural Areas	1.32	1.40	1.72	2.02	2.18
Sum of Cities	2.45	2.41	3.27	3.50	3.31
District Total	2.14	2.14	2.86	3.11	3.03

When poor relief administrations undertook unemployment counts it was not surprising to find that they exhibited less interest in the number of jobless individuals per se than in the degree of unemployment and the accompanying hardship or need. With this factor in mind, we might mention that an 1891 survey placed the number of unemployed in Berlin at approximately 34,000. During the

1890's, a series of counts were made in major German cities including Hamburg, Munich, Nuremberg, Stuttgart, Cologne, Hannover, Elberfeld, Duesseldorf, Erfurt, Stettin, Aachen, Kassel and Dortmund. A sample of the kinds of data on unemployment collected by those whose primary interest was poor relief can be gleaned from the following table.[117] The occupational breakdown on unemployment leading to poor relief indicated a high proportion of domestic servants and workers engaged in manufacturing, construction and commerce.

OCCUPATIONAL AND GEOGRAPHICAL DISTRIBUTION OF PERSONS SUPPORTED BY POOR RELIEF DUE TO UNEMPLOYMENT
(From April 1, 1896 to March 31, 1897)

No.	Occupation	Sex	Frankfurt a. M.		Altona		Straßburg		Mannheim		Darmstadt		Frankfurt a. O.		Freiburg i. B.		Summe	
			e.	m.a.	e.	m.a.	e.	m.a.	e.	m.a.	e.	m.a.	e.	m.a.	e.	m.a.	e.	m.a.
1.	Agriculture	m	3	1	1	—	—	—	—	—	1	—	—	—	5	2	10	3
		f																
2.	Fishing & hunting																	
3.	Mining, foundries & saltworks																	
4.	Stone & earthworks	m	—	1	—	—	—	—	2	—	1	—	—	—	3	—	6	1
		f													1	—	1	—
5.	Metal working	m	7	2	1	—	—	—	5	1	—	—	—	—	2	1	15	4
6.	Machinery & tools	m	2	2	—	—	—	—	2	—	1	—	—	—	—	1	5	3
7.	Chemical industry																	
8.	Forestry byproducts																	
9.	Textiles	m	1	1	2	—	—	—	1	—	—	—	—	—	1	1	5	2
10.	Paper	m	—	—	—	—	—	—	—	—	—	1	—	—	2	—	2	1
11.	Leather	m	2	—	—	—	—	—	—	—	—	—	—	—	2	—	4	—
		f													—	1	—	1
12.	Wood	m	1	1	2	—	—	—	2	1	1	—	—	—	—	1	6	3
13.	Food	m	—	1	4	—	—	—	1	1	2	—	—	—	6	1	13	3
14.	Clothing	m	4	2	2	—	—	—	1	1	—	—	—	—	1	—	8	3
		f	7	9	5	—	—	—	—	—	2	—	—	—	1	1	15	10
15.	Construction	m	9	4	8	—	—	—	2	—	1	1	—	—	8	4	28	9
16.	Polygraphic Trades	m	1	—	—	—	—	—	—	1	1	—	—	—	1	—	3	1
17.	Artists		—	—	1	—	—	—	3	—	—	—	—	—	—	—	4	—
18.	Factory workers	m	21	10	—	—	—	—	9	4	—	—	—	—	1	—	31	14
		f	7	5	—	—	—	—	—	—	1	—	—	—	—	—	8	5
19.	Commerce	m	8	4	2	—	—	—	7	1	3	—	—	—	2	—	22	5
		f	3	—	2	—	—	—	—	—	—	—	—	—	—	—	5	—
20.	Insurance	m	—	—	1	—	—	—	—	—	—	—	—	—	—	—	1	—
21.	Communications	m	3	3	—	—	—	—	—	—	—	—	—	—	1	—	4	3
22.	Restaurants & Hotels	m	5	2	—	—	—	—	—	—	—	—	—	—	1	—	6	2
23.	Domestic service	m	1	1	36	—	—	—	6	—	1	—	4	1	14	1	65	3
		f	16	9	17	—	—	—	—	—	—	—	—	—	1	—	33	9
24.	Free professions	m	7	8	2	—	—	—	1	—	1	—	—	—	—	—	11	3
		f	—	—	—	—	—	—	1	—	—	—	—	—	1	—	2	—
25.	No occupation	m	3	2	19	—	—	—	—	—	—	—	—	—	—	—	22	2
		f	16	14	—	—	—	—	—	—	—	—	—	—	—	—	16	14
			127	77	107	—	6	—	33	11	22	2	3	—	54	14	357	104

While the poor relief statistics cited here revealed the existence of unemployment, they consistently registered illness as the single most common cause of need. In this context, it is worth reiterating the belief that claims for assistance based on illness, accidents or disability frequently camouflaged a certain amount of unemployment. The fact that those suffering from physical ailments were excused from work and subsidized by the state under Bismarck's social insurance led to potential abuse by the able-bodied unemployed lacking recourse to alternate support. The increase in applications for relief based on sickness during periods of economic distress could be attributed to totally spurious claims. Or one could presume that those marginally incapacitated preferred to work when the economic incentives were favorable and only resorted to subsidized idleness when acceptable remunerative employment became unavailable. The contemporary estimate of the relationship between claims based on sickness and unemployment was spelled out in a 1905 article published in Reichsarbeitsblatt. Relying on statistics for sickness insurance collected in 1894, the article explained how to derive a scale of average unemployment in various trades from the Krankenkassen figures.[118]

> In der damaligen Bearbeitung findet sich ein Versuch, zu einer solchen Durchschnittsskala zu gelangen, der von der fingierten Annahme ausgeht, dass die in dem hoechsten Mitgliederstand der Kassen zur Erscheinung gekommene Zahl Arbeitsfaehiger in der Tat waehrend des ganzen Jahres vorhanden sei. Unter dieser fingierten Voraussetzung kann man aus der Differenz des hoechsten

Mitgliederstandes mit dem durchschnittlichen Mitgliederstand ablesen, wie gross in Prozenten der Gesamtzahl der Arbeitsfaehigen die Arbeitslosigkeit durchschnittlich das Jahr hindurch--ungefaehr--gewesen ist. Die Differenz zwischen dieser Hoechstzahl und der monatlichen Mitgliederzahl der Ortskrankenkassen wird dann als die Zahl der in dem betreffenden Monat arbeitslos gewesenen Arbeitsfaehigen betrachtet.

According to the example provided, this theoretical construct worked as follows:[119]

Vergleicht man z.B. mit der hoechsten Monatsziffer 3 510 809 die durchschnittliche Mitgliederzahl 3 327 753, indem man bei der Berechnung der letzteren den Mitgliederstand am 31. Dezember mitberuecksichtigt, so findet man, dass von den arbeitsfaehigen Personen im Kreise der Ortskrankenkassen 5,2% im Jahres durchschnitt arbeitslos gewesen sind.

In looking at figures on health insurance, it is important to emphasize that those groups affected by unemployment and those suffering from physical disability were not necessarily coterminous to any extent. Not all unemployed were ill--and according to our definition of the term, only those physically able to work would be counted. Nor were all disabled persons unemployed--some held parttime jobs and others worked normal shifts. So in looking at this problem, it is necessary to differentiate among those who were: Physically able to work but unemployed, physically handicapped but employed, or unemployed due to some physical disability. The physical incapacity could be temporary or permanent and subsidized or not, regardless of the individual's employment status.

The problem of distinguishing among these groups was complicated by imprecise records, spurious claims and the attachment of unemployment funds to organizations whose primary function was the administration of health insurance. In 1899 for example some five million persons were covered by local health insurance programs administered by more than 13,000 funds with varying regulations on unemployment benefits. In the general debate over unemployment insurance, it was hotly contested whether such assistance was to be attached to health insurance which covered 8,750,000 persons by 1901, to invalid insurance which covered 12,000,000 or to accident insurance which covered 19,000,000. The amorphous relationship between unemployment coverage and other forms of social insurance was one result of Bismarck's initial foray into state-subsidized protection of German workers which persisted throughout our period and beyond. With regard to the use of statistics outlining the extent of membership in social insurance programs as determinants of unemployment, one contemporary observer provided this analysis:[120]

> Diese Zahlen lassen in ihren Schwankungen Schluesse auf den Gang der Beschaeftigung zu....Dass das Schwanken der Zahl der Versicherten in der Differenz keineswegs die Zahl der Arbeitslosen bezw. der wiederbeschaeftigten Arbeitslosen ergiebt, wurde wiederholt hervorgehoben. Dieser Statistik so gut vermieden werden, wie bei jeder anderen.

THE UNEMPLOYMENT PROBLEM AS REFLECTED IN THE 1895 CENSUS

As we have seen in analyzing quantitative data, the overall extent of unemployment recorded during our period remained relatively small. Less than three percent of the potential labor force was unemployed at any given time during good years and even during bad years such as 1892 or 1901, rates in excess of six percent were rare. In fact, estimates of unemployment in 1901 indicated that although large cities suffered rates between seven and ten percent, the empire as a whole experienced a 4.8% rate of idleness among the labor force.[121] During the subsequent economic downturn of 1907-08, Germany once again suffered a "major" outbreak of unemployment with an estimated four percent of the population being affected.[122]

With the possible exception of the interval between 1876 and 1879 in large cities such as Berlin, we have no evidence that unemployment ever approached epidemic proportions during our period. Nevertheless, qualitative reactions to unemployment did assume major dimensions. Expressed in institutional forms ranging from Arbeits-nachweise to increasingly sophisticated surveys and relief measures, the reaction frequently vented itself in explicit statements about the revolutionary potential of work short-ages. Because such anxiety was not borne out by the reality reflected in aggregate unemployment statistics, we must turn to a more detailed examination of the patterns of job scarcity which evolved in the German labor market.

One particularly useful tool for assessing the economic situation is the 1895 census which contained the only nationwide unemployment count undertaken in Germany between 1873 and 1913. With the help of that survey we shall try to determine the extent of vulnerability to unemployment which various segments of the labor force evinced. We shall attempt to analyze the distribution of unemployment by occupation, skill, region, age, sex and marital status. In addition, we shall consider the duration and frequency of joblessness, trying to evaluate the degrees of risk--real and imagined--which confronted certain sections of the population on a daily basis. While we rely primarily on the 1895 figures because of their comprehensive nature, an effort has been made to correct for idiosyncracies of that survey through reference to subsequent counts. In analyzing these figures we strive to portray in theory what never existed in historical fact--a "typical" unemployed German industrial laborer. In a socio-economic context, we shall delineate an ideal type of jobless worker and assess his dilemma which loomed disproportionately large on the contemporary horizon.

The 1895 Census

In general terms, the economic outlook in 1895 was better than it had been during the preceding years of our period. Business conditions in most sectors of German industry were improving, much-lamented overproduction was on the decline and prices were regaining their pre-deflation upward momentum. Employment opportunities in commerce and industry were expanding and reduced hours or lay-offs were resorted to less frequently. The economy had begun its long-awaited recovery by the mid-Nineties and this was evident in the labor market conditions registered in the 1895 census.

In contrast with unemployment data published between 1903 and 1913 in the Reichsarbeitsblatt, the census figures gave due weight to the plight of seasonal workers. Unorganized labor in agriculture and the building trades which accounted for such a high proportion of jobless workers in 1895 were virtually excluded from subsequent tallies and this factor must be taken into account when comparing the census figures with other estimates of the unemployment problem. Here it is also worth noting that during the ten years after the Reichsarbeitsblatt began publishing unemployment statistics,[123] the annual nadir and zenith of those numbers frequently occurred at times other than June and December. An approximate idea of the general dimensions of the unemployment problem could be gleaned from the data compiled during those months. But it is important to emphasize that the June figures probably failed to reflect the minimum level of unemployment during 1895 and the December figures failed to indicate its absolute maximum. It is more likely that unemployment reached its low in September and its peak in January.[124]

Germany's first nationwide unemployment survey was conducted in two parts to allow for seasonal variations in the labor market. Separate counts were conducted on June 14 and December 2 of 1895. On both dates an effort was made to enumerate able and willing workers who were without jobs for economic reasons. Persons physically unfit for employment and others whose idleness stemmed from non-economic sources were to be excluded from the final tallies. Here it is worth noting that in June forty percent of the reported unemployment was due to illness while in December only 28 percent of the problem was attributable to sickness. Among agricultural workers, the percentage of unemployment due to illness in winter was less than half the summer figure.

The difficulty in arriving at workable criteria and the novelty of the entire undertaking produced results which must be interpreted with caution. To cite an example, 12% of those registered in Berlin and 31% of those registered in Stuttgart were erroneously designated as unemployed. This considerable margin of error serves to remind us of contemporary vagueness about quantifiable measures of unemployment. One would therefore do well to take all of the following figures as rough reflections rather than precise indicators of the unemployment situation in Germany.

Of those counted as unemployed, the overwhelming majority--consistently more than 90%--were laborers. Consider the following figures:

	Total Number of Unemployed		Unemployed Due to Illness		Other Unemployed	
	June 14	December 2	June 14	December 2	June 14	December
Men	218,603	553,584	85,866	153,561	132,737	400,017
Women	80,749	217,421	34,482	63,804	46,267	153,623
Total	299,352	771,005	120,348	217,365	179,004	553,640

As percentages of a total working population slightly in excess of 22 million, the figures translated into unemployment rates of 1.35% for June and 3.46% for December. The numbers for _Arbeitnehmer_ or employees were somewhat higher, with 1.85% unemployed in summer and 4.78% in winter.[125] The census indicated that employees, numbering 16,146,671, constituted 31.2% or almost one-third of the total population.

More than three-quarters of the entire difference between the unemployment rates for June and December could be traced to the seasonal nature of work in five basic occupational categories: Agriculture, the building trades, mining, commercial trades, hotel and restaurant industries. Almost eighty percent of the discrepancies between the two surveys were attributable to unemployment in these five sectors. The predictability of unemployment in these areas and the supposedly higher wages paid to seasonal workers were presumed to enable those affected to save for lay-offs during the inevitable slack periods. As we shall see, however, personal and private remedies for unemployment came to be recognized as impractical with the result that collective solutions to the problem were grudgingly developed.[126]

Occupation as a Factor in Unemployment

One of the most important determinants of unemployment was occupation, and workers in various sectors evinced widely differing susceptibilities to loss of their jobs. In the broadest terms, the figures looked this way:

Occupational Category	Unemployed Workers		Percentage of Workers Unemployed		For Every 100 Unemployed in June, the December Figure Was
	6/14	12/2	6/14	12/2	
Agriculture and Forrestry	19,204	162,472	0.33	2.81	846.03
Industry	97,782	274,625	1.53	4.18	280.85
Commerce	26,180	41,994	1.75	2.78	160.40
Domestic Service	30,907	68,423	1.74	3.82	221.38
Public Service and Professions	4,931	6,126	0.76	0.93	124.23
TOTALS	179,004	553,640	1.11	3.40	309.29

The extraordinarily low levels of unemployment in the agrarian sector during June were surpassed only by civil servants and clerics. The discrepancy between summer and winter figures was predictably much higher for agricultural work, a seasonally related occupation. While industry and commerce registered higher unemployment levels year round, their rates increased between two and three times where that of agriculture multiplied almost ninefold. Looking exclusively at the Prussian example, we find that agriculture accounted for almost one-third of all unemployment during December--31%--but it contributed less than half that amount--15%--during the summer. Conversely, while Prussian industry was responsible for 56% of the unemployment in June, its percentage dropped to 48% in the winter survey.

In addition to agriculture, mining and the building trades, occupations utilizing large numbers of unskilled workers evinced the greatest susceptibility to seasonal variations in unemployment. We might take a closer look at the census results in this context. Of the 553,640 workers who were counted as unemployed in December, 347,000 were attached to jobs regularly interrupted by weather. They included 158,340 engaged in gardening or agriculture, 145,121 involved in the building trades, an additional 11,603 in the transport and shipping industries, 20,615 from the stone, clay and brickmaking industries, plus 11,838 from the lodging and refreshment industry. Those five seasonally related occupations accounted for almost two-thirds of the total number of unemployed workers in December.[127] The winter rates of unemployment in the above industries ranged from 6.75 to 8.5 times the summer rates.

Within the context of seasonal variations in employment, we should also look at the wide discrepancies between June and December figures for day laborers and unskilled workers. In the summer of 1895, factory hands, workmen and nondescript assistants reported 2.55% unemployment while the winter survey indicated that 18.19% of these essentially interchangeable employees were without jobs. Among day laborers, conditions were even worse with 5.87% jobless in June and 20.83% in December. In addition to the census data, statistics from the relief works at Duesseldorf during the first decade of the twentieth century reflect the high proportion of unskilled laborers among the unemployed. During 1901-02, unskilled labor accounted for

75% of the unemployment; that percentage increased in 1902-03 to 77.1 percent. Although the absolute number of unskilled workers who were without jobs expanded significantly during the economic downturn between 1907 and 1909, their percentage of the total unemployed labor force dropped to 62% during that recession. One contemporary observer offered an explanation of the high proportion of unskilled workers among the unemployed by pointing to their connection with skilled labor. He noted that in industries with volatile labor markets such as printing or lithography, the lay-off of a single skilled workman almost invariably resulted in the simultaneous dismissal of several unskilled assistants who had functioned as a support staff.[128]

In order to get a clearer picture of the distribution of risk, we might consider the chart on the following page which averages June and December figures for individual occupations to arrive at a ranking of jobs in ascending order of rates of unemployment.[129] Here it is important to emphasize that more than two-thirds of the entire German labor force worked in occupations which reported less than 2% unemployment on the dates of the 1895 census. It is significant that in the relatively prosperous year of the survey when the economy had already gathered the momentum which moved it from a long period of deflation to recovery, those working in the most essential large industries were exposed to the lowest rates of unemployment. Particularly conspicuous in this context were the chemical, textile, paper, mining, machine and tool industries.

The chart shows that the first group, which contained occupations with less than one percent unemployment, accounted for slightly more than 2.5 million employees or about 16% of the total labor force.

1. Berufe, welche durchschnittlich weniger als 1% Arbeitslose hatten.

Berufsarten	Von den Arbeitnehmern waren arbeitslos durchschnittlich
C 11. Post- und Telegraphenbetrieb	0,13
C 12. Eisenbahnbetrieb	0,16
E 3. Kirche, religiöse Anstalten	0,23
E 4. Erziehung und Unterricht	0,32
E 6. Privatgelehrte	0,42
E 2. Staats-, Gemeindedienst	0,46
B 121. Torfes?	0,46
B 1. Erzgewinnung	0,47
B 19. Spielwaaren aus Porzellan, Glas	0,51
B 2. Hüttenbetrieb	0,51
B 3. Salzgewinnung	0,51
B 4. Stein- und Braunkohlen ꝛc.	0,53
B 11. Lehm- und Thongräberei	0,53
B 35. Eisendrahtzieher	0,57
B 77. Bleicherei, Appretur	0,58
B 51. Schwarz- und Weißblech	0,64
B 36. Stifte, Schrauben, Ketten	0,65
B 72. Weberei	0,65
B 73. Gummi- und Haarflechterei	0,66
B 70. Spinnerei, Spulerei	0,67
B 42. Eiserne Kurzwaaren	0,67
B 25. Spielwaaren aus Metall	0,67
B 39. Zeug-, Messerschmiede	0,72
B 18. Spiegelglas u. Spiegelfabrikation	0,72
B 60. Farbematerialien	0,75
C 2. Geld- und Kredithandel	0,77
B 74. Strickerei und Wirkerei	0,80
B 118. Essigfabrikation	0,83
B 16. Glashütten	0,83
B 69. Zubereitung von Spinnstoffen	0,84
B 14. Feine Thonwaaren	0,86
B 119. Tabaksfabrikation	0,85
B 63. Gasanstalten	0,85
B 81. Papier und Pappe	0,89
B 61. Zündwaaren	0,93
B 100. Spielwaaren aus Holz, Horn	0,93
B 124. Ausstattung von Puppen	0,95
B 33. Blechwaaren	0,97

2. Berufe, welche durchschnittlich 1–2% Arbeitslose hatten.

Berufsarten	
C 14. Straßenbahnbetrieb	1,00
B 43. Nadel-, Drahtwaarenfabrikation	1,04
B 58. Chemische, photogr. Präparate	1,04
B 15. Fayence und Porzellan	1,04
B 84. Lohnmühlen	1,05
B 48. Wagenbauanstalten	1,05
B 17. Glasveredelung	1,05
B 129. Handschuhmacher	1,07
B 62. Abfälle, Düngstoffe	1,09
E 5. Gesundheitspflege	1,10
C 5. Zeitungsverlag ꝛc.	1,11
B 94. Grobe Holzwaaren	1,12
B 51. Sonstige Musik-Instrumente	1,12
B 55. Pianoforte, Orgelbau	1,13
B 40. Schwerenschleifer	1,13
B 21. Gold- und Silberschläger	1,15
B 7. Steinbrüche	1,16
B 87. Wachszug, Zwirnereien	1,17
B 9. Ries, Sand, Kalk, Cement	1,18
B 65. Öle, Fette, Firniße	1,18
C 10. Versicherungswesen	1,16
B 89. Spielwaaren aus Kautschuk	1,21
B 30. Eisenschnitterei	1,27
B 24. Zinnnerzerei	1,27
B 76. Färberei	1,28
B 97. Steinwaaren	1,29
B 27. Erzgießer, Glockengießer	1,31

Berufsarten	
B 71. Tuchmacher	1,33
B 103. Bürstenmacher	1,35
B 113. Wasserwerke, Mineralwasser	1,35
B 67. Ölmühlen	1,37
B 109. Rübenzucker	1,39
B 45. Maschinen, Werkzeuge	1,41
B 112. Animalische Nahrungsmittel	1,41
B 75. Häkelei, Stickerei	1,47
D 1. Häusliche Dienste	1,45
B 110. Vegetab. Nahrungsmittel	1,45
B 66. Lichte, Seifen	1,46
C 13. Posthalterei, Pers.-Fuhrwerk	1,47
B 93. Holzzurichtung	1,48
B 29. Metalllegirungen	1,52
D 78. Posamentenfabrikation	1,53
A 1. Landwirthschaft	1,54
B 85. Gerberei	1,57
B 41. Feilenhauer	1,57
C 3. Spedition, Kommission	1,58
B 104. Säcke, Schirme	1,56
B 82. Spiele aus Papiermaché	1,59
B 114. Mälzerei	1,61
B 20. Goldschmiede, Juweliere	1,63
B 102. Kammacher	1,66
B 64. Küblerei, Holzschuhe, Harz	1,67
B 116. Branntweinbrennerei	1,68
B 132. Schuhmacher	1,70
B 10. Cementwaaren, Gipsdielen	1,72
B 88. Gummiwaaren	1,73
B 47. Stellmacher, Waaner	1,75
C 16. Räderei, Schiffsbefrachtung	1,76
C 21. Leichenbestattung	1,77
C 7. Handelsvermittelung	1,82
B 79. Seilerei	1,82
A 4. Forstwirthschaft	1,83
B 155. Farbendruckerei	1,84
B 51. Schumacher (ohne Flickschuster)	1,86
B 59. Apotheker	1,82
C 9. Versicherung, Stellenvermittelung	1,87
B 91. Spielwaaren aus Leder	1,87
B 101. Dreh- und Schnitzwaaren	1,87
B 44. Schreibfedern aus Stahl	1,87
B 26. Verarbeitung unedl.Metalle(oh.Eisen)	1,93
B 159. Musterzeichner, Kalligraphen	1,93
B 151. Schriftgießerei, Holzschnitt	1,94
B 37. Grob- (Huf-) Schmiede	1,96

3. Berufe, welche durchschnittlich 2–3% Arbeitslose hatten.

Berufsarten	
B 34. Nagelschmiede	2,02
A 3. Thierzucht	2,04
B 125. Künstliche Blumen	2,06
B 130. Kravatten, Hosenträger	2,08
B 99. Drechslerei	2,09
B 23. Roth- und Gelbgießer	2,11
C 6. Hausirhandel	2,15
B 52. Uhrmacher	2,17
B 80. Leder, gearbt, lackirt	2,17
B 8. Feine Steinwaaren	2,19
B 57. Electrotechnik	2,19
B 28. Gürtler, Bronzeure	2,21
B 153. Graveure, Modelleure	2,21
B 60. Lampen	2,22
B 6. Buchbinderei, Kartonagenfabrikation	2,25
B 100. Getreidemühlen	2,29
B 95. Tischlerei	2,29
B 96. Böttcherei	2,30
B 63. Abdecker	2,31
B 5. Torfgraberei	2,31
C 4. Buch-, Kunst-, Musikalienhandel	2,31

Berufsarten	
B 153. Stein- und Zinkdruckerei	2,31
B 117. Schmalz-, Obstweinfabrikation	2,32
B 126. Hutmacherei	2,33
B 32. Klempner	2,34
B 154. Kupfer- und Stahldruckerei	2,34
B 15. Fracht- und Rollfuhrwerk	2,34
B 55. Physikalische, chirurgische Apparate	2,35
B 113. Brauerei	2,35
B 38. Schlosserei, Geldschrankfabrikation	2,56
C 1. Waaren- und Produktenhandel	2,60
B 152. Buchdruckerei	2,56
B 160. Künstlerische Berufe	2,63
B 121. Schneider, -innen	2,64
B 99. Flechterei von Holz, Stroh	2,77
C 20. Dienstmänner, Botenanlager	2,79
C 22. Beherbergung, Erquidung	2,80
B 142. Glaser	2,82
B 155. Badeanstalten	2,83
E 8. Musik, Theater ꝛc.	2,91
B 127. Rüßenmacherei	2,92

4. Berufe, welche durchschnittlich 3–5% Arbeitslose hatten.

Berufsarten	
B 19. Hafen- und Lootsendienst ꝛc.	3,01
B 133. Barbiere	3,07
B 6. Steinmetzen, Steinhauer	3,11
B 80. Netze, Segel, Säcke	3,19
B 90. Riemer und Sattler	3,19
B 49. Schiffsbau	3,22
B 134. Friseure, Perrückenmacher	3,22
B 22. Kupferschmiede	3,42
B 108. Konditorei	3,42
B 105. Spiegel-, Bilderrahmen	3,61
B 128. Kürschner	3,64
B 138. Bauunternehmung	3,7
B 46. Mühlenbauer	3,7
A 2. Kunst- und Handelsgärtnerei	3,4
B 150. Schornsteinfeger	3,86
B 12. Ziegelei, Thonröhren	3,91
B 50. Büchsenmacher	3,91
B 1. Fleischer (Schlächter)	4,01
A 6. Binnenfischerei	4,02
B 13. Töpferei	4,02
B 136. Wäscherei, Plätterei	4,04
B 122. Kleider-, Wäschekonfektion	4,16
B 156. Photographie	4,46
B 147. Brunnenmacher	4,49
B 148. Gas-, Wasser-Installateure	4,69
B 139. Feldmesser, Kulturtechniker	4,93

5. Berufe, welche durchschnittlich über 5% Arbeitslose hatten.

Berufsarten	
B 141. Zimmerer	5,74
B 123. Buchmacherei	5,75
E 7. Privatsekretäre, Schreiber	5,78
B 149. Eisenleer	5,80
C 18. Bummenmischer	6,09
S. Hülfsgewerbe des Handels	7,06
A 5. See- und Küstenfischerei	7,90
B 92. Tapezierer	8,11
B 157. Maler, Bildhauer	8,78
B 145. Quadecker	9,07
B 144. Stukateure	9,65
B 151. Stubenmacher	9,97
B 140. Maurer	10,75
B 161. Gewerbl. Arbeiter ohne näh. Bez.	10,90
B 146. Steinleger	11,50
D 2. Lohnarbeit wechselnder Art	15,70
C 17. See- und Küstenschiffahrt	19,40

Public employees, churchmen, tutors and journalists were among the 878,761 workers with the smallest risk of unemployment. Also belonging to jobs with less than one percent unemployment were wage laborers involved in mining, smelting, saltworks, cutlery, tin and iron production. Workers in the paint industry, glass and porcelain manufacturing, tobacco and paper industries, and money or credit handling rounded out those occupational categories least susceptible to unemployment.

A second group of occupations with unemployment rates ranging from one to two percent on the dates of the census included most of the workers engaged in the primary sectors of agriculture and forestry. It also consisted of domestic servants, shoemakers, tanners, blacksmiths, engineering workers, iron founders, cloth makers, cutlers, lace makers, embroiderers, dyers, haberdashers, quarry workers. In addition, this group was comprised of lime, cement, gypsum, faience and porcelain manufacturers; sugar beet and brandy makers; forwarding agents; insurance and commission agents; brush and basket makers. This hodgepodge of skilled, semi-skilled and menial occupations which reported between one and two percent unemployment accounted for 8,779,856 workers or 54.5 percent of all employees in the German economy. In other words, mid-way through our period more than half of the labor force was involved in occupations which subjected them to very low levels of unemployment.

A third category registering unemployment rates between two and three percent included traders in housewares and home produce, truckers and freight carriers, pub and inn employees, carpenters, locksmiths, plumbers, lathe turners, glaziers, tailors and dressmakers, bookbinders, printers, lithographers, zinc etchers, brewers, coopers, hatmakers, watchmakers, and theatrical workers. With the exception of vendors, transport workers and hotel or restaurant employees, this group included a high proportion of skilled craftsmen among the 2,293,320 workers which represented 14.2% of all German employees.

A fourth category with unemployment rates ranging from three to five percent included a large number of construction workers and clothing makers. It consisted of stonemasons, brickworkers, pipe makers, butchers, seamstresses, clothing and linen manufacturers, furriers, leather workers, harness makers, launderers, barbers, wig makers, potters, horticulturists, florists, bakers, pastry makers, ship builders and coppersmiths. Totalling 1,387,052 persons, this category contained eight percent of the labor force.

The fifth category with the highest rates of unemployment--in excess of five percent--numbered 1,123,986 or 6.9% of all workers. This group encompassed milliners, clothes cleaners, stenographers, stove fillers, joiners, paper hangers, painters and sculptors, house painters, roofers, stucco workers, masons and stone setters. Also included were: Inland, sea and coastal shipping employees, commercial assistants; wage earners with changing sources of income and workers whose jobs had no precise designations-- two big groups likely to encompass high proportions of unskilled, interchangeable and frequently itinerant laborers.

The following chart provides an encapsulized look at the distribution of unemployment among the five categories described above.

Group	Absolute Number of Employees	Percentage of Labor Force	Unemployed		
			Absolute Number		Average Unemployment Level
			June	December	
1	2,562,477	15.9	12,419	14,656	under 1%
2	8,779,856	54.4	55,669	210,112	1-2%
3	2,293,320	14.2	49,720	68,250	2-3%
4	1,387,052	8.6	29,166	75,267	3-5%
5	1,123,966	6.9	32,030	185,355	over 5%
SUMS	16,146,671	100.0	179,004	553,640	2.27%

Seventy percent of those counted as employees worked in occupations which experienced unemployment rates between one and three percent on the dates of the 1895 count. Fifteen percent belonged to categories which reported negligible unemployment levels of less than one percent, and an approximately equal number were engaged in jobs registering more than three percent unemployment.

Based on the above figures, we might conclude that the "typical" German employee worked in an occupation that exposed him to low levels of unemployment, affecting less than three percent of his co-workers at any given time. We might also deduce that those most susceptible to unemployment were likely to be involved in seasonally related areas

such as the building trades or shipping industry. In
addition, it is worth noting that workers without specific
job skills were especially vulnerable to loss of employment
because their lack of training made them almost interchangeable and therefore susceptible to frequent replacement. Workers in highly mechanized industries were also
prone to unemployment if continuity of output was dependent
on the technology of machines rather than the training of
labor. Almost all occupations which reported unemployment
rates in excess of five percent in the census were either
seasonally related, required low levels of skill, or both.
As a general rule, job security tended to increase with the
level of training required to perform the work. Predictably, those engaged in handicrafts occupied a middle
position between unskilled and highly trained technical
workers and this was reflected in the intensity of unemployment among their ranks.

Figures on itinerant workers collected by the
German labor colonies during the years after 1895 serve to
reinforce the data outlined above. Between 1896 and 1910
the colonies assembled statistics on the occupations of
their inhabitants. The job categories which consistently
appeared in substantial numbers included agriculture, the
building trades, metal working, commerce, wood working, food
processing, clothing and cleaning. Each of these occupations suffered disproportionately from unemployment.
However, the single largest category, continually outstrip-

ping all others by two to four times the number of workers, was that of Arbeiter ohne naehere Angabe.[130]

In addition to findings of the labor colonies, articles on unemployment which were published by the Reichsarbeitsblatt after 1903 mirrored the census conclusions. A comparison between the occupational risks of unemployment in various trades during 1895 and the early years of the twentieth century is instructive in this context. The organized trades which were most often cited in the Reichsarbeitsblatt as suffering from conspicuously high levels of unemployment included the moulding workers or Bildhauern; bakers and cooks; printers, lithographers and photographers plus their assistants; paperhangers; glaziers; and hairdressers' assistants. It is significant that all of these professions with high rates of unemployment supplied the luxuries rather than necessities of life, providing products whose consumption could be drastically curtailed during hard times. With the previous comments in mind, let us consider the following comparison between the risks of unemployment in 1895 and the early years of this century.[131]

Die Arbeitslosenziffer betrug am Quartalsschluss im Durchschnitt der Quartale (30. September 1903 bis 30. Juni 1905) bei den Verbänden

unter 1%
Schuhmacher
Tischler
Klempner und Metallarbeiter

1-2%
Kaufleute
Handels- und Transportarbeiter
Töpfer, Ziegler
Schiffszimmerer
Maschinenbau- und Metallarneiter, Schmiede
Glasarbeiter
Porzellanarbeiter
Bauhandwerker

2-3%
Lederarbeiter
Brauereiarbeiter
Buchbinder
Graveure und Formstecher
Hut- und Filzwarenarbeiter
Zigarrensortierer

3-5%
Graphische Berufe, Maler, Buch- und Steindruckereihilfsarbeiter, Lithographen
Photographengehilfen
Mühlenarbeiter
Handschuhmacher
Bildhauer (Gewerkverein)

über 5%
Konditoren
Bäcker
Buchdrucker
Bildhauer (Zentralverein)

Von den Arbeitnehmern waren nach den Zählungen vom 14. Juni und 2. Dezember 1895 Durchschnittlich arbeitslos Prozente in folgenden Berufsarten

unter 1%
Eisendrahtzieher
Schwartz- und Weissblechherstellung
Stifte, Schrauben, Ketten, Nägel, Nieten, Drahtseile, soweit nicht zum Gewerbe der Nagelschmiedegehörig
Eiserne Kurzwaren
Spielwaren aus Metal
Zeug-, Sensen- und Messerschmiede
Spiegelglas und Spiegelfabrikation
Geld- und Kredithandel
Glashütten
Feine Tonwaren
Blechwarenfabrikation

1-2%
Näh- und Stecknadeln
Drahtwarenfabrikation
Fayence-Porzellanfabrikat
Handschuhmacher
Verfertigung von Holzwaren. Dreh- und Schnitzwaren
Eisengiesserei
Verfertigung von Maschinen, Werkzeugen und Apparaten
Spedition und Kommission. Handelsvermittelung. Reederei. Schiff befrachtung
Schuhmacherei

2-3%
Graveure und Modelleure
Buchbinder
Tischler
Stein- und Zinkdrucker
Hutmacherei und Filzwarenfabrikat
Klempner
Brauerei
Buchdruckerei

3-5%
Schiffsbau
Firsuere
Kupferschmiede
Konditoren
Bauunternehmung
Bäckerei
Ziegelei
Töpferei
Photographie

über 5%
Maler
Bildhauer
Maurer usw.

When calculating the amounts of unemployment which affected members of various occupations, there were a number of approaches for arriving at a statistical verdict. The disparate impressions conveyed by numbers purporting to measure unemployment may be illustrated with reference to figures published in the Reichsarbeitsblatt during the final year of our period. The first set of statistics reflects the percentage of unemployment reported at the end of the last week in each month by members of participating unions. The second set of figures represents the frequency or number of individual instances of unemployment for each 100 union members during an entire quarter. While the former statistics reveal the amount of unemployment at a single point in time, the latter show how many persons were affected over the course of a longer interval.[132]

Ende	1903	1904	1905	1906	1907	1908	1909	1910	1911	1912	1913
Januar	.	.	.	.	1,7	2,9	4,2	2,6	2,5	2,1	3,2
Februar	.	.	.	.	1,6	2,7	4,1	2,3	2,2	2,3	2,9
März	.	.	2,0	1,6	1,1	1,3	2,5	3,5	1,3	1,9	1,4	2,3
April	.	.	.	.	1,3	2,3	2,3	1,3	1,3	1,7
Mai	.	.	.	.	1,4	2,8	2,8	2,3	1,6	1,9
Juni	.	3,2	2,1	1,5	1,2	1,4	2,9	2,8	2,0	1,2	1,7
Juli	.	.	.	.	0,3	1,4	2,7	2,5	1,9	1,4	1,8
August	.	.	.	.	0,7	1,4	2,7	2,3	1,7	1,8	1,7
September	.	2,3	1,8	1,4	1,0	1,4	2,7	2,1	1,3	1,7	1,3
Oktober	.	.	.	.	1,1	1,3	2,9	2,3	1,6	1,3	1,7
November	.	.	.	.	1,1	1,7	3,2	2,0	1,8	1,7	1,3
Dezember	.	2,6	2,4	1,3	1,6	2,7	4,4	2,6	2,1	2,4	2,8

	1903	1904	1905	1906	1907	1908	1909	1910	1911	1912
1. Viertelj.	.	7,9	8,6	6,4	6,5	9,2	12,7	8,7	9,1	9,0
2. "	8,6	7,9	7,0	6,1	6,1	9,4	9,5	8,0	6,6	6,9
3. "	8,2	7,4	7,2	5,4	6,9	9,6	8,5	7,1	7,1	6,9
4. "	7,8	8,6	6,3	5,7	7,1	11,2	8,4	7,2	7,0	7,4

Marked as the variations were for Fachverbaenden as a whole, the discrepancies were even more pronounced and noteworthy within certain occupations. Figures from 1904, for example, indicate that although a relatively small percentage of union members were unemployed at the conclusion of any given quarter, substantial numbers suffered from idleness at some time during the three-month period. The following chart reveals that percentages measuring the frequency of unemployment per 100 members during a quarter were between two and eight times greater than percentages reflecting levels of unemployment at the conclusion of that period. The numbers reported by the glaziers, bookbinders and moulding workers' unions were particularly illustrative in this context. [133]

Gewerbe	Zahl der Mitglieder		4. Quartal 1903				1. Quartal 1904			
			Zahl der				Zahl der			
	Ende 1903	Ende 1904	Arbeits-losen am Schluß	%	Gäste	%	Arbeits-losen am Schluß	%	Gäste	%
Verband der Porzellan- und verwandten Arbeiter, Charlottenburg (Gewerkschaft)	8 613	8 722	226	2,6	301	3,5	150	2,1	269	3,7
Verband der Metallarbeiter, Stuttgart (Gewerkschaft)	158 548	181 328	3 148	2,0	11 644	7,3	2 297	1,4	13 054	8,2
Deutscher Buchbinderverband, Stuttgart (Gewerkschaft)	13 672	16 843	235	1,7	1 645	12,0	283	2,0	1 857	13,1
Zentralverband deutscher Brauereiarbeiter, Hannover (Gewerkschaft)	13 591	19 371	213	1,5	825	7,5	292	1,4	902	5,4
Zentralverband der Glaser, Karlsruhe (Gewerkschaft)	3 734	4 231	120	3,5	743	19,7	342	9,2	1 257	33,7
Verband der deutschen Buchdrucker, Berlin (Gewerkschaft)	31 807	38 219	1 947	6,0	5 487	15,4	1 405	4,0	4 383	12,4
Zentralverein der Bildhauer Deutschlands, Berlin (Gewerkschaft)	3 928	4 580	644	16,4	2 202	56,1	341	8,3	1 784	43,2
Zentralverband der Handels-, Transport- und Verkehrsarbeiter Deutschlands, Berlin (Gewerkschaft)	29 411	40 314	709	1,8	1 551	5,2	31	1,1	47	1,5

Gewerbe	2. Quartal 1904				3. Quartal 1904				4. Quartal 1904			
	Zahl der				Zahl der				Zahl der			
	Arbeits-losen am Schluß	%	Gäste	%	Arbeits-losen am Schluß	%	Gäste	%	Arbeits-losen am Schluß	%	Gäste	%
Verband der Porzellan- und verwandten Arbeiter, Charlottenburg (Gewerkschaft)	92	1,2	195	2,4	123	1,6	193	2,4	160	1,8	318	4,2
Verband der Metallarbeiter, Stuttgart (Gewerkschaft)	394	2,7	1 826	12,4	250	1,2	1 012	7,4	353	2,3	2 425	14,4
Deutscher Buchbinderverband, Stuttgart (Gewerkschaft)	2 489	1,6	11 422	7,1	2 430	1,5	11 882	7,6	3 221	1,5	12 627	7,4
Zentralverband deutscher Brauereiarbeiter, Hannover (Gewerkschaft)	365	2,4	991	6,3	369	2,6	852	5,6	285	1,4	862	5,1
Zentralverband der Glaser, Karlsruhe (Gewerkschaft)	141	3,8	981	25,4	16	0,6	1 039	25,7	112	2,7	972	23,0
Verband der deutschen Buchdrucker, Berlin (Gewerkschaft)	2 375	6,4	4 893	14,4	3 039	8,1	6 686	18,1	1 707	4,5	5 653	14,8
Zentralverein der Bildhauer Deutschlands, Berlin (Gewerkschaft)	282	6,3	2 205	49,4	355	7,4	2 044	42,6	739	16,3	2 537	55,4
Zentralverband der Handels-, Transport- und Verkehrsarbeiter Deutschlands, Berlin (Gewerkschaft)	401	1,2	1 515	5,3	415	1,1	1 320	4,3	603	1,5	2 160	5,4

These numbers are important because they demonstrate that although the level of unemployment at any single point in time might appear low, a significant portion of the populace could still be affected by loss of work over the course of longer intervals. And here it should be emphasized that we have been looking at figures on organized laborers which for reasons alluded to earlier were likely to suffer far lower rates of unemployment than their non-union competition.

An additional point needs to be made at this juncture. Discrepancies between the percentage of jobless workers at the end of a quarter and the frequency over an entire quarter was attributable in small measure to multiple cases of unemployment suffered by isolated individuals. Figures published after 1903 indicated that relatively few workers were subjected to successive instances of unemployment within any given three-month period. The data was gathered by members of the Zentralverein der Bildhauer, the only union to regularly report such numbers in the Reichsarbeitsblatt. The Bildhauer consistently suffered the very highest rates of unemployment throughout the first decade of this century. Even among their members, however, an average of almost three-quarters of those counted as unemployed lost their livelihoods only one time during any quarter. At various intervals, fractions ranging from five to nine percent of the total number of unemployed Bildhauer lost their jobs three or more times during the preceding ninety days. Considering the unusually high susceptibility

of this profession to unemployment, their experience suggests that instances of repeated work loss were probably not
very great. Apparently, the onus of unemployment was more
widely distributed, with a succession of new individuals
rather than the same workers serving as victims. Figures
from the first quarter of 1906 when the average frequency of
unemployment was 6.6% suggest that in many occupations, loss
of work was likely to affect large numbers of persons for
short periods of time.[134]

Verband	1. Quartal 1906	1. Quartal 1905	4. Quartal 1905
Zentralverein der Bildhauer	45,0	52,1	48,0
Friseurgehilfen	34,7	35,6	44,8
Tapezierer	34,6	32,3	23,0
Kupferschmiede	31,2	40,9	22,2
Glaser	32,0	30,3	22,3
Bäcker	24,8	20,3	22,6
Konditoren (Hamburg)	22,5	15,9	13,1
Photographengehilfen	18,1	18,3	12,7
Holzarbeiter	15,3	14,3	13,3
Böttcher	13,7	6,6	11,3
Bergolder	13,0	18,7	10,8
Sattler	12,9	14,1	13,7
Buchbinder	12,7	13,2	15,4
Gutarbeiter	11,6	8,3	13,2

The following figures showing the average frequency of unemployment and the average duration of support during the
second quarter of 1905 reinforce the impression created by
the preceding chart. Both indicate the high proportion of
persons affected by unemployment over time--a fact frequently camouflaged by other statistics.[135]

	Der Verband hatte Mitglieder	Es kamen auf 100 Mitglieder Fälle von Arbeitslosigkeit	Die durchschnittliche Unterstützungsdauer betrug Tage
Kupferschmiede	8 655	45,4	15,2
Zentralverein der Bildhauer	4 794	41,0	14,7
Friseurgehilfen	1 434	30,0	9,5
Tapezierer	6 747	28,8	10,3
Glaser	4 552	21,0	10,4
Bäcker	8 754	19,9	15,2
Arbeiter in Hut- und Filzwaren	5 000	17,5	12,8
Photographengehilfenverband	836	15,3	18,4
Sattler	5 400	15,0	12,4
Holzarbeiter	114 100	13,6	12,1
Notenstechergehilfen . . .	331	13,4	4,6
Konditoren (Hamburg) . .	1 952	12,5	19,6
Vergolder	1 760	12,6	10,7
Graveure	2 312	12,5	7,8
Schmiede	15 700	12,1	10,4
Buch- und Steindruckereihilfsarbeiter	6 766	11,9	10,1
Buchbinder	16 057	11,7	17,8
Buchdrucker	40 000	11,5	19,1
Lithographen und Steindrucker	11 700	9,3	13,0
Maschinisten und Heizer .	10 000	7,5	13,8
Gewerkverein deutscher Bildhauer	437	7,3	16,0

The Duration of Unemployment

In trying to analyze the duration of unemployment, the 1895 census-takers were instructed to determine how long jobless individuals had been without work on the date of the survey--as of June 14 and December 2. No provisions were made for follow-up inquiries about subsequent idleness. Therefore the following figures do not necessarily reflect the total number of days without employment. Since it is highly improbable that all unemployed laborers returned to work on either June 15 or December 3, the next chart would tend to underrate the ultimate duration of joblessness. The statistics register days of unemployment for reasons other than sickness up to the time of the census.

Duration of Unemployment on Day of Survey	Unemployed			
	Absolute Number		Percentage	
	June 14	Dec 2	June 14	Dec 2
1 day	2,104	15,791	1.17	2.85
2-7 days	17,471	70,589	9.76	12.75
8-14 days	39,659	155,206	22.16	28.03
15-28 days	19,782	98,180	11.05	17.74
29-90 days	39,398	132,810	22.01	23.09
more than 90 days	25,256	39,051	14.11	7.05
unknown	35,334	42,013	19.74	7.59
TOTALS	179,004	553,640	100	100

As these figures reveal, the most common span of unemployment lasted for periods between one and two weeks. Significantly, from two-thirds to three-quarters of all those without work experienced intervals of idleness longer than seven days but less than three months.

Some specific local inquiries conducted in the aftermath of the nationwide June and December counts shed further light on the duration of unemployment. For example, a Berlin survey of the period between July 9 and September 20, 1895, revealed that the average length of unemployment in the capital was 28 days. The Berlin count also showed that three months after the June 14 census, 31.6% of those unemployed on that day were still without work. A Stuttgart poll undertaken after the winter census showed that 19.1% of those registered as unemployed on December 2 had found work again within ten days. However, of that nineteen percent, only three-quarters re-entered the Stuttgart job market in positions for which they had originally been trained. The rest were forced to take whatever work they could find regardless of background or preference. Even during a mild winter such as that at the end of 1895, a large number of workers were reduced to seeking employment in occupations other than those for which they were best qualified.[136]

Returning to the census itself, we find rather different summer and winter breakdowns on the duration of unemployment in broad occupational categories. Significantly, workers with the highest incidence of unemployment --the greatest number of persons without work--did not necessarily experience the longest duration of idleness. Among those unemployed in agriculture and gardening, for example, only 11.3% had been idle for more than 90 days in June and only 4.2% for that period in December. The building trades, which accounted for the second largest contingent of unemployed, reflected similar conditions with 15.4% reporting idleness in excess of three months on June 14 and 3.1% on December 2. In all instances, the relative duration of unemployment in German industry was closely alligned with that of the labor force as a whole.

Noteworthy also is the small number of persons who were jobless for long periods of time--less than 15% reported being without work for more than three months in June and fewer than half that number counted themselves as unemployed for 91 days or more on December 2. By far the most common stretches of idleness ranged from one to two weeks or one to three months--relatively short intervals if one considers the large proportion of seasonal occupations among the unemployed. The registered duration of unemployment in winter would probably have increased if the census were conducted later in the season. Here it is important to emphasize that those without work for more than one year on the date of the surveys were not included in the final figures. The rationale was that they probably were unfit for work and ought to be classified as "Arbeitsunfaehige" or unemployable rather than "Arbeitslose" or unemployed.

Because figures on the hard core unemployed were not collected even in 1895, it is impossible to get a definitive fix on their number. One comes away from the literature, however, with the vague feeling that truly long-term unemployment--idleness in excess of one year--was rare during our period and confined to very few persons. The deterioration of skills, loss of self-esteem and family crisis frequently attendant upon prolonged inactivity had a limited impact on German laborers because so few of them were subjected to unemployment for excessive periods. Writing at a time when work scarcity existed on a larger scale, the twentieth-century economist A.G. Pigou made the following observations about the personal and social ramifications of the duration of unemployment. Referring to various professional and personal tragedies associated with the loss of employment during the 1930's, Pigou noted:[137]

> Evils of this kind do not follow from small doses of unemployment spread over many men, even though the aggregate amount is large. They are the fruit, in the

main, of large concentrations of unemployment upon a
small number of especially unfortunate people. It
should be noted, however, that, while from this point
of view, a distribution of unemployment that involves a
moderate number of long spells is certain to be much
more injurious than one that involves a large number of
short spells, a very small number of very long spells
is not necessarily worse than a moderate number of long
spells. For it is arguable that, say, a year's continuous unemployment does nearly as much damage to
industrial and human quality as two or even ten years
could do. If this be so, it may be a less social evil
to have the same 10,000 persons unemployed continuously
for five years than to have an equal number of man
years of unemployment spread over 50,000 people in
continuous spells of one year each.

As we noted above, unemployment in excess of a year was
deemed to be synonymous with unfitness for work and inappropriate for inclusion in the 1895 census. It was apparently rare at the time.

DURATION OF UNEMPLOYMENT ACCORDING TO OCCUPATION

Absolute Numbers of Unemployed for Specified Amount of Days

Occupation	On June 14						On December 2					
	1	2–7	8–14	15–28	29–90	91✓	1	2–7	8–14	15–28	29–90	91✓
Agriculture	322	2007	3235	1492	2636	2171	3969	16804	45968	36077	38813	6868
Industry	1078	10119	23060	12191	21116	13572	8145	40320	83993	45296	61239	18200
Commerce	277	2208	5265	2522	7295	5196	1275	4662	8219	5313	13633	6679
Domestic Service	401	2906	7291	3179	6865	3360	2243	8352	16192	10797	16915	6052
Church, Government and Professions	26	231	808	397	1484	957	159	451	834	697	2210	1252
TOTALs	2104	17471	39659	19782	39398	25256	15791	70589	155206	98180	132810	39051

Relative Numbers

Of Every 100 Unemployed Persons, The Number Jobless Since _____ Days

Occupation	1	2–7	8–14	15–28	29–90	91✓	Not Kn'wn	1	2–7	8–14	15–28	29–90	91✓	Not Kn'wn
Agriculture	1.68	10.45	16.84	7.77	13.74	11.30	38.22	2.44	10.34	28.29	22.21	23.89	4.23	8.06
Industry	1.10	10.35	23.58	12.47	21.60	13.88	17.02	2.97	14.68	30.58	16.49	22.30	6.63	6.35
Commerce	1.06	8.43	20.11	9.63	27.87	19.85	13.05	3.04	11.10	19.57	12.65	32.46	15.91	5.27
Domestics	1.30	9.40	23.59	10.29	22.21	10.87	22.34	3.28	12.21	23.66	15.78	24.72	8.85	11.50
Services and Professions	0.53	4.68	16.39	8.05	30.09	19.41	20.85	2.59	7.36	13.61	11.38	36.08	20.44	9.54
TOTALS	1.17	9.76	22.16	11.05	22.01	14.11	19.74	2.85	12.75	28.03	17.74	23.99	7.05	7.59

In the preceding chart the occupational category
agriculture included animal breeding, forestry, gardening
and fishing. Industry included mining, smelting and construction while domestic service contained those designated
as working at "Lohnarbeit wechselnder Art". The total
number of persons who were unemployed for unknown periods on

June 14 was 35,334, of which approximately half worked in industrial occupations. On December 2, 42,013 persons did not know how long they had been without work and slightly more than 17,000 of them were from industry. The pattern which emerged in Germany prior to 1913 seemed to be one best calculated to minimize the negative impact of unemployment. Throughout our period, relatively large numbers were subjected to short intervals of idleness usually resulting from a change of jobs or predictable seasonal interruptions of economic activity. This fact is borne out by the 1895 census and other less comprehensive unemployment surveys.

Aside from the census, there were two other sources of information on the duration of unemployment which merit consideration. Some of the most important statistics on the tenure of unemployment during our period were collected by unions and thus give an overview of conditions within wide geographical but narrow occupational parameters. During the 1890's another body of data about the extent of idleness began to emerge in various cities which reversed the aforementioned trend by enumerating unemployed workers of all trades who were resident within their limited jurisdiction. Because these surveys included unorganized as well as union labor, they tended to reveal somewhat longer intervals of unemployment. Those stemming from the early Nineties reflected depressed conditions in the German economy which exacerbated the duration of idleness. Figures published in Soziale Praxis, for example, indicate that in

Elberfeld-Barmen during the month of July, 1894, 955 persons were unemployed for a total of 17,088 weeks or an average of 17.9 weeks. While two-thirds of the unemployed were without jobs for less than four months, a significant percentage remained inactive for longer stretches.[138]

As we noted in a different context, a slightly earlier survey had been conducted in the wake of the cholera epidemic which swept through Hamburg and the surrounding area during 1893. That survey which polled about a third of that city's residents showed that on February 11, 18,891 persons were unemployed. They had been idle for a total of 191,013 weeks, an average per unemployed individual of 10.37 weeks. Of the Hamburg unemployed, 5084 had been without work for less than five weeks and 8741 had been jobless for six to ten weeks. Only 2167 individuals had been unemployed for more than five months. If one looked at unemployment over the course of the preceding year rather than figures which applied on the date of the survey, the average inter-val of idleness escalated to 16.41 weeks or approximately four months, a figure quite close to the Elberfeld-Barmen average. The suburb of Altona generally duplicated the Hamburg results while the neighboring district of Ottensen registered somewhat shorter intervals of unemployment.

Moving into the twentieth century, continuous data on the circumstances of unemployment begins to emerge with increasing frequency. The city of Dresden, for example, collected statistics on the duration of unemployment between 1902 and 1912.[139]

PERSONS UNEMPLOYED FOR SPECIFIED NUMBER OF DAYS

Year	1-7	8-14	15-28	29-60	61-90	91-180	181-360	Over 360	Unknown
1902	722	1265	1031	980	497	723	437	271	716
1903	666	1443	1001	1003	507	689	403	146	645
1904	593	1093	747	666	387	480	254	108	485
1905	537	914	692	599	330	423	206	62	314
1906	430	706	555	440	241	322	180	35	294
1907	293	843	466	377	184	256	189	28	596
1908	543	1089	890	748	342	571	278	56	413
1909	416	1007	737	630	470	423	342	42	421
1910	457	869	520	473	249	339	195	35	415
1911	395	714	473	447	237	326	174	11	336
1912	341	732	463	430	228	269	158	10	332

The high figures for the first year are the product of the recession which affected German trade and industry at the beginning of the twentieth century. During 1908 and 1909 when business conditions once again went into a slump, all intervals showed increases but idleness in excess of three months underwent the largest proportionate expansion. In other words, during hard times, not only did more people experience unemployment, the average span of inactivity also increased, compounding a severe existing problem. Most cities which reported on unemployment during the last decade of our period--a time of general economic prosperity-- indicated that one to two months was the average duration of idleness. Although periods of one to two weeks were common, anything in excess of eight weeks was considered long and anything in excess of six months, a rarity.

Figures collected by various unions during the years between 1903 and 1913 tend to reinforce impressions created by the 1895 census and subsequent municipal surveys. We might, for example, look at the mercantile unions which consisted primarily of membership in four major organizations--Verein deutscher Kaufleute, Deutsch-nationaler Handlungsgehilfenverband, Buchhandlungsgehilfen and the Kaeufmannischer Verband fuer weibliche Angestellte. These unions experienced slightly longer stretches of unemployment during the last six years of our period than the 1895 census would lead one to anticipate. The mercantile unions reported that the average duration of unemployment among their members ranged from six weeks to two months between 1907 and 1912. The time frame for union support averaged five to six weeks. Despite their relatively lengthy intervals of idleness, members of these unions suffered less than might be expected because the incidence of unemployment was comparatively low in the commercial trades. During the second quarter of 1907, their situation was described in the following terms:[140]

> Wie immer zeigt sich auch diesmal die langste durch-
> schnittliche Dauer der Arbeitslosigkeit bei einigen
> kaufmaennischen Verbaenden. Sie steigt auf 42,4 Tage
> bei dem Zentralverband der Handlungsgehilfen, auf 32,4
> Tage bei dem kaufmaennischen Verein fuer weibliche
> Angestellte, allerdings ist die Haeufigkeit der Ar-
> beitslosigkeit hier sehr gering.

In addition to the commercial unions, some seasonally related trades such as mining and construction were subjected to intervals of unemployment which were relatively long. During the first quarter of 1907 when all Fachver-baenden surveyed reported that thirteen days was the average length of unemployment, the building trades averaged 25.7 days and the miners and smelters averaged 30.4 days.

When looking at any figures on unemployment which purport to represent large segments of the labor force during our period, it is important to read them with the understanding that they probably camouflaged significant variations stemming from occupational and regional differences. With this in mind, it is worth noting that after 1903 the average length of unemployment was two to three weeks in the Fachverbaenden which reported such data to the Reichsarbeitsblatt. Two points deserve to be made in this context. First, since all unions imposed waiting periods upon their members prior to the commencement of relief payments, many cases of unemployment were too brief for compensation. In instances where union funds were paid out, the average duration of unemployment relief consistently fell within the range of two to three weeks.[141]

Here a second point merits consideration. Occupations which suffered frequent instances of unemployment were not necessarily synonymous with those which experienced the most protracted periods of idleness whenever work losses occurred. Once again figures published in the Reichsarbeitsblatt during the closing years of our period help to illustrate the point. As we have seen, the organizations most consistently reporting numerous instances of unemployment included the unions of Bildhauer, Friseurgehilfen, Tapezierer and Glazer. Even during intervals when one quarter to one half of their entire membership was subjected to unemployment, these unions experienced durations of idleness which were generally below average. During the second quarter of 1910, for example, the average duration of unemployment in all reporting unions was fifteen days and in the fourth quarter of 1913, it was seventeen days. Data on the length of unemployment in those unions with unusually high incidences of work loss was as follows:

Union	Cases of Unemployment per 100 Members		Average Duration of Unemployment	
	2nd Quarter 1910	4th Quarter 1912	2nd Quarter 1910	4th Quarter 1912
Bildhauer	47.8	44.6	14	13
Tapezierer	24.9	28.6	10	11
Glazer	32.2	31.1	15	10
Friseurge-hilfen	46.3	30.8	15	9

At the same time there were organizations of workers in the porcelain, glass and metal industries which experienced cases of unemployment that were exceptionally few in number but of conspicuously long duration. The fact that there was no apparent correlation between the frequency and duration of unemployment in any single occupation is borne out by figures in the Reichsarbeitsblatt. For Fachverbaenden as a group, however, there was a general tendency for changes in the duration and frequency of unemployment to move in the same direction. When one increased or decreased, the other usually did the same.

AVERAGE NUMBER OF DAYS FOR UNEMPLOYMENT SUPPORT IN FACHVERBÄNDEN
WITH FREQUENCY SHOWN IN PARENTHESES

	1903	1904	1905	1906	1907	1908
1st Quarter	---	19.2 (7.9)	17.5 (8.6)	16.4 (6.4)	17.0 (6.5)	18.9 (9.2)
2nd Quarter	19.6 (8.6)	16.7 (7.9)	16.5 (7.0)	15.9 (6.1)	15.4 (6.1)	18.9 (9.4)
3rd Quarter	19.1 (8.2)	16.6 (7.4)	17.2 (7.2)	15.1 (5.4)	16.4 (6.8)	18.7 (9.8)
4th Quarter	17.0 (7.8)	17.5 (8.6)	15.4 (6.3)	14.2 (5.7)	15.7 (7.1)	19.1 (1.2)

To summarize our findings on the duration of unemployment, we might conclude that short intervals of less than three months were consistently the rule at least during the second half of our period. Findings from the 1895 survey indicate that one to two weeks and four to twelve weeks were the most common intervals of unemployment. The census figures did not deviate far from the norm. Similar results were reported during the economically severe years of the early Nineties. An 1893 survey of workers in 31 cities with 2.5 million inhabitants reported that 42,000 unemployed with 40,000 dependents were without work for an average ranging from ten to 103 days. Figures from the area around Hamburg which in 1893 was doubly hard-hit by economic recession and cholera suggest that even under adverse circumstances the average duration of unemployment rarely exceeded four months. Union figures, which admittedly dealt with an elite, suggest that the six to eight week intervals of unemployment experienced by members of the commercial trades were atypically long. Data for Fachverbaenden between 1903 and 1913 show that two to three weeks was more representative of the duration of unemployment for organized labor as a whole. As we have seen, those unions with the greatest frequency of unemployment did not necessarily coincide with occupations which experienced the longest duration of idleness. This meant in general terms that the onus of work scarcity rarely fell on a single group with unrelenting severity. That fact plus the relatively short duration of idleness which seemed to prevail during much of our period went far to mitigate the impact of unemployment on German labor before 1913.

Age Distribution of the Unemployed

The distribution of Germany's population by age resembled a regular pyramid with young children forming the broad base and senior citizens comprising the narrow apex. This basic geometric structure reflected the chronological makeup of the Reich populace in 1882 and 1890 as well as 1895. Of the 51,770,284 persons counted during the latter year, 43 percent were employed. That percentage, however, varied considerably with age. The same person over the course of a single lifetime was apt to progress from dependent to worker to pensioner. Typically very few very young children were employed but some persons under fourteen years of age worked in family businesses or cottage industries. The peak years of employment appear to have been the twenties during which 65 percent of the population had jobs. High percentages of employment persisted up to age 60 when a marked decline began followed by a precipitous drop off among those over 70 years old. As we shall see, there were differences between employment patterns for male and female workers with the latter most likely to hold jobs before marriage and after loss of a spouse. These general contours of the population at large should be kept in mind as we consider the age distribution of Germany's unemployed.

Looking at the ages of those who were subjected to unemployment in 1895, we find the highest incidence among elderly workers. With a few notable exceptions limited to various service and professional occupations where experience and seniority were more valued than sheer stamina, those over fifty years old suffered rates of unemployment well in excess of younger employees. The approximately 30 percent of those over 70 who worked were particularly vulnerable to unemployment in all jobs except the public sector. The high rate of unemployment among older persons may be attributed at least in part to their greater suscep- tibility to illness. It is also important to note that older people were less resilient in the event of unemploy- ment which affected them more adversely than percentages alone would indicate. While elderly members of most occupations were generally vulnerable to loss of work, there were also instances in which youth was a liability. Unlike other sectors, the highest rates of unemployment in government-related jobs occurred among the youngest em- ployees. Workers under 20 who had least seniority were most prone to lose public positions and those between 20 and 30 fell close behind.

At this juncture, we might consider the age distribution in some of the occupational categories used in the census. The total work force counted in the five broad categories of agriculture, industry, commerce, domestic service and public service on June 14, 1895, was 15,931,658 persons. Of approximately 16 million workers, 28 percent were between ages 14 and 20; 31 percent were between ages 20 and 30; 28 percent were between ages 30 and 50; 12 percent were between ages 50 and 70 and one percent was more than 70 years old. Looking at figures showing the overall distribution of the labor force by age, we find that the youngest group--from 14 to 20 years--was underrepresented among the unemployed. At the opposite end of the chronological spectrum, persons over 70 accounted for only one percent of population but more than twice that amount of unemployment. For the intervening age categories, we find that unemployment among those between ages 30 and 50 came out almost exactly proportional to their number in the work force at 28.98 and 28 percent respectively. Those between 20 and 30 represented 31 percent of the labor force and 33 percent of the unemployed, a relatively small variation. For the group aged 50 to 70, which constituted only 12 percent of the workers, slightly advancing age meant elevated representation among the unemployed--they comprised 15.39 percent of the jobless.

It is significant that agriculture provided a high proportion of employment for very young and even more particularly for very old workers. Many of those in their economically most productive years--between ages twenty and fifty--worked in industrial occupations where jobs were relatively scarce. Employees in less demand because of their age tended to find work more readily in agriculture where labor was a scarce resource during the 1890's and indeed throughout most of our period.

With reference to specific occupations it is worth noting the high rates of unemployment in the polygraphic trades and among factory workers for those under 30. The category designated as "Fabrikarbeiter, Gesellen und ohne naehere Bezeichnung" contained a large proportion of un- skilled laborers who were consistently subjected to the very highest rates of unemployment. The only double digit rate of unemployment--a whopping 17.34 percent--was recorded for workers in this category who were over 70 years of age. The second largest rate of unemployment was 8.46 percent among seasonal workers in the building trades. Other jobs in which laborers of advancing years suffered abnormally high levels of unemployment were: Metal working, tool making, the leather and wood industries, chemicals, the food indus- try, polygraphic trades and artistic professions.

Scattered findings collected by various municipal unemployment projects during the course of our period help to put the 1895 census figures into perspective. Data gathered in Magdeburg during December of 1902 and January of 1904 reproduced the census results for the large age cate- gories between 20 and 40 which accounted for approximately half of the unemployed. But the Magdeburg figures revealed significant differences in the patterns of unemployment at both ends of the chronological spectrum. Whereas the 1895 returns indicated an underrepresentation of very young workers and a disproportionately large number of workers over 40 years old among the unemployed, the later returns presented an even more exaggerated picture.[142]

BREAKDOWN OF THE MAGDEBURG UNEMPLOYED BY AGE ON DATES SPECIFIED

	Jan. 24,1904	Dec.7,1902	June 14,1895
up to 20 years	14.89%	14.01%	23.46%
20 to 30 years	28.93%	30.53%	28.90%
30 to 40 years	18.73%	20.76%	23.69%
40 to 50 years	21.68%	20.06%	14.16%
50 to 60 years	12.52%	10.72%	6.98%
over 60 years	3.27%	3.92%	2.81%
Totals	100.00%	100.00%	100.00%

In June of 1895, Magdeburg reported that 23 percent of its unemployed were under 20 years old and approximately the same percentage was over 40. In 1902 and 1904, only 14 percent of the unemployed fell into the first age category while workers over 40 comprised roughly 36 percent of the city's jobless.

The economically severe conditions which prevailed in much of the German labor market during 1908/09 prompted additional municipal unemployment surveys. Data gathered in Cologne showed that of the 1991 persons who were hired by the city's relief works, the age distribution was as follows:

Age	Absolute Number	Percentage	
to 20 years	183	9.2	
20 to 25 years	285	14.3	
25 to 30 years	370	18.6	32.9
30 to 35 years	350	17.6	
35 to 40 years	226	11.3	28.9
over 40 years	586	29.0	

In 1896 when Cologne introduced its insurance coverage against unemployment in winter, more than half of those who initially enrolled--117 out of 220--were over 40 years of age. This at least in part reflected the fact that older workers considered themselves more vulnerable to unemployment and were more anxious than younger persons to protect themselves against that eventuality. In contrast with this example, we might note that figures collected by a Berlin relief organization between 1893 and 1911 indicated that more than one-quarter--24,313 out of 82,136--of those registered as unemployed were under 21 years old. This fact and the large number of unemployed between 21 and 30 years of age that expanded disproportionately during economic recessions are noteworthy in the table that follows.[143]

Statiſtik über das A l t e r d e r A r b e i t s l o ſ e n,
die ſich an den Verein „Dienſt an Arbeitsloſen" in Berlin wandten.[1])

Jahr der Zähl.	—14	14—16	17—20	21—30[2])	31—40	41—50	üb. 50	o. Ang.	Zuſ.
1893/1894	—	70	326	85	19	7	—	31	538
1894/1895	—	63	624	468	230	158	71	855	2469
1895/1896	—	133	565	491	247	154	74	112	1776
1896/1897	—	55	523	566	223	161	93	53	1674
1897/1898	—	21	505	645	320	200	142	50	1883
1898/1899	—	133	631	700	417	206	141	48	2276
1899/1900	—	110	697	851	409	241	168	48	2524
1900/1901	—	84	1106	1408	647	441	224	97	4007
1901/1902	—	91	1356	2124	744	689	190	114	5308
1902/1903	—	62	1441	2098	702	441	265	25	5034
1903/1904	—	71	1475	2082	833	496	268	56	5281
1904/1905	—	99	1700	2523	930	510	69	343	6174
1905/1906	80	962	1418	1726	964	627	312	21	6110
1906/1907	24	150	1612	2100	1243	729	405	305	6568
1907/1908	1	124	1658	2981	1452	805	430	51	7502
1908/1909	5	188	2201	3536	1422	819	384	27	8582
1909/1910	2	148	1899	3267	1408	745	407	1	7877
1910/1911	3	189	1717	2487	1157	607	401	1	6553
	115	2744	21454	30138	13367	8036	4044	2238	82136

[1]) Nach den Jahresberichten XII bis XXIX des Vereins.
[2]) Vom Jahr 1898/1899 an ſind die Gruppen von 20—25 und 26—30 getrennt ge-
zählt; danach entfallen durchſchnittlich zwei Drittel auf die Jahre von 20—25.

Because the bulk of the labor force was between 20 and 40 years old, these age categories repeatedly registered the highest absolute number of unemployed workers. Between one-half and sixty percent of all jobless individuals consistently fell into that twenty-year chronological span. However, relative to their number in the labor force, there seemed to be an inverse relationship between age and vulner-

AGES OF UNEMPLOYED WORKERS IN MAJOR OCCUPATIONAL CATEGORIES

Absolute Numbers

Occupation	Unemployed on 6.14.95 Age in Years					Unemployed on 12.2.95 Age in Years				
	14-20	20-30	30-50	50-70	70+	14-20	20-30	30-50	50-70	70+
Agriculture	4656	8273	10734	12139	2636	35771	52764	57296	53866	7077
Industry	35614	55710	50621	22688	2376	76031	120031	128297	61551	4761
Commerce	7672	15819	10730	2866	223	11195	24343	17487	5131	326
Domestic Service	11553	17036	12736	7556	940	20132	30698	30812	20371	1905
Public Service	1286	2537	1939	819	93	1699	3363	2215	971	119
TOTALS	60781	99475	86760	46068	6268	144798	231999	238107	141913	14188

Relative Numbers: Of 100 Unemployed, The Distribution by Age Categories

	14-20	20-30	30-50	50-70	70+	14-20	20-30	30-50	50-70	70+
Agriculture	12.08	21.73	27.85	31.50	6.84	17.13	25.27	28.40	25.81	3.39
Industry	21.32	33.36	30.31	13.59	1.42	19.42	30.87	32.77	15.72	1.22
Commerce	20.56	42.40	28.76	7.68	0.60	19.14	41.63	29.90	8.77	0.56
Domestic Service	23.19	34.19	25.56	15.17	1.89	19.37	29.54	29.65	19.60	1.84
Public Service	19.27	38.01	29.05	12.27	1.40	20.02	40.34	26.57	11.64	1.43
TOTALS	20.30	33.23	28.98	15.39	2.10	18.78	30.09	30.88	18.41	1.84

DISTRIBUTION OF LABOR FORCE BY AGE ON JUNE 14,1895

Occupation	Age in Years				
	14-20	20-30	30-50	50-70	70+
Agriculture	1710246	1599361	1368414	800161	110660
Industry	1726956	2016744	2050464	620332	45082
Commerce	341122	500753	501263	140075	6445
Domestic Service	623490	609912	314288	167152	21652
Public Service	64261	164879	286760	120661	11525
TOTALS	4466075	4891649	4521189	1857381	195364

PERCENTAGE OF UNEMPLOYED AMONG AGE CATEGORIES

	Age in Years				
	14-20	20-30	30-50	50-70	70+
	0.27	0.52	0.78	1.52	2.38
	2.06	2.76	2.47	3.61	5.27
	2.25	3.16	2.14	2.05	3.46
	1.85	2.79	4.05	4.52	4.43
	2.00	1.53	0.68	0.68	0.81
	1.36	2.03	1.92	2.48	3.21

ability to unemployment. The scattered figures which we have suggest that with few exceptions, young workers who were generally without health problems and perhaps willing to accept lower wages, suffered the lowest rates of unemployment. For the bulk of the labor force between ages 20 and 50, unemployment rates corresponded quite closely with the overall percentage of working persons in this category. During the middle years of one's economic life, age apparently was not a factor in unemployment. But for workers over 50, advancing age posed an increasingly severe threat to individuals who wanted to hold jobs. Senior citizens, in other words, were disproportionately vulnerable to unemployment. (See previous page.)

Sex and Marital Status of the Unemployed

Turning from considerations of age to figures on the marital status and sex of unemployed persons, perhaps the most striking fact to emerge is the discrepancy between rates of joblessness among single and married or widowed women. In most occupations, single females experienced rates of unemployment which were about one and one half times greater. In the charts which follow, the higher proportion of joblessness among widows and widowers reflects the advanced age associated with the loss of both spouses and work.

MARITAL STATUS OF THE UNEMPLOYED ACCORDING TO OCCUPATION AND SEX

Absolute Numbers

Occupation	Sex	June Unemployed Workers			December 2 Workers			Total Number of Unemployed		
		Single	Married	Widowed	Single	Married	Widowd	Single	Married	Widowd
Agriculture	M	9834	13174	2089	37232	57851	7733	2106554	1107258	103937
	F	6361	3017	4063	56294	27930	22257	1618905	568587	218785
	Sum	16195	16191	6152	93526	85781	29490	3725459	1675845	322722
Industry	M	77581	57573	5004	170914	162213	13023	2756997	2512110	105725
	F	19347	3636	3868	31201	6590	7530	822039	195144	114830
	Sum	96928	61209	8872	202115	168803	20553	3579036	2707254	220555
Commerce	M	20602	10126	756	31573	17702	1356	560812	538390	18760
	F	5393	174	259	7059	310	482	289570	73932	13490
	Sum	25995	10300	1015	38632	18012	1838	850382	612322	32250
Domestic Service	M	7221	9119	1015	18724	26805	2771	80896	134051	9036
	F	26811	1441	4214	40382	5269	9967	1385641	39867	122312
	Sum	34032	10560	5229	59106	32074	12738	1466539	173918	131350
Public Service and Professions	M	2966	1396	147	4199	1785	206	180287	310225	17561
	F	1665	154	346	1602	139	409	121963	7601	11062
	Sum	4631	1550	493	5798	1924	615	302350	317826	28663
TOTALS	M	118204	91388	9011	262639	266356	24589	5685546	4602034	255361
	F	59577	8422	12750	136538	40238	40645	4238120	885131	480479
	Sum	177781	99810	21761	399177	306594	65234	9923666	5487165	735640

Relative Numbers

		Cf 100 Unemployed						Of 100 Employees Number Unemployed on June 14		
Agriculture	M	39.19	52.49	8.32	36.39	56.54	7.07	0.47	1.19	2.0
	F	47.32	22.45	30.23	52.87	26.23	20.90	0.39	0.53	1.8
	Sum	42.03	42.01	15.96	44.79	41.08	14.14	0.43	0.97	1.9
Industry	M	55.35	41.08	3.57	49.38	46.86	3.76	2.81	2.29	4.7
	F	72.05	13.54	14.41	68.84	14.54	16.62	2.35	1.88	3.3
	Sum	58.04	36.65	5.31	51.63	43.12	5.25	2.71	2.26	4.0
Commerce	M	65.44	32.16	2.40	62.36	34.96	2.68	3.67	1.88	4.0
	F	92.57	2.99	4.44	89.91	3.95	6.14	1.86	0.24	1.9
	Sum	69.67	27.61	2.72	66.06	30.80	3.14	3.06	1.68	3.1
Domestic Service	M	41.61	52.54	5.85	38.76	55.50	5.74	8.93	6.80	11.2
	F	82.58	4.44	12.98	72.61	9.47	17.92	1.93	3.61	3.4
	Sum	68.31	21.20	10.49	56.88	30.86	12.26	2.32	6.07	3.9
Public Service and Professions	M	65.78	30.95	3.26	67.82	28.85	3.33	1.65	0.45	0.8
	F	76.51	7.11	15.98	74.51	6.47	19.02	1.37	2.03	3.1
	Sum	69.39	23.22	7.39	69.54	23.08	7.38	1.53	0.49	1.7
TOTALS	M	54.07	41.81	4.12	47.44	48.12	4.44	2.08	1.99	3.5
	F	73.78	10.43	15.79	62.90	18.51	18.69	1.41	0.95	2.6
	Sum	59.39	33.34	7.27	51.77	39.77	8.46	1.79	1.82	2.9

Another question arises in conjunction with the marital status and number of persons affected by unemployment. At a time when income was measured largely in terms of the family rather than the individual wage earner, loss of one livelihood had varying repercussions. In instances where heads of households were without work, unmarried persons almost invariably lacked the supplementary wages generated by family members. When married laborers became unemployed, their families might supply alternate assets if spouses or children held jobs. However, dependents might also represent unwelcome burdens to an unemployed worker if they failed to produce income and continued to require maintenance. In all of these instances, the family situations of unemployed persons went far to determine the number of individuals affected by loss of work and the extent of suffering which that loss entailed.

Recognizing this fact, the 1895 census tried to enumerate not only unemployed heads of households, but also non-working married women, children under fourteen years of age and other dependent family members. Let us look at one specific example of the extent to which dependents complicated the unemployment picture. A Berlin survey reported 23,985 unemployed workers with 15,837 non-working dependents in contrast to 3,042 employed dependents who were able to ameliorate the circumstances of a family member's loss of a job. Of 6,344 unemployed married men, 793 could fall back on the earnings of a working wife. In 773 cases the number of working persons in the family of an unemployed male was at least as great as the number not holding a paid position. In 550 instances there was one more non-working person. And in 2327 cases, there were two more non-working persons than gainfully employed residents of households presided over by unemployed males. Among unemployed females, about half resided in relatives' homes, primarily because the vast majority of women active in the labor force were unmarried. The following chart summarizes the situation in Berlin during the mid-Nineties.

Relationships	Men		Women	
	Unemployed	Dependents	Unemployed	Dependents
Unemployed without Dependents	11,011	--	5,585	--
Unemployed with Only Non-working Dependents	4,712	11,292	590	1,071
Unemployed with Working* and Non-working** Dependents	1,428	2,153* 3,167**	162	232* 307**
Unemployed with Working Dependents	336	423	161	234
TOTALS	17,487	17,035	6,498	1,844

In a related context, we must consider the impact of secondary employment which provided supplementary income for a number of workers. Unfortunately for our purposes, the 1895 census failed to enumerate loss of secondary positions. Married women and dependent family members were frequently engaged in such activities either to augment incoming wages or minimize outgoing expenditures for work performed by hired assistants. In addition to traditional small family business ventures such as inns, shops or farms, various kinds of cottage industries came into play as sources of secondary and usually part-time employment. While the absolute number of those involved in cottage industries as a primary occupation had undergone substantial contraction between 1882 and 1895, the number engaged in such work on a secondary or part-time basis actually increased. The increase was particularly strong among women working at home--their number grew by almost 75 percent between the 1882 and 1895 censuses. Cottage industries in 1882 employed 175,440 men and 164,204 women as a primary occupation plus an additional 15,743 men and 16,441 women as a secondary occupation. By 1895, the full-time employees numbered 157,002 men and 130,387 women while part-time workers included 18,559 men and 28,216 women.[144]

The 1895 census results for both summer and winter indicated that a majority of the unemployed were single.[145] This was not surprising in view of the fact that unmarried persons predominated among wage earners as a whole, many of whom were relatively young. The following statistics provide an overview of the situation.

THE DISTRIBUTION OF UNEMPLOYMENT

Marital Status	June 14, 1895			December 2, 1895		
	Male	Female	Total	Male	Female	Total
Single	118,204	59,577	177,781	262,633	136,544	399,177
Married	91,388	8,422	99,810	266,356	40,238	306,594
Widowed	9,011	12,750	21,761	24,589	40,645	65,234

Of Every 100 Unemployed, Number Who Are Married, Single and Widowed

	Male	Female	Total	Male	Female	Total
Single	54.07	73.78	59.39	47.44	62.80	51.77
Married	41.81	10.43	33.34	48.12	18.51	39.77
Widowed	4.12	15.79	7.27	4.44	18.69	8.46

Single persons comprised 59.39 percent or almost three-fifths of the unemployed in June and slightly over half--51.77 percent--in December. Married individuals accounted for 33.34 percent in the summer count and 39.77 percent in the winter. Widows and widowers constituted the remainders, just over seven percent in the first survey and eight percent in the second. The distribution of unemployment among married and single men was approximately equal while single women far surpassed both married and widowed jobless females. As we mentioned earlier, the overwhelming majority of working women were unmarried. Single women were therefore exposed to the danger of unemployment in far greater numbers than their wedded counterparts who had typically withdrawn from the labor market at the time of their betrothal.

According to the census, on June 14, 1895, the distribution of unemployment among each 100 employees was as follows:

Marital Status	Men	Women	Overall
Single	2.08	1.41	1.79
Married	1.99	0.95	1.82
Widowed	3.53	2.65	2.96

Here the disproportionately large percentage of widowed workers who were unemployed can probably be attributed to the advanced age and the small aggregate number of employees who had lost a spouse.

Contemporaries generally believed that unemployment affected heads of households, fathers and married women far more adversely than single workers. In cases where unemployment compensation was paid, adjustments were frequently made for dependents. Married persons were also given priority in filling public works positions. Although no specific quantitative evidence is available, one suspects, largely on the basis of other forms of preferential treatment, that married men with families were discharged less readily than other employees. There clearly was some prejudice against single persons when it came to hiring and firing practices as well as the disbursement of unemployment relief. Municipal unemployment statistics collected during the early twentieth century consistently show a majority of men, mostly married, among the jobless. And the reason for this preponderance becomes clear when one looks at figures for public works, insurance and other forms of municipally funded relief. Assistance almost invariably went to male heads of households with disproportionately large numbers of dependents. Since such individuals were most likely to benefit, it is not surprising that they were most prone to register as unemployed. The result was that women were undercounted by municipal authorities and large families headed by men were probably overrepresented.

With regard to the number of dependents affected by unemployment, the 1895 census produced some interesting results. The June survey showed that slightly more than a third of all unemployed persons, including the sick, were heads of households. This meant that 104,250 persons-- 88,110 men and 16,410 women--who were without work occupied independent residences. To the households of these 104,250 unemployed individuals were attached 67,625 spouses, 126,750 children under fourteen years of age and 18,816 non-working dependents of variable description. The December figures showed that 266,525 men and 50,730 women--more than two-fifths of the unemployed--were heads of households. The 317,282 unemployed persons who headed families in December were responsible for 217,727 spouses, 426,280 children under fourteen and 59,239 assorted other dependents. Looked at somewhat differently, this meant that for every 100 unemployed household heads, there were averages of 121 children plus eighteen other dependents in June and 134 children plus nineteen others in December. In an age when average family size was far greater than today, these figures were not cause for particular alarm. Adding dependents to the number of jobless persons, we might conclude that on December 2, 1895, approximately one and a half million persons suffered from unemployment.

In fact, contemporaries ought to have been consoled by the realization that unemployment among persons with large numbers of dependents was relatively rare. As we noted earlier, municipal surveys tended to overrate unemployment among men with large families. Figures from Braunschweig, Oldenburg and Bremen reflect that unemployment among heads of households with three or more children averaged around twenty percent of the total in June and about 24 percent in December. Perhaps workers with greater responsibility were more careful to seek employment in stable sectors of the economy--avoiding, for example, seasonal occupations. There is evidence that they received preferential treatment from employers, unions and public agencies. Ultimately, the fact remains that the impact of unemployment on the population at large was mitigated by the small proportion of joblessness among those with excessively large families. A more detailed breakdown on the occupational distribution of unemployed heads of households is given in the following table which also shows the number of dependents affected.[146]

Berufsabtheilungen und Berufsgruppen	Am 14. Juni 1895						Am 2. December 1895					
	Beschäftigungslose Haushaltungsvorstände			deren nicht erwerbsthätige			Beschäftigungslose Haushaltungsvorstände			deren nicht erwerbsthätige		
	männlich	weiblich	zusammen	Ehefrauen	Kinder unter 14 Jahren	sonstige Fam.-Ang.	männlich	weiblich	zusammen	Ehefrauen	Kinder unter 14 Jahren	sonstige Fam.-Ang.
A. Landwirthschaft ꝛc.	13 849	4 954	18 803	9 815	17 012	3 645	59 913	27 292	87 205	45 225	90 255	15 732
B. Industrie ꝛc.	54 698	5 553	60 251	42 718	81 386	11 074	160 752	10 801	171 553	134 956	250 672	34 467
C. Handel ꝛc.	9 689	468	10 157	7 789	13 229	1 703	17 345	778	18 123	14 608	24 512	3 153
D. Häusliche Dienste ꝛc.	9 659	4 995	14 654	6 793	13 601	2 603	26 861	11 363	38 224	21 665	42 718	5 577
E. Öffentlicher Dienst, freie Berufsarten	1 712	425	2 137	974	1 579	350	1 681	496	2 177	1 304	2 049	372
Summe A–E	88 710	16 410	104 529	67 625	126 750	18 816	266 552	50 730	317 282	217 727	426 280	59 250
I. Landwirthschaft, Gärtnerei u. Thierzucht	12 571	4 886	17 457	8 748	16 110	3 415	57 168	26 839	84 607	42 900	92 310	14 327
II. Forstwirthschaft u. Fischerei	778	68	846	597	202	230	2 745	453	3 198	2 325	3 925	205
III. Bergbau, Hüttenwesen ꝛc.	3 534	58	3 592	3 115	7 992	992	5 002	110	5 112	4 483	9 830	1 253
IV. Industrie d. Steine u. Erden	3 340	110	3 450	2 637	5 552	723	13 028	376	13 404	11 152	23 485	2 854
V. Metallverarbeitung	6 057	81	6 138	4 805	8 709	1 263	7 509	65	7 574	6 262	11 599	1 236
VI. Maschinen, Werkzeuge ꝛc.	2 992	40	3 032	2 388	4 318	553	4 026	49	4 075	3 343	5 524	739
VII. Chemische Industrie	713	55	768	573	1 129	133	742	84	826	613	1 311	148
VIII. Forstwirthschaftliche Nebenproducte ꝛc.	418	18	436	338	641	76	510	27	537	441	795	72
IX. Textilindustrie	4 335	1 269	5 604	2 926	6 013	891	4 788	1 420	6 208	3 491	7 269	1 077
X. Papier	699	151	850	516	1 057	144	730	218	948	612	1 253	173
XI. Leder	1 220	48	1 268	961	1 829	225	2 077	58	2 135	1 717	3 074	342
XII. Holz- und Schnitzstoffe	5 148	147	5 295	4 105	7 523	908	7 405	136	7 542	6 053	11 055	1 374
XIII. Nahrungs- u. Genußmittel	4 202	327	4 529	3 159	6 976	764	5 629	516	6 145	4 442	8 569	928
XIV. Bekleidung und Reinigung	2 158	3 075	5 234	1 602	4 646	737	3 808	7 046	10 854	2 993	9 315	1 529
XV. Baugewerbe	18 233	65	18 298	14 384	23 975	3 319	100 723	210	100 933	85 478	159 713	21 729
XVI. Polygraphische Gewerbe	958	57	1 015	755	1 305	181	1 004	73	1 077	802	1 335	172
XVII. Künstler f. Lohn-Gewerbe	126	1	127	96	146	25	285	3	288	226	304	41
XVIII. Fabrikarbeiter, welche ꝛc.												

Demography and the Geographical Distribution of Unemployment

We have tried to analyze the unemployed by breaking their number down into its component parts on the basis
of occupation, duration of idleness, age, sex and marital
status. One additional factor merits consideration at this
juncture--the geographical distribution of Germany's unemployment problem. In order to evaluate this factor, population trends must be examined since they played a large role
in determining the contours of the labor market.

During the period with which we are dealing, the
German population increased steadily but unevenly. Between
the 1882 and 1895 occupational censuses, population expansion was directly proportional to existing population
density--gains were greatest in the most thickly populated
areas of the nation and smallest in the least populated

regions. While Berlin added almost forty percent to its residential base, the old Hanseatic cities registered increases approaching thirty percent and the two Reuss districts grew by 26 and 30 percent respectively. At the same time, the Kingdom of Saxony grew by 25 percent, the Rhineland by 23 percent and Westphalia by 29 percent. Although international and overseas migrations produced net declines in the population of a few districts such as Koslin, Sigmaringen and Jagtkreis, rural areas as a whole registered gains, ranging from 5.47 and 4.23 percent in both Mecklenburgs to 3.78 percent in Pommerania and 2.77 percent in East Prussia.

Overall, urban areas expanded most rapidly and rural areas most slowly. While Germany as a whole increased its population by 14.48 percent between 1882 and 1895, large cities with more than 100,000 persons grew by 111.29 percent. Medium cities with 20,000 to 100,000 persons grew by 29.62 percent. Small towns with 5,000 to 20,000 persons grew by 29.62 percent and villages with 2,000 to 5,000 persons grew by 10.16 percent. Taken as a group, all cities--urban areas with more than 2,000 inhabitants-- increased by 36.47 percent while population in rural areas increased a mere 1.31 percent between 1882 and 1895. During the thirteen years under consideration, Germany added fourteen cities whose population exceeded 100,000 and the nation assumed a more urban character as those living in large cities increased from 7.36 to 13.58 percent of the total population.

The trend toward a more urban society continued throughout our period. The growth of cities in excess of 100,000 persons registered a 400 percent increase between 1875 and 1910. The number of major cities in the German Empire was as follows:

Year	1875	1885	1895	1905	1910
Major Cities	12	21	28	41	48

In terms of smaller urban clusters, we know that 23.7 percent of the population lived in towns with more than 5,000 inhabitants in 1871 while 4.8 percent of the population lived in the four German cities whose residents numbered more than 100,000. By 1910, 48.8 percent of the populace lived in towns of 5,000 while the Reich's 48 major cities accounted for 21.3 percent of the citizenry. The most highly urbanized area of Germany in 1910 was the Rhine province where almost three-quarters of the people lived in cities.[147]

Significantly, the areas which experienced the most pronounced population increases coincided exactly with those which were most thoroughly industrialized. The Kingdom of Saxony, Berlin, Westphalia, the Rhineland, Saxony-Altenburg and both Reuss districts were the most industrial areas of Germany in 1895. As we have seen, these were also the regions with the greatest population growth. Predictably, the labor force in Germany's large cities was employed almost exclusively in commercial or industrial as opposed to agricultural pursuits by the middle of our period. The areas most dependent upon commerce were the old Hanseatic cities where between 28 and 35 percent of the residents were engaged in commercial ventures and Berlin where one-quarter of the population was thus employed. The rapid expansion of the population base from which industrial manpower was drawn had a pronounced effect on the labor market. Whenever the working age population increased more rapidly than the number of available jobs, the net result was usually unemployment. There was also a direct correlation between population density and non-agricultural employment as the following rankings based on the entire country show.

	A	B		A	B		A	B
Berlin	1	1	Reuss aelterer Linie	5	6	Rhineland	8	7
Hamburg	2	2	Saxony	6	5	Westphalia	9	11
Bremen	3	3	Reuss jungerer Linie	7	8	Anhalt	10	12
Luebeck	4	4				Saxon-Altenburg	11	9

POSITION IN NATIONAL RANKING ON THE BASIS OF A INDUSTRIAL AND COMMERCIAL DEVELOPMENT AND B POPULATION DENSITY

These figures suggest that population shifts were closely linked to the availability of economic opportunities which directly impacted the demand for labor. People tended to move where they thought employment prospects were greatest and their movement in turn influenced the local markets in which they functioned as both producers and consumers. The period under consideration was one of substantial relocation for large segments of the German populace. This fact is borne out by patterns of overseas and internal migration which correlated with the relative position of business conditions in various regions.[148] High emigration rates just prior to the beginning of our period declined sharply after the crash of 1873 but resumed with a vengeance during the following decade when almost 1.5 million persons left the Reich. Although overseas migration tapered off after 1893, it was an important factor in alleviating unemployment throughout the economically depressed Eighties and early Nineties.

In addition to emigration, the uncertain business conditions which followed the 1873 crash induced considerable internal resettlement. Prior to 1885 short distances were typical of movement which contributed to increasing urbanization. After 1895 longer distances were traversed as the pull of cities such as the capital and industrial centers of the Ruhr drew population from further away than immediately adjacent rural areas. A general lack of economic opportunity in the agrarian East led many young, single, landless agricultural workers to move west in search of better jobs. Most of those laborers left intending to seek employment in nonagricultural occupations, with males likely to end up working in mining or manufacturing and females in domestic service. Urban, industrial regions with high wage rates were the primary beneficiaries of the relocation process while districts dominated by large agrarian estates were the most obvious losers. Between the time of the unemployment census and the turn of the century, the predominantly rural areas of Prussia suffered a population loss in excess of one million persons. One problem which complicated a clear-cut delineation of urban as opposed to rural population was the considerable body of workers who moved back and forth based on seasonal or cyclical changes in the labor market.

Accompanying the tendency toward urbanization was a pattern of increasingly industrial employment for the German labor force. While Berlin and Nuremberg were the only cities with more than half of their populations employed in industry as late as 1882, by 1895 thirteen additional cities had a majority of industrial workers. Bremen with almost three-fourths of its workers engaged in industry had the single most highly industrialized labor force in 1895. But in Krefeld, Chemnitz, Elberfeld and Dortmund approximately two out of three workers were involved in industrial occupations. Berlin, Breslau, Duesseldorf, Cologne, Aachen, Nuremberg, Dresden, Leipzig and Braunschweig all employed 50 to 60 percent of their work force in industrial jobs in 1895. On the average, by 1895 half of the labor force in urban areas was involved in industrial pursuits and another 20 to 25 percent was engaged in commerce, leaving the remainder in various forms of public, domestic or other service categories.

We know that a surplus labor supply was a necessary prerequisite for industrial expansion and that people tended to congregate where perceived economic opportunity was greatest. Not surprisingly, therefore, the ongoing processes of industrialization and urbanization advanced together. And in the minds of many contemporaries, industrialization, urbanization and unemployment became an inextricably linked triad. There were those who looked at the discrepancy between unemployment rates in agriculture and industry during 1895 and deduced that "the industrialization of the Empire and the increasing danger of unemployment go hand in hand."[149] The census figures were frequently used to demonstrate the connection between unemployment and urbanization.

An estimate published in _Soziale Praxis_ during 1896 indicated that eighty percent of all industrial unemployment was concentrated in large and medium cities. To show the correlation between joblessness and urbanization the following data is helpful.

Size of Cities	Inhabitants		Absolute No. of Unemployed		Percentage of Unemployed in Population	
	June	December	June	December	June	December
More than 100,000	7027790	7272400	116557	176770	1.66	2.43
10,000 to 100,000	8524363	8771439	67734	139587	0.79	1.59
Less than 10,000	36218131	36202750	115061	454648	0.32	1.26

The differences between urban and rural rates of unemployment were more pronounced during the summer of 1895 when five times as many workers per 100 residents were without jobs in cities. The urban to rural ratio in winter was only two to one but that fact reflected the seasonal nature of

agricultural employment which predominated in the countryside. A census conducted ten years after the one under
consideration here produced entirely similar results, with
large cities reporting unemployment rates four times greater
than the rest of Germany. And again, under the economically
severe conditions which prevailed during 1908, another
survey revealed that large and medium cities--those whose
populations exceeded 100,000 and 20,000 respectively--
consistently registered the highest rates of
unemployment.[150]

A different way of looking at the geographical
distribution of unemployment may prove helpful at this
juncture. Of every 100 unemployed persons, the number
living in variously populated areas was as follows:

	6/14/1895	12/2/1895
Major Cities with 100,000 plus	44	21
Districts with 10,000 to 100,000	22	16
Areas with less than 10,000	34	63

The medium and large cities contained two-thirds of all
Germany's unemployed during the summer but only 37 percent
during the winter. Inverse relationships applied during
alternate seasons, with agricultural pursuits accounting for
much of the difference between the June and December ratios
for urban and rural areas. Germany's two largest cities
reflected the situation in miniature: Berlin contained 15
percent of the nation's unemployed in summer and 7 percent
in winter; Hamburg 7 percent in summer and only 2.5 percent
in winter. Together, the two cities were home for 22

percent of all unemployed in summer but only 9 percent in winter. The capital and the great Hanseatic ports had the highest unemployment rates in the country during both seasons. At the opposite end of the spectrum, a few cities reported unusually low unemployment rates in 1895. These included: Dortmund, Barmen, Krefeld, Strassburg and in winter, Chemnitz.[151]

In general terms, it's possible to conclude that unemployment was significantly higher in the northern districts of Germany than in the more agrarian South. Areas which were heavily industrialized and urbanized were particularly prone to high unemployment rates as were those with large numbers of agricultural workers during the winter. Seasonal unemployment posed problems in northern port cities which were dependent upon the weather for trade. Even more serious, however, was the situation in rural areas where indigenous labor problems were compounded when workers employed elsewhere during the summer returned home to idle away the cold, inactive months of every year.

Significantly, it was in the southern states which had a more heterogeneous economic base and a heritage of more liberal municipal government that insurance measures were initially adopted to cope with unemployment. One major concern of those urban officials who administered local relief was the origin of unemployed persons. For cities which were equipped to provide public relief exclusively to bona fide residents of some duration, the importance of this question was obvious. The dimensions of the residence problem can be illustrated with a few examples. In Stuttgart it was discovered that a majority--52.7 percent-- of those who were counted as unemployed in the city had residences which qualified them for support elsewhere. In Dresden that number was less, with 41 percent of those designated as unemployed living some place else and 59 percent of those registered actually domiciled in the city itself. In other metropolitan areas including the capital, fluctuations in places of residence made it difficult or impossible to pinpoint the origins of persons registered as unemployed. The high proportion of non-resident unemployed indicated in the Dresden and Stuttgart examples posed problems for municipal authorities seeking to administer relief.

Historically, residence had been a primary criterion of charitable support through the parishes which administered poor relief. The collection and disbursement of secular funds also came to be tied to residence requirements. It was economically essential for local administrators of public works projects, insurance programs and labor exchanges as well as poor relief to determine which individuals fell within their jurisdiction. With a large proportion of all unemployed persons officially domiciled in one place and commuting to work in another, this distinction presented frequent dilemmas. It remained a recurring headache throughout our period because public unemployment relief continued to be the exclusive domain of local government. Not surprisingly, municipal unemployment counts reported that an overwhelming majority of those workers within their jurisdiction who claimed to be unemployed also claimed to be residents. Here it is important to remember, however, that procuring relief was of far greater interest to the unemployed than the impersonal gathering of accurate statistics. It is highly unlikely that workers with nothing to gain would even bother to respond to municipal surveys.

As a footnote to this discussion about the roots of the unemployed, it is interesting to add that most non-resident respondents in 1895 had come relatively short distances. Looking again at Stuttgart, we find that only 29 persons or 2.23 percent of the unemployed were of non-German origin. Of all those without work in Stuttgart, 17.5 percent came from someplace other than Wurttemberg, leaving the vast majority as citizens of that state. The situation was quite similar in the Kingdom of Bavaria where in December of 1895, 2.6 percent of the unemployed were non-Germans and 5.2 percent were non-Bavarian Germans. Significantly, however, non-Bavarians were over two times more plentiful among the unemployed than among the population as a whole. The states contributing to Bavaria's unemployment problem included Prussia with 829 persons, Wurttemberg with 750, Saxony with 321, Baden with 326 and Hesse with 176. Among foreigners, the overwhelming majority came from other German-speaking areas with Austria-Hungary contributing the largest contingent and Switzerland coming next. A survey conducted in Munich ten years after the census indicated that its results were not unique. Ninety percent of Munich's unemployed during 1905 had been born in Bavaria and an approximately equal percentage made their homes either in the city itself or in the surrounding area. This pattern remained in effect throughout Germany's major cities, with the vast majority of unemployed registered in municipal tallies claiming resident status and the programs systematically denying relief to all those considered non-residents.

By way of conclusion to our discussion of geographical determinants of unemployment in 1895, we might turn to some statistics from the highly volatile building trades. The primary movement of construction workers from rural to urban settings took place during the years immediately preceding the unemployment census. Of every 100 construction workers, the distribution at designated intervals was as follows:

Year	Land	Small and Medium Cities	Large Cities
1882	50.1 (35.4)	39.3 (52.9)	10.6 (11.7)
1895	39.5 (28.9)	41.3 (51.1)	19.2 (20.0)
1907	36.9 (24.8)	41.8 (50.7)	21.3 (24.5)

Although 1882 marked a recovery from a seven-year slump in the index of production for the building trades, the twenty-year interval between 1875 and 1895 was one of general stagnation in this sector. The substantial increase in urbanization of the building trades during the period prior to the 1895 census and the much smaller movement, approaching a standstill, during the subsequent interlude are noteworthy in view of the slump.[152] It is also worth mentioning that throughout the years under consideration, construction workers maintained a slightly less urban profile than the industrial labor force as a whole (whose distribution is shown in parentheses in the preceding chart). The discrepancy was especially pronounced in Germany's small and medium cities, although the gap between construction and other industrial workers in these areas tended to narrow as the period progressed. It seems that during the peak season for construction, which usually fell between April and October, small and medium cities reported the lowest relative amounts of unemployment while large cities suffered the highest. This pattern was more than offset however during the transitional months of November, December and March plus the dead months of January and February. During the off season, things were so much better in large cities that the year-round average gave them a decisive edge on employment among workers in the building trades.

As a general rule, the tendency to build through the winter whenever weather permitted increased with the size of the city. While construction in non-industrial, non-urban areas was confined almost exclusively to single-family dwellings and limited commercial buildings, different patterns emerged in large cities. The substantial capital outlays required to finance the erection of apartment houses and major industrial plants necessitated the earliest possible completion dates. Financial imperatives imposed deadlines which frequently meant working beyond the summer months. The tendency for building to continue through the winter in urban, industrial areas and cease entirely in rural, agrarian districts produced significant regional variations within this sector as the following data shows:

Province	Dead Months	Transitional Season	Building Seas
East and West Prussia, Posen	66.7	19.5	7.5
Pommerania	58.1	12.9	4.9
Mecklenburg	69.1	19.7	7.1
Rhine Province	16.5	11.0	7.1
Westphalia	25.9	8.2	4.9
Saxony	37.8	11.0	5.2

The extent of variation may also be gauged from the fact that on January 27, 1912, Mecklenburg reported 79.1 percent unemployment among construction workers while the Rhineland reported only 17.8 percent.

Despite the general impression that the building trades suffered higher rates of unemployment in agrarian than industrial areas, it should be noted that there were significant exceptions. In January of 1912, for example, 83.7 percent of all Berlin construction workers were without jobs. The annual average of unemployment during 1912 shows that for every 100 members of the various building unions, the following number were unemployed:[153]

	Total	Without Sickness
Brandenburg	22.5	19.8
Mecklenburg	20.9	18.2
East and West Prussia, Posen	20.1	17.4
Bavaria excluding Rhinefall	19.6	16.9
Silesia	18.3	15.6
Alsace-Lorraine	17.6	14.9
Pommerania	15.4	12.7
Schleswig-Holstein, Hamburg and Luebeck	13.5	10.8
Saxony, Thuringia and Anhalt	12.3	9.6
Hesse-Nassau and Hesse Grand Duchy	11.5	8.8
Saxony	11.2	8.5
Hannover, Oldenburg, Braunschweig, Bremen	11.1	8.4
Wurttemberg, Baden and Bavarian Rhinefall	10.7	8.0
Rhine Province	9.3	6.6
Westphalia, Lippe, Waldeck	8.6	5.9
EMPIRE AVERAGE	14.2	11.5

The figures suggest that in sectors particularly susceptible to economic swings which induced work stoppages, regional factors such as urbanization and industrialization levels went far to determine the extent of unemployment. Climate of course was another regional variable in unemployment which impacted seasonal occupations and its role will be considered in the next chapter. But with reference to the building trades, it is perhaps sufficient at present to note that unemployment levels in the same sector differed by as much as 300 percent between heavily industrialized and predominantly rural regions of Germany. This example suggests that aggregate statistics for the nation as a whole camouflaged significant regional variations which cannot be ignored if one seeks an accurate assessment of unemployment.

Summary

Having considered the separate characteristics of Germany's unemployed, let us conclude this discussion with a summary of traits shared by workers most prone to loss of their jobs. In occupational terms, persons employed in seasonally related work were vulnerable to predictably recurring periods of idleness. Agricultural laborers, those engaged in the building trades and some parts of the transportation industry were subjected to the highest rates of unemployment. An additional factor in this context was the degree of training required for a particular occupation. As a vague guideline, the occupational risk of unemployment was inversely proportional to the amount of skill needed to perform a given task. Unskilled workers who were plentiful and basically interchangeable could be dismissed and rehired with minimal effort. They were therefore subject to far greater risks of replacement than highly skilled workmen.

Here, however, a telling point must be made. Although the unskilled worker was more likely to lose his job, once that eventuality occurred he was frequently in a more advantageous position to reenter the labor force than a highly trained colleague. Unless the latter were willing to forego use of his training out of desperation and take any job, he was hampered in searching for employment by the limited number of available positions requiring his particular skills. In this context, highly trained laborers in sectors undergoing rapid expansion were invariably in demand but those with training in industries experiencing contraction had very different prospects. When such workers refused to retrain or accept work in other areas or when employers labeled these persons "overqualified" and refused to engage them, they became the hard-core unemployables which Germans regarded with aversion and fear.

In terms of age, those most susceptible to unemployment were elderly workers. Individuals over 50 years old were more vulnerable than younger persons and those still working after age 70 suffered the very highest rates of unemployment. Because population distribution dictated a majority of young people in the labor force, they accounted for the largest contingent of unemployed. If one looks at relative rather than absolute numbers, however, it becomes clear that susceptibility to unemployment in most occupations increased with age. Males as a group were more prone to unemployment than females. And single persons who predominated in the labor force as a whole were affected more frequently than married workers. At a time when family size was considerably larger than it is today, statistics show that surprisingly few dependents were affected by unemployment among heads of households. Those workers who were unfortunate enough to lose their jobs in 1895 were most likely to reenter the labor market within the relatively short interval of eight to fourteen days. Reflecting the large number of seasonal workers, those who were idle for longer stretches typically resumed employment after one to three months of inactivity.

In geographical terms, unemployment was concentrated most heavily in large cities where industrialization and population growth went hand in hand. Two important factors linked together by the physical mobility of large numbers of people worked to alleviate the unemployment which contemporaries associated with the spread of urban, industrial centers. Prior to 1895, the short distances traveled by landless workers leaving agrarian districts to pursue industrial employment in Germany's cities permitted their return to the countryside with relative ease. There is considerable evidence that potential movement between urban jobs and rural families worked as a sort of safety valve for victims of industrial unemployment. This pattern prevailed at least until the mid-Nineties when the longer distances which came to be traversed between a worker's agrarian origins and industrial livelihood made it more difficult to move back and forth between the two. In addition to the internal migration which characterized this period of German history, the years between 1880 and 1893 also witnessed emigration abroad on an unprecedented scale. The movement of persons from labor markets with limited economic opportunity to those with more potential for satisfactory employment went far to mitigate what might have been a truly horrendous scarcity of jobs. Although recurring problems flared up after the turn of the century, large-scale foreign and domestic relocations were unnecessary after 1895 because the prolonged recessions which dominated the first half of our period did not recur.

As we shall see, another factor which helped to alleviate a potentially serious situation during the 1870's and 1880's was the effort of employers to curtail wages and hours rather than resort to lay-offs during periods of slack demand. This combined with policies which took into account the family circumstances of laborers, primarily the number of dependents, helped to minimize the impact of unemployment on the working classes.

If there was a typical unemployed industrial laborer in Germany at the time of the 1895 census, he would have been male, single, unskilled, working in a seasonally related occupation, probably in a large city. In all likelihood he would have arrived at both his work and residence fairly recently and would not belong to a union or any other institution whose collective means gave members leverage in a shifting labor market. His work would provide the primary motivation for his choice of location and when threatened with unemployment, he might decide to move on. Although he might very well be old, he was unlikely to belong to the working class elite which was more highly skilled, organized and firmly entrenched in society through long-standing communal and family ties.

The quasi-itinerant status of many unemployed industrial laborers was made quite clear in an 1893 article which detailed conditions in the Berlin Asyl fuer Obdachlose. The article pointed out that of the institution's inmates a mere 10 percent were born in the capital and of those, only one-sixth made their home in the city. The following explanation indicated why such a small proportion of the destitute were long-term residents of the area and why newcomers were far more apt to find themselves without a livelihood and consequently in need of public assistance.[154]

> Auch das kann nicht wunder nehmen, da die geborenen Berliner, selbst Soehne von Berliner Arbeitern, bei ihrer besseren Kenntniss der gewerblichen Verhaeltnisse meist in die best-bezahlten und staendig arbeitenden Gewerbe gehen, und da das Vorhandensein von Verwandten und Freunden, und vor allem die Unterstuetzung der kraeftigen Arbeiterorganisationen, die in den lohnenden Industrien bestehen, diese nicht oft bis an die aeusserste Grenze des Elends kommen lassen. Bei den Zugewanderten dagegen treffen Ueberwiegen der Saisongewerbe, Unkenntniss der Konjunkturen, Huelflosigkeit in der fremden Umgebung zusammen, um sie zahlreichen aufs Pflaster zu werfen.

As the preceding statement implied, there was a price which Germany's mobile labor force paid for relocation. They tended to find work in occupations which subjected them to significantly higher risks of unemployment than their more settled colleagues. On the one hand, they were likely to be engaged in low-paying jobs which afforded scant opportunity to practice the virtues of self help espoused by their betters. They were also apt to work in seasonal occupations which by definition increased the probability of their eventual idleness and almost without exception cut them off from union protection. Without organized assistance, lacking family ties in newly relocated, impersonal urban settings, frequently cut off from municipal unemployment assistance by residence requirements, the multitude of workers who came to industrial cities in search of opportunity formed the core of a potentially undesirable Lumpenproletariat. They were the very opposite of the working class elite from whom they were separated by innumerable subtle distinctions within a variegated and highly stratified social order.

Based on the data which has been collected, it seems fair to postulate that the more privileged elements within the working class--married men with families, union affiliations, stable residences, and a modicum of job skills--were not subjected to inordinate amounts of unemployment between 1873 and 1913. Precisely because these pillars of the lower eschelon establishment remained immune, there was no real unemployment crisis during our period. The social implications of unemployment were minimized because even those directly affected by loss of work were rarely threatened with economic extermination. Furthermore, their inactivity had limited repercussions due to the fact that their dependents were apparently not too numerous, and were occasionally able to compensate for lost income. As we saw with reference to the Bildhauer's union, recurring instances of unemployment within very short intervals were probably scarce. Nor was there any demonstrable direct correlation between the frequency and duration of idleness. Jobless workers were given sufficient opportunities to regain their economic composure--neither the tenure of their inactivity nor the immediate prospect of its recurrence was sufficient to destroy their productive potential. Add to this the observation that the unemployed were the most economically impotent members of the community--factors including occupation, age, skill, family status, tenure of residence and lack of organization all worked to their disadvantage. Finally, the political apathy of the unemployed should be noted in passing.

Despite the jobless workers' lack of economic or political power, their potential as drop-outs fueled fears of revolution among the more fortunate classes. As we have attempted to show, these fears were totally unrealistic before 1913. Too few people were affected--both in terms of unemployed individuals and their dependents--for too short a period of time. They had too many alternatives and too little unity to resort to political violence. Because they were idle for such brief intervals and in relatively small numbers and because those who held any semblance of power through collective institutions escaped virtually untouched, there was no real danger of an upheaval. During our period, unemployment was confined almost exclusively to the least powerful segment of the labor force and affected them in ways with which they could learn to live. As we shall see, this meant that solutions to unemployment problems could be sought in terms of half-measures such as temporary reloca-tion, limited access to labor exchanges or public works projects and aborted discussions of insurance schemes.

There was no real risk of political upheaval although there was a very real concern over that eventuality because contemporaries remained poorly informed about the uneven impact of unemployment on the German population. What we are left with is a gap between the reality and perception of unemployment. This discrepancy derived in large measure from the inadequate data which was used to encourage unfounded fears of revolution and piecemeal efforts to cope with work shortages.

DETERMINANTS OF AGGREGATE UNEMPLOYMENT LEVELS

Among theoretical explanations of the causes of unemployment, overproduction was the most frequently articulated source of trouble. Between 1873 and 1913 excess supply rather than insufficient demand was considered the primary factor in work shortages by most contemporaries. Only a few nineteenth-century observers recognized that lack of aggregate demand for goods and services also produced periodic diminutions of job opportunities. Reduced rates of economic growth such as Germany experienced in the late 1870's and early 1890's might have been alleviated by policies calculated to increase aggregate demand but measures such as tax cuts were not adopted during our period.

In addition to explanations of unemployment which attributed the situation to imbalances between the supply and demand of goods and services, there were those who focused more directly on the labor market itself. Structural unemployment was the result of mismatching between job seekers and job opportunities. Factors such as population distribution, urbanization, labor mobility, expectations about the terms of employment, the location of industries and the educational level of the work force came into play here. A complex of interrelated factors impinged on the job market: Employers' demand for workers, real-wage rates stipulated by potential employees, the distribution of labor and its mobility. The relationship among these factors at any given point in time went far to determine the extent of mismatching which resulted in structural unemployment. This type of unemployment could be remedied by improved dissemination of information in the labor market which was the avowed function of Arbeitsnachweise after 1890. It could also be alleviated by efforts to augment the qualifications of potential employees through additional training or education. Only sporadic efforts in this direction were forthcoming between 1873 and 1913.

A third source of unemployment which derives from technological change relates to both demand shortages and mismatching in the labor market. Whenever machines facilitated the expansion of available goods and services more rapidly than demand required, the lack of synchronization was conducive to unemployment. Technology which increased the output per worker without simultaneously increasing consumption led to unemployment. Technological advances which rendered existing job skills obsolete and required additional training compatible with the operation of new machinery frequently produced displacement at least on a temporary basis.

In addition to theoretical explanations of the causes of unemployment, there were efforts to determine the actual sources of idleness in particular situations. As we have seen, the subject of these inquiries assumed variable parameters ranging from individual occupations and geographical boundaries to trade unions. They also varied in terms of the specificity of causes used to categorize the unemployed. The most frequent distinction was between those who were unemployed for health-related reasons and those who were unemployed for other non-physical reasons. The 1895 census excluded the permanently disabled and showed that in June two-fifths of the unemployed were idle because of their unfitness for work and three-fifths were jobless for other reasons. In December the discrepancy became even more obvious with only one-fifth of the unemployment attributable to illness. Another common distinction during our period isolated individuals who had lost their jobs due to their own grossly inappropriate behavior. These persons plus the lazy and those who simply refused to work were consistently presumed to constitute a small minority of the unemployed.

At this juncture, we might briefly re-examine a few of the more representative efforts to explain the sources of unemployment in specific instances. Those in seasonal trades attributed their unemployment variously to unfavorable weather, scarcity of materials, traditional seasonal shutdowns, and lack of effort among discouraged job-seekers to find alternate employment in the face of repeated rejection. An unemployment survey conducted in 1909[1] by the Zentralverband der Maurer Deutschlands divided unemployed bricklayers into three categories based on the cause of their idleness. The sources of unemployment were work scarcity, atmospheric conditions and illness. What is significant in the pattern that emerged is not only the correlation between unemployment caused by weather and job scarcity but also the way in which sickness fits into the overall picture. During the period of peak unemployment-- the months of January and February--illness was also at its zenith--above 4%--and during the transitional months of November, December and February it remained about one-third higher than during the active summer months. These figures suggest what is also indicated elsewhere, namely that illness as a source of unemployment tends to increase as labor market conditions deteriorate.

In addition to unions representing individual occupations, a number of cities made attempts to determine the cause of unemployment among their residents. We might briefly consider one of the most important of these which took place in Dresden between 1903 and 1913. During the first year of inquiry, the most common causes of unemployment were seasonal work, bad business practices and operational shutdowns. While only a tenth of the unemployed had been dismissed by their employers, between one-sixth and one-seventh were idle due to illness. Many of the latter got well and returned to work within a relatively short time.

It is interesting to note that health-related problems including sickness and pregnancy accounted for a far higher proportion of the unemployment among Dresden's female population. Between 23% and 46%--or an average of 30%--of the unemployment among women during the ten years from 1903 to 1913 was attributable to physical ailments.

During the same interval, health problems accounted for between 10% and 18%--or an average of 14%--of the unemployment among men.[2] The general trend during the decade surveyed was toward diminished unemployment for both sexes as the German economy recovered from the crisis following the turn of the century.

Richard Herbst, a moving force behind the national network of labor exchanges, attributed the high unemployment in Dresden during 1902 and 1903 to work shortages or lay-offs initiated by employers in the wake of a general economic downturn. Between 1908 and 1909 the abrogation of tariff and trade agreements combined with cyclical sectoral downswings to elevate unemployment levels again until new treaties were negotiated in 1910 and 1912. In 1913 another crisis compounded by political considerations, poor business conditions, diminished building activity and strong contractions in the labor market stimulated unemployment in Dresden and throughout Germany. With the noteworthy exceptions just enumerated, the period between 1902 and the Great War was characterized by a sound economic recovery and a decline of unemployment in Dresden.[3]

Like Dresden, a number of other German cities undertook surveys which sought to explain the cause of unemployment. In Magdeburg between 1902 and 1904, for example, 1341 cases were attributed to work shortage, 103 to atmospheric conditions, 96 to employees' notice, 35 to employers' notice, 54 to sickness and old age, 30 to operational shutdowns. 86 offered no explanation, and the remainder attributed their idleness to variable causes such as strikes or disputes over wages. In Hannover during the same years vaguer distinctions were made among 1089 fully unemployed persons with 151 cases attributable to illness, 291 to "Kuendigung", 634 to "sonstigen Grunden". In the adjacent jurisdiction of Linden similar results were forthcoming: Of 244 unemployed men, 47 were idled by illness, 81 by "Kuendigung" and 116 for other reasons. In Munich explanations included "Mangel an Arbeit, Beendigung der Saisonsstelle, Krankheit und Unfall". More than 70% of Munich's male unemployed were without jobs due to work shortages. Among these, many were inactive because of inclement weather and seasonal shutdowns. Wage disputes and other differences of opinion between employers and employees were responsible for six percent of the unemployment and a comparable percentage was attributed to accidents or illness.[4]

In addition to municipal surveys, there were union tallies which attempted to determine the causes of unemployment among broad sections of organized labor. During the winter of 1892/93, as we have seen, the Social Democratic unions undertook an unemployment survey in a number of major German cities. The results showed that approximately seven percent of their members were without work for an average of ten weeks per unemployed individual. At various intervals over the next twenty years, reasons ranging from illness to weather, military drills and bad business conditions were held accountable for unemployment among Germany's union-affiliated work force.

Many persons leaving particular positions did so voluntarily to seek other preferred employment. One estimate during the 1890's indicated that approximately five million non-agricultural employees changed jobs in the course of an average year. In the process of such changes, workers typically experienced two to three weeks of unemployment.[5] A 1912 survey conducted in Saxony suggested that half of the unemployed had left jobs of their own volition. One quarter had gone at the management's request, and something in excess of ten percent departed as a result of the termination of seasonal employment. More than 80% of the unemployment stemmed from these broad but admittedly vague sources.[6]

A Munich survey conducted on February 11, 1912, reported a total of 7006 unemployed[7] of whom more than three-fourths--76.1%--attributed their idleness to former employers' notice. Of the 5334 persons without jobs due to dismissal, 5051 had been discharged because of insufficient work. Four percent of all unemployed had been dismissed for other unspecified reasons. Fourteen percent had given notice of their own accord--a far lower figure than that recorded in the Saxon survey cited above. Sickness and accidents accounted for 6.4% of Munich's unemployment, strikes a mere 0.1% and miscellaneous reasons about 3.5%.

Overall, the surveys conducted between 1910 and the end of our period suggested that one-half to three-quarters of the unemployed lacked positions for reasons which were classified as economic. The balance were idle primarily for personal reasons.

The preceding effort to highlight both general and specific causes of unemployment suggests that contemporaries had rather vague notions about theoretical and actual sources of the problem. In the sections which follow we shall consider how a multitude of factors interacted to determine aggregate unemployment levels. These included seasonal fluctuations, technological change, political policy decisions, the emergence of collective protection, mobility, internal factors in the labor market and micro-economic variables. Separately and cumulatively, these forces went a long way toward establishing prevailing rates of unemployment in German industry between 1873 and 1913.

SEASONAL UNEMPLOYMENT

As we saw with regard to the 1895 census, a good deal of Germany's unemployment during our period was seasonally related. The census takers themselves recognized this fact and divided their inquiries accordingly, with the December tally recording significantly more unemployment than the June survey. Much of the difference between the summer and winter rates was attributable to seasonal shutdowns in agriculture, transportation and the building trades. Geographically, seasonal differentials were greatest in major ports, large cities and agrarian areas. Regional variations between northern and southern, eastern and western provinces were frequently pronounced due to divergent patterns of economic development as well as climatic differences.

Weather-related factors contributing to unemployment ranged from frozen waterways to frost, snow-cover and inhospitable drops in temperature which prohibited outdoor activity. Lack of natural resources during certain seasons in industries such as food processing were conducive to unemployment. Tourism which affected Germany's hotel and restaurant business was frequently seasonal. In addition to regularly recurring seasonal changes, the threat of natural disasters such as floods, hurricanes, droughts and crop failures were unpredictable hazards which plagued those who depended on nature for their livelihoods.

As we have seen with reference to the 1895 census, seasonal variations in the labor market were not confined to the agrarian work force. Nor were factors which influenced the demand for agricultural workers without import for the industrial economy. The primary sector provided the raw materials for industrial production and consumed much of its output. Throughout our period and particularly during the early years, agriculture exerted a powerful influence on the industrial labor market and was a major determinant of unemployment in all sectors of the economy.

One crucial difference between seasonal and other sources of unemployment is the predictable nature of the former which entailed a foreseeable period of idleness each year. Cyclical forms of economically induced unemployment depend on variable business conditions, shifts in demand or overcrowding of certain occupations. Random chance plays a large role and any semblance of regularity is rare. Seasonal unemployment involves climatically dictated annual ceilings on the number of work days which can be expected in trades such as agriculture, construction or shipping. The variation from year to year is minimal, thus allowing a certain amount of planning for and preliminary adjustment to the inevitable interlude of inactivity. The most severe impact of seasonal change on the German economy was felt in the three occupations alluded to above. As we already noted with regard to the 1895 census, two-thirds of the unemployment registered in December was attributable to seasonal shut-downs in the building trades and agricultural production.

In general terms, weather and natural causes dictated that unemployment peaked at the beginning and end of each calendar year. Unemployment rates typically began a gradual ascent in October or November and underwent a slow but steady retraction in February or March. This tidy generalization about overall conditions admittedly obscures considerable variations among industries and regions. Although differing markedly in intensity, most industries experienced some sort of dead season at some time during the average year. One observer in 1912 pointed out that statistics collected during the preceding decade indicated there had always been a month in which one great industry underwent its worst difficulties while another experienced its highest prosperity.[8]

Lack of synchronization was an essential factor in the health of the German economy since it prevented business activity from coming to a complete halt during the winter months. Even though winter idleness was widespread, a staggered pattern of seasonal unemployment was conducive to minimizing its impact on the entire economy. It provided the opportunity for alternate employment plus continued production and consumption in sectors not experiencing seasonal contractions. When exceptionally severe weather coincided with poor business conditions, however, the toll in terms of unemployment could be devastating. In the agrarian sector which was subjected to a prolonged depression during the first half of our period, bad winters or poor harvests proved extremely troublesome.

Among those whose employment was regularly and predictably interrupted by winter weather were gardeners,[9] agricultural laborers, plumbers, street pavers, canal builders and inland navigators. In the building trades, carpenters and masons worked short days during winter until the arrival of frost curtailed their activity to the point of extinction. Workers engaged in the fashion industry including the manufacture of ready to wear apparel such as coats, or yard goods such as draperies, had their seasons from fall to Christmas and from March to June. During both January and February and the hot summer months, this sector worked with a diminished labor force, if at all. In custom goods industries which employed hundreds of thousands of craftsmen including leather workers, cabinetmakers, plastics workers, threshers and paper workers, production was geared to the export market. Employment was therefore at its peak from the beginning of summer until shortly before Christmas. But in the middle of December, demand for such output underwent a precipitous decline with the result that a large part of the labor force was left without employment for several months.

In the printing trades, the dead season typically fell between April and October. Printers frequently suffered three times more unemployment during the month of

August than during the season when production was at its peak. In August of 1893, for example, printers' assistants estimated that about 9000 of their number were unemployed. Like the printers, the brewers experienced inactivity during the summer months. The pastry chefs and Pfeffer-Kuechlern were busiest during October and November but usually without work during the period immediately before and after Christmas. The tobacco workers had their season from mid-March through the beginning of December. As the following remarks indicate, many contemporaries felt that at some point during the year seasonal unemployment was inevitable:[10]

> Kurz eine sehr grosse Zahl von Produktionszweigen hat mit der Thatsache zu rechnen, dass in einem Theil des Jahres ueberschuessige Arbeitskraefte auftreten. Das ist bei den klimatischen Verhaeltnissen, den Modeneigungen und den waehrend des Jahres wechselnden Beduerfnissrichtungen nicht zu aendern; da hilfs aller und auch der beste Arbeitsnachweis nicht; wo keine Arbeit ist, kann er keine ermitteln.

In the hatmakers union, different seasonal employment patterns emerged on the basis of sex. In 1912 the organized hatmakers who numbered around 10,000 were evenly divided between male and female members. Women, however, experienced significantly higher unemployment rates because they worked in the manufacture of straw hats, a product in purely seasonal demand. Over 40% of all female hatmakers were unemployed in the summer of 1912 with idleness decreasing from the end of September through March. For men working in the same industry the pattern was rather different. The lowest unemployment rates among organized male hatmakers came between the end of July and October, with idleness increasing significantly at the end of both November and December, and beginning to taper off by late January. The lower unemployment rates among men engaged in hatmaking stemmed from male predominance in the manufacture of felt hats whose peak production was in summer. Even during the less active early part of each year, most male hatters were able to find work. Chronic seasonal unemployment among hatmakers was apparently confined primarily to those who worked with straw, and as we have indicated, a majority of them were female.[11]

To the extent that industrial revolutions have been defined in terms of man's harnessing the power of nature to further his economic objectives, the persistence of seasonal unemployment must be considered a shortcoming in the process. Despite the level of industrial development which Germany had achieved by 1873, men in pursuit of livelihoods remained at the mercy of weather which they could neither predict nor control. One of the most conspicuous testaments to the imperfection of industry's ability to control its environment was provided by the building trades. On December 2, 1895, for example, approximately 150,000 construction workers were unemployed. That number continued to swell over the course of the winter until it peaked sometime during the following January or February.

The most active building season typically occurred between April and October when less than ten percent of the trade was likely to be affected by unemployment. During the transitional months of March, November and December, a quarter of the work force was usually idle. And during the final dead season of each year, something approaching two-thirds of all construction workers were without jobs. As we noted earlier, the number of insurance claims based on illness tended to vary inversely with the demand for labor and directly with unemployment. As we also indicated, unemployment in the building trades varied with the size of the labor market directly during the summer and inversely during the winter. While unemployment among construction workers in major cities was almost twice as great as in rural areas during the summer months, population and unemployment were inversely proportional during the winter.[12]

Apparently, union membership in the construction trades also varied inversely with unemployment rates. The lowest membership levels were recorded at the end of the first quarter of each year. A period of expansion followed during the second and third quarters with membership reaching its annual zenith at the end of the third quarter. After that it usually declined until the end of the year. The pattern of union affiliation reflected the fact that jobless workers were hesitant to commit themselves to organizations which offered scant benefits but solicited unwelcome fees from employed members. The Gewerkverein der

Bauhandwerker, for example, offered unemployment relief only between April and November. During the dead season which occurred each winter no unemployment funds were available.

In this regard, the construction workers' unions were typical. Their intent was to compensate members for unemployment caused by the economy and exclude seasonally related claims. Both the Free Trade Unions and the Christian Unions made some provision for seasonal unemployment in their compensation programs. But most organizations whose members belonged to a seasonal trade continued to exempt the dead period from unemployment coverage unless they offered a self-help program in the form of savings or deferring income earned during active months.

Recognizing the seasonal disparity between unemployment levels over the course of a single year, one of the first municipal efforts to combat unemployment confined its relief payments exclusively to the cold months. This tended to fill a void in union coverage of the unemployed during off-seasons and benefited construction workers more than any other single group.[13] The city of Cologne established its unemployment fund in 1896 specifically to offset the effects of winter idleness among male residents. Membership in the fund was strictly voluntary and although a public subsidy was forthcoming, administration and organization of the project retained an essentially private character. The subscribers never numbered more than a couple thousand and constituted a very small segment of the city's labor force.

Available figures suggest that there was some justification for the seasonal limitations of the program since unemployment in winter ran from one and one-half to three times higher than summer rates. The largest figures were recorded during the recession which prevailed throughout the first months of both 1908 and 1909.

Although the Cologne insurance plan was unusual in the extent of its focus on the seasonal factor in unemployment, other cities also found that the need for assistance in winter was far greater than during the summer. In Strassburg, for example, January was typically the month of highest unemployment and June or July the lowest. Between two-thirds and three-fourths of all claims were made during the winter--from October to March of the following year. Despite widespread recognition of distress during winter, some municipal insurance funds such as that established in Stuttgart specifically exempted seasonal unemployment from their coverage. This rationale focused on the availability of other means of assistance including higher wages conducive to saving for foreseeable intervals of inactivity. A few advocates of unemployment relief for seasonal occupations suggested a schedule of rebates for those contributing to funds but not withdrawing from them over a period of several years.[14]

In addition to municipal statistics, data from assorted relief organizations bears testimony to the seasonal nature of Germany's unemployment problem. Figures from Herbergen zur Heimat suggest a direct correlation

between economic conditions, unemployment and numbers of

occupants. In the words of one contemporary observer:[15]

> Wie sehr durch diese Arbeitslosigkeit, von der
> bestaendig Tausende heimgesucht werden, das Wandern
> befoerdert wird, geht aus der Tatsache hervor, dass der
> Wanderverkehr in Zeiten groesserer Arbeitslosigkeit
> stets dementsprechend anschwillt. Dieses ist in allen
> schlechten Jahren beobachtes wordern und zeigt sich in
> jedem Winter von neuem.

A report from the labor colony at Carlshof printed on

February 2, 1888, outlined in some detail the relationship

between seasonal change, unemployment and the numbers in

need of assistance. Carlshof was situated in East Prussia,

an agrarian district with no significant industry and a

short growing season. Contemporaries estimated that the

area typically experienced six or seven months of good

weather during which the demand for labor almost invariably

exceeded the supply. This picture contrasted sharply with

the situation in the West where German farmers benefitted

from nine or ten months of favorable climatic conditions.

In East Prussia, during the entire interval between November

and the middle of April, the economic activities which pro-

vided employment for the bulk of the labor force came to a

virtual standstill. Agricultural pursuits ceased while

cutbacks in railroad construction and "Festungswerken" in

the city of Koenigsberg compounded the unemployment problems

of local citizens. The fact that there were surplus jobs in

the summer and a severe shortage each winter was reflected

in the occupancy rate of Carlshof. That labor colony was

virtually empty when warm weather encouraged economic
activity in the surrounding countryside. But when cold
temperatures prevailed, the number of inhabitants surpassed
300.

As we noted with reference to the 1895 census,
unemployment during the winter was likely to be especially
great in areas with high concentrations of agricultural
laborers. Urban centers and industrial districts also
suffered unusually high unemployment rates but the cause was
rarely linked to seasonal change. In certain areas such as
Lippe, unemployment in winter was aggravated by the return
of local residents who worked outside the district as
seasonal laborers during the summer and then came home to
idle away the cold months. In major ports, seasonal unemployment stemmed from diminished activity in the harbors,
docks and grain elevators. But as a general rule, urban
unemployment was greater in summer and rural unemployment
most significant in winter. Rates of idleness on the
average were greater in the North of Germany than in the
South.

In terms of the seasonal movement between town and
country, large cities such as Berlin or Breslau tended to
attract numerous job-seekers in February, substantially
fewer in March and an escalating number as the weather
warmed in April. The following figures are interesting in
this context. They show monthly breakdowns on the relationship between available positions and job applicants at the

Berlin labor exchange between 1890 and 1896. Almost without exception that ratio was most favorable during the month of March when the influx of workers from the country was in temporary abeyance. For each 100 places, the following number of applicants registered at the central labor exchange in the capital. Note the high figures during transitional months as the economy adjusted to seasonal changes.[16]

	Jan	Feb	Mar	Apr	May	June	July	Aug	Sept	Oct	Nov	Dec
1890	191_6	179_9	93_3	141_6	149_5	149_5	139_1	104_5	120_2	155_0	186_2	148_2
1891	216_9	180_5	118_3	194_6	201_2	253_8	182_8	130_7	112_4	162_9	192_7	159_2
1892	189_8	237_0	121_5	167_5	166_2	152_9	150_4	96_5	106_2	95_7	198_8	111_7
1893	147_9	157_0	108_0	160_5	189_8	168_6	173_0	129_4	123_5	162_1	183_8	135_1
1894	206_2	144_7	104_5	173_0	190_2	183_2	157_7	136_4	112_5	143_1	184_5	148_8
1895	172_7	115_2	120_0	175_5	154_0	145_6	141_6	106_3	110_0	129_1	140_4	113_9
1896	157_0	117_5	100_9	135_3	135_4	159_5	103_4	125_8	109_8	115_3	132_6	114_5
AVERAGE	183_2	161_7	109_4	164_0	169_0	171_3	149_7	118_6	113_5	137_7	174_1	133_1

In addition to the capital, the southwest was a particularly attractive target for would-be employees during the late 1890's. Cities all the way from Cologne to Nuremberg registered noteworthy population increases.

One source of recurrent disagreement related to seasonal unemployment involved the question of whether those affected were compensated at sufficiently higher levels to enable them to save for the inevitable dead season. A number of contemporaries extolled the virtues of thrift and self-help as solutions to Germany's unemployment problem. However, most publicists sympathetic to labor's plight maintained quite rightly that the workers' wages relative to their cost of living rarely permitted the preservation of any "excess" earnings.

Oddly enough, relatively mild winters were often a greater problem than more severe ones. When snow and frost were plentiful enough to halt regular economic activity but too scant to provide widespread employment through public assistance projects designed to facilitate their removal, workers were doubly hard hit. As we shall see in the fourth section of this study, municipally funded public works projects, local insurance programs and relief institutions were adopted with increasing frequency after 1890 to ameliorate seasonal unemployment.

One final point needs to be made with reference to seasonal work shortage. Not only did it remain a frequent source of idleness affecting a variety of occupations throughout our period. Its widespread impact was intensified by the fact that unemployment during the winter was generally of longer duration.[17] Since most seasons lasted several months and since many more idle workers were competing for a diminished number of scarce jobs, seasonal unemployment was likely to be a matter of longer tenure. Other varieties, as we have seen with reference to the 1895 census, rarely lasted more than a few weeks or a single month.

TECHNOLOGICAL CHANGE AS A SOURCE OF UNEMPLOYMENT

Questions about the nature of the relationship between technological change and unemployment were not resolved during our period and even today different perspectives on the issues involved persist. Whether technology produced a net loss or gain for the German unemployed between 1873 and 1913 is perhaps less important than the structural changes in the labor force which occurred in its wake. For even more than other phenomena associated with industrialization, technological change influenced the economy unevenly. To cite one obvious illustration, introduction of the Bessemer converter had far greater repercussions for employment in the iron and steel industries than in other parts of the economy. Related industries such as coal mining were also affected, and the system-wide repercussions of such an important technological advance eventually exerted indirect pressures on labor requirements of seemingly unrelated industries such as railroads. The ultimate impact of any innovation was determined by the sectoral and geographical points at which the change was introduced into the economy and by the pattern of linkages between industries that were directly affected and the rest of the market.

Because large-scale technological change was invariably costly and required significant infusions of capital, one side effect was to make employers hesitant to shut down production entirely. There is evidence[18] that producers throughout the first half of our period were anxious to keep highly capitalized plants operating even if that meant selling their output at reduced prices. If the immediate and obvious effects of improved technology were increased productivity, fewer men required to manufacture more goods, lay-offs and a diminished demand for labor, the long-range impact was likely to be rather different. Formerly, unskilled workers were considered interchangeable, subject to lay-offs and easily replaced when demand for their output warranted rehiring. But with technology came an increased need for more highly skilled, scarce and specifically trained labor. That combined with capital investments which made it unprofitable to cease production led to new employment practices during the last quarter of the nineteenth century. Rather than dismissing workmen when the economy went into a temporary slump, alternative production patterns were developed. Reduced hours and wages, stockpiling inventories, lowering profit margins, opening up export markets and selling at reduced prices became preferable alternatives to laying off employees and ceasing production.

Technology in conjunction with other forms of economic innovation was a major factor in the relative abilities of individual firms to compete in the German marketplace. Those producers who failed to keep pace with the competition were ultimately forced out of business by entrepreneurs more willing and better prepared to eliminate inefficient, outdated or unproductive methods and equipment. The result was reflected on a macroeconomic scale in the occupational surveys conducted in 1882, 1895 and 1907. A growing percentage of inefficient operations disappeared so that the total number of enterprises declined and the number of employees per firm increased.

As Shulamit Angel-Volkov has suggested for artisans, craftsmen and shop owners, the small, independent businessmen were among those most adversely affected between 1882 and 1895 by this process of concentration. In large cities where industrial employment was most readily available, the change in their status was likely to be from independent workmen to dependent employees. In the textile industry, the transition frequently entailed unemployment[19] and deterioration in the overall economic position of those directly involved. In the building trades,[20] which were both more responsive to shifts in the economy and less affected by technological change, expansion rather than concentration led to unemployment, loss of independent status and impoverishment for workmen during hard times. Technology played a major role in redefining the demand for labor and the structure of the German work force. Both the contentration and expansion which came in its wake heralded the eclipse of the independent craftsman plus the proletarianization of many artisans and shopkeepers.

The process of concentration such as that which occurred in the electrical industry made finding jobs potentially more difficult. As numerous small and medium firms were absorbed or driven out of business by conglomerates, the range of employment options diminished. A multiplicity of producer-employers offered jobless individuals a better chance of reentering the labor market. This was particularly true of workers whose physical mobility was limited by family considerations. When large numbers of laborers were dependent on a single employer for their livelihood as in so-called company towns, the economic implications of shut-downs could assume calamitous proportions.

While contemporaries were attuned to the question of technologically based unemployment, there were some who felt that the problem had been exaggerated.[21] In conjunction with concern for displaced workers came recognition of the new employment prospects opened up by technological innovations. Technological change could have one of two effects on the working population.[22] On the one hand it could render labor obsolete by replacing men with machines. Vulnerability to this pattern and the resulting unemployment tended to increase with the division of labor. If, on the other hand, laborers and craftsmen were flexible enough to conform to the demands of economic change, they could be retrained and their skills adapted to the new technology plus the job opportunities it created.

There was growing recognition of society's responsibility to make the workers' readjustment to technological change as easy as possible. Assistance was to take the form of education, training and mobility to enable otherwise unemployable individuals to reenter the labor force as productive members of a prospering economy. Through schools, unions, and labor exchanges every effort was made to facilitate the smooth flow of manpower with upgraded skills across occupational, industrial and geographical boundaries. In reality the two effects--adaptation and obsolescence--were not mutually exclusive choices. Some were forced to adapt their job skills to changing technology and managed to do quite well. Others, for a variety of reasons ranging from age to lack of opportunity, were unable to make the necessary transition. Frequently, these individuals ended by disappearing from the economic mainstream and joining the ranks of unemployables.

One's perspective on the impact of technological change became increasingly tied to the vantage point from which the situation was surveyed. Those who represented workers victimized by technologically related shifts in demand tended to abhor the innovations which inaugurated their constituents' loss of employment. Shifts in the composition of demand for labor which inevitably accompany technological change generally resulted in diminished employment opportunities for persons with scant or outdated training. The fact that highly skilled workers, men involved in retraining the labor force and individuals servicing the new technology benefited did not help others who lost their jobs because machinery erased the need for formerly marketable skills.

Looking at technology as a panacea for those who bend it to their will, employers frequently saw it as a source of increasing productivity, efficiency and growth. They pointed with pride to the fact that technology created more jobs in new industries than it destroyed in old sectors of the economy. Ultimately, the question came down to one of assessing social costs and economic gains. While the burden of technological unemployment descended on specific elements within the working class, the benefits of increased productivity accrued primarily to the middle and upper echelons of the economic hierarchy.

Throughout much of the nineteenth century technology by expanding productivity and efficiency as it promotes economic growth freed labor to pursue both leisure interests and better occupations. Service industries tended to expand as machinery liberated men from the drudge work which formerly occupied them in agricultural or industrial jobs. The problem, of course, was that new and improved economic opportunities did not automatically translate into jobs for displaced workers. Those with blue collar mentalities were not transformed overnight into white collar personnel. While some gained from the process of industrial change, others lost and society had to find a way to more equitably distribute the costs of technological unemployment.

Consider the situation among weavers whose security was so profoundly affected by technological change during the last quarter of the nineteenth century. Between 1873 and 1880, for example, the highly industrialized city of Chemnitz reported a decline in the number of handlooms from almost 3000 to less than 1850.[23] Their disappearance was part of a more general phasing out of unproductive and antiquated methods in the wake of the worst recession during our period. In addition to domestic competition from technologically advanced firms, German producers had to compete with foreign operatives, many of whom relied on the cheap labor of women and children to undercut textile prices on the international market. Weavers in addition to being vulnerable to foreign competition, automation, and cyclical economic changes were also susceptible to seasonal variations in demand. An 1886 report from Duesseldorf clearly suggests that while most handloom weavers were employed during the summer months, winter heralded the idleness and economic disappearance of many. Enough persons were affected in the mid 1880's so the government established a fund to ease the transition of displaced handloom weavers to other kinds of work.[24]

The plight of the weaver is set out in bold relief in an 1896 article from Soziale Praxis. The article outlines conditions over the preceding 25-year period in the textile industry which dominated the district around Schweidnitz. An area rich in cotton, linen, wool and other textiles, Schweidnitz witnessed a 500% increase in the number of powerlooms between 1870 when there were 1206 and 1894 when there were 6733. An increasing pattern of concentration marked the emergence of large-scale operations with the majority of firms employing in excess of 100 looms by 1894. Despite this growth, a considerable number of handloom weavers survived in the district. While hand operatives were not entirely phased out, their number in the area declined by more than 50% between 1871 and 1895. The decline was gradual until the late 1880's at which point it accelerated until 1892 when it leveled off.[25]

1871 -- 15326 handloom weavers	1892 -- 7658
1876 -- 14047	1893 -- 7707
1881 -- 11752	1894 -- 7703
1886 -- 12878	1895 -- 7562

Between 1871 and 1895, the number of masters declined by 50.3% while the number of assistants including married women and children who worked as weavers declined 51%. Significantly, the handloom weavers in the district who had no secondary occupation declined by 54.9% between 1871 and 1895. But during the same interval the number of handloom operators who had supplementary work diminished by only 20.3%. As percentages of the total population, handloom weavers during the early 1890's accounted for anywhere from 1.5% to 5.5% of the whole. Data from Schweidnitz and elsewhere in Germany confirms that with the arrival of power driven machinery, the number of hand operatives declined. However, they did not disappear altogether and those with

secondary occupations seemed best able to withstand mechanization as well as the advent of large-scale producers.

Unemployment resulting from technological change
was perceived as a serious problem during our period. An
1894 article from the publication Die Volkswohl lucidly laid
out contemporary wisdom on the relationship between technology and unemployment:[26]

> Fasst jede neue technische Erfindung, welche Menschen-
> kraft spart und die Leistungsfaehigkeit der Maschine
> erhoeht, schafft voruebergehend Arbeitslose. Dieselben
> suchen sich sofort anderen Erwerbszweigen zuzuwenden.
> Aber da der technische Fortschritt in Grossgewerbe ein
> allgemeiner ist, so Stossen Sie auch hier wieder auf
> die Maschine. Der steigende Mitbewerb treibt auch hier
> zur Vervollkommnung der Technik, um billig erzeugen zu
> koennen, auch hier schafft die Technik Arbeitslose.
> Herrscht eine Zeit aufsteigender Geschaeftsthaetigkeit,
> so bekommt von diesen durch die Moderne Technik aus dem
> Kreis fester Verhaeltnisse losgeloesten Arbeitern ein
> Teil irgendwelche Beschaeftigung, ein anderer Teil
> bleibt ueberfluessig. Wo es ihm gelingt, durch unter-
> bieten der Loehne Beschaeftigung zu erhalten, verd-
> raengt er andere aus ihren Stellungen; die Personen
> wechseln, aber die Zahl der Arbeitslosen bleibt. Sie
> sind ein Opfer des Unterschiedes, der zwischen der
> schnellen Entwickelung der Technik und der Entwickelung
> des allgemeinen Verbrauchs und der Ausdehnung unserer
> Absatzgebiete herrscht.

THE IMPACT OF POLITICAL POLICY DECISIONS

In addition to seasonal and technological changes which periodically affected the level of unemployment, there were predictable attempts at planning and government-initiated controls formulated to impact the labor market. Policy decisions may be broken down for analytical purposes into two categories--federal and local--which remained both separate and different in nature throughout our period. On the national level, unemployment policy rarely went beyond the stage of heated debate and very little in the way of practical results emerged from the imperial government. As we saw with reference to unemployment statistics, the distribution, duration and absolute quantities of work shortages during our period were such that they could be tolerated by society at large. The unemployed were for the most part few in number, idle for brief intervals and confined to the least powerful elements in the socio-economic order. And as we shall see, even those elements were prevented from going outside the system to seek reso-lution of their dilemma.

Although in theory unemployment was viewed as a potentially revolutionary force, between 1873 and 1913 the following factors worked to minimize a danger whose extent was grossly exaggerated by ill-informed contemporaries: General acceptance of the inevitability of seasonal idle-ness; technological change and entrepreneurial innovations which opened up new opportunities as they phased out obsolete positions; continuation of industrial expansion, albeit at reduced rates; emergence of new firms as old ones disappeared; efforts on the part of employers to avert layoffs by resorting to alternatives ranging from stockpiling inventories to reducing wages and hours; emigration; returning to rural family homes to wait out intervals of idleness; union assistance programs and local government efforts to mitigate the effects of work shortages. Together these decentralized measures were reasonably effective. Consequently, for the nation as a whole,[27] the pattern of unemployment between 1873 and 1913 never posed unmanageable social or economic problems which required broad political solutions.

Because the socio-economic order was able to contain the unemployment which occurred throughout our period, the federal government could refrain from direct intervention in the labor market. The _Reich_ continued to abrogate its responsibility to formulate anti-cyclical employment policies well beyond 1913. There were vigorous debates among members of the _Reichstag_, political parties, academic circles, the union leadership, and journalistic cadres about the relative merits of various unemployment policies. But in terms of concrete programs, far more was actually accomplished on the local level or through private initiative. Given the tendency for federal unemployment policy to be limited to debate and local measures to result in action, we shall begin our assessment of the German government's role in the labor market on a theoretical level and proceed to a consideration of actual plans adopted by various municipalities. The latter, as we shall see, instituted piece-meal programs aimed at containing the consequences, rather than eradicating the causes, of work shortages.

The question of what role the state was to play in combating unemployment was inextricably connected with contemporary views about its causes. As late as 1907, economic liberals maintained that the nation had a twofold interest in alleviating job scarcity. First of all, it was necessary for the recently unified state to minimize unemployment because it had been a contributing factor in almost all modern revolutions.[28] In addition, the government would benefit by eliminating idleness because national production was the sum total of individual citizens' output. Whenever loss of work removed producers from the labor force, total production and the competitive advantage of Germany vis-a-vis other nations declined.[29] So both politically and economically the state had reasons to pursue policies that would minimize unemployment.

Throughout our period, there were divided opinions on the question of labor's culpability for unemployment. There were many who persisted in blaming job shortages on individual failures, with aversion to work most frequently cited as the source of idleness. Economic liberals preached that work was readily available for all those who sought

employment. But by the turn of the century, there was a
growing awareness of the role which impersonal forces played
in causing unemployment. The following excerpt from a 1909
publication reflects the dichotomy of opinion which persisted on this question:[30]

> Die Gruende der Arbeitslosigkeit koennen in der Person
> des Arbeitslosen oder in wirtschaftlichen Verhaelt-
> nissen liegen.
>
> Von Gruenden in der Person sind insbesondere zu nennen
> Arbeitsscheu, Arbeitsunfaehigkeit, Krankheit, Unfall,
> Invaliditaet, Streik, Aussperrung freiwillige Aufgabe
> einer Arbeitsstelle, Nichtannahme angebotener Arbeit.
>
> Die wirtschaftlichen Ursachen der Arbeitslosigkeit
> koennen dauernder, voruebergehender oder periodisch
> wiederkehrender Natur sein. Dauernd durch Niedergang
> einer Industrie (z.B. Handweberei) oder durch Stilleg-
> ung von Betrieben (z.B. Zechen); hier kann nur Ubergang
> der Personen zu anderen Beschaeftigung oder Wegzug
> helfen. Voruebergehend durch arbeitsparende Maschinen,
> wirtschaftliche Krisen, Wechsel der Mode, Zeitweise
> Ueberfuellung des Berufes, Betriebsstoerungen durch
> Beschaedigung von Maschinen oder durch Feuer, Wetter-
> verhaeltnisse und der gleich. Periodisch wiederkehrend
> in den Saison Industrie (z.B. Konfektion), wo arbeits-
> reiche und stille Zeiten wechseln; in Berufen, deren
> Ausuebung von den Wetter Verhaeltnissen abhaengig ist
> (Landwirtschaft, Baugewerbe, Binnenschiffahrt); ferne
> in Berufen mit Gelegenheitsarbeit.

The view which one adopted on the causes of
unemployment obviously influenced the policies espoused for
its elimination or control. If one presumed that the
individuals affected were to blame for their own malaise,
the state could not be held accountable and self-help would
be the preferred remedy. If, on the other hand, economic
forces indiscriminately threatened the security of innocent
persons, then society as a whole would be obliged to assume
the role of intermediary. State intervention would be

necessary to eliminate job scarcity and alleviate its consequences. To take that argument a step further, the level of state intervention reflected German views on the relative blame assignable to individual as opposed to impersonal features inherent in the capitalist system.

It was during our period that the government first acknowledged that the source of unemployment lay in the industrial economy. At the same time, the state began to assume tentative responsibility for victims of unemployment. Without formulating policies for dealing effectively with the problem, it laid the foundation for the electorate attributing blame to both the economic system and the political regime. Recall that adoption of Bismarck's social legislation in the mid 1880's constituted prima facie recognition of the state's obligation to the elderly, the sick and the disabled. The obvious exception was the unemployed, and their practical exclusion will be considered in the context of a theoretical right to work. For the present, let us turn to a fuller account of proposals for federal unemployment assistance that emerged between 1873 and 1913.

In the most general terms, there were three types of unemployment policies which were considered on a national scale. These aimed respectively at preventing, controlling and relieving unemployment. Preventive measures included monitoring production, increasing the educational level of the labor force, regulating the number of apprentices, restructuring the organization of industries, adjusting wages and hours to minimize lay-offs, equitably distributing available work and stockpiling inventories. Many of these preventive measures were successfully introduced at the micro-economic level and did a great deal to contain unemployment rates within manageable limits. However, very little was forthcoming from the federal government by way of macro-economic measures specifically designed to combat unemployment. A true anti-cyclical economic policy never came out of Berlin prior to 1913.

The second category of measures to combat unemployment on the policy level was confined during our period almost exclusively to the introduction of labor exchanges. During the late 1890's, a nationwide network of exchanges emerged as part of an effort to alleviate unemployment stemming from faulty dissemination of information in the labor market. As we shall see, public works projects were also used to combat unemployment although they did nothing to root out its causes. They did provide a source of activity and income for workers without jobs in the private sector and there was some talk of using the state's role as an employer to combat idleness. But here as elsewhere much more was accomplished on the local than the national level. Consideration was given to tariff policies and resettling urban industrial workers in depopulated rural areas but little in the way of practical results was forthcoming. Short-term policies calculated to increase the demand for labor by progressively raising tariffs, funding public works projects or subsidizing industries simply were not within the purview of federal bureaucrats.[31]

The third and most prevalent variety of unemployment policy aimed at alleviating the consequences of work loss. Nationally, the greatest discussion was generated by unemployment insurance. As we noted earlier and shall see further in the next chapter, no program was adopted until the Weimar Era. Here the problem of inertia was compounded by ignorance of the extent of persons and expenditure involved. As a prelude to insurance, any number of deliberative bodies ranging from the Reichstag and the Prussian Abgeordnetenhaus to lesser diets were able to concur that the collection of unemployment statistics was a necessary and desirable undertaking. The uncertainty born of ignorance, poor statistical methods, and the perennial difficulty in precisely forecasting unemployment precluded the adoption of any federal insurance plan during our period. Chancellors from Bismarck to Bethmann- Hollweg remarked during recurring parliamentary debates that such a scheme was premature.[32] A limited number of municipalities did adopt insurance programs, many of which were tied to union affiliates.

There were also networks of institutions for dispensing charity and public welfare which emerged at unpredictable intervals to assist the unemployed. Various measures of support and insurance were aimed at averting

poor relief and protecting the idled worker from the deleterious effects of begging, diminished skills and living off
of public charity. Unlike poor relief recipients who were
assumed to be totally destitute and dependent, the unemployed were not to be denied a feeling of economic independence or viability. Rather than charity for perpetual
economic nonentities, temporary benefits were to assist
workers in their own efforts to regain a footing in the
labor market. In the case of insurance it was important to
emphasize that workers themselves contributed to the fund.
They were, therefore, at least in part self-insured and
entitled to draw payments in the event of unemployment.[33]
There was an element of deferred savings inherent in insurance which enabled beneficiaries to collect when the eventuality against which they purchased protection--
unemployment--actually materialized.

As this fact dawned on contemporaries, blame for
unemployment gradually shifted from the affected individuals
to impersonal economic forces. Consequently, the stigma
associated with loss of work tended to decline. An increasing number of persons began to recognize that the state
acting as the agent of society at large had a duty to
institute policies aimed at alleviating work shortages.
Unfortunately, however, lack of sophistication in the area
of federally formulated unemployment policy persisted
throughout our period.[34] As late as August 1913[35] publicists were still complaining about the dearth of centralized

planning and the resultant anarchy in the German labor
market. They called for controls to regulate wages, the
geographic and sectoral distributions of labor, the number
of foreign and female workers, seasonal employment and
secondary occupations. Suggestions were made that the
federal government establish agencies to reassign idle
workers from areas of high to low unemployment. Such
thinking reflected a change in perception of the proper role
of the state in the German economy since 1873.

Historically, according to Hans-Juergen Puhle,[35a]
the old liberally interpreted state had aimed at preserving
the social _status quo_. It had confined its activities to
such supposedly neutral functions as levying taxes, raising
an army and preserving public order. Each of these functions indirectly affected the level of unemployment. Armies
and prisons withdrew potential employees and idlers from the
labor market, thus improving the ratio between available
positions and jobseekers. As we found earlier, one observer
noted that without this type of government action in 1895
the average rate of unemployment would probably have doubled-
--from 3.5% to 6%--or increased by some 400,000 persons.[36]
Taxes by affecting the amount of money which producers and
consumers had to spend also exercised a considerable influence on the demand for labor and its output.

In addition to inaugurating fiscal policy, the
federal government affected unemployment levels in its
capacity as an employer. In terms of its role as a sta-

bilizing influence in the labor market, consider the impact of anti-cyclical public works projects plus the relatively constant number of bureaucrats working as public servants. Federal postal and telegraph authorities, national railroad employees, military personnel, shipping officials, diplomats and parliamentary staff were rarely subject to vicissitudes in employment. While those working in the private sector lived with the fear of unemployment during recessions, persons holding government jobs were rarely discharged for purely economic reasons. More, however, was expected from the federal government than merely providing stable employment for a fortunate minority.

As contemporary discussions about unemployment policy indicate, there was a growing tendency to demand state intervention in regulating the relationship between the economic system and the forces of society. Rather than adopting a neutral posture, the late nineteenth-century state began to assume the role of policy maker and planner. Unlike England where federal labor programs emerged, unemployment initiatives in Germany were delegated to local and occasionally state governments.[37] At the municipal level, demands for unemployment relief by the working class had to be balanced against the bourgeoisie's efforts to procure state intervention on their own behalf. The interest groups representing German industry wanted public assistance in coping with problems of foreign competition, technology and labor. They were very effective in jockeying for power within the local administrative bodies which inaugurated unemployment remedies.

One of the outstanding features of the German response to unemployment during our period was the failure of the federal government to pursue consistent anti-cyclical economic policies. There were however a number of ways in which the government deliberately or inadvertently affected the aggregate level of unemployment. As an employer, consumer, administrator, legislator and entrepreneur the federal government exerted considerable influence in the labor market. Whenever the government hired or dismissed employees on a permanent basis or as part of public works projects, changes in unemployment occurred. State and local construction projects were used during the downswing of the 1870's to provide jobs for workers who would otherwise have competed in the private sector or been unemployed. During the early years of our period, recessions caused by over-production or underconsumption could have been ameliorated by increased federal spending. There is however little evidence to suggest deliberate initiatives to stimulate employment by the German government in its capacity as a consumer.

In the realm of legislation, laws stipulating the hours, wages, plus the minimum and maximum age of employment worked to control the number of persons in the marketplace and the amount of labor they could legally expend over a given period. In addition laws regulating tariffs, trade and migration affected the levels of industrial unemployment in Germany. As an entrepreneur, one of the most conspicuous roles of the government was in its control of the nationalized rail system. By building canals, maintaining roads and operating the railways the German government exerted a tremendous impact on transportation costs. This in turn had effects which reverberated throughout an economy dependent on the movement of persons and produce for its very existence. Government power in the field of domestic transportation gave the state important leverage with major clients such as the representatives of heavy industry in the Ruhr. Unfortunately, the federal government was either unable or unwilling to coordinate its powers in the pursuit of an anti-cyclical full employment policy. Throughout our period, measures were aimed at containing the effects of unemployment rather than eliminating its causes.

Local Unemployment Policies and Programs

If federal policy and its administrators had an impact on unemployment in Germany between 1873 and 1913, it was largely confined to the realm of attitudes and ideas. In concrete terms most of the practical steps designed to alleviate unemployment were undertaken on a regional or municipal level. Insurance, for example, was adopted in Cologne, Dresden and Strassburg[38] long before the Reich was prepared to move beyond debate on the subject. Public works projects were also the result of municipal rather than federal initiatives. Labor exchanges evolved from the

ground up, emerging on a local level and then superimposing
a national structure by linking existing institutions. Even
more punitive organizations designed to discourage begging
and inculcate industrious work habits had a distinctly
regional flavor.

By the end of our period, there was explicit
acknowledgment of the role which local anti-cyclical labor
policies could play in curtailing unemployment. A composite
report of public works projects in 43 cities between 1894
and 1908 was published by Soziale Praxis. It reflected the
fact that municipal governments were using engineering
projects to combat unemployment during recessions. When
economic slumps set in, the level of publicly funded employment expanded to compensate for contraction in the
private sector. The graph shows cumulative albeit interrupted growth of public projects between 1894 and 1908 with
rapid increases during years of peak private unemployment
and plateaus or slight declines following economic
recessions:[39]

> Sie steigern ihre Unternehmungen in den Jahren des
> allgemeinen guten Geschaeftsganges, der allseitigen
> vollen Beschaeftigung, um mit dem Eintritt der De-
> pression, des Mangels an Arbeitsgelegenheit ebenfalls
> mit ihren Unternehmungen und Auftraegen zurueckzuhalten
> und sich einzuschraenken.

The assumption was that wherever practicable local authorities should schedule work to coincide with periods of
economic decline or maximum unemployment to benefit as many

individuals as possible and ameliorate reduced demand for labor in the private marketplace.

During the winter of 1894/95, for example, the city of Frankfurt am Main undertook a public works schedule designed to alleviate both unemployment and the exorbitant demands which it had placed on agencies for poor relief. The jobs included work as stonecutters, gravel diggers, navvies or street cleaners at 20 Pf. per hour for eight hours per day. Employment was limited to 474 residents referred by the poor relief administration, all but 13 of whom accepted the work. Preference was given to married men with families so that of those hired only 13 were widowed and 13 single. Their ages were as follows: seven were less than 16 years old; 40 were between 16 and 20 years; the remainder were more than 20 years old. Two-thirds of those engaged were unskilled including large contingents of day laborers and construction workers. Only a tenth of the persons hired for public work were from non-seasonal, skilled occupations.[40]

Whether state and municipal officials deliberately or consistently adopted anti-cyclical full employment policies after 1894 is questionable. However, by the end of our period, there were specific demands that public agencies act to schedule work in a manner consistent with minimizing unemployment.[41]

Die oeffentlichen Koerperschaften sollen also einen der Auf- und Abwaertsbewegungen des Wirtschaftslebens entgegengesetzten Unternehmungszyklus, der der regelmaessigen Wiederkehr der als Folge der Wirtschaftkrisen auftretenden Arbeitslosigkeit entspricht, beobachten.

This linking of unemployment with periodically recurring economic crises which could be countermanded by government policy was a rather sophisticated approach to both the cause and resolution of the problem. Further suggestions for state intervention were forthcoming. In addition to using its role as employer to mitigate the impact of cyclical changes on the labor market, the government was urged to use its management of public resources to offset recurrent crises. Labor exchanges were implemented to fill public as well as private positions during boom and depression periods. Insurance was to provide for those unable to find work due to purely economic factors beyond the control of either government or private agencies. Unfortunately, this fairly comprehensive outline of public unemployment policies was never fully executed during our period.

One reason for the gap between theory and practice can be traced to the hesitancy of government officials at all levels to assume responsibility for the unemployed. The idea of individual accountability, the notion of self-help as a practical alternative to public assistance and the persistence of laissez faire attitudes with regard to government interference in the labor market all worked to contravene the development of comprehensive federal policies to combat unemployment. In virtually every area of unemployment relief, the Reich abrogated its role to the communal and state governments, allowing institutions to evolve at the grassroots level first.

There were certain common restrictions on public relief agencies which made local governments hesitant to adopt unemployment policies and at the same time made them easy prey for potential critics. In the case of public works, for example, there was widespread agreement that such projects were never to compete with private enterprise. This meant in many instances that the public undertakings could not be operated at a profit and from a purely economic viewpoint that they were unfeasible. Because many of the unemployed possessed very limited job training and because public projects were geared to the lowest common denominator in terms of skills, most cities confined relief work to menial labor. Highly skilled workers such as tailors whose employment required specific types of manual dexterity which might be impaired by the strenuous physical exertion involved in typical public jobs like snow removal posed problems. In such instances, efforts were made toward the end of our period to find more suitable alternate employment.

Most public projects were viewed as a service, not altogether different from poor relief but with the added moral advantage inherent in working for subsistence. In terms of social benefits, contemporaries believed that government-subsidized jobs tended to ameliorate the political unrest and criminal offenses thought to accelerate during periods of high unemployment. One important aspect of local public works projects was that they were confined to residents of a specified duration. There was a genuine aversion to supporting non-residents in any form through poor relief, insurance or public employment. As a general rule, outsiders were viewed as undesirable contributors to unemployment and social unrest. They were not encouraged in migrating to cities where they swelled the ranks of the unemployed and competed with residents for both jobs and relief.

Despite good intentions there were limitations on the role which any regional government could play in controlling unemployment. Georg Adler suggested in 1895 that state and municipal authorities could do only three things for the unemployed. First of all, they could create otherwise non-existent employment opportunities in the public sector on either a permanent or temporary basis. Secondly, they could make the unemployed aware of previously existing positions which went unfilled due to prior lack of information. Thirdly, they could provide relief for those who were unable to find work in either public or privately funded jobs. The first service could be rendered through temporary public works projects or long-term civil service employment; the second through labor exchanges and the third primarily through insurance. To varying extents in different geographical areas, all three means were adopted during our period by local German authorities.

If one moves beyond the local level, the pervasive attitute toward unemployment during our period was a general concensus on the need for a policy whose specific contours remained vague. Agreement was forthcoming on the desire for improved labor statistics and for the development of additional employment opportunities. Inexpensive labor exchanges were enthusiastically embraced. With regard to unemployment insurance, however, the attitude of the Prussian Abgeordnetenhaus in the wake of the economic downturn during 1908 was typical--scant enthusiasm for a project whose time had not yet come.[42] Content to specify that job creation was more important than insurance, the legislators enumerated unresolved problems with various insurance schemes and demurred when it came to providing relief in that form altogether.

Objections to unemployment insurance plans were legion. The shortcomings of various proposals were sufficient to deter most agencies from acting at all--by the end of our period only a handful of cities had instituted programs. And even municipalities which had pioneered in this area expressed reservations about the feasibility of their good intentions. This attitude was not uniquely German. As we noted, the Swiss city of St. Gall abandoned an existing insurance fund because skilled, hard-working, fully employed laborers were unwilling to support their less fortunate comrades. Much of the objection to unemployment insurance plans stemmed from the popular refusal to differentiate between relief in the form of public charity and true insurance. This prejudice was compounded by ignorance of the probable extent of unemployment and by exaggerated fears about the expense involved in underwriting relief programs.

One particularly vocal opponent of unemployment insurance represented employers in seasonal trades such as construction. A delegation to the Reichstag in November of 1905 vehemently attacked the imposition of the financial burdens entailed in funding unemployment benefits. They objected to all new costs or to anything which encouraged labor's ability to strike and thereby shortened the building season. They claimed that seasonal unemployment did not justify insurance because it was predictable and workers were compensated at sufficiently higher rates to enable them to save for the inevitable dead season. Insurance was intended to protect against exceptional economic crises, not against seasonally recurring, foreseeable idleness. Those able-bodied persons employed in seasonal occupations during part of each year were supposed to make their own arrangements for work during the remaining months. According to employers, it was not society's responsibility to provide for the unemployed except in extreme instances.

A further argument against insurance focused on the question of control or how to guarantee that the mass of unemployed workers would reenter the labor market at the earliest possible opportunity rather than continue to live

off public largesse. This problem along with other potential abuses of the non-existent system was thought to be
especially acute for unorganized workers. The role of
unions in the administration of insurance was a hotly
debated point throughout our period. Detractors maintained
that the more state and local government devoted to unemployment insurance, the more union funds were freed up to
support strikes and agitation for higher wages.

Theoretically, by attracting workers to cities,
municipal insurance contributed to rural depopulation and
forced agrarian employers to rely on foreign labor. It
was therefore perceived as a double-edged threat to the
national welfare. Insurance advanced the cause of unions at
the expense of employers. It also undermined both the
distribution and the composition of the labor force by
fostering the growth of urban idleness and the infusion of
undesirable foreign elements into rural areas.[43] Opponents
of unemployment insurance administered by unions also emphasized that such plans did nothing for the vast majority of
shopkeepers, self-employed artisans and workers who were not
affiliated with labor organizations.

There were numerous proposals for various types of
communal unemployment insurance and we can do no more here
than outline the most important ones. Before the turn of
the century the German Volkspartei supported a plan for
mandatory insurance in major cities. Administrative costs
were to be funded by the states, and the legal intricacies

were to be legislated by the Reich. But the cities would retain the flexibility to adopt programs to local needs within specified guidelines. The administration of the insurance program was to be conducted by a commission composed of laborers and employers, presided over by non-partisan municipal bureaucrats.[44] This variation of the Ghent system was opposed by those who believed it cumbersome to combine public funds with union administration. The Wurzburg professor Georg Schanz stated that one had to turn the matter of insurance over to the unions entirely or opt for a plan of general compulsory savings. Schanz also pointed out that insurance did nothing to eliminate unemployment. In its stead, he advocated wide-ranging measures such as labor exchanges, labor colonies, public works projects plus controls over institutions ranging from cartels to apprenticeships.

The long list of policy disputes over municipal unemployment insurance included disagreements about statistics, coverage, abuses, seasonal variations, culpability of jobless individuals, voluntary or compulsory participation, the role of employers, the extent of public subsidy, cooperation with labor exchanges, government jurisdictions and occupational differences. The possible combinations of resolutions on these diverse issues rendered agreement on a single policy for the Reich beyond the resources of contemporary bureaucrats. Differences of opinion persisted with the result that a half dozen cities adopted isolated insurance programs after 1896 which left the vast majority of workers unprotected.

Despite the failure to agree on the specifics of a federal insurance program, discussions indicated widespread recognition of the need for a national or even international unemployment policy. By 1911, _Soziale Praxis_ was publishing articles which asked the _Bundesrat_ and _Reichstag_ to require nationwide insurance for certain occupations. During the final years of our period, the feeling was explicity stated that unemployment through individual municipal governments had come as far as it could. The implication was that previous experiments had failed and nothing further could be learned by multiplying examples at the local level. The notion of approaching the problem of unemployment insurance on an occupational rather than geographical basis was also gaining acceptance by 1913.[45] In addition to calls for national insurance measures, there were a growing number of international conferences on unemployment and an increasing array of studies on foreign efforts to cope with the problem. Belgian municipal subsidies, programs in Swiss cantons and French state funding were examined by those who advocated public supplements for existing private insurance programs. However, none of these efforts succeeded in reaching the vast majority of German workers who remained unorganized and unprotected throughout our period.

The Unemployment Policies of Political Parties and Their Leaders

If little in the way of protection through insurance was forthcoming from federal, regional or local government, perhaps the reason lay in the unemployment policies of political parties and their leaders. We might begin our consideration of partisan policies by examining the attitudes of the most influential personality of the era, Otto von Bismarck. The social legislation enacted under his tutelage conspicuously omitted unemployment benefits from the insurance package designed to win the loyalty of the German labor force for the newly unified state. Nevertheless, when Bismarck addressed the Reichstag during the early 1880's, he specifically and repeatedly adluded to a "Recht auf Arbeit" or a right to work. That single phrase generated heated, lengthy discussions and various interpretations over the next three decades.

In a bid to rob enemies on the left of their natural political base, Bismarck sought to demonstrate the good will of his government toward the working classes. He did this through legislation aimed at protecting those unable to work from financial disaster. The Chancellor sought to eliminate or at the very least minimize the impact of elements such as accidents or sickness which contributed to the economic fears of the working class. In reality, his insurance directly affected a relatively small number of workers who suffered from nearly chronic disability. For those whose idleness was attributable to economic circumstance rather than physical disorders, Bismarck was not prepared to assume liability. Rather than unemployment insurance, he advocated a theoretical right to work and government responsibility for providing jobs during periods of exceptional need.

Bismarck's vision of a right to work was intended to eliminate mass unemployment during severe recessions and prevent economic downswings from assuming a political dimension. The Chancellor wanted to minimize the qualitative uncertainty of working-class life in industrial society. He recognized the political wisdom of alleviating fears of unemployment which could lead to proletarianization or an inability to work due to loss of skills. By using the state to guarantee economic stability, Bismarck hoped to win broad loyalty for his government and prevent the masses from turning to socialist demagogues during future crises. In practical terms, his avowal of a right to work translated into occasional public works projects to avert severe crises.

When Bismarck affirmed the right to work in the Reichstag during May of 1884, the arch-conservative Heinrich von Treitschke pointed out that the Chancellor had just conceded the issue over which the 1848 Revolution was fought in Paris. Treitschke further indicated that Bismarck's affirmation would involve the government in massive enterprises necessary to provide employment for all able-bodied workers and change the existing system into one which closely resembled state socialism. Brushing aside this outrageous contention, Bismarck cited the Prussian Landrecht as precedent for his position. Confusion was injected into the debate by deliberately obscuring the difference between a right to charitable handouts and a right to employment, if necessary in the public sector.[46] The effort of Bismarck to win adherents for the state through proclamations about the right to work was apparently successful. Even after the Iron Chancellor's departure, a number of appeals addressed to the Kaiser asked him to provide work for the unemployed in the same spirit which had motivated recent social legislation.

Under Bismarck's tutelage, public works projects such as canal building were to be undertaken to alleviate unemployment. That plus rhetoric was to assure the loyalty of the laboring classes by demonstrating the state's good will. Beyond this, Bismarck was unwilling to interfere with the free enterprise system--he had no intention of using government agencies to tip the balance between management and labor in favor of the latter. He wanted to avoid measures which entrepreneurs would view as freeing the working class to pursue strikes, wage increases and other benefits. His intent was never to liberate union unemployment funds by subsidizing workers through public insurance.

As with other forms of exceptional need due to illness or accident, Bismarck was prepared to offer limited protection against unemployment. His concept of a right to work formed the basis for instituting temporary public works projects in times of widespread distress rather than national labor exchanges or federally funded unemployment insurance. Unfortunately, fighting socialism took priority over eliminating work shortages. Because the relationship between the two was so confused in the public consciousness, the federal government ultimately played a limited role in translating Bismarck's right to work into viable employment policies. Nor did matters improve once he was out of office.

With the abatement of earlier economic crises and the onset of politics dominated by interest groups ranging from conservative agrarians to big business, little in the way of social legislation was forthcoming during the 1890's. Bismarck's successor Caprivi presided over an ultimately reactionary era in which the demands of labor were hampered by outmoded organizational apparati stemming from restrictions imposed during the anti-socialist period. In an era of so-called organized capitalism, big labor in the form of centralized union representation was non-existent. Scattered representatives of the working class were no match for major agricultural entrepreneurs, industrial cartels and other well orchestrated interest groups. With unions struggling to regain a foothold in the marketplace and recoup losses incurred under repressive legislation, the political arm of the labor movement--the SDP--was left to lead the battle for a coherent federal unemployment policy.

As we shall see, however, the socialist leadership was ambivalent about unemployment.

Apparently, resolution of the unemployment issue was not a top priority item for any party. There was no consistency in efforts to enact legislation which would have eliminated or even alleviated unemployment on a permanent basis. Instead, both the Reichstag and regional legislative bodies appear to have taken up the question of relief as a cyclical regimen which predictably coincided with economic crises. After the 1895 survey had established statistically that unemployment existed in manageable proportions during years of relatively normal economic activity, only severe slumps occasioned debate over public policy in this area. Accordingly, glimpses of party attitudes toward unemployment were afforded in 1901-02 and 1907-08 when assorted voices were raised on behalf of the victims of economic recessions.

Among the federal remedies proposed by Social Democrats in the Reichstag were construction and other public works projects, labor exchanges, warming halls, federal labor bureaus, improved nationwide unemployment statistics, eight-hour work days, six-day work weeks, a ban on labor for children under 14 years old, and formation of a special commission to study insurance against unemployment. Reports of debates published in Soziale Praxis[47] indicate that the Social Democratic leadership failed to pursue their unemployment resolutions with sufficient vigilance. They typically relied on second-rate speakers and no statistical materials beyond what was already available in newspapers. This was unnecessary because their ranks included eminently qualified people with solid backgrounds combining statistics, economic policy and publishing. Here it is worth noting with regard to unemployment insurance that socialist authors lagged behind their bourgeois colleagues by almost a decade, taking up the issue only around the turn of the century. Despite the new-found and vociferous enthusiasm of socialists for federal unemployment relief after 1900, they managed to achieve very little by speaking out in the Reichstag. In responding to socialist demands the government indicated a willingness to use its role as an employer to minimize unemployment during 1901 through such agencies as the post office, railroad, military and marine administrations.[48]

In terms of labor's attitude toward social insurance, there seemed to be a desire for government intervention to control the vicissitudes of the marketplace. This was particularly true of workers in seasonal trades such as construction. Organized representatives of the building trades argued that if the resources and energy of healthy workers could be diverted from searching for work, they would be able to provide for their own sickness, disability and old age. In their opinion, provision of public insurance had no impact on the attraction of Social Democracy because it was the physically and economically fit workers rather than the disabled who were politically involved.[49]

Furthermore, one could not assume that all politically active laborers were automatically drawn to support the Socialist Party. Many of the demands enumerated by Socialist candidates were embraced by other parties.

The National Liberals, who represented the interests of heavy industry, advocated public works projects, improved statistics and communal labor exchanges to offset unemployment during 1901. In the Hessian House of Representatives they also supported an insurance proposal.[50] We have already noted the demands for federal legislation requiring communal unemployment insurance which were forthcoming from the German Peoples Party. The *Volkspartei* favored unemployment insurance through towns with more than 10,000 inhabitants. But we should not convey the impression that all parties wooed labor with their support of unemployment relief.

The Catholic Center Party represented the essentially conservative interests of the peasantry and independent lower middle class. Their attitudes toward unemployment were predictably defensive. Small independent agricultural or business operatives who would not benefit from unemployment programs had no desire to finance relief for the urban labor force. The Center's posture clearly reflected this fact. Finally, we might consider the practical attitudes of Conservatives who represented agrarian interests. Although generally opposed to expensive insurance plans, they introduced legislation in the Prussian House of Representatives

to relieve unemployment through publicly funded and regulated labor exchanges. They also recognized the advantages
of Verpflegungsstationen. Their initiatives came during
periods of relative prosperity when both the urgency and
cost of implementing such measures were minimal.

The Right to Work

As we have seen, German interest in the idea of a
right to work originated with a speech of Bismarck's to the
Reichstag. However, the notion that it was society's
obligation to provide the unemployed with jobs rather than
alms can be traced back much farther than Otto von Bismarck.
The seventeenth-century English philosopher John Locke
suggested that men had the right to earn a subsistence wage
through their own work rather than reliance on charity.[51]
Recognizing that unemployment was attributable to both
overproduction and underconsumption, late-nineteenth century
publicists like Heinrich Herkner also spoke of a right to
existence in conjunction with a right to work.[52] The
capitalist marketplace required not only producers of goods
but a mass base financially able to consume the output of
labor. The need to maintain Germany's working class as a
source of consumer demand was seen as the inseparable
correlate of labor's need for both work and a steady income.
Maldistribution of income resulting in insufficient demand
was as conducive to underconsumption and unemployment as
overproduction. However, the latter factor received more

attention in an age when the former connection smacked of Marxist ideology.

The idea that all able-bodied beneficiaries of public largesse should work for a living was reflected in institutions ranging from English poor houses to German Verpflegungsstationen, labor colonies, labor yards and Herbergen zur Heimat. With the growing number of industrial unemployed came recognition that most instances of idleness were attributable to impersonal economic forces rather than individual shortcomings. This combined with the secularism of the nineteenth century made the state the logical recipient of the mantle of social protection which had once fallen to religious and private charitable institutions.

In such a setting the right to work remained suspect because contemporaries were reluctant to guarantee employment opportunities for those unable to find jobs in the private sector. The debate over a "Recht auf Arbeit" was soon translated into a heated dispute as to whether the state or government at any level should acknowledge its obligation as an employer of last resort. Because of exaggerated notions about the extent of unemployment, governments hesitated to recognize theoretical responsibilities which would saddle them with undetermined but potentially significant long-term financial obligations. This attitude was reflected in every discussion of plans for federal unemployment insurance and resulted in forestalling any written legal affirmation of the right to work during our period.

One further point about the historical evolution of the concept of a right to work needs to be stressed at this juncture. For Bismarck and his generation, we should recall the role which the right to work had played in France during the 1848 Revolutions. The specter of hungry jobless workers parading through the streets demanding employment was something more than a reactionary's invention. It had actually played a part in past revolutionary upheavals and the theoretical association between unemployment and political unrest during our period was undoubtedly lent credence by recent events in Paris. The fact that the level of unemployment and its causes were quite different in Germany between 1873 and 1913 was not sufficient to dispel the fear born of this association. As we noted with reference to Treitschke, the appearance of conceding revolutionary demands by adopting unemployment insurance was at least a tacit argument against that particular form of social legislation.

Discussions of a right to work produced disagreement over whether society at large or a single segment of the working class would benefit from its recognition. The most strident portion of the disagreement tended to focus on the role of socialism. The official socialist posture toward recognition of a right to work was that the government ought to affirm the principle by adopting a series of measures against unemployment.[53] Social Democrats in approaching the issue of a right to work took considerable pains to emphasize that their constituents were not asking for charity, but merely for an opportunity to earn their own sustenance. They wanted jobs not alms, and were anxious to work for a living if society through state agencies would undertake to provide employment when private industry failed to do so.[54] A communique issued by the Prussian ministry of the interior in 1894 emphasized that it was the obligation and duty of municipal as well as state governments to use their role as employers to combat job scarcity.

These measures were adopted against a backdrop of socialist advocacy of principles averring a right to work. Affirmation of that right represented common ground on which moderate socialists and the liberal working class could agree. It contrasted sharply with the negative extremism of Marxists like Karl Kautsky who saw the workhouse and public charity as the only alternatives to unemployment under German capitalism. Kautsky noted that insufficient demand for goods due to reduced purchasing power during recessions made public as well as private jobs an inadequate remedy for unemployment. The uncertainty of economic life under capitalism was inherent in the system and orthodox Marxists rejected the notion of eliminating unemployment without discarding the entire economic structure.

If the right to work had been an idea whose implementation were purely in the interest of labor, it

would never have received the amount of attention it generated during our period. It came into prominence precisely
because the question was formulated in terms which encouraged society at large to believe that acknowledgment of a
right to work was necessary for Germany's general wellbeing.
The evangelical trade unions' pronouncement on the subject
in 1895 reflected widespread belief of the notion that the
right to work was "ein Urrecht eines Christenmenscher". And
conversely for laborers the duty to work was "eine heilsame
Gottesordnung".[55]

In addition to executing a divine plan which
ordained that good Christians should work, nineteenth-
century social theorists maintained that it was the duty of
the state to guarantee all able-bodied citizens the opportunity to work. Because society prohibited men from steal-
ing or begging, it was obliged to afford them the chance to
earn a living by working. As the collective agency of
society, the state was the only institution with the duty,
the mandate and the means to provide employment for those
unable to find work in the private sector. And ours was not
an age which put much store in individual as opposed to
collective remedies for major social problems.

Despite recognition of the need for public action,
the right to work during our period never received tangible
affirmation. Those who opposed its formal acknowledgement
advanced the same kinds of arguments as adversaries of other
unemployment relief. Either it would cost too much, or

benefit one class at the expense of society or free both organized labor and Social Democrats to agitate for other advantages in their battle against the bourgeoisie. Furthermore, it would be difficult to establish qualifications and prevent abuses. For these and other equally spurious reasons, a number of short-sighted critics objected to the notion that all individuals had a right to expect jobs which would enable them to support themselves and their families at subsistence levels.

Criticism persisted despite the fact that society suffered from the loss of potentially productive members through starvation, migration or the equally insidious unfitness for work derived from prolonged idleness. Instead of theoretical validation through legislation guaranteeing everyone a job, the federal government deferred its responsibility to communities which took piecemeal action to avert consecutive economic crises. Here as in so many other areas of social concern, the Second Reich failed to move beyond the vision and pronouncements of its founder Bismarck.

Prior to our period, social theorists would have been more familiar with the notion of a duty to work than with the idea of a right to work. In contrast with the punitive nature of the work house and labor yards which were designed to extract effort from supposedly recalcitrant inmates, new forms of benevolent and less demeaning assistance were forthcoming after 1873. For the first time, recognition of a two-way responsibility between the individual and society was emerging. While each person still had an obligation to work, society haltingly undertook to guarantee him an opportunity for employment. The idea that individuals were entitled to rely on collective institutions to buffer them against the ravages of economically induced unemployment was not far away. During an era when laborers preferred work or self-help programs to charity, they were prepared to assert that it was the inherent right of every citizen to expect protection against crises from the government.

The Role of Women and Children in the Labor Market and Its Impact on Employment Policies

It is significant that in the area of public unemployment relief, many benefits were confined to jobless adult males. In the realm of municipal assistance this was certainly true as an 1896 article published by Soziale Praxis indicated. The fact that the city of Colmar i. E. had undertaken to support jobless female residents with dependents was deemed newsworthy. The program which was implemented between December 16, 1894, and March 16, 1895, enabled unemployed women to receive a low wage for doing washing and general housekeeping chores. The indoor nature of the jobs is significant when contrasted with the heavy outdoor physical labor exacted from males in comparable circumstances. This allocation of tasks by gender was actually a great step forward for otherwise destitute female heads of households. Unfortunately, the Colmar experiment was not widely emulated.[56]

During the years between 1873 and 1913 women in the labor force made significant advances. Working-class women first emerged as an important factor in the industrial marketplace and middle-class women made initial forays into the professions, certain political arenas and the educational establishment.[57] As we noted in another context, the majority of working women during our period were unmarried and usually quite young (pre-marriage age) or rather old (widowed). Nevertheless, then as now, an increasing number of married women were finding that scarce and expensive housing, food and other essentials made it necessary for them to supplement their husbands' earnings. Frequently, it was also necessary for children to contribute to family incomes as well.

The tradition of family-oriented enterprises was well established in rural areas where agricultural undertakings, cottage industries and shopkeeping were joint ventures. When rural unemployment and lack of economic opportunity stimulated an exodus to urban industrial centers, women and children played an important role in the formation of a new industrial labor force. In sectors such as the textile, tobacco and food industries, female and young workers constituted a large part of the labor supply from the very beginning. As producers in these industries made the transition from cottages to factories, women and children frequently provided a link with agriculture where the family's primary breadwinner continued to work. The role of women and children in the industrial labor force most closely represented that of proletarians--usually they worked in the most undesirable jobs requiring least skills under the worst conditions for the lowest wages. Within the highly stratified German working class, they occupied the lowest stratum.

Because women and children were among the least skilled and most vulnerable segments of the labor force, they were frequently willing to work for sub-standard wages. There were numerous instances in which dependents worked virtually without salaries in family businesses. Particularly among handicraft and poor artisan families the role of spouses and youngsters helping out in shops was an essential source of free labor exploited to the hilt during hard times.[58] In addition to family situations, the employment of women and children throughout the nineteenth century was recognized by unscrupulous and stereotypically greedy employers as highly profitable. Particularly in the old craft industries where strict hierarchies continued to predominate, young apprentices from rural areas were at the mercy of new-found urban masters.[59] Given the abuses which inevitably arose from this system, the government was prevailed upon to redress the worst grievances through legislation during the early 1890's.

Although little was done to improve the plight of adults, measures were enacted to protect young people in the industrial labor force. The precise hours and terms of employment including starting times, quitting times, holidays and pauses were spelled out for youths along with restrictions as to the work place. Changes in the Gewerbeordnung placed limitations on the number of hours which workers under sixteen years of age could be employed. Children under twelve were not to be engaged in factories at all while children under fourteen were to work a maximum of six hours per day. Education was not to be subordinated to employment and those with school obligations had to receive a minimum of three hours' daily instruction. Those between the ages of fourteen and sixteen could be employed in factories up to ten hours per day. Legislation enacted in 1884 instituted a maximum eleven-hour workday for women. As an apparent afterthought, it was stipulated that pregnant women were not to work during the three weeks immediately following delivery. Despite the good intentions of the Kaiser and others who pushed for these regulations in June of 1891, slack enforcement procedures enabled some employers to perpetuate abuses. As long as female and child labor remained profitable and inspectors few in number, manipulative employers would continue to rely on cheap young workers rather than more independent and expensive adult males.

By the turn of the century an estimated four million youngsters worked in German industry while about half that number was engaged in agriculture. The impact which these figures had on adult unemployment is difficult to estimate with precision. But it is clear that if all young people could have been kept in the classroom, conscripted into military service or otherwise prevented from entering the job market, the labor surplus even during periods of economic crisis would have dwindled into insignificance. Combine this with the effect of actually confining married women to the home and the unemployment problem would have disappeared entirely. The probable result would have been to transform a labor surplus into a severe shortage if the source of marginal workers which women and children constituted had been eliminated. By the turn of the century there were simply not enough adult males to do all the work in Germany's expanding industrial economy. An industrial labor shortage never arose, however, because the poor wages which men earned made it necessary for dependent women and children to work in order to subsist at a decent level.

The Role of Foreign Competition in Unemployment

In an increasingly international marketplace, the level of unemployment in Germany came to be seen as a function of foreign competition. Concern over the impact of non-German competitors in the domestic labor market developed two basic foci. The first emphasized the role of foreign products and sought to eliminate undesirable advantages through protective tariffs. The second stressed the role of foreign laborers both at home and abroad with particular emphasis on relative wage rates or labor as a cost factor in production. A growing demand for the "protection of national labor" became an umbrella term covering both aspects of the role of foreign competitors in unemployment.

It is significant that Germany went through the worst years of recession and unemployment with a policy of *laissez faire* economic liberalism and free trade. It took the severe slump of the 1870's to demonstrate to Bismarck and his supporters that state intervention in general and protective tariffs in particular were needed as anti-cyclical weapons against on-going economic crises. With interest groups ranging from large agrarians to small craftsmen and major industrialists clamoring for tariffs, a new era in German trade policy began during 1878. A great deal has been written about the so-called alliance between rye and iron. Rather than rehash the details here, we shall attempt to outline the two-way relationship between tariffs and unemployment.

Pro-tariff arguments designed to lend a competitive advantage to domestic industries consistently referred to the benefits which would accrue to German laborers. Whenever the government could advance the mutual interests of both labor and management, it was prepared to act in the hope of receiving support from the broad mass of workers as well as the smaller but more powerful coterie of major employers. Unfortunately, the issue of foreign competition did not break down so conveniently in every instance. There was, for example, the inherent conflict of interest between workers seeking to maximize their wages and employers seeking to minimize product costs in order to compete successfully in a free market situation. The bottom line here of course was unemployment--if manufacturers were not competitive due to unreasonable labor costs, they would have to cease production and dismiss their work force.

There is evidence that German producers under the free trade agreements which prevailed throughout the depressed years between 1873 and 1879 were willing to sell their goods abroad for less than at home. To avert shut downs, they were prepared to accept minimal profits, preferring to stay open despite falling domestic and international prices. By glutting already abundantly supplied markets, they contributed to the significant price declines which characterized that period. According to Martin Kitchen,[60] heavy investments in plant and equipment combined with improved methods of production made employers hesitant to curtail output. In the short run this tended to minimize unemployment, but the resulting reduction in industrial profits had a long-term effect on the expansion of demand for labor over the following decades.

As foreign markets consumed a growing percentage of German output, domestic producers found themselves increasingly at the mercy of an unstable, frequently unpredictable world price structure. At home too the question of tariffs was crucial in terms of the relative costs of German-made goods and imported merchandise. Naturally, all manufacturers favored a government policy calculated to expand their markets by imposing substantial duties on imported competitive products while pressuring foreign governments not to retaliate in kind. High protective tariffs at home and low import duties abroad were the ideal which each interest group sought for its output. The question of tariffs cut two ways because additional taxes meant increased costs for domestic consumers as well as protection for domestic producers. When Bismarck's conservative government had to make a choice between the interests of management and labor, it typically opted for the former. There was recognition of the fact that the more Germany relied on exports or became involved in international trade, the more susceptible the domestic economy became to fluctuations in the world marketplace.[61]

In fact, the tariff issue was largely responsible for crystallizing the formation and alignment of power groups on the basis of interests. Cooperative organizations of entrepreneurs in both heavy and light industries emerged to play prominent roles in policy decisions during the 1870's. Agrarians subsequently united to form their leagues and by the time the economy recovered in the mid-1890's, consolidated interest groups were an important factor in the formulation of federal economic, trade and labor policies.

The high tariffs which were introduced in 1879[62] remained in effect until the 1890's. At that point, Bismarck's successor Caprivi opted to accede to the demands of big industry in a two-step process by reducing duties despite the protests of German agriculture. In 1902 Chancellor von Buelow introduced the first agrarian subsidies, evoking socialists' outrage over high grain prices.

Bismarck had encouraged the formation of interest groups as bases of support for the government and used the theme "protection of national labor" to rally major industrialists such as Kardorff and Stinnes to the cause. Relying on their interest in international trade and tariff policy, he created a vehicle for agricultural and industrial magnates to directly influence economic policy until 1913. During the 1880's the tariff issue had been supplanted by another facet of Bismarck's effort to protect the German labor force through social insurance. The interest groups which had coalesced to influence tariff policy counseled the Chancellor to proceed cautiously in this area. They pointed out that the costs of insurance added to their disadvantage vis-a-vis foreign producers whose prices were not inflated by taxes to support social programs. Many were reluctant to bear the expense of additional insurance even during the most prosperous times and when the economy turned bad, they were shrill in their opposition to paying for exorbitant social benefits. Industry's spokesmen argued that the best way to protect national labor was to refrain from overtaxing

the resources of big business. According to Ruhr industrialists, if the costs of social insurance became too
great, labor would ultimately suffer through cutbacks, wage
reduction and lay-offs.[63] A final phase in the theme of
protecting German workers began to eclipse the social
insurance angle during the last decade of our period when
armaments became the focal point of those still claiming to
safeguard labor and the national interest.[64]

Although the interests of agriculture and industry
appeared to coincide during 1879 with the common front
pushing for protection, it was not long before the marriage
between rye and iron gave way to a mutually satisfactory
divorce. By the time the economic recession of 1901 hit,
agriculture was pushing for subsidies, tariffs and protection while German industry felt able to compete in a free
international market. Rather than safeguarding national
labor through tariffs, which were no longer in its own
interest, industry advocated other types of unemployment
protection by the turn of the century. While many agrarian
conservatives continued to prefer protective tariffs as a
means to combat unemployment, this ran counter to their
general opposition to government at any level assuming
responsibility for the jobless. Proponents of savings and
other self-help measures, the agricultural bloc was not
willing to pay additional social insurance premiums for the
unemployed.[65]

In undertaking to protect German industrial laborers from foreign competition, government policy looked to internal as well as international threats. During the late 1870's note was taken of the fact that laws restricting child labor in Germany made it difficult for domestic producers to compete against manufacturers in countries where fewer restraints were imposed on the supply of cheap labor. Belgian spinners, for example, were able to turn out yarn which lessened the demand for German production both at home and abroad. In 1877 at a time when the textile industry was hard hit--facing high unemployment and cut-backs in hours amounting to one-third--critics laid blame squarely on the terms of trade with which domestic producers had to contend. French, English and Belgian manufacturers benefited from cheaper raw materials, lower freight costs, better bank discounts, and greater freedom to employ younger, less expensive laborers for longer hours. The result was that they were able to undercut German sellers by about five percent. Demand reflected the price differential, with foreign-made textile goods outselling German products by as much as ten times in certain areas.[66]

Both factory owners and laborers resented the competitive advantages of those working abroad during periods of high unemployment such as the late 1870's. Their complaints were, however, less common than efforts to eradicate the impact of foreigners resident within the Reich. The fact that Germans resented foreign nationals who were perceived to take jobs away from citizens in domestic markets was a recurring theme in the unemployment literature. In order to assess the seriousness of the problem, data on the number of foreigners living in Germany during our period is helpful. In 1871 there were approximately 207,000 foreigners in the Empire. By 1875, their number had increased to 290,000; by 1885, 370,000; by 1895, 486,000; by 1905, 1,030,000 and by 1910, 1,260,000. Slightly more than 40% of these aliens resided in the Kingdom of Prussia throughout our period. Men seemed to predominate over women by a margin of three to two. Particularly when unemployment was a threat--during slack periods, seasonal slowdowns or the recessions of 1901 and 1908, resentment ran high against foreign workers usurping German jobs.

Near the end of our period in November of 1913, employers in the building trades were taking note of the large number of foreign construction workers. Many of them had been attracted to jobs in large cities where high wage rates assured a steady stream of new arrivals--usually enough to guarantee a labor surplus during periods of normal building activity. The result of this surplus during recessions was a clarion call to once again protect German labor from foreign competition. In Westphalia during 1902 the province funded public building projects with terms of employment which explicitly discriminated against foreigners. Construction jobs were to be limited to those who belonged to the _Reich_ and spoke the German language as their mother tongue.[67] The situation after the turn of the century was apparently even worse with northern and central Germany reporting large numbers of unemployed Bohemians, Croats and Slovenes looking for work. Swelling their number elsewhere were Italian and Czech construction workers whose presence led to requests for preferential treatment of German nationals during hard times.

Many believed that foreigners, in addition to being barred from publicly subsidized jobs or benefits should be the last hired and first fired by private employers. There was apparently fierce resentment when domestic jobs were filled by non-Germans during periods of substantial unemployment. The following proviso was in no sense atypical of the measures which ensued from this mentality:[68]

> Ein Beschaeftigungsverbot slavonischer Arbeiter in Grossherzogtum Baden hat das badische Ministerium des Innern erlassen, indem es die Bezirkaemter anwies, dass slawonische Arbeiter bis zum 20 Februar 1909 nicht beschaeftigt werden duerfen, weil die Arbeitslosigkeit unter den unheimischen Arbeitern zu gross sei.

Since most public unemployment benefits were administered through local agencies which imposed residence requirements, foreigners were automatically excluded from relief programs. In addition, they were routinely barred from jobs wherever numerous German workers were unemployed. The needs of fellow countrymen came first as evidenced by measures to protect national labor at home through priority employment and abroad through the terms of trade. Rather than uniting an international proletariat against bourgeois employers, unemployment turned worker against fellow laborer, splitting interests along national as opposed to class lines during our period.

COLLECTIVE PROTECTION AGAINST UNEMPLOYMENT

One of the major consequences of the ongoing
processes of urbanization, industrialization and modernization was to challenge the efficacy of individual initiative.
The major problems such as unemployment which came in the
wake of rapid socio-economic change seemed too overwhelming
to be resolved through isolated personal effort. The de-
humanizing impact of life in an urban slum or work in a
highly mechanized factory definitely took its toll on the
self-esteem of labor. Recognition of the impersonal nature
of economic forces led men to look for collective strength
in combatting mutual problems through sheer numbers.

East German historians have referred to our period
as an era of state monopoly capitalism and West Germans have
developed the term organized capitalism to describe essentially the same phenomenon. As an alternative, collectivist
capitalism seems a more appropriate designation for the
emergence of unions, cartels, syndicates and interest groups
which came to play an increasingly important role in all
aspects of economic life under the Second _Reich_. The following excerpt from a 1902 article on unemployment insurance
summed up the collectivist approach of German labor during
the preceding decades:[69]

> Drei Ideen von eminenter sozialpolitischer Wichtigkeit
> arbeiten in den letzten zwei Jahrzehnten in der deuts-
> chen Lohnarbeiterschaft: die Organisation der Produ-
> zehnten zu grossen Gewerkschaften, die Organisation der
> Konsumenten zu Genossenschaften, die Organisation des
> Arbeitsangebots und der Arbeitsnachfrage in central-
> isirten Arbeitsnachweisen. Alle drei Gedanken haben

etwas Wesensverwandtes an nachwiesen. In ihnen pulst naemlich die Grundidee: mehr Ordnung, mehr Richtung und Regelung in das Gewirr unseres Wirthschaftsleben hineinzubringen.

The notion that collective action could bring more order, more direction and regulation to bear on the confusion of economic life was widespread. The seemingly random nature of economic forces, plus the insecurity, uncertainty and fear aroused by unpredictable elements of industrialization led men with mutual interests to seek mutual assistance. In the realm of unemployment, it was clear that individual remedies such as savings programs or migration were neither adequate nor feasible alternatives.

It is extremely significant that claims exonerating workers from culpability for their own unemployment referred specifically to their number as proof of innocence.[70] The thinking of the day seemed to indicate that unemployment was a problem demanding social and state intervention only when large numbers of persons were affected. Human suffering as well as individual solutions received surprisingly little attention during our period. Contemporaries seemed very concerned about the collective ramifications of unemployment but almost criminally insensitive to its personal repercussions. The morality of unemployment and its impact on workers themselves were discussed far less frequently than revolutionary socialism's appeal to the discontented or the loss of national output which resulted from idle hands. Almost all advocates of unemployment relief tried to convince those who would bear the expense that it was in their own best interest and in the interest of society at large to provide the assistance.

An 1896 excerpt from Soziale Praxis is typical of efforts to persuade employers, governments and laborers themselves to share the cost of unemployment protection. In this case the argument was tailored to the needs of the construction industry. Everyone was supposed to benefit from insurance paid for through regular savings by building workers supplemented with contributions from employers plus communal and state agencies.[71] The reason why each of these parties should contribute was the opposite of altruism--it was described as pure self-interest. Workers would benefit by receiving assistance without the demoralizing influence of accepting charity. Employers who needed a ready supply of labor during the building season had to protect its source during slack periods. The state, city and Reich would benefit by maintaining social peace and avoiding poor relief or the cost of prosecuting the unemployed for crimes requiring the assistance of additional police and court officials.

The severe economic conditions of the first half of our period went far toward convincing former economic liberals of the benefits which might accrue from state intervention. So-called Kathedersozialisten such as Lujo Brentano, who had been a staunch opponent of anything which smacked of Marxism, came to support the idea of organization and planning as an alternative to overproduction. Regulation of production through publicly orchestrated coordination was seen as a possible remedy for unemployment. It would prevent manufacturers from glutting the marketplace with goods for which there was insufficient demand.[72] Arguably, the first step toward collective protection came at the end of the economically disastrous seventies with Bismarck's coalition for tariffs. Informal associations of persons with like interests had existed earlier. But the crises which recurred during the first half of our period were conducive to increasing demands for public assistance against economic disaster. Antipathy to state intervention and unfair restraint of trade gave way to the necessities of survival which seemed to confirm the wisdom of cartelization and government control. Solidarity among manufacturers, collectivism among workers and close cooperation with public authorities were the order of the day for German industry after 1890.[73]

The Role of Interest Groups in a Collectivist Age

One of the most effective and rapidly proliferating mechanisms for the dissemination of collective pressure between 1873 and 1913 was the interest group. Persons with common concerns joined together to exert influence derived either from their number or from their prominence in the economy, society or government. The former type of association included labor unions which will receive separate consideration and organizations such as the Agrarian

League. The second type of association consisted of powerful conglomerates of industrial entrepreneurs such as the
Centralverband Deutscher Industrieller which represented
heavy industry in the Ruhr. Recently Wolfram Fischer has
suggested that these organizations of like-minded persons
were formed to exert influence on German politics at three
levels: On public opinion, on parliamentary legislation,
and on the administration as the executive and legal pre-
paratory branch of government.[74] It is important to emphasize that interest groups were anxious to affect more
than the central administration and frequently went to
considerable lengths in their efforts to influence the
Reichstag and provincial legislatures.

The present concensus in West German historiography seems to be that interest groups emerged into the
political limelight during the 1870's as part of the response to dual stimuli. The combined impact of a severe
economic recession and Bismarck's effort to build an
effective coalition in support of his tariff program brought
many groups with common interests into being. The groups
saw themselves as partners of the state in formulating
economic policies tailored to their specific regional or
sectoral needs. Organized factions seeking to influence the
state as representative of the nation came to equate their
own interests with those of society as a whole. It was not
uncommon for large manufacturing or banking concerns to
employ high civil servants in important positions as con-

duits for their interests. Nor was this reliance upon collective influence a one-way street. Bismarck was certainly not above using his contacts with major industrialists to drum up support for programs included under the umbrella term of protecting national labor.

Beginning with tariff and tax matters in the 1870's, an increasing array of large and small associations came to exert a growing influence on German politics. Interest groups proliferated to such an extent that by the turn of the century, major questions such as unemployment insurance were likely to elicit a multitude of statements from organized coalitions. Competing for the attention of the press, legislature and administration, these groups advanced the claims and counterclaims of citizens whose collective concerns they represented. By 1900 rather than dealing with individual requests, bureaucrats were typically faced with a whole series of conflicting demands from organizations hoping to be included in formulating policy. These organizations constituted a source of unified support for the state in matters of international importance such as tariff, fleet and colonial policy. Conflicting economic needs, however, frequently divided interest groups in domestic matters. Competition between agriculture and heavy industry was reflected in divergent views on issues ranging from wages to employment and other questions relating to the labor market.[75]

Little has been written about the role of the unemployed within the matrix of interest groups that dominated German politics during our period. We noted earlier that unemployment tended to be concentrated among the least powerful members of society and that it rarely existed in sufficient quantity to make numbers alone a source of strength. It seems reasonable to conclude that those subjected to the threat of potential unemployment exercised greater collective influence than actual victims. Suffering from lack of confidence and loss of independence, most jobless individuals were passive and apathetic. Failure to consolidate their position by coming together to advance their common interest meant that the only organized representatives of their needs were the unions and the SDP. The need for an organization which would enable unemployed workers to exercise influence from below on the public, the parliamentary bodies, and the administration was never fully appreciated. By failing to coalesce along lines of mutual advantage, the unemployed suffered a severe handicap in an era of blatant political and economic influence peddling.

To the extent that the unemployed relied on organizations to alleviate their plight, it was frequently through institutions such as labor exchanges. Informal channels of information through union contacts frequently enabled unemployed members to get early notice of available positions by word of mouth. Having access to some source of group support gave the unemployed a distinct advantage over non-affiliated workers in the competition for reentry into the labor force.[76] Georg Schanz has suggested that this type of access was one of the most effective recruiting weapons in the arsenal of socialist unions whose numerous members were well situated to inform colleagues about potential employment opportunities.

Within the labor market itself, collective efforts had well-established precedents by the early years of our period. Historically, workers with similar interests had organized in associations ranging from medieval guilds to trade unions. In order to counterbalance the emerging front of organized labor, associations representing employers' interests came into being during the 1870's. Dealing with demands for better wages and hours, frequently within the confines of a single industry, these associations almost invariably condemned proposals for subsidized unemployment benefits. Using the unemployment issue to attack their avowed enemy--socialism--industrialists during the late 1870's supported Bismarck's contention that left-wing agitators had caused unemployment by undermining business confidence.[77]

Willing to take a harsh line whenever escalating unemployment rates made workers more than normally vulnerable, employers' associations found their adversaries meager competition after 1879. Between Bismarck's anti-socialist legislation and the recurring economic crises, most representatives of organized labor were so involved in fighting for their existence that they had scant opportunity to pose serious threats to industrial magnates. The primary impetus for collectivist action among employers after 1890 was channeled into the formation of cartels and syndicates. Like other forms of collective protection, these conglomerates were designed to prevent falling prices stemming from oversupply or insufficient demand during economic recessions. By controlling production and maintaining prices, they would be able to avert unanticipated lay-offs, stabilize the labor market and eliminate unemployment.

After the turn of the century when prosperity was more prevalent, employers seemed to demonstrate a renewed interest in joining together to oppose the consolidated front of organized labor. When the last economic downturn of the period passed in 1909, political realities began to supercede economic interests as a focal point of collective activity. Broadening the electoral base and achieving mass support for associations whose interests paralleled the organization of political parties became the order of the day. Alongside the conservatives' Agrarian League and heavy industries' Centralverband Deutscher Industrieller, distinctly liberal interest groups such as the Hansabund began to emerge. Alliances between Conservatives were joined by forces like the Catholic peasants' league and cartels. At the same time, the Hansabund, National Liberals and Freisinnige Party were augmented by Christian trade unions in pushing for social reform just prior to the Great War.

More and more parties became the mouthpieces of special interests, frequently organizing along class lines and making no pretense of addressing the needs of the nation as a whole. Bismarck's system of so-called negative integration--winning the loyalties of disparate groups for the state by uniting them into a coalition against internal enemies such as socialists--aimed at preserving the status quo until 1912. It precluded real social change or the adoption of federal measures to eliminate unemployment. Although permitting economic improvements including higher wages and safer working conditions, the Bismarckian system denied labor social or political equality. An effort was made to use potential opposition forces such as social democracy to discipline the protest potential of labor over unemployment and add to the stability of the system.

Not only did the unemployed fail to emerge as a revolutionary tool in the hands of socialists except as a grossly exaggerated threat concocted by conservative alarmists, jobless workers never materialized as a political force at all during our period. Political activism to achieve economic ends was beyond their purview because they lacked the cohesion and organization necessary to function effectively in an era of collectivist values. As subsequent studies of the political behavior of unemployed individuals have shown, apathy rather than involvement was the typical response.[78] Even during periods when unemployment reached extreme levels, political discontent rarely went beyond registering disgruntlement by voting for extremist candidates.

Economically disenfranchised workers failed to evolve creative channels for circumventing a system which remained unresponsive to their needs. They were also unable to work effectively within the governmental structure to achieve a well-formulated unemployment policy. At a time when the organized representatives of industrial interests functioned as the primary opponents of publicly funded unemployment benefits, the jobless worker had no comparable forum in which to respond. The obvious institutional mechanism for combating such attacks would have been the trade unions. But as we shall see, organized labor for a variety of reasons attached a relatively low priority to resolving the unemployment problem.

Labor Unions' Unemployment Policies

It needs to be emphasized at this juncture that there was a striking contrast between the public pronouncements of those representing the collective interests of large industrial employers and individual management decisions. While organizations such as the CDI were among the most vociferous opponents of unemployment insurance, many entrepreneurs adopted measures to protect their employees from lay-offs. There were even a few well-publicized instances in which individual employers sponsored specific unemployment programs for their workers.[79] In addition to providing special unemployment benefits, which were rare, companies adopted a variety of measures designed to avert lay-offs. With this in mind, let us turn to an examination of the actual and perceived role which trade unions played in determining the level of unemployment and the policies adopted to control it.

As representatives of labor's interests on the unemployment issue, unions were poorly equipped to handle the challenge posed by management's collective power. There were two primary reasons why unions were unequal to the task of functioning effectively as an interest group for the unemployed. First of all, keep in mind that organized labor throughout our period never represented a majority of the work force. Most of the time, trade union members constituted less than a quarter of German labor, essentially an elite. It is indeed arguable that those most vulnerable to industrial unemployment fell totally outside the jurisdiction of unions because they remained unaffiliated with any organization. Beyond this lies a second related point. Because many union members were subject to relatively low levels of unemployment, they tended to place greater emphasis on other priorities such as health insurance, wages and working conditions.

A recent article[80] on self-help through unions as a form of labor solidarity suggests that programs fell naturally into two broad categories--one defensive in nature and the other offensive. The former included such social assistance programs as accident, invalid and life insurance while the latter had a more aggressive tone, providing strike and travel supplements. To a certain extent this division mirrored a split within the labor movement itself. Unions couldn't decide whether to adopt a strict Marxist approach by appealing to the class interest of the proletariat or a more reformist line by appealing to the rising material expectations of German workers.

Both moderate and radical elements within the labor movement cited Marx as justification for their attitude toward union unemployment benefits. Radical spokesmen opposed any measures which would delay the inevitable revolution by making the injustices inherent in the capitalist system more palatable to the working class. They were therefore against union unemployment insurance and all other palliative measures which were assumed to undermine the inevitable class struggle. They saw union members as the elite core of revolution with no need to contaminate their ranks by attracting infiltrators from the industrial reserve army.

Moderates who were less sanguine about the imminent demise of capitalism envisioned a more long-term confrontation. They felt that unemployment benefits were a powerful recruiting tool for unions--the center of the Marxist movement and root of future revolutions. Until the system could be overthrown, they strove to make the lives of workers as free from hardship as possible. Their ability to provide a semblance of security was intended to exercise a powerful attraction on potential members. Less elitist than the radicals, moderate factions sought to expand their unions by all possible means, and if unemployment insurance provided a suitable lure they were willing to use it.[81]

Different unions put together packages of benefits with varying emphases on offensive and defensive means of achieving solidarity. Unemployment funds presented a special case since they were used offensively to attract new members to the union cause and free potentially militant workers from the threat of punitive dismissals. They were also, however, seen as a defensive mechanism designed to prevent privation among those unable to find work in much the same way as disability or health insurance.

One measure of union priorities is the relative expenditure of resources for support to members with dif-fering needs. How much was spent on relief for the unem-ployed as opposed to maintenance of disabled or striking men? In order to put such figures into perspective, data on the membership of various unions is necessary to give some idea of per capita outlays. In 1891, the three largest unions--Free, Christian and Hirsch-Duncker--had memberships totaling 344,000. Over the course of the next four years, due to declines in the Free Unions, membership actually decreased. At the time of the 1895 census, only 332,000 workers belonged to Germany's three largest unions. From 1896 onward, with the economy prospering, membership began to increase rather steadily. It is significant to note, however, that there were declines during 1901 and 1908 when recessions hit German industry. The growth of union membership and economic prosperity appear to have gone hand-in-hand.[82] By 1900, there were 849,000 members of the three major unions and by 1905 that number had doubled. In 1910, membership was 2,435,000 and in 1913, 3,024,000. At the end of our period an estimated 3.2 million members of all trade unions were protected by unemployment insurance--a huge advance over conditions in 1873.[83]

There were of course significant variations in emphasis among labor organizations. In 1913 for example the socialist unions reported expenditures of eight million Marks for unemployment support, 18 million Marks for strikes and six million Marks for agitation and organization.[84] The basic revolutionary orientation which these allocations reflected was consistent with the socialist tendency to emphasize disruptive activities such as strikes more than defensive subsidies to unemployed members. Contrast this with figures for the Hirsch-Duncker unions. Between 1909 and 1913 those unions spent almost half their subsidies on defensive programs such as sickness benefits while less than a quarter of their funds were set aside for more aggressive means. With reference to benefits paid to jobless members, the highest percentage was allocated by the Free Unions whose outlays for travel and unemployment were substantially larger than those of other labor organizations. The Christian unions tended toward a more balanced expenditure of funds targeted for members, with unemployment benefits receiving less emphasis. In terms of total expenditure and per capita support, the Hirsch-Duncker and Free Unions were competitive with both far in advance of the more frugal Christian unions.

Evolution of union unemployment programs occurred gradually during the first half of our period. At the beginning, only a handful of organizations with highly skilled members such as the printers union offered any form of unemployment subsidy. The printers continued to lead the way in terms of unemployment benefits, consistently offering some of the highest levels of support. Between 1868 and 1890 the printers allocated one-fourth of their funds for unemployment benefits and an equal amount for travel subsidies. As a rule, the Hirsch-Duncker unions were conspicuous for their innovative approaches to unemployment benefits. Predictably, union unemployment expenditures varied with economic conditions, peaking during recessions and subsiding during boom periods. Aggressive activities such as strikes were inversely proportional to unemployment.

By 1891, of the 58 affiliated Free Unions with 277,659 members, only ten organizations with 32,267 members provided unemployment benefits amounting to some 44,000 Marks. Around the turn of the century, great advances were made in this area. By 1900, of the same 58 Free Unions whose membership had expanded to 680,000, 20 affiliates with 226,000 members spent in excess of a half million Marks for unemployment. By 1902, 26 Free Unions extended unemployment assistance to their people. These gains in protection resulted in unprecedented coverage for idle workers during the recession which began in 1901. During that year more than a third of the Free Unions' aid to its members was earmarked for unemployment and travel.

Although considerable progress was made during our period, less than one-quarter of the labor force was organized and not all unions provided unemployment coverage. As late as 1907, when the economy was entering the last major recession before 1913, one-third of all Free Unions provided no unemployment protection of any kind nor did they anticipate the introduction of such benefits. Characteristically, many of those who remained unprotected were most in need of unemployment funds because they worked in seasonal occupations or jobs which periodically subjected them to lay-offs. During 1907 when Free Unions expended an average of five Marks per member on unemployment, the Christian unions were doing even less--spending a mere 0.25 Marks per capita on unemployment. Only 1.6% of the Christian unions' outlays went to help the unemployed and more than a quarter of their membership remained unprotected in 1907. Occupying an intermediate position, the Hirsch-Duncker Associations spent 136,143 Marks or 1.15 Marks per capita for unemployment benefits to its 118,508 members in 1906. This represented 9.7% of its annual budget. As these figures suggest, there was a significant range of union priorities reflected in unemployment expenditures.

In order to place the German situation in perspective, a brief comparison with other European countries might prove instructive. We know, for example, that in 1907, unions in 13 countries spent 17 million Marks or 16.66% of their annual budget for unemployment benefits. While English unions allocated 21.5% of their resources to unemployment and the Netherlands 1.2%, German unions devoted 14% of their funds to jobless members. A total of 4,845,365 German union members received per capita unemployment subsidies of 3.53 Marks. The highest expenditure was 6.74 Marks in England, while Denmark was second and Germany ranked a distant third with 2.88 Marks. Between 1897 and 1906 the 100 most important English unions devoted an average of 22% of their resources to unemployment benefits, an amount well in excess of their German colleagues during most years. In 1907, for example, the Free Unions in Germany allocated 15% of their funds to the unemployed, a sum slightly above the national average but well below England.[85]

Unemployment Subsidies of Trade Unions
in 13 European Nations in 1907

Country	No. of Organized Workers	Total Annual Expenditure	Annual Expenditure for Unemployment in Marks	%age of Exp. Devoted to Unemp.	Total Exp. per Member in Marks	Exp. per Member for Unemp.
England	2,106,283	39,956,990	8,594,357	21.51	31.36	6.74
Netherlands	128,845	695,450	8,315	1.20	21.55	0.25
Belgium	181,015	1,041,441	116,943	11.22	7.69	0.85
Denmark	109,914	1,797,615	315,078	17.52	17.15	3.00
Sweden	239,000	2,058,843	95,481	4.58	10.93	0.51
Norway	48,215	859,790	46,006	5.35	22.18	1.18
Finland	32,000	81,506	400	0.49	3.23	0.01
Germany	2,446,480	47,914,202	6,729,926	14.04	20.57	2.88
Austria	501,094	5,956,442	956,279	16.05	11.88	1.90
Hungary	142,030	1,528,363	218,093	14.26	10.76	1.53
Serbia	5,434	64,685	7,147	11.04	11.90	1.31
Bulgaria	10,000	14,098	1,789	12.69	9.34	1.18
Switzerland	135,377	805,437	19,644	2.44	11.92	0.29
	6,088,687	102,774,853	17,109,458	16.66	21.21	3.53

In any discussion of unions and unemployment, the role of the so-called Ghent System must be considered. Essentially an insurance scheme based on the experience of the Belgian city for which it was named, this plan entailed pooling the resources of public funding and union administration. Widely adopted in Belgian and French communities, this arrangement was also used with some modifications in Norway, Denmark and Luxembourg. Opponents in Germany were loud in denouncing the program both for its admitted failure to cover unorganized labor and its supposed subsidy of union interests. It should be noted that the most vociferous antagonists of the Ghent system were the organized associations representing employers' interests. Predictably, unions were the most vocal supporters of the system.

In order to allay fears that the Ghent system would subsidize labor agitation, every effort was made to use public monies to fund purely defensive self-help programs such as unemployment. Precautions were taken to guarantee that no assistance was given to further labor's struggle against employers. The Ghent model amounted to a public acknowledgment of the inadequacy of governmental organization which was felt to be unequal to the task of administering unemployment insurance. It had the advantage of coordinating public and private coverage, eliminating both duplication of benefits and the ever-feared abuses of the system by those out to defraud the government.

To a certain extent, unions, by agreeing to

cooperate with local government in an effort to alleviate unemployment, became part of the establishment. Rather than functioning as aggressive organizations devoted exclusively to furthering labor's class struggle, they became a partner in the state's social insurance program. This was viewed with mixed feelings by those who recognized it as a major step toward the integration of the labor force into the rest of industrial society.[86] It was tacitly assumed by moderates that such integration would strengthen the unions' position, but radicals who believed that revolutionary means were preferable to working within the system remained skeptical.

Not surprisingly, the Ghent format was most warmly applauded by the Free Unions which welcomed state assistance in meeting the high cost of their generous subsidies to members. The Social Democrats were less enthusiastic about accepting monies from and cooperating with government officials who were perceived with what we might term justifiable paranoia as the enemy. Because most unions were organized along occupational or industrial lines, unemployment concentrated in certain sectors could rapidly dissipate entire insurance funds. This kind of narrow economic base made unions vulnerable to acute, focused sectoral recession. That in turn made it attractive for many labor organizations to seek some form of back-up support in the guise of public unemployment subsidies under the Ghent system.[87]

Union attitudes toward the Ghent system in particular and unemployment in general varied widely. Basically labor organizations sought to provide protection for their members through a combination of self-help and collective measures. The proposal of the evangelical unions which was adopted during the recession of 1901-02[88] is fairly typical of the means which workers were prepared to use in the battle against unemployment. The resolution supported establishment of obligatory labor exchanges in towns with more than 10,000 persons and a centralized superstructure to coordinate local activities. It also advocated voluntary self-insurance programs within the unions as a transitional step to a national law requiring obligatory unemployment insurance organized along occupational lines. In addition, the proposal called for a savings program for young workers, provisions for destitute itinerants, and assistance for those changing jobs.

On a local level, similar suggestions were advanced concurrently by spokesmen for the Christian trade unions and other labor organizations in Mannheim. They favored eight-hour days for public employees, elimination of overtime and double shifts, scheduling public works projects to coincide with periods of peak unemployment, banning child labor and certain specific wage controls. They also requested that the city make available to the unemployed at its cost necessities such as food, shelter and fuel. Priority whenever possible was to be afforded local resi-

dents. At every point they stressed the need to differentiate clearly between what the unemployed required--
Nothstandsunterstutzung--and what the chronically poor
received--Armenpflege. One comes away with the impression
that unions felt they were entitled to receive public
assistance in their attempt to help unemployed members
through temporary difficulties. The union leaders were in
effect soliciting a partnership with local officials in
coordinated efforts to resolve mutually unsatisfactory labor
problems. They strove hard to differentiate between charity
and aid for individuals who were in a sense self-insured.
As a result, society was beginning to give credit to jobless
workers who were doing everything possible to help themselves.

During the closing years of the century the German
Volkspartei came to champion a plan which would involve
union, public and entrepreneurial participation in unemployment insurance. The Hirsch-Duncker Associations opposed
this plan because they felt that a totally impartial organization ought to administer insurance. And they believed
that workers would not receive fair treatment in the proposed tripartite program. Since Max Hirsch had advanced the
idea in the 1880's, the unions bearing his name preferred an
inter-occupational form of insurance which would provide a
broader economic base from which to draw compensation for
unemployed members. The practical problems involved with
this plan included the small total membership of these

associations, the frequent lack of professional unity and the reluctance of workers in occupations with low unemployment rates to be lumped together with those who regularly experienced a far greater incidence of idleness.

Free Unions which observed the strictest occupational separation among their members offered the highest unemployment benefits. Compensation usually amounted to between one and two Marks per day after a considerable waiting period and continued for a limited duration. Professionally oriented unions with well-paid members who had invested in prolonged training tended to provide the best subsidies while labor organizations representing unskilled, seasonal or quickly trained workers paid the least. There seemed to be a direct correlation between the level of job training and unemployment compensation in German unions, particularly during the 1890's.[89]

We might conclude this discussion of union unemployment benefits with an analysis of the travel subsidies which frequently preceded payments to non-itinerant members. A conspicuously high proportion of union subsidies was devoted to travel benefits during the 1890's. Its relative decline after the turn of the century was due to a rapid expansion of other forms of support rather than any reduction in mobility. Relocation as a remedy for unemployment was a time-honored tradition which became feasible as soon as the broad mass of workers obtained the personal and occupational freedom to move in search of jobs. As we shall see in the next section of this study, demography was a major factor in determining the extent of unemployment.

Even prior to the beginning of our period, unions such as the printers offered members the opportunity to change their residence and place of employment by subsidizing travel. The instability of employment relationships which came with rapid industrialization necessitated mobility for industrial workers as well as craftsmen. Neither Wanderlust nor a desire for professional and social advancement but material need and lack of work provided the primary incentives to relocate during the first half of our period. Impending starvation in the wake of non-existent job opportunities and insufficient savings induced many union members to accept travel subsidies as a means of entering more hospitable, less crowded labor markets. As a recruiting device, travel funds were definitely more appealing to the single, youthful, and adventuresome worker who did not reject mobility as an alternative to idleness.[90]

A FREE LABOR FORCE: MOBILITY AND UNEMPLOYMENT

One of the major determinants of unemployment was the supply of labor, which was a function of demographic shifts and population distribution. The number of would-be workers relative to the number of available jobs was a primary factor in establishing the prevailing rate of unemployment in any given labor market. Responsiveness of workers to the demand for their services was dependent on the effective transmission of information through institutional mechanisms such as labor exchanges and less structured channels which included word of mouth.

Assuming that employment information was available, two crucial innovations of nineteenth-century social legislation facilitated the free, mass movement of labor. The Bauernbefreiung and the Gewerbefreiheit laws were essential preconditions for geographical and occupational mobility on the scale necessary for sustained industrial development. A free labor force simultaneously paved the way for mobility and unemployment. Both were increasingly prevalent among urban workers who rented rather than owned their places of residence and depended upon continuous employment for their hand-to-mouth subsistence.[91] Cut off from the kind of support network available to agricultural laborers and craftsmen under the old guild systems, the propertyless urban proletariat was uniquely vulnerable to unemployment. At the same time, however, the urban industrial laborer, by virtue of his lack of roots, was less restricted from moving to resolve his economic dilemma.

Along with the occupational and geographical impediments to mobility which were legislated out of existence prior to our period, physical barriers began to disappear after the coming of the railroad. During the years of construction, railroads provided an invaluable source of employment for itinerants who would otherwise have been idle. Displaced workers ranging from handloom weavers to rural day-laborers, apprentices and urban idlers were hired to build the German railways.[92] During our period, however, the rail network was virtually complete and the transportation industry filled a more important and far-reaching need of the unemployed. No longer a source of jobs for transients, railroads offered a means of physical mobility. This in turn opened up the exploration of new labor markets as an alternative to immobile idleness. Recognizing the potential of railroads in this area, German authorities in the southern and eastern provinces actually requested restrictions on mobility to prevent their districts from being overrun by train-hopping itinerants looking for jobs.[93]

In addition to the physical barriers to mobility, there were numerous sources of friction which arose in connection with employment changes. The legal restrictions which were eliminated with the introduction of Gewerbe-freiheit by no means guaranteed smooth transitions between jobs. The feasibility of transferring or substituting skills had to be dealt with on an individual basis each time a person made occupational decisions. Employers' flexibility in terms of minimum requirements were limited by the type of product being made, the manufacturing process and the capital involved. Technological sophistication, mechanization and long periods of training tended to minimize the potential for substitution of alternate experience in positions which required highly specific skills. As these factors impinged with increased frequency on the German labor market, unemployment caused by a mismatching of employers' needs with employees' abilities became chronic in certain sectors.

Fortunately, however, there were economic forces working simultaneously to reduce the impact of mismatched opportunities. These included conditions which enabled workers to adapt with greater speed to the structural changes affecting the labor market during our period. We have already alluded to the improved opportunities for geographic mobility afforded by the railroads. There were also more educational options providing new skills for those whose training had become obsolete. Another factor which worked as a sort of safety valve on unemployment was the process of entry into and exit from the work force.[94] In most theoretical models, both during our period and later, mobility of labor was seen as a primary corrective to unemployment.[95] Every effort to minimize the cost, time and lack of information which were deterrents to effective utilization of this weapon against unemployment worked to the advantage of the German labor force.

In terms of looking at the persons who actually availed themselves of the opportunities afforded by mobility, one salient feature stands out. Unmarried laborers consistently outnumbered heads of households among those who were prepared to uproot themselves and move in search of jobs.[96] Despite the understandable hesitancy of married men with family responsibilities, contemporary estimates indicated that about five million non-agricultural workers changed positions annually and in the process experienced brief intervals of unemployment.[97] An average annual turnover of 74,000 jobs in Stuttgart[98] alone was estimated and figures from the Berlin chemical and metal industries during the early 1890's suggest that the tenure of employment in the same job was frequently less than a year.[99]

Granting the theoretical benefits of mobility as an alternative to unemployment, there were drawbacks which made workers hesitant to move if viable options were available. The cost of relocating was one deterrent. Even if the travel expenses were covered by union or public subsidies, setting up a new residence was seldom a cost-free proposition. The fact that movement did not necessarily guarantee employment was an additional disincentive. Several protracted stints of job hunting might leave the seeker unemployed and even more destitute after his fruitless excursion. For seasonal workers without alternate job skills, travel was not likely to eliminate idleness and they accounted for a large contingent of the unemployed. To put matters very simply but in terms which must have seemed very real to the individuals involved, it was frequently a question of whether to leave a familiar environment for an unknown one. The latter choice was full of uncertain opportunities and risks; the former offered whatever comforts home, family and stability held for the unemployed.

One crucial point needs to be restated in this context. The only public unemployment relief which existed during our period was contingent upon residence of some duration. While local authorities believed this condition was essential to protect them from the onus of supporting hordes of alien freeloaders, residence requirements were also a built-in disincentive to leave saturated labor markets. Potential loss of benefits must have made workers hesitate before resorting to movement as an alternative to idleness. For those fortunate few who belonged to unions, travel benefits became increasingly available along with unemployment funds which rarely had to be sacrificed for mobility since national labor organizations made transfers reasonably routine.

Population Aggregates

In addition to mobility which affected population distribution, the aggregate number of workers in the labor market exercised a profound influence on unemployment levels. Before looking more closely at specific mobility patterns which affected the unemployment situation in Germany, we might consider aggregate population changes which impacted the industrial labor market. At the time of unification, the <u>Reich</u> populace was slightly more than 41,000,000. Four decades later, in 1910, the population had expanded to almost 65,000,000, having experienced an annual growth rate of 1.18%. The number of German residents increased by 26,000,000 between 1871 and 1913 and the labor market had to absorb the impact or suffer unemployment. This population growth, unlike that after 1913, was "largely independent of area changes".[100] Rather than attributing aggregate population gains to higher birth rates, contemporaries tended to explain the expansion in terms of lower mortality rates.[101] Although birth rates actually declined, mortality rates dropped even more rapidly between 1870 and 1910.[102] The declining death rates have been attributed to higher income levels, and the attendant opportunities for better housing, safer working conditions plus greater expenditures for health and hygiene.

In addition to birth and death rates, another factor which had a decisive impact on demographic change was migration. This self-adjusting mechanism, enabling the working population to respond to demand in the labor market, exercised a profound influence on unemployment levels in Germany. Figures compiled by W.G. Hoffmann on the years between 1817 and 1959 show that the largest single loss over the course of almost one and one-half centuries was recorded during the 1880's when emigration swelled. The same data indicates that a net gain resulted from migration between 1898 and 1907--the first time a positive figure had occurred since the 1830's.[103]

Another important factor in determining the impact of population on the labor market was age. Throughout our period, approximately 62% of the German people were between 14 and 65 years old.[104] They were therefore at least theoretically of working age. After 1873 there were a number of factors tending to raise the average age at which workers entered the labor force. Restrictions on child labor, increasingly lengthy compulsory schooling and expanding educational opportunities all worked to defer entrance into the industrial labor market. Health-related factors came into play with regard to retirement age which also affected the proportion of the overall population holding jobs. W. G. Hoffmann has estimated that between 43% and 44% of the German people were employed from 1850 to 1880. During the years between 1880 and 1914, that percentage expanded to 46 out of every 100 persons working, a proportion not again sustained until the economic miracle of the 1950's. Significantly, while population expanded an average of one percent per year between 1850 and 1913, the number of employed persons grew at an annual rate of 1.2%. According to Hoffmann: "Die Differenz der beiden Zuwachs-raten von 0.1% ist damit der Erhoehung der Erwerbsquote zuzurechnen."[105] The German economy during our period was called upon to employ a growing percentage of an expanding population.

Overseas Migration

Emigration played an important but variable role in determining the level of industrial unemployment in Germany between 1873 and 1913. By diminishing the number of potential wage earners in a given market, it placed a ceiling on unemployment. When the prospect of finding work in a particular locale dwindled, people were free to move elsewhere in search of jobs. And, in fact, the German labor force opted for physical mobility over idleness in record numbers during our period. We shall consider the impact of internal migration presently but first we must look at the aggregate results of emigration. As John Garraty points out in Unemployment in History, each person who emigrated either left behind a job for somebody else or if they were without work reduced the number of Germany's unemployed by one.[106] Although somewhat simplistic, this formula helps us appreciate the crucial difference which emigration made in unemployment levels, especially during the interval between 1880 and 1893.

Emigration figures suggest that departures from the Reich were substantial during 1872 and 1873 but dropped off sharply when the crash occurred and remained low until the end of the decade. Despite the severe economic conditions and the probable existence of substantial pockets of unemployment, only about 32,000 persons left Germany each year between 1874 and 1879. An astonishing increase in emigration occurred between 1880 and 1884 when an estimated 173,000 persons per year left the country. The annual average abated to around 100,000 between 1885 and 1889 and picked up again with the third major economic recession which was in full swing between 1890 and 1893.[107] More than 220,000 residents left the Reich in 1881 and a total of 1,400,000 emigres departed over the course of the 1880-89 decade. The following data from the 1904 edition of the statistical yearbook of the Reich suggests the contours of emigration.[108]

Overseas Emigration from Germany 1884-1903

Year	Number	% of Population
1884	149,065	3.22
1885	110,119	2.36
1886	83,225	1.77
1887	104,787	2.20
1888	103,951	2.16
1889	96,070	1.97
1890	97,103	1.97
1891	120,089	2.41
1892	116,339	2.31
1893	87,677	1.73
1894	40,964	0.80
1895	37,498	0.72
1896	33,824	0.64
1897	24,631	0.46
1898	22,221	0.41
1899	24,323	0.44

If these individuals had remained in Germany, continued to occupy jobs, to reproduce, or to require public relief because they couldn't find work, they would have exercised a profound influence on unemployment levels. This would have been particularly evident during the recessions between 1882 and 1886 and in the early 1890's.

The years prior to our period had also witnessed a significant exodus with an estimated 1,000,000 Germans emigrating during the decade after 1864. It is not unreasonable to postulate that the recession which began in 1873 would have been far worse in terms of unemployment if a million persons had failed to leave the country. Many of those who emigrated between 1871 and 1873 came from non-industrial areas--39% from the Northeast, 25% from the South and 15% from the Northwestern regions of Schleswig-Holstein, Hannover and Oldenburg. Agrarian conditions had a far greater impact on emigration during the early Seventies as evidenced by the geographical origins of the overwhelming majority of participants. Not a single major highly industrialized province was listed among the regions contributing most heavily to emigration during this phase.

The years between 1875 and 1879 resembled the early 1840's in terms of the levels of emigration, with a total of about 143,000 going overseas. Substantial increases between 1880 and 1893 resulted in the departure of 1,800,000 Germans, with about a third leaving between 1881 and 1883 and 100,000 going abroad annually for the next decade. The following economic reasons have been suggested for this mass exodus.[109]

> Zwar wirkten sich weniger akute Notlagen (push-Effekt) aus, zumal durch die Ausweitung des Arbeitsplatzange-bots im sich beschleunigenden Industrialisierungs-

> prozess die relative Ueberbevolkerung weitgehend
> abgebaut war, aber agrarische Bevoelkerungsueber-
> schuesse folgten eher der Chance bauerlicher Siedlung
> in Uebersee (pull-Effekt) als dem Angebot industrieller
> Arbeit in Deutschland.

After 1895 with the termination of free land grants by the American government and with the overall improvement in the German economy, overseas emigration fell to an annual rate of about 27,000. During the entire period between 1895 and 1913, only slightly in excess of half a million persons left the Reich. Many of these moves were motivated by a speculative search for improved business opportunities.

Certain demographic and social distinctions among the waves of German emigration had a pronounced influence on the extent to which departures impacted unemployment. Prior to the mid-1860's, for example, entire families moved and many of these came from the class of independent peasants and artisans. The second phase of emigration which is most important from our vantage point lasted until 1895 and contained a growing contingent of single individuals. Emigrants during this period were drawn from lower social origins--sub-peasant groups of agrarian day-laborers and Insten plus dependent members of the lower middle class. After the turn of the century, single persons, including unmarried women and industrial workers, were even more strongly represented among emigres. As a general rule, the ratio of three men to two women remained fairly typical of those who left the country.

The ages of those migrating naturally underwent some changes as the proportion of families declined and single individuals increased. Between 1884 and 1890 about a quarter of the emigres were less than 14 years old but between 1901 and 1910 only one in five was that young. During the same period, the percentage of 14 to 21 year olds sank from 21% to 19%. At the opposite end of the chronological spectrum, those in excess of 50 years represented 6% of all emigres between 1884 and 1890 and 5% between 1901 and 1910. This data suggests that the percentage of working age adults was expanding and that there was an increasingly close correlation between emigration and reductions in unemployment levels.

It is of course doubtful whether each individual who emigrated actually reduced the number of unemployed by one. This notion ignores the fact that every person has a dual economic function--workers acted as consumers as well as producers. It is fair to assume that those who left diminished the demand for many other commodities besides jobs. Nevertheless, it is probably true that overseas migration provided a welcome alternative to severe unemployment in Germany during the 1880's and first half of the Nineties. By easing the pressure of sheer numbers in the labor market, it went far to ameliorate what might have been acute work shortages. Exporting many of its actual and potential cases of unemployment, Germany was able to contain the problem and defer the formulation of policies designed to root out its causes.

As a footnote to this discussion of emigration, mention should be made of the reverse process--namely, the immigration of foreigners into Germany. While the largest contingent of German emigres--more than 5,000,000 between 1820 and 1910-went to the United States, the overwhelming majority of foreigners in the Reich came from European countries or their colonies. A sprinkling of North and South Americans plus a handful of Asians and Africans accounted for negligible percentages--all of them together totaling about 2% of non-German residents. Between 1900 and 1910, the number of foreign persons living in the Reich increased from approximately 780,000 to about 1,260,000. As we have indicated, they were openly resented for taking jobs away from citizens and discriminated against whenever possible in administering unemployment relief.

Internal Migrations, Regional Variations and Population Distribution

Although emigration abroad declined markedly after 1893 and Germans never duplicated the exodus of the preceding decade, the internal migration which had begun simultaneously persisted throughout our period. The domestic resettlement which occurred between 1873 and 1913 constituted one of the greatest mass movements in German history.[110] To lend some perspective to the situation, it is worth citing the 1907 census which indicated that 48% of the population resided in a community other than their birthplace. Some 15,000,000 persons or three times the number of emigrants had crossed state and provincial borders in search of new homes between 1860 and 1914. Estimates suggest that by the end of our period every second citizen had participated in some phase of the massive relocation process which accompanied industrialization.

Mobility enabled the labor force to maximize its opportunities, abandoning areas of slow growth for more vital economic climates. Prior to 1880, internal migration had typically been confined to short moves between adjacent districts. After the 1870's, however, new patterns began to evolve with migrants traveling longer distances, most frequently from east to west. During the last two decades of the nineteenth century, more than 1.3 million persons migrated from the eastern provinces to other parts of the Reich. The result was a severe agricultural labor shortage in many East Elbian districts, with the areas dominated by large landholdings suffering the most. As one might anticipate, both the productivity of the region and the number of independent landholdings tended to be negatively correlated with emigration. This process continued after the turn of the century, although the rate of relocation subsided somewhat. The primary beneficiaries of migration in terms of expanded labor supplies and local markets were Berlin and the surrounding area of Brandenburg plus the western industrial districts of the Rhineland and Westphalia. Since the rate of economic expansion was not always rapid enough to permit the immediate absorption of numerous new arrivals, the public began to see unemployment, urbanization and industrial development as parts of the same process.

The individuals who resorted to internal migration were typically single, young, landless agrarian laborers of both sexes. Males frequently moved from positions as artisans' assistants into mining or manufacturing jobs. Females often ended up in domestic service in large industrial cities[111] on a temporary basis until they found husbands and then withdrew from the labor force to raise children. Migration affected the demography of areas involved as contributors and recipients of mobile populations. Both in terms of the proportion of working age persons and the ratio between the sexes, significant variations occurred. While 24.8% of the Reich populace consisted of males between 16 and 30 years of age in 1900, 26.3% of residents in the Rhineland and Westphalia but only 21.7% of the people in the northeastern Prussian provinces fell into this category. Men were slightly more mobile than women with seven males migrating for every five females. As a result, significant regional variations in population distribution occurred. For every 100 men, there were 103 women in Germany as a whole, but there were 107 women in the northeast and only 97 in the western part of the country.[112] The percentage of people in the work force was considerably higher among those who migrated than among stationary residents. Jobs in both the primary and secondary sectors were over-represented among occupations obtained by migrants, a disproportionate number of which ended up as common laborers.[113]

Most of those who came from agrarian backgrounds sought and found employment outside of the primary sector. Industrial expansion, urbanization and the lure of higher wages were all forces which tended to attract migrants in increasing numbers after 1880. The following table shows which areas gained and lost population as a result of domestic relocation during our period.[114]

Net Changes in Population Owing to Migration in
Administrative Districts of Prussia, 1849-1910,
Expressed as Percentages of Population

	(1) 1849-1866	(2)e 1867-1885	(3) 1867-1870	(4) 1871-1873	(5) 1874-1879	(6) 1876-1880	(7) 1881-1885	(8) 1886-1890	(9) 1891-1895	(10) 1895-1900	(11) 1900-1905	(12) 1905-1910
1. East Prussia	1.3	—10.4	—1.2	—1.9	—2.8	—1.7	—4.1	—6.7	—4.5	—7.3	—4.4	—4.7
2. West Prussia	0.7	—17.3	—1.9	—2.6	—4.7	—3.4	—7.0	—7.0	—4.7	—4.7	—4.3	
3. Posen	—5.0	—18.3	—2.8	—3.1	—4.8	—3.1	—6.7	—6.9	—5.1	—7.0	—4.9	—5.3
4. Brandenburg	—5.6	—6.1	—2.3	—0.1	—1.0		—2.1					1.2
a) Frankfurt	—6.5	—13.5				—2.7	—4.8	—3.9	—3.1	—5.0	—3.4	
b) Potsdam	—4.9a	—1.1				—1.0	0.2	8.5	10.7	10.0	15.0	
5. Berlin						9.0	11.7	14.1	1.0	7.8	3.7	10.5
6. Pomerania	—6.8	—22.0	—4.9	—3.6	—4.4	—2.7	—8.5	—6.1	—3.6	—3.5	—3.8	—4.4
7. Silesia	—1.3	—6.1	—1.0	—0.9	—1.8	—1.5	—2.1	—3.0	—1.8	—1.7	—1.2	(d)
8. Prussian Saxony	—4.9	—6.5				—0.9	—1.5	—1.1	—2.7	—2.4	—1.7	—3.1
9. Schleswigb						—1.9	—4.1	—0.3	—1.4	—0.2	—0.7	0.4
10. Hanoverb						—1.1	—3.0	—1.0	—0.3	—0.8	—0.8	—0.5
11. Westphalia	—3.4	1.0	0.0	1.0	0.1		—0.2					2.1
a) Münster	—6.5	—3.4				1.0	—0.4	2.4	3.4	7.7	5.6	
b) Minden	—15.9	—13.8				—2.3	—3.4	—1.7	—1.4	0.7	1.4	
c) Arnsberg	7.2	10.1	4.0	4.0	1.6	1.4	1.8	3.0	1.9	9.0	1.2	
12. Hesse-Nassaub						0.6	2.4	0.5	—0.4	0.6	1.7	0.2
13. Rhineland	0.4	—0.6	0.0	0.2	0.2		0.4					1.7
a) Koblenz	—8.1	—8.0				—0.6	—3.1	—2.9	—3.4	—2.0	—1.3	
b) Düsseldorf	8.3	7.4	2.5	2.1	1.5	0.0	1.9	3.9	1.9	8.0	4.1	
c) Cologne	—0.5	1.9				—0.1	1.2	3.2	2.2	4.4	3.1	
d) Trier	—5.8	—9.5				—2.0	—3.6	—2.1	—0.4	—0.4	0.3	
e) Aachen	0.0	—7.4				—1.9	—2.1	—2.4	—2.3	—3.0	—1.7	

The east Elbian and other agrarian provinces were the most conspicuous losers. The big winners were the Rheinish-Westphalian cities of the Ruhr, Berg and Mark; the central

German Silesian industrial districts including Saxony; the aggregation around the Capital; the north German coastal cities of the old Hanseatic League; the Saar, Lorraine and the area along the Rhine-Main river axis.

Prior to 1870, Saxony had the highest population density of any area in Germany, tied in some measure to the labor surplus which ran its impressive textile industry. During our period, however, textiles experienced sluggish growth and increased population in the Rhineland, Westphalia and urban centers like Berlin or Hamburg began to outstrip Saxony. Many of the Ruhr mining centers such as Bochum owed their existence to the astronomical population expansion associated with migration after 1880. Unfortunately, the agrarian revolution which facilitated this exodus from east to west, from countryside to city and from agriculture to industry had not gone far enough to avert acute labor shortages in many rural areas. Nor had the industrial revolution sufficiently advanced to assure all comers a smooth transition into essentially urban labor markets.

Observers including Gustav Schmoller began to question whether the process was going too far. They pointed accusing fingers at industrialization for depopulating rural areas in the east and saturating urban labor markets in the west to the point where unemployment became chronic and inevitable. The solution, it was suggested, lay in a perfectly mobile and free labor force able to move at its members' rather than its employers' discretion. By the turn of the century, substantial numbers of jobs annually traded hands on a voluntary basis. Due to personal ambition rather than compulsion, large segments of the labor force routinely changed positions because they sought better terms of employment. During prosperous periods, moves at the initiative of employees were typical and severence imposed by employers became rare exceptions.

Urbanization

One of the primary results of internal migration in the Reich was the increasingly urban nature of German industrial society. The most rapid phase of urban development coincided with the industrial expansion which characterized our period. In 1871 less than a quarter of the German people lived in communities with more than 5,000 inhabitants and less than 5% of the population resided in major cities. By 1910 almost half the nation was domiciled in municipalities with more than 5,000 residents, more than a fifth of the country lived in major cities and the highly industrialized Rhineland had about three-fourths of its population in urban settings.[115] As we noted earlier, cities such as Berlin, Halle and Krefeld experienced population growth many times the national average. At various intervals, this astonishing growth was reflected in unemployment levels. Data from the 1895 census plus other public and private sources suggests that unemployment was significantly higher in large cities than in less urban areas.

Indeed in the minds of many contemporaries, urbanization came to be seen as a cause of unemployment. They believed that maldistribution of the population in general and urbanization in particular were to blame for a significant share of Germany's unemployment. The real and imagined attractions of urban living were among the most powerful incentives for internal migration. Many attributed the much-lamented rural depopulation to the almost magical lure of big cities. In fact, the number of major cities increased sixfold during our period and the number of urban residents tripled. Migration rather than any significant alteration in birth or mortality figures accounted for the extent and rate of this expansion.

The classes which contributed most heavily to the new urban labor force were apprentice and journeyman artisans, landless peasants, agricultural workers, obsolete leftovers of cottage industries and a motley array of domestic servants. Despite the diversity of their backgrounds, the difficult conditions frequently encountered in the process of being transplanted from a rural community to an urban society gave these workers a shared sense of being outsiders. To a certain extent this alienation might have been ameliorated by the fact that the scale of enterprise in Germany remained relatively small. More than one-half of the labor force worked in shops of less than five men during the first half of our period. The urban environment, however, was far more impersonal, tending to separate the workplace and residence more completely than rural areas. Persons transplanted from the protected life of an agrarian community to the overwhelming vista of rapidly expanding industrial cities had either to defend old values or adapt abruptly to essentially alien circumstances. The institutional mechanisms designed to facilitate this transition were insufficient to buffer the new arrivals who often had problems finding adequate housing and employment.

Between the disintegration of the old guild system and the development of trade unions, these persons must have felt lost indeed. Although the apprenticeship system had once encouraged a temporary period of wandering in search of experience for many artisans, the craftsmen eventually established professional and personal roots. A new class of permanently mobile job-seekers evolved during our period, accepting employment when and where it was available and then moving on.[116] Urbanization was not only the result of this process, it was also in part the cause. Large cities provided far more diverse employment opportunities than rural labor markets, enabling workers to move from one type of occupation to another without necessarily changing residence.

In addition to more flexible job situations, big cities offered potentially higher wages which apparently induced many migrants to seek out urban employment. Tending to undervalue the hidden perquisites of rural residence and looking solely at wage rates, workers blithely exaggerated the advantages and ignored the costs of adopting an urban lifestyle. Those who arrived without specific job skills often found themselves disillusioned overnight. When industry was unable to absorb the newcomers thronging to urban centers in the hope of economic advancement, the migrants became prime candidates for induction into Germany's industrial reserve army. Although theoretically necessary for continued expansion, this labor surplus in major cities was particularly lamented by those who noted the simultaneous shortage of labor in agricultural districts.[117]

The recommended remedy was a program to encourage the resurgence of handicrafts in Prussia which was intended to stem the flow of population out of rural areas. This notion gained adherents in the early 1880's and persisted until the end of our period.[118] The problems created by maldistribution of labor due to precipitous urbanization became pronounced during interludes of severe seasonal or cyclical unemployment. Some critics advocated higher agricultural wages calculated to keep workers in rural areas and pointed out that their overabundance in urban markets would have a depressing effect on industrial wage rates.[119] As we shall see, rural depopulation frequently enabled highly mobile urban laborers to return to the countryside and wait out periods of industrial unemployment with greater ease than in the cities.

The threefold process of mobility which characterized German society during this period played an absolutely crucial role in containing the level of industrial
unemployment during successive downswings. Because labor
could move from areas of lesser economic opportunity to
districts where their services were in demand, unemployment
rarely assumed ominous proportions in any given locale.
Emigration, by reducing the total number of would-be employees during the crucial years between 1880 and 1893, contributed significantly to easing potentially severe unemployment problems. Internal migration by allowing for a
redistribution of the German population from agrarian to
industrial districts averted a surplus labor force in the
wake of an agricultural revolution and played a major role
in industrialization. Although in certain areas the process
may have gone too far and caused temporary labor shortages,
the voluntary redistribution of workers seems to have
responded rather well to the demands of a free market
system. In addition to emigration and internal migration,
the urbanization process had a great impact on supply and
demand in the labor market during our period. Associated
with the concentrated manpower needed to staff burgeoning
industries, the rapid growth of cities was frequently viewed
as a cause of unemployment rather than an alternative to
economic stagnation.

While all three forms of mobility were lamented by
various segments of the population at different times, each

played an essential role in limiting unemployment. By guaranteeing individuals the freedom to respond to the workings of an expanding industrial labor market, Germany was able to avert unemployment crises in the midst of recurring economic recessions. Given the legal right to move, the information provided by labor exchanges, and assistance in the form of union travel benefits or public half-way houses, the population distributed itself in a manner well calculated to ensure its economic survival through work. The fact that unemployment rates were not higher is impelling testimony to the popular willingness to perceive economic opportunity and then act on that perception. Perhaps more than any other single factor the individual ability to move wherever jobs were to be found explains the low levels of unemployment during our period.

With a mobile population approaching 50% of the labor force, maldistribution was rarely a cause of unemployment for very long. It is worth recalling that before passage of the so-called Freizugigkeitsgesetz on November 1, 1867, this type of flexibility would have been impossible. Just six years prior to the beginning of our period, the mobility that we are considering here would have been precluded by law. Certain elements of stability and predictability would have been substituted for the freedom of movement and opportunity which faced contemporaries between 1873 and 1913. Under such conditions, unemployment in general and its industrial component in particular would have posed a very different set of problems.

INTERNAL CONDITIONS IN THE LABOR MARKET AND UNEMPLOYMENT

Dissemination of Information in the Labor Market

One of the most telling criticisms of mobility as an antidote to unemployment was also an indictment of the effectiveness of labor exchanges. Noting the aimless nature of much wandering, observers complained that the job-seeker was not able to go from a location of previous employment to a specific destination where he had reason to believe work would be available. Instead he was forced to resort to a haphazard search, roaming from place to place and looking for jobs with no real guide to their availability. To improve the itinerant unemployed's prospect of success, a national repository of information about the labor market was essential.

Unions to a certain extent filled this need. But their labor exchanges were essentially private, limited to members and covered only a small range of employment opportunities. In addition to formal institutional mechanisms, unions provided an informal communications network enabling their people to exchange job information simply by word of mouth. This was not an insignificant advantage in situations where work was scarce and potential applicants plentiful. Indeed during recessions any competitive edge no matter how small could make a decisive difference in determining who was hired and who remained unemployed.

Here mention should also be made of labor exchanges sponsored by employers. Although relatively few in number, some provided a valuable source of information about job opportunities. But others abused their power by black-listing or seeking to impose sanctions against recalcitrant labor through the exchanges. As a corrective for abuses, a few joint employer and employee ventures in this realm proved successful and these will be discussed in Part Four. The crucial shortcoming of these private enterprises in addition to their bellicose tendencies was their lack of any interlocking network among local organizations.

While unions and entrepreneurs confined their employment efforts to specified trades, public labor exchanges were available to a much broader spectrum of job-seekers. Most public exchanges were organized on a municipal basis, although after 1898 there was a federal superstructure which linked local bodies. This potential network constituted the most important source of information about employment prospects in Germany. Reaching across assorted boundaries, it broadened the scope of the labor market, at least in theory, enabling both employers and employees to reach beyond local barriers to place the right man in the right job. Although not without shortcomings, labor exchanges proved to be the most effective institutional mechanism to prevent unemployment.

The first labor exchanges predate our period by nearly a decade, but it wasn't until the 1890's that they began to exert an important influence on the German labor market. The spread of municipal exchanges was necessary

because of the high job turnover, particularly among unskilled workers. Figures from Stuttgart in the 1890's
suggest that seven or eight months was the average tenure of
employment for most "Arbeiter und Dienstboten".[120] With
thousands of persons changing jobs on a regular basis, the
following were the traditional means of procuring a new
position: "Umschauen, Wandern und direktes Anfragen nach
Arbeit, sowie in Folge von Zeitungsinseraten oder oeffentlichen Anschlagen".[121] Few would deny that there was a need
for a public agency to augment these rather haphazard means
of seeking work. And as we have seen, even stalwart opponents of costly unemployment relief such as insurance tended
to acknowledge the wisdom of establishing labor exchanges.

The municipal authorities who undertook to involve
themselves as intermediaries between laborers needing jobs
and employers needing men occasionally went too far. One
example of their zeal was provided in Krefeld where in
September of 1894 an office which opened for two hours each
day published lists of available workers and open positions.
Since the city was to serve as a go-between anyway, it took
advantage of the opportunity to legislate all "agitatorische
Thaetigkeit" out of existence, thus settling the issue of
strikes once and for all. Despite such excesses, the
municipal exchanges served a vital need which became especially obvious during economic downswings. In 1908, for
example, an article published in Soziale Praxis noted that
the most recent recession offered German labor a distinct

advantage over earlier periods--"Die Berichterstattung ueber den Arbeitsmarkt und die Organisation der Arbeitsnachweise ist weit besser ausgebaut als vorden."[122]

Of course, the labor exchanges experienced varying degrees of success over time and geographical boundaries. The Verbandes Deutscher Arbeitsnachweise made noteworthy strides in the number of positions they filled between 1900 and 1912.[123] Filling some 350,000 vacancies in 1900, the public labor exchanges expanded their volume of successful placements by 264.7% during the first twelve years of the century. Although there were setbacks attributed to conditions in the labor market in 1908, 1909 and 1912, an impressive record of progress was recorded. Between 1900 and 1902, the number of placements expanded by 26.5%; between 1902 and 1904 by 40.2%; between 1904 and 1906 by 32.8%; between 1906 and 1908 by 8.9%; between 1908 and 1910 by 20.4%; between 1910 and 1912 by 16.2%. In 1912, almost 1.3 million persons were able to find work through public labor exchanges.[124]

Theoretically, labor exchanges were designed to limit unemployment to an irreducible minimum. Aside from the work-shy and incapacitated, all unemployment except that stemming from insufficient economic opportunity would vanish when labor exchanges functioned at 100% efficiency. At that point, every person looking for work would have knowledge of each opening and conversely, every employer would have information about all job-seekers. Frictional unemployment due to mismatching between employers and employees would be reduced to the amount of time necessary to establish physical contact between the two parties. Exchanges were never intended to create employment and they did nothing to increase the number of available jobs. They did however eliminate what we might term waste in the labor market by diminishing the number of existing jobs which remained vacant because qualified applicants knew nothing of them.

The labor market was in many ways unique--unlike other commodity markets it was influenced by a number of complicated and shifting determinants of supply as well as demand. Factors such as technological progress, increasing professional specialization, the changing composition of demand, population growth, and industrialization all had profound effects on the German labor market. Under the impact of ongoing changes, Arbeitsnachweise were viewed by contemporaries as a means of returning some semblance of order to the newly reorganized labor situation. They also provided a means of capitalizing on the unprecedented mobility of the work force, turning it into an asset in the battle against unemployment. Particular emphasis was placed on the role of the federal network of exchanges. By consolidating many separate labor pools into one large source of supply, the Verband Deutscher Arbeitsnachweise was intended to overcome geographical barriers and previous distribution problems which contributed to unemployment.

Structural Change: The Impact of Agriculture on the Industrial Labor Market

Up to this point our attention has been focused on the non-agricultural segment of the German labor force. But now it is time to assess the impact of agriculture and structural change on industrial unemployment. Just as the German economy did not operate in a vacuum, so its various components were not totally independent of each other. This fact should not be ignored despite our effort to analyze agricultural and industrial labor separately for heuristic purposes. As we noted earlier, mobility played a key role in determining the nature of the relationship between agriculture and industry. When the pool of surplus labor became too great in either sector there was a marked tendency to alleviate the problem at least temporarily through relocation.

The primary focus of most demographic studies has been to trace the flow of labor from rural agrarian districts into urban industrial centers. However, the frequently neglected movement in the opposite direction was also a significant factor in determining the rate of industrial unemployment. In this context, two salient points bear repeating. First, it is important to remember that prior to 1880 internal migration occurred across relatively short distances, often between adjacent areas. This made it possible for migrants to return to rural homes in order to wait out periods of industrial unemployment. And that was an attractive prospect because it usually entailed less expense than urban living. Both housing and food were likely to be far cheaper in the countryside, especially if established family ties existed between the recent urban transplant and his rural roots.

There was the additional potential for rural employment, even on a temporary basis. And this point brings us to a second major consideration. Particularly after 1890, there were acute labor shortages in many of Germany's agricultural areas. That made it feasible for the industrial unemployed to return to agrarian districts with some hope of finding work. The susceptibility of agriculture to seasonal unemployment posed problems in this regard as did the influx of foreigners who were admitted to ease the demand for scarce farm labor during the summer. All of these considerations must be weighed as we examine the impact of agriculture on the industrial labor market. Three basic aspects of agriculture's complex role in unemployment merit close scrutiny: Its role as a source of manpower for industry, its role as a source of jobs for industrial laborers and its role in nurturing cottage industries.

To a large extent we have already considered agriculture's contribution to the industrial labor force in the context of internal migration and urbanization. Typically, higher wages in urban industries attracted large numbers of unskilled and semi-skilled workers from agriculture during boom years such as those just prior to 1873. When economic recessions set in, these recent transplants epitomized the cliche--"last hired, first fired". Many of those laid off from industrial jobs returned to agriculture in search of more stable employment. During the economically depressed early years of our period, agricultural conditions sporadically encouraged waves of migration either abroad or to Germany's industrial cities.[125] Mechanization and increasingly intensive cultivation pulled in the same direction, requiring fewer hands to work a given acreage and causing unemployed agricultural laborers to migrate into other geographical and occupational areas. The trend was particularly noteworthy among propertyless workers who lacked an acreage which might have given them a greater personal stake in the primary sector. It is important to emphasize that rural depopulation was due to migration. An exodus more than compensated for the fact that Prussia's rural birth rates consistently outstripped urban rates during the crucial years between 1882 and 1895.

As a general rule, the percentage of the labor force engaged in agriculture was inversely proportional to population density. Agriculture was concentrated in rural areas and claimed only a small portion of the urban populace. The relative and absolute decline of agriculture over the course of our period was one of the most pronounced structural changes of the nineteenth century. Along with the corresponding expansion of German industry, it accounted for a virtual revolution in the distribution of the work force. These changes should not however obscure the fact that agriculture remained one of the largest employers in the Reich well beyond the First World War.

One important footnote in this context is the role which agriculture played in the employment of women. Increasingly sophisticated census data suggests that women formed a far higher percentage of the agrarian work force than its industrial counterpart. Whereas the typical pattern for urban women was to withdraw from the labor market at the time of their marriage, a different scenario prevailed in rural areas. In many instances, farms were run as family businesses and women played a crucial role in providing the inexpensive labor needed to make the operations economically feasible. Working alongside spouses and children, wives as well as single women formed an important contingent of the agricultural labor force. While men predominated among industrial laborers throughout our period, women made significant relative and absolute gains in agrarian employment.[126] Differences in counting female agricultural laborers among occupational census takers at various intervals make their precise progress difficult to trace. This problem was compounded by the fact that many women sporadically contributed their time and energy for little or no remuneration.

The contributions of unpaid family members were particularly crucial during recessions. Whether caused by cyclical downswings, crop failures or low prices, the typical agrarian reaction to hard times varied considerably from industry's response. While industralists frequently met crises by retrenching, cutting back employment and production, many farmers reacted by taking on additional hands and working them even harder.[127] This policy of redoubled effort brought little relief to the bulk of agricultural laborers at the end of the 1870's when declining incomes and rising costs combined to undermine their buying power.[128]

Because few agricultural producers during our period responded to recessions by reducing production or employment, and because seasonal slowdowns were an accepted part of agrarian life, rural attitudes toward unemployment were seldom sympathetic. A spokesman for agriculture at a Baden conference on unemployment in 1909 summed up agrarian attitudes by saying he had no interest in supporting insurance. Rural residents were unwilling to assume financial responsibility for urban workers and opposed the idea of federal or state subsidies for the unemployed. Unemployment relief was deemed to be the exclusive concern of cities and industries, not agricultural districts or their populations. Much like large industrialists who opposed the notion of subsidizing the working class, rural magnates, peasants and agricultural laborers resented paying for benefits in which they had no visible share or stake. Noting that unemployment was many times higher in industrial than agrarian districts, and that consecutive census figures showed a declining proportion of agricultural workers, one contemporary concluded that "...the industrialization of the Empire and the increasing danger of unemployment go hand in hand."[129] Or phrased differently "The growing danger of unemployment in Germany, as elsewhere, is in the main due to the process of industrialization".[130]

Unemployment was only one of the evils which a vocal group of anti-modern spokesmen attributed to industrialization during our period. Particularly in the 1890's there was strong public sentiment in favor of halting further industrial growth and fostering policies calculated to revitalize a rural, agrarian economy for the Reich. This reactionary view of progress, yearning for an idyllic, pastoral and largely illusory past presaged similar strains in ideology during the next century. The notion that unemployment was the result of urban, industrial growth and that its elimination lay in a return to agriculture had a distinctly anti-modern component. Along with anti-socialist sentiment this attitude toward unemployment which repeatedly surfaced during our period offered limited practical results.

In terms of unemployment, one of the most important functions of German agriculture was to provide sustenance for persons who had been laid off from jobs in other sectors of the economy. There was a general tendency for agriculture to relinquish laborers for industry during boom periods and reabsorb them during slumps.[131] Throughout our period, the primary sector played an important role in minimizing the scope and impact of urban industrial unemployment. It provided a sort of safety net by permitting recent migrants to return to family residences and wait out short intervals of idleness with greater ease in familiar country surroundings. This option was particularly important during the downswing after 1873 which conclusively demonstrated the bonds between unemployed industrial workers and their rural origins. Particularly among recently arrived unskilled workers, who were dismissed in substantial numbers, there was a marked tendency to revert to agricultural jobs.[132] Richard Herbst, one of the most influential forces behind the formation of labor exchanges summarized the situation this way:[133]

> Ausserdem erfolgt im Winter des oefteren eine Abwanderung der zur Sommerszeit in den Grossstaedten beschaeftigten Arbeiter nach der Heimat, um der Unterstutzung durch die Wohnsitzgemeinde teilhaftig zu werden und in Anbetracht des in der Provinz billigeren Lebensunterhaltes die Zeit der Beschaeftigungslosigkeit dort leichter zu ueber dauern.

In certain instances an influx of idle industrial workers compounded already high winter unemployment rates due to seasonal shutdowns in agricultural districts. But overall this method of waiting out unemployment in an area with family ties, seemed preferable to remaining near the source of previous employment. Industrial areas provided jobless workers with little more than a costly and essentially alien environment.

Using agriculture as a backup for the industrial unemployed was possible during much of our period because the average duration of idleness was short and because cases of truly chronic unemployment were rare. It is important to emphasize that this pattern of returning to the countryside as a temporary alternative to unemployment appears to have resulted from individual initiative. Personal decisions rather than a collective movement enabled rural ties to ameliorate hard times among industrial workers with agrarian origins. The feasibility of this alternative tended to decline as the geographical distance between industrial jobs and rural roots grew. It also diminished with the passage of time. As industrial workers became acclimated and more firmly entrenched in their new surroundings it was increasingly difficult for them to move back and forth between town and country. There was a span during the early years of our period when the industrial labor force was essentially fluid and one could move in and out with relative ease. But as German industry became more structured, the labor force ossified to a certain extent and mobility became more difficult.

Although most efforts to use agriculture as an alternate source of employment were the result of individual decision-making, there were a number of social critics who advocated public policies along similar lines. Noting the disparity between labor surpluses in urban industrial centers and labor shortages in rural agricultural districts, they advocated measures to redistribute the population. To cite one example, asylums for the poor began training unemployed residents as agricultural laborers so that they would not have to remain idle if positions in their chosen field were closed.[134] In another context, schemes were suggested for placing industrial operations in proximity to agrarian districts so that unemployment could be averted.

Various efforts to close the gap between industrial and agricultural laborers by essentially fusing the two groups were suggested. Small plots of land were to be given all workers and each person was to have temporary employment in both agriculture and industry. As a last resort, state-sponsored cultivation of wasteland was advocated as an occupation for the unemployed during slumps in industrial production.[135] The notion that surplus industrial labor could be diverted into agricultural jobs was popular during the 1890's when suggestions for government intervention at all levels were forthcoming.[136] But as in many realms of public policy during our period, nothing came of grandiose proposals for alleviating industrial unemployment through subsidized agriculture.

In conjunction with traditional agricultural jobs theoretically available to industry's unemployed, we should consider a number of innovations which emerged during our period to compensate for labor scarcity. Because there seemed to be a direct correlation between the size of agricultural estates and the shortage of labor, contemporaries concluded that one way to stem migration was to give workers their own plot to cultivate. As a result, in the northwest a number of day laborers were provided with two to five hectares of land which they could work for their own profit. In exchange for the right to cultivate that land, the recipient owed between 20 and 60 days of work per year.

In addition to this effort to give day laborers a vested interest in agricultural employment, the agrarian labor shortage produced a new class of itinerant field hands. Necessitated by the increasing cultivation of root crops during the last quarter of the nineteenth century, large numbers of workers were in demand during planting and harvesting seasons. Sugar beet crops attracted itinerant pickers from the poorer districts of the east into central Germany. After 1890 substantial contingents of Poles and other foreigners--many of them women--swelled the ranks of the itinerent agricultural labor force. This as we noted raised protests against foreign usurpers of German jobs during periods of high unemployment.

Despite the theoretically simplistic notion that unemployed industrial laborers could smoothly take up agricultural jobs, there were some real barriers to be overcome. Even if industrial employees were willing to swallow their pride and accept low status positions as agricultural laborers, there were deterrents. Many were physically unable to withstand the grueling toil of field work despite the best of intentions. Aside from endangering their health, some workers faced deterioration of hard-earned job skills if they substituted prolonged agricultural labor for their chosen occupation.[137]

Perhaps the area where agricultural and industrial employment overlapped most completely was in cottage industries. A report from Aachen dated April 12, 1886, suggested the kind of symbiotic relationship which characterized agriculture and domestic industries during the early stages of industrialization.[138]

> Von den Hauswebern der Sammt- und Seidenindustrie ist noch immer der grossere Theil ohne Beschaeftigung. Die Weber werden nach und nach wieder Beschaeftigung als landwirtschaftliche Arbeiter suchen muessen. Es wird das den Landwirthe nicht unerwuenscht sein, da dieselben in den Weberdistrikten ueber Mangel an Arbeitskraeften zu klagen hatten.

Cottage industries in textiles and other sectors evolved as an adjunct to seasonal occupations in agriculture. In many cases they took up the slack occasioned by cessation of outdoor work during the winter. For years expanding industries both at home and in factories had supplied income and activity for agriculture's seasonal unemployed. Later when industrialization had proceeded farther and provided the primary source of employment for many of Germany's most able, skilled and highly paid workers, the situation was reversed. Those unemployed in industry turned to look backward, recalling a day when a subsistence living had been eked out by putting together whatever combinations of agricultural and industrial jobs were available. The emphasis had shifted, with industry gaining the ascendant position, but the basic combination continued to provide an attractive alternative to idleness, social stigma and starvation. Without the cushion of agrarian jobs, the plight of the industrial unemployed would probably have been far more severe and more difficult for federal policy makers to ignore.

Cottage Industries

The occupational census data compiled during our period reflects an overall decline in the absolute and relative importance of cottage industries. Both the number of operations and individuals employed steadily diminished: In 1882 there were 386,000 operations with 476,000 workers; in 1895, 343,000 operations with 458,000 persons continued to function; by 1907, 316,000 operations with 405,000 employees remained. These aggregate figures camouflage significant variations. For example, there were precipitous drops in the number of spinners and weavers working in cottage industries which claimed a declining proportion of the employment in shrinking textile markets.

At the same time, slightly different trends were manifest in occupations previously organized along handicraft lines. There also cottage industries were losing ground to factory production although they made temporary gains as an intermediate step in the modernization process. Technology, division of labor and changing market conditions dictated the increasing concentration of industrial production. For several decades cottage industries flourished among trades such as carpentry and shoemaking which were in transition between handicraft and factory production. Ultimately, however, cottage industries in these trades also began to decline. They served as a sort of temporary half-way house for semi-skilled workers waiting to be absorbed into the new factory system.

Few contemporaries lamented the decline of the cottage system which many felt was conducive to abuse. The more easily regulated and inspected production in factories was hailed as progressive. Cottage industries frequently relied on the contributions of cheap female and child labor particularly in the old agrarian districts where such industries were family enterprises. The difference between a true cottage industry and the factory system lay in the organization of production. In the former, the laborer provided his own material, his own work place and contracted with a single entrepreneur to supply a specified product. This type of small-scale independent contractor was very different from the factory employee who worked for a wage with materials and in an environment supplied by an employer.

Cottage industries declined conspicuously in Germany's small and medium cities although they proved more tenacious in traditional agricultural areas such as the central highlands. Surprisingly, the region of greatest vitality for home production proved to be urban areas.[139] According to the 1895 census, big cities had the highest concentration of cottage industries, with small villages next and strictly rural areas trailing well behind. There were of course regional variations from the national norm. In Saxony where cottage industries flourished, medium and small towns as well as rural districts had three times more domestic production than big cities. Small Saxon villages had thriving cottage industries during the mid-1890's and similar patterns revailed in Silesia, the Thuringian states, Saxony-Weimar, Saxony-Gotha, both Schwarzburg and both Reuss districts. Among the cities with the most highly developed cottage industries were Krefeld, Elberfeld and Barmen which formed the core of such production in the lower Rhineland. At the opposite end of the spectrum, Charlottenburg, Dortmund, Braunschweig and Duesseldorf were conspicuous for the paucity of cottage industries within their boundaries in 1895.

Between 1882 and 1895 cottage industries in the central German districts where it was most highly concentrated underwent a noticeable contraction. On the periphery of this area were districts where the decline was trivial as in Breslau or Erfurt and others where gains were registered as in Oppeln or Oberfranken. Declines in cottage industries between 1882 and 1895 were evident in the lower Rhine area around Duesseldorf and Aachen as well as in the southwest with the exception of Sigmaringen and the Pfalz. Significant gains in cottage industries between 1882 and 1895 were visible in Berlin, Breslau, Munich and Stettin in the north and in the southeast district of Upper Bavaria. Losses occurred in five cities: Bremen, Strassburg, Dresden, Hannover and Danzig.

In addition to data on the geographical distribution of cottage industries, the 1895 census provides fascinating insight into the role of dependents in the labor force. According to the census, the participation of family members was greatest in the primary sector, next highest in trade or commercial ventures and lowest in industrial production. The likelihood of family involvement tended to diminish as the size of the enterprise increased. In cottage industries, family participation was the predominant pattern, and indeed striking differences in the role of women were evident.

With an increasing number of wives and daughters engaged in cottage industries producing for commercial markets rather than domestic consumption, purchasing patterns of households also changed. Women who entered the labor market as producers, devoting their time and energy to creating output sold to strangers, were increasingly forced to become commercial consumers themselves. Formerly consigned to weave, bake, sew and clean to meet their domestic needs, women began to elevate these household chores into paid jobs, doing the work for employers rather than their own families. Particularly as women moved away from cottage industries to work outside the home, they began to rely on commercial suppliers of food, clothing and convenience products. On a different but perhaps parallel scale, contemporaries faced the same kinds of changes which are occurring today as a result of increasing numbers of women in the labor force.

Whole new markets were opening up between 1873 and 1913. The extent to which households were self-contained units producing and consuming largely for their own needs diminished sharply as married women turned their attention beyond the traditional vistas of hearth and home. According to the figures for June 14, 1895, approximately a quarter of Germany's 26,000,000 females were in the labor force--the same figures indicated that two-fifths of the male population was working.[139a] An admittedly wide gap was gradually beginning to close. But these statistics included females who remained in cottage industries which kept them as physically tied to their homes as more traditional "women's work". Both married women and underage daughters continued to form a large contingent of the labor force which produced for in-house operations.

Predictably, areas with large concentrations of cottage industries reported exceptionally high proportions of dependent family members in the labor force. In districts including Berlin, Silesia and Saxony, the strong representation of cottage industries gave deceptive contours to the working population, exaggerating the number of independent producers in the 1895 census. As a general rule, the population of an area varied inversely with the number of enterprises and directly with the size of enter-

prises. Cottage industries were by their very nature
composed of numerous smaller operations, with the overwhelming majority--in excess of 98% in 1895--employing less
than five persons.

By far the strongest contingent of cottage production was devoted to textiles and clothing. These accounted
for almost four-fifths of all employment in cottage industries in 1895, with the remainder divided among wood, metal,
food and luxury items. The overall decline in cottage
industries noted earlier was attributable in large measure
to sharp drops in demand for domestic spinning and weaving.
With textiles and clothing comprising such a large part of
cottage output and with increasing competition from mechanized factory production, contractions in this sector of the
economy might have had an even greater impact on cottage
industries.

A word about the chronological distribution of
those engaged in cottage industries is perhaps in order.
The 1895 census indicated that especially high proportions
of older workers--over 60 years of age--were employed in
that capacity. The primitive nature of the production
process in most domestic enterprises lent itself to reliance
on certain marginal categories of industrial labor. The
technical simplicity and unusually light physical demands of
cottage industries enabled them to employ individuals who
were no longer fit for jobs in handicrafts or factories.
The number of single persons engaged in cottage production

was below that in other branches of industry and the number of widowed persons was significantly higher. Marital statistics also reflected the underrepresentation of young persons and the overrepresentation of older workers in cottage industries.

At this juncture we might insert a word about the role of child labor. The 1895 census revealed that approximately 215,000 children under the age of 14 worked in cottage industries. Eighty-one percent of these youngsters were between the ages of 12 and 14, and about 40,500 were less than 12 years old. Approximately two-thirds of those under 14 were engaged in agriculture, while roughly 18% or some 38,000 worked in industry. The ethics of child labor are a moot point but the obvious argument can be made that underage workers were better off in a domestic setting than in a factory.

In addition to hiring women and children, cottage industries provided a source of employment for certain types of laborers who were subject to dismissal during recessions. To cite a specific example, reports from Osnabruck in 1875 suggest that workers laid off from a cigar factory were able to avert unemployment by taking up piecework in their own homes.[140] This is just one of numerous instances in which cottage industries enabled workers unemployed in more conventional modes of production to eke out a livelihood during hard times.

By providing an alternate source of income for the unemployed, cottage industries tended to alleviate the problems associated with lay-offs. By supplying work for older persons and those just beginning their productive employment, cottage industries absorbed two groups which were particularly vulnerable to dismissal. By diverting these workers from the industrial mainstream it opened up jobs for other laborers and diminished unemployment. At the same time, cottage industries freed the most capable segment of the working population for employment in the expanding secondary sector, using marginal labor to perform simple but necessary tasks. Employing married women and children who were thereby removed from the ranks of the jobless, cottage industries provided an important source of family income. The supplementary contributions of wives, children and other dependents were crucial, particularly if the principal breadwinner were subjected to periodic intervals of unemployment. The role of cottage industries as a primary occupation has been our sole concern here but in the sections which follow we shall see that they were also an important source of secondary employment. As such they provided a buffer between the person laid off from primary employment and impoverishment.

Industrialization as a Factor in Unemployment

Despite the fact that the first half of our period has been characterized as a great depression, the economy in general and the industrial sector in particular continued to expand. The rate of economic growth slowed somewhat after 1873 relative to the preceding decades, but industrialization persisted. Throughout the years between 1873 and 1913 employment statistics testify to the vitality and resilience of German industry in the face of successive economic crises.

As we noted earlier, an expanding percentage of the population began to work for a living during our period. Whereas 44% of Germany's 35,000,000 residents were gainfully employed in 1850, 46% of 67,000,000 residents worked by 1913. During that interval the number of jobs in mining, industry and handicrafts increased 400%. In terms of the value of output, industry first surpassed agriculture during the 1890's. But in terms of employment it wasn't until the years just prior to 1913 that the secondary sector surpassed the primary sector.

The Structure of Employment in Percentages

Period	Primary (Agriculture, Forestry, Fishing)	Secondary (Industry, Handicraft, Mining)	Tertiary (Trade, Commerce, Service, Public Service)
1861/71	51	28	21
1878/79	49	29	22
1880/89	47	31	24
1890/99	41	35	24
1900/04	38	37	25
1905/09	36	38	26
1910/13	35	38	27

Employment in industry and handicrafts experienced an annual growth rate of 1.9% over the years between 1850 and 1913. During the same interval industry and handicrafts' share of

GNP doubled--from approximately one-fifth to two-fifths of the whole. But its share of employment in relation to the total population expanded by a much smaller percentage--from 24% to 35%. The impressive increase in labor productivity was largely a result of capital investment and technological advances. By 1907, approximately one-third of the working population was engaged in factory production. During the same year, about one-half of the residents of the Reich belonged to the working class and about 20,000,000 or one-third of the total population comprised the industrial labor force.[141]

In addition to changes in the relationship among broad sectors of the economy, our period witnessed alterations within each occupational category. In the case of industry and handwork, the early predominance of employment in the textile, clothing and leather industries declined precipitously. More gradual contractions occurred in other consumer goods industries. At the same time, expanding employment opportunities were available in construction, transportation, metals, mining, chemicals and public utilities. Government employment opportunities increased as did the number of jobs in trade and hotels. About halfway through our period metals replaced textiles as the largest employer among German manufacturers. Particular note should be taken of the growth rate in gas, water and electricity which increased 6.3% between 1875 and 1913. Graphic trades grew 4.4%, chemicals 3.9%, construction 3.6%, metal working 3.4% and paper 3.4%. These figures were well in excess of the industrial averages computed by W. G. Hoffmann and far in advance of such sluggish older industries as textiles which expanded a mere 0.6% during the same years.[142]

Although occupational categories are perhaps the most crucial divisions for an analysis of unemployment, note should also be taken of certain social distinctions which contemporaries considered important. On the basis of the 1895 occupational census, Gustav Schmoller assigned German families, whose number he estimated at 12 million, to one of four categories. The criteria he used were occupation, property, income and social position. The results were as follows: 250,000 families were classified as aristocratic --large landowners and entrepreneurs, members of the highest civil service, doctors, artists and rentiers. 2,750,000 families belonged to the upper middle class--middle-range landholders and entrepreneurs, most upper level civil servants, plus many members of the liberal professions. 3,750,000 families comprised the lower middle class--small peasants, hand workers, craftsmen, small shopkeepers, lower civil servants, foremen, better paid members of the labor force. Finally, 5,250,000 families formed the lower class, basically wage laborers and lower level clerks, poorer craftsmen and small peasants. Despite this four-part division, Schmoller recognized the increasing danger of polarization posed by industrialization--a wide gulf separated the independent, propertied capitalists from the dependent, propertyless proletariat.

In addition to occupational and social changes in the wake of industrial development, important alterations in the size of individual units of production affected the labor market. As a general rule, the size of enterprises was steadily expanding during our period. In 1875, 64% of 18,600,000 workers were employed in operations with a maximum of five persons. During the next 30 years, the percentage was cut in half and by 1907, less than a third of the labor force worked in small businesses. Some industries like mining were organized in large units from the beginning of our period when more than 90% of the labor force already worked in enterprises employing in excess of 50 men. In contrast to mining, other industries and handicrafts continued to have decentralized organizations--with almost 90% of the businesses employing less than five men as late as 1907. While the number of small businesses in industries and handicrafts decreased only slightly during our period, the decline in terms of persons employed was precipitous. There was a steady shift in employment away from small operations to medium firms with 6 to 50 employees and even more notably toward large firms which employed more than 50 persons.[143] Between 1882 and 1895, the average size of all industrial enterprises increased from 2.6 to 3.7 persons. The depression years were not conspicuous, however, for any

441

increase in the size of small shops among traditional urban handicraft occupations.

Perhaps the most outstanding feature of the so-called Great Depression was the precipitous drop in prices particularly during its first phase between 1873 and 1879. Deflation had a decided impact on the size of firms and the ability of small producers to compete with large-scale entrepreneurs. In general, larger firms had greater flexibility, were more competitive and better able to withstand falling prices. There were in addition structural changes which tended to eclipse the role of small operators and thrust large enterprises into the forefront of industrial production. With the decline of the consumer goods industry and the increasing importance of heavy industry after 1873, the large industrial producer took on a new prominence. Protective tariffs, government contacts, domestic markets, sources of raw materials, cartelization plus an immensely powerful leadership elite worked to give heavy industry a dominant role in the German economy. Small firms diminished in importance as a result of the depression, the decline of consumer goods industries, the ascent of heavy industry and the structure of recently legislated tariffs.[144]

The alliance between big agriculture and big business which formed the basis for Bismarck's new political coalition in 1879 also consolidated the role of the German upper middle class as pillars of the established order.

Rather than working as a force for social or political change to parallel industrialization, they adopted the posture of the agrarian elite and allied themselves with the forces of anti-modernism. As a group they consistently opposed federally funded unemployment relief and vociferously denounced the expenditures associated with other forms of social insurance. This was their attitude despite their outspoken fear of socialism and revolution in the wake of widespread labor discontent associated with unemployment.

A great deal has been written about the concentration of German industry during the late nineteenth century. General discussions of cartelization and syndicates, state monopoly capitalism, organized capitalism, and protective collectivism have proliferated during recent years. Faced with falling prices in the 1870's, many of the larger heavy industrialists moved to consolidate their positions by banding together to control production and price levels through monopolistic organizations. Although cartels antedated the crash of 1873, the ensuing crises accelerated the consolidation process, encouraged the emergence of a collectivist mentality and heightened the agitation for government intervention in the economy.

An alliance among financial, industrial and government interests was established to combat the effects of deflation and the Great Depression. The consolidation process in heavily industrialized areas like the Rhineland or Westphalia tended to bring increasing numbers of em-

ployees into a diminishing number of rapidly growing enterprises. Concentration in mining emerged along with price
cartels in the cement and chemical industries. Syndicates
also formed to control iron and coal production. A movement
which began as a defensive response to falling prices in the
1870's came to full fruition in the 1890's. It flourished
long after the economic conditions which originally justified its existence had dissipated.

The Ruhr enterpreneurs who devised cartels and
syndicates as mechanisms for price control viewed them as a
positive response to cyclical fluctuations. They considered
price stability as a means of restoring some semblance of
order to an essentially chaotic marketplace. And by identifying their own needs with those of the economy, industrialists moved ahead self-righteously convinced that they were
acting in the national interest. Reports to Berlin during
the mid-1880's reflect the popular acceptance of this
posture along with the mistaken belief that the collective
approach would persist only as long as the crisis.

Unlike the temporary alliance between rye and iron
which split apart when competing economic interests dictated
divergent paths for agriculture and industry, many organizations of major producers within single sectors endured.
Some were powerful enough to control production, prices and
to a certain extent employment within large segments of the
economy. To the extent that cartels and syndicates thrived
beyond the mid-Nineties, their continued operation was in

the economic interest of their participants.[145] One contemporary view of the impact of cartels on the labor force and unemployment was voiced by Karl Oldenburg in 1895:[146]

> Man wuerde z.B, einen grossen Arbeitgeber, der seinem Personal dauernde Beschaeftigung sichert und, wie dies schon jetzt vorkommt, bei Arbeitsstockung doch einen Teil des Lohnes weiterzahlt, etwa in der Benutzung des Arbeitsnachweises freier Stellen, andererseits zur Arbeitslosenkasse den einzelnen Arbeitgeber nach dem Masse der von ihm jaehrlich vorgenommenen Personalentlassungen heranziehen. Der weiter unten zu erwaehnenden Anonymus hebt derartiges mit Recht hervor. Bei ganz grossen Arbeitgebern und namentlich bei kartellierten Industriezweigen wuerde aus einer privaten Fuersorge der bezeichneten Art von selbst eine Art Versicherung (Selbstversicherung) gegen Arbeitslosigkeit werden. Ein dringendes Beduerfnis bleibt dagegen die foermliche Versicherung bei der Kleinindustrie.

While industrial conglomerates generally opposed government unemployment benefits, they were in a better position than most individual producers to protect their employees from the vicissitudes of economic fluctuations. Through labor exchanges, unemployment funds, and stockpiling inventories, large employers had greater latitude than small businessmen in devising alternatives to lay-offs and preserving prized caches of skilled labor. Despite the supposedly impersonal nature of large-scale operations, many major industrialists developed a combination of huge resources and paternalistic attitudes which enabled them to infuse an element of stability into their employment policies. Small producers could rarely afford to match these options.

As we shall see, despite theoretical conjectures about an era of organized capitalism, it was on the microeconomic level that daily decisions about hiring and firing continued to be made. The most effective practical means for combating unemployment were worked out on an individual basis by single laborers and employers responding to the needs of the moment. In a negative way, however, the organization of industry had a powerful effect on attitudes toward unemployment. Major industrialists used their joint influence along with agricultural interests to lobby against insurance. Their collective efforts must be seen as a contributory factor in the federal government's failure to cope with unemployment on a policy level. Industrial interest groups worked together to contain unemployment, to downplay its dimensions, and to fan the fears of those who associated loss of work with socialist revolutions. In an age of organized capitalism,[147] decentralized entrepreneurial decisions free of government intervention were the means clearly favored by industrial magnates who addressed themselves to the problems of unemployment.

Although we have discussed industrial development as a whole, it was hardly a monolithic process. Shifts in employment within various sectors proceeded at different rates. For the broad category of manufacturing, mining and building trades, the labor force expanded by more than two-thirds between the census years of 1882 and 1907. While this was far more impressive than agriculture in relative terms, it lagged well behind the phenomenal expansion of the tertiary sector during the same period. The breakdown within the industrial sector was as follows:[148]

Employment in Major Manufacturing Industries, Mining, and Transportation, Selected Years, 1882-1939

Year	Mining	Stone and Clay	Metal-working	Chemicals	Building	Textiles	Clothing	Leather	Foods and Tobacco	Wood	Paper and Products	Printing	Railroads	Shipping	Total
						NUMBER (thousands)									
1882	427	307	573	106	372	572	386	70	522	239	85	61	305	58	4,081
1893	528	504	902	161	854	758	499	96	717	368	124	105	415	68	6,097
1903	740	642	1,412	237	1,127	874	684	119	865	522	177	167	560	94	8,220
1913	1,047	650	2,209	327	1,458	995	862	148	1,222	601	243	231	787	125	10,905
1929	1,064	648	2,482	540	1,482	1,113	878	113	1,203	722	262	313	713	117	11,650
1939	963	744	4,326	794	2,184	1,355	972	144	1,359	762	312	336	966	133	15,350
						INDEXES (1882 = 100)									
1882	100.0	100.0	100.0	100.0	100.0	100.0	100.0	100.0	100.0	100.0	100.0	100.0	100.0	100.0	100.0
1893	123.7	164.2	157.4	151.9	229.6	132.5	129.3	137.1	137.4	154.0	145.9	172.1	136.1	117.2	149.4
1903	173.3	209.1	246.4	223.6	303.0	152.8	177.2	170.0	165.7	218.4	208.2	273.8	183.6	162.1	201.4
1913	245.2	211.7	385.5	308.5	391.9	174.0	223.3	211.4	234.1	251.5	285.9	378.7	258.0	215.5	267.2
1929	249.2	211.1	433.2	509.4	398.4	194.6	227.5	161.4	230.5	302.1	308.2	513.1	233.8	201.7	285.5
1939	225.5	242.3	755.0	749.1	587.1	236.9	251.8	205.7	260.3	318.8	367.1	551.0	316.7	229.3	376.1
						PERCENT OF TOTAL EMPLOYMENT									
1882	10.5	7.5	14.0	2.6	9.1	14.0	9.5	1.7	12.8	5.9	2.1	1.5	7.5	1.4	100.0
1893	8.7	8.3	14.8	2.6	14.0	12.4	8.2	1.6	11.8	6.0	2.0	1.7	6.8	1.1	100.0
1903	9.0	7.8	17.2	2.9	13.7	10.6	8.3	1.4	10.5	6.4	2.2	2.0	6.8	1.1	100.0
1913	9.6	6.0	20.3	3.0	13.4	9.1	7.9	1.4	11.2	5.5	2.2	2.1	7.2	1.1	100.0
1929	9.1	5.6	21.3	4.6	12.7	9.6	7.5	1.0	10.3	6.2	2.2	2.7	6.1	1.0	100.0
1939	6.3	4.8	28.2	5.2	14.2	8.8	6.3	0.9	8.9	5.0	2.0	2.2	6.3	0.9	100.0

In the preceding chart, the relative expansion of employment in the metalworking, building, chemical, and printing industries should be noted. Although they never employed more than a small percentage of the total labor force, chemicals, utilities, graphic trades and the highly concentrated electrical industries were conspicuous for expansion averaging 4% over the entire period between 1850 and 1913. The single largest contingent--about one-third--of the industrial labor force was employed in clothing and food production. If one adds those engaged in providing housing as well, approximately one-half of the entire industrial labor force during our period worked to supply the basic necessities of life as late as 1913.[149] This was true despite the sluggish growth rate in agriculture and textiles during our period.

If we look at the key position of the metal
industry which had strong forward and backward linkages, we
find a tenfold expansion in employment between 1850 and
1913. With coal and the highly concentrated mining industries on one side plus machine building and metalworking on
the other, metals lay at the very core of the capital goods
industry. Benefitting from high rates of technical progress
and increasing labor productivity, metals played a key role
in the expansion of many other related industries. It came
as close as any to a "leading sector in the increasingly
concentrated heavy industry". The high rates of capital
investment in many of these industries called for a correspondingly well-trained labor force with a high proportion
of skilled workmen.[150] An abundant labor supply due to high
birth rates and declining death rates facilitated the
expansion of employment in the capital good industries. The
incentive for greater employment in these industries has
been attributed to high levels of demand which led entrepreneurs to increase output by reinvesting profits.[151] Particularly after emigration tapered off during the early 1890's,
the working population increased rapidly enough to insure
against labor shortages and facilitate growing employment.

While expansion was occurring in the metal trades
which had accounted for a mere 10% of the industrial labor
force in 1861, lethargic growth and contraction were predominant in older industries such as textiles. Statistics
from the Zollverein in the year 1861 show an estimated 40%

of the industrial labor force in textiles. With the acceleration of factory production and the unprecedented reliance on mechanical equipment, employment in certain branches of the textile industry underwent absolute as well as relative declines. Even in the increasingly important cotton industry, for example, employment was virtually cut in half between 1850 and 1913. Declines in the linen industry and sluggish growth in the once predominant wool industry did little to brighten the outlook for employment in textiles. Mechanization played a crucial role in this sector of the German economy, rendering old skills obsolete and substituting a diminished number of newly trained personnel for hand operatives in both spinning and weaving. Particularly in the latter instance we have a stereotypical case of technological unemployment with handloom weavers unable to adapt to competition from more efficient power-driven machinery.

Although hardly a leading sector, textiles showed impressive resillience throughout our period and continued to employ a significant segment of the industrial labor force. The same was true of various handicrafts in an age of increasingly mechanized, factory-organized production. Surprisingly, handicrafts overall managed to keep pace with other industries, expanding at about the same rate as population. Admittedly, the number of small independent masters which had increased steadily from the 1840's until the beginning of our period began to decline after 1875.

However, the number of dependent employees in the handicraft industry continued to climb in the face of the Great Depression. After 1896, improved economic conditions accelerated expansion of this group even further. In the building trades which were organized along handicraft lines, four times as many people were employed in 1913 as in 1849. This should be contrasted with the fact that overall employment in the secondary sector expanded only 2.2 times during the same period. In Prussia during the middle of the nineteenth century, some 660,000 persons were employed in handicrafts. By 1895 that figure had grown to more than 1.5 million. Although industrialization during our period meant increasing concentration and mechanization, it did not preclude more traditional forms of growth. And the continued importance of employment in trades organized along handicraft lines should not be underestimated.

Before abandoning this cursory treatment of industrialization it is important to note regional as well as sectoral differences in development. Hans-Ulrich Wehler has suggested in Deutche Kaiserreich that industrialization was a regional phenomenon. Confined primarily to the Ruhr, the Saar, Saxony and Upper Silesia, it left other parts of Germany with their essentially preindustrial economies intact. Whether it makes more sense to focus on regional as opposed to national development, it is obvious that industrialization in different parts of the country proceeded at varying rates with variable results. It is also important to remember that even within highly industrialized districts such as Saxony there were pockets of intense development adjacent to backward districts. Particularly in the case of industrial unemployment one could argue that due to regional variations it made more sense to look at local rather than either regional or national labor markets.

Mobility to a certain extent negates this premise and it along with industrialization played a key role in establishing unemployment levels throughout our period. Industrialization as an ongoing process enabled the German economy to expand and absorb an increasing percentage of a growing population even during the so-called Great Depression. By creating a greater demand for labor it worked toward preventing economic stagnation and unemployment at a time of falling prices. While mobility enabled workers to move to the geographical source of need for their services, the original stimulus for employment was inherent in Germany's persistent economic growth. The kind of pauperism, starvation and unemployment which prevailed during the Hungry Forties did not recur after 1873 and the reason lay within the industrialization process itself. Providing an impetus for economic expansion, albeit at a temporarily slower rate, ongoing industrial development enabled the German labor force to weather three successive economic crises during 23 years with levels of unemployment which could either be tolerated or absorbed.

Secondary Occupations and Alternate Employment

One of the best hedges against unemployment for the individual laborer lay in holding several jobs. In the event that the worker was laid off from his primary occupation, he would have a second income to rely on. The greatest security was afforded when the two positions were in totally unrelated areas since that minimized the chance of both being eliminated simultaneously by shifting market conditions. Holding multiple jobs was not of course unique to the industrial labor force. Historically many agricultural laborers had divided their time between tilling their own small plots of land and working the larger estates of their neighbors. As we noted earlier, cottage industries provided agricultural families with an opportunity to diversify their sources of income and played an important role in German economic development.

Census data suggests that the number of persons engaged in secondary occupations declined between 1882 and 1895. It should be kept in mind that both surveys counted the number of positions in each secondary occupation and that persons holding multiple jobs were enumerated once for each place of employment. Overall, the number of secondary positions declined approximately 3.6%--by some 184,000 jobs.[151a] In the industrial and service sectors, men tended to hold independent positions as secondary occupations while women worked as dependents. Members of both sexes who chose independent secondary employment in industry also tended to be independent in their primary occupation which was most frequently agriculture. By contrast, those choosing independent agricultural jobs as secondary occupations tended to hold dependent positions in their primary employment. Among independent contractors working in cottage industries as a secondary occupation, the vast majority of men held independent primary jobs, largely agricultural, while women had dependent status.

Midway through our period in 1895, there were slightly less than five million secondary positions enumerated in the occupational census. Approximately three million secondary employees had primary employment, 200,000 were "berufslose Selbstaendige" and approximately 1.5 million were servants and dependents without primary occupations. The latter were almost overwhelmingly female-- married women and daughters assisting the head of their household by doing part-time work. In 1895 two-thirds of the secondary occupations were filled by men and one-third by women. This represented a considerable increase in the proportion of women since the 1882 ratio had been three males for each female.

Data from 1895 shows almost three-fourths of all secondary positions were in agriculture and forestry. Furthermore, secondary occupations accounted for more than 30% of all employment in the agrarian sector. Many of those whose primary and secondary employment both lay in agriculture were day laborers who supplemented their wages by working a small parcel of land for themselves on the side. Most other agricultural workers sought secondary employment in industry. By contrast, 20% of the jobs in the service sector were attributable to secondary occupations. A mere 7% of all positions in industry were due to secondary employment with cottage industries having the highest contingent--15% of the total. Only domestic and public service undercut the industrial sector in terms of the proportion between secondary and primary positions.

Of those whose primary employment was in agriculture at least 45% chose secondary occupations in agriculture as well. Between 1882 and 1895 those whose main employment was agricultural showed a diminished tendency to have multiple occupations. With the single exception of independent farmers who increasingly sought secondary employment, every other agricultural group registered significant absolute declines in the number of persons with more than one job. Agricultural laborers tended to rely on secondary work closely allied with their primary agrarian jobs. Mining, forestry and construction were popular choices as secondary fields for agricultural workers. Very few sought supplementary employment in urban jobs such as the polygraphic trades, artistic fields or insurance.

Most industrial workers who had secondary occupations chose independent agricultural employment to augment their primary income. In each of the following sectors, more than 80% of those with second jobs chose agriculture as an auxiliary pursuit: Mining and smelting, stone and earthworks, metalworking, machinery, chemicals, luminous matter, textiles, leather, wood, clothing and cleaning, construction, food supplies and household luxuries, nondescript and industrial professional personnel, commercial trades, lodging and refreshment. Of the groups with high proportions of workers choosing secondary employment in agriculture, the overwhelming majority had strong roots in small towns and rural villages. As a general rule, multiple occupations were less prevalent in major cities than in less urban areas. A disproportionately low percentage of those working in distinctly urban professions opted for agricultural jobs as secondary occupations.

Between 1882 and 1895 the number of secondary positions in agriculture declined by almost half a million. The majority of secondary positions which disappeared belonged to independent operatives--their number diminished by about twice the amount of increase among dependent agricultural workers. In view of the overall decline in agricultural population, this setback was not surprising. Among those involved with cottage industries, basket makers, carpenters, weavers, shoemakers and tobacco workers were most likely to have additional occupations.

The relative proportion of female employees in an industry was inversely proportional to its significance as a secondary field. Occupations conspicuous for the lowest level of secondary employment coincided precisely with those designated as women's areas. Clearly, most women with secondary occupations worked in a dependent rather than independent capacity--perhaps as an assistant to a spouse---in their second job. Only in the clothing and cleaning trades were women with secondary occupations working independently rather than for someone else. While the number of men with secondary occupations declined between 1882 and 1895, the number of women in both primary and secondary jobs increased. Nine out of every ten women with secondary occupations in agrarian production, industry and commerce were employed in agriculture, trade, restaurants, or pubs. If one added women employed in clothing and cleaning, food and luxury items plus textiles, they would account for 98.35% of all females with secondary occupations. As industrialization increased, so did the number of industrial workers with secondary occupations. Particularly noteworthy was the number of female servants who took jobs as laborers. The only decrease in 1895 occurred among women with primary occupations and male workers who pursued independent secondary positions in "Industrie fuer eigene Rechnung".

There were a number of areas, most notably independent agricultural production in which secondary employment was more prevalent than primary. The following occupations were among those in which independent secondary employment predominated, accounting for the designated percentage in 1895: Animal-breeding 75.2%, oil manufacturing 74.5%, wood finishing 66.9%, insurance 63.7%, distilleries 62.4%, coarse sand production 59.8%, public health care administration 54.2%, brickworks 53.4%, waterworks and mineral water processing 50.7%.[152] Approximately one-third of those who worked in agriculture and had secondary occupations chose industrial jobs as supplementary employment. Most of those from the agrarian sector who chose secondary occupations in industry and other non-agricultural areas were independent farmers.

Given this breakdown of secondary occupations, it was no surprise to find reports of industrial layoffs indicating that dismissed personnel were able to reenter the labor market almost immediately. Even during depressed periods they had the option of seeking employment as field workers, construction workers, stone breakers or factory hands. Shop clerks who were subject to periodic fluctuations in the demand for their services frequently had secondary occupations to fall back on and so did many of their wives.

Regional data on the decline of handloom weavers in three districts between 1871 and 1895 suggests that workers with secondary occupations were better able to withstand attrition in their field than those without an additional source of employment. The number of handloom weavers without secondary occupations in the districts of Reichenbach, Schweidnetz and Waldenburg decreased more than twice as much as the number with secondary positions during the first half of our period.[153] A very common pattern in the textile industry was to combine spinning or weaving in the winter with agricultural labor in the summer. There is every reason to believe that those with secondary occupations had greater flexibility. They could adapt more readily to the kind of competition which mechanization posed for handloom operatives. Secondary occupations provided the unemployed individuals and members of their families with supplementary incomes which enabled them to survive temporary layoffs or transfers to different occupations. Occasionally, secondary jobs could also become the primary focus of employment when previous opportunities disappeared.

In addition to the above-mentioned benefits, secondary work afforded an antidote for seasonal unemployment in occupations such as the building trades. Among skilled bricklayers a substantial number regularly left construction for employment in road building and forestry during the late fall and winter months. Those construction personnel most prone to seek secondary occupations included building assistants, bricklayers and carpenters. Roofers were slightly less active in secondary positions while glaziers, painters and stucco workers trailed far behind. The latter were perhaps deflected from pursuing alternate employment by the fact that they could practice their trade indoors during the winter.

Between 1882 and 1895 a decline in secondary employment occurred among construction workers overall. To a certain extent, construction itself served as a secondary occupation, accounting for 4.8% of employment in 1895 and 4.6% in 1907. Here also a decline occurred between 1882 and 1907. Of 100 workers whose primary occupation was in construction, 31.6% in 1882, 18.9% in 1895 and 17.7% in 1907 had secondary occupations. We know that in both 1895 and 1907 an overwhelming majority of those construction workers who sought secondary employment found it in agriculture. Despite decreases in secondary occupations among construction workers between 1882 and 1907, alternate employment was not an insignificant factor in seasonal occupations. In addition to improved economic circumstances during the last half of our period, the decline in secondary employment may be attributable to the previously noted tendency of construction projects to proceed year-round in urban areas.

Before terminating our discussion of secondary occupations, a word about their geographical distribution is in order. Those with primary occupations in industry and commerce who sought secondary employment found it in the agricultural sector. The following table shows the breakdown of independent persons and laborers with secondary occupations whose primary work was industrial. The ranking of regions in ascending order of secondary employment among laborers is shown in parentheses. On the average slightly more than a third of the independent industrial operatives had secondary occupations. 12% of the industrial laborers, 28.9% of the independent commercial operatives and 11% of the commercial workers pursued secondary occupations.

Unter je 100 haben Nebenerwerb

	Selbständige	Arbeiter	Selbständige	Arbeiter
	der Berufsabtheilung B		der Berufsabtheilung C	
1. Waldeck	60,35	(2) 26,95	(13) 37,22	(18) 13,35
2. Hohenzollern	55,17	(10) 19,14	(3) 51,28	(2) 28,32
3. Schaumburg-Lippe	54,89	(1) 41,65	(5) 49,11	(1) 29,59
4. Lippe	54,32	(4) 24,10	(1) 57,75	(3) 24,13
5. Oldenburg	52,87	(9) 19,19	(2) 53,72	(5) 23,34
6. Westfalen	52,04	(3) 26,67	(4) 50,53	(4) 23,91
7. Schwarzburg-Sondershausen	51,71	(5) 23,73	(6) 47,17	(8) 18,51
8. Hannover	49,07	(8) 21,05	(7) 42,82	(6) 21,95
9. Württemberg	46,81	(25) 11,75	(16) 34,70	(14) 14,32
10. Sachsen-Meiningen	46,18	(18) 14,68	(9) 40,78	(11) 15,62
11. Hessen-Nassau	45,47	(13) 17,81	(25) 31,74	(22) 11,77
12. Schwarzburg-Rudolstadt	45,04	(11) 18,94	(10) 40,41	(17) 13,65
13. Provinz Sachsen	44,71	(6) 22,10	(12) 38,01	(13) 14,65
14. Reg.-Bez. Pfalz	43,99	(20) 13,51	(8) 41,24	(7) 18,72
15. Mecklenburg-Schwerin	42,91	(12) 18,51	(11) 39,00	(10) 16,15
16. Baden	42,14	(24) 12,01	(23) 32,45	(16) 14,14
17. Reg.-Bez. Oberfranken, Mittelfranken, Unterfranken	40,72	(32) 9,64	(32) 28,43	(31) 9,69
18. Elsaß-Lothringen	40,29	(17) 14,72	(15) 34,73	(15) 14,32
19. Sachsen-Coburg-Gotha	40,01	(16) 14,73	(27) 30,79	(24) 11,38
20. Großherzogthum Hessen	39,15	(26) 10,72	(30) 30,29	(26) 11,76
21. Pommern	37,30	(23) 12,08	(24) 32,25	(25) 11,83
22. Braunschweig	37,29	(14) 16,67	(28) 30,79	(23) 11,60
23. Rheinland	37,27	(15) 16,20	(14) 35,66	(20) 13,67
24. Sachsen-Weimar	37,19	(21) 12,34	(21) 33,03	(27) 11,01
25. Anhalt	37,02	(7) 21,27	(20) 33,10	(9) 17,21
26. Schleswig-Holstein	36,06	(28) 10,35	(31) 30,03	(30) 10,13
27. Brandenburg	35,03	(22) 12,13	(26) 31,03	(19) 13,13
28. Posen	33,35	(29) 10,25	(18) 33,91	(12) 14,69
29. Ostpreußen	32,56	(33) 8,84	(22) 32,76	(32) 9,63
30. Westpreußen	32,50	(30) 10,13	(17) 33,98	(21) 11,80
31. Oberbayern, Niederbayern, Oberpfalz, Schwaben	32,09	(35) 6,04	(37) 22,91	(35) 5,39
32. Mecklenburg-Strelitz	32,03	(19) 14,12	(19) 33,53	(29) 10,15
33. Lübeck	28,17	(27) 10,63	(33) 28,35	(33) 8,90
34. Reuß jüngerer Linie	24,55	(36) 5,75	(35) 23,24	(36) 5,02
35. Schlesien	24,33	(31) 9,91	(34) 25,37	(34) 8,41
36. Sachsen-Altenburg	24,03	(34) 8,21	(29) 29,66	(28) 10,72
37. Reuß älterer Linie	22,20	(39) 3,71	(36) 23,02	(39) 2,69
38. Königreich Sachsen	16,67	(38) 4,44	(38) 18,70	(37) 4,61
39. Bremen	7,88	(37) 4,85	(39) 8,92	(38) 3,03
40. Hamburg	5,56	(40) 1,52	(40) 6,02	(40) 0,83
41. Berlin	3,61	(41) 0,94	(41) 3,93	(41) 0,69
Reichs-Durchschnitt	34,31	12,65	28,90	10,64

In the cases of independent industrialists and even more notably industrial laborers, secondary occupations abounded in districts with good access to small-scale agricultural holdings and small commercial operations. In the following areas where small-scale agricultural and commercial establishments were both plentiful, we find the highest density of secondary employment: Waldeck, Hohenzollern, Schaumburg-Lippe, Lippe, Oldenburg, Schwarzburg-Sondershausen, Wuerttemberg, Sachsen-Meiningen and Hesse-Nassau. Secondary occupations were also popular among industrial operatives where large commercial establishments predominated as in Westphalia and Hannover. Secondary employment was significantly less prevalent in regions where the economy was dominated by large-scale peasant holdings and great estates in combination with small commercial ventures. This was the pattern in Mecklenburg-Strelitz, Oberbayern, Niederbayern, Oberpfalz, Swabia, West Prussia, East Prussia, Posen, and Schleswig-Holstein. In districts where large-scale industrial and commercial ventures co-existed with large estates, we find the lowest rates of involvement in secondary occupations--in Hamburg, Bremen, Luebeck, Saxony, Saxony-Altenburg, both Reuss districts and Silesia.

The percentages of those independently pursuing secondary occupations who chose agriculture is shown by district below:

Agriculture Most Strongly Represented
As Independent Secondary Occupations

Westphalia	62.13%
Anhalt	61,07%
Saxony (Province)	59.63%
Rhineland	57.94%
Schleswig-Holstein	53.01%
Pommerania	51.14%
Brandenberg	50,49%
Hannover	49.20%
Westpreussen	48.06%
Hesse-Nassau	47.46%

Agriculture Most Weakly Represented
As Independent Secondary Occupations

Hamburg	6.58%
Berlin	8.74%
Hohenzollern	21.98%
Saxony (Kingdom)	23.77%
Oberbayern	27.50%
Oberfranken	29.70%
Bremen	29.77%
Wuerttemberg	30.37%
Baden	30.53%
Reuss juengerer Linie	30.70%
Sachsen-Altenburg	31.63%

A variety of workers sought secondary employment in industry where the density of agricultural populations made transfers to other occupations imperative. This was the case in Wuerttemberg, Baden, Hohenzollern, Oberfranken, Mittelfranken and Unterfranken. Other pockets of major secondary employment in industry occurred where strongly represented cottage enterprises afforded both the encouragement and opportunity for development. This was the pattern in Silesia, the Kingdom of Saxony, Saxon-Weimar, Saxon-Meiningen, Saxon-Altenburg, Saxon-Coburg-Gotha and both Reuss districts.

The kinds of secondary occupations which workers found in the private sector were frequently not that different from the public works projects designed to alleviate unemployment. Both generally required more physical exertion than job training because they had to match the lowest common denominator in the labor market. The existence of secondary occupations often obscured the unemployment issue. It was hard to determine when a person holding more than one job should be counted as unemployed. In order to qualify as unemployed, did an individual have to lose his primary position, his secondary job or both? The ratio between his incomes from the two positions would certainly have been a factor and there were admittedly degrees of both unemployment and underemployment. But subtle distinctions blurred neat divisions on which those administering unemployment relief typically relied.

To the extent that it's possible to generalize, we might conclude that secondary occupations were an effective alternative to total unemployment during a period of transition from agricultural to industrial production. Secondary occupations thrived in areas where smallscale operations were still economically feasible in both agrarian and commercial ventures. They were apparently not a viable option when large-scale production predominated in regional markets. Small towns and rural rather than urban settings lent themselves to secondary employment.

Economic Crises and the Impact of Overproduction

The periodically recurring economic crises associated with above average unemployment rates came to be recognized as an inherent feature of the mature capitalist marketplace. The crises during our period which contemporaries attributed to overproduction were fairly recent phenomena coinciding with the shift from local to world markets and from precisely identifiable to virtually anonymous consumers. Under the old order, producers had been able to estimate the demand for their output with reasonable precision because they were familiar with the local economy and personally acquainted with many of their customers. Skilled craftsmen frequently created custom-made articles designed to individual specifications and sold in advance of production. This was a far different type of business from that of factory owners who mass-produced articles for an indeterminate number of faceless individuals in farflung regions which they would never see. Without any concrete knowledge of their competition, independent producers could easily overestimate demand and the collective result of their individual decisions would be to flood the market with unwanted goods. Falling prices in the face of surplus commodities would force cutbacks in production, perhaps spawn a few bankruptcies and many innocent victims of unemployment.

This was the scenario which contemporaries evolved to explain economic crises--overproduction rather than underconsumption was squarely branded as the culprit. In a time before governments tried to stimulate consumer demand through manipulative tax incentives or other anti-cyclical policies, overproduction was the primary focus of analysts trying to understand unemployment and cyclical fluctuations. Indeed those such as Wehler who have written more recently about our period still discuss economic crises in terms of the overproduction inherent in industrial capitalism. The following description is instructive in this context: "die im Banne der Konjunktur, aber auch angesichts der fehlenden Transparenz des Marktes, der Immobilitaet des fixen Kapitals und der Ungewissheit langfristig wirksamer Nachfrage permanent zu Ueberinvestitionen und Krisenanfaelligkeit neigte."[154]

During our period there were a variety of explanations of economic crises which shed considerable light on the parameters of contemporary conceptualization about the industrial marketplace. In addition to proponents of simple overproduction theories, there were analysts who stressed the necessity for a precise balance between the total volume of output and the total volume of demand. Without such a delicate balance, such economic luminaries as Turgot, J.B. Say, and James Mill maintained that crises could not be averted. Another group among which Malthus and Sismondi were preeminent saw the origins of crises in the conflict among increases in wealth, population and income. A different explanation advanced by John Stuart Mill, Max Wirth and Julius Wolf focused on productive relations, attributing crises to the diminution of circulating capital. Among National Economists like Lujo Bentano other productive relations such as the distribution and consumption of available land was of primary interest. The group which included Godwin, Proudhon and Rodbertus believed crises originated in mismatching between the purchasing power of society on one side and productive resources on the other. Louis Blanc, Henry George, Adolf Wagner and Karl Marx explained crises in terms of the historical evolution of capitalism, focusing on the capitalist organization of production. Various theorists emphasized monetary, exchange or credit relationships. But the majority of Germans who wrote about unemployment attributed the underlying crises to overproduction which led to excessive supplies vis-a-vis consumer demand.

Believing that the source of economic crises and attendant increases in unemployment lay in a chain reaction consisting of overproduction, falling prices, bankruptcies plus work stoppages, contemporaries sought a solution in institutions designed to control output. During our period, this usually meant cartels, syndicates or other price-fixing oligarchic organizations which maintained prices by curtailing supplies that might otherwise glut saturated markets. In an article on unemployment published in Conrad's Jahrbuch during 1895, Georg Adler expressed the popular view that through industrial reorganization cartels could eliminate overproduction and the crises which ensued in its wake. He recognized the impracticality of forceably imposing a solution which would thwart the individual entrepreneurial spirit that lay at the very heart of German capitalism. But Adler maintained that its voluntary introduction would not occur in the foreseeable future since concentration ran contrary to prevailing national and international interests. His conclusion was that without cartels cyclical fluctuations, crises and unemployment were likely to continue well into the future.[155]

As we noted earlier, the first cartels in the Reich emerged during the 1870's in an effort to prevent falling prices by controlling production.[156] A number of East Germans have expressed great interest in these cartels which they view as the epitome of the economy's transition to "state monopoly capitalism." Nineteenth-century liberals and twentieth-century Marxists shared the notion that economic crises could be eliminated through centralized planning and control of production. Whereas liberals sought salvation in cooperation among leaders of the private sector, Marxists welcomed such collective efforts with state sanctions as a transition toward government control over the economy. Cartels were viewed by both as a means to eliminate the overproduction which ended in crises. Beyond that, however, socialist historians regarded concentration under private initiative as an intermediate stage, a higher form of capitalism and a step closer to the centrally planned, government-regulated economy they favored.

Unlike nineteenth-century capitalists who accepted crises as an inevitable byproduct of unpredictable consumer demand, Marxists argued that centralized planning and reorganization of the means of production under state ownership would eliminate crises. The fact that cartels and privately run monopolies set the stage for high prices and inordinately large profits without government sanctions did not go unnoticed by left-wing historians. They applauded cartelization as a step toward the inevitable downfall of capitalism. They also maintained that the government cooperated with entrepreneurs by erecting artificial tariff barriers to eliminate foreign competition and by sanctioning cartels which devastated non-participating domestic producers. According to their paradigm, the state, acting in the interest of an industrial elite rather than society at large, assured virtual monopolies to select groups of extremely powerful magnates.

Despite Marxist rhetoric, measures such as tariffs were intended to produce stable employment and eliminate the periodic retrenchment necessitated by recurring intervals of overproduction, falling prices and labor surpluses. The fact that crises continued to recur even in areas where production was organized along monopolistic lines led a few economists to question whether demand rather than supply factors were determinants of prosperity. Even those advocating regulation of production acknowledged that consumption remained an inherently decentralized process in the capitalist marketplace. Unfortunately, the notion that insufficient demand rather than excessive supply is the source of crises never gained widespread currency during our period.

After Marx, economic analysts recognized intermittent crises as an inherent part of the capitalist system. Because workers rarely received an adequate share of the profits from their labor, frequent slowdowns stemming from underconsumption occurred. Cutbacks in output and employment resulted at least in part from reduced consumer demand. Lay-offs plus further reductions in consumption were the results. In an escalating series of vicious circles, consumption, production and employment were reduced, driving the market progressively further into a severe slump until the downward trend bottomed out and expansion resumed. In a capitalist economy which failed to recognize the right to work, unemployment was inevitable when low wages forced workers to curtail consumption. This in turn led to surplus goods flooding the market plus cutbacks in production and subsequently diminished employment.

With increasingly international markets for various commodities, a number of external factors could also impinge on the German economy. During the early 1890's, for example, the existing crisis was attributed to a whole range of factors including poor harvests, cholera, the Panama

Canal scandal plus state bankruptcies in Argentina, Portugal and Greece. Contemporaries believed that all of these events contributed to the increase in savings and reduction in consumption which in combination with German tariff policies made domestic producers vulnerable to international pressures.

With fluctuations in demand, a number of unprofitable ventures were driven out of business during severe economic crises. Bankruptcies and take-overs were common occurrences and consolidation was frequently the only alternative to a total loss for uncompetitive small businesses. Records of the period show a number of old firms going under and new ones opening which produced divergent results in terms of unemployment. The banking industry was particularly noteworthy in this regard, with giant concerns emerging from the crises during the first half of our period. Although the crisis years were marked by deflated prices, unemployment, and limited production, the impact of the so-called Great Depression was variable. While some suffered, others such as the big "D" bankers survived and even expanded.

Just as high unemployment is frequently taken as a symptom of depression, so too is a decrease in consumption. Throughout our period the years labeled as crises tended to show declines in the rate of expansion in consumer demand and producers' output. Certain conspicuous instances of actual contraction are well known. But neither massive unemployment nor total shutdowns of major segments of German industry were forthcoming. A slower rate of growth rather than absolute retrenchment was typical of industry between 1873 and 1896. Thereafter the pace of expansion accelerated until the First World War. With a growing population and a developing economy, Germany never experienced a spiral of diminished demand, excess supplies, overproduction, or cutbacks in output and employment on a scale that approached the Depression of the 1930's.

If one put any stock in eyewitness reactions to the economic declines associated with unemployment, the obvious conclusion would be that between 1873 and 1913 contemporaries experienced a series of crises which varied in intensity. To a certain extent, the crises became progressively less severe in scope but increasingly ominous in their cumulative impact on the collective psyche. The most severe recession opened our period, lasted from 1873 until 1879 and was characterized by a dramatic deflationary trend that persisted in abated form for two decades. Although data is scant, unemployment was probably at its peak during this first slump. The Eighties were an interval of incomplete recovery, characterized by high levels of emigration which helped minimize unemployment rates between 1882 and 1886. The first half of the Nineties saw a third economic crisis which began to ebb in 1894 and gave way to rapid recovery after 1896. Although the second half of our period saw an end to the severe deflationary trend of the early years, briefer recessions recurred in 1901 and 1907. While the intensity of the setbacks steadily diminished between 1873 and 1913, they were sufficiently frequent and severe to foster an undeniable crisis mentality. A certain sense of insecurity was the result and this combined with fears of socialism lent the German unemployment situation a potentially revolutionary dimension. In the realm of job scarcity, concern was focused on the unpredictable nature of who would be affected, when, and for how long.

Wages and Prices

One of the most obvious byproducts of an overproduction crisis was a shift in the wage and price structures of German industry. If we look at work as a commodity and at wages as the prevailing price in the labor market, we can see the variable impact of supply and demand on payscales. Wages in turn were inextricably connected to the rate of unemployment. During the late 1870's, for instance, serious deflation combined with excessive production led to decreased demand in many industrial sectors. Producers responded to problems of surplus goods and falling prices by stockpiling inventories, curtailing output, dismissing employees, lowering wages or adopting some combination of these measures.

Recent studies have suggested that the only substantial decline in money wage rates during our period occurred in the first decade. Predictably, this coincided with the timespan for which evidence of significant but scattered unemployment has emerged. During subsequent crises wage rates exhibited sluggish growth, retardation or minor declines which "conformed fairly well to major cyclical changes in general business conditions."[157] Research has shown that there was a consistent time lag in the response of wage rates to "cyclical changes in business conditions." All of these facts have led to the conclusion that German wage rates exhibited a "pronounced downward rigidity."[158]

The retarded growth and contraction which accompanied economic slumps constituted the reverse side of the process set in motion during boom periods. When times were good employers frequently raised wages in an effort to attract more and better employees. The relationship between the rate of expansion of the labor supply and the tempo of industrial growth determined the impetus for wage increases. Greater employment and higher wages usually entailed heightened consumption which in turn drove up prices, production and profits. Higher prices pushed up the cost of living which led to demands for still higher wages. According to A.V. Desai, the impact on real wages "depended on the growth in the demand for consumer goods on the one hand and the opportunities for innovation and expansion in their production on the other."[159]

Real wages in German industry expanded rapidly during the Reichsgrundung period, fell markedly between 1873 and 1880, rose distinctly during the following decade and more slowly during the Nineties. Weekly wages for the country as a whole doubled between 1871 and 1913, while the average number of hours worked declined significantly. As a general rule, movement of the cost of living indices tended to parallel fluctuations in real wages. Available data suggests that wages in capital goods industries with strong linkages to railroads were most profoundly affected by cyclical changes. According to A.V. Desai, the prosperity just prior to our period was accompanied by simultaneous increases in employment, money wages and productivity. Conversely, the slump and "wage reductions after 1873 were occasioned by declines in productivity and profits and pushed through with the help of reductions in employment."[160] Although it is difficult to generalize about national trends because labor markets in the short run were limited in geographical scope, over longer periods mobility and substitution of skills "create the semblance of a national market."[161]

Among the indices traditionally associated with prosperity are full employment, plus high or rising levels of real income produced and consumed.[162] Depressions on the other hand entail idle resources including labor and low volumes of per capita production and consumption. At least in theory depressions and other periods of high unemployment are conducive to reductions in money wages. Even in the German economy, where wages during the first half of our period showed considerable downward rigidity, there were many individual employers who responded to declining demand and low prices by reducing wages. Wage reductions were often part of employers' initial response to falling prices. Among small producers whose wage rates typically lagged behind those of major enterprises, further declines encouraged employees to seek other jobs. If labor was scarce employers were generally reluctant to risk losing good men by reducing wages; on the other hand, if unemployment was high and surplus labor was available, that risk was minimized. Most workers preferred lower wages to the almost certain prospect of unemployment.

As we shall see, lower wages and fewer hours were introduced by individual entrepreneurs as an alternative to lay-offs. It is theoretically possible that if wages were allowed to fall continuously, unemployment could have been eliminated almost entirely. Of course this was not an acceptable resolution of the problem as far as German labor was concerned.[163] In fact, efforts were made to resist wage reductions wherever possible. As an alternative to falling wages, a revival of investment was the means favored to end overproduction or underconsumption crises and the attendant unemployment. This investment was to be financed by dishording or by new bank credit supplied largely through the big "D" banks which played a major role in the revival and expansion of German industry.

Although hard data is lacking, it seems reasonable to postulate that unemployment during the deflationary years of our period would have been far worse if wages had not been allowed to decline. Given the international scope of the so-called great depression, lower wages were probably a decisive factor enabling Germany to avoid truly chronic unemployment and severe cutbacks in production.[164] Despite the widespread deflation, German industry continued to expand between unification and the end of the century. Benefitting from this progress, the labor force experienced a general rise in real earnings during those years.

Average weekly earnings followed the general business cycle rising after 1871, falling until the early 1890's, then rising rather sharply and finally tapering off. According to recent estimates, real earnings were lower in 1881 than they had been ten years earlier.[165] Similarly, the plateau established in 1900 was not surpassed for more than a quarter of a century. Money wages increased during the later years of our period, but those gains were largely offset by parallel increases in the cost of living. Although prosperity had returned by 1896, the years between 1900 and 1913 witnessed a "gradual leveling off in the upward trend of weekly real earnings" occasioned by a "declining rate of production growth."[166] While changes in weekly income represented only slight advances for the average worker, shorter work weeks typically meant higher hourly wages. Much of the benefit was to be measured in terms of gains in leisure time rather than spendable income.

Wages did not always respond to economic stimuli as a single unit, and there is evidence that they varied on the basis of both sex and skill. The sparse information available on sex differentials suggests that women continued to earn less, often for the same work. To compound the injustice, females tended to make less rapid advances in earnings than their male co-workers. It has been suggested that the difference between the wage rates of skilled and unskilled workers increased during the first half of our period and lessened during the last half.[167] According to data compiled by both Gerhard Bry and Juergen Kuczynski, the wage differentials between skilled and unskilled workers ranged from 25% among cotton spinners and construction workers to 60% among coal miners in Upper Silesia. In terms of quantity, the 1907 census showed that there were an estimated 4.9 million skilled workers and 3.5 million unskilled workers in the German industrial labor force. Autobiographies suggest that frequent job changes accompanied by brief intervals of unemployment were typical for unskilled industrial laborers.[168]

Reflecting variations in the value of their output and demand for their services, the wages of workers in different branches of German industry fluctuated independently. They responded to the general business cycle with varying time lags and intensity. In looking at developments after 1873, one must keep in mind the phenomenal expansion of real wages during the preceding Reichsgrundung era. It is against this background of meteoric rises that the declines of our period have been measured and as a result they appear more drastic than would otherwise be the case. The pre-1873 expansion was stimulated largely by railroad construction and wage fluctuations were most pronounced in industries with strong linkages to rails.

The recession during the last half of the 1870's was severe enough to cause wage decreases in all investment goods industries except machines. In the textile and printing trades this interval produced stagnation and a barely perceptible increase in real wages which persisted into the 1880's. In other investment goods industries, the early Eighties were years of renewed expansion in real wages, followed by a more gradual rise during the next decade. In the highly organized printing trades, money wages remained stable between 1873 and 1875, declined slightly during 1876 and 1877, fell somewhat more rapidly in 1878 and then tapered off until 1886 when they returned to the level achieved at the beginning of our period. In the building trades which were more immediately responsive to changes in the business cycle, the decline between 1873 and 1879 was steady and cumulatively much more significant. While printers' money wages declined about 6%, construction workers lost almost 20% of their earnings. Even more extreme was the situation among coal miners whose annual earnings dropped from a remarkable average high of 1172 Marks in 1873 to 593 Marks in 1878. Steelworkers' money earnings fell 26% between 1874 and 1880 while machinery manufacturers sustained relatively good earnings during most years. Among those working to make machines, earnings continued to rise until 1875 and fell off sharply rather late--between 1884 and 1886. In the textile industry variations were slight--between 1873 and 1886, the lowest money wages were recorded during the first year, the highest during 1876. The next chart provides a more detailed look at annual earnings in major sectors during the later years of our period when gradual but steady expansion of wages was characteristic of German industry as a whole. The single exception which occurred during 1892 when unemployment rose significantly and wages declined slightly should be noted in this context.[169]

Annual Earnings in Major Industries, 1888 to 1913
(1913 = 100)

Year (1)	Mining (2)	Stone and Clay (3)	Metal-working (4)	Chemicals, Gas, Water (5)	Building (6)	Textiles (7)	Clothing (8)	Leather (9)	Food and Tobacco (10)	Wood (11)	Paper and Products (12)	Printing (13)	Railroad (14)	Shipping (15)	Total (16)
1888	52.2	60.4	59.7	64.4	59.9	62.8	58.9	57.4	63.2	65.0	62.4	84.8	63.7	52.5	58.9
1889	55.4	62.1	61.2	65.3	62.2	63.6	61.2	57.4	64.3	64.7	63.6	88.8	65.7	59.7	60.7
1890	60.4	60.4	62.1	67.5	62.2	64.7	61.7	59.0	65.6	65.8	65.7	93.9	68.1	60.3	61.5
1891	61.9	62.6	63.1	68.5	62.5	65.4	64.4	60.0	67.4	67.8	66.9	85.3	69.0	61.8	63.5
1892	59.9	62.1	62.2	68.9	62.6	65.6	64.6	60.2	67.7	66.9	65.6	84.9	70.5	61.8	63.2
1893	58.9	61.8	62.7	69.2	61.9	68.2	66.4	59.8	68.4	66.8	64.4	82.7	71.5	62.4	63.4
1894	59.4	62.2	63.0	68.8	62.1	68.3	65.9	60.7	68.2	67.2	64.4	79.5	71.8	61.7	63.6
1895	59.9	61.8	63.5	69.9	62.9	68.9	69.3	62.9	67.9	66.1	66.9	80.9	72.1	59.1	64.0
1896	62.6	61.5	65.2	70.7	65.0	70.2	70.0	62.3	70.7	68.5	69.2	77.6	73.2	60.1	65.7
1897	65.5	65.0	65.8	71.9	66.1	71.4	71.4	63.7	72.3	70.7	71.8	83.3	74.6	60.9	67.4
1898	66.3	68.1	69.1	73.3	69.1	72.6	71.3	67.2	73.5	72.5	73.7	87.6	71.3	62.1	69.1
1899	69.7	69.5	70.1	73.6	71.0	74.1	71.3	67.7	75.8	74.9	73.7	85.8	74.0	64.0	70.9
1900	74.2	71.0	71.3	75.4	74.1	75.6	72.0	69.6	77.4	75.7	75.4	88.2	75.1	67.0	72.9
1901	71.3	72.9	69.9	75.4	73.3	76.9	73.6	71.5	78.4	77.8	75.4	83.3	75.9	63.8	73.1
1902	69.8	74.4	72.7	75.4	74.1	78.1	74.9	73.0	75.8	78.8	76.2	85.4	76.6	75.3	73.6
1903	72.5	75.6	74.2	78.0	74.9	78.9	79.5	75.3	77.6	80.2	78.4	83.3	77.3	77.9	75.2
1904	73.5	79.5	76.2	78.9	76.5	80.3	82.4	76.3	77.6	80.2	80.0	84.1	78.5	83.2	77.0
1905	74.6	81.8	78.6	80.5	79.0	81.0	83.9	78.6	79.0	82.7	81.8	85.3	79.6	84.2	78.9
1906	81.5	85.1	81.5	84.1	84.0	85.0	87.3	83.6	81.6	86.5	84.9	87.5	82.1	85.4	83.2
1907	88.7	88.9	87.3	85.5	87.1	85.8	91.8	87.2	86.1	88.8	88.3	93.1	85.5	87.1	87.2
1908	88.2	89.2	87.6	87.3	86.5	87.0	92.1	88.9	87.3	89.3	89.5	93.4	77.3	90.0	88.0
1909	83.4	89.4	88.3	87.9	88.9	89.2	93.2	90.0	88.4	89.9	90.3	94.0	92.6	90.6	88.4
1910	84.7	91.7	91.5	90.0	91.4	91.3	95.4	92.7	90.1	93.0	92.3	95.3	94.1	90.6	90.8
1911	87.9	94.7	95.1	93.9	95.6	92.9	95.1	94.8	93.8	95.7	94.7	96.3	95.9	91.8	93.8
1912	94.8	97.3	98.4	96.9	97.7	96.6	97.1	98.1	95.3	99.4	97.7	99.8	99.8	92.9	97.0
1913	100.0	100.0	100.0	100.0	100.0	100.0	100.0	100.0	100.0	100.0	100.0	100.0	100.0	100.0	100.0

The following chart reflects two estimates of the movement of wages during our period--the first column of

figures is the work of Ashok V.Desai who derived his statistics from the second set of numbers compiled by Juergen
Kuczynski.[170]

| | Desai | | | Kuczynski | | |
Year	Gross Money Wages	Standard of Living	Real Wages	Gross Money Wages	Standard of Living	Real Wages
1871	70	106	66	78	95	82
1875	98	113	87	97	104	93
1880	82	104	79	82	104	79
1890	98	102	96	100	103	97
1895	100	100	100	100	100	100
1900	118	106	111	115	105	110
1910	147	124	119	139	126	110
1913	163	130	125	153	137	112

Although there are significant discrepancies toward the end
of our period, the most substantial disagreements arise over
real wages and the standard of living during the late
1870's. The initial disparity between the two estimates of
money wages in 1871 can be attributed to Desai's exclusion
of the chemical and woodworking industries owing to inadequate data. With this exception, both estimates of money
wages concur until 1885, after which Desai's index acceler-
ates more rapidly than Kuczynski's. Because Desai's cost of
living figures decline more in the Seventies and climb less
after the turn of the century, his "index of real wages
shows a much larger increase between 1871 and 1875, falls
less in the next five years, and rises more rapidly after
1900."[171] While western historians paint a picture of
gradual contraction between 1875 and 1880, Marxist re-

searchers like Kuczynski see this period as one of steeper declines in both employment and real wages.

As we noted earlier wages tended to rise during booms when employers were prepared to offer higher salaries in order to attract more workers. Conversely wages contracted during depressions when decreasing demand for labor and higher unemployment made it possible to buy plentiful help at a far lower price. Although precise correlations are difficult to establish, sharp declines in wage rates such as those during the late 1870's usually signalled above average labor surpluses and higher unemployment.

Industrial Production, Labor Productivity and Unemployment

As we saw with regard to employment statistics, standards of living and wages, there are significant differences of interpretation among eastern and western historians. This also applies to the relationship among industrial production, unemployment and labor productivity. According to Hans Mottek,[172] employment tended to increase along with production and vary inversely with productivity. Mathematically, Mottek has postulated that the quantity of employment equalled the amount of production in a given time period divided by labor productivity. Or production was equal to the quantity of employment multiplied by labor productivity. Looking at the handloom weavers, Mottek indicates that their decline coincided with an acceleration of average productivity. That increased productivity was accompanied by stable production levels and diminished employment. At the same time many machine operatives were forced out of work by cutbacks in production so that the total volume of output decreased and employment grew even more sluggish. Mottek cites parallels in related and separate industries where declining production or increasing labor productivity boded ill for employment.

According to Mottek, one of the primary means of increasing labor productivity after 1873 was to modernize existing operations. Many entrepreneurs reported that employees worked more industriously as the depression and the accompanying threat of unemployment loomed larger. Apparently a selection process was under way, with employers weeding out less productive workers and retaining only those who performed well. Mottek maintains that both the exploitation and efficiency of labor increased during the depression.

With regard to technological progress during the depression, Mottek made distinctions between industries which he felt Kuczynski's data overlooked. In his study of overproduction crises, Kuczynski had argued that industrial production increased more than 50% during the 17 years between 1871 and 1888.[173] Mottek maintained that cost cuts and decreases in investment applied primarily to large enterprises which had previously sought to expand their capacity. While such concerns curtailed expenditures, other entrepreneurs continued to upgrade existing capacities with negative results in terms of employment. Mottek cited a number of heavy industries in which productivity increases and production cutbacks were large. Typically, these industries were dominated by a few big concerns and rarely included sectors where small operators accounted for a large share of total production. In other words, industries where small-scale operations were significant appear to have been more resistant to simultaneous increases in productivity and cutbacks in production during the first phase of the Great Depression. The textile, paper, cement and mining workers fared better in this period than the more highly concentrated machine building and foundry operatives. Mottek's findings are important for our purposes because they are used to substantiate claims of extreme curtailments in employment between 1873 and 1879. On the basis of gains in productivity and cutbacks of non-agricultural production, he estimates that employment declined at least 11% between 1873 and the end of the decade.

At this juncture,[174] Mottek began to calculate not unemployment per se but underutilization of the potential labor supply. Noting demographic factors such as population increases and migration, he estimated that the number of expendable work hours between 1873 and 1879 increased by 7%. Mottek argued that 82.3% of available employment was being utilized, leaving an underemployment rate of 17.7% for the seven-year period. Given the population shifts occurring during these years, Mottek calculated that the expansion of industrial labor increased the Reich's employment potential some 14%. Accordingly, between 1873 and 1879 underemployment in German industry amounted to an estimated 22.1%.

This was not to say that unemployment affected more than a fifth of the labor force but rather that the theoretical potential of industrial workers was underutilized by that amount. Alternatives to unemployment do not effectively enter into Mottek's calculations. His interest appears to lie in documenting the severity of this particular crisis of the German capitalist system. Profit-hungry entrepreneurs were not of interest when they sought to minimize unemployment by resorting to other expedients. As we shall see in the next section of this paper, their individual decisions went far toward containing the number of lay-offs and converting potential unemployment into diminished utilization of the available labor supply. In Mottek's scheme, labor's only interest in productivity was its impact on employment. And the bourgeoisie's sole concern was with the impact of productivity on business declines resulting from the sudden fall in prices during the recession. This monolithic, oversimplified view of economic motivation in the capitalist marketplace seriously distorts the Marxist analysis of unemployment during our period.

Figures published by West German historians do not generally lend support to Mottek's contention that employment and labor productivity were inversely proportional. Recent data from the Handbuch deutschen Wirtschafts- und

Sozialgeschichte[175] indicates that annual growth rates of employment, production and labor productivity between 1850 and 1913 tended to move together and at approximately parallel rates. Those industries which experienced the largest increases in employment also had the highest growth rates in both production and labor productivity. The economic historian W.G. Hoffmann has assembled data which suggests that for certain branches of German industry employment and production did not vary directly or at the same rates as Mottek hypothesized.[176] In his study of German wages, Bry has shown that the movement of industrial production and real earnings corresponded quite closely during the last three decades of the nineteenth century. Likewise the "decline in the rate of production growth and the more pronounced cyclical fluctuations between 1900 and 1913 coincide with the gradual leveling off in the upward trend of weekly real earnings."[177] Other historians such as Volker Hentschel[178] have used aggregate production figures from W.G. Hoffmann to question the validity of sharply differentiating between a boom before 1873 and a crisis thereafter. Noting that total production grew until 1875 and peaked after the beginning of the so-called depression, Hentschel proceeds to cite additional evidence on industrial production and net investment which challenges the validity of the Great Depression concept.

With regard to German handicrafts, contributors to the Handbuch[179] cited above have suggested that increased capital investment and use of mechanical power facilitated expanded labor productivity and production in conjunction with stable employment after 1895. In view of growing labor shortages between 1895 and 1907, such investment was needed to accelerate production and meet the demands of a prosperous economy. With labor becoming both more scarce and more productive, wages increased. In addition to handicrafts the agrarian order bequeathed to the modern economy two essential preconditions for growth: An expanding population and agriculture with a limited absorption capacity. Both industrial production and productivity were able to increase during our period because agriculture could supply the necessary food and raw materials without monopolizing labor required by more expansionary sectors of the economy.[180]

With regard to improvements in productivity, contemporaries questioned whether labor shared adequately in the benefits. The tendency toward more intensive capital investment could make things easier or more difficult for employees. If machinery and technological innovation substituted mechanical energy for human toil without eliminating too many jobs, workers were probably better off. The terms of employment could improve with technological advances, making certain jobs less physically taxing or hazardous. On the other hand, most of the economic advantages of technological improvements or increased capitalization accrued to management.

Workers rarely shared in the profits attributable to heightened productivity. If employees were expected to exert more effort or submit to work in a dangerous environment they were seldom rewarded with additional compensation for their sacrifices. Occasionally they were able to work fewer hours when demand failed to keep pace with expanded output.[181] But overall, entrepreneurs who could capitalize on enlarged production, cheaper methods of operation and perhaps smaller payrolls benefitted far more than workers from increased productivity. Contemporaries noted that once higher levels of productivity were achieved, entrepreneurs tended to expect that they be sustained permanently. Management viewed the resultant increases in output as its legitimate gain and considered itself shortchanged whenever performance failed to measure up to heightened expectations.[182] In any dispute over who was entitled to the profits of greater productivity, the advantage almost invariably lay with employers rather than labor or its organized representatives.

MICRO-ECONOMIC VARIABLES IN UNEMPLOYMENT

The Hiring and Dismissal Practices of Individual Entrepreneurs

The extent to which labor was able to influence unemployment policies varied with prevailing ethical considerations, perceptions of economic alternatives, and configurations of political influence. In addition, the manner in which divergent groups viewed the impact of unemployment on its victims and on their own interests affected their willingness to negotiate with labor.[183] The fact remains that as our period progressed, an increasing number of employers were seeking responses to economic crises other than lay-offs. In areas such as Wuerttemberg, a capable labor force had been perceived as a scarce and valuable commodity since the beginning of industrialization.[184] Growing recognition of the value of well trained workers was making itself felt among entrepreneurs. They began to realize that the best way to ensure an adequate labor supply during prosperous years was to retain the services of their employees even during recessions. Employers learned to hoard skilled workers in particular, and in the process, they evolved creative ways to circumvent discharging other laborers when demand for their products declined temporarily. The last word became the operative factor in their calculations. Recognition of the temporary nature of crises and the inevitable return of prosperity motivated employers to seek alternatives to unemployment.

Although aggregate unemployment statistics are sorely lacking for the early years of our period, scattered clues suggest something other than a monolithic response of the German labor market to economic crises. There appear to be time lags in unemployment and ample evidence of efforts to avert lay-offs even during severe slumps in economic activity. In a recent article on prosperity and crisis in Wuerttemberg, for example, Volker Hentschel has indicated that there was a demand for good workers well beyond the economic downturn in 1873 and that even wages continued to climb until 1875. Figures from the coal industry in Dortmund also suggest a time lag with employment dipping significantly only in 1877 and then continuing to rise until 1885. While there were gradual gains, the 1876 level was not surpassed until 1881.

Typically, much bleaker analyses of unemployment during crises have come out of East Germany. Take for example Kuczynski's estimate of the crisis during the early Nineties. Beginning with a calculation that actual unemployment in 1890 amounted to 1%, he proceeds to postulate a decline in employment of 5% and a simultaneous increase in population of more than 3%. This leads to a revised unemployment rate of 6%. To that he adds reduced hours plus the diminution of overtime to conclude that wages declined by 10%.[185] And bad as this was, things continued to deteriorate, getting progressively worse in 1891 and finally bottoming out in 1892. Citing annual figures on the total number of workers employed in Saxon factories between 1883 and 1893, Kuczynski estimates a decline in employment of almost 2% during 1892, the only year for which negative net losses were recorded.[186] In response to the subsequent economic crisis of 1901, Kuczynski suggests a parallel development--unemployment reached 7% and wages declined 10%.[187] These unemployment rates were calculated on the basis of questionable labor exchange statistics and other unspecified data.

Evidence gleaned from quarterly reports presents a complex and occasionally confusing picture of German entrepreneurs' responses to economic crises. While it is easy to look at their reports and cite numerous instances of lay-offs during the years between 1877 and 1879, in 1892 and in 1901, this represents only part of the picture. There were also instances of expansion during those years, with employment in many firms remaining stable, with new firms emerging and with employers finding ways to avert lay-offs. In addition to state and local expenditure for public works projects and other forms of unemployment relief, a 1901 article in Soziale Praxis cited the following measures to avoid firing workers in various branches of German industry:[188]

> In vielen Gewerben versucht man, durch forcirte Verkaeufe ins Ausland, durch Herabsetzung der Arbeitszeit, durch Einlegung von Feiertagschichten das Schlimmste, die Entlassung von Arbeitern zu verhuten. In anderen Industrien bestehen Tarifgemeinschaften, die den Arbeitern in Zeiten geschaeftlicher Depressionen einen Schutz gewaehren.

During 1894 the mayor of Essen commented on the unemployment situation as portrayed in the Social Democratic or ultramontane press. According to him, the so-called crisis was a pure fabrication of extremist groups who hoped to create a false sense of need and discontent among the working class to further their own corrupt political ends.[189]

Perhaps the best overall picture of aggregate changes in employment has been offered by W.G. Hoffmann. Although we noted earlier that employment statistics do not easily translate into estimates of unemployment, the following figures give some idea of the macro-economic consequences of micro-economic decisions about hiring and firing.[190]

The Annual Growth Rate of Employment

1873	1.9%	1883	1.2%	1893	0.7%	1903	1.9%
1874	1.8%	1884	1.2%	1894	1.5%	1904	1.8%
1876	1.3%	1886	1.9%	1896	2.1%	1906	1.9%
1878	0.9%	1888	1.6%	1898	1.8%	1908	0.7%
1880	0.4%	1890	1.3%	1900	1.9%	1910	2.3%
1881	0.5%	1891	0.5%	1901	0.3%	1911	2.1%
1882	1.1%	1892	0.5%	1902	1.0%	1912	1.7%
						1913	1.4%

These figures say nothing about population increases or distribution and tell us little about variable unemployment rates. Based on other evidence, it is however reasonable to surmise that whenever the annual growth rate of employment approached one percent, the labor market was tight and whenever it fell below that level, unemployment was likely to be unusually high. It is also worth noting in passing that the lowest annual rate of growth in employment came not during the so-called Great Depression but well after the return to prosperity--during the crisis of 1901.

One of the primary reasons why employment continued to expand (albeit at slower rates) during recessions was that individual entrepreneurs developed alternatives to dismissing their labor force in times of crisis. As we shall see, one of the most commonly adopted practices to avoid laying off employees was to reduce wages, hours or both. On numerous occasions such cutbacks produced what entrepreneurs referred to as a voluntary exodus of workers. There is evidence to suggest that such responses occurred even during periods of supposedly chronic unemployment such as Mottek believes prevailed in the late 1870's. A report dated January 7, 1878, for example, indicates that workers voluntarily left their jobs at the mechanical weaving firm of H.Stroink in Nordhorn when the company cut their workday by three hours and reduced their piece rates by 25 Pfennigs or 20%.[191] Obviously evidence of such independence was far more common during periods of less severe economic hardship, but this and other examples suggest that even at its worst, German unemployment never reached levels extreme enough to foreclose the possibility of alternatives. Workers could not have left even poorly paid employment if the size of the surplus labor force made it impossible for them to believe they could find other jobs.

In addition to laborers who left on their own initiative, there were many employees who were dismissed when entrepreneurs perceived that low prices, overproduction or slack demand made such action necessary. In this context, there is evidence to suggest that some employers used economic crises to weed out unproductive laborers and upgrade the quality of their work force. A report from a needle factory in Aachen during 1890 indicated, for example, "dass sie die schlechten Arbeiter allmaehlig entlassen".[192]

Certain categories of workers were particularly vulnerable to dismissal. Women, however, occasionally benefitted from economic crises on a temporary basis. Because they were willing to work for lower wages female laborers were sometimes hired as a cost-saving measure. In areas of international competition such considerations apparently weighed heavily.[193] But persons hired to minimize expenditures during crises did not always retain their positions when prosperity made other employees more attractive. Women were not the only ones who faced discrimination in employment policies. Evidence suggests that there was an effort to take the economic circumstances of employees into account. In the Osnabrueck Bergwerks und Huttenverein, for example, 300 unmarried workers were laid off between 1872 and the end of 1875.[194] We have already indicated that foreign workers were dismissed before German laborers. Those who fared best over the long haul were married men with families, well-established residences and union affiliations.

According to communist historians like Kuczynski employers discriminated against all union men and agitators in particular during crises. Not out of any humane concern for the superior benefits of union unemployment funds, but out of vindictiveness Kuczynski would have us believe bourgeois capitalists dismissed organized proletarians. Contrary to Kuczynski's assertions, more highly skilled, organized and contractually protected union members were probably less susceptible to lay-offs than other workers. Obvious troublemakers of any sort would be natural candidates for dismissal but East German historians have failed to present convincing proof that employers used the threat of lay-offs during recessions to discriminate against organized labor and discourage employees from belonging to unions.

Regardless of the individual victims, there is reason to conclude that dismissals were selective and not random. Workers who were least productive, efficient, reliable or tenured and perhaps most troublesome were among the first to be laid off. Recent agricultural employees with little seniority or experience were especially vulnerable--the last hired were frequently the first to be discharged. So too were single workers--an effort was made to keep on married men with children in preference to unmarried men or any women. Female employees took precedence over males only when their retention was economically advantageous due to lower wages. In times of crisis, employers sought to upgrade the efficiency of their operations out of necessity by cutting labor costs and maximizing output per employee.

During every crisis which occurred in our period, employers took pains to point out that former workers who had been laid off found jobs elsewhere rather than joining the ranks of the unemployed. From the 1870's to the Great War, agriculture provided one of the primary sources of employment for those discharged from the industrial sector. Supplying labor for industry during boom periods, agriculture managed to reabsorb much of the industrial surplus when recessions curtailed wages and diminished the demand for workers. Regional differences were a major factor in determining the extent to which agriculture eased the industrial unemployment situation. In Wuerttemberg during the 1870's, for example, agriculture played a key role in alleviating unemployment resulting from industrial lay-offs.[195]

Agriculture traditionally provided work for a variety of laborers who were especially vulnerable to unemployment. These included construction workers suffering from seasonal unemployment and weavers hard hit by structural changes deriving from mechanization. In the case of handloom operatives, cyclical unemployment was complicated by threatened obsolescence through more efficient power driven machinery. The problem of the handloom weaver had to be approached by finding ways to translate their skills into other types of work.[196] Scattered evidence suggests that agriculture provided employment for textile workers throughout the recurring crises which comprised the Great Depression. Masters who owned small parcels of land around the town of Lingen, cotton spinners in the district of Osnabrueck and weavers working in cottage industries in the vicinity of Aachen were among those who turned to agricultural employment to get through the successive recessions of the 1870's, 1880's and 1890's.[197]

Situations varied in Germany's major cities. During the 1870's in Berlin, Mottek's figures suggest that agriculture could not absorb the overflow of idle industrial workers. During the crisis of 1901, however, Kuczynski points out that the Hansa ports were spared major concentrations of unemployment because the surrounding agrarian districts were able to alleviate conditions in Hamburg and Bremen. Proximity to agricultural areas seemed to provide an ongoing source of unemployment "insurance" for highly industrialized districts during economic crises. Agricultural jobs were not, however, the only alternative to unemployment for urban workers laid off from industrial positions. Especially after the turn of the century, public employment provided an escape from idleness. Although most public works projects during our period were conceived and executed at the local level, there were a number of ways in which the federal government could take up slack in the industrial labor market.

With regard to private industry there were numerous instances even during recessions when employers rehired the same individuals who had been recently discharged. Occasionally entrepreneurs resorted to euphemisms such as extended vacations--"vorlauefig beurlaubt"--to avoid acknowledging the more permanent situation implied by the term lay-off or "Entlassung". If jobs were not available in certain occupations, workers frequently found employment in related areas. To cite one example, in the Osnabrueck district of Papenburg during 1876 there was a recession which severely affected the local wood industry. When the demand for wooden railroad cars and ships declined, between 50 and 100 workers were diverted for "die Loschung und Verpackung der Holzer".[198] This type of diversion was fairly commonplace. Rather than creating unemployment, slack demand in many cases produced new ways to retain the services of labor until the return of economic prosperity reinstated output of traditional products. In addition to finding employment in related industries in the same district,[199] workers typically had the option of mobility as an alternative to unemployment.

Evidence from towns such as Wetzlar in the vicinity of Wiesbaden, from Dortmund, Breslau and other manufacturing centers suggest that crisis periods were conspicuous for the instability of industrial operations. The emergence and disappearance of firms in given geographical areas make it difficult to accept scattered reports on lay-offs as conclusive proof of overall declines in employment or rises in unemployment. While some firms were dismissing workers or closing down production completely, others were hiring labor forces, absorbing competitors, and commencing operation for the first time. This process was at the very heart of Germany's industrial expansion and it continued uninterrupted but at variable speeds throughout the slumps and booms which characterized our period. The result of the emergence, absorption and disappearance of firms may have been a wash in terms of aggregate employment statistics but it lent an element of vitality to the economy. Pockets of growth, even in the face of overall contraction, were an important antidote to stagnation in the labor market and the economy as a whole.

As we noted earlier, ours was a period of unprecedented labor turnover with brief intervals of unemployment typically accompanying job changes. The mobile, fluid quality of employment in German industry helped to prevent any but a few isolated cases of chronic structural unemployment. It also insured that the channels for finding work never became so clogged by industry's rejects that they were functionally impassable or altogether inoperative. As we have attempted to demonstrate here, one of the most important reasons why unemployment failed to become widespread during our period is that entrepreneurs averted lay-offs whenever it was economically feasible. We shall turn next to a consideration of the micro-economic alternatives adopted to avoid industrial unemployment. But let us close this discussion of workers' options in the event of lay-offs with a contemporary analysis of the situation during the crisis of the 1880's.[200]

> Da viele der vorwaehnten Arbeitseinschraenkungen erst im Fruehjahre eingetreten sind, so gelang es dem grossten Theile der beschaeftigungslos gewordenen Arbeiter sehr bald wieder bei der Feldarbeit, dem Baugewerbe, in Steinbruechen, auch in anderen Fabriken vorlaeufig ein Unterkannen zu finden. Freude, frueher zugezogene Arbeiter kehrten vielfach wieder nach ihrer Heimath zurueck, und sind infolge diesen allgemeinere, in die Augen fallende Nothstuende ebensowenig, wie Unordnungen oder Ruhestoerungen hervorgetreten.

Short Time as an Alternative to Unemployment

One of the most common alternatives to lay-offs as a means of cutting both expenses and production during periods of slack demand was to curtail the hours worked. Either by adopting a shorter workday or diminishing the number of days worked each week, employers sought to limit the total time an employee spent on the job. This enabled entrepreneurs to preserve their labor supply while instituting economically necessary cutbacks in production during crises. Reduced hours also provided a way of spreading the burden of work shortages more equitably. They were frequently preferred to the alternative of dismissing some workers in order to maintain full shifts for the smaller labor force. This type of underemployment became increasingly popular with entrepreneurs who were reluctant to relinquish the services of good workers that might be difficult to rehire with the inevitable return of prosperity.

Contemporaries recognized that unemployment rates would have been higher during recessions if management had failed to substitute fewer hours for lay-offs. This sort of industrial underemployment was nevertheless the subject of heated discussion. Not everyone applauded reduced hours as an altruistic innovation by entrepreneurs to ward off unemployment. Twentieth-century socialist historians, for example, point to this practice as an additional means of oppressing the broad mass of workers. They see it as an adjunct to unemployment, supplementing the misery of total idleness and insuring its spread throughout the working class.

Despite such contentions, the Social Democratic Party and its leader August Bebel fought for the eight-hour workday which they hoped would lead to an increased demand for labor in German manufacturing. Bebel, it should be recalled, saw rising unemployment as evidence of impending revolution. And that presented a dilemma for socialists who had to balance conflicting commitments to improving the short-term conditions of the working class and accelerating the overthrow of capitalism. The range of thought within German socialism on the relationship between reduced hours and unemployment has been described by Vernon Lidtke in these terms:[201]

Moderates such as Auer, Grillenberger and Viereck maintained that by setting legal maximums on working hours unemployment would be reduced significantly. Using Marx's Capital Liebknecht argued that although desirable, the normal working day could not solve unemployment because employers would intensify the work load--technological advances would make increased production possible without employing more workers.

The question of efficacy aside, there were numerous advocates of shorter hours both as an antidote to unemployment and as a means of increasing efficiency. An 1893 speech delivered by a member of the Center Party in the Reichstag criticized the eight-hour day as a contributory factor in increasing rather than diminishing unemployment. Professor Hitze made this argument on January 21, 1893, when the economy was in the midst of a severe recession:[202]

> ...wenn die Herren immer auf dem achtstuendigen Arbeitstag bestehen, so erblicke ich darin keine Massnahme, der Arbeitslosigkeit entgegenzuwirken, sondern ich sehe indem allgemeinen schablonenhaften achtstuendigen Arbeitstag den sichern Weg zu allgemeiner Arbeitslosigkeit: entweder zur Herabsetzung des Lohnes--was die Herren doch wohl selbst nicht wollen--oder aber, wenn die Loehne bleiben zum Verlust des auslaendischen Marktes und damit zu groesserer Arbeitslosigkeit.

Among the least controversial measures designed to reduce the length of the workday were proposals to limit the employment of women and children. In 1884 a maximum eleven-hour workday for women was instituted. Minimum age requirements were adopted and parameters established for the hours during which child labor was permissible. Efforts were also made to eliminate overtime and night work which were believed to aggravate the unemployment problem during economic crises.[203] By the 1890's some of the more progressive unions such as the printers were negotiating nine-hour workdays for their membership. One of the major trends affecting industrial unemployment levels between 1873 and 1913 was the decline in hours spent at work. Because Germany began the industrialization process relatively late, workers at the beginning of our period were still laboring under "the long hours customary in agricultural work and common in early industrialization".[204] Although the eight-hour day which Social Democrats advocated wasn't adopted until 1918, our period witnessed significant reductions in the average length of time spent on the job.

During the 1870's a twelve-hour workday was probably typical. There were however significant varia-tions, with organized labor in major cities working less than ten hours and those toiling in rural cottage industries putting in up to fifteen hours each day. While it is difficult to generalize, employees in urban areas and large-scale operations frequently worked fewer hours.[205] Shorter hours were a major objective of organized labor throughout our period and after 1890 reductions began to occur. Recognizing occupational differences, W. G. Hoffmann estimated a decline in average weekly hours from 64 in the 1890's to 57 by 1914. Hans-Ulrich Wehler has suggested that the weekly average declined from 72 hours in 1872 to 62 hours by 1900 and 57 by 1914. According to Gerhard Bry, the average workday in 1897 was between 10 and 10 1/2 hours.

Labor contracts in 1913 stipulated workdays slightly in excess of 9 1/2 hours.[206] According to Hoffmann's estimates,[207] the average annual work time declined from 3,780 hours in 1875 to 3,290 hours by 1913.

It is worth noting in passing that municipal public works projects entailed days which averaged from eight to nine hours. Although days were as short as 6 3/4 hours in Danzig and as long as 10 1/2 hours in Freiburg i.B., the 8 1/2 hour day was typical because most public projects had to be executed during daylight.[208] The duration of time spent on public jobs is important because it reflected popular views on what constituted an acceptable workday. In addition to providing temporary sustenance for the unemployed, public jobs were supposed to inculcate values of industrious behavior and esteem for hard work. While they were not intended to compete with the private sector, public works set certain precedents which did not go unnoticed by German industrialists. In the realm of employment, there was clearly a trend in both the public and private sectors toward reduced hours.

As our period progressed, Sunday labor increasingly became a thing of the past. Six-day work weeks were typical in most industries, but the average number of working days per year varied from one occupation to the next. Although regional differences also entered the picture, the following figures from the statistical yearbook of the city of Berlin gave some indication of occupational

variables. Members of the building trade worked an estimated 220 days per year; inland navigators worked 270 days;
food manufacturers worked 315 days and those employed in
bathing establishments or meat markets almost never had a
day off. The overall annual average came out to approximately 300 working days.[209]

Of course, general economic conditions affected
these averages significantly. During prosperous periods of
full employment the so-called average was likely to be
greater than it was when business conditions were conducive
to both lay-offs and reduced hours. To cite an example used
by Juergen Kuczynski who looks at the "crisis of 1891",
unemployment increased from two to six percent between 1890
and 1892 while work time decreased a full ten percent during
those years.[210] The following quotation is indicative of
labor's response when slack demand confronted workers with a
choice between lay-offs for some or fewer hours for all:[211]

> Die Elberfelder Industrie habe im allgemeinen eher
> Mangel an tuechtigen gelernten Arbietern. Daher
> erklaerte es sich auch, dass sie in Zeiten schlechter
> Konjunktur lieber die notwendige Beschraenkung der
> Produktion durch Verkuerzung der Arbeitszeit mit Erhal-
> tung des vorhandenen Arbeiterstammes, als durch
> Entlassung von Arbeitern vornehme.

The distinction between lay-offs for a few and shorter hours
for many was not always clear-cut. During recessions, for
example, the class of "Aushilfsarbeiter" working as waiters,
hairdressers, cooks or musicians stood halfway between
unemployed and underemployed laborers.[212]

Perhaps the most interesting aggregate figures on the relationship between unemployment and reduced hours were compiled during and after the economic crisis of 1901-02. The first table shows that at the specified dates and places the overall ratio of partially to totally unemployed was 699 to 1,000. The second table shows a ratio of 616 partially unemployed to 1,000 totally jobless individuals. During 1902 when the German trade cycle was at its nadir there were 702 partially unemployed persons for each 1,000 totally idled workers. In December of 1902, 28.5% of those responding to a questionnaire indicated that their work week had been reduced by six hours or less; 23.3% of the respondents worked from seven to 12 hours less each week; 34.1% worked 13 to 18 fewer hours; 10.9% worked from 19 to 24 hours less and 3.2% worked a week diminished by 24 or more hours.

(Except as to Stuttgart, February 15, 1901, which is from *Arbeitsmark* Jahrgang VL., No. 9, pp. 162, 1 3, the particulars given below are fror *Correspondenzblatt*, March 3, 1902, p. 144.)

Date.	Place.	Number of Persons Unemployed.		Percentage of partially Unemployed to wholly Unemployed.
		Wholly.	Partially.	
1901. February 15	Stuttgart	1,127	748	62·1
October (end of)	Breslau and suburbs	1,133 (1)	—	—
November	Leipsic	1,017 (3)	—	—
"	Rixdorf	2,263	—	—
December (beginning)	Hanover	3,590	—	—
" "	Crimmitschau	187 (3)	308	134·4
" "	Quedilnburg	112	—	—
December	Mühlhausen, i. Th.	418	—	—
"	Bernburg	300	224	74·7
"	Dantzig	1,120	—	—
"	Halle-on-Saale	2,429	—	—
"	Gotha	400	About 300	75·0
1902. January	Munich	9,377 (4)	—	—
"	Nuremberg	4,391	—	—
"	Fürth	1,069	1,605	150·1
"	Dresden and suburbs	10,170	—	—
February	Berlin and suburbs	73,820	32,501	69·1
"	Hanover	About 6,000	—	—
"	Calbe	283	—	—
February 29	Stuttgart	1,405	778	55·3
TOTALS AND MEAN PERCENTAGE		124,211	56,463	63·9

(Except as to Stuttgart, Nov. 10, which is from *Arbeitsmarkt*, Jahrgang VI., No. 9, p. 163, the particulars given below are from *Correspondenzblatt*, April 25, 1903, p. 271.)

Date.	Place	Number of Persons Unemployed.		Number of Hours lost per Week by those Partially Unemployed, so far as particulars are available.					Total Number of persons as to time lost who were partially or wholly unemployed.	Percentage of partially unemployed to wholly employed.
		Wholly.	Par- tially.	6 or less.	7-12.	13-18.	19-24.	Over 24.		
1902.										
November 10	Stuttgart	737	338	—	—	—	—	—	—	45.9
„ (end of)	Hildesheim	95	269	—	—	—	—	—	—	35.2
December (beginning)	Brandenburg	688	218	118	37	35	16	14	218	31.7
December 2	Rathenow	105	23	—	—	—	—	23(1)	23	21.7
„ 7	Magdeburg	3,125	2,580	291	737	956	262	73	2,472	73.8
„ 14	Offenbach	305	103	—	—	—	—	—	—	35.4
„ 20	Halberstadt	343	601	601(1)	—	—	—	—	601	175.2
„ 21	Bürgel a. M.	83	21	8	5	—	9	—	22	73.7
„ 21	Neuruppin	119	—	—	—	—	—	—	—	
„ 28	Oggersheim	97	17	—	—	—	—	—	—	17.5
„ 23	Zeitz	330	223	—	—	223(1)	—	—	223	65.3
1903.										
January 4	Bunzlau	366	214	—	—	—	—	—	—	58.7
„ 4	Gotha	237	111	—	—	—	—	—	—	46.8
„ 11	Bielefeld	1,041	1,772	—	—	—	—	—	—	170.2
„ 11	Gera	688	115	—	—	—	—	—	—	7.2
„ 11	Stassfurt	218	229	229(1)	—	—	—	—	229	105.0
„ 11	Wolfenbüttel	215	31	—	—	31(1)	—	—	31	14.4
„ 18	Dresden and suburbs.	3,289	—	—	—	—	—	—	—	
„ 18-20	Karlsruhe	436	—	—	—	—	—	—	—	—
„ 25	Burg	233	—	—	—	—	—	—	—	—
„ 25	Luckenwalde	95	—	—	—	—	—	—	—	—
„ 23	Offenbach	365	—	—	—	—	—	—	—	—
February 1	Crimmitschau	457	159	—	—	—	—	—	—	34.8
„ 1	Frankfurt on Main.	3,030	853	—	853(1)	—	—	—	853	28.3
„ 3	Ludwigshafen	453	268	—	—	—	—	—	—	59.3
„ 3	Kolberg	103	—	—	—	—	—	—	—	—
„ 15	Brunswick	1,374	—	—	—	—	—	—	—	—
„ 15	Offenbach	258	61	—	—	—	—	—	—	23.8
„ 15	Ohrdruf	63	11	—	—	—	—	—	—	17.5
March ?	Freiberg	387	—	—	—	—	—	—	—	—
TOTALS AND MEAN PERCENTAGE*		19,942	8,335	1,245	1,687	1,245	387	113	4,677	81.8

(1) Average.
* For the places which returned both totally and partially unemployed.

According to "Handel und Wandel" by Richard Calwer[213] which appeared in 1901, the practice of reducing hours as an alternative to curtailing the number of employees was widespread in Germany. This was believed to be in the common interest of the individual laborer, the working class and the unions, because it minimized the contraction of employment and the attendant repercussions. By spreading the hardship of diminished demand, reducing hours came to be seen as a more equitable means of dealing with work shortage than unemployment. A preference for underemployment over lay-offs was far more common in Germany than in other industrial nations such as England. Rather than cutting hours, English industrialists tended to dismiss superfluous workers during recessions with the result that British unemployment rates were generally higher than German rates. The fact that the latter frequently failed to reflect widespread reductions in hours of employment should not be overlooked.

Data from German trade unions compiled during the summer of 1903 indicated that for every 100 persons counted as unemployed an additional 66 were affected by reduced hours. An estimated reduction of one-third of the normal worktime was deemed to have occurred. This meant that the unions surveyed experienced unemployment rates which were nearer to 3.9% rather than the 3.2% figure which did not take shorter hours into account. The preceding calculations were called into question by the assumption that reduced hours were unique features of recessions and by the fact that the 1901 crisis had abated before the middle of 1903[214]. And indeed figures on the Wuerttemberg economy suggest a much less equitable ratio between totally unemployed and underemployed workers during 1903.[215]

The point needs to be made that statistics which failed to consider reduced hours probably underestimated the extent of unemployment. This was especially true during recessions when German industrialists were increasingly prone to curtail hours rather than dismiss valued employees. As we shall see in the next section, one of the most inevitable and obvious by-products of shorter hours as an alternative to unemployment was wage reductions. For in addition to curtailing output, employers sought to cut expenses by minimizing wage outlays. The extent to which workers suffered from lower wages introduced as cost-cutting measures by employers has been a major source of contention between East and West German historians.

Lower Wages as an Alternative to Unemployment

If we again look at wages as the prevailing price of labor, it makes sense to recognize that the cost increased when the supply declined relative to demand. Like any other commodity, labor was valued in proportion to its scarcity and wage rates reflected this fact. With high unemployment, it would seem to follow that labor surpluses drove wage rates downward. During the recessions which occurred between 1873 and 1913, increases in unemployment were part of a scenario which also included price reductions, production cutbacks, declines in investment, fewer hours of work and lower wages. Although shorter hours and lower wages invariably went together as a means of cutting costs during recessions, the situation was rather different during periods of prosperity. When the economy was thriving, organized labor repeatedly chose to press management for a combination of fewer hours and higher wages. What then was the nature of the relationship between wages, hours and unemployment in Germany during our period?

Classical economists have maintained that if wages were infinitely elastic in the downward direction, unemployment could be eliminated entirely. It is of course theoretically possible to argue that under any given economic condition there was a wage rate which if established would yield full employment. If laborers were willing to work for practically nothing, one can surmise that it would be profitable for employers to engage their services even if prices and consumer demand for their products were also low. In reality, it was the relationship among wages, prices, mobility, the elasticity of demand for labor and consumption which affected the level of unemployment.

German workers in general and organized labor in particular strongly resisted wage cuts as a means of enabling entrepreneurs to cope with diminished demand. Wages were therefore rigid in the downward direction, and industrial unemployment was seldom averted during recessions. Economic theorists have postulated that the rate of change of money wages was faster when unemployment was declining than when unemployment was on the rise. Money wages fluctuated more when unemployment was low than when it was high. This relationship occurred because employers were both willing and able to increase wages during prosperity. Workers on the other hand tenaciously resisted cuts in pay during recessions.

According to John Garraty's general observations on Unemployment in History, organized labor in the nineteenth and twentieth centuries "usually preferred to see some of their members discharged rather than to share the loss by having all work for lower wages."[216] The unhappy choice between a large number of workers with low incomes or a smaller number with higher incomes was seldom made by trade unions rather than employers. But the willingness of organized labor to accept lower wages as an alternative to lay-offs was likely to be influenced by who paid the cost of unemployment insurance. If public agencies picked up the tab for the unemployed, unions were more free to insist on the maintenance of high wages. If on the other hand, benefits came out of union funds, a different attitude toward acceptable levels of unemployment and wages might prevail.[217]

The situation in Germany varied among regions, unions and occupations. But as a general rule unions were more successful in advancing demands for higher wages during booms than in preventing reductions of members' earnings during recessions. As a practical matter, there not much to be done when employers offered lower wages and large pools of surplus workers were willing to accept the proffered compensation. Resistance to wage reductions varied with the size of the proposed cuts--objections generally increased with the amount of the reductions. Most of the evidence suggests that employers instituted wage rollbacks which were less than a quarter of employees' earnings. And labor in turn frequently accepted such cuts for lack of a preferable alternative during recessions.

Classical theory implies that decisions about wages inevitably entail consequences in the form of unemployment. During recessions when labor surpluses tend to depress earnings, artificially inflated wage rates were automatically accompanied by higher unemployment. Only when the real demand for labor pushed wages up during prosperity---reflecting the need for a scarce commodity--were high wage rates compatible with low unemployment. The relation between wages on the one hand and the demand for labor on the other was crucial in determining the rate of unemployment. By opting to reduce wages during recessions, German employers either deliberately or inadvertently lessened unemployment. And workers to the extent that they insisted on the maintenance of high wage rates for a reduced labor force during crises increased unemployment.

As we noted earlier, German money wages were generally rigid in the downward direction. Although slight declines were common and often sufficient to curtail rising unemployment, the only substantial decrease during our period occurred in the first decade.[218] One reason why unemployment wasn't higher during the Seventies must be sought in the deflated prices which accompanied the economic crisis. In an era of deflation, reduced earnings retained more of their purchasing power than in an inflationary period. This in part eased the burden of significantly lower income from 1876 to 1884 when real eages rose for those who continued to work. Unemployment during those years would have been much greater had wage rates been artifically prevented from falling. Lower wages in other words were probably more acceptable to German labor because deflated prices made money go farther and because already high levels of unemployment made alternatives even less appealing.

In Berlin where East German historians have postulated extremely high levels of both unemployment and underemployment during the early years of our period, wages fluctuated as follows: The years between 1870 and 1875 were characterized by rapid increases, with average annual incomes rising from 508 to 627 Marks. From 1875 to 1882, these gains were entirely wiped out, falling back to 500 Marks before beginning another ascent. As we noted earlier, police reports in Berlin indicated a drastic decline in employment between 1875 and 1878 and then a rise until 1881. Between 1883 and 1891 average income in the capital in-creased steadily according to estimates published in Soziale Praxis.[219]

Looking at Germany as a whole and adjusting real wages for income lost through diminished overtime, unemployment and reduced hours, Kuczynski sees a much more critical situation during 1874 and 1875. Loss of work during those years in proportion to 1872 was estimated at 10% and 12% respectively. Net real wages which in 1872 had been 80% of the level reached in 1900 fell to 70% of that level in 1874. The 1874 figure represented the absolute nadir of net real wages during the entire depression, although a comparable low was recorded in 1877 according to Kuczynski.[220] For the 1880's East German historians emphasized the role of emigration in containing the glut on labor markets which characterized other crises. According to Kuczynski, net real wages declined 14% between 1890 and 1892 while hours of work dropped by 10% and unemployment increased from two to six percent.[221] Again during the crisis of 1901 significant reductions in both hours of employment and earnings accompanied rising unemployment.[222] Although reduced wages frequently coincided with shorter hours which many regarded as inadequate compensation for lower earnings, the two responses to crises were not always linked. As Kuczynski noted with reference to a machine factory in Elbing during 1875, employers were capable of reducing wages by 20% and expecting employees to work with "iron-like diligence and consistent precision".[223]

Perhaps more than the issue of unemployment per se, unions capitalized on the workers' desire for higher pay in their recruiting efforts. Fewer hours and higher wages were the objects of numerous strikes during prosperous periods. The benefits for which unions negotiated were powerful recruiting tools that attracted many new members to labor organizations when times were good. The brief interval between 1889 and 1890 plus the prolonged upswing after 1896 were conspicuous for substantial gains in union membership and simultaneous rises in wage rates. Despite organized labor's efforts to advance industrial wages through strikes and other more conciliatory means, workers' real wages increased by no more than one percent annually between the late 1880's and 1913.[224] Even after a prolonged upswing, German industrial labor received lower real wages than their co-workers in the United States, United Kingdom, France and Sweden.[225]

It is clear from numerous reports submitted by entrepreneurs over the course of our period that cutting costs by reducing wages was a typical response to recessions. In addition to reduced hours and cutbacks in production this means of retaining a full complement of labor at a lower price was widely adopted. As an alternative to unemployment, it was severely criticized by the nineteenth-century socialists and their twentieth-century intellectual heirs. Seen as a means of exploiting labor unfairly and dangerously reducing the proletariat's already low standard of living, wage cuts have been unreservedly condemned. But it must be acknowledged that reduced wages in the face of falling prices plus declining demand for both labor and its output prevented unemployment from skyrocketing during recessions.

As an alternative to layoffs along with reduced hours, wage cuts helped to distribute the loss derived from work shortages more equitably among the laboring classes. One may argue that the middle and upper classes deserved to share more of the burden accruing from such shortages. But if under the capitalist system the lower orders were forced to bear the brunt of hardship, it was perhaps preferable that many rather than only a few divide the expense. Reduced wages as an alternative to unemployment implemented by individual entrepreneurs at the micro-economic level made that broadly-based division possible in Germany.

Willingness to Work

At the beginning of this study, we specified that those designated as unemployed had to be willing and able to work and without jobs through no fault of their own. However, eagerness to work was a relative rather than absolute attribute, a variable rather than constant response to changing conditions in the labor market. As wages, hours and other terms of employment changed with overall business conditions, so too did the motivation to seek work. We have seen how employers responded to economic crises in ways which limited the extent of unemployment. Now we must consider how alternately recurring crises and booms affected the willingness of the potential labor force to participate in the job market. For those individuals at the margins of the laboring populace what were the terms of employment which would induce them to work?

Contemporaries who wrote about unemployment were extremely concerned with work-shy individuals and potential abuses of relief programs. There was almost a tacit assumption that laziness was an instinctive trait and industriousness something which had to be deliberately and painstakingly cultivated because it ran contrary to human nature. Habits of steady work were hard to inculcate in people used to numerous interruptions in the form of religious holidays, seasonal shutdowns in agriculture, wars, plagues and variable business conditions. This was the heritage of pre-industrial society to an economy which required constancy of its labor force. Unemployment itself was viewed as a source of laziness among those who believed that idleness in any form bred sloth.

Critics of unemployment insurance objected to various proposals on the grounds that they would undermine the willingness to work and create a class of public pensioners. By enabling potential laborers to refuse some jobs or search less eagerly for work, insurance and other forms of public relief were considered counterproductive. Since the unemployed were valued solely in their capacity as producers, nineteenth-century critics failed to weigh the positive impact their consumption would have on the economy. Consequently unemployment insurance payments were seen by some not as a stimulus to production but as a substitute for hard work.[226] From the perspective of employers in the building trades, for example, unemployment insurance exercised a demoralizing influence on those too lazy to work.[227]

Popular attitudes did not require the unemployed to accept just any type of proffered work. Unions were particularly sensitive to the suitability of employment which their jobless workers were expected to take. None of the trade unions paying unemployment benefits required its members to work outside of their occupations.[228] Certain criteria particularly for skilled laborers were considered essential. The person had to be mentally and physically able to perform the task at hand without impairing his health or other job skills. Despite this apparent leniency those who refused to work because wages, hours or subjective aspects of available jobs were unsatisfactory, received scant support if they wound up unemployed.[229] Many did not consider unemployment involuntary if laborers refused prevailing wage rates. In that case, they were deemed to have withdrawn from the labor market and were not counted as unemployed. Nor were they entitled to any unemployment compensation.

The practical ramifications of variable willingness to work can be illustrated by reference to the problem of absenteeism. With workers holding tedious or otherwise unpleasant jobs, the tendency to alleviate boredom by taking unscheduled vacations was commonplace. If the economy was healthy and unemployment relatively low, absenteeism was a problem immediately following weekends or pay days. If work was scarce and workers put their livelihoods at risk by arbitrarily failing to report, absenteeism was not much of a temptation. The point with regard to absenteeism and overtime which workers used to make up for lost wages is that attitudes varied tremendously. Some laborers were eager to work full shifts and put in for overtime to supplement their incomes when the opportunity was available. Others were anxious to skip work whenever possible with the stipulation that neither their jobs nor their earnings would be jeopardized. This range of attitudes and variable willingness to work made it difficult to establish specific guidelines for the unemployed.

An article published in Soziale Praxis during 1896[230] laid down standards of culpability for unemployment. Workers were responsible for their own unemployment and probably ineligible for compensation when they voluntarily left jobs due to deterioration of wages or hours. They were also responsible when dismissed for laziness, drunkenness, debauchery, incompatability or insubordination. The long and variable list of culpable offenses also included repeated absenteeism, tardiness, negligence or poor performance. Those fired for supporting striking colleagues were frequently but not always considered guilty. Membership in a union or political party was not acceptable grounds for firing and workers who lost jobs for such reasons were almost without exception entitled to whatever compensation was availble. The typical case of "unverschuldet" unemployment however sprang from purely economic reasons, taking the form of dismissals attributable to cutbacks and work shortages.

Despite growing recognition that unemployment was a problem which legitimately demanded a social rather than individual solution, concern with abuses of relief programs persisted. The time-tested means of separating the lazy from the hard-working idle was to provide employment. And indeed many felt that public works projects were preferable to insurance or other "handouts". It was however difficult to quickly establish and efficiently administer publicly funded projects without competing with private enterprises during recessions. There were in addition the instances of idle persons not eager for employment. For those who were "Arbeitsscheu"--able but unwilling to work--and expecting to live off of public charity, harsher measures were adopted. As we shall see in the next chapter, a rigid division between those who were "arbeitslos" and those who were "arbeitsscheu" was developing. This worked to the clear advantage of the unemployed who could be treated by society as guilt-free while leaving the work-shy to the tender mercies of the police.

The public was becoming increasingly sophisticated in its dealings with those who were not working. Differentiating among persons unable to work for physical reasons, those unwilling to work due to moral turpitude, and individuals unable to find jobs for purely economic reasons represented a major step forward. This differentiated approach lay at the very heart of evolving modern methods for coping with industrial unemployment. And it took place in Germany during our period largely as the result of the confluence of three historial events: Bismarck's social legislation, the so-called Great Depression and the ongoing process of industrialization. By the time of the 1895 census, those unable to work had become the province of poor relief or social insurance administrators. Those unwilling to work were dealt with by the police, Labor Houses and other legal or correctional authorities. And with the proper classification of individuals, the way finally became clear to put into place the institutional apparatus necessary for coping with problems generated by economically induced unemployment. In the next chapter we shall see how Germans during our period came to organize and implement institutions such as Arbeitsnachweise, labor colonies, Verpflegungsstationen and insurance to deal with unemployment.

In examining aggregate unemployment levels, we have seen how seasonal variations, technology, policy decisions, collective protection, mobility, endogenous labor considerations and micro-economic changes affected German industry. Because the perceived and real sources of unemployment were so diverse, few multi-causal explanations of work shortages were forthcoming. Lack of a comprehensive theory of unemployment which took into consideration the complexity of underlying causes played a major role in limiting contemporary efforts to resolve attendant problems. In conjunction with insufficient quantitative data, which blurred the details of the dilemma, this failure to grasp its broad contours precluded formulation of effective countermeasures. The result, as we shall see in the fourth and final part of this study, was a fragmented effort to contain rather than eliminate industrial unemployment.

PART FOUR: MEASURES TO ALLEVIATE INDUSTRIAL UNEMPLOYMENT

A large portion of the periodical literature devoted to unemployment between 1873 and 1913 outlines contemporary remedies for dealing with the problems of German industry's jobless laborers. That literature and society's corresponding efforts to cope with those out of work can be divided into several discrete but related categories for analytical purposes. The first line of defense against the perils of unemployment was the individual worker himself who was urged to be diligent on the job and parsimonious with the fruits of his labor. In addition to proponents of self-help, there were many who advocated private efforts of a collective nature either through employers' organizations or, on the employees' side, through trade unions. Others attempted to deal with unemployment through legislation and viewed the issue as part of the larger problem of social welfare. In a related vein, there were men who concurred that the public bore responsibility for families which could not support themselves. During the relatively short-lived Second Reich, their concern focused on the form rather than the substance of relief--they argued about administrative jurisdictions and whether unemployment was the proper concern of local, state or national governments.

Beyond that, there were debates over the efficacy of specific public institutions which had evolved to deal with the unemployed. Among the more conspicuous were tramp prisons, labor colonies, work houses, employment offices and public works projects. Although each of these institutions was discussed in print at some length, none of them elicited the avalanche of verbiage generated relatively late in our period by schemes for unemployment insurance. Finally, there was some discussion about alternate employment and here as elsewhere it is interesting to note the practical and concrete rather than theoretical bent of the literature. Short-term solutions for dealing with the immediate problems generated by unemployment--providing food, shelter and perhaps a temporary alternative to idleness or begging--were the order of the day. Very slight attention was given to long-range problems like education, structural shifts in the economy, or changing patterns of demand. Dealing with the industrial unemployed was seen as a social, political and moral problem as well as an economic dilemma and the solutions which will be examined here in some detail reflect this fact.

SELF-HELP: INDIVIDUAL VERSUS COLLECTIVE EFFORTS TO COPE
WITH UNEMPLOYMENT

At a time when German society was called upon to respond effectively to the rapidly increasing demands of economic modernization,[1] collective rather than individual action seemed most likely to achieve results. In approaching the unemployment problem, many contemporaries expressed serious doubts about the efficacy of individual effort. Nevertheless, conservative voices asserting that self-help alone would suffice struck a responsive chord in certain sectors of the economy.

The most vociferous advocates of self-help were mouthpieces of employers' associations. Although some companies[2] provided unemployment benefits for their workers, employers as a group were slow to recognize their responsibility in this area. The following disclaimer by the consistently negative <u>Deutscher Arbeitgeberbund fuer das Baugewerbe</u> appeared as late as 1913: "Wir erkennen ein Beduerfnis, die Arbeiter gegen die Folgen der Arbeitslosigkeit zu schuetzen, nicht an."[3] This statement denying any obligation to those without jobs was part of a larger argument against public unemployment compensation. Given comparable attitudes among most employers, surprisingly few voices called for individual measures like private savings accounts as correctives for unemployment. Instead it was assumed that collective efforts in the form of union or cooperative[4] self-help were necessary if workers were to make realistic strides toward solving their own problems. Employers generally expressed the opinion that the first line of defense against unemployment ought to be labor's collective reserves accumulated through voluntary or automatic savings programs during periods of full employment.

Although there were important differences, employers and would-be reformers shared a common outlook on certain issues related to work shortages. For example, those who argued that relief was a communal responsibility, also placed limitations on the administration of public aid. There was a concensus that only unemployment arising from purely economic causes was of general concern. Those out of work due to illness, accidents, strikes, sloth or military service were not to be dealt with under the same heading as the unemployed. And every effort was made to avoid spurious claims derived from overlooking this distinction. Most articulate advocates of relief also recognized the fact that a certain amount of unemployment was inevitable and therefore stipulated that the problem could only excite general interest when "excessive" numbers were without jobs. Despite the nation's loss of output, most Germans feared extreme social reforms and unlimited demands on the public purse more than they feared the economic or personal ramifications of unemployment.

An article published in the 1906 edition of Reichs-arbeitsblatt reflected this attitude.[5] The author maintained that workers were organizing to defend themselves against unemployment through trade unions and consumers' associations. To supplement self-help projects, all members of society rather than a few innocent victims were called upon to share the costs. Public relief was to augment the private efforts of all economically dependent persons who were to be offered the chance to participate in insurance programs. According to the article cited here, liberal arguments in favor of general unemployment compensation would if carried to their logical conclusion, result in a large dole approaching the modern welfare state.

While reformers feared that state socialism would be the consequence of too much assistance, employers feared that revolutionary socialism would result from too little public interest in unemployment relief. The following comments reflect employers' general preference for a hands-off attitude and their simultaneous reservations about the dangers inherent in this posture.[6]

> Mit der zunehmenden Industrialisierung der Wirtschaft nimmt diese Arbeitslosigkeit zeitweise einen Umfang an, der vordem ungeahnt war. Laenger andauernde Arbeitslosigkeit erzeugt neben schweren wirtschaftlichen und sittlichen Nachteilen fuer die Betroffenen auch Gefahren fuer die oeffentliche Wohlfahrt und Ordnung. Daher tritt die Frage, wie diesem Uebelstand zu begegnen sei, mehr und mehr in den Vordergrund des oeffentlichen Interesses.

As the statement indicates, even employers determined to do as little as possible for the common man believed that they ran a considerable risk by attempting to ignore or contain rather than resolve the unemployment problem. By deferring its costs, they risked increasing the consequences of widespread labor unrest during periods of high unemployment.

In addition to political ramifications, unemployment raised serious economic questions about how to finance relief. Who was to pay the bill for whatever form of compensation society adopted? A wide range of answers to this question were forthcoming. As a corrective to seasonal fluctuations, Otto Most suggested higher wages and a program designed to instruct workers to "lay by something for regularly recurring unemployment".[7] In times of less predictable joblessness stemming from widespread economic distress, the triple solution of public "Vorbeugung, Bekaempfung und Fuersorge"[8] was advocated. Another proposal suggested that savings contributed by workers and employers be supplemented by public funds in times of emergency.

Aside from begging, many felt that the only independent solution for workers was a voluntary or mandatory savings program or some form of insurance. Thrifty workers had access to ordinary savings banks and some availed themselves of plans offered by cooperative consumers' or building societies. A few benefitted from employers' funds. The problem with every form of savings-- as opposed to other unemployment remedies--was that the accumulated reserves were frequently spent by the time that the jobless individual needed them most. Given this drawback, many preferred a system of compensation which provided small but regular payments over a longer period of time rather than savings accounts which gave workers access to their entire reserve all at once.

Weighing the relative advantages of savings as opposed to insurance, the next passage is revealing in terms of contemporary attitudes toward alternate forms of unemployment relief.[9]

> Der Einwand, dass die Verweisung auf die Selbsthilfe den Arbeiter zu Unrecht belaste, wird auch erhoben gegen den Sparzwang, der als Ersatzmittel der Arbeitslosenversicherung und im Gegensatz zu dem Prinzip der Versicherung "all fuer einen" auf der Grundlage des individualistischen Grundsatzes "jeder fuer sich selbst" zu einer Sicherstellung gegen die Folgen der Arbeitslosigkeit vorgeschlagen worden ist.
>
> Alle Vorschlaege sind darin einig, und alle praktischen Erfahrungen haben ergeben, dass von wesentlicher Bedeutung fuer jede Form einer Arbeitslosenunterstuetzung oder Versicherung das Vorhandensein und die Vervollkommung der Arbeitsvermittelung ist.

Many advocates of general assistance for the unemployed worker proposed that the government cover the cost of compensation. Recognizing the social dimension of the unemployment problem, Dr. Richard Freund maintained that the citizenry as a whole should bear the expense of relief which was to be administered through the individual states.[10] Because public expenditures for poor relief and security police would be reduced by controlling unemployment, general revenues could be diverted to supplement private funds for those without work. The crucial point here was that unemployment is not exclusively a problem of individuals--it had an undeniable social component. And by the twentieth century, proposals to eliminate the problem clearly reflected its social dimension, at least as much as its personal ramifications.

One of the main arguments in favor of public support and against self-help through private savings programs derived from the belief that it was impossible for workers to put aside enough money to get by during periods of prolonged unemployment. This being the case, innocent victims in the form of dependent wives and children would suffer when their breadwinner failed to provide an income--presumably through no fault of his or their own. The following plea on behalf of the sacrosanct institution of the German family is typical of this kind of attitude toward self-help as a defense against unemployment.[11]

> Es muss in hohen Grade trostlos sein, gerade im Winter, der an die Schaffenskraft des Familienoberhauptes stets erhoehte Anfordernisse stellt, bei ruestiger Kraft arbeitslos zu sein und mit bestem Willen es nicht aendern zu koennen, dass Frau und Kinder dem Hunger, die Kaelte, dem Elend preisgegeben sind.
>
> Man wende nicht ein, dass solche Faelle nur vereinzelt dastehen; die staben nicht vereinzelt da, sondern sind fuer Hunderttausende in Deutschland--speciell im Winter fuer das Baugewerbe--die Regel.
>
> Auch sage man nicht, dass der Arbeiter im Sommer genuegend hohen Verdienst habe, um fuer den Winter einen Nothpfennig zuruecklegen zu koennen...

Most pleas for relief from the effects of unemployment start with the assumption that society as a whole has a stake equal to that of individuals in eliminating the problem. The implication here is that when personal problems are multiplied many times they assume a social dimension. The subsequent analysis by Dr. Georg Schanz begins with the impact of unemployment on various types of workers and traces the results from demoralization, begging and prostitution to general social disorder.[12]

> Die Arbeitslosigkeit ist eine furchtbare Geissel fuer die Arbeiterbevoelkerung, sie bringt dieser die Gefahr des materiellen und moralischen Ruins. Die Mehrzahl der Menschen wird durch den regulaeren Gang der Beschaeftigung und des Einkommens auf dem Wege des Guten gehalten, sie strauchelt, sobald dieser Gang unterbrechen wird und die Noth an die Thuere pecht. Die besten Charaktere erweisen sich schwach gegenueber dieser Gewalt. Auf Viele wirkt es schon sehr anstumpfend, wenn sie in Folge laengerer Arbeitslosigkeit almosengenoessig werden. Selbstgefuehl und Scham erleiden nicht selten Einbusse. Die unverheirateten Arbeitslosen gerathen leicht ins Wandern, gewoehnen sich ans Nichtsthun und Betteln, kommen in den Kleidern herunter, verfallen dem Alkoholgenuss und der Unreinlichkeit und sinken so allmaehlich in die Klasse der Stromer und Vagabunden, um nicht selten als Verbrecher zu enden, Die unverheirateten weiblichen Arbeitslosen sind der Ausbeutung der Vermittelungsbureaux und der Prostitution ausgesetzt. Auch die verheirateten Arbeitslosen und mit ihnen ihre Familien vorkommen. Der Mann, der wochenlang nichts zu thun hat, wird zum Muessinggaenger und Wirthshausbesucher. Oft ist es in solcher Lage nur noch die Frau, welche die Familie und damit den Mann durch ihre Arbeit erhaelt, und auch das wirkt leicht demoralisirend auf den Mann. Reicht das von der Frau Verdiente nicht aus, sind die allenfalls vorhandenen kleinen Ersparnisse verzehrt, dann kommen Schulden fuer noethigsten Beduerfnisse des Lebens und Miethzinstueckstaende und schliesslich, wenn der Kredit erschoepft ist, die bitterste Noth. Zur Arbeitslosigkeit gesellt sich bald die Wohnungslosigkeit und wenn die Familie einmal auf der Gasse ist, dann ist der vollstaendige Zerfall derselben kaum mehr zu verhindern. Man darf sich nicht wundern, wenn dann den Betreffenden der Muth sinkt, wenn sie sich gaenzlich gehen lassen und wenn sie auf der abschluessigen Bahn allmaehlichen Verkommens dauernd der Gemeinde zur Last fallen. Nicht selten endet aber, ehe es so weit kommt, die durch die Arbeitslosigkeit und Noth zur Verzweiflung gebrachte Familie unter erschuetternden Scenen in gemeinsamen Tod.

Ultimately, the unemployed became a menace to society,

ending either as public pensioners, idlers or disgruntled demonstrators.

The previous emotional appeal to the national conscience was representative of a number of arguments[13] against self-help which adopted a very strong moral tone. Many of these discussions focused on the deleterious effect of charity or begging as a way of coping with unemployment. The beggar was subject to evils of "Muessigang, Arbeits- scheu, Landstreicherei" while dangers to the public included "Drohung, Erpressung, Diebstahl".[14] Compensation and insur- ance provided preferable alternatives to handouts which demoralized destitute recipients. The following attempt to differentiate unemployment assistance from poor relief is especially noteworthy because it acknowledged the workers' aversion to charity. Throughout our period, the unemployed had a difficult time convincing society that they were eager to work and preferred jobs or self-help programs to alms. Every effort was necessary to communicate the desire of most displaced workers to be independent of public largesse.[15]

Das Herabsinken in die Armenpflege soll gerade ver- hindert werden. Der grundsaetzliche Unterschied ist, dass die Armenpflege die voellige Mittelosigkeit, die Beduerftigkeit zur Voraussetzung hat. Die Arbeitslos- enunterstuetzung hat die Mittelosigkeit nicht zur Voraussetzung, im Gegenteil, sie will verhindern, dass dieser aeusserste Zustand eintritt, der bereits die wirtchaftliche Vernichtung einer Existenz bedeutet. Aber auch auf die Wohltaetigkeit will der Arbeiter nicht verwiesen werden. Die Wohltaetigkeit gibt Almosen. Aber selbst wenn private oder oeffentliche Wohltaetigkeit grosser Arbeitslosigkeit gewachsen waere--der ohne sein Verschulden arbeitslos gewordene Arbeiter wuenscht nicht Almosen zu erhalten, sondern,

soweit er sich nicht selbst zu helfen vermag, einen
Anspruch auf Hilfe erheben zu duerfen.

The preceding position was moderate relative to
those which denounced unemployment insurance in equally
strong moral terms. According to Dr. Alfons Fischer,
insurance would also undermine a worker's acquired sense of
responsibility and desire to earn his own living.[16]

> Das weiteren wurde gesagt, dass die Arbeitslosenver-
> sicherung demoralisierend wirken wuerde, denn dem
> Menschen sei der Hang zur Arbeit nicht angeboren, durch
> die Aussicht auf die Arbeitslosenunterstuetzung wuerde
> das eigene Beantwortungsgefuehl gemindert werden.

An entirely similar concern was expressed among those who
hoped to preserve the will to work by providing nothing
beyond a subsistence level of compensation for the unemployed: "Die zu zahlenden Unterstuetzungen sollen auch
nicht so hoch sein, dass sie etwa die Arbeitslosigkeit
beeintraechtigen koennten. Sie sollen nur den notdurftig-
sten Unterhalt ermoeglichen".[17]

The primary concern here was that society pay
enough to keep the unemployed alive without robbing them of
their incentive to work. This involved an assumption about
the nature of the working class which was far from flattering. The prevailing attitude toward labor seemed to have
been simultaneously tinged with fear and condescension. The
essence of it was that workers if left to their own devices
would not choose to work at all--they were presumed to be
inherently lazy and in need of conditioning to resist their
natural inclination toward idleness. Excessive support was

to be avoided as a deterrent to prolonged voluntary unemployment. Despite evidence of labor's preference for jobs over hand-outs, this prejudice persisted.

To avoid competition with employers, compensation for being out of work was never to exceed the lowest wages received for labor. And as for those unwilling to take available jobs, there were many who felt that "those who would not work were not entitled to eat." In addition to the generally acceptable notion that every German had a duty to support himself by his own labor, there were some who believed that every German willing to work had a right to a job.[18]

> Das Recht auf Arbeit ist zwar zur Zeit nur ein imaginaerer Begriff; es wird gesetzlich nur insofern anerkannt, als derjenige, welcher gegen die Pflicht zu arbeiten, groeblich verstoesst, Strafe zu gewaertigen hat. Dennoch wird jeder nicht weniger bedauernswerth erscheinen, der von dem Willen beseelt, durch redliche Arbeit sich und den Seinigen das taegliche Brot zu verdienen, an der Bethaetigung dieser Pflicht lediglich durch Einwirkung hoeherer Gewalten behindert wird.

The alternative to finding employment for those unable to come up with jobs on their own was not very appealing. It involved hunger, demonstrations, social disintegration and ultimately political radicalism which would result in social democracy. In other words, unemployment in addition to its demoralizing effect on individuals posed a fundamental threat to the very fabric of German society.[19]

> ...heute ist die Arbeiterkneipe die Stelle, wo noch am ehesten Arbeitsgelegenheit zu hoeren ist und so pilgert denn der Arbeitslose Mann von Bau zu Bau, von Strasse--

> von Kneipe zu Kneipe--Tage lang, oft Wochen und ja
> Monate lang und nirgends war Arbeit zu finden und zu
> Hause Weib und Kind, die nach Brot verlangen. Ist es
> da ein Wunder, dass der Arbeiter mit solchen Verhaelt-
> nissen unzufrieden ist und seiner Unzufriedenheit
> dadurch Ausdruck gibt, dass er sich als Socialist
> geirt?
>
> Dem gefunden, nicht dem kranken Arbeiter muss in
> der Folge die groessere Fuersorge des Staates zu Theil
> werden, wenn anders Wandelung eintreten soll, denn
> Arbeitslosigkeit ist das Grab jeden Familienglueckes,
> die wahre Nahrmutter der Sozialdemokratie.

So once again the bottom line of concern about the political

implications of unemployment was the exaggerated socialist

menace. As we have seen, this threat was of paramount

importance to opponents as well as benefactors of working-

class causes.

Presumably, measures for the relief of unemploy-

ment worked to the advantage of the labor force and the

theoretical disadvantage of other groups who would share the

cost of providing compensation. Many felt that unemployment

relief was unfair because it benefitted only a single

segment of the population and did so at the expense of all

others. Particular animus was reserved for compensation

administered through trade unions which worked to the

supposed detriment of employers. With regard to the plight

of entrepreneurs during periods of widespread economic dis-

tress, the following statement is revealing:[20]

> Da Arbeitslosigkeit bekanntlich in erhoehtem Masse
> meist nur in Zeiten wirtschaftlichen Niederganges
> eintritt, die Arbeitgeber unter der Ungunst der Kon-
> junkturen aber mindestens eben so leiden, wie die
> Arbeiter selbst, gerade in Zeiten wirtschaftlicher

> Depression zahlreicher Existenzen von Arbeitgebern zu
> Grunde gehen, so duerfte es die Grenze des Moeglichen
> bei weitem ueberschreiten, wenn Mann gerade auf diesem
> Gebiete den Arbeitgebern noch besondere soziale Lasten
> auferlegen wollte.

Given this perspective, it is not surprising that business-men hard-pressed to keep their operations afloat should resent being asked to provide unemployment protection for workers who reserved their gratitude for the trade unions. Particular offense was taken by opponents of the Ghent system who resented the use of public funds to support union administered unemployment relief. This system was portrayed as benefitting "the bitterest enemies of the employer, the trade unions and Social Democracy."[21]

Nor were employers the only ones to oppose the kind of privileged treatment which most unemployment compensation plans afforded organized urban laborers.[22]

> Der Vertreter der Landwirtschaftskammer hatte betont
> dass das Land keine Interesse an der Arbeitslosenver-
> sicherung habe; auf dem Lande gebe es auch im Winter
> keine Arbeitslosigkeit. Das Land koenne keine Lasten
> fuer die in der Stadt lebenden Arbeiter ubernehmen
> zumal da es schon jetzt unter der Leutenot leide. Also
> der Stadt duerfte die Arbeitslosenkasse nicht unter-
> stuetzen; dies sei vielmehr Aufgabe der Staedte, da
> diese ein Interesse an der Ausdehnung der Industrie
> haben. Aber die Staedtevertreter aeusserten die
> schwersten Bedenken gegen die Arbeitslosenversicherung.

This statement implied that industrial management in addi-tion to all of rural, agrarian Germany resented the idea of unemployment benefits paid for by everyone but paid exclu-sively to union-affiliated urban workers. The main problem here involved where to draw the line when subsidizing the needy--once society undertook the support of organized industrial laborers who couldn't find work, wouldn't others acquire an equally legitimate claim on the public's resources? Contemporaries feared that every economically vulnerable group would be entitled to similar treatment. Craftsmen and employers, for example, would be discriminated against by being disqualified from the benefits received by unemployed laborers. The prohibitive cost and political ramifications of the quasi-socialist state which would ensue from general unemployment coverage were obviously to be avoided. Since coverage could not be provided for all classes, no one class was entitled to special treatment.[23]

Class considerations aside, how far should the state have gone to protect and help those unable to take care of themselves? On the interrelationship among self-help, organized labor and state aid, these comments are revealing:[24]

> Die Elmschen Gedankengange beruhen auf der Anschauung; dass es grundsaetzliche und primaere Pflicht des Staates und der Gesellschaft sei, fuer die Arbeitslose zu sorgen, sie "gegen die Folgen der kapitalistischen Wirtschaftsordnung zu schuetzen". Der Grundgedanke der geltenden Wirtschaftsordnung ist dagegen, dass das einzelne Individuum, sei es allein oder durch genossenschaftlichen Zusammenschluss, zunaechst sich selbst zu helfen hat, und dass der Staat, abgesehen von seinen polizeilichen Aufgaben, nur insowiet eingreifen soll, als oeffentliche Interessen, sei es der Volksgesundheit, der Wehrfaehigkeit oder andere es erfordern und als die Selbsthilfe bei normalen Anforderungen nicht imstande ist, von sich aus diesen Interessen Rechnung zu tragen...Nur wo die Selbsthilfe versagt kommt ergaenzend die Staatshilfe in Betracht.

The thrust of this argument was that the state should intervene on the unemployment issue only where self-help failed to protect a majority of individuals against the hardships imposed by a capitalist economy. If the general social welfare were threatened by the extent of distress, society as a whole would be expected to stand as a buffer between certain of its members and unemployment. The state, in other words, was to function as an additional defense against the vicissitudes of economic fluctuations. But it was to intervene only when private efforts failed to avert economic disaster for a large portion of the population.

In addition to political and moral issues, there were a number of more purely economic concerns generated by German society's need to cope with the unemployed. First of all, there was the realization that a certain amount of frictional unemployment was necessary and even healthy in an industrial economy. Writing in 1910, Otto Most expressed this viewpoint quite clearly:[25]

> Unemployment is a problem which affects all classes, yet all forms of unemployment, however painful their effects may be for the individual, cannot be regarded, from an economic standpoint, as regrettable and calling for a remedy. On the contrary, in the labour market, as in all others, a certain excess of supply over demand must be constantly present if business is not to stagnate. A certain number of unemployed, a reserve of labour, is an absolutely indispensable condition of economic progress.

An acceptable level of unemployment by Dr. Most's standards was one percent in summer and three percent in winter.

In the popular consciousness, unemployment went hand in hand with urbanization. As we have seen, newly arrived unskilled workers were among those most susceptible to the ravages of urban work shortages. Their plight was particularly grim in the wake of seasonal or cyclical downswings. The following estimate of unemployment placed the urban industrial nature of the problem in bold relief: "...Im Winter jenes Jahres stellten das weitaus grosste Kontingent der Arbeitslosen die Fabrikarbeiter mit 35,66 Proz. und demnaechst der baugewerblichen Arbeiter mit 15,61 Proz., waehrend die beschaeftigungslosen Landarbeiter nur 3,62 Proz. ausmachten."[26]

Despite such confident estimates of high unemployment among urban members of the industrial labor force, there were some who questioned the seriousness of the problem altogether. Arguing against additional measures to relieve the unemployed and pointing to railroad construction, Arbeitsnachweise plus various subsidies, there were a surprising number of authors who believed that anyone really looking for a job could find work--and find it on his own without travelling long distances.[27] Given this attitude and the firm belief that published statistics frequently exaggerated the amount of distress, there was some comfort to be derived from the popular notion that unemployment was a proper matter for public concern only when it was sufficiently widespread to affect the entire community.[28]

It was, of course, difficult to determine what constituted an excessive level of joblessness and this difficulty was further complicated by inadequate statistics and the issue of culpability. There was general agreement

among those who wrote about unemployment that only individuals out of work through no fault of their own deserved
help. As we noted earlier, drunkenness, strikes or a taste
for leisure resulting in loss of jobs were not to be compensated under the guise of unemployment relief. But in
many instances, the employer and employee were not of one
mind as to the cause of termination and then questions arose
over the legitimacy of applications for aid.

Another source of conflict over unemployment
compensation involved the wage scales in seasonal trades.
The issue here was whether wages were sufficiently inflated
to compensate employees for predictable periods of idleness,
usually necessitated by natural causes such as weather.
There were many who argued that higher pay for seasonal
labor was intended to encourage the worker to save something
for months when he would have to seek alternate employment
or, failing that, live without an income. As we have seen,
Otto Most's solution[29] to the problems of seasonal workers
was to pay them well and urge labor unions to teach their
members about saving enough of their salaries to get by
during the inevitable slack periods. Others proposed more
general economic solutions tailored to the specific cause of
unemployment.[30]

While insurance or other temporary support would
help in some instances, more permanent remedies involving
the long-term transfer of personnel were necessary to combat
structural changes which led to the decline of entire

occupations or the closing of specific firms. Surprisingly, there were very few instances when the logical expedient of shifts in the labor force was suggested as an alternative to unemployment compensation. The author cited below also distinguished himself by outlining a broad range of solutions to a problem which many contemporaries tried to cope with by advancing a single measure.[31]

> Die Bekaempfung der Arbeitslosigkeit durch vorbeugende und repressive Massnahmen bildet nicht den eigentlichen Gegenstand der hier zu gebenden Darstellung. Es gibt eine Reihe solcher Massnahmen. Hier sind vor allem zu nennen die Regelung des Lehrlingswesens usw., sowie die Vermittelung vorhandener Arbeit und die Arbeitsbeschaffung (Notstandsarbeiten).

THE ROLES OF EMPLOYERS' AND EMPLOYEES' ORGANIZATIONS

Among those who demanded that the unemployed solve their own problems, self-help was frequently the preferred solution. However, when individual effort proved inadequate, a second line of defense was to be found among organized coalitions of employers and, more often, employees. Although associations like trade unions and management cooperatives were not without detractors, the population at large came to accept the initiatives of private interest groups in the realm of unemployment relief as a preferrable alternative to a comprehensive system of public welfare.

We have seen that the specter of welfare leading to socialism was repeatedly thrust forth as the inevitable result of broadly based public unemployment assistance. In view of this pervasive attitude, it is perhaps surprising to recall the relative disinterest which the Social Democratic Party exhibited toward the entire unemployment problem.[32] The fatalism of Marxist orthodoxy and the inevitability of historical change made it difficult for theoretically oriented Social Democrats to concern themselves with reforms which would improve the daily lives of the industrial labor force. While their attention was riveted on political growth and survival, responsibility for economic improvements was delegated to the relatively apolitical trade unions. Even in the more radical unions with Social Democratic affiliation, members looked to cooperative efforts between the state, community and private sources to resolve the dilemmas created by unemployment. At a time when organized Social Democrats were spending twenty-two million Marks for strikes, agitation and organization, only eight million Marks were allocated for unemployment benefits. Given the priorities reflected by these expenditures, the trade unions, with little more than tacit party approval, made significant strides during the early Reichsgrundung years. Organized workers began to benefit from a wide range of welfare funds which could be drawn on to sustain them through illness, strikes, disability and even death. Although typically their organizational links with Social Democracy were tenuous, many of the unions' gains evaporated with the advent of Bismarck's anti-socialist legislation.[33]

With regard to unemployment rates, there is absolutely no reason to assume that union members were more susceptible to economic fluctuations than their unorganized counterparts. Figures on work shortages published in the Reichsarbeitsblatt failed to indicate that any significant disparity existed between the unemployment levels of organized and non-union workers.[34] However, the question naturally arises whether the unorganized worker was as visible, accessible or responsive to those who counted the unemployed. A negative answer would be difficult to document although one suspects that the less articulate non-union workers who had nothing to gain by registering as unemployed were even more susceptible to the vicissitudes of the labor market. As we have seen, the advantages which unions offered their members were often indirect but significant, especially during the Bismarckian era.

Although a few unions like the _Deutsche Buchdrucker Verein_ established funds for members who needed to travel in order to find work, it was not until the 1890's that even the more progressive unions gave serious consideration to general unemployment compensation. And according to published estimates,[35] the average level of unemployment among organized workers from 1890 until the end of our period hovered around three or three and a half percent, lasting for a period of about two weeks. So by the time unions came around to providing compensation for lost wages, unemployment was a less pressing problem than other reforms whose introduction earned the loyal support of many industrial workers.[36]

In fact, the number of unions offering unemployment compensation remained relatively small throughout the nineteenth century. Paul Berndt noted that as late as 1897 only fifteen out of fifty-six unions surveyed were offering unemployment benefits to their members. The General Commission of German Trade Unions justified this low level of support by referring to the perils which continued to plague organized labor even after the repeal of the socialist law.[37]

> Den Gewerkschaften fehlt jede sichere Basis. Von jedem Polizeibeamten koennen sie aufgeloest und in ihrer Entwickelung gehindert werden(!). Staendige Sorge haben die Leiter der Organisationen des Vermoegen derselben vor der Konfiskation sicher zu stellen.

> Unter solchen Umstaenden koennen die Gewerkschaften nur
> mit groesster Vorsicht groessere Vermoegen, wie sie
> fuer solche Unterstuetzungseinrichtungen erforderlich
> sind, ansammeln. Erst gewaehre man den Arbeitern das
> Recht, sich frei zu Vereinigen und an der Kommunal- und
> Staatsverwaltung teilzunehmen, dann wird der Weg fuer
> die Arbeitslosenversicherung frei sein und von den
> Gewerkschaften auch beschritten werden.

With the memory and ever-present threat of confiscation, it is perhaps not surprising that many labor leaders wanted to establish a secure footing for their organizations before risking the formation of large funds whose seizure could wipe out their reserves. Prior to the turn of the century, relatively few union members were covered by unemployment protection.[38] This situation changed during the last ten years of our period when the more secure German trade unions began to supply unemployment benefits through mutual insurance programs.

By 1908, forty out of the sixty Independent Federations granted unemployment compensation which usually included travel and severance allowances. Seventy-two percent of their total membership or 1,314,243 individuals qualified for this coverage. Comparable figures applied to the smaller Christian trade union movement where 192,443 workers--73% of the membership--in fourteen of the twenty unions qualified for unemployment compensation. An even higher percentage of coverage was achieved by the Hirsch-Dunker Associations where 97% of the membership--slightly more than 100,000--received support for travel and unemployment. In all of the above cases, participation in unemployment insurance programs was compulsory for union members.

As a footnote to any discussion of compensation by trade unions, mention should be made of approximately 350,000 shop assistants, clerks and salesmen who benefitted from the unemployment plans of commercial associations. Also noteworthy was the effort of the "Produktion" of Hamburg, the only cooperative society which succeeded in setting up a program for unemployment insurance. This group of about 42,000 members had access to an emergency fund which could be drawn on (regardless of an individual's accumulated input) to purchase merchandise from the Society during periods of unemployment.

The cost of compensating jobless members was substantial particularly during recessions. In 1908, for example, unions spent almost nine times the amount laid out by Arbeitsnachweise to alleviate unemployment. During that year alone, the independent unions spent 8,100,000 Marks with travel benefits consuming 1,200,000 Marks and removal allowances amounting to 29,000 Marks. The Hirsch-Dunker Corporative Associations spent 288,068 Marks on unemployment during 1908 with 18,241 Marks going for travel benefits. Of the existing commercial associations, nine shop assistants' groups distributed 226,250 Marks to unemployed members while four groups of clerks and commercial travellers gave 6,651 Marks and five associations of higher grade clerks paid out 67,096 Marks. Fourteen of the twenty Christian trade unions, with a membership of 192,443 or 73% of the total, paid unemployment and travel benefits which amounted to 134,453 Marks in 1908.[39]

Looking back, we find that during the eighteen years between 1908 and 1891 the independent trade unions spent approximately 27,500,000 Marks on unemployment compensation. The amounts paid out varied with the economic fluctuations from one year to the next. Unions which spent a half million Marks on unemployment relief in 1900 paid out more than twice that amount when a recession struck the following year.[40] Paralleling the growth of the independent trade unions, the Hirsch-Dunker Associations by 1894 had a total membership of 67,000 to whom they paid 73,000 Marks for all forms of unemployment compensation. Five years later in 1899, the total expended on unemployed members had increased by more than a third, amounting to 105,000 Marks.

Predating other union efforts, special note should be taken of the Verein Deutscher Kaufleute which as early as 1885 had established an insurance fund for unemployed members who could receive a monthly stipend ranging from thirty to forty-five Marks for a period of up to six months. After 1890, the size and duration of the stipend were adjusted to correlate with the length of membership: After one year, compensation was limited to 30 Marks for three months; after five years, members received 37.50 Marks and after ten years, they were eligible for the maximum 45 Mark payment for each of six months. Between 1885 and the turn

of the century, this coverage cost the <u>Verein</u> <u>Deutscher</u>
<u>Kaufleute</u> a total of 63,608 Marks.

The amount of compensation paid for unemployment
varied considerably among divergent professional groups.
The frequency and duration of unemployment as well as the
length of waiting periods before compensation began reflected differences in unions. The length of compensation
and the stipend per jobless worker were other widely ranging
variables which affected the total cost of supporting
unemployed workers. After the turn of the century, most
unemployment among union men was of relatively short duration, with overall quarterly averages ranging consistently
between two and three weeks. But some unions had unemployment which typically lasted no more than a day or two while
others reported joblessness which stretched out for periods
in excess of five weeks. Almost all unemployment funds
imposed waiting periods on their subscribers which meant
that no compensation was paid in cases where the duration of
a worker's idleness was not sufficiently lengthy to qualify
for aid. Despite waiting periods, during times like the
economically depressed early months of 1907, the unions
spent more than a million Marks on unemployment compensation
during a single quarter.

As an alternative to union funds, the government
occasionally provided relief for the unemployed. One
indicator of the cost involved in this type of extraordinary
unemployment benefit may be gauged from the fact that a 1909

tax on tobacco involved legislation which provided a four million Mark indemnity for tobacco workers who would lose their jobs as a result of decreased production attributable to the tax. Six months after the passage of this provision--by January 1, 1910--46,000 men had already collected more than 1.6 million Marks.

In addition to plans that merely advocated public expenditures, there were a number of proposals floating around which dealt with how to apportion the costs. National, state and local governments, employers, cooperative societies, unions, and individual workers were among those expected to share whatever expense was involved in alleviating unemployment. The fractions assigned to each varied predictably with the interests of those assessing the obligation. One comprehensive suggestion for apportioning responsibility advanced the persuasive argument that more individuals could be helped by the government if public agencies worked to supplement private efforts.

Establishing a national labor exchange, subsidizing union relief funds, sponsoring public works projects for construction workers in winter and encouraging non-union skilled labor to organize were four ways to combat unemployment. Relief was recognized as a financial issue and the proper role of the state was thought to be subsidizing the meager benefits paid by existing unions, trade associations and insurance funds. In this way the government could alleviate the suffering of jobless workers who received "too little to live and too much to die."[41]

Analyses such as this notwithstanding, there were severe limitations which characterized both public and private expenditures on unemployment throughout our period. Despite the restrictions which unions placed on unemployment benefits paid to members, we should note from the outset that their efforts were more successful than others. They were also more numerous than comparable undertakings on the part of employers who tried to help the people that worked for them.[42] Although many trade unions and private associations provided an increasing amount of protection against unemployment during the early twentieth century, attention must be paid to the criteria which continued to limit compensation.

In this context, the relationship between unemployment and strikes was a delicate issue for union members and separate funds had to be maintained for each. Typically, there were two ways in which strikes led to unemployment. In the first instance, the worker might lose his job as the result of a strike in which he was not participating. He would then be entitled to claim benefits from his union's unemployment fund. In the second case strike participants might find themselves unable to return to work after the end of a labor dispute. Even when strike benefits ceased, workers under such circumstances were frequently denied unemployment coverage. Unemployment relief for those without jobs due to economic reasons was paid without question. But loss of work due to personal reasons, including union affiliation, remained a grey area in terms of compensation.[43]

The further troublesome question of responsibility for an employee's loss of work was repeatedly raised and here the prevailing opinion was that support should go exclusively to those afflicted by "unfreiwillige und unverschuldete Arbeitslosigkeit". Obviously, it was often difficult to determine whether employees were in any way culpable for their own lack of work. These rather vague outlines were suggested in an article published in Soziale Praxis on March 21, 1901: "Schuldig ist der Arbeitnehmer an der Arbeitslosigkeit insbesondere in folgende Faellen: a) Grundloses Verlassen der Arbeit b) Verlust der Arbeitsgelegenheit in Folge Kuendigung des Arbeiters c) Verlust der Arbeitsgelegenheit in Faellen der Gewerbeordnung."[44] Unfortunately, these amorphous pronouncements did not go very far toward clarifying qualifications for compensation in individual cases. And this in practice was the crucial point.

In addition to determining responsibility for unemployment, a judgment had to be made as to whether union regulations permitted coverage in each instance. In some industries, the problem of seasonal fluctuations in the labor market was a chronic complication for those trying to design a program of unemployment compensation.[45] Unions arrived at various solutions, designed to deal with the divergent problems of their trades. While the building artisans confined coverage to the months between April and November, neither the Free Unions nor the Christian Unions exempted seasonal unemployment from their relief programs.[46] Further questions arose about the requirements which unions could make on unemployed members with regard to travel and work outside of the trade. As a general rule, single men were expected to be geographically mobile if finding a job dictated a change of residence. Less pressure was placed on married men with families to move and virtually no member was required to accept a position "ausserhalb des Berufs, Arbeit schlechthin anzunehmen".[47]

The general public attitude toward union control over their unemployed members hinged less on the question of administration than on the source of support. If public funds were used to supplement members' contributions, conservative interests resented union control. Much of the controversy centered around the Ghent system of proportional indemnity for unemployment. The first German city to try this plan was Strassburg which introduced coverage of resident organized laborers during 1907. In rapid succession, a number of other cities copied this model. The Ghent system was so successful that cities like Cologne with municipal unemployment insurance seriously considered initiating changes which would subsidize union unemployment funds.

Despite the advantages of drawing on existing union administrative apparati, the Ghent system posed serious drawbacks according to its numerous detractors. Many saw the system as a means of strengthening the unions directly by increasing their hold on organized labor and indirectly by making membership a precondition for equal benefits. Since the unions would administer compensation and naturally favor their own members, the Ghent System tended to lure non-union members into the more powerful labor organizations. Nevertheless, unions were not always enthusiastic supporters of the system. Labor leaders repeatedly denied that the introduction of unemployment relief would cause unions to lose ground in the class struggle. They advanced the claim that unemployment coverage would tie members to labor organizations and insure their continued support. According to the following excerpt, unemployment relief did not drive men out of unions which provided coverage but worked to advance the cause of organized labor.[48]

> Sie sehen ihre Hauptaufgabe in der Verbesserung der Lohn und Arbeitsbedingungen ihrer Mitglieder. Die Arbeitslosenunterstuetzung ist fuer sie kein Hemmschuh in diesem Streben, sondern ein vorzuegliches Mittel zu rascherem Vorwaertskommen. Die Arbeitslosenunterstuetzung fesselt die Mitglieder an die Organisationen, was am besten dadurch bewiesen wird, dass trotz aller Muehe zahlreiche Bauarbeiter nicht zum Ubertritt aus den Verbaenden mit Arbeitslosenunterstuetzung in unsern Verband zu bewegen sind. Die Arbeitslosenunterstuetzung traegt zur Erhaltung der Kampffaehigkeit der Arbeiter bei.

In view of the advantages which accrued exclusively to organized labor, many critics of the Ghent System argued that it was absurd to expect society as a whole to subsidize the union unemployment funds.

As we noted earlier, there were very few instances during the nineteenth century in which individual firms tried to provide unemployment protection for their employees.[49] By 1910, only a handful of companies had established employers' funds which provided compensation for those facing unemployment. One of the few examples of any significance was Carl Zeiss' Optical Instrument Works in Jena. There compensation took the form of severance pay for any worker who was involuntarily dismissed. In many cases, the amounts paid were substantial, sometimes approaching six months' wages and a quarter of an entire pension. Even though an imperial act made indemnities to discharged workmen increasingly common, very few companies provided adequate unemployment protection for their employees during our period. Slow to act individually, employers as a group were also loathe to assume financial responsibility for workers unable to find jobs. As a typical example, it is worth recalling employers in the building trades who feared that unemployment funds would be used to strengthen unions, support strikes, aggravate class struggles and rob management of its "Herr im Hause" role.[50]

Presumably, a major cause of unemployment was widespread distress among industrial firms. And during times when business conditions required employers to curtail their work force they were in no position to give away money. They resented supporting unemployment compensation with Marks which they could not afford to pay out for wages. Furthermore, to complete a circle, they argued that the more employers were forced to pay in unemployment compensation, the less they would have to meet payrolls. Hence, the fewer employees they could engage and the more unemployment there would be. Employers admittedly faced problems during economic downswings but they had certain advantages over the men and women who worked for them. If the latter made bad employees, others were almost always available as replacements. And during times of economic trouble, reduced hours and wages or layoffs were options exercised at the employer's discretion. Meanwhile, those workers out of a job due to seasonal changes or depressed business conditions frequently lacked attractive alternatives.

Certain periods in given geographical areas were particularly inauspicious for those seeking support among industrialists for unemployment measures, as these remarks from a 1909 conference in Baden indicate.[51]

> Indusrielle weisen darauf hin, dass Zeit jetzt unguenstig sei, man leide unter der Zollpolitik und auch durch die neue Reichsverischerungsordnung drohten den Arbeitgebern weiters grosse Ausgabe. Fernen wurde betont, dass die industriellen Verhaeltnisse in Baden, das weder Eisen noch Kohlen besitzt und weit vom Moore liegt, keineswegs besonders guenstig seien und andererseits gerade hier die Arbeitslosigkeit im Vergleich zu anderen Aeras keinen grossen Umfang genommen habe.

Here as elsewhere there seemed to be a reluctance and even resentment at being asked to pay for benefits which would not yield any direct return to the individuals sharing their expense. This resentment tended to coalesce along geographical as well as class lines--making it doubly unlikely that employers in areas like Baden would embrace schemes for national unemployment compensation. This was apparent at a conference convened by the ministry of interior on November 12, 1909, in Karlsruhe. Included were leading representatives of "grosseren Staedten, Handelskammern, Handwerkskammern, Arbeitgeber- und Arbeiterverbaenden". However, it was the arguments set forth by the Verband suddeutscher Industrielle in a plea to the Baden government which best defined the position of those opposed to unemployment insurance:[52]

> Als Gruende gegen die geplante Versicherung macht die Eingabe unter anderen die folgenden geltend: In Deutschland und Baden koenne von einer positiven Arbeitslosigkeit nicht gesprochen werden, solange in der Landwirtschaft und auch in einzelnen Gewerben und Orten Arbeitermangel herrsche. Von der Versicherung sei zu befuerchten eine Herabsetzung des Selbstverantwortlichkeitsgefuehls der Arbeiter, eine zunehmende Verweichlichung der ungelernten Arbeiterschaft, die schon jetzt die schwereren arbeiten Auslaendern ueberlasse, eine Hemmung des Zurueckstroemens der Arbeiter auf das Land in Zeiten schlechten Geschaeftsganges der Industrie, ein Aufhoeren der jetzt durch zahlreiche Industrielle erfolgenden Weiterbeschaeftigung von Arbeitern in Zeiten des Tiefstandes, eine weitere finanzielle Belastung der Arbeitgeber und eine Herabsetzung der Exportfaehigkeit der badischen Industrie. Das Genter System insbesondere bedeute eine Stellungnahme des Staates und der Gemeinden im wirtschaftlichen Kampfe zugunsten der organisierten Arbeiter. Als Massregeln zur Bekaempfung der Arbeitslosigkeit und ihrer Folgen empfiehlt die Eingabe die Foerderung der Spartaetigkeit, insbesondere auch Unterstuetzung der Plaene der Vereinsversicherungsbank fuer Deutschland (Volksversicherung), Ermoeglichung der Einrichtung von

Zwangssparkassen fuer Jugendliche, die frueher bei
verschiedenen badischen Betrieben bestanden haetten,
aber auf Grund der Gewerbeordnung aufgehoben worden
waeren, endlich die Ueberlassung von Ackerland seitens
der Gemeinden an die Industriearbeiter und uberhaupt
Landerwerb durch diese.

In addition to private schemes involving entrepreneurs in remedies for the unemployment problem, there were a
number of quasi-public plans which required their cooperation in varying degrees despite reservations such as those
outlined above. Municipal projects to provide work for the
unemployed reflected the kind and extent of employer involvement which was forthcoming. In numerous instances,
German cities contracted with private industry to engage
unemployed workers on either a part time or full time
basis.[53] This was especially necessary in situations where
the municipalities could not employ all available hands in
traditional public works projects. Employers were urged to
find work for previously jobless individuals as a public
service and as a substitute for alms which only encouraged
sloth among the laboring poor. Every effort was made to
find an alternative to charity for the sake of the workers
themselves and society as a whole.[54]

As we have indicated, there were numerous examples
of individual entrepreneurs who did more to alleviate
unemployment than merely hiring new workers. Many firms--
particularly those dependent on skilled labor--tried to
avert unemployment by reducing hours and wages rather than
resorting to lay-offs. Some efforts in this direction were

so successful that resentful employees "voluntarily" left their jobs rather than work under conditions necessitated by a cut-back in production. In situations like this, an increasing number of workers came to rely on the services of labor exchanges as an alternative to coping with underemployment or total joblessness.

Among private exchanges, there were three types, the first of which was managed by employers. Through Employers' Associations, 114 labor exchanges filled more than 510,000 jobs in 1909. And about half that number was filled by Trade Guilds through 2400 exchanges across Germany. The second type of labor exchange, which functioned primarily in large cities, owed its existence to associations of workers which by 1908 were filling about 300,000 vacancies. The third type of operation, under the joint management of masters and men, frequently evolved out of agreements to transform employers' or employees' exchanges into jointly run enterprises. These offices were most successful in smaller industries like the printing trade. Sixty jointly managed exchanges in 1904 filled an estimated 51,000 jobs while the 47 offices which survived until 1908 managed to fill almost 90,000 vacancies. In addition to the three types of private exchanges, there were a growing number of public employment agencies after 1890. When the collective but private efforts of employers or employees failed to cope with the unemployment situation, it became necessary for the state to intervene. As we shall see next, this intervention frequently took the form of legislation or the inauguration of welfare programs.

THE ROLE OF THE STATE: PUBLIC MEASURES FOR DEALING WITH
UNEMPLOYMENT THROUGH WELFARE AND LEGISLATION

The welfare system which began to emerge during
our period was greatly influenced by the bundle of factors
grouped under the umbrella term modernization. Despite
conditions unique to the late nineteenth century, however,
it is worth noting that welfare in the form of state intervention in the economy had historical antecedents of long
standing in Prussia. For many centuries, the full employment of individuals had been identified with the common good
and sought as a means to promote the economic power of the
state.

According to R.A. Dorwart's monograph on the roots
of the early modern welfare state,[55] one can trace its
origins back to the middle ages. The crucial but rather
amorphous trait that Dorwart sees as common to the Prussian
welfare state throughout its development was the exercise of
its legal police power to promote public wellbeing. Sharing
this goal, three stages of evolution can be discerned.
During the later middle ages, the state usurped the welfare
functions performed by the Catholic Church and secularized
them. Between 1500 and 1800 the notion of welfare was
gradually transformed from a moral or religious concept into
an economic one. Medieval paternalism gave way to dynastic
mercantilism accompanied by doctrines which stressed economic growth as the best means to enhance the power of the
state. During the last half of the eighteenth century, the

Prussian state rejected paternalistic intervention, preferring the Enlightenment, political democracy, liberalism and
ultimately nineteenth-century _laissez_ _faire_ doctrines.
Finally, during the 1870's and 1880's, a new stage in the
evolution of a welfare state began when Bismarck's social
legislation revitalized the desire for state intervention
which shaped German attitudes toward welfare into the
twentieth century.

During the years which separated the _Reichsgrun-_
dung from the French Revolution, the functions of the state
had undergone a transformation which differentiated the old
preindustrial form of government from its modern counterpart. Hans-Juergen Puhle distinguishes between the planning
functions of the new state charged with supervising change
and the old state whose primary objective was to preserve
the status quo. Puhle describes the structural and func-
tional differences between the modern state as policy maker
and its predecessor limited to operating as a politically
neutral instrument. Rather than confining its activities to
collecting taxes, raising an army and preserving peace, the
modern German state was prepared to intervene decisively in
order to regulate social and economic development.[56]

To understand the welfare policies which emerged
under Bismarck, it might be helpful to recall certain
carryovers from the early part of the century. One legacy
of Napoleonic rule in the German states was a system of
decentralized authority which left political and judicial

power firmly entrenched in the hands of the Staende elite that historically exercised local control over government administration. Even after 1871, the heirs of the old order reorganized in political parties and economic interest groups retained power and the reigns of administration which were reserved for federal bureaucrats in countries like England. As economic development proceeded, the new representatives of big business were grafted onto the old agrarian power structure under Bismarck's benevolent eye. In the political arena, the increasingly urban, industrialized masses were also organized into pseudo-democratic parties which encouraged artisans, shopkeepers, proletarians and bourgeoisie alike to demand state intervention in the new depression-prone economy.

As modernization proceeded, two competing views of political democracy engaged in an uneven contest for support in Bismarckian Germany. The older view had its roots in the Anglo-Saxon Herrschafts-principle of sovereignty and the writings of John Locke. This view stressed that ownership of property provided the basis for freedom, emancipation and participation in politics. The liberals who embraced this posture saw the primary function of the state in protection of property and assigned a lower priority to participation than political education. A second more radical view of political democracy won socialist support. Its intellectual forbears were adherents of anarchism, Marxism and English Utilitarianism. In their scheme of things, the state's primary function was to introduce equality through frequent intervention and a policy which placed highest priority on political participation. Given this dichotomy, one could interpret Bismarck's suffrage program as implementing the former view in Prussia. But in Germany, the Chancellor usurped certain aspects of the latter view, robbing the true radicals of their popular appeal at the same time that he persecuted them as internal enemies of the state.[57]

Under Bismarck state intervention supplied a sophisticated back-up system on which big business or big agricultural concerns could rely. It came into play when the efforts of party organizations and interest groups failed to provide sufficient control over the vicissitudes of a rapidly developing economy. If self-help was the first line of defense against unemployment and private associations were the second, the state was looked to as a third and final bulwark against economic disaster. Doctrines of laissez faire and economic liberalism didn't suffice to protect industrial workers or employers from the uncertainties which were produced by the crash of 1873 and compounded by subsequent slumps during a period of rapid change. Between 1873 and 1913, the government was looked to as a last resort to limit the spread of discontent due to joblessness. Its function in this context was to protect property and preserve the political order. During our period the state was given a mandate to keep a tight reign on the parallel processes of industrialization and political

democratization. By 1913 and subsequently during the
economic crises at the end of the 1920's, ostensibly conservative governments played a radical role in implementing the
goals of a true modern welfare state. Under the Weimar
Republic, however, even more extreme measures were required
to cope with the severe depressions of a more mature economy
and a more democratic political system.

During our period, Otto Most pointed out that the
state automatically exercised a certain amount of control
over the labor market by performing such mundane tasks as
arresting vagabonds, raising an army and administering poor
relief. Dr. Most estimated that of the half million en-
listed men in the German army, 200,000 were drawn from the
civilian working class. He also calculated that even under
normal conditions there were at least a quarter of a million
convictions each year for vagabondage. And he concluded
that if the workers detained by the prisons and the military
"were thrown on the labor market at the date of the census
in December, 1895, the number of the unemployed would be
very nearly double, rising from 3 1/2 percent of the entire
working class to over 6 per cent."[58]

Neither prisons nor large armies were creations of
the Second Reich. For centuries, the state had been coping
with the problems of protecting society from enemies,
foreign and domestic. Under the latter headings, beggars,
vagabonds and the poor posed difficulties nearly as ancient
as they were pervasive. As early as 789, Charlemagne had

legislated against roving "waremongers and hucksters" whose crooked practices were conducive to an itinerant lifestyle. Despite legislation, the number of vagabonds in the German states underwent a substantial increase after the Crusades. A large mobile population preyed on respectable citizens during the thirteenth century and by 1400 they constituted a well-organized menace in the territories east of the Rhine. During the fifteenth century, gypsies began to arouse public animosity which over the years was compounded by the antics of unemployed soldiers, highwaymen, jobless servants and robbers of every description thriving on the spoils of vulnerable travellers and isolated villages.

Widespread violence and extortion were the frequent companions of early modern Germany's marginal itinerant population. And to make matters even worse, vagabonds were not above taking advantage of Catholic religious precepts which encouraged individual charity. In addition to tithing, parishioners were expected to give alms for the support of honest but impoverished wayfarers ranging from pilgrims and students to mendicant friars. The Church did not regard begging as less than respectable and prior to the Reformation it was common for the clergy to solicit and redistribute charitable donations. Unfortunately, this practice led to fraud and deception among selfishly motivated predecessors of modern solicitors of spare change.[59]

The problem then as now was to separate legitimate claims of the needy from spurious requests of those who were vagrants and thieves by choice. In varying degrees, poverty has been a given of western civilization ever since men began keeping historical records and probably long before that. So when governments undertook to secularize the powers and responsibilities of the medieval Church, the state naturally inherited its role in the administration of poor relief as part of the bargain. In the decentralized German states local charities were established to care for those unfortunate few who were truly unable to support themselves. Poor relief was necessary for the survival of wounded veterans, orphans, the old, the sick and those unable to find work. In a secular age, it was up to the government to provide relief for persons who genuinely needed it and at the same time to discourage bogus requests for help from the professional beggars and vagabonds who preyed on respectable citizens.

In pursuance of this goal, a police ordinance of 1515 had specifically charged magistrates with the administration of public poorhouses and offices. On a theoretical level, the seventeenth-century political philosopher Seckendorf attributed the following responsibilities to German princes: Guarantees of economic livelihood, poor relief, care in poor houses and protection from beggars and idle wayfarers. In 1687, the Hohenzollerns adopted a more utilitarian attitude toward the criminal and vagrant poor who fell under their jurisdiction. All those capable of productive activity--including a motley array of beggars, prostitutes, unmarried women and loiterers--were put to work spinning and those who refused were sent to prisons or houses of correction. The scarcity of spinners which threatened to depress Prussia's wool industry during the seventeenth century was to be alleviated by teaching idle hands how to spin and employing them for the mutual benefit of manufacturers and the state. By the end of the seventeenth century, in the central provinces of Brandenburg, Pommerania, Magdeburg and Halberstadt, the mercantilist Hohenzollern electors had established spinning houses for local paupers and issued edicts to drive foreign beggars out of their dominions.

Finally, in 1703 legislation was enacted which established a system of poor relief that remained in effect throughout Prussia for over two centuries. According to the edict, the poor were required to register in order to be screened for need and organized for work if they were capable. We are told that many tried to avoid the proffered employment, preferring the leisure of begging or even prison life to the activity of the workhouse. It is interesting to note here that this pattern prevailed until the late nineteenth century at which time the Hohenzollerns still favored publicly subsidized work programs rather than charity as a remedy for unemployment.[60] By that time it should have been clear that most unemployed persons preferred work to alms, but the idea that sloth was the natural inclination of the lower classes was not easily dispelled.

Although this brief discussion of poverty, vagabonds and charity is rather sketchy, it constitutes an
important element of the prehistory which helped to shape
attitudes toward the unemployed during our period. Prior to
the nineteenth century, most legitimately needy alms-seekers
stayed close to home partly because of inadequate transportation but primarily because poor relief had been made a
local responsibility by a Prussian edict of April 1696.
With the advent of industrialization, however, the size of
the labor market expanded, physical movement was facilitated
by improved transportation, and the impediments to job
mobility associated with guilds had disappeared.

Travel thus became a frequent component of and
corrective for unemployment. However, centuries of sus-
picion against itinerants generated by the kinds of abuse
outlined above did not disappear overnight. Unemployed
travellers had been identified with lazy, drunken, immoral
and even illegal behavior for generations. It is highly
probable that the prejudices of their forefathers continued
to affect Bismarck's contemporaries as they sought to cope
with the old problem of unemployment in a new industrial
age.

The social legislation which Bismarck introduced
during the 1880's marked a subtle but distinct departure
from anything the state had done in the past for the labor
force. Workers were insured against physical inability to
perform work, but they were not protected against an econo-

mically-induced inability to find jobs. Despite Bismarck's patronizing statements about a "right to work", no unemployment insurance was forthcoming as part of his social legislation. Nor were any measures enacted which placed the state in the role of intermediary between employers and their hired hands. Labor's priority demands for higher wages and better working conditions were not sympathetically received by the government.

Although legislation helped to reduce the uncertainties and attendant anxieties of an industrial worker's existence, it did not eliminate them entirely. The repeated downswings which followed the crash of 1873 retained ample latitude for wreaking havoc in the lives of German laborers despite the efforts of Bismarck to woo them through his limited program of social insurance. Unfortunately, the Chancellor was simply not willing to assume the full burden of the role he toyed with by trying to transfer working class support from the persecuted trade unions to the state. Posing as a protector of the proletariat, the Bismarckian state recognized a limited obligation to give assistance to its weaker citizens as well as the right to take money from them in the form of taxes or service in the form of military duty.

It was not in the public interest that unemployment be allowed to reach proportions which caused starvation or open rebellion and measures were taken to control the impact of economic recessions. During unusually severe cyclical downswings, discussions of general unemployment relief were numerous. Although efforts were made to alleviate the results of unemployment through severance pay, reduced hours and institutions ranging from tramp prisons and employment offices to labor colonies, no preventive federal legislation was forthcoming during our period. Given the recent and tenuous nature of unification and Germany's long-standing tradition of decentralized authority, it was probably unrealistic to look for federal unemployment relief under Bismarck.

Perhaps more surprising than the lack of a nationally administered program was the sluggishness of government initiative in the individual states. Historically, public efforts to deal with the problems of the industrial unemployed evolved on the municipal level and connections across broader geographical areas developed relatively late. Most of the public discussions and programs were generated by economic necessity--concern about unemployment appeared to be short-term, with demands for new programs surfacing and disappearing in direct proportion to the urgency of the problem itself. In Imperial Germany, unemployment compensation, much like poor relief in preceding centuries, came to be seen as a municipal service-- public works projects, employment offices, insurance programs all had grass roots origins. They did not filter down to local communities as innovations from above; federal and state agencies were slower to respond to the needs of the unemployed than local bureaucracies. Measures to alleviate unemployment were instituted on a communal basis first and then an effort was made to establish an organizational network by linking local offices together.

At every administrative level public unemployment relief had definite limitations placed on its scope. Municipal as well as state and federal officials wanted to do no more than was absolutely necessary to alleviate the immediate symptoms of the problem. A 1913 Hannover newspaper article indicated that although many recognized that the public interest was best served when the state acted to avert large-scale unemployment, no level of government was willing to acknowledge an inherent responsibility to eliminate work shortages by guaranteeing jobs for the unemployed. Although a blanket promise to provide jobs was not forthcoming, communities were increasingly willing to act when economic crises created exceptionally large numbers of unemployed.[61]

Many aspects of German plans for unemployment relief were copies from earlier programs which evolved in neighboring communities.[62] As a case in point, mention has already been made of the Ghent system. Most organized workers favored this system and saw it as the state's duty to supplement union unemployment funds. During a 1908 convention in Munich, the Generalversammlung des Zentralverbandes der Handlungsgehilfen und Gehilfinnen boldly asserted that it was the responsibility of all levels of government--federal, state and local--to guarantee adequate unemployment protection for the entire working population.[63] Despite this view of public responsibility, not everyone approved of plans to introduce the Belgian system into the Reich. Equally important was the influence of the Swiss cantons. Although certain aspects of programs originating at Bern and St. Gall were widely emulated in German cities, there was one important difference. Unlike Switzerland where every canton functioned as an independent state, obligatory unemployment insurance in Germany was precluded until each governmental jurisdiction enacted appropriate legislation. This perhaps helps to explain why municipal insurance remained on a voluntary basis and why it made relatively slow progress.

Given the local nature of most unemployment relief programs and the substantial regional variations within Germany, broad comparisons are difficult. More discrete analyses will therefore be deferred to the section dealing with specific institutions. For now, we might note that the greatest need for unemployment assistance was felt in the industrial urban centers of northern Germany and in areas with a high concentration of agricultural laborers. Seasonal changes were a particular problem and as one would expect, the most intensive periods of unemployment occurred during the winter months.

The efforts which individual areas made to cope with their unemployed residents were too numerous to cata-

logue separately but some of the more significant innovations merit at least passing reference. Despite the
importance of the Reich unemployment census of 1895, few
local efforts to duplicate the example were forthcoming. As
late as 1903, when unions were systematically gathering
quarterly statistics, only Stuttgart and Dresden published
communal unemployment figures on a regular, annual basis.
By far the most common means of coping with unemployment on
the local level was to establish municipal labor exchanges.
The rationale behind such public organizations was outlined
in these terms:[64]

> Wenn auch eine Verpflichtung der Stadtgemeinden, den
> Arbeitslosen, insbesondere den von ausserhalb angezo-
> genen durch Beschaeftigung mit kommunalen Arbeiten zu
> dem nothwendigen Lebensunterhalt zu verhelfen, nicht
> besteht, so erachten ich es doch fuer eine der vernehm-
> sten Aufgaben der staedtischen Behoerden, die Personen,
> die faehig und willig sind, ihnen zu uebertragende
> Arbeiten zu verrichten, die Moeglichkeit zu bieten,
> sich und ihre Familienangehoerigen ohne Inanspruchnahme
> der oeffentlichen Armenpflege zu ernaehren. Dieses
> Ziel wird in zweckentsprechender Weise nur dadurch
> erreicht werden koennen, wenn Seitens der Stadtge-
> meinden eine oder mehrere Arbeitsnachweisestellen
> eingerichtet werden.

A less pervasive but much discussed form of unemployment
relief was through municipal insurance. As late as 1909,
there were only four German cities which had communally
funded and administered unemployment insurance--Cologne,
Strassburg, Erlangen and the Berlin suburb of Schoeneberg.
Leipzig had a private insurance program and Muelhausen
introduced a variation of the Ghent System at the end of
1910. Many other municipalities were considering[65] various

insurance proposals. However, at the very end of our period only six German cities had developed comprehensive unemployment insurance programs and a few others had instituted plans which provided partial relief.

PUBLIC INSTITUTIONS FOR THE RELIEF OF UNEMPLOYMENT

There were five basic public institutions for the relief of industrial unemployment which merit careful consideration. We have already mentioned Arbeitsnachweise, or labor exchanges. In addition to taking a more careful look at these offices, we shall now consider public works projects plus efforts to isolate and employ work-shy or jobless individuals in tramp prisons, labor colonies and work houses. The primary objective throughout all of these public efforts to cope with unemployment was to design measures which would prevent the formation of idle habits by keeping the workers occupied.

During the 1870's labor houses were available to quarantine the contaminated idlers, cure them of sloth and rehabilitate them to join the work force. During the Eighties labor colonies performed essentially the same function on a longer-term voluntary basis in a more rural setting. At the same time the Verpflegungsstationen and Herbergen zur Heimat plus the Wanderarbeitsstaetten provided limited relief in kind to the unemployed in exchange for manual labor. During the 1880's and 1890's Arbeitsnachweise tried to alleviate the unemployment problem by facilitating contact between employers and employees in the private sector. After the turn of the century public works projects were designed to employ jobless members of the community usually on a seasonal basis with as little disruption as possible. In all of these institutions, an effort was made to separate the unworthy idler and confirmed loafer by choice from the worker who was unemployed through no fault of his own. Writing about vagabonds during 1884, one contemporary observer had this to say:[66]

> Um den professionsmaessigen Stromer von dem wirklich nothleidenden und vielleicht unverschuldet arbeitslosen Reisenden zu unterscheiden, empfiehlt es sich die Anweisung auf eine Unterstuetzung nur nach einer entsprechenden Arbeitsleistung fuer die Gemeinde, wie Strassenreinigung Schneeschoepfen Holzspalten und zu erteilen.

The test then for determining whether an unemployed laborer merited relief was to offer him work of any kind and be sure he was willing to do it rather than anxious to avoid it.

Arbeitsnachweise

The history of public labor exchanges in the German cities began well before Bismarck united the Second Reich. As early as 1816 the poor relief administration in Bavaria was performing many of the functions later filled by municipal Arbeitsnachweise. The first German community to establish a labor exchange was the Prussian town of Minden. During 1864, the town added an employment office to the existing Verpflegungsstation, a refuge which gave relief in kind to unemployed workers. A second, more important exchange was founded in Stuttgart during the following year.

These early examples of municipal efforts to procure employment for local residents were not emulated with regularity until the 1880's and 1890's. Among the Arbeitsnachweisestellen which came into being between 1880 and 1893 were: 1880 in Neisse, Goest; 1883 Berlin; 1884

Bublitz, Querfurt, Arnsberg, Iserlohn; 1885 Petershagen, Oeynhausen, Altona; 1886 Hattingen, Lippstadt; 1887 Thorn, Carlshafen, Hofgeismar; 1888 Fehrbellin; 1889 Hannover, Haynau, Herford; 1890 Duesseldorf; 1891 Pankow; 1892 Zellerfeld, Gutersloh; 1893 Paderborn. During the following year, there were an unusually large number of exchanges which emerged for the first time. In 1894, these cities established exchanges: Heilbronn, Wiesbaden, Augsburg, Esslingen, Frankfurt a. M., Nordhausen, Trier, Erfurt, Elberfeld, Ravensburg, Muenchen, Bamberg, Ulm, Fuerth, Mainz, Ludenscheid, Krefeld, Duisburg and Dessau added new employment agencies. At the same time projected Arbeitsnachweise were being planned in Leipzig, Nuernberg, Wuerzburg, Halle, Bremen, Metz, Chemnitz, Solingen, Braunschweig, Barmen, Remscheid and Breslau.

Part of this activity was due to the economy but in Prussia there was a more compelling reason for the sudden increase in labor exchanges. Under a decree of the Prussian trade ministry in September of 1894, towns with more than 10,000 inhabitants were charged with the duty of establishing Arbeitsnachweise. During March of 1893 the Regierungspraesident Von Liegnitz Prince Handjery wrote to the magistrates of his district in cities with more than 10,000 residents noting the increase in laborers unable to find work. He attributed much of the problem to industrial development and urbanization which concentrated labor surpluses in Germany's major cities. In order to give workers a chance to support themselves and their families, labor exchanges were seen as an indispensible supplement to inadequately funded public works projects.[67] The decade after 1894 produced many changes in Arbeitsnachweise in addition to a general improvement in the economy and the condition of the labor force. Following the initial spurt of development, labor exchanges evolved at a slower rate. Regional organizations in areas such as Westphalia and Alsace-Lorraine plus the use of railroads and telephones made the work of coordinating job-seekers with available positions more effective. Progress was steady but uneven, with exchanges in the South better developed than in the North of Germany.[68]

Perhaps the most important event during the decade after 1894 came when a majority of the public labor exchanges were organized into a national network. In 1898 the Verband Deutscher Arbeitsnachweise was founded under the leadership of Dr. Richard Freund. Over 200 of the more than 450 public labor exchanges in the Reich belonged to this central union by 1910. Of the existing exchanges that year, 325 were municipal and their services were generally gratuitous. When such exchanges were functioning properly, they were exempt from competition with private employment agencies. Under an imperial act of 1910, licenses were to be refused all private ventures in areas where a public exchange was already operating effectively.

Among the various types of exchanges, we have previously considered only the private organizations of unions and industrial management. Of the public employment agencies affiliated with the central association, 84 municipal and 15 voluntary exchanges were jointly managed by employers and employees in 1910. At the same time, 47 municipal and 16 voluntary exchanges were directed by designated authorities without the participation of either interested party. These bureaucratically controlled offices were in a distinct minority and their number tended to decline toward the end of our period. The officers of the jointly-managed public exchanges were generally appointed by local officials and held accountable to municipal authorities ranging from council members to boards of guardians and even public health administrators. The work of labor exchanges was frequently coordinated with relief efforts. The administrative advantages of this kind of coordination were spelled out by the president of the Verband Deutscher Arbeitsnachweise in a discussion of the relationship between unemployment insurance and labor exchanges. He maintained that:[69]

> die Durchfuehrung der Arbeitslosenversicherung im innigsten Anschluss an die Organisation des Arbeitsnachweis nicht nur moeglich, sondern geradezu notwendig ist.... Arbeitslosigkeit ist ueberall da nicht vorhanden, wo dem aus einer bestimmten Beschaeftigung getreten Arbeiter eine andere angemessene Stelle offen steht; der Arbeiter, der sich ohne Grund weigert, eine solche Stelle anzunehmen, hat keinen Anspruch auf die Leistung der Arbeitslosenversicherung.

According to Dr. Freund, coordination also enabled relief agencies to use the Arbeitsnachweise as an institutional check on spurious claims for unemployment benefits.

Looking at organizational aspects of the exchanges, contemporaries found that certain specialized employment agencies which catered to all members of a single trade posed administrative problems stemming in large part from job mobility. Unskilled laborers who worked at a variety of odd jobs and moved from one exchange to the next were a constant source of headaches for administrators of unemployment insurance programs and Arbeitsnachweise.[70] Among the exchanges serving a multitude of industries, the busiest offices were organized to contain separate registration desks for each trade. Their waiting rooms served the dual purpose of providing shelters for the unemployed and premises for the interviews between potential employers and employees.

Several systems of registration were in use at the exchanges. At Colmar in Alsace, for example, a group system was developed. Other offices used lists of names, personal slips or combinations of the two. In addition to the local and national organizations, municipal offices benefitted from affiliations with a dozen territorial Unions which extended more comprehensive geographical coverage to those looking for work. It's possible to differentiate among four basic groups of employment bureaus, listed in decreasing order of labor participation and control: 1) professionally managed exchanges such as servants' registry offices, 2) self-help organizations through unions, professional associations or other labor institutions, 3) bureaus attached to charitable organizations such as Herbergen zur Heimat, or 4) exchanges established by public authorities.[71]

In order to gauge the overall effectiveness of the public exchanges, it is worth noting that near the end of our period agencies affiliated with the national organization were filling almost a million vacancies per year. During 1907-08 the number of jobs filled amounted to more than 930,000 and although that number decreased to 860,000 during the trade slump of 1908, both figures accounted for an overwhelming majority of the success achieved through public offices. This contention is borne out by the fact that only 53,000 jobs were found by public exchanges not participating in the Verband during 1908-09. For comparative purposes, we might also recall that employees' exchanges filled approximately 300,000 positions while employers' associations were handling almost twice that volume of jobs. In absolute terms the volume of business conducted by the Verband exchanges far surpassed that handled by employers' bureaus. However, the average number of situations filled by each individual agency was approximately the same--somewhere around 7500--for both types of operation.

Both the effectiveness and the clientele of exchanges varied considerably from one region of the country to another. An effort was made to place unskilled as well as skilled workers and apparently with equal success. However, very few agricultural laborers benefitted from the exchanges and women in all branches of the economy fared less well than men who availed themselves of the services of public employment agencies. Some effort was made to place reservists and in the south German states considerable emphasis was put on finding situations for apprentices. The exchanges, in attempting to be fair to the public they served, tried to fill jobs primarily on merit. If there were more than one qualified applicant for a position, preference would be given to permanent residents or married men and beyond that to the earliest candidate. It is worth noting that during strikes or lock-outs, the public exchanges carried on business as usual, merely informing their clients of the existing situation. Since these exchanges were dependent upon the cooperation of both employers and employees, a neutral posture in case of disputes was essential.

Although a comprehensive examination of individual Arbeitsnachweise lies beyond the scope of this study, we might take a brief look at a few statistics from some of the more important public exchanges. The labor exchange of the Berlin Zentralverein, for example, filled 401,941 vacancies between its founding in 1883 and January 1, 1905. Of these jobs, more than ninety percent went to men. Also catering to the needs of male workers and apprentices, the Stuttgart employment bureau dated back to 1865. During its first thirty years of operations, the situation was described as follows: "der Arbeitssuchenden 246,581 nebst 4329 Lehrlingen; den auswaertigen Stellen wurden 15,481 Personen zugewiesen."[72] The Bureau charged membership fees of twenty Pfennigs for workers and up to fifty Pfennigs for employers. The Hannover labor exchange founded in 1889 was used mostly by Handwerksgesellen. During its fourth year of operations, 4464 workers and 3233 employers registered with the exchange; slightly more than 3400 places were filled. Also founded in 1889, the Anstalt fuer Arbeitsnachweise in Mulhausen filled 1931 vacancies during 1892-93 by coordinating the skills of 3841 employees with the needs of 2563 employers.

At Krefeld the city took over the function of intermediary between employers and employees, banning agitation and bringing the parties together by establishing a list of workers seeking positions and employers seeking help. Unfortunately, the office posting positions, which was founded during September of 1894, was open for business a mere two hours per day. At Karlsruhe an exchange serving twelve unions was founded during 1891. In the following year 3418 workers registered of which 1124 were able to find places. And by 1894 more than 93% of the nearly 5000 workers using the exchange found jobs. During its first seven months, the exchange serving Freiburg im Breisgau registered 1818 employers and 2023 workers out of which 1329 were placed (in 1892). Of the 2884 male laborers registered in 1894, 2054 found jobs while 1319 of the 1492 female domestic servants and 78 out of 141 apprentices secured positions.

Exchanges were founded at Darmstadt and Mannheim during August of 1893. In the course of that year, the former placed 300 out of 817 unemployed registrants. The latter during its first seventeen months, helped find work for 7656 of the more than 24,000 job applicants. Erfurt's exchange, established in 1885 to discourage door to door begging, filled 220 vacancies in 1893-94 from among its pool of largely unskilled workers. Also consisting primarily of unskilled laborers like char- and washerwomen, 4192 workers (1140 males and 3052 females) were placed with 3633 employers by the Dresden exchange in 1892. During the fifteen years following its founding in 1880, the labor exchange in Siegen had more than 57,000 workers pass through its offices and 3252 positions were filled from a group of 6820 ardent job seekers. In 1894, 140 of the employees looking for work found positions; almost 5600 workers frequented the Siegen premises that year.

Founded in 1885, the Dortmund exchange filled 1501 out of 1847 vacancies from among 2343 laborers during 1890-91. A slight decline occurred during 1893-94 when 886 workers registered for 1296 available jobs and 685 were placed. The decline was attributed to "der anhaltenden grossen Geschaeftsflauheit und Konkurrenz der Innungs-Arbeitsnachweise." One could go on multiplying examples but this brief list illustrates the variable track records of the public exchanges over time and geographical area.[73]

The kind of worker who availed himself of the services of a public labor exchange was reflected in figures from the Central-Arbeitsnachweisestelle fuer Rheinland und Westfalen during the economically grim year of 1893. The level of job skills in the enumeration which follows is particularly noteworthy. While 461 persons had been placed during 1892 when unemployment was unusually high, 739 applicants got jobs through the exchange in 1893. These included: 188 "Arbeiter und Auslaeufer", 49 "Haus-Knechte, Diener, Waertes, Pfleger und Portiers", 78 "Kutscher, Acker-und Fuhr-Knechte und Landarbeiter", 389 "Handwerker"; 22 "Schreiber, Comies, Reisende und Buchhalter" and 13 "Dienst und Fabrikmaedschen."[74] Of the 739 workers, 87 were married and 652 single. These and other figures suggest that the typical unemployed worker who turned to the Arbeitsnachweise for help in industrial areas during the early 1890's was male, single and moderately skilled.

The effectiveness of the exchanges in finding work for those who sought help was called into question by a conference of the "Volkswirtschaftliche Sektien des Freien Deutschen Hochstifts" which met on October 8, 1893, in Frankfurt am Main.[75] According to reports from that conference, the effectiveness of all types of labor exchanges was grossly overestimated. Despite such misgivings, it must be noted that from a financial viewpoint, Arbeitsnachweise provided an excellent return on monies invested. During 1908, for example, labor exchanges affiliated with the Verband Deutscher Arbeitsnachweise spent 943,411 Marks of which slightly more than a quarter came from public subsidies. The return on this outlay was highly satisfactory-- the exchanges managed to fill a vacancy for almost every Mark expended. In addition to their role in finding jobs for the unemployed, Arbeitsnachweise served a humanitarian purpose through auxiliary organizations which supplied temporary lodgings and food for the wandering poor in return for their labor.

As the scattered statistics cited above indicate, the public labor exchanges provided a basic grass roots system for alleviating unemployment. Although they were unable to create new jobs, the exchanges diminished the likelihood of unemployment stemming from a lack of communication between employers and employees. They facilitated the more perfect dissemination of information in the labor market and thus reduced the probability of frictional unemployment. Gauging their actual impact on the employment picture as a whole, however, would be a risky calculation at best. Unfortunately, not all of Germany's unemployed sought jobs through the public or private labor exchanges and at the same time many currently employed workers seeking to change positions availed themselves of the services of the Arbeitsnachweise. As a general rule, exchanges enumerated persons seeking jobs without regard to their current employment status. Those positions and workers not registered with exchanges were of course not included in the statistics at all. The data produced by labor exchanges also had a polemical dimension and was used to justify specific institutions. For all of these reasons, it is extremely difficult to establish more than the vaguest type of correlation between statistics from the exchanges and unemployment.

Public Works Projects

Although there was already talk of alleviating industrial unemployment through public works projects during the 1870's, it wasn't until after the turn of the century that such undertakings became commonplace. The first definition of this concept from a 1905 publication which is cited below linked extraordinary ventures by all levels of government directly with the objective of hiring the unemployed during periods of joblessness.[76] The second definition, written two years later, elaborated on the objective and depicted publicly subsidized work as the primary alternative to outright charity and the moral corruption of its recipients.[77]

> Unter Notstandsarbeiten verstehen wir die von oeffentlichen Gemeinwirtschaften (Gemeinde, Bezirk, Provinz, Staat) veranlassten aussergewoehnlichen Arbeiten mit den ausgesprochenen Zwecke der Beschaeftigung Arbeitsloser in Zeiten von Arbeitslosigkeit.

> Unter Notstandsarbeiten versteht man solche Arbeiten, die die Gemeinde oder der Staat in Zeiten der Arbeitslosigkeit einrichtet, um seine Mitbuerger nicht der Armenpflege anheimfallen an lassen, sondern um durch ihre Arbeit in der Zeit des sinkenden Geschaeftsganges volkswirtschaftliche und moralische Werte zu schaffen.

While the moral component of arguments in favor of alleviating unemployment through work rather than charity varied, everyone from publicists to Bismarck to the crown prince and later Kaiser Wilhelm II agreed that providing employment was the preferred solution.

The creation of labor colonies, work houses and other institutions which virtually incarcerated the laborer as a precondition for sustenance were far more disruptive of a normal life than public works projects. The latter enabled seasonally unemployed married men with dependent children, for example, to remain in their places of residence and by working for the government make it through the predictable dead season with a minimum of dislocation. Through public works projects, the laborer did not learn to depend on demoralizing handouts but was able to survive the slack period with his self-respect and finances in tolerable condition. When an old job became available again, the worker was free to return to normal employment in the private sector.

The city, in addition to helping unemployed individuals directly, benefitted indirectly from public works projects which were used to maintain municipal streets, grounds, utilities and other services essential for the well-being of all citizens. Not everyone took equally benevolent attitudes toward those who relied on public works during the slow season in the private sector. A few critics invariably resented temporary public employees who abandoned municipal projects when more attractive employment became available.

A brief overview of the divergent opinions about unemployment relief through public works is afforded by the programs adopted in various cities. In response to the economic crisis of 1901/02, the city of Essen decided not to engage the unemployed in relief works. At the same time, officials in Goerlitz maintained that extraordinary public works projects had been unnecessary since 1894 because urban growth had created a demand for navvies and street maintenance people which provided ample employment. In contrast to such attitudes, municipal jobs were made available in Erfurt and Mannheim during the early years of the twentieth century. And in Dortmund where public works projects had been considered unnecessary for the last fifteen years, a number of unemployed residents were engaged during 1902 for urban improvements.[78]

Given the diversity alluded to here, it is difficult to arrive at an accurate comparison of relief works in German cities. The problem is rendered even more difficult by variations in the total number of unemployed and those participating in public works projects. While most government officials and social reformers saw the solution to the unemployment problem as a municipal responsibility, there were a few toward the end of our period who assumed a much broader perspective.[79]

> Besonders wichtig ist die Bemerkung der Verwaltung,
> dass mit den Notstandsarbeiten die Arbeitslosenfrage
> nicht geloest sei, dass diese vielmehr als interna-
> tionale Angelegenheit einer internationalen Loesung
> beduerfte.

This kind of enlightened recognition of the pervasiveness of
the unemployment problem resulted in a series of international conferences during the years immediately prior to
World War I.

Cooperation on an international scale was, however, hardly a typical approach to coping with unemployment
during the earlier decades of our study. The bureaucratic
red tape which made coordination between various levels of
government so tedious is illustrated in the following early
reference to unemployment relief through public railroad
construction. This exchange took place in 1877, at a point
when there was some resistance to the idea of public works
projects and bureaucratic questions begot additional inquiries rather than answers.[80]

> Landdrostei zu Osnabrueck. Berlin 3. Februar 1877:
> Mit Bezug auf meinen Erlass von 23. d. Mts., betreffend
> die Beschaeftigung der Arbeiter "Bevolkerung in den
> Kreisen Waldenburg, Neurode, Reichenbach und Glatz
> durch die Eisenbahn Verwaltung, veranlasse ich die
> koenigliche Regierung zu einer schleunigen Aeusserung
> darueber, an und in wie weit Schritte geschehen sind,
> um der arbeitslosen Bevoelkerung der bezeichneten
> Kreise Gelegenheit zur Beschaeftigung der Chaussen und
> Wegebauten zu gewaehren worueber der Bericht von 10. d.
> Mts. Nichts enthaelt." Osnabrueck 16. Februar 1877:
> Indem wir den Obrigkeiten unseres Verwaltunsbezirks
> vorstehend Abschrift einer Verfuegung des Herrn Han-
> delsministers vom 3. d. Mts. zur verlaeufigen Nach-
> richt und Beachtung zusehen lassen, wollen wir gleich-
> zeitig einer baldigen Anzeige der ueber entgegensehen,
> 1.ob fuer die dortige Arbeiter-Bevoelkerung schon jetzt
> keine genuegende Beschaeftigung mehr vorhanden ist,
> eventl. ob eine Arbeitslosigigkeit fuer dieselbe in

naechsten Zeit zu erwarten steht, 2.wie hoch der augenblickliche Tagelohn durchschnittlich sich stellt, 3.ob im Falle der Bejahung unserer Anfrage sub 1 etwa durch in Aussicht stehende groessere Arbeiten von Privaten Verbaenden oder Gemeinden genuegende Beschaeftigung der Arbeitern wird dargeboten werden, oder gar noch Zuzug von Aussen noethig sein moechte.

It is worth noting the interest which the government officials expressed in ascertaining the potential of private sources for providing sufficient employment and thus measuring the need for public projects. The obvious implication here is that private remedies were preferable to public programs for unemployment relief.

In addition to general concerns about the necessity of relief projects, there was resentment over foreigners who benefitted from programs aimed at limiting assistance to local residents of long standing. The anonymity and wage scales accompanying urbanization plus the recurring difficulties of seasonal unemployment combined to make this a particular concern in the building trades. The problem for construction workers was one of distribution with too much of the labor force concentrated in urban areas where wages were highest. Suggestions were made that municipal building projects be undertaken to provide employment when private construction was inadequate. Efforts were to be made to coordinate public projects with labor's needs through unions and guilds. In order to minimize unemployment among urban construction workers during the winter, relocation in rural areas was recommended although this might displace foreign labor. The implication was clear that German workers' unemployment warranted government intervention while idleness among foreign residents could remain a low priority item.[81]

In order to limit the number of claims for relief, there were restrictions placed on individuals seeking to qualify for employment through public agencies. Surprisingly, as late as 1905, only twelve cities had imposed restrictions based on age in administering public works. An area of greater concern was the cause of unemployment and as in other forms of relief, there was an aversion to unworthy applicants. Public employment was not established to reward the miscreants of the private sector and culpable workers had to be dealt with differently from those unemployed through no fault of their own. This point was made with reference to specifics in the following discussion.[82]

> Als Faelle der gedachten Art nennt Coeln: Trunkenheit sowie ungebuehrliches Benehmer gegen den ueberwachsenden Beamten, letzteres auch Offenbach renitentes Verhalten der Arbeiter. Frankfurt a. M.und Mainz erwaehnen in fast woertlicher Uebereinstimmung: Nichtannahme anderer geeigneter Arbeit, Unterlassung der Angehoerigenfuersorge und unentschuldigtes Ausbleiben, Ungehorsam, Stoerung der Ruhe und Ordnung auf der Arbeitsstelle, mit dem Hinzufuegen, dass in solchen Falle eine Wiedereinstellung des Entlassenen bei den in dem betreffenden Winter veranstalteten Notstandsarbeiten ausgeschlossen ist. Von Frankfurt a. M., wo, wie in Strassburg, auf diese Weise ausgeschlossene Personen hoechstens noch bei der Armenverwaltung Beschaeftigung finden koennen, wird als Grund zu sofortigen Entlassung auch unentschuldigtes Ausbleiben um Falle der Bestellung zu Schneeraeumungsarbeiten erwaehnt.

In addition to restrictions arising from the cause of unemployment, there were other criteria used to determine the merit of workers seeking public jobs. As we noted with regard to the building trades, there was sentiment which favored limiting public employment to resident or native jobseekers--administering public works projects much as poor relief was doled out. This of course presented deterrents to geographical mobility and aggravated the unemployment problem it was intended to alleviate. Additional restrictions on applicants for public jobs in 46 cities during 1905 limited employment to workers with dependents. This in effect meant married men. In areas where single workers were hired, their wages were adjusted downward to reflect their obligations. This kind of attitude toward pay-scales for public works projects was expressed in terms which foreshadowed the subsequent Soziallohn:[83]

> Als ein weiteres fuer die Verguetung von Notstandsarbeiten charakteristisches Moment ergibt sich bereits aus dem bisher Gesagten, dass die Hoehe den Arbeitslosen bezahlten Lohnes nicht immer ausschliesslich nach dem Quantum tatsaechlich geleisteter Arbeit, sondern vielfach zugleich nach dem jeweiligen Grade der Unterstuetzungsbeduerftigkeit bemessen wird.

A further control on wages for public employment was the prevailing pay-scale in the private sector. As with other types of unemployment relief, public works projects were to pay less than private jobs to assure that the government was not competing for labor which could be utilized elsewhere. The daily wages for public jobs in 1905 ranged from a low of 90 Pfennigs for boys under 16 in Goerlitz to a high of 3,10 Marks for adult males with dependent children in Frankfurt a.M. Wages fluctuated with age and skill within these parameters but the average hovered between one and two Marks per day. Total costs ran into many thousands of Marks each year, the amounts varying with the number of workers and kinds of projects in which they were employed.[84]

If the government had attempted to alleviate all unemployment reported during the 1895 census by paying each jobless individual one Mark per day in exchange for participating in a public works project, estimates projected a total annual expenditure of 144 million Marks. If the subsidy per individual were increased to a more equitable wage of two Marks per day, the outlay would have approached 280 million Marks during a year which contemporaries believed was better than average in terms of unemployment. Although that amounted to less than a third of the sum spent on the army and navy, it was more than most taxpayers were willing to allocate for unemployment relief.[85]

Paralleling variations in the cost of public works projects were differences in the work time. The range of hours spent on the job went from a low of 6 3/4 per day in Danzig to a high of 10 1/2 in Freiburg i.B. Eleven cities--Duesseldorf, Elberfeld, Erfurt, Frankfurt a.M., Fuerth, Giessen, Halle, Luebeck, Mainz, Mannheim, and Muenchen-Gladbach--had adopted eight-hour work days for their public projects by 1905. Of these cities, Duesseldorf, Elberfeld, Frankfurt a.M., Halle and Mainz allowed one hour for breaks, while two hours were permitted in Elberfeld, Fuerth and Mannheim. Giessen, Luebeck and Muenchen-Gladbach allocated 1 1/2 hours per day. The other cities arranged for interruptions in the work day which varied in length with the total number of hours spent on the job. Eight and a half hour days were the rule for public works projects in Barmen, Bochum, Dresden, Ludwigshafen, Magdeburg, Muenchen, Nuernberg and Stuttgart. Up to nine hours of employment were required in Bielefeld, Koeln, Koenigsberg, Ulm, Augsburg, Hannover and Leipzig. This gives some idea of the expectations of municipal authorities using the services of unemployed workers to improve their communities.

At first glance, the relatively short hours look rather progressive and lenient but one must remember that most public works projects operated out of doors. They were by their very nature dependent upon daylight and the vast majority were conducted during the winter months when the hours of sunlight were at a minimum. This seasonal nature of many projects, rather than any liberal tendency on the part of officials dealing with the unemployed, goes far to explain the relatively brief workday. The short season of most projects also deserves comment. In most cases, projects commenced at the end of November or the beginning of December and continued through early to mid-March. A particularly early project started on October 13 in Nuernberg and an unusually late one ended on May 30 of the following year in Leipzig. The average duration of employment through public works projects was about 16 weeks with

some running for as little as two months and others stretching out through half the year. As a general rule, skilled
workers required public jobs for shorter periods of time
than unskilled laborers. Regardless of training, however,
most workers left public employment voluntarily. This fact
is reflected in statistics on the duration of employment and
the causes of termination from a 1903 article on deutschen
Fachverbaende. The article reported a brief tenure of
employment, with no workers staying more than three months
and only eight percent remaining in excess of 60 days. Of
those who were employed for less than ten days, only six
percent attributed their departure to involuntary causes.[86]

At this juncture, it would be appropriate to
consider another variation in public works projects--namely,
the kinds of tasks performed. The projects ranged from
street maintenance and cleaning to erecting buildings,
macadamizing roads, gardening, canal digging and railroad
construction. The diversity of undertakings inaugurated in
the guise of public works was hinted at in a list of projects at Mannheim. The distinction between ordinary
services--Notstandsarbeiten in the narrow sense--and extraordinary measures initiated to alleviate unemployment was
especially telling. The former tended to include long-range
maintenance while the latter was confined to one-time
projects whose implementation could be made to coincide with
high rates of unemployment.[87]

Was die Art der Arbeiten anlangt, so waren vorgesehen
als A.Notstandsarbeiten in engeren Sinne: 1. Schot-
terschlagen und eventuell Strassenreinigungsarbeiten.
2. Die Anlegung vom Baumgruben in der oestlichen
Stadterweiterung. 3. Veranderung des Sportplatzes im
Luisenpark. 4. Umwandlung des Neckarauer Waldes in
einen Park. 5. Abhub der Schlossplaetze und Anlage
einer Strasse durch der Schlossgarten.

B. Ausserordentliche Arbeiten zur Beschaeftigung
Arbeitsloser: 6. Herstellung des Luisenparks. 7.
Neupflanzung grosser Baeume in der oestlichen Stadter-
weiterung. 8. Umgraben der Anlageflaechen an der
Augusta-Anlage. 9. Humusandecken in der Luisenparks.
10. Verbreiterung der Stephaniepromenade.

Public works projects such as those outlined above were
relatively scarce during the 1890's but they became almost
commonplace immediately after the turn of the century.[88]

Before concluding our discussion of public works
projects, mention should be made of certain administrative
differences among the municipalities. Some cities coordinated their programs with the poor relief administration;
others were mindful of the programs administered by the
local labor exchanges and still others performed their
operations in conjunction with municipal offices. Essen,
for example, used the existing Board of Works as an employment office while Offenbach involved the mayor's office
in hiring and the Board of Works in allocating and compensating public employees. In Darmstadt the poor relief
administration engaged laborers who then came under the
jurisdiction of offices overseeing actual maintenance or
construction. An increasing number of cities tended to
allow determinations about the distribution of labor to be
made by the agencies using its services.

As a supplement to public works projects, other options were needed to keep jobless industrial workers in the labor force. Drawing on past experience, a few authors recognized that additional forms of alternate employment were necessary. During the transitional stages from an agrarian to a predominately industrial economy, cottage industries had provided supplemental incomes for family members too numerous to sustain themselves through agriculture alone. Particularly during the winter months when it was too cold to work in the fields and when farm income was at its annual nadir, piecework in the home provided a welcome respite from idleness and hunger.[89]

> Ausserdem erfolgt im Winter des oefteren eine Abwanderung der zur Sommerzeit in den Grossstaedten beschaeftigten Arbeiter nach der Heimat, um der Unterstuetzung durch die Wohnsitzgemeinde teilhaftig zu werden und in Anbetracht des in der Provinz billigeren Lebensunterhaltes die Zeit der Beschaeftigungslosigkeit dort leichten zu ueberdauern.

By the beginning of our period, this situation had reversed itself. Industrial workers unable to find jobs in the urban economy returned to recently familiar agrarian communities in order to ride out predictable periods of unemployment as well as possible. Some were sufficiently disheartened with their experiences of life in the industrial labor force to remain on the land but many returned to urban jobs when work again became available. As we indicated in the previous chapter, mobility between agriculture and industry was quite common throughout the period between 1873 and 1913.

With the advent of railways, whose construction
and operations provided employment for many that might
otherwise have been jobless, physical mobility became
possible on a large scale. There were, however, persistent
deterrents to effective job mobility. The terms of unemployment relief which invariably imposed residence requirements on recipients created problems as did the limited
power of public and private agencies to compel workers to
accept alternate employment when it became available. The
difficulties presented by an occupationally immobile labor
force became acute when structural changes shook the
economy. During periods of rapid economic development,
unskilled workers had greater flexibility than highly
skilled laborers whose training was job-specific. Many
skilled artisans, shopkeepers and craftsmen of previous
generations could neither compete nor adapt as readily as
circumstances demanded. As a result, they often sustained
conspicuous losses from industrialization. Automatic
mechanisms which might have prevented the market from being
glutted with handloom weavers were no more effective during
the last century than they are today. The occupations in
distress have changed but the inability to predict the
relationship between supply and demand has remained equally
problematic.

In view of this persistent dilemma and the apparent inevitability of unemployment, Pastor von Bodelschwingh
offered the following advice to those seriously looking for

work. Using the familiar "du" form of address, he urged the unemployed to stay on the main thoroughfares and avoid the small villages where no work or relief would be available, particularly during the winter. He recommended the use of labor exchanges, gave tips about obtaining appropriate documents and counselled against illegal activities such as begging. For those who could not find employment of any kind, he suggested reliance on public agencies ranging from Wanderarbeitsstaetten to poor relief. To this he added the following list of suggestions:[90]

Das U.W.G. (Unterstuetzungswohnsitzgesetz), dessen 28 Dir einen Rechtsansprunch auf Gewaehrung von Obdach, Nahrung, noetiger Kleidung, erforderlichenfalls Krankenhauspflege, durch den Ortsarmenverband Deines Aufenthaltsortes gewaehrt, gilt im ganzen deutschen Reiche mit Ausnamhe von Bayern und Elsass-Lothringen.

1. Frage nach dem Rathaus, Burgermeisteramt, Amtshaus, Schultheissenamt, Gemeindevorsteher, Ortsvorsteher-Kreisarzt, Armenarzt; Krankenhause.
2. Tritt bescheiden aber bestimmt auf. Frage nach dem Beamten, der die Armenverwaltung abweisen. Frage nach seinem Vertreter. Du wollest weder betteln noch stehlen, faendest keine Arbeit, habest kein Obdach und keine Nahrung, seiest gezwungen, armenrechtliche Unterstuetzung zu erbitten.
3. Wirst Du dennoch ab- und hinausgewiesen, so frage den Betroffenden, wor er sei, (Name und Amtsstellung) Du muessest Dich bei seiner vorgesetzten Behoerde ueber ihn beschweren; wer die naechste vorgesetzte Behoerde sei?
4. Kannst Du diese nicht gleich erreichen, so suche eine der in dem Ministerial-Erlass genannten Personen, einen Geistlichen oder ein Vorstandsmitglied der Herberge auf, zeige Deinen Wanderschein mit dem Schutzzeugnis vor und bitte, dass sie sich fuer Dich verwenden. Du muesstest sonst betteln oder eine andere strafbare Handlung begehen und muesstest sie vor Gericht als Zeugen dafuer verschlagen, dass Du vergeblich bei der Ortsbehoerde Dein Recht gesucht haettest.
5. Kannst Du schreiben oder findest Du einen, der bereit ist, fuer Dich zu schreiben, so schreibe einen Brief an den Unterzeichneten, worin der thatsaechliche

Hergang kurz und streng-wahrheitsgemaess angegeben ist, mit Deinem Namen, Beruf, Gebuts-Ort und -Tag und Namen und Stand derjenigen, an welche Du Dich vergeblich um Hilfe gewendet, mit genauer Angabe des Ortes, des Tages und der Tagezeit, und gieb an, wie Du Dir dann selbst geholfen hast.

    6. Hast Du kein Papier und keine Freimarke, so bitte den Hausvater der naechsten Herberge zur Heimat oder sonst jemand darum; ich werde ihm, wenn er mich darum bittet, da Porto erstatten.

    7. Stets bleibe bescheiden, und streng bei der Wahrheit! Sonst wuerdest Du Gefahr laufen, wegen Betruges bestraft zu werden, und unserer Fuersprache Schande machen.

This lengthy guideline for behavior contained the advice best calculated to minimize the impact of unemployment according to the popular wisdom of the day.

Labor Houses

For those who ignored Dr. von Bodelschwingh's advice or were unable to find work for some other reason, labor houses provided one of the less attractive alternatives to starvation. As we noted in another context, the precedent of using labor houses for the dual purpose of public and personal relief from the problems of unemployment was established in Prussia long before the 1870's. As early as the third quarter of the eighteenth century, the Hohenzollerns adopted a policy of eliminating sloth, mendicancy and vagrancy by committing idlers to detention houses where they could work for their keep. With the advent of the Second Reich, the Imperial Penal Code under sections 361 and 362 included the following offenses as cause for confinement in a labor house: Vagabondage, begging, gambling, drunkenness, idleness, prostitution, sloth and homelessness. Under an amendment to the penal code which was adopted in June of 1900, procurers and <u>souteneurs</u> were added to the list which in practice also included juvenile delinquents.

As one might surmise from this hodgepodge, a potential problem with the whole system was that it indiscriminately threw together minor moral offenders and the confirmed dregs of German society. What was more significant from the vantage point of our study, however, was the frame of mind which this mix reflected. Not only was begging no longer regarded as an honorable act of charity- -it had become a punishable criminal offense. Furthermore, prostitution and intoxication were placed on a par with laziness and the corrective for social ills of every stripe was simply reduced to hard work.

Efforts to inculcate the virtue of industriousness in the lower orders formed a major part of the labor houses' mandate. In addition, they served to separate the work-shy from the legitimately unemployed. On a very basic level, labor houses were set up to protect workers against their own instinctive tendencies toward idle dissipation. The success of the ongoing battle between the good forces of hard work and the evil influence of sloth might be gauged from a few relevant statistics. The figures dealing with arrests for begging in major cities were indicative of the proportions the vagrancy problem reached during the early years of our period.[91]

So betrug die Zahl der wegen Bettelei und Obdachlosig-
keit in Polizeigewahrsam Genommenen in Berlin im Jahre
1875: 8688, 1876: 13 192, 1877: 21 407, in Breslau im
Jahre 1875: 4748, 1876: 6166. Die Verhaftungen wegen
Bettelns, Landstreichens und dgl. beliefen sich bei der
Polizeidirektien in Dresden im Jahre 1875 auf 2683,
1876 auf 3967, 1877 auf 5298, 1878 auf 6634.
Nach einer weitern Berechnung des Saechsischen statistischen Bureaus ueber das Jahr 1879/80 ergab sich, dass
gerade die Berufsklassen, die in der Wirtschaftsstock-
ung am meisten gelitten hatten, das groesste Kontingent
zu   jenen Bestrafungen   stellten: Von 26 547   im
Koenigreich Sachsen vom 1. April 1879 bis 31. Maerz
1880 wegen Bettelns und Vagierens Bestrafen Personen
entfielen auf
die Gewerksgehilfen oder Arbeiter ohne
    naehere Bezeichnung   5665
die Textilindustrie   3385
die Nahrungs- und Genussmittelindustrie   3268
die Gewerbe der Metallverarbeitung   2966
die Gewerbe der Bekleidung und Reinigung   2241
das Baugewerbe   2159
Das sind insgeamt 19 684 oder 74 Prozent aller
    Besraften.

Repeated offenders for begging and vagrancy were committed

to labor houses in growing numbers between 1877 and 1881,

rising from 220,000 to 320,000 during that interval. It's

important to recall the steady, sharp increases during the

economically depressed years of the late seventies and the

apparent tapering off with the improvement which came after

1879. During the swing year of 1892, police records from

the city of Berlin showed that arrests of beggars and

paupers in the capital alone numbered in excess of 10,000

each.[92]

During the administrative year 1907-08, 15,495

persons were detained in all the Prussian labor houses.

With the number of releases approximately equal to the

number of new commitments, their inmates worked out to an

average of 7528. Of these 7500 individuals, about 25% were domestic servants and "casual laborers" while 3,000 listed their occupations as laborers in industry, mining and the building trades. More than 5,000 were adult males between the ages of 30 and 60 while about 10% were female. More than two-thirds of all these workers were committed for begging. Those detained in labor houses represented a mere fraction of the total number of persons apprehended, prosecuted and convicted for begging--only about half of those apprehended were actually convicted for their offense. According to available statistics, there was a tendency for the incidence of mendicancy to decline toward the end of our period in absolute numbers and even more dramatically in relative terms.

This was encouraging, but one could question whether the salutary effect of diminished begging during the early twentieth century were attributable to the labor houses. A negative conclusion was supported by the high recitivism rate reported by Prussian labor houses. Looking still at the figures for 1907-08, more than 80% of those detained had been in prison. Almost two-thirds of the inmates in Prussian labor houses were at least second offenders while one-third had been convicted three times. Eighteen percent had been recommitted to a labor house within a year of their last discharge. According to estimates of officials at the labor houses, about 25% of the inmates were thoroughly reformed while between one-third and one-half of the total number improved without being totally rehabilitated.

These figures must have been something of an embarrassment to those who administered labor houses since every effort was made to reintegrate the released offender into the labor market. When an inmate was freed, local authorities at the destination of his choice were notified to prepare for his arrival. Either the police, the clergy or members of philanthropic societies were supposed to assist the newly repentant miscreant in finding housing and a job. Despite the high recitivism rate, labor houses did a great deal to confirm the notion that tramps, beggars and idlers of every description could be induced to work when given the proper supervision. Unfortunately, however, when the imposed restraints of the labor house were eliminated, many rejected the virtues of an industrious lifestyle and returned to habits of leisurely dissipation.

The activities undertaken in the labor houses were designed to inculcate diligence in their inmates. By living what was deemed to be a good moral existence, it was hoped that the lazy would reform their ways and learn to be useful members of society. The keynote of activity in labor houses was hard work, most of which was directed at self-maintenance of the houses and their inhabitants to avoid competition with the free market. Much of the work was conducted out of doors and dependent upon natural lighting.

The typical workday thus ranged from ten to twelve hours, allocated as follows:

Rise	5:45 a.m.	
First breakfast	6:00	
Work	6:15 to 9:00	(2 hours, 45 min)
Second breakfast	9:00 to 9:30	
Work	9:30 to 12:00 noon	(2 1/2 hours)
Dinner and rest	12:00 to 1:30 p.m.	
Work	1:30 to 5:00	(3 1/2 hours)
Supper	5:00 to 5:30	
Work	5:30 to 6:45	(1 1/4 hours)
Rest	until bedtime	
Bedtime	7:00 p.m.	

On the basis of this schedule, ten hours were devoted to work in four unequal installments punctuated by food and a single brief rest.

The kinds of jobs assigned to inmates included farming, construction, earth works, building maintenance, domestic service, culinary work and industrial labor within the confines of the institutions themselves. In addition to jobs performed for the labor houses per se, some inmates were assigned to work for provincial administrations, for officers of the labor houses and even for private agricultural or industrial concerns. Over the years covered in this study, there was a steady decline in the proportion of inmates employed by private industry. Just prior to the beginning of our period in 1869, 73 percent of the inmates were used by industrial entrepreneurs. That percentage had declined to slightly more than half--52.6 percent--by 1896 and fell to 40.4 percent by the turn of the century. In 1903 the percentage was down to 27.2 and it continued to drop as the amount of work undertaken inside the labor houses increased. The aim of this activity was to make the workers diligent and the houses economically self-sufficient.

There was usually enough surplus from annual production to afford the inmates a small wage. That provided the "carrot" part of the program while prison-like discipline supplied the attendant "stick". The inmates of labor houses led a spartan existence. Even such luxuries as cigars were frowned upon and reprimands were meted out to those who failed to complete their daily quota of work due to laziness or insubordination. Punishments ranged from reproofs and suspended visiting privileges through dietary restrictions and curtailed earnings to cell detention and strict imprisonment. For genuinely severe misbehavior, straight jackets and chains were available. Although in theory the houses were not designed as punitive institutions, commitment was involuntary and aimed at correcting laziness by inculcating the virtues of industry.

The maximum period of confinement was two years but many individuals were discharged after a much shorter term. About half the convictions were for a period of six months to two years. A quarter of the inmates served terms of three to six months and a final 25 percent received the maximum sentence of a full 24-month confinement. As with all institutions of this kind, genuine reform depended at least as much on the individual as on the program he was subjected to during his stay in the labor house. Working under imposed conditions was no guarantee of diligence in a free market situation and that, in the final analysis, was the test of the long-range impact of labor houses on workers unemployed due to their own lack of enterprise.

Alternatives to Begging: Labor Colonies, Verpflegungsstationen, Herbergen Zur Heimat, Wanderarbeitsstaetten

During the first half of our period, contemporary estimates placed the number of destitute unemployed job-seekers wandering across Germany in excess of 200,000. Mobility on this scale had been facilitated by reforms which occurred earlier in the century--society underwent ongoing changes in response to the liberation of the peasantry and the introduction of occupational freedom of choice. During the last quarter of the nineteenth century, the impact of these reforms was compounded by recent economic and political developments. Together they lifted the barriers between states and lured an increasingly large percentage of the labor force into urban industrial centers. Changes began to intrude upon the stable, predictable existence of earlier decades when most laborers knew from birth exactly what jobs they would do and where they would live out their lives.

Uncertainty and insecurity rather than order shaped the expectations of those who made up the ranks of the industrial working classes. Where and when work would be available and for how long were questions of vital concern to laborers who could find only intermittent employment during the years between 1873 and 1896. Lured into abandoning rural, agrarian lives during the phenomenal boom which immediately followed the founding of the Empire, many of the new industrial laborers were subjected to the vicissitudes of an economy which underwent a crash followed by three major downswings during the next twenty-three years. The economic crises of the late nineteenth century left thousands fearing poverty and unemployment. To a surprising extent, that fear of economic hardship produced many of the same repercussions during our period that its realization evoked later in the twentieth century.

During the initial years of our study, the institutional means of administering relief to the unemployed were sorely lacking. Rather than starve, many destitute workers turned in desperation to an itinerant lifestyle, often accompanied by begging or theft. During the 1870's, society by and large left its unemployed to the mercies of labor houses or police authorities. But due in part to the magnitude of the problem, there was growing recognition of the fact that not all those who resorted to wandering the countryside were worthless idlers. Many were legitimate job-seekers and during the 1880's, the public began to show an increased willingness to deal fairly with the unemployed by differentiating between them and confirmed beggars, vagrants or thieves. As we have seen, work-shy individuals were detained in labor houses and the sick or disabled unemployables were cared for in hospitals. This left the bulk of able-bodied willing job-seekers to be handled separately. Those who had pursued an itinerant lifestyle for a considerable time without locating any prospect of employment were cared for in labor colonies where, if necessary, they could remain for relatively long periods until work became available.

For impoverished laborers with more immediate job prospects, there were a series of loosely affiliated institutions designed to provide cheap food and lodging, often in exchange for work. The labor yards, refuges and inns were all set up to afford short-term relief for those who preferred to earn their keep rather than ask for a hand-out as they passed through an area looking for work. All of these institutions were devoted to helping unemployed laborers avoid the pitfalls of living as an itinerant beggar lurking on the fringes of respectable society. By getting them through jobless periods with their self-respect and willingness to work intact, relief agencies helped avoid the fate outlined in graphic terms below:[93]

> ...sehr viele wegen Stellenlosigkeit auf die Wanderschaft gehen. Dadurch wird ihre Lage in vielen Faellen noch schlimmer. Sind sie auf sich allein angewiesen, und finden sie nicht zeitig neue Arbeitsgelegenheit, so stellt sich bald die bitterste Not ein. Diese zwingt schliesslich zur Verpfaendung oder zum Verkauf der bessern Kleider usw., so dass die aeussere Erscheinung mehr und mehr einem Landstreicher aehnlich wird. Die Aussicht auf dauernde Arbeit wird immer geringter, da ein Arbeitgeber nicht leicht einen "Vagabunden" einstellt. Kein Wunder, wenn in dem Ungluecklichen allmaehlich tiefe Erbitterung Platz greift und er seine Sorge durch Alkohol zu betaeuben sucht. Noch haelt ihn der letzte und festeste Damm, sein Ehrgefuehl, vor der Abgrunde zurueck. Aber die Not hat ihn bereits in die Gesellschaft der untersten Menschenklassen gefuehrt. Bald wird er selber dazu gehoeren. Hat er erst einmal

seine Hand nach der Bettelgabe ausgestrockt und die
Verachtung der Offentlichkeit ueber sich ergehen
lassen, so beginnt sich zwischen ihm und der menschlichen Gesellschaft eine Kluft aufzutun, die sich
immer mehr vertieft. Er faengt an, gegen seine Lage
gefuehllos zu werden. Es geht mit Riesenschritten
bergab. Gar bald hat er sich an das erbetelte oder
gestohlene Brot gewoehnt, das ihn ohne Arbeit so bequem
leben laesst, und die Arbeit, die er frueher vergebens
gesucht hat, ist ihm jetzt gleichgueltig und verhasst.
Er verschwindet in der Masse der Verlorenen.

Wenn schon die Armut an sich, sobald sie an fremde
unentgeltliche Unterstuetzung gewoehnt ist, sehr leicht
die Liebe und Bereitwilligkeit zu geregelter Arbeit im
Menschen ertoetet, so noch viel eher und nachhaltiger,
wenn zur Armut das traege Wander- und Herbergleben
hinzukommt. Dieses wirkst direkt erschlaffend und
entnervend auf den innern und aeussern Menschen und
fuehrt geradeswegs zur Arbeitsscheu. In vielen Faellen
tritt dann noch Trunk, Diebstahl und aehnliches hinzu,
wodurch der Rueckweg immer mehr verlegt wird.

Labor Colonies

Founded during the 1880's under the moral leadership of the Protestant clergyman Friedrich von Bodelschwingh, the labor colonies were designed to provide work
and shelter for the wandering unemployed. In March of 1882
the original colony was founded at Wilhelmsdorf in Westphalia and during the succeeding years a number of imita-
tions began to appear through the active efforts of
Bodelschwingh and the financial assistance of the royal
family. Both Bodelschwingh and his friends in high places
envisioned the labor colonies as an alternative to charity
in dealing with unemployment. For the well-being of society
and the unemployed, begging was to be strictly discouraged
and work offered as a substitute for handouts to those who
could not find regular paying jobs.

In order to get the unemployed wanderer through his difficulty without begging, a chain of labor colonies was to be established across Westphalia and the Rhine provinces where the need was greatest. The colonies were to provide temporary relief for legitimate job-seekers and here, as elsewhere, the test of legitimacy was willingness to work. Labor was to be performed in exchange for food and shelter and those too lazy or proud to work were to be accorded punishment elsewhere rather than assistance through colonies. The following anecdote which Bodelschwingh related in a speech to the Herrenhaus on February 26, 1908, was representative of the kind of thinking behind efforts to sustain and expand labor colonies.[94]

> Auf einer der groessten Wanderstrassen der Welt, naemlich von Berlin nach Koeln, auf der in der gegenwaertigen Notzeit bis zu 50 Arbeitslose taeglich an jede Tuer, wo sie ein Stueck Brot fuer den Hunger erhoffen, anklopfen (denn Arbeit ist weit und breit nicht vorhanden), habe ich dicht vor der Tuer meines Pfarrhauses, an einen Abhang des Teutoburger Waldes, einen kleinen Steinbruch angelegt, versehen mit den noetigen Werkzeugen und unter die Aufsicht eines fleissigen Vorarbeiters gestellt. Dieser Steinbruch bietet zunaechst das sichere Scheidewasser zwischen allen arbeitswilligen und arbeitsscheuen Wanderarmen der Landstrasse. Nur gegen eine Stunde fleissiger Arbeit in demselben wird eine Mittagssuppe dargereicht. Das gab auf der Stelle einen wunderbaren Wandel: von 20 an die verschiedenen Kuechen unserer Anstalten Anklopfenden bleiben hoechstens immer nur 2; die uebrigen koennten ohne Arbeit bei mitleidigen Bauern Mittag speisen. Kein Bettler ward seit der Zeit mehr an meiner Tuer gesehen und alles arbeitsscheue Gesindel war verschwunden. Dagegen war die Kunde, dass man hier gegen Arbeit Brot erhalten kann, schnell ins Land gedrungen; und nun stellten sich bald diejenigen Arbeitslosen ein, die leiber ihr Brot erarbeiten als erbetteln wollten.

Here, as in the labor houses, the inhabitants included a random mix of criminal, immoral and unfortunate types. The colonies served a more mobile population, however, and were sought out or entered on a voluntary basis.

One of the primary advantages of the labor colonies was that they helped to keep the unemployed worker active rather than idle during layoffs in private industry. And as Bodelschwingh's last sentence implies, there were many unemployed individuals who preferred to work for their own support rather than submit to the humiliation of accepting handouts. On this point, most contemporaries agreed that putting the unemployed to work was in the best interests of employers, society and the laborers themselves. In order to occupy the urban unemployed, suggestions were made for the reclamation of wasteland which had certain advantages over programs designed to support the industrial reserve army in costly idleness.[95]

> Die Arbeitslosen der Grosstaedte sollen beschaeftigt
> werden bei der Urbarmachung des deutschen Moor- und
> Oedlandes. Nicht den schon heruntergekommenen, sondern
> den arbeitsfaehigen, durch Saisonarbeit und Krisen
> arbeitslos Gewordenen soll durch lohnende Beschaeft-
> igung Gelegenheit zu gesunder Lebenshaltung geboten
> werden. Die betraechtlichen Mittel die bisher von
> Behoerden, Gemeinden, Gewerkschaften, Wohltaetig-
> keitsvereinen und Privatpersonen zur Unterstuetzung
> Arbeitsloser und deren Angehoerigen unproduktiv aus-
> gegeben werden sind, sollen nutzbringend angelegt
> werden. Der Industrie und dem Gewerbe soll die not-
> wendige Reservearmee arbeitsfaehig erhalten, der
> Landwirtschaft neue Gebiete erschlossen werden.

The idea that an industrial economy required a surplus labor supply was central to many institutional efforts to cope with unemployment.[96] Social reformers maintained that work had to be supplied by extra-economic means when industry failed to provide enough jobs for its boom-time labor force. They believed that idleness corrupted labor, making it unfit for use in the private sector and thus dependent upon public subsidies.

In addition to affording temporary employment, the function of colonies was to provide jobless workers with a means of getting from one labor market to another without resorting to begging. A chain of stations was to perform a dual service for the local communities and the unemployed wanderers. The former would be freed from the nuisance of itinerant beggars and the latter would benefit by simultaneously avoiding the demoralizing influences of mendicancy, the formation of lazy habits and an addictive dependence on handouts. The unemployed laborer could earn his shelter and food by staying in a succession of labor colonies as he moved across the country in search of a permanent job. The labor colonies and their affiliates filled a need in the lives of unemployed workers who were destitute, prohibited from begging and without any claim on the districts they passed through looking for work. In human terms, their objective was described this way:[97]

> In ersten Linie sind diese Anstalten ja keineswegs
> errichtet, um einen moeglichst grossen landwirt-
> schaftlichen, oder sonstigen pekuniaeren Gewinn zu
> erzielen: arbeitslosen doch arbeitswilligen Armen eine,
> wenn auch vorubergehende Beschaeftigung zu gewaehren,
> Arbeitsentwoehnte wieder mit dem Segen geregelter
> Arbeit vertraut zu machen, den von ihren Mitmenschen

> Abgewiesenen, an sich und der Welt Verzweifelnden den
> Glauben an die stets zu helfen bereite Liebe und
> Selbstvertrauen wieder einzupflanzen--das ist die erste
> Aufgabe der Arbeiter-Kolonien.

The importance attached to the colonies as an alternative to idleness and begging stemmed from the conviction that it was easier to prevent the formation of bad habits than to rehabilitate offenders. According to popular wisdom, the trap of poverty entailed its own vicious circle.[98]

> Nun gehoert aber--und das ist einer unserer Haupt-
> gruende der groesste Theil der huelfsbedurftigen
> Wanderer der Klasse der Landarmen an. Die meisten
> derjenigen, welche sich dem Wanderleben ergeben haben,
> entstammen von vornherein Verhaeltnissen, die keine
> Dauer haben, und ihr Wandertrieb verhindert sie, selbst
> wenn sie feste und gute Arbeit finden, an einem Orte
> dauernd zu beliben. Entweder sind die Kinder von
> Landarmen, oder sie werden bald Landarmen, und mit
> wenigen Ausnahmen bleiben sie Landarm, wenn sie es
> einmal geworden sind.

Labor colonies were intended to help workers avoid this snare and escape from the clutches of poverty.

The philosophy which motivated those who worked to establish labor colonies had a mixture of moral and religious underpinnings. Men like Bodelschwingh believed that it was their duty to instill the old virtues of the Protestant eithic into the lower orders of society. The following paraphrase of a story printed by the labor colonies in an 1888 publication illustrated the kind of values they hoped to inculcate in the working classes.[99]

> An unemployed artisan wandered the streets of Berlin
> thinking of the wife and two hungry children waiting
> for him to return to their shabby dwelling with some
> food. Despite his efforts to find work, he would have
> to go home without a penny in his pocket. On the way
> back, he found a briefcase lying on the pavement.

Inside were the owner's name and address plus many large-denomination bills. Elated over his good fortune, the worker purchased bread and meat for his family with the money he had found. When he reached home, he didn't tell his wife where he had gotten the money to buy food since he knew that she'd rather starve than take anything that wasn't rightfully theirs. As the family sat down to its first good meal in months, the six year old son said this prayer: "Come Jesus, be our guest and bless this gift that you have given us." As the worker tried to eat, a terrible voice whispered in his ear that the money was no gift and he was no better than a thief. Without a word and despite the late hour, the man left his home to seek out the owner in order to return the briefcase. He openly explained why he had taken a small part of the money and told how his son's prayer had led him to return the rest. The owner was a rich, compassionate man who decided that the parents of a child that prayed must be good people. He understood that only desperate need had led the worker to take some of the money and on the very next day he found the fellow a job in his factory and promised to help educate and rear the small devout son.

Two points stood out in this uplifting narrative. First, it wasn't necessary for the worker to steal and secondly, the reward for his honesty was not a monetary handout but a job--the opportunity to provide for his own family's subsistence.

According to officials in the labor colonies, there was apparently none of the aversion to work that inmates in labor houses exhibited. Therefore, from the workers' perspective as well as the colonies', a job offer such as the one in the preceding story would have been a most welcome, highly satisfactory and fitting reward for honesty. Until a laborer found regular employment, he had to be prepared to work as long as he stayed in one of the colonies. Out of a sense of pride and aversion to begging, most inhabitants of labor colonies welcomed the opportunity to earn their keep.[100] It was assumed that the voluntary residents of labor colonies already recognized the value of hard work which the labor houses tried to teach their unwilling inmates through strict discipline. Unlike the idlers who were committed to labor houses for reform, those working in labor colonies were prepared to take jobs but unable to find them for a variety of reasons. Before looking at the relationship between the colonies whose organization was not equipped to line up jobs in the private sector and the Arbeitsnachweise, a word about the kinds of job-seekers attracted to the colonies might be helpful. They came from diverse backgrounds and occupations as the following statistics showed. Note in particular the relatively large numbers of seasonal workers and "Arbeiter ohne naehere Angabe" plus the increase in residents following economic recessions.[101]

Statistik der Berufe derjenigen Wanderer, die in den
Jahren 1896 bis 1910 in die deutschen Arbeiterkolonien
aufgenommen wurden.

Berufsgruppen	1896	1897	1898	1899	1900	1901	1902	1903	1904	1905	1906	1907	1908	1909	1910
1. Landwirtschaft, Gärtnerei, Forstwirtschaft	536	546	563	750	797	790	1059	1202	1160	947	865	1029	1074	1163	1175
2. Fischerei	7	5	7	7	10	13	12	16	14	15	10	21	12	8	8
3. Bergbau	37	28	48	53	49	72	98	69	85	67	42	56	67	85	71
4. Industrie der Steine und Erden	173	200	203	168	175	217	200	182	181	183	172	174	246	230	212
5. Chemische Industrie, Farb.	45	27	48	77	72	82	64	75	95	94	70	79	121	77	117
6. Baugewerbe	655	664	659	579	687	768	834	918	799	801	804	949	1132	1111	1082
7. Holz- und Schnitzstoffe (Lackierer u. Vergolder)	308	330	274	290	353	399	413	359	386	414	404	375	567	652	543
8. Beleuchtung, Heizung .	22	19	20	18	18	20	26	27	36	33	22	35	51	46	55
9. Maschinen, Werkzeuge .	44	109	109	121	193	241	253	251	254	228	196	202	245	301	337
10. Instrumente, Uhren . .	27	31	36	41	35	39	22	41	44	65	51	56	71	63	54
11. Metallverarbeitung . . .	561	431	464	426	457	654	795	705	620	554	513	538	695	770	623
12. Textilindustrie	187	170	203	194	209	280	211	219	247	210	202	183	220	196	201
13. Bekleidung u. Reinigung .	579	487	587	517	421	471	504	504	504	530	497	508	523	512	537
14. Nahrungs- und Genuß-mittel	530	518	496	489	431	449	519	517	520	544	529	474	607	611	599
15. Beherbergung und Er-quickung	105	93	73	84	81	83	90	152	181	176	130	191	220	237	222
16. Verkehrsgewerbe	36	55	41	48	54	58	69	56	65	70	60	86	135	166	111
17. Schiffahrt	79	55	71	72	85	91	89	98	74	72	54	95	113	85	89
18. Handel	467	488	395	357	368	448	545	600	593	589	569	563	679	654	634
19. Papier und Leder . . .	149	159	140	178	184	178	229	193	204	154	166	174	194	235	176
20. Buch- und Kunstdruck .	83	61	66	64	61	88	90	95	69	72	88	68	112	80	90
21. Literatur und Presse . .	10	6	19	21	20	14	9	20	12	16	9	18	17	12	17
22. Künstlerische Betriebe für gewerbliche Zwecke . .	13	13	20	25	14	42	31	35	38	52	32	64	40	44	45
23. Kunst und Wissenschaft	27	19	16	8	25	29	21	32	32	35	26	35	28	27	23
24. Fahrende Kunst	16	31	22	20	29	11	23	15	24	24	19	30	28	17	42
25. Beamte, Feldmesser, In-genieure	173	164	170	153	150	150	161	118	125	142	129	108	143	143	141
26. Heilpersonal, Barbiere, Friseure	105	93	99	73	88	92	94	116	103	112	115	134	157	152	211
27. Persönliche Dienstleistung.	65	50	52	63	46	66	97	108	56	94	76	89	163	128	162
28. Arbeiter ohne nähere An-gabe	2434	2210	2210	2173	2212	2749	3138	2911	2826	3246	2772	3103	4298	4557	4272
29. Alle übrigen Berufe . .	168	142	222	175	170	215	341	564	472	470	491	414	524	524	424
Zusammen	7640	7191	7353	7244	7494	8823	10046	10307	9819	10009	9113	9856	12587	12575	12363

In view of this disparate clientele, one might
assume that the differences vastly outweighed the similarities among those who passed through labor colonies. But the
following remarks focused on shared characteristics of
wanderers who availed themselves of the services the colonies provided.[102]

Dem Einwande aus Gegenden, wo sich Mangel an Arbeits-
kraeften fuehlbar macht: dass jeder, der arbeiten
wolle, auch Arbeit findet koenne, und dass sonach fuer
die betreffende Gegend sie Arbeiterkolonie keinen prak-
tischen Werth habe, wird mit Recht entgegengehalten,
dass die Kolonie hauptsaechlich der Aufnahme solcher
Elemente bestimmt sei, welche einer geregelten und ans-
trengenden Arbeit bereits seit laengerer Zeit entwoehnt
und meist auch in ihrem Aussern soweit heruntergenommen

seien, dass sich kaum Jemand dazu verstehen werde, sie in diesem Zustande in Arbeit zu nehmen, und die somit durch einen laengeren Aufenthalt in der Kolonie erst wieder zu geordneter Thaetigkeit und zu brauchbaren Gliedern der menschlichen Gesellschaft erzogen werden sollen, soweit dies uberhaupt noch moglich ist.

Many of the workers who landed in labor colonies had not had steady jobs for a long time--upon their departure this pattern changed for some, but not all, of the alumni. As with labor houses, much of the success depended on the original state of the workers entering the colonies rather than on any experiences during their stay. Working with a wide range of inmates, the colonies could offer only limited assistance to the uneven population drawing on their re-sources. In addition to the unemployed workers looking for jobs, the labor colonies attracted cripples, semi-invalids, drunks and foreigners of assorted descriptions. As variable as the workers were in quality, they also differed in quantity over time.[103]

Even during the peak of their operation during the late 1880's, the labor colonies were only equipped to handle a small percentage of the itinerant poor. Of the estimated 200,000 job seekers roving the highways in search of employ-ment, only about 4000 could be accommodated by all of the labor colonies in Prussia (which, incidentally, was better equipped to deal with the itinerant unemployed than any other German state). The greatest number of wanderers seeking work and temporary sustenance entered the colonies during the winter months, and the vast majority departed as the weather warmed. Seasonal fluctuations in the number of residents at any given labor colony were considerable and these differences were compounded by regional variations across Germany.[104]

The evolution of the German labor colonies was described in an article published during 1888 which noted the increase in the number of colonies over the preceding four years--from seven to sixteen. Colonies were spreading across Prussia, Bavaria, Posen and Thuringia by the late 1880's. An unbroken chain of colonies encompassing the entire Reich was eagerly anticipated because a national network would at least in theory enable itinerant job seekers to travel around the country in search of work without resorting to begging.[105] A significant decline in the latter offense had been recorded since the founding of the first colony in 1882. The officials who ran the colonies were eager to receive credit for the improvement and welcomed state subsidies in recognition of their contribution. But economic fluctuations independent of their services had a great deal to do with statistical changes in the incidence of vagrancy and begging.

Verpflegungsstationen and Herbergen zur Heimat

If labor colonies deserved credit, the decline of mendicancy must also be partially attributed to the introduction of Verpflegungsstationen, or refuges where the unemployed received relief in kind. These refuges were equipped for ministering to the needs of wandering job seekers over shorter periods of time than the labor colonies. The refuges provided food and overnight quarters rather than long-term relief to those passing through the area in search of work. Like the labor colonies, the Verpflegungsstationen also catered to a dual constituency. The stations served those who were legitimately unemployed, averse to begging, and in need of inexpensive lodging as they looked for work. The second group of individuals were chronic beggars and tramps whose temporary incarceration was intended as a deterrent and a social service.[106] The extent of the stations' activities in various regions was reflected in statistics from the economically perilous years between 1882 and 1887. During 1882, 320 of Prussia's 535 Kreise had Verpflegungsstationen and 215 did not. In 1882, there were 24,000 persons in Prussia's correctional institutions. Five years later, that figure had fallen to 15,000. The following figures attempt to demonstrate the correlation between crime and the availability of stations.[107]

> Die Provinzen I nach der Zahl der Kreise mit Stationen und II nach der Verminderung der Corrigenden prozentualiter klassificiert, ergiebt folgendes Resultat: I. 1) Sachsen 91% 2) Pommern 90% 3) Westfalen 87% 4) Brandenburg 83% 5) Hessen-Nassau 79% 6) Ostpreussen 64%. II. 1) Pommern 63% 2) Brandenburg 58% 3) Hannover 57% 4) Westfalen 52% 5) Rheinland 52% 6) Ostpreussen 45%. I. 7) Schleswig-Holstein 59% 8) Rheinland 50% 9) Hannover 49% 10) Schlesien 44% 11) Posen 24% 12) Westpreussen 19% II. 7) Schleswig-Holstein 44% 8) Hessen-Nassau 41% 9) Sachsen 38% 10) Posen 32% 11) Schlesien 28% 12) Westpreussen 25%.

In the typical case, the unemployed laborer combed areas between refuges looking for work. Since the labor colonies were only equipped to deal with about 4,000 residents, the vast majority of wandering unemployed were left to seek food and shelter in institutions geared to short-term help.

As the next set of figures indicates, the number of Verpflegungsstationen along with the number of individuals using their facilities tended to decline during the 1890's, reflecting the overall improvement which the economy had made since the preceding decade.[108]

Bezirk	Zahl der Verpfleg.-Stationen			Von 1890 — 1898 hat sich die Zahl verm. vermindert		Verabfolgte Nachtquart.		Zunahme der Nacht- quartiere	Abnahme der Nacht- quartiere
	i. J. 1890	i. J. 1896	i. J. 1898	um	um	i. J. 1890	i. J. 1898		
Kgr. Preußen	951	612	547		404	1 076 466	705 022		371 444
Kgr. Bayern	239	340	279	40	—	237 798	493 732	255 934	—
Kgr. Sachsen	144	40	63		81	111 118	101 047		10 071
Kgr. Württemberg	130	38	34		96	83 618	43 178		40 440
Grht. Baden	335	157	140		195	163 314	95 739		67 575
Grht. Hessen	40	18	23		17	60 446	58 167		2 279
Grht. Meklenb.-Schwerin	—	—	—		—	—	—	—	—
Grht. Meklenb.-Strelitz	7	7	7		—	14 053	12 287		1 766
Grht. S.-Weimar-Eisenach	31	19	17		14	47 143	31 202		15 941
Grht. Oldenburg	3	3	2		1	4 941	1 706		3 235
Hrzt. Anhalt	9	6	4		5	31 429	11 993		19 436
Hrzt. Braunschweig	8	2	2		6	10 233	11 197	964	—
Hrzt. Sachsen-Altenburg	14	10	10		4	20 470	15 808		4 662
Hrzt. S.-Coburg-Gotha	18	9	8		10	19 295	6 952		12 343
Hrzt. Sachf.-Meiningen	3	13	4	1	—	6 174	6 498	324	—
Frft. Lippe	5	1	1		4	6 076	1 483		4 593
Frft. Schaumburg-Lippe	1	1	1		—	1 635	3 450	1 815	—
Frft. Reuß ältere Linie	—	1	2	2	—	—	5 721	5 721	—
Frft. Reuß jüngere Linie	3	2	1		2	5 872	4 569		1 303
Frft. Schwarzburg-Rudolft.	5	5	7		3	7 746	4 234		3 512
Frft. Schwarzburg-Sonderh.	5	2	2		3	10 663	1 807		8 856
Frft. Waldeck	4	1	1		3	3 452	1 597		1 855
Freie Stadt Bremen	1	—	—		1	13 739	—		13 739
Freie Stadt Hamburg	—	—	—		—	—	—	—	—
Freie Stadt Lübeck	—	—	—		—	—	—	—	—
Reichsl. Elfaß-Lothringen	1	—	—		1	410	—	—	410
Deutsches Reich	1957	1257	1150	43	— 850 + 43 — 807	1 936 091	1 617 389	264 758	— 883 499 + 264 758 — 313 702

The administration of relief took on a certain added sophistication during the Nineties as the refuges began to make greater use of centralized organizational methods. The procedure for handling new arrivals was indicative of how refuges dealt with itinerant job seekers by the turn of the century. An initial determination was made about the immediate employment prospects of each individual. If no work was likely to be available in the district, the person was rerouted to a main station situated on major thorough-fares. Presumably a position would open up in the vicinity of the main station where unemployed itinerants could remain for several days. In the interim, their behavior would be observed resulting in assessment of their abilities and industriousness.[109]

In conjunction with the labor colonies and Ver-pflegungsstationen, there were a number of shelters desig-nated as Herbergen zur Heimat where the unemployed stranger could find cheap lodging and intermittent work. By 1899 the Herbergen or inns were doing more than any other institution in terms of sheer numbers to alleviate the problems of the wandering poor--they were serving in excess of two million laborers. The exact number of their visitors that year was 2,024,000; in 1901 it reached 2,690,000 and by 1902 it climbed to 2,936,000. During the next five years there was a gradual but steady decline which reflected improvements in the economy: In 1903 the number passing through Herbergen zur Heimat was 2,618,000 and that had fallen to a figure of 2,032,000 by 1907. During the downswing of 1908 and 1909 the numbers again rose to 2,587,000 and 2,694,000 respectively.

The correlation between overall bad times and the number of travelers seeking sustenance in inns or refuges was even more clearly reflected in the figures on "mittelosen Stationsgaeste": They numbered approximately 507,000 in 1899, 759,000 in 1901 and 834,000 in 1902. With economic recovery came a rapid decline to 436,000 until 1907. Then in 1908 with another recession, 716,000 destitute guests used the facilities and the following year 704,000 availed themselves of the same opportunity.[110] During 1908, more than 450 Herbergen zur Heimat accommodated almost two million paying customers for an average stay of two nights; in addition they provided lodging for about 700,000 unemployed workers from the Verpflegungsstationen. People seeking help from the inns and refuges were those anxious to avoid begging or charity and eager to earn as much of their own subsistence as possible.[111]

Despite certain similarities between Herbergen zur Heimat and the Verpflegungsstationen, there were distinct differences between the institutions and the clientele they attracted. While the inns provided lodging in exchange for cash, the refuges offered food and shelter to those willing to work. One contemporary observer differentiated between the institutions in these terms:[112] "Herbergen zur Heimath duerfen sich nicht mit Verpflegungsstationen fuer Mittellose einlassen; erstere sind fuer ordentliche Wanderer, letztere fuer Bummler da." Apparently paying for services with money was considered more respectable than reciprocating with work. The existence of an interlocking network of inns, refuges and colonies catering to the basic needs of the itinerant job seeker did much to solve the most immediate problem of unemployment--subsistence per se. Although after

1882 workers in search of employment could stay alive without an income or charity, the institutional chain described here had an important missing link.

All shelters were directed toward preventing begging among those who were between jobs, but none of them was adequately equipped to secure long-term employment for the individuals that needed work to solve their problem on a meaningful level. The meager success of these institutions in placing job applicants could be judged from the fact that of two million persons taking advantage of the services of Herbergen zur Heimat during 1908, the inns managed to find positions for less than 140,000. As we might expect, the percentage of persons finding placement was significantly lower during recessions. Comparing data from the prosperous year of 1899 with statistics from 1902, we find that 31% more persons used the Inns but 18% fewer patrons secured jobs during the latter year. While one out of 20 residents of Herbergen zur Heimat found employment in 1904, one out of 22 succeeded in 1903 and only one in every 27 got a job in 1902.

Similar figures suggest that the same thing on a smaller scale occurred in German labor colonies. Of the 12,878 individuals who passed through the colonies during 1909, only 2003 or 15% left because they had found work. More than half of all residents voluntarily left the labor colonies without any definite prospect of employment. Even more distressing than this was the fact that among the relatively small group which had jobs when they left the colonies, many soon found themselves out of work and again seeking employment through an itinerant existence. It was therefore not surprising to find workers entering labor colonies on a repeat basis. During 1886, 20% of the individuals had been in colonies before; in 1891 that percentage climbed to 46.3%, and by 1910 it had reached 61.5%. These figures were indicative of the fact that the colonies and other institutions under consideration here alleviated but did not eliminate the unemployment problem because they failed to provide adequate job placement facilities.

An appallingly small percentage of success in eliminating unemployment was typical of institutions which lacked connections with a labor exchange, the only truly effective procurer of work in the private industrial sector. The importance of this connection was so overwhelming in the minds of those actively involved in relief efforts that this guideline was adopted: "Wo kein Arbeitsnachweis moeglich, da in der Regel auch keine Verpflegungsstation noetig."[113] Comments from an 1888 publication revealed that the potential effect of labor exchanges affiliated with refuges was impressive. In Prussia during that year, there were 503 stations associated with labor exchanges with a tremendous opportunity for the placement of itinerant jobseekers. Admittedly, the extent to which labor exchanges fulfilled their potential was variable.[114]

Part of the reason why the services of a labor exchange were so necessary may be attributed to society's tendency to attach a stigma to those who availed themselves of the hospitality of inns, refuges or labor colonies. Employers frequently had to be persuaded that alumni of these organizations deserved a stable job, humane treatment and the chance to reenter respectable society. Among many employers, there was some question as to whether individuals who wound up in public institutions were serious job seekers. Popular wisdom held that artisans and laborers really looking for work would avoid roaming the highways because with few exceptions the railroads were cheaper and more conducive to a successful job search. Given this assumption, the less time one spent in the kinds of places considered here, the more employable he was likely to be. Those who sought employment on foot were therefore encouraged to give up their itinerant lifestyle as soon as possible and return to a permanent position.

Wanderarbeitsstaetten

In addition to the Verpflegungsstationen and Herbergen zur Heimat, there were a number of Wanderarbeitsstaetten or labor yards where unemployed workers could do manual chores in exchange for room and board. The labor yards were frequently established in proximity to major cities where they provided an important service. In Berlin, for example, assistance was rendered to approximately 7,000 persons annually near the end of our period. The labor yards, like the refuges and inns, catered to itinerant job seekers and had close ties with Arbeitsnachweise.[115]

> Die Verbindung von Arbeitsnachweise und Wanderarbeits-
> staette ist eine sehr innige. In den Staedten, wo
> oeffentliche Arbeitsnachweise sind, finden die Wanderer
> in der Arbeitsstaette nur Aufnahme, wenn sie beim
> Arbeitsamt vergeblich Arbeit nachgesucht haben. Wo
> kein Arbeitsnachweis vorhanden war, ist ein solcher in
> den Wanderarbeitsstaette selbst eingerichtet.

The connection with employment offices was important to labor yards because they too were set up to aid the itinerant job seeker and protect him from "dem schlechten Einflusse der Landstrasse und vor den Gefahren der Arbeitslosigkeit."[116] Their concern was to provide alternatives to hunger and begging for the wanderer willing to work but unable to secure immediate employment on his own. The labor yards were not corrective institutions--they envisioned their function as preventive and tried to avert the formation of dissolute behavior patterns rather than reform inveterate tramps. Government support of this effort was formalized in a law of June 29, 1907, which outlined a mechanism for the establishment of administrative links between the labor yards and local communities. With the approval of a two-thirds majority of the provincial diets, rural and urban districts could be required to introduce, support and maintain Wanderarbeitsstaetten. Their mandate was to provide work for needy, able-bodied males who were traveling in search of employment.[117]

Despite the good intent and the successes of Wanderarbeitsstaetten and all the other institutions we have discussed here, the everpresent prospect of an itinerant existence had a disruptive impact on the industrial labor force.

Unemployment was dreaded by the working classes and by society at large as the prelude to a transition from respectability to degeneracy. Workers without jobs were thought to undergo some dark transformation from productive members of society into useless prototypes of a despicable Lumpenproletariat. The fear of unemployment leading to poverty, a dependence on charity and loss of respectability made the mere prospect of losing one's job a traumatic experience for the laboring classes. The discomfiture of anticipation was heightened by the unpredicability of its onset--at least with the seasonal unemployment which had plagued agriculture for centuries, there was an element of regular recurrence. But in the case of most industries, contemporary knowledge was not sufficiently sophisticated to predict the irregularly recurring cyclical downswings which resulted in major shutdowns and frequent unemployment. Even if a particular recession wasn't severe enough to result in the loss of one's job, a worker never knew when a minor setback or a major catastrophe might engulf his vulnerable family.

In addition to periods of unemployment, changes in employment had a disruptive effect on the workers who were forced to move from one job to another and on those who had to adjust when their firms changed management. An economy in a state of flux such as Germany had during the years between 1873 and 1913 wreaked psychological havoc on the lives of the industrial labor force despite the efforts of public institutions to avert the degeneration of workers into beggars and paupers. A more palatable approach to unemployment toward the end of our period seemed to lay in the introduction of insurance schemes which would give a worker greater security without adding to the degredation or disruption of his existence.

INSURANCE

Most schemes for unemployment insurance limited coverage to able-bodied, willing employees who were without work due to economic conditions. The lazy, the destitute, the incapacitated and self-employed were all routinely excluded from insurance protection. The primary function of insurance was to shield those who qualified from the economic hardships of unemployment and thereby avert the deterioration of their lifestyle to a dependence on hand-outs. Insurance admittedly did nothing to prevent the onset of unemployment, nor did insurance contribute to the elimination of that condition once it had occurred. Like most forms of unemployment relief considered above, insurance programs tried to provide an alternative to alms-giving which was reserved for totally destitute individuals who had accepted "die wirtschaftliche Vernichtung einer Existenz". The following remarks about the differences between insurance and other forms of compensation reflected popular attitudes toward unemployment during the first decade of this century.[118]

> Die Arbeitslosenunterstuetzung geht von der Tatsache der Arbeitslosigkeit aus, ohne Ruecksicht, ob sich ihr Eintritt voraussehen liess oder nicht, ohne Beruecksichtigung der Wahrscheinlichkeit ihres Eintritts und ihrer Dauer. Unter Versicherung versteht man auf Gegenseitigkeit beruhende wirtschaftliche Veranstaltungen zwecks Deckung zufaelligen schaetzbaren Vermogensbedarfs. Legt man diese Begriffsbestimmung auch fuer die Versicherung gegen die Folgen der Arbeitslosigkeit zugrunde, so ergibt sich, dass der Versicherungsfall (Arbeitslosigkeit) ein zufaelliger sein muss, dass seine willkuerliche Herbeifuehrung durch denjenigen, dem Ersatz geleistet werden soll, moe-

glichst ausgeschlossen sein soll, dass ferner der Bedarf nicht bei allen Teilnehmern gleichzeitig und in gleicher Hoehe eintreten darf. Es gehoert aber auch begrifflich zur Arbeitslosenversicherung, dass jeder Teilnehmer ein Recht auf die Deckung seines Vermoegensbedarfs hat. Wo kein Recht besteht, sondern nur die Hoffnung auf Gewahrung nach freiem Ermessen, da liegt Versicherung nicht vor.

Many insurance plans including Bismarck's national coverage of sickness and old age entailed an element of subsidy as well as self-help. Unlike other forms of compensation, insurance was dependent on an ability to predict the incidence, extent and duration of unemployment. It presupposed that not all subscribers would be in a position to press claims at the same time but guaranteed the individual participant a right to expect payment when he presented a legitimate claim. In exchange for that right, participants were required to remit regular premiums--they were in effect buying protection so that when the contingency arose they were entitled to demand the coverage for which they had already paid. In terms of preserving the workers' self-respect, insurance was deemed to be further removed from hand-outs than other forms of compensation and therefore had much to recommend it.

There were a variety of unemployment insurance schemes contemplated and introduced on a trial basis in various parts of Germany during the latter half of our period. An article published in the Reichsarbeitsblatt divided the unemployed who had claims on national insurance programs into six groups. They had coverage under self-help programs through 1) labor unions, 2) national health insurance legislation, 3) professional associations, 4) national invalid insurance, 5) mutual specialty exchanges and 6) communal funds.[119] In various contexts we have already considered each of the groups alluded to with the exception of the last one--those who had insurance claims through local communities.

To recapitulate, we have touched on mutual insurance schemes available through trade unions and commercial associations. We have examined the scattered efforts of enlightened employers to provide benefits for their employees. We have considered Bismarck's social legislation which extended coverage to the sick and invalid members of society but did nothing to protect workers from the vicissitudes of purely economic change. In this context it would be worth recalling that subsequent efforts to introduce national unemployment insurance failed to evoke a favorable response during the early twentieth century. We have also looked at the role of Arbeitsnachweise in solving the unemployment problem and will therefore concentrate primarily on the communal insurance programs here.

Three basic kinds of subsidized unemployment insurance were offered in German cities after 1896. A fourth form, compulsory unemployment coverage, didn't exist in Germany during our period. The first type of plan, involving optional funds, was adopted at Cologne and Leipzig. The earliest fund, inaugurated in Cologne during 1896, insured only against seasonal unemployment. Although it was one of the more active efforts it did not obviate the need for municipal public works projects. After thirteen years of operation, a total of 1957 subscribers had paid premiums which equalled 42.7% of the claims: 82.9% of the insured individuals had suffered from unemployment. The less active Leipzig fund which came into being during 1905 had insured fewer than 250 persons after four years. It was not however limited to seasonal unemployment. Unlike Cologne which was dependent upon municipal financing, its primary means of support was a private charitable foundation.

A second type of plan which involved proportional indemnity was named after the Belgian town of Ghent where it originated. Among the German cities which experimented with various adaptions of this system were Munich, Mainz and Wernigerode where supervision of unemployed organized workers was entrusted to the trade unions. Similar programs were tried in the Berlin suburbs of Charlottenburg and Schoeneberg as well as Strassburg and its environs. The Strassburg system limited coverage to union men and correlated its activities with municipal relief works and labor exchanges. In Strassburg during 1909 approximately 29,000 Marks were expended on unemployment compensation through the cooperative efforts of the city and the labor unions. Among the 335 individuals receiving a total of 8095 days of public compensation, 164 were metal workers who received 1853 days worth of support; 139 printers collected relief for 2197 days; 121 woodworkers were awarded benefits for 1095 days and 111 carpenters were compensated for a total of 1212 days. While the city provided protection for slightly more than 8000 days, unions assumed responsibility for more than 15,000 days of unemployment compensation.[120]

Two years after its inception--during the period alluded to above--the program had more than 5000 affiliated members of 32 trade unions as participants. The surrounding communities of Schiltigheim and Bischheim as well as the city of Freiburg established funds similar to Strassburg's during the years immediately after 1907. Each community instituted minor variations in adapting the plan to its particular needs--Freiburg, for example, paid premiums to thrifty subscribers much like Ghent. Meanwhile, an alternate type of proportional indemnity system was tried in Erlangen where every unemployed male who had been a resident of the town for three years could receive help if he did not participate in relief-works. In Erlangen there was no requirement that those applying for aid subscribe to an insurance fund. Instead, the city voted a credit in 1909 to support unemployed residents. Finally, a third type of insurance combined proportional indemnity with optional funds. This combination of the Cologne and Ghent systems was recommended to municipalities by the south German governments of Baden and Bavaria toward the end of our period.

Having outlined the broad contours of local unemployment insurance in Germany, we might now afford a few of the programs somewhat closer consideration. The early models for German unemployment insurance schemes were derived from prior experiments in neighboring Belgian and Swiss communities. The Ghent system, which originated in Belgium during 1901, was adopted in Scandinavia and France as well as towns like Strassburg. The system supplemented trade union unemployment funds and tended to heighten existing differences between organized and unskilled workers. Although somewhat less emulated, the oldest municipal insurance programs in Europe came from Switzerland--the city of Bern introduced a voluntary program in 1893 and during the following year the canton of St. Gall experimented unsuccessfully with compulsory unemployment insurance. The former ultimately provided the prototype for the program adopted in Cologne while the latter was much discussed in Duesseldorf and other cities but never adopted in Germany during our period. The compulsory St. Gall program ultimately failed even in Switzerland. As we noted earlier, it had to be abandoned because many of the more skilled and industrious workers resented what they regarded as subsidies for their less fortunate colleagues. Despite setbacks of this kind in adjacent countries, municipal unemployment insurance thrived in most German cities where it was introduced during the first decade of this century. By 1909, the following cities had some form of insurance already operative or under consideration: Strassburg, Erlangen, Braunschweig, Frankfurt am Main, Hessen, Altenberg, Munich, Rixdorf, Luebeck, Nuremberg, Leipzig, Elberfeld, Cologne, Ludwigshafen, Mainz, Remscheid, Muelhausen, Muenchen-Gladbach, Regensburg, Dessau, Duesseldorf, Chemnitz and Aachen.

At first glance, the above list might look rather impressive, but in fact there were substantial differences in the programs inaugurated or contemplated in various communities. The limitations of the progress made during our period were reflected in comments produced by a commission which met in Cologne during 1909 to discuss unemployment in the great German industrial centers. That commission indicated that only a handful of major cities had actually put insurance programs into operation.[121] This limited progress was disappointing to organizations like the Zentralverbandes der Handlungsgehilfen und Gehilfinnen which had met the previous year in Munich and declared "dass es eine Pflicht von Reich, Staat und Gemeinde sei, den Angestellten und Arbeitern bei Arbeitslosigkeit Unterstuetzung zu gewaehren, und zwar in Form eines Zuschusses an jene Berufsvereine, die statuarische Arbeitslosenversicherung zahlen."[122] Despite such claims, we have already indicated that the national and state governments preferred to leave unemployment insurance to local initiatives. Furthermore, on the municipal level, most insurance programs were severely limited in terms of coverage. Qualifying criteria included stipulations about sex, residence, marital status, age, occupation, season, level of skill, union affiliation, health, waiting periods and cause of unemployment.

To take a specific example, we might look at the earliest and one of the most important municipal insurance plans--Cologne's "Versicherungskasse gegen Arbeitslosigkeit im Winter". Based on the Swiss model at Bern, the Cologne program was privately controlled but after 1902 received an annual subsidy of 20,000 Marks. Participation was voluntary and cost unskilled workers 25 Pfennigs and skilled workers 35 Pfennigs per week. To qualify, a person had to be more than eighteen years of age, regularly employed and a resident of the city for at least one year. Coverage was limited to males and specifically excluded "Personen ohne regelmaessige Beschaeftigung, Gelegenheitsarbeiter und dauernd Arbeitsunfaehige". The insurance provided compensation exclusively for unemployment during the period between December 1 and March 1 of the following year. Unmarried participants without dependents in Cologne were required to accept employment outside of the city when it became available and transportation costs were covered. In order to gain a brief overview of the cost and extent of support offered by Cologne's insurance against unemployment in winter during the first ten years of operation, these figures should be considered.[123]

Geschäftsjahr	Zahl der abgeschlossenen Versicherungsverträge	Zahl der Versicherten, deren Arbeitsverhältnis gemäß § 6 der Satzung erlosch (von der / in der Rechnung)	Von den bei der Unterstützten Versicherten wurden erwerbslos	Zahl der Tage, an denen die erwerbslosen Versicherten unterstützt wurden *)	Zahl der Tage, wofür Tagegelder gezahlt wurden	Gesamtbetrag der ausgezahlten Tagegelder		Von den eingezahlten Tagegeldern trachten die Verpflegten durch Rückerstattung ein		
						ℳ	₰	ℳ	₰	ℳ ‰
1896/97 . .	220	88	—	96	2 181	1 408	2 355	—	1 000	50	42,3
1897/98 . .	324	88	—	151	2 646	2 197	3 495	37	2 213	25	63,3
1898/99 . .	347	65	—	144	2 857 ½	2 025 ½	3 313	21	2 444	75	73,1
1899/1900 .	266	30	—	154	3 703 ½	2 772 ½	4 708	38	2 009	50	42,7
1900/01 . .	571	35	—	411	6 478 ½	12 638 ½	19 337	73	4 561	75	23,6
1901/02 . .	1 205	100	52	612	15 853	18 238 ½	30 046	—	12 434	95	41,6
1902/03 . .	1 355	90	27	1 008	28 946 ½	16 814 ½	25 507	—	14 878	85	49,7
1903/04 . .	1 631	123	29	1 151	26 713 ½	22 910	33 915	—	19 772	90	49,5
1904/05 . .	1 717	121	25	1 271	22 648 ½	25 051	42 832	—	20 762	29	48,5
1905/06 . .	1 610	147	21	1 057	28 713 ½	13 414	13 635	—	21 651	85	91,7

A closer look at statistics from a single year indicated that from April 1, 1902, to March 31, 1903, the number of insured persons increased from 1205 to 1355. Of the 1355, 311 were unskilled and 1044 were skilled workers. Of the monies paid out that year 6605.50 Marks went to 214 unskilled workers who received an average of 30.87 Marks while 22,202 Marks were allocated to 750 skilled laborers, an average of 29.60 Marks. The total expended that year was 28,807.50 Marks on 964 insured persons who received a combined average of 29.88 Marks, as compared with the previous year's average of 37.46 Marks. The breakdown of expenditure among skilled workers was as follows: 264 masons received a total of 5751 Marks or an average of 21.78 Marks; 290 plaster and stucco workers received 8065 Marks, an average of 27.81 Marks; 17 joiners and carpenters received 668.50 Marks, an average of 39.32 Marks; 117 painters and paperhangers received 5508.50 Marks, an average of 47.08 Marks; 51 pavers and soil rammers received 1660 Marks, an average of 32.55 Marks; 11 other skilled workers were allocated 549 Marks, an average of 49.91 Marks.

The seasonal nature of the Cologne program accounted in large part for the overwhelming predominance of the construction trades, whose organized representatives had no unemployment insurance through their unions. Although their need was somewhat less marked at the beginning, construction workers and other members of seasonal trades had been the primary beneficiaries of the program ever since its inception. Of the 220 men who participated in the insurance fund during its first year of operation in 1896, the breakdown by profession was: "29 Anstreicher, 1 Dachdecker, 1 Dreher, 2 Fassbinder, 11 Gaertner, 28 Maurer, 1 Schlosser, 7 Schreiner, 1 Stellmacher, 1 Stukkateur, 122 Tageloehner, 1 Tapezierer, 11 Verputzer und 4 Zimmerleute".[124] Of this group, 45 persons were between the ages of 18 and 30; 58 were between 31 and 40; 66 were between 41 and 50; 42 were aged 51 to 60; and nine were between 61 and 70 years of age. 176 of the insured men were married while 44 were unmarried. From this beginning, the insurance program went on to serve an increasing number of workers.[125]

During the 1907/08 business year, 1505 individuals subscribed to the Cologne insurance fund; of these, 1127, or 81.5%, were unemployed. The 1500-plus workers had jobs for a total of 20,042 days and received 48,670 Marks worth of insurance for a period of 28,899 days. Of the amount paid out, weekly premiums covered 20,663 Marks or 42.5% of the compensation. The figures for the following year showed that the fund attracted 1957 men of whom 82.9%--1481 persons

--suffered from unemployment. During 1908/09 almost 2000 laborers found intermittent work, which left 37,971 days worth of claims totaling 61,934 Marks. Of that, 42.7% or 26,439 Marks were paid into the fund by its participants. These figures represented a significant advance over those for 1896. Despite the gradual increase in subscribers, the Cologne insurance fund never came close to extending unemployment coverage to a majority or even a significant minority of the city's labor force. This was the case throughout Germany where municipal experiments with unemployment insurance consistently failed to attain major proportions in terms of coverage before World War I.

Part of the reason why unemployment insurance programs were unable to attract large numbers of subscribers during our period stemmed from organizational idiosyncracies. In trade unions, unemployment funds were self-help measures organized along professional lines with a treasury held separately from monies allocated for sickness and strike support. The first program was established in 1879 by the German Buchdruckerverband and the movement won adherents during the 1890's. But it was not until the early decades of the twentieth century that the drive for union unemployment insurance really gained momentum. At the same time, public insurance began to emerge at the municipal level. This tended to evolve along two lines--the Ghent system and the kind of subsidized insurance plan adopted in Cologne to combat seasonal unemployment. Another type of unemployment insurance--mandatory programs set up by a few scattered employers for their employees during the late nineteenth century--never amounted to much. Employers' organizations consistently opposed public unemployment insurance in general and plans to adopt the Ghent system in particular.

The problem with unemployment insurance in Germany was two-fold: 1) Leaving aside the relatively insignificant number of employers' funds, the private programs which achieved comprehensive coverage in a territorial sense were limited to union members organized along occupational lines. 2) The public programs which achieved comprehensive coverage across professional lines failed to attain sufficient geographical scope to be truly effective. Contemporaries suggested that skilled workers would benefit from professional organizations while unskilled labor might find territorial organizations preferrable. Regional backwardness and variable unemployment risks were problems which had to be overcome in resolving the administrative barriers to broadly based unemployment insurance.[126]

Although the state governments of Baden and Bavaria showed some interest in unemployment insurance after 1909 and the question of a national insurance program was raised in the _Reichstag_ during 1902, 1906, 1908 and 1913, nothing significant beyond the municipal level was introduced.[127] On a national scale, people were willing to settle for, and even seemed to prefer, protection of especially vulnerable laborers such as construction workers, navvies and miners. We have already noted popular fears about the Ghent system and resentment of using public funds to strengthen union causes. If such opposition had been overcome, this might have provided a way to surmount the choice between protection organized along geographic or professional lines. As a result of residence requirements and the limited geographical base of support for unemployment insurance which evolved in Germany, many workers who might have left their hometowns to find employment elsewhere were detained by the need to qualify for public relief.

Unemployment during our period was not a local problem nor was it a problem which affected only a few well-organized professions. In an increasingly complex industrial society, work shortages reached across arbitrary territorial and occupational boundaries to touch a multitude of individuals. A successful insurance program needed to be organized along comprehensive lines--public and private efforts would have had to be coordinated to achieve adequate coverage on a national level. What was missing in Germany was a network of interlocking institutions. Such a network could have linked municipal insurance programs to form a national system of public unemployment coverage for non-union members. A complementary private system organized along union lines could have been coordinated to extend protection to all occupations. The programs which did exist in the public and private sectors were unsuccessful precisely because they lacked the institutional apparatus to extend their coverage to a meaningful share of the working classes. This lack of administrative expertise and coordination was typical during an era which some historians have characterized as an age of organized capitalism.

A related problem which at least in part stemmed from organizational deficiencies involved controls needed to administer unemployment insurance programs. Much of the difficulty derived from the fact that insurance had to protect its subscribers not only against an absolute lack of work but also against an absence of work suited to the personal circumstances of the individual. The cause of unemployment and any culpability which might be attached to the insured were difficult and frequently impossible to determine. With the exception of a few liberal Hirsch-Dunker unions, the Workmen's Unemployment Insurance Societies coped with this problem by ignoring the question of personal fault. Instead, they substituted strict supervision over the extent and duration of unemployment itself. Societies which involved fewer men tended to have an easier time checking on the causes of unemployment. In the public sector, cities like Erlangen, Freiburg, Muelhausen and Strassburg--where the Ghent model was in force--used a testing system which involved the trade unions as well as municipal councils. In cities like Cologne and Leipzig, which offered optional insurance programs utilized almost exclusively by small numbers of seasonal workers, frequent registration requirements were implemented as a check on the unemployed.

Another measure for improving municipal control over existing insurance programs was to establish closer ties with Arbeitsnachweise. Certain remarks by Richard Freund were indicative of this line of thinking.[128] According to Freund stronger linkages between labor exchanges and unemployment insurance were absolutely necessary to eliminate waste in the job market. Such connections would help to identify and reject workers who advanced insurance claims after refusing available positions. Those who contemplated national unemployment insurance advocated[129] the creation of a federal network which could be built on communal insurance funds. Controls would be easier to maintain where such funds were already in existence and tied in administratively with organizations such as labor exchanges or trade unions. One of the greatest obstacles to a federal insurance program was the unorganized labor force whose supervision during unemployment was almost impossible because there was no existing administrative apparatus to monitor their activities and prevent them from abusing the system. Unlike France where the state governments provided supervision or Belgium where the communities fulfilled the same function, the public contribution to unemployment insurance in Germany was generally limited to subsidizing trade union funds.

To summarize the difficulties, the three areas of

control which seemed to be of most widespread concern to those evaluating unemployment insurance were: 1) determining whether the cause of unemployment legitimately entitled the insured to compensation, 2) ascertaining through a system of frequent registration whether unemployed subscribers were cheating the system by working on the side while collecting benefits, and 3) finally, making sure that the insurance payments were sufficiently meager and the waiting periods sufficiently lengthy to encourage unemployed workers to return to the labor force as soon as jobs became available. None of these problems was satisfactorily resolved during our period and each contributed to the public's apprehension about insurance. By themselves, however, inadequate administrative controls might not have been enough to squelch plans for a comprehensive insurance program.

In addition to abuses and the problems envisioned by their control, opponents of publicly subsidized insurance raised a series of objections against its effectiveness in combating unemployment. One of the more interesting arguments against relying exclusively on insurance to resolve the unemployment problem placed that solution within the broader context of policy decisions affecting the labor market.[130]

Als Ergebnis der Darstellung ist zunachst hervorzuheben, dass die Bekaempfung der Arbeitslosigkeit selbst nicht im Wege der Versicherung zu erfolgen hat, sondern

> dass die Bekaempfung teils durch vorbeugende Massnahmen allgemeinen Charakters. (Regelung der Produktion, allgemeine Wirtschaftspolitik, Hebung der Volksbildung, Regelung des Lehrlingswesens usw.), teils durch Vermittlung vorhandener Arbeit und durch Arbeitsbeschaffung (Notstandsarbeiten) geschieht, waehrend die Versicherung nur eine Sicherstellung gegen die aus der Arbeitslosigkeit sich ergebenden Folgen bietet.

Rather than proposing alternate policies to cope with unemployment, there were a number of critics who were more interested in delineating the drawbacks of insurance per se.

In another context, we have already noted one such detractor--the organization of entrepreneurs which called themselves the Verband Suddeutscher Industrieller. Their reasons for opposing unemployment insurance were comprehensive and precise. To begin with, they pointed out that the level of unemployment was usually too low to warrant such action. Furthermore, they noted the dangers of destroying the workers' feelings of self-reliance and pampering the unskilled German laborers who were already in the process of abandoning unpleasant jobs to less selective foreign workers. The industrialists also hinted that insurance would undermine entirely sufficient existing correctives to unemployment in two ways: 1) by deterring workers from returning to the land when industry suffered a slump and 2) by encouraging additional lay-offs on the part of conscientious employers who had previously refused to dismiss their help when times were bad--even at great sacrifice to their operations. The implication here was that public insurance would obviate the need for private measures to avert unemployment which would thus be increased. The industrialists also feared that insurance would place an unfair added financial burden on employers, diminish the competitive position of their products, and under the Ghent system intervene on the side of organized labor in the economic struggle between masters and men. As an alternative to insurance, the entrepreneurs advocated the predictable old standby of various savings plans to which they appended a proposal for the "Ueberlassung von Ackerland seitens der Gemeinden an die Industriearbeiter und ueberhaupt Landerwerb durch diese".[131]

Other frequently repeated arguments which were added to this already formidable list against unemployment insurance stressed its demoralizing impact on workers. Laborers would be robbed of their freedom of occupational choice and compelled to accept any available job. According to its opponents, insurance would tend to lure people away from agriculture, thereby compounding the related problems of urbanization and depopulation of rural areas. That was one side of the argument against unemployment insurance; the reverse side of the same logic focused not on the labor force but on those soliciting its services. Insurance was unfair to employers because it would heap additional expenses on a group already overburdened with taxes. Worse still, it would strengthen unions, the class enemies of management, and encourage demands for increased wages, strikes and Social Democracy. This type of thinking led one jurist later affiliated with the chemical industry to the inspired conclusion that more jobs rather than insurance would provide the proper solution to the unemployment problem.[132]

> Ein besonderes Interesse fuer die Arbeitslosenver-
> sicherung haben bis jetzt nur die Gewerkschaften
> gezeigt, die in ihr ein wichtiges Mittel zur
> Durchfuehrung ihrer Lohnkaempfe erblicken. Je mehr
> Staat und Gemeinde die Kosten der Arbeitslosenver-
> sicherung uebernehmen, um so mehr sind die Gewerk-
> schaften in der Lage, ihre Mittel fuer Streikunter-
> stuetzungen bereitzustellen. Eine staatliche Arbeits-
> losenversicherung unterstuetzt demnach dem gegen die
> Arbeitgeber gerichteten Kampf der Gewerkschaften. Sie
> wird aber weiter die Wirkung haben, dass der Zustrom zu
> den grossen Staedten staerker zunimmt und dem Lande
> noch mehr Arbeitskraefte entzogen werden. Die beson-
> ders infolge der Landflucht notwendige Beschaeftigung
> grosser Mengen auslaendischer Arbeiter bedeutet eines
> Gefahr, die nicht durch Einfuehrung einer
> Arbeitslosen-Versicherung noch vergroessert werden
> darf. Aus allen diesen Gruenden kann die Fuersorge
> fuer die Arbeitslosen nicht auf dem Wege der Ver-
> sicherung erfolgen, sondern nur durch die unmittelbare
> Bekaempfung der Arbeitslosigkeit durch geeignete
> Massnahmen der Arbeitsvermittelung, Arbeitsverteilung
> und Arbeitsbeschaffung.

Unfortunately, Dr. Moldenhauer never enlightened his contemporaries by delineating how the jobs he proposed were to be created. And that, in the final reckoning, was what had to be resolved before unemployment could be eliminated rather than merely contained.

CONCLUSION

By way of conclusion, we might summarize a few of the more important assumptions about unemployment which affected policies aimed at alleviating the attendant problems. In a certain sense, unemployment measures were designed to fill the gap created during the 1880's when Bismarck's social legislation failed to include protection against economically induced disasters for the industrial labor force. Almost without exception, the remedies for joblessness considered here were to apply exclusively to unemployment which was excessive and whose onset occurred due to cyclical fluctuations in the economy rather than any fault of the individual employees. These measures were preferred to alternate employment because popular wisdom held that Germany had to maintain a surplus labor supply if it was to continue its rate of industrial expansion.

In this context, a strong anti-modern bias came into play. A reactionary strain manifested itself by portraying urbanization and industrialization as the twin sources of unemployment and Social Democracy as its primary beneficiary. Assumptions about the nature of the potentially revolutionary working class were not very flattering, although they improved somewhat over the course of our period. During the Bismarckian era, many authors and reformers proceeded on the basis of a dual assumption—first, that sloth was the natural proclivity of the labor force and second, that it was easier to avert the formation of bad habits than to rehabilitate practiced offenders. Institutions for the prevention of idleness and begging ranging from the rather punitive labor houses to the voluntary labor yards, colonies, refuges and inns were products of this line of thinking.

After the 1880's, the public showed an increased willingness to accept responsibility for unemployment and a tendency to remove the stigma attached to that condition. A few perceptive analysts began to acknowledge labor's preference for work rather than charity. Quarantine-like separation of the jobless gave way to less disruptive public works projects and private savings programs were supplemented by municipally subsidized insurance schemes after the turn of the century. In each of these undertakings, however, there was evidence of a firm conviction that private measures were preferable whenever possible. And every effort was made to avoid placing the unemployed worker in competition with the market mechanisms of private industry.

It is crucial to note that all of these programs were intended to contain the problems created by unemployment--they were aimed at helping affected laborers get through jobless periods as well as possible. Of the policy decisions considered here, only those related to labor exchanges were able to effectively curtail and eliminate unemployment by helping workers find permanent jobs. However, not even Arbeitsnachweise were equipped to expand the number of positions available to those looking for work.

Measures specifically designed to create additional employment of a nontemporary nature either in the public or
private sectors were simply not forthcoming during our
period.

In the final analysis, there was a two-fold
benefit to policies of containment which ensured the continuation of a controlled level of unemployment: 1) The
threat of unemployment leading to Social Democracy contributed to the internal enemies strategy which lent
cohesion to the newly unified German state; 2) A certain
amount of unemployment was the inevitable companion of the
kind of surplus labor supply which contemporaries envisioned
as a precondition for continued economic growth and industrial development. Unemployment was accepted in limited
quantities as the handmaiden of a pseudo-democratic political system and a developing industrial economy--it was quite
simply an integral component of the ongoing modernization
which affected the lives of workers in Germany during the
years between 1873 and 1913.

EPILOGUE

Looking at Germany between 1873 and 1913, we have traced the definition of industrial unemployment, the collection of data as a prerequisite for policy decisions, contemporary understanding of the source of work shortages and remedies designed to alleviate attendant problems. At every step along the way, the German response to unemployment constituted a series of stop-gap measures enabling contemporaries to contain rather than eliminate the phenomenon. There was an unfortunate and persistent tendency to deal with unemployment only when directly confronted by the problem. As we have seen, the years between 1873 and 1896 subsumed the single major industrial depression prior to the 1930's. These years therefore provided Germany's sole opportunity to evolve a workable unemployment policy before the Great Depression of the twentieth century.

The era with which we are dealing marked a transitional phase between pre-industrial and modern methods of dealing with unemployment. Attitudes were formed and institutional mechanisms were developed which conditioned subsequent responses to widespread idleness. Our period was a time for experimentation, a time for trial and error, and ultimately, a time for missed opportunities. The brief interval of intense but contained unemployment during the late seventies, the major shifts in population both internally and internationally, three successive economic downswings without sufficient intervals of recovery, compounded by inaccurate and incomplete quantitative data, produced a climate of fear and anxiety about unemployment which was totally out of proportion to its aggregate dimensions.

Motivated by unfounded fear in the absence of a hardcore unemployment problem, public and private innovators produced some positive institutional mechanisms for dealing with jobless workers. The collectivist means for coping with work shortages which emerged around the turn of the century included labor exchanges, refuges for both itinerant and non-mobile unemployed, public works projects and assorted insurance schemes. All of these institutional remedies were introduced at the grass roots level as part of municipal and union efforts to alleviate local problems. The creation of a national superstructure was forthcoming during our period in the case of labor exchanges although it was delayed in more costly instances such as insurance.

If we look at relief institutions as part of the effort to control unemployment and its consequences, we see once again that the greatest success was achieved at the lowest level of organization. Individual entrepreneurs were more effective than employers' cooperatives like the Centralverband der Industrieller in combating unemployment. Individual laborers willing to capitalize on their mobility to find jobs were more effective than any union in averting unemployment. And municipal officials were far more successful in conceiving, organizing and implementing unemployment policies than federal bureaucrats. Throughout our period, the tendency was to construct a solution from the ground up. Single employers, migrants, municipal administrators, local union officials and regional census-takers did more to limit unemployment rates than their counterparts at higher levels of organization.

Evidence indicates that the personal decision-making process was at least as important as collective policy-making in affecting unemployment between 1873 and 1913. While members of the Reichstag debated endlessly about the pros and cons of unemployment insurance, indi-vidual entrepreneurs cut wages and hours rather than dis-missing their labor force. While Bismarck stirred up theoretical controversies over a Recht auf Arbeit, indi-vidual workers decided to migrate to centers with greater employment opportunities rather than remaining rooted to familiar environments. At the federal level, there was a real failure to come to grips with the unemployment problem in a meaningful way. Ultimately, the lack of anything resembling a national anti-cyclical full employment policy constituted one of the major failures of the Imperial government. Because local authorities and creative entrepreneurs in private industry responded intelligently to economic crises and unemployment never assumed unmanageable proportions, the consequences of this failure were not immediately apparent prior to World War I.

The legacy of the Second Reich to its successors in the area of unemployment policy contained a major gap at the federal level. Simply stated, there was no proven national program for dealing with unemployment during economic crises. Between 1873 and 1913, federal policy-makers had responded to the needs of workers only under duress-- when rising unemployment rates were immanent. When prosperity returned, the few remaining pleas for a federally conceived and executed unemployment policy fell on deaf ears. In this context, let us look at John Garraty's analysis of German responses to unemployment.

> Most German academic economists remained...wedded to classical theory:...state intervention would stifle initiative, and in any case the task was too complicated for any organization to manage efficiently. Essentially, they believed that the way to restore prosperity and thus to reduce unemployment was to enable producers to make profits, and that the way to make production profitable was to reduce the cost of labor. Their proposals thus required [wage reductions and] further deflation...
>
> The counterargument of their critics was inflationary, although not always so stated. The more sophisticated of these critics called for dealing with unemployment by trying to stimulate consumption rather than production. If consumption could be increased, demand would come into balance with supply. Business profitability could then be restored by raising the prices of goods rather than by lowering the costs of making them.[1]

This assessment of unemployment policies goes on to speak of plans to resettle surplus workers in rural areas, of romanticizing the pre-industrial past and of disillusionment with both cartelization and urbanization. It was written as a description of conditions in Germany during the 1930's. Significantly, however, it described contemporary attitudes between 1873 and 1913 as well. Every one of these ideas affecting unemployment policy during the Thirties had been advanced at some point during our period. A few of the deflationary measures had actually been implemented and gave the illusion of adequacy as long as the rate of unemployment was low. And it must be emphasized that during the years we have considered unemployment rates paled in comparison with the dimensions of the problem during the Thirties. Measures to contain isolated, intermittent outbreaks of unemployment on the local or regional level sufficed during our period. But they were not readily adapted to deal with massive work shortages on a national scale.

The moderate approach and efforts to work within the system through mechanisms such as insurance, labor exchanges or public works projects were tailored to meet the needs of limited unemployment which Germany experienced prior to World War I. As we have seen, there were a number of factors at work during our period which combined to minimize the level of industrial unemployment. The ongoing process of industrialization was among the most important forces for sustained growth in the German labor market. While the rate of industrial expansion slowed markedly during the early deflationary years, it never came to a complete standstill. Another impetus for economic development was population growth. In conjunction with mobility and migration, Germany's increasing populace provided an adequate and flexible labor supply plus a larger consumer market. Although the role of the working class as consumers rather than producers was frequently underestimated, an expanding population base exerted a powerful influence on industrial production.

In this context, two safety valves which set a ceiling on industrial unemployment in Germany during our period merit recall. The first was emigration and internal relocation which enabled labor to move from geographical centers of saturated demand to areas where their services were needed. Particularly during the 1880's, mobility of the labor force was a crucial component in a chain of spontaneous individual initiatives to avert unemployment. In addition to overseas migration and redistribution of the domestic labor supply, mobility enabled agriculture to exercise a salutary effect on industrial unemployment. By relinquishing hands to industry during prosperous years and reabsorbing excess labor during recessions, German agriculture provided an invaluable cushion for marginal elements within the working class. Mobility, by facilitating permanent migration and temporary resettlement on the basis of variable demand for labor, enabled agriculture and industry to allocate a growing workforce with a minimum of unemployment.

Another factor tending to contain the level of unemployment involved the hiring and firing practices of individual entrepreneurs. As our period wore on, employers showed a distinct preference for maintaining a stable labor force whenever that was economically feasible. Rather than automatically resorting to lay-offs during crises, they began to reduce wages and hours in conjunction with production cutbacks designed to combat falling prices on saturated markets. The effort of employers to retain the services of their better workers during recessions was a major deterrent to unemployment.

Despite the low levels of joblessness which prevailed nationwide, there was a gap between the perception and reality of Germany's unemployment situation. Like many aspects of the emerging modern economy, industrial unemployment was a novel phenomenon in 1873. It was moreover one which was perceived to contribute to labor's lack of stability, security and control over its own economic destiny. The unpredictable, almost random nature of unemployment was conducive to widespread fear among the working class and overreaction among the rest of society. Uncertainty about the quantity of industrial unemployment, about its causes and about the most expedient remedies bred a fear of the situation which was totally disproportionate to the actual extent of the problem during our period.

Given the pattern of recurrent economic downswings without sufficient intervals of recovery between 1873 and 1896, the climate was ideal for nurturing anxiety about conspiracies. The list of internal enemies included Jewish, socialist, Catholic and unemployed revolutionaries. Fear of imaginary upheavals and domestic rebels was aggravated by the precarious equilibrium of Germany's newly unified national state. The need to adapt simultaneously to industrialization, national unification, and social modernization during an era of economic crises had a major impact on the response to unemployment. The additional pressures of demographic shifts plus the increasing demand for political participation made the extent of change in German society seem intermittently overwhelming. The complexity of adjusting to these unsynchronized but simultaneously progressing changes made it very difficult to evolve an effective means of coping with industrial unemployment during periods of economic stress.

In all of the above areas the years between 1873 and 1913 marked a transitional phase between the old predominantly agrarian order where unemployment was seasonal and the new industrial order where seasonal change was just one of many sources of unemployment. Just as there were no adequate statistics to determine with accuracy precisely how much unemployment existed, so there was no generally accepted theory or explanation of the causes of work shortage which informed policy decisions. Most analysts attributed unemployment to overproduction and called attention to the supply side of the problem. Rather than seeking the source of diminished demand, contemporaries focused on surpluses in the supply of commodities, including labor. Instead of trying to stimulate new demand, the preferred treatment was to control output by regulating wages, prices and the distribution of products through cartels or syndicates.

Various publicists attributed unemployment to seasonal change, technological improvements, government policy decisions, demographic shifts or general market conditions stemming from overproduction. The inability to determine either the extent or causes of unemployment had a marked effect on contemporary remedies. Without accurate information about the exact quantity or precise sources of unemployment, it was not possible to work out viable measures to combat the problem over extended periods of time. A pattern of stop-gap, decentralized efforts to contain the situation emerged in lieu of a consistent federal policy.

Unfortunately, there was one area where a national concensus had been achieved in relation to the unemployment problem. And that involved the identification of high levels of unemployment with left-wing revolutions. Throughout our period, anxiety about job scarcity and its victims was stirred up by and focused on the notion that socialist agitators would be the primary beneficiaries of idle disgruntled laborers. Fear of losing one's livelihood combined with fear of violent political upheavals on the left were the legacy of the years between 1873 and 1896 to those who lived through the Great Depression of the twentieth century.

It is important to recall that during the 1890's Germany had produced groups such as the _Bund der Landwirte_ which cultivated both extremist political views and the machinery of a broadly based mass movement. This did not seem particularly ominous at the time because contemporaries had no reason to fear right-wing organizations. Since Bismarck, anxiety over the political perils attached to unemployment had been channeled almost exclusively into anti-socialist sentiment. The tendency to link work shortages and revolutionary socialism in the popular imagination was firmly established during our period. Although economic circumstances failed to produce levels of unemployment which fanned fears stemming from this connection, the bond persisted in the public consciousness.

Fear stemming from a lack of knowledge about the extent of unemployment between 1873 and 1913 had produced institutional mechanisms for working within the system plus a new radical ideology. However, when unemployment assumed truly epidemic proportions during the early Thirties, the expedient of working within established institutions failed to achieve satisfactory results. There were no federal policies, no sophisticated statistics, comprehensive theories or national organizations adequate to meet the challenge of widespread unemployment because none had evolved under the Second Reich. Nor were there subsequent opportunities to close this gap because Germans dealt with unemployment only during economic crises and our period contained the sole industrial depression prior to the 1930's. As we have seen, the radical left was convincingly branded by Bismarck and his successors as exploiters rather than ameliorators of labor problems. Once voters had dismissed institutions at the center of the political spectrum as ineffective and left-wing parties as revolutionary, the far right was the logical place to look for a solution to the unemployment problem.

Prior to 1913, few ventured to point out the threat from the right associated with unemployment. Nor was much attention given to radical sentiments such as anti-Semitism which were beginning to assume disturbingly modern forms by the end of the century. When the economic reality of largescale work shortage was finally confronted, the time-honored connection between unemployment and revolution in conjunction with anxiety over lost earnings, humiliation and impoverishment led people to turn to a drastic political remedy. During the Weimer years, Communists succeeded in organizing unemployed members of the working class who were desparately seeking to regain their livelihoods. But disgruntled members of the lower middle class threatened by loss of employment and seeking to hold on to what they had, did not flock to the international proletarian banner. Anxious to maximize the distance between themselves and their social inferiors, they embraced the semi-respectable, bigotry laden dogma of groups on the far right. In the final analysis there was an unanticipated direct correlation between levels of unemployment and votes registered for National Socialists during the early 1930's. The fact that both unemployment and popular enthusiasm for right-wing candidates appeared to peak in 1932 encouraged Hitler to make a decisive bid for power before his support was eroded by economic recovery. The connection between socialist revolution and unemployment which was firmly established during our period set a precedent for the subsequent anxiety, bigotry and hatred exploited by the radical elements on both the left and right when aggregate levels of joblessness reached significant dimensions. Followed by unforeseen traumas including the Great War, the Versailles Treaty, the Sparticist Uprising and the hyperinflation of the Twenties, our period left behind a shaky foundation on which to build viable unemployment policies.

The heritage left behind by leaders in the area of labor policy between 1873 and 1913 was deficient in at least two crucial respects. No nationally tested or workable solutions to large-scale unemployment problems had been devised despite ample opportunities. Instead, the series of individual and local initiatives which had evolved to contain work scarcity deferred resolution of the attendant social, political and economic issues. Second, disproportionate fear of both unemployment and revolution from the left emerged with such consistent and convincing fervor that it was assimilated into the popular consciousness almost without question. Remaining virtually unchallenged, this learned response of fear at the prospect of losing one's job drove many unemployed workers to support extremist candidates during the Weimar period. Given the unpredictable onset of unemployment, those who continued to hold their jobs during the early Thirties were not exempt from the same kind of paranoia. Being only too well aware of the supposed danger on the left and totally oblivious to the threat from the opposite end of the political spectrum, they also voted for radical programs in response to the threat of unemployment. When job shortages occurred, all of the extremist parties gained support at the polls.

It is unfortunate that the solution to unemployment problems worked out during the formative years of modern Germany's political and economic development was called upon to meet the demands of a more complicated era. While the national state was in the process of consolidation and the industrial economy was in the early stages of maturation, unemployment typically remained below five percent. The reactions to limited unemployment and the methods used to resolve attendant problems proved singularly ill-suited to the needs of a mature industrial economy presided over by a faltering democratic experiment. And yet they seemed to define the parameters of available options during the late Weimar years. Why Germans of the 1930's failed to evolve viable alternatives to their far more serious unemployment problems is not the proper concern of our study. It has rather been our purpose to delineate the circumstances, causes and solutions of the unemployment problem which existed between 1873 and 1913. Beyond that we have attempted to retrace the contours of those solutions in order to suggest tentatively why they proved inadequate for subsequent generations.

During our period, there was a unique opportunity to develop a consistent federal policy and institutional apparati for dealing with industrial unemployment while the quantitative parameters of the problem were still within manageable bounds. Regrettably, this opportunity was wasted because an insurmountable gap between the perception and reality of unemployment persisted from 1873 to 1913. Ignorance derived from a lack of experience, reliable statistics and a comprehensive theory led Germans during those years to exaggerate the extent of unemployment and the present dangers.

On a theoretical level, the resulting tendency was to respond by overreacting to inflated estimates of the late nineteenth-century unemployment situation. On a practical level, initiatives were confined to poorly coordinated, badly timed and insufficiently funded measures which contained the immediate consequences but ignored the ultimate causes of industrial unemployment. In the realm of rhetoric and theory, radical and uniformly negative responses were tailored to address fears of revolution based on erroneous perceptions of the actual extent of work shortage. In the realm of policy and practice, collective, institutional and individual responses were tailored to the reality of limited job scarcity. The practical programs proved adequate to the needs of our period, but piecemeal, stop-gap measures were insufficient to cope with the large-scale unemployment of later years. This combination of

extreme rhetoric and inadequate policy subsequently dovetailed to burden the established order and help pave the way
for a takeover by the radical right. In the final analysis,
the Great Deflation left behind a legacy of inadequate
policies in conjunction with ignorance, prejudice and fear
of revolution which proved disastrous when unemployment
engulfed over six million Germans during the Great Depression of the twentieth century.

APPENDIX: UNEMPLOYMENT IN THE PRINTERS UNIONS

The printers union could trace its origins back to 1866 when 34 delegates representing 3187 colleagues in 85 cities were sent to a conference held in Leipzig between May 20 and 22. That was the first Buchdruckertag. When a second conclave met in Berlin during April of 1868, 5000 members were represented and the first steps were taken to establish support funds for needy members through an Invalidkasse. In addition to advancing such funds, the printers devoted their efforts to fighting for a ten hour day, opposing Sunday labor and improving the relationship between apprentices and masters. By the time the third Buchdruckertag convened in Frankfurt am Main in September of 1871, the printers unions had managed to double their membership. With their expanded affiliation, much union effort during the 1870's was devoted to the struggle for higher wages. Despite the imposition of restrictive legislation, membership continued to increase and at a meeting in Stuttgart on August 29, 1882, an estimated 10,000 organized printers were represented.

The relationship between apprentices, or "Lehrlingen" and "Gehilfen", or assistants, remained fairly stable during the early years of the organization with the former being outnumbered by a ratio of approximately two to one. In 1869 an estimated 9000 "Gehilfen" and 4000 "Lehrlingen" belonged to the printers union while in 1881 the numbers were 14,958 and 7429 respectively.

Between 1868 and 1890, the printers unions paid out 5,612,069 Marks in relief to members who were unable to work either because they were physically incapacitated or unable to find jobs.

Year	Unemployment On basis of wage rates	Benefits On basis of regulation [1] since 1880	Travel Subsidies since Oct. 1875	Invalid Benefits since 1880	Sickness Payments since July 1881
1868/69	11,280				
1870	7,952				
1871	1,042				
1872	21,946				
1873	124,746				
1874	43,090				
1875	45,082		28,737		
1876	5,617		120,250		
1877	66,711		44,017		
1878	6,963		47,871		
1879	1,038		62,005		
1880	9,590	16,806	52,500	102	
1881	1,605	14,156	64,974	829	13,351
1882	9,035	24,619	114,651	2,314	147,992
1883	22,024	28,532	132,191	8,882	226,947
1884	34,252	34,832	125,584	15,404	239,145
1885	18,355	35,763	107,081	22,231	271,813
1886	21,874	56,448	92,237	50,670	320,942
1887	266,344	130,861	147,418	75,349	329,396
1888	26,282	76,687	83,496	68,954	305,399
1889	17,664	56,512	62,421	78,648	300,377
1890	36,514	56,394	86,190	83,661	347,424
TOTALS	799,006	531,610	1,371,623	407,044	2,502,786

As the second column shows, a fund was established to help itinerant unemployed members in 1875 and a second one emerged for subsidies to permanently located individuals in 1880. The first fund which was associated with a labor exchange expended a total of 420,357 Marks between 1875 and 1882. The second fund initially limited benefits for non-mobile workers to a period ranging from ten to forty weeks. The estimated rate of unemployment due to scarcity of work opportunities for printers between 1875 and 1882 was an average of six percent of the organized labor force. As the preceding figures showed, approximately one Mark in five spent to improve needy members' lives went for unemployment relief during the years between 1868 and 1890. If travel benefits were added to the unemployment expenditure, almost half of the more than five million Marks were allotted to those members who were without work.

Speaking of an army of unemployed and incapacitated laborers and affirming every member's right to work, the printers union on the occasion of the 25th anniversary of its founding advocated shorter hours as a means of combatting job scarcity. Like Brentano, the printers saw protection against unemployment as a crucial prerequisite to other kinds of labor insurance such as coverage for invalid and ill members. It is interesting to add as a footnote that while union regulations exempted unemployed members from payment of fees, Bismarck's social legislation enacted on April 4, 1884, required that every member--including the unemployed--pay a weekly stipend into the sickness insurance fund. This stipulation cost the central treasury of the printers union an estimated 62,281 Marks between 1884 and its withdrawal at the end of September, 1895.

Let us briefly turn to a consideration of the printers' expenditure on travel benefits related to unemployment for the years between 1880 and 1901. The first table reflects more than a four-fold increase in average membership over the 21-year period. It also shows "Angaben ueber die zu staendig arbeitslosen oder reisenden Mitgliedern umgerechneten arbeitslosen Tage, den zur Deckung der Ausgaben notwendigen Jahres und Wochenbeitrag des einzelnen Mitglieds". Finally, it provides an accurate indication of the number of printing shops where union members were present during a given year.

Year	Average Number of Members	Number of Travel Days	Reduced to Permanent Travel		Sum of Travel Support	Share of Subsidy/Member		Printing Shops With Members
			Absolute	Percent		Mk/Yr	Pf/Wk	
1880	6959	86142	236	3.39	80558.75	11.59	22.29	400
1881	8403	95303	261	3.11	89241.25	10.62	20.42	501
1882	9108	141266	387	4.25	133492.50	14.66	28.19	555
1883	10118	141721	388	3.83	134572.25	13.30	25.58	588
1884	10818	153902	422	3.90	140278.40	12.97	24.94	563
1885	11739	109560	300	2.56	97650	8.32	16	576
1886	12868	129486	355	2.76	111051.45	8.63	16.60	548
1887	11724	126301	346	2.95	110350.15	9.41	18.10	569
1888	11233	98539	270	2.40	87341.55	7.78	14.97	587
1889	11902	74551	204	1.71	64719.20	5.44	10.46	557
1890	15864	89320	245	1.54	75761.25	4.78	9.19	650
1891	17410	80805	221	1.27	68665.75	3.94	7.58	617
1892	15387	120390	330	2.14	101703.75	6.61	12.71	715
1893	15852	112223	307	1.94	95269.85	6.01	11.56	703
1894	17262	129697	355	2.06	109164.50	6.32	12.15	774
1895	19166	123818	339	1.77	106313.50	5.55	10.67	837
1896	21410	150885	413	1.93	135060.75	6.31	12.13	865
1897	22830	146887	402	1.76	132741.50	5.81	11.17	899
1898	24331	121996	334	1.37	110387.75	4.54	8.73	960
1899	26049	116492	319	1.22	110729.00	4.25	8.17	963
1900	28506	137636	377	1.32	151834.75	5.33	10.25	981
1901	30696	218291	598	1.95	241051.75	7.85	15.10	1045
Totals		2705211		2.32	2487939.50		14.86 Pf.	

Compare the preceding figures on benefits paid to traveling unemployed members with the following numbers reflecting the printers' subsidies for stationary unemployment during the same period.

Year	Average Member-ship	No. Days with Sta-tionary unemploy-ment	Reduced to permanent stationary unemploy-ment Absolute	%-age	Sums of benefits to sta-tionary unemployed	Share of subsidy per member Mk/yr	Pf/wk	Print shops employing members
1880	6959	16393	45	0.65	16393	2.36	4.54	400
1881	8403	20332	56	0.67	20332	2.42	4.65	501
1882	9108	27666	76	0.83	27666	3.04	5.85	555
1883	10118	32154	88	0.87	32154	3.18	6.12	588
1884	10818	37536	103	0.95	37536	3.47	6.67	563
1885	11739	40328	110	0.94	40328	3.52	6.77	576
1886	12868	69991	192	1.49	69991	5.44	10.46	548
1887	11724	111077	304	2.59	111077	9.47	18.21	569
1888	11233	79991	219	1.95	79991	7.12	13.69	587
1889	11902	58746	161	1.35	58746	4.94	9.50	557
1890	15864	56261	154	0.97	56261	3.61	6.94	650
1891	17410	39843	109	0.63	39843	2.29	4.40	617
1892	15387	146337	401	2.61	146337	9.51	18.29	715
1893	15852	89831	246	1.55	89831	5.67	10.90	703
1894	17262	99763	273	1.58	99763	5.78	11.12	774
1895	19166	95044	260	1.36	95044	4.96	9.54	837
1896	21410	126484	347	1.62	126484	5.91	11.37	865
1897	22830	132331	363	1.59	132331	5.80	11.15	899
1898	24331	139903	383	1.57	139903	5.75	11.06	960
1899	26049	139482	382	1.47	156358.75	6.00	11.54	963
1900	28506	181896	498	1.75	267087.50	9.37	18.02	981
1901	30696	349790	958	3.12	513549.25	16.73	37.17	1045
Totals		2091179		1.46	2357006.50		11.04 Pf.	

Combining the results of the preceding two tables we find that during the 22 years between 1880 and 1901, organized German printers' assistants were unemployed for a total of 4,796,390 days or 13,140 years, 9 months and 17 days. Computed on the basis of an average weekly wage of 24 Marks, this represented lost income amounting to 16,399,728 Marks. If the cost of compensation--4,844,946 Marks--is added to this figure, we come out with 21,244,674 Marks as the cost of unemployment to organized printers in Germany for the years between 1880 and 1901.

Jahresausweise über Unterstützung an Arbeitslose auf der Reise und am Orte.

Jahr	Mitglieder (Durchschnittszahl)	Zahl der arbeitslosen Tage u. der Reise u. am Orte	Auf ständig Arbeitslose (auf d. Reise u. a. Orte) reduziert		Summe der Unterstützung f. Arbeitslose auf der Reise und am Orte	Auf jedes Mitglied entfallender Beitrag		Zahl der Druckorte, i. denen Mitglieder
			absolut	in Prozenten		pro Jahr Mt.	pro Woche Pf.	
1880	6959	102535	281	4,04	96951,75	13,95	26,83	400
1881	8103	115635	317	3,78	109573,25	13,04	25,07	501
1882	9108	168932	463	5,08	161158,50	17,70	34,04	555
1883	10118	173375	476	4,70	166726,25	16,48	31,70	588
1884	10818	191433	525	4,85	177814,40	16,44	31,61	563
1885	11739	149868	410	3,50	137978,—	11,84	22,77	576
1886	12888	199477	547	4,25	181042,45	14,07	27,06	548
1887	11724	237378	650	5,54	221427,15	18,88	36,31	569
1888	11233	178530	489	4,35	167332,55	14,90	28,66	587
1889	11902	133297	365	3,06	123465,20	10,38	19,96	557
1890	15861	145531	399	2,51	132022,25	8,39	16,13	650
1891	17410	120648	330	1,90	108506,75	6,23	11,98	617
1892	15387	266727	731	4,75	248040,75	16,12	31,00	715
1893	15852	202054	553	3,49	185160,85	11,68	22,46	703
1894	17262	229160	628	3,64	208927,50	12,10	23,27	774
1895	19166	218362	599	3,13	201357,50	10,51	20,21	837
1896	21410	277359	760	3,55	261544,75	12,22	23,50	865
1897	22830	279218	765	3,25	265072,50	11,61	22,32	899
1898	24331	261899	717	2,94	250290,75	10,29	19,79	960
1899	25649	255974	701	2,89	267087,75	10,25	19,71	963
1900	28566	319532	875	3,07	418922,25	14,70	28,27	931
1901	30636	553081	1556	5,07	754691,—	24,53	47,27	1015
		4796390		~ 3,78 %	4844946,10		~ 25,90 Pf.	

Before leaving our analysis of the unemployment figures compiled by the printers unions, we might consider the extent to which their jobs were dependent upon seasonal changes. In doing so, the table on the following page is extremely helpful because it provides a comprehensive comparative view of the labor market on a monthly basis over a twenty-two year period. The month of each year which offered most work opportunities for printers was designated by a 1; the month of each year which registered the highest level of unemployment by a 12. Note the degree of consistency over this long and economically diverse interval. On the average, March seemed to offer the best job prospects for those employed in the printing trades and publishing, while October was the worst month. Seasonally, the months of February, March and April were consistently the best in terms of employment both for itinerant and stationary workers while July, August, September and October were the worst. To cite Karl Oldenburg, "The season of the printing trade begins in November and ends in April."

COMPARATIVE TABLE SHOWING MOVEMENT OF THE LABOR MARKET IN INDIVIDUAL YEARS AND MONTHS

	TRAVELING												STATIONARY											
Year	Jan	Feb	Mar	Apr	May	Jun	Jul	Aug	Sep	Oct	Nov	Dec	Jan	Feb	Mar	Apr	May	Jun	Jul	Aug	Sep	Oct	Nov	Dec
1880	3	2	1	4	5	7	9	11	12	10	8	6	2	1	4	3	5	7	10	11	9	12	8	6
1881	4	2	1	3	5	7	9	12	11	10	8	6	11	2	1	6	4	3	5	7	8	12	9	10
1882	3	1	2	4	6	8	9	11	12	10	7	5	7	2	1	4	5	9	10	11	12	8	3	6
1883	4	2	1	3	6	8	9	12	11	10	7	5	4	1	3	2	5	9	7	11	12	10	6	8
1884	5	2	4	3	7	8	10	12	11	9	6	1	6	2	3	1	8	9	7	12	10	11	5	4
1885	4	2	1	3	7	8	10	12	11	9	6	5	4	2	1	3	5	6	8	12	10	11	7	9
1886	4	3	1	2	5	6	8	9	10	11	12	7	6	3	1	2	4	5	11	9	10	12	8	7
1887	6	3	1	4	7	8	10	12	11	9	5	2	8	2	1	6	3	4	9	11	12	10	7	5
1888	5	2	1	4	7	8	10	11	12	9	6	3	8	3	2	1	5	10	9	12	11	7	4	6
1889	5	4	1	3	6	8	10	12	11	9	7	2	10	6	2	1	4	8	9	12	11	7	5	3
1890	2	3	1	4	7	8	10	12	11	9	6	5	5	1	2	3	6	7	9	12	11	10	8	4
1891	3	1	2	4	5	6	7	9	8	-	-	-	4	2	1	3	5	6	7	9	8	-	-	-
1892	-	-	2	3	5	6	9	10	8	7	4	1	-	-	1	6	4	5	7	10	9	8	3	2
1893	3	1	2	4	7	8	10	12	11	9	6	5	5	4	1	2	3	9	10	11	12	8	6	7
1894	1	2	3	5	7	8	10	12	11	9	6	4	5	1	3	2	7	12	9	10	11	8	4	6
1895	4	2	1	3	6	8	10	12	11	9	7	5	5	3	1	2	4	8	6	11	12	10	9	7
1896	3	2	1	4	6	8	10	12	11	9	7	5	6	3	1	2	8	7	9	12	10	11	5	4
1897	5	3	1	2	7	8	10	12	11	9	6	4	8	2	1	4	6	7	11	12	9	10	5	3
1898	5	2	1	4	7	8	10	12	11	9	6	3	8	2	1	3	5	7	10	12	11	9	4	6
1899	5	3	1	4	7	8	10	12	11	9	6	2	7	2	1	3	4	8	9	11	12	10	5	6
1900	3	1	2	4	6	8	10	12	11	9	7	5	5	3	1	2	4	6	8	10	12	11	9	7
1901	3	2	1	4	6	8	10	12	11	9	7	5	4	1	2	3	5	8	9	12	11	10	7	6
Average:	4	2	1	3	6	8	10	12	11	9	7	5	7	2	1	3	4	8	9	12	11	10	6	5

NOTES: PART ONE

1. For all employment-related definitions and concepts, see John A.Garraty, Unemployment in History: Economic Thought and Public Policy. New York: 1978.

2. Ibid., p. 4.

3. Ibid., pp. 234-5.

4. Ibid., pp. 234-5.

5. This term appears frequently in the unemployment literature of our period and was in no way confined to Marxist interpretations.

6. Richard Herbst, Die Methoden der deutschen Arbeitslosen-Statistik. Leipzig und Berlin: 1914. Page 3.

7. Garraty, op. cit., p. 5.

8. Reichsarbeitsblatt, Nr. 6, 1906, s. 518.

9. See in particular Alexander Gerschenkron's lengthy review of Rosenberg's book in Journal of Economic History XXVIII: 154 (1968).

10. Ibid.

11. For an excellent discussion of the controversy, see reviews of Rosenberg's book and for England S.B. Saul, The Myth of the Great Depression 1873-1896. London: 1969.

12. This applies to our subject despite the economic dimensions of German unemployment.

13. Alexander Gerschenkron, Continuity in History and Other Essays. Cambridge, Mass.: 1968. Pages 33-34.

14. Simon Kuznets' early work is noteworthy in this context. See, for example, Economic Change: Selected Essays in Business Cycles, National, Income and Economic Growth (New York: 1953).

15. See Hans Rosenberg's first chapter in Grosse Depression und Bismarckzeit Wirtschaftsablauf, Gesellschaft und Politik im Mitteleuropa. Berlin: 1967.

16. Joseph A.Schumpeter, "The Analysis of Economic Change," Review of Economic Statistics, XVII, No. 4, page 4.

17. Ibid, page 5.

18. According to Kondratiev, the first long wave which can be historically documented ran from 1783 to 1842, the second from 1842 to 1897 and the third began in 1897, running beyond his present of roughly 1920.

19. Schumpeter, "Analysis", page 8.

20. Joseph A.Schumpeter, Business Cycles: A Theoretical, Historical and Statistical Analysis of the Capitalist Process. New York and London: 1939. Page 6.

21. According to Hans-Ulrich Wehler, the outbreak of war in 1912 caused the number of German soldiers to increase from five million to eleven million or from 7.5% to 16.5% of the total population. See Das deutsche Kaiserreich, page 203.

22. Schumpeter, Business Cycles, page 13.

23. Schumpeter, "Analysis", page 8.

24. Ibid, pages 8-9.

25. Ibid, page 9.

26. The comments of Chr. R.Jansen and Erik Korr Johansen, The Study of Unemployment; Remarks Based on Unemployment Research in Nineteenth Century Denmark. XIV International Congress of Historical Sciences, San Francisco, August 22-29, 1975, would be very useful for a comparative perspective of the unemployment problem.

27. Schumpeter, Business Cycles, page 170.

28. Ibid, pages 396-97.

29. Wolfram Fischer, Wirtschaft und Gesellschaft im Zeitalter der Industrialisierung. Goettingen: 1972. Pages 183-84.

30. Ibid, page 181. As in this footnote, translations of quotations cited in the text have been inserted where appropriate. "It is generally valid in an economy with technical branches with the highest growth rates in labor productivity, that the number of workers does not grow at the same rate as production. In times of crisis during the nineteenth century, the number of workers was quickly reduced in order to save costs at the same time that technical innovations were necessary so that renewed expansion of the volume of labor occurred only gradually."

31. This observation is also supported by the Danish findings alluded to in Note 26.

32. Richard J.Evans, editor, Society and Politics in Wilhelmine Germany. New York: 1978. Pages 227-28.

33. Ibid, pp. 226-227 and Fischer, op. cit.

34. See Vernon L.Lidtke, The Outlawed Party. Princeton: 1966 for a full discussion of this point.

35. See Fischer, op. cit.

36. Dr. Rosenfeld, Der Beobachter, Nr. 294, 14. Dezember 1907. See also Die Arbeitslosigkeit: ihre Bekaempfung und Statistik; Inaugural-Dissertation der hohen philosophischen Fakultaet der Vereinigten Friedrichs-Universitaet Halle-Wittenberg zur Erlangung der Doktor wuerde vorgelegt von Paul Berndt. Halle: 1899. Page 15 has a discussion of the contemporary view of recurrent economic crises and unemployment. "Suddenly there stands on one side great capital sums invested in products. The crisis is there, and thousands and tens of thousands of workers are unemployed. One can compare this process with the self-cleansing of a river and name it the self-cleaning of the stream of production."

37. See Garraty, op. cit., pages 104-07.

38. Ibid.

39. See Wilhelm Abel, Massenarmut und Hungerkrisen im vorindustriellen Deutschland. Goettingen: 1972.

40. See Betty G.and Leo Fishman, Employment, Unemployment and Economic Growth. 1969. Page 81.

41. See Dr. Otto Most, The Problem of Unemployment in Germany, London: 1910. Page 4.

42. Abel, op. cit., pages 8-24.

43. Ibid, p. 24.

44. Ibid.

45. According to Abel (see Massenarmut, page 74) the latter figure contrasted with an increase approaching 5 percent during the remarkable growth of the 1950's in West Germany.

46. See Garraty, op. cit. on this.

47. We shall return to this point at length in the last chapter of the study which follows. It is also dealt with by Garraty and by R.A. Dorwart in The Prussian Welfare State before 1740.

48. Abel, op. cit., pages 15-16.

49. Garraty, op. cit.

50. Ibid, p. 29.

51. Ibid.

52. Schriften des Deutschen Werkmeister-Verbandes Heft XIII Fuersorge fuer Stellenlose Duesseldorf. "Arbeitslosen-Versicherung", von Dr. Otto Most, page 4. "The sources of unemployment and lack of a position are not only physical (want of a fitness for work), not only in the narrower sense ethical (want of a willingness to work), but also prominently economic (want of an opportunity to work). And to be sure the last factor dominates the foreground the more the economy loses the stable forms of the past and the more its well-being becomes tied in with fluctuations of the world economy. With the growing industrialization of the German economy, unemployment due to economic reasons temporarily assumes a size which one had previously not anticipated, and which entails difficult economic and moral disadvantages for those affected plus considerable dangers for the public welfare and order."

53. Ibid, page 6.

54. Ausschnitt aus der Zeitschrift fuer Versicherungswesen Nr. 36, Mittwoch den 16. September 1908 "Das Problem der Arbeitsversicherung".

55. This notion recurs throughout our period and reflects the anti-modern bias of many contemporaries.

56. On this point see also Osnabrucker Zeitung 16. September 1913 Nr. 12730 "Arbeitslosenversicherung". The quotation was taken from the article cited in Note 54. "Major urban unemployment is not only a phenomenon associated with modern economic life. It was rather already prominent in the old cultural states of Greece and Rome where it occurred in great volume."

57. Georg Schanz, Zur Frage der Arbeitslosen-Versicherung. Bamberg: 1895, pages 3-4. "I recommend relief works in the larger cities, which certainly have to contend with many difficulties and often bring only shifts in unemployment; I

recommend domestic colonisation in order to reduce the excessive influx of population into industrial centers; I recommend investing in a regular process of assistance for industrial cartels, production, and employment; I recommend assistance for the worker by discouraging overtime, short-ening work hours, regulating piecework, diminishing overtime of apprentices in specific professions (printers, shop clerks, etc.), facilitating the absorption of the excess labor force through maintenance of wages, diminishing underconsumption of the masses and thereby preventing overproduction along with its repercussions; I do not recommend the value of shorter warning periods through which the latitude for obtaining a new place would be increased; I commend the efforts of employers who in times of poor business conditions instead of resorting to definitive lay-offs prefer to discontinue work on certain days or to regularly rotate superfluous laborers who would only tempo-rarily be without work and be paid a waiting stipend so that the effects of recessions would be shared by all and more easily borne. One calls particular attention to a better organization of the labor supply."

58. Verein fuer soziale innere Kolonisation Deutschlands. E. V. 18. August 1913.

59. See Shulamit Angel, "The Emergence of Popular Anti-Modernism," unpublished PhD dissertation, University of California, Berkeley.

60. See Der Beobachter Samstag 24. Mai 1884 "Deutschlands soziale Gefahren II. Die industriellen Verhaeltnisse".

61. Evans, op. cit., page 274.

62. See Garraty, op. cit., pages 148-49.

63. Hans-Ulrich Wehler, Das deutsche Kaiserreich 1871-1918. Goettingen: 1973.

64. Evans, op. cit., page 22.

65. See in particular Kuczynski's chapter entitled "Beschaeftigung, Arbeitslosigkeit, Auswanderung, Einwander-ung, Gewerkschaftliche Organisation", pages 253-94 of Darstellung der Lage der Arbeiter in Deutschland von 1871 bis 1900 Teil II Die Geschichte der Lage der Arbeiter.

NOTES: PART TWO

1. See Niedersaechsischen Staatsarchiv Osnabrueck Dep 3b V Fach 45/46 No. 32, ss. 193-95. Deutscher Arbeitgeberbund fuer das Baugewerbe E.D. Berlin 20 Nov. 1913 Eingabe gegen die Einfuehrung der Oeffentlichen Arbeitslosenunterstuetzung.

2. Soziale Praxis V.5 1895-6 No. 39 S.1039. "Those considered culpable for being unemployed included persons who were jobless as a result of voluntary exodus, as a result of giving up places due to wage disputes, as a result of lay-offs attributable to laziness, debauchery, quarrelsomeness, insubordination or drunkenness. Hence the worker who is dismissed because he refused the required deterioration of the terms of employment (longer hours, lower wages) has become unemployed through his own fault."

3. Campbell R.McConnel (ed.), Economic Issues: Readings and Cases (New York: 1963) Council of Economic Advisers, Economic Report of the President, pp. 81-83.

4. Soziale Praxis, V.21 1911-12, S.694.

5. Ibid., s. 696. "Between both classes stands still the class of workers' assistants which only with difficulty can be made to convey the idea of one or the other and strictly constructed, requires a separate treatment. To them belongs an army of assistant waiters, barbers, cooks, musicians, which vacillate between full unemployment and makeshift employment."

6. Soziale Praxis, V.22 1912-13, S.905.

7. Ibid., S.554. "The existence of the evils of unemployment no longer needs to be demonstrated; the experiences of the labor exchanges clearly show that the "industrial reserve army" is present, that even in regular times, it is not always idlers or incompetent workers who cannot find jobs. The controversial question, whether the number of unemployed is greater than in the previous year, has relatively subordinate interest."

8. Soziale Praxis, V.17 1907-08, S.491.
9. John A.Garraty, Unemployment in History, Economic Thought and Public Policy. New York: 1978, p. 168.

10. Frank B.Tipton, Jr., Regional Variations in the Economic Development of Germany During the Nineteenth Century, Middletown, Connecticut: 1976. p. 163.

11. Handbuch der deutschen Wirtschafts- und Sozialgeschichte, Bd. 2. Stuttgart: 1976. S.619.

12. Ibid., S.613.

13. See Richard J.Evans, ed., Society and Politics in Wilhelmine Germany. New York: 1978.

14. Hans Mottek, "Die Gruenderkrise. Produktionsbewegung, Wirkungen, theoretische Problematik" Jahrbuch fuer Wirtschaftsgeschichte 1966 Teil II Berlin: 1966. S.103.

15. Ibid.

16. Martin Kitchen, The Political Economy of Germany, 1815-1914 Montreal: 1978. P.157.

17. Soziale Praxis, V.18 1908-09, S.131.

18. Mottek, "Grunderkrise", S.105.

19. Ibid. "It has however remained decisive that the deep depression 1873 to 1879 was connected with a mass unemployment, that led to a strong decline of real income for the working class."

20. See Borchardt's article in the Handbuch on this point. "To be sure we have no statistical proof for this, nevertheless contemporary evidence demonstrates this just as consideration makes plain the assumption of a relatively high unemployment."

21. Ibid, S.264.

22. Volker Hentschel, "Prosperitaet und Krise in der Wuerttembergischen Wirtschaft", VfSuW 63. Bd. Heft 3 (1976) S. 347. "The inherently not unjustified attempt to be able to formulate everything in Marks and meters, tons and quotas, has two dangers. The one I have named after the example of the work of Hoffmann--the calculation becomes laden with so many premises, which to be sure are logical in themselves, that their product is a fiction. The second seems to me not less unfortunate. Economic history research becomes confined to an area which insists on sufficient quantitative material for order. The calculations suffice, the conclusions are right--only the relation between consumption and historical significance has been destroyed."

23. This statement underscores the subjective nature of statistical interpretations and shows that contemporaries recognized their potential for manipulation. Despite this fact, most of those dealing with the unemployment problem were obsessively concerned with the compilation of objectively accurate quantitative data. "The worker needs no lecture to the effect that unemployment is large; he knows it, sees it daily around himself; for him no numerical proof

is necessary; without knowledge of the number of his suffering colleagues, he feels the enormous size of the need."

24. Tipton, op. cit., p. 162.

25. Walter G.Hoffmann et al, Das Wachstum der deutschen Wirtschaft seit der Mitte des 19. Jahrhunderts Berlin: 1965. S. 531.

26. Ibid.

27. Ibid., S.26.

28. Population shifts will be discussed in greater detail in the next chapter.

29. Handbuch, S.248.

30. Ibid, S.613.

31. Juergen Kuczynski, Studien zur Geschichte der Zyklischen Ueberproduktionskrisen in Deutschland 1873 bis 1914. Berlin: 1961. S.26. "Let us take as new losses vis-a-vis 1872 through shorter hours relative to the end of overtime and unemployment:"

32. Juergen Kuczynski, Darstellung der Lage der Arbeiter in Deutschland von 1871 bis 1900 Bd. 3 Die Geschichte der Lage der Arbeiter unter dem Kapitalismus. S.266.

33. Mottek, "Grunderkrise", S.102. "Collectively the growth of possible employment of the potential of labor in industry must have amounted to about 14 percent and the underemployment in industry given these assumptions must have amounted to about 22.1 percent."

34. Hans Mottek, Wirtschaftsgeschichte Deutschland. S.175.

35. Mottek, "Grunderkrise", S.103. "According to statements of the police president of Berlin, there was a decline of employment identified with 22 to 28 analyzed branches of industry. A further increase of unemployment through lay-offs followed in 1876 in Berlin where a decline of employment in the area included by the factory inspectors amounted to 14 percent. In the year 1877 a further decline of approximately 6.3 percent was registered, while unemployment in the years 1878 and 1879 decreased rather than increased. Altogether Roessler came to the conclusion 'that with the commencement of the socialist legislation around 25 to 28 percent of the Berlin workers in the sector of industry and the productive handicrafts had become unemployed.'"

36. Vernon L.Lidtke, The Outlawed Party: Social Democracy in Germany, 1878-1890. Princeton: 1966, p. 178.

37. See Ashok V.Desai, Real Wages in Germany 1871-1913, Oxford: 1968. And Gerhard Bry, Wages in Germany 1871-1945. Princeton: 1960.

38. Desai, op. cit., p. 42.

39. Ibid. p. 43.

40. Ibid.

41. Ibid., p. 44.

42. Ibid., p. 98.

43. Particular emphasis was placed on industries with linkages to railroads since the 1873 boom was largely associated with speculative rail construction and the ensuing bust attributed to its abrupt curtailment. Desai relied on capital goods industries related to railways where the increase in real wages during the 1880's was much higher than in sectors such as textiles or printing.

44. See Desai's discussion on this point.

45. Desai, op. cit., pp. 118-19.

46. Soziale Praxis, V.4 1894-95, No. 15, SS. 173-174.

47. Ibid. "The resultant picture shows the narrow connection of popular nutrion with periods of economic decline which in Berlin have proceeded quite analagously."

48. Ibid.

49. Ibid.

50. Ibid.

51. Ibid. "The last year shows a remarkably strong decline for all four drinks, and this in connection with the similar conforming fact, that the profits of industry in their consumption have likewise rapidly decreased, with the further fact that unemployment in the year 1892 notoriously strongly increased, leads to the fairly certain conclusion that this year, with the recession of industry, a strong drop in the income and the purchasing power of the entire Berlin population also began simultaneously."

52. Herbst, Methoden, SS. 98-99. "1. Counts from house to house 2. Public requests for self-registration (Stuttgart

or south German method, registration system) 3. Public requests for entry in a publicly issued list 4. Public requests for self-registration through the lord mayor 5. Indirect enrollment on the basis of the legal status for tax purposes (Saxon method) 6. Filling out a census card for each jobseeker registered with a labor exchange 7. Identification of job seekers who could not be placed through municipal labor offices 8. Registration with the bureau for relief works 9. Random sample survey in 31 premises, which according to information of the statistical bureau of the city of Charlottenburg can really not be taken into consideration as an unemployment census 10. Control surveys of cities in both national unemployment counts on June 14 and December 2, 1895 11. Inquiry through the police agencies 12. Inquiries through poor relief."

53. As we noted earlier, the primary disadvantage of relying on labor exchanges for unemployment statistics derived from the disorganization of those institutions. In towns where there was more than one exchange, insufficient safeguards were adopted to prevent duplicate registrations.

54. Soziale Praxis, V.2 1893, S.80.

55. See Frankfurter Zeitung 6.11.1897.

56. "Die Gewerkvereine und der Versicherung II", Leipziger Zeitung, 20.9.82.

57. Ibid., 21.9.82

57a. Soziale Praxis v. 11, 1901-02, Nr. 17 pp. 424-26 and Nr. 20, pp. 502-503.

57b. Moritz Wagner, Beitraege zu der Arbeitslosenfuersorge in Deutschland, Berlin-Gruenewald: 1904, S.322.

58. Ibid.

59. Keeping the above criteria in mind, consider the example of the large group of union shop clerks in Germany represented by the Vereine der Handlungsgehilfen. During the early 1890's when all German Arbeiterfachvereine had a membership thought to number around 400,000, the shop clerks claimed approximately 100,000 persons or almost a quarter of the total. Within the shop clerks' union, the Verein der deutschen Kaufleute was the first to offer unemployment protection. Between its introduction in 1885 and 1890, their insurance against "Stellenlosigkeit" paid relief amounting to between 30 and 45 Marks per month for a period of six months. After 1890, a one year membership requirement was introduced along with a graduated schedule of benefits based on seniority. Having been a union member for

one year, an unemployed individual became eligible for three monthly payments of 30 Marks each; after five years of union affiliation, the payments were 37.50 Marks per month and after ten years, 45 Marks. Until the end of 1899, an estimated 63,608 Marks were paid out for "Stellenlosigkeit" by the Kaufleute Verein. The Berlin chapter of this organization which led the way toward unemployment relief on October 4, 1884, made participation in their unemployment fund mandatory by 1889. The following amounts were paid out by the Berlin shopkeepers' union:

Year	Out of General Support Fund		Out of Special Division	
	Cases	Marks	Cases	Marks
1891	9	432	6	702
1900	112	6343	28	3009
1905	401	21970	115	9384
1908	639	35917	175	14249

Following the example of the Berlin local and the national shopkeepers' union, the parent organization--the German National Shop Clerks' Union--adopted measures to provide unemployment relief in 1898.

60. Moritz Wagner, op. cit., S.321.

61. Following this example, the carpenters adopted a mandatory union unemployment fund.

62. "Zum Problem der Arbeitslosenversicherung", Deutsch Krankenkassen-Zeitung. Berlin 25. Oktober 1902.

63. Versicherung gegen die Folgen der Arbeitslosigkeit, SS. 448-49. "In the year 1904, 38 of 62 central unions had introduced unemployment protection, all Hirsch-Duncker Associations had adopted this kind of protection, and of the Christian unions the butchers, woodworkers, shoemakers, leather workers, metal workers and the graphic trades went ahead with its introduction. The same development occurs with the independent unions and the professional divisions of the association of Catholic labor unions."

64. Moritz Wagner, op. cit., S.322.

65. Versicherung gegen die Folgen der Arbeitslosigkeit, SS. 448-9. "A connection between unemployment and strikes occurs primarily in two cases: the one instance is, where someone who is himself not striking becomes unemployed as a result of the strike (because, for example, a coal shortage occurs), in which case he would be dealt with as unemployed; the second instance is that after a concluded strike someone who is no longer striking and also no longer receiving

strike subsidies, finds no employment. This situation is not touched upon at all in most statutes. One would be supported as unemployed, possibly under the guise of punishment because intercession is in the interests of the union."

66. Posener Zeitung, 2.10.1887.

67. Rheinischer Kurier, Wiesbaden, 13.12.1892.

68. Sozialpolitisches Centralblatt, Berlin 8. Mai 1893, "Die Arbeitslosigkeit des letzten Winters" No. 32, V.2.

69. Deutsche Versicherungs-Presse. Organ fuer das gesammte Assekuranzwesen, Nr. 23 XXIV Jhrg. Berlin, den 21. Juni 1896, S. 219.

70. Dr. E.Hirschberg, Die Massnahmen gegenueber der Arbeitslosigkeit, Berlin: 1894, S.14.

71. Soziale Praxis, V.7 1897-98, S.847.

72. Correspondenzblatt der General Kommission der Gewerkschaften Deutschlands, Statistische Beilage Nr. 6 vom 13. August 1910, S.184 und Statistische Beilage Nr. 6 vom 30. August 1913, S.194.

73. Soziale Praxis, V.1 1892, S.128.

74. These figures were reported regularly in publications ranging from newspapers to journals such as the Reichsarbeitsblatt and Soziale Praxis.

75. Herbst, Methoden, S.40.

76. Soziale Praxis, V.2 1893 No. 2, S.14.

77. Ibid., S.58. "First and Last names? Residence? Street Number? Floor? Occupation? Do you work at home, in a factory or workshop? How old are you? Years. Married or Single? Number of gainfully employed family members? Are you currently unemployed? Since when have you been unemployed? Are other family members who contribute to the support of the household unemployed? Were they in the course of the year, before the epidemic, unemployed? How many weeks? How many hours per day do you work under normal business conditions? How many hours per day do you work now? How long have you worked shorter hours? How much do your weekly wages total? With normal business conditions? Marks and Pfennigs. Now? Marks and Pfennigs."

78. "Hamburger Arbeitslosenstatistik", Vorwaerts No. 194, 22.1.93. "Bakers and pastry cooks 40, barbers and hairdressers 24, construction and earth workers 147, bleachers,

launderers 33, brewers 63, bookbinders 24, book printers and typesetters 69, factory and commercial assistants and workers 80, hotel assistants 185, casual laborers 843, harbor workers 336, fishermen 112, longshoremen 27, inspection personnel 42, grainery workers 90, shop clerks 35, retailers, newsmongers, grocers 80, house boys and clerks 85, firemen and machinists 85, coopers 22, coachmen 61, painters and lacquer workers 253, plumbers and mechanics 48, locksmiths and machine builders 152, smiths 99, musicians 66, shipwrights 80, seamstresses 141, shoemakers and quilters 52, wheelwrights and millwrights 32, cigar makers 122, cigar sorters 39, carpenters 267, potters 35, timber workers and joiners 192."

79. Hirschberg, op. cit., S.5. "One knows neither exactly the industries nor the places, which are affected or exempt, neither the sources nor the consequences of unemployment, neither its volume nor its nature."

80. Shulamit Angel-Volkov, "The Decline of the German Handicrafts--Another Reappraisal" VSWG 61/2; p. 181.

81. Vierteljahrschrift fuer Sozial und Wirtschaftsgeschichte, Bd. 64 Heft 2 (1977), S.172.

82. Sozialpolitisches Centralblatt, Berlin 7. Jan..1895 Nr. 15 IV. Jhrgng S.176.

83. Hentschel, op. cit., S.381. "The data of labor exchanges has always been so imprecise and inconsistent-- tendencies which they surely also reveal. In 1875 there were 8,349 work offers registered in Stuttgart, in 1877 there were still only 5,040. The number of job seekers remained the same at around 9,400. Instead of 1,875 unemployed 9,088 were supported. In 1878 it was 11,650."

84. Soziale Praxis, V.6 1896-97, S.882.

85. Paul Berndt, Die Arbeitslosigkeit Ihre Bekaempfung und Statistik Halle: 1899, S.36.

86. Sozialpolitisches Centralblatt IV. Jhrgng. Nr. 12 Berlin 17. Dezember 1894, S.140. "In 45 Berlin exchange places approximately 50,000 positions have been filled while 115,000 applicants have registered. In 39 unions, 44,000 vacancies were registered, of which 32,000 were occupied; in 35 of them alone 82,000 applicants were present."

87. Versicherung gegen die Folgen der Arbeitslosigkeit, Teil II, SS. 220-222.

88. Central Arbeitsnachweis-Einrichtungen als Private Unternehmungen gemeinnutziger Vereine, S.33. "The job-

seekers numbered 246,581 including 3,357 apprentices, the number of the required labor force was 188,981 including 4,329 apprentices; the estimated places would be assigned to 15,481 persons."

89. Versicherung gegen die Folgen der Arbeitslosigkeit, Teil II, S.55.

90. Arbeiter-Kolonie, 5. Jhrgng Nr. 2, Feb 1888, S.35. "The number of delivered male correctional assignees in the years from 1884 to 1887 fell from 1321 to 1175-922-766. Of these the number of first offenders in the designated years came to: 573-355-252-215, that is in four years a decrease of 62.5%; on the other hand, repeat inmates declined: 748-820-670-551, that is in the year 1885, which relative to 1884, the opening year of the colony, represented a growth of 2,634 total support days; an increased recitivism of only 110% occurred with a decrease of first offenders of about 30%; from there on a decline also of these backsliders took place but only about 22% relative to the year 1884."

91. Versicherung gegen die Folgen der Arbeitslosigkeit, Teil II. Berlin: 1906, Anhang, S.271.

92. See the fuller discussion of labor colonies in the fourth part of this paper.

93. Versicherung gegen die Folgen der Arbeitslosigkeit, Teil II, S.265.

94. Ephrem Rickling, Die deutschen Wanderarbeitsstaetten Muenchen Gladbach: 1912, S.139.

95. Ibid., S.140. 54 stations failed to report during the former period and 6 stations did so during the latter interval.

96. Germania, Zeitung fuer das deutsche Volk und Handelsblatt. Berlin, Dienstag den 22. Januar, 1901.

97. Rickling, op. cit., S.141.

98. Arbeiter Kolonie 5. Jhrgng Nr. 5, Mai: 1888, S.137.

99. See Rickling, op. cit.

100. See Rickling, op. cit.

Vergleichende Statistik der deutschen Verpflegungsstationen aus den Jahren 1890, 1896 und 1898

Bezirk	Zahl der Verpfleg.-Stationen			Von 1890—1898 hat sich die Zahl vermehrt um	vermindert um	Verabfolgte Nachtquart.		Zunahme der Nacht-quartiere	Abnahme der Nacht-quartiere
	I. J. 1890	i. J. 1896	I. J. 1898			i. J. 1890	i. J. 1898		
Kgr. Preußen	951	612	547	—	404	1 076 466	705 022		371 444
Kgr. Bayern	239	340	279	40	—	237 793	493 732	255 934	—
Kgr. Sachsen	144	40	63	—	81	111 118	101 047		10 071
Kgr. Württemberg	130	38	34	—	96	83 618	43 178		40 440
Grht. Baden	335	157	140	—	195	163 314	95 739		67 575
Grht. Hessen	40	18	23	—	17	60 446	58 167		2 279
Grht. Meklenb.-Schwerin	—	—	—	—	—	—	—	—	—
Grht. Meklenb.-Strelitz	7	7	7	—	—	14 053	12 287		1 766
Grht. S.-Weimar-Eisenach	31	19	17	—	14	47 143	31 202		15 941
Grht. Oldenburg	3	3	2	—	1	4 941	1 706		3 235
Hrzt. Anhalt	9	6	4	—	5	31 429	11 993		19 436
Hrzt. Braunschweig	8	2	2	—	6	10 253	11 197	964	—
Hrzt. Sachsen-Altenburg	14	10	10	—	4	20 470	15 808		4 662
Hrzt. S.-Coburg-Gotha	18	9	8	—	10	19 295	6 952		12 343
Hrzt. Sachs.-Meiningen	3	13	4	1	—	6 174	6 498	324	—
Frst. Lippe	5	1	1	—	4	6 076	1 483		4 593
Frst. Schaumburg-Lippe	1	1	1	—	—	1 635	3 450	1 815	—
Frst. Reuß ältere Linie	—	1	2	2	—	—	5 721	5 721	—
Frst. Reuß jüngere Linie	3	2	1	—	2	5 872	4 569		1 303
Frst. Schwarzburg-Rudolst.	5	5	2	—	3	7 746	4 234		3 512
Frst. Schwarzburg-Sondersh.	5	2	2	—	3	10 663	1 807		8 856
Frst. Waldeck	4	1	1	—	3	3 452	1 597		1 855
Freie Stadt Bremen	1	—	—	—	1	13 739	—		13 739
Freie Stadt Hamburg	—	—	—	—	—	—	—	—	—
Freie Stadt Lübeck	—	—	—	—	—	—	—	—	—
Reichsl. Elsaß-Lothringen	1	—	—	—	1	410	—		410
Deutsches Reich	1957	1287	1150	43	—850 +43 —807	1 936 091	1 617 389	264 758	—533 460 +264 758 —318 702

¹) Nach den Protokollen der 4. und 6. ordentlichen Versammlung des Gesamtverbandes.

101. As this data from the source cited in note 91 suggests, the greatest placement success came during years of relatively low unemployment and was almost inversely proportional to occupancy of the inns.

102. See Rickling, op. cit.

Statistik der deutschen Herbergen zur Heimat und der mit denselben verbundenen Verpflegungsstationen von 1899—1910

Jahr	Zahl der Herbergen z. H.	Davon hatten eine Verp. i. St.	Durchreisende Herbergsgäste Bettfremd.		Stationsgäste		Gesamt-zahl der Durch-reisenden	Auf je eine V.-St. kamen		pro Stat. Tag (Ver...)	Kosten der Verpflegungsstationen		In Arbeit wurden gebracht (Herbergs-u.St.-gäste)	
			Personen	Verpfleg.-Nächte	Personen	Verpfl.-Nächte		Ver-pflegte	Verpfl.-Nächte		insge-samt	pro Station	ins-gesamt	pro 100
1899	457	250	1 516 377	2 424 142	507 889	475 068	2 024 266	2032	1900	5.5	285 259	1141.20	132 891	6.56
1900	457	237	1 601 536	2 538 942	553 000	526 017	2 154 536	2333	2219	6.3	318 710	1356.32	125 789	5.84
1901	462	240	1 931 575	2 866 980	759 057	723 274	2 690 632	3163	3014	8.6	430 453	1793.60	108 505	4.03
1902	462	231	2 101 231	3 073 076	834 788	795 564	2 936 069	3614	3444	9.9	464 486	2010.76	109 306	3.72
1903	459	237	1 937 636	2 935 776	680 571	650 820	2 618 207	2872	2746	7.8	368 598	1555.26	117 154	4.47
1904	461	222	1 805 089	2 858 353	575 164	553 779	2 380 253	2591	2517	7.1	316 182	1424.24	122 042	5.13
1905	452	210	1 734 103	2 828 377	536 880	519 367	2 270 983	2557	2473	7.0	303 635	1445.94	137 130	6.03
1906	461	213	1 602 708	2 752 577	441 957	435 083	2 044 665	2075	2043	5.7	256 819	1205.72	159 110	7.78
1907	452	216	1 596 245	2 812 374	436 584	437 444	2 032 829	2021	2025	5.5	275 749	1276.61	158 500	7.79
1908	454	216	1 871 271	3 088 357	716 273	711 121	2 587 544	3316	3292	9.1	441 755	2045.17	138 088	5.38
1909	449	217	1 959 604	3 313 123	704 975	708 002	2 694 579	3249	3263	8.9	449 662	2072.18	133 899	4.97
1910	447	215	1 917 252	3 305 726	585 717	593 233	2 502 949	2724	2759	7.5	392 162	1824.00	159 111	6.36

¹) Nach den Jahresberichten. „Der Wanderer" XVII bis XXVIII.

103. Soziale Praxis, V.2 1893, S.18.

104. Ibid.

105. It is noteworthy that these figures show the highest incidence of per capita need during the warm summer months and a decline during the cold season.

106. Funfundzwanzigster Jahres-Bericht des Berliner Asyl-Vereins fuer Obdachlose, 1893, S.6.

107. William Harbutt Dawson, The Vagrancy Problem, London: 1910. Pp. 177-78.

108. Hirschberg, op. cit., S.6.

109. See Victor Boehmert, Die Ergebnisse der saechsischen Armenstatistik in der Jahren 1880, 1885 und 1890.

110. Ibid., S.121. "The cases of support due to unemployment, insufficient wages, etc. divide themselves fairly uniformly into prolonged and temporary support. The long-term support reicpients of these categories belong in the main part to those which due to weakened labor power can no longer earn the means of subsistence for themselves and their dependents; to the short-term support recipients on the other hand are assigned more who to be sure are fully capable of work but due to temporarily deficient work opportunities require charity."

111. "Armenstatistik", Social-Correspondenz, Organ des Centralvereins fuer das Wohl der arbeitenden Klassen. 8 Jhrgng. No. 10, Dresden: 1883. "The Saxon poor statistics show that the industrial areas, in which one usually presumes there are the most proletarians, in no way as a rule exhibit a high number of poor but that much more the richest cities are the worst. The industries care for their poor through miners' relief and other funds and also give to the weaker elements the opportunity for work. Lazy individuals are less tolerated there, even less than in the countryside; on the other hand one often tends to provide alms in rich cities superabundantly and thereby attracts the needy from near and far."

112. Schanz, op. cit., S.91. "35427 heads of families and single persons (as well as 60041 married women and children under 14 years old)"

113. Ibid., S.205.

114. See Boehmert, op. cit., S.140.

115. See Boehmert, op.cit. and Sozial-Correspondenz Organ des Centralvereins fuer das Wohl der arbeitenden Klassen. "Armenstatistik" 8. Jhrg. Nr. 10., Dresden: 1883.

116. Sozial Correspondenz, 8 Jhrg. No. 10, Dresden: 1883 "Armenstatistik".

117. Deutsches Zentralarchiv I, Potsdam Reichsministerium des Innerns, Armenwesen No. 2, Adh. 2. Vol. 2 Acta betreffend die Armenstatistik 7. Juli 1883 und 31. Januar 1888.

118. Reichsarbeitsblatt III. Jhrgng Nr. 9 1905, S.761. "In the current treatment there is an attempt to reach such a scale of averages which starts with an imaginary hypotheses, that in the highest membership of the fund lies the actual number of able-bodied workers during the whole year. Under this fictitious hypothesis one can determine out of the difference between highest membership and the average membership, approximately how great in percentage of the total number of able-bodied workers the employed have been on average during the year. The difference between this highest number and the monthly membership number of the local health insurance fund will then be considered the number of formerly able-bodied workers which became unemployed in the respective month."

119. Ibid. "If one compares for example the highest monthly figure of 3,510,809 with the average membership number of 3,327,753 (in which one considers the membership on December 31 along with the computation of the latter), one finds that of those persons capable of work in the district of the local health insurance fund an annual average of 5.2% have been unemployed."

120. Soziale Praxis, V.5 1895-96, Nr. 2, S.36. "These numbers in their variations suggest conclusions about the course of employment. . . . It will be repeatedly emphasized that fluctuations in the number of insured in no way produced differences in the number of unemployed relative to the rehired jobless. These statistics will be dealt with just like any other."

121. Soziale Praxis, V.11 1901-02, Nr. 11, SS. 283-84.

122. Otto Most, The Problem of Unemployment in Germany, p. 22.

123. See Reichsarbeitsblatt, V.11 1913 Nr. 1, S.31.

124. Soziale Praxis, V.6 1896-97, Nr. 13, S.316.

125. Here we might recall Otto Most's estimate that the December figures would indicate that six rather than 3.5 percent of the entire working class was unemployed if those removed from the labor market by military service and prisons were included.

126. Other factors contributing to the higher unemployment rates during December were the greater registration of vagabonds and the large number of workers with secondary occupations like piece work to supplement seasonally conditional income. In the latter context it is worth noting that those with agrarian jobs or in home weaving would not show up in the June figures but would register in December.

127. Many union figures fail to include agriculture or the building trades where a great deal of unemployment was concentrated, especially during winter.

128. Dr. M.Wagner, "Neues zur Arbeitslosenversicherung", Reformblatt fuer Arbeiter-Versicherung IV. Jhrgng Nr. 16 1908 August II.

129. Statistik des Deutschen Reichs, Neue Folge, Band III, Die Berufliche und Sozial- Gliederung des Detuschen Volkes. Berlin 1899, S.249.

130. Rickling, op. cit., S.134.

131. Reichsarbeitsblatt III. Jhrgng 1905, Nr. 9, S.759. "Zur Frage der Berufsrisikos der Arbeitslosigkeit".

132. Reichsarbeitsblatt XI Jhrgng 1913, Nr. 4, S.269 and Nr. 1, S.32.

133. Reichsarbeitsblatt III Jhrgng. 1905, Nr. 1, SS. 18-19.

134. Reichsarbeitsblatt IV Jhrgng 1906, Nr. 4, S.305.

135. Reichsarbeitsblatt III Jhrgng.1905, Nr. 7, S.571.

136. Soziale Praxis, V.6 1896-97, Nr. 3, S.60.

137. A.G. Pigou, The Theory of Unemployment, London, 1933, P.16.

138. Soziale Praxis, V.3 1893-94, S.609.

139. Herbst, Methoden, S.86.

140. Reichsarbeitsblatt V.Jhrgng 1907, Nr. 7, S.623. "As always the longest average duration of unemployment occurs this time also in some retailers associations. It climbs to 42.4 days with the central association of clerks, to 32.4

days with the commercial association for female employees, though the frequency of unemployment here is very small."

141. Reichsarbeitsblatt VI. Jhrgng 1908, Nr. 10, S.915.

142. "Arbeitslosigkeit...Arbeitslosenzahlungen in deutscher Staedten" Reichsarbeitsblatt II. 1904, Nr. 2, SS. 104-121.

143. Rickling, op. cit., S.137.

144. Soziale Praxis, V.6 1896-97 Nr. 1, S.9.

145. It is however difficult to generalize and we must note that subsequent municipal surveys showed a predominance of married unemployed. Whether this reflected limitations of assistance programs or the real distribution of unemployment is worth considering.

146. Statistik des Deutschen Reichs, N.F. Bd. 111, Berlin: 1899., S.258.

147. Handbuch der deutschen Wirtschafts- und Sozialgeschichte Bd 2., S.22.

148. See Tipton, Regional Variations, p. 88.

149. Most, op. cit., p. 23.

150. Reichsarbeitsblatt VIII Jhrgng, 1910 Nr. 1, SS. 24-31.

151. Soziale Praxis, V.6 1896-97, Nr. 13 SS. 317-18.

152. Angel-Volkov, op. cit., p. 168.

153. Arbeitslosigkeit im Baugewerbe nach Landesteilen und Ortsgrossenklassen sowie Arbeitsmarkt politik der Gewerkschaften 21. Oktober 1913.

154. Soziale Praxis, V.3 1893-94, S.233. "Also it's no wonder that native Berliners, themselves sons of Berlin workers, with their superior knowledge of trade relations go mostly into the best paid and steadily working trades; and the presence of relatives and friends, and above all the support of powerful labor organizations which continue in the lucrative industries, do not often let them come to the outermost limits of need. The transients on the other hand encounter the excesses of seasonal trades, uncertainty of the business cycle, helplessness in foreign surroundings."

NOTES: PART THREE

1. An earlier survey of the <u>Maurers</u> union in the 1890's provided a breakdown of the causes of unemployment as follows:

Unemployment resulting from:	1890	Oct. 1, 1891 to Oct. 1, 1892
Arbeitsmangel	154,950.75	85119
Unguenstiger Witterung	209,959.50	74879
Krankheit	41,778.50	16160
Streiks	57,675.25	1582
Militaer. Uebungen	---	127
in Ortsschaften	202.00	99
Auf je 1 Arbeiter, der sich an der Zaehlung betheiligten kamen wegen Arbeitsmangel u. unguenstiger Witterung arbeitslose Tage	50.50	57

Georg Schanz, <u>Zur Frage der Arbeitslosen-Versicherung</u> Bamberg: 1895, S.229.

2. See Richard Herbst, <u>Die Methoden der deutschen Arbeitslosenstatistik</u>, Lepzig und Berlin: 1914.

3. <u>Ibid.</u>, SS. 86-87.

4. <u>Reichsarbeitsblatt</u> 1905 Nr. 1, SS. 38-43.

5. Schanz, <u>op. cit.</u>, S.7.

6. <u>Reichsarbeitsblatt</u> II: 1913 Nr. 11, SS. 833-36.

7. <u>Reichsarbeitsblatt</u> 10: 1912, SS. 587-95.

8. <u>Soziale Praxis</u>, V.22 1912-13, S.356.

9. Gardeners were often fully employed during the planting seasons each spring and fall. During the height of both summer and winter, they experienced an off-season. See Dr. H.Post, <u>Untersuchungen ueber dem Unfang der Erwerbslosigkeit innerhalb der Einzelnen Berufe und Berufsgruppen</u> Jena: 1914, SS. 12-13.

10. Schanz, <u>op. cit.</u>, S.8. "A very great number of production branches have to reckon with the fact that during a part of the year a surplus labor force appears. That is not to be changed given the climatic relations, tastes and changing directions of demand during the year; there the best labor exchange does not help at all; where there is no work, it can find none."

11. See Post, op. cit., SS. 102-103.

12. Soziale Praxis, V.20 1910-1911, SS. 507-08.

13. Reichsarbeitsblatt, IV Nr. 9, SS. 803-808.

14. See, for example, the discussion of building trades in Soziale Praxis, V.5 1895-96, No. 34, S.920.

15. See Ephrem Rickling, Die Deutschen Wanderarbeits-staetten. Muenchen-Gladbach: 1912. "How much this unemployment will advance migration among stable thousands who become afflicted, can be judged from the fact that itinerant traffic regularly increases proportionately in time of greater unemployment. This has been observed in all bad years and shows itself anew each winter."

16. Soziale Praxis, V.6, 1896-7, S.882.

17. Reichsarbeitsblatt 10: 1912, SS 587-595. "Neuere Arbeitslosenzaehlungen in Deutschland".

18. Martin Kitchen, The Political Economy of Germany 1815-1913, London and Montreal: 1978, P.157.

19. Shulamit Angel-Volkov, "The Decline of the German Handicrafts--Another Reappraisal," VSWG 61/2, P.181.

20. Ibid., p. 182.

21. Paul Berndt, Die Arbeitslosigkeit Ihre Bekaempfung und Statistik. Halle: 1899, S.14.

22. Ibid. SS 17-18.

23. Kitchen, op. cit., p. 156.

24. See Staatsarchiv Koblenz, Abt. 403 Nr. 8322, SS. 151-54. Acta des rheinischen ober-Praesidiums betreffend: Die Lage der Industrie, Arbeiterentlassungen, Arbeitsein-stellungen 1886-Juli 1887.

25. Soziale Praxis, V.5 1895-96, No. 1, S.15.

26. Die Volkswohl, No. 4, 4.10.94. "Die Versicherung gegen Arbeitslosigkeit." "Almost every new technical discovery which conserves manpower and increases the efficiency of the machine creates temporary unemployment. The displaced persons at once try to transfer to other lines of work. But where the technical progress in major trades is more general, they are driven out again by the machine. The increasing competition also promotes the perfection of technique, in order to be able to produce cheaply, here also technology

creates unemployment. If a time of rising business activity prevails, out of the circle of stable situations, through modern technology, one part of the detached workers receives some employment, another part remains superfluous. Where it succeeds through lowering the wages in maintaining employment, it drags others out of their positions; the persons change, but the number of unemployed remain. They are a sacrifice of the difference which prevails between the rapid development of technology and the development of the general use and expansion of our market outlets."

27.   See   Handbuch deutschen Wirtschafts- und Sozialgeschichte, SS. 270-71.

28.   The French experiences of 1830, 1848 and 1871 were not lost on German conservatives, nor was the role which unemployment had played in those upheavals.

29.   Hauptstaatsarchiv Stuttgart E150-Stuttgart E150-1768. See Dr. Rosenfeld in Der Beobachter Nr. 294, 14. Dez. 1907.

30.   Hauptstaatsarchiv Stuttgart E150-1768. Denkschrift ueber die Arbeitslosenversicherung, Karlsruhe 1909. "The causes of the unemployment could lie in the person of the unemployed or in economic relationships..
    "Among causes in the person, the following are especially noteworthy: laziness, inability to work, sickness, accident, invalid status, strikes, lock-outs, voluntary departure from a work place, refusal to accept an available job.
    "The economic causes of unemployment can be of a permanent, temporary or periodically recurring nature. Permanently through decline of an industry (for example, hand weaving) or through shut-down of operation (for example, mines); here only transfer of people to other occupations or migration can help. Temporarily through labor saving machinery, economic crises, change of fashion, temporary overfilling of the occupation, interruption of production through damaging of machines, or through fire, weather and the like. Periodically recurring in the seasonal industry (for example, ready-made clothing), where times of plentiful and scarce work change; in occupations whose practice is dependent on weather relationships (agriculture, construction, coastal shipping); further in occupations with casual labor."

31. A.G. Pigou, The Theory of Unemployment, pp. 250-53.

32. This much quoted statement was indicative of the delaying tactics preferred by many politicians who were anxious to defer action on volatile issues like unemployment insurance.

33. See _Reichsarbeitsblatt_ IV 1906 Nr. 6, SS. 518-21.

34. However, it became painfully clear at a most inopportune juncture during the early 1930's. With appalling numbers unemployed, the union response was to advocate measures designed to diminish the quantity of workers by eliminating prospective student, female, elderly and foreign job-seekers from the German labor market.

35. _Arbeitsmarkt-Correspondenz_, Nr. 3205, Calwer, 16. August 1913.

35a. See Ritter, _op. cit._, pp. 31-35.

36. Otto Most, _The Problem of Unemployment in Germany_, P.6.

37. Puhle sees this as a carry-over from the French tradition of decentralized authority which had persisted in some states since Bonaparte. See Hans-Juergen Puhle, "Von Wohlfahrtsausschuss zum Wohlfahrtsstaat", in Ritter, _op. cit._, s 35.

38. _Reichsarbeitsblatt_, 11: 1913 Nr. 3, S.188.

39. _Soziale Praxis_, V.22, 1912-13, S.387. "They increase their enterprises in the years of generally good business activity, of full employment on all sides, also in order to curb and stop the need for work opportunities through their enterprises and commissions with the onset of the depression."

40. _Soziale Praxis_, V.5, 1895-96, No. 10, S.265.

41. _Soziale Praxis_, V.22, 1912-13, S.388. "The public corporations should also observe the upward and downward movement of economic life opposite business cycles, whose regular recurrence as a result of economic crises matched emerging unemployment."

42. _Soziale Praxis_, V.18, 1908-09, S.302.

43. Niedersaechsischen Staatsarchiv Osnabrueck 3b V Fach 45/46 No. 32. See comments by Dr. jur. Moldenhauer made at the conference in Cologne.

44. See _Soziale Praxis_, V.9, 1899-1900, S.18 and V.7, 1897-98, SS. 579-580.

45. _Soziale Praxis_, V.20, 1910-11, S.1590.

46. See records of the _Reichstag_ debate from May 9, 1884.

47. See _Soziale Praxis_, V.11, 1901-02, Nr. 20, S.502-503.

48. _Ibid._, Nr. 17, SS.424-25.

49. "Die Organisation der Arbeit", _Zeitschrift fuer das deutsche Baugewerbe_, 6.7.88.

50. See _Soziale Praxis_, V.11, 1901-02.

51. Georg Adler "Arbeitslosigkeit", S.32 in _Conrads Jahrbuch_ 1895.

52. _Soziale Praxis_, V.1, 1892, SS. 128-29.

53. _Soziale Praxis_, V.19, 1909-10, SS. 1425-26.

54. See Deutsches Zentralarchiv I, Potsdam, Reichsamt des Innern: Acta betreffend: die Statistik ueber Arbeitslosigkeit vom 25. Oktober 1892 bis Juni 1906. Vol. 1, S.1044 Arbeiterversicherung No. 7.

55. K. Oldenburg, "Kleinere Mitteilungen. Arbeitslosen statistik, Arbeitsvermittelung und Arbeitslosenversicherung" _Schmollers Jahrbuch_ 1895 1.2 Leipzig SS. 258-69.

56. _Soziale Praxis_, Nr. 51, V.Jhrgng, 17. Sept. 1896, S.1333.

57. Evans, _Society and Politics in Wilhelmine Germany_, p. 204.

58. See Shulamit-Angel Volkov, "The Decline of the German Handicrafts--Another Reappraisal", _VSWG_ 61/2.

59. See Hall, "Youth in Rebellion" in Evans, _op. cit._

60. See _Political Economy in Germany_, p. 157.

61. _Soziale Praxis_, V.18, 1908-09, S.192.

62. Agrarian tariffs were raised in 1887.

63. Wolfram Fischer, _Wirtschaft und Gesellschaft im Zeitalter der Industrialisierung_ Goettingen: 1972, SS. 188-195.

64. A sophisticated predecessor of the mentality which gave us such twentieth-century equivalents as "what's good for General Motors is good for the nation" reflected the attitudes of groups trying to use the state to advance their own interests.

65. See, for example, Soziale Praxis, V.11, 1901-02, Nr. 17, S. 426.

66. Staatsarchiv Koblenz Abt. 403 Nr. 8319. Aachen 12. Jan. 1878. An den K.Staatsminister, Minister fuer Handel, Gewerbe und oeffentliche Arbeiten Herrn Dr. Achenbach.

67. Soziale Praxis, V.11, 1901-02, Nr. 9, S.227.

68. Soziale Praxis, V.18, 1908-09, S.379. "The Baden Ministry of the Interior has issued a prohibition against the employment of Slavic workers in the Grand Duchy of Baden, in that it instructs the district bureaus that Slavic workers can not be employed until February 20, 1909, because unemployment among the uneasy workers is too great."

69. Deutsche Krankenkassen-Zeitung, Berlin, 25. Oktober 1902 "Zum Problem der Arbeitslosenversicherung". "Three ideas of more eminent importance for social policy worked on the German wage labor force during the last two decades: the organization of producers in great trade unions, the organization of consumers in associations, the organization of labor supply and demand in centralized labor exchanges. All three ideas have evinced something organically related. In them pulses namely the basic idea: more order, more direction and regulation should be brought to bear on the confusion of our economic life."

70. Soziale Praxis, V.5 1895-96, No. 45, S.1198.

71. Ibid., No. 34, SS. 918-20.

72. See Juergen Kuczynski, Studium Uberproduktionskrisen, S.172.

73. Martin Kitchen, Political Economy, p. 155.

74. W.Fischer, Wirtschaft und Gesellschaft, SS. 198-99.

75. Ibid., S.211.

76. Georg Schanz, Zur Frage der Arbeitslosen-Versicherung. Bamberg: 1895, S.37.

77. Kitchin, op. cit., pp. 173-74.

78. John Garraty, Unemployment in History, pp. 179-187.

79. Soziale Praxis, V.7 1897-98, S.712 or S.44-45 provides examples.

80. Klaus Schoenhoven, "Selbsthilfe als Form vom Solidaritaet. Das gewerkschaftliche Unterstuetzungen im Deutscher

Kaiserreich bis 1913", _Archiv fuer Sozialgeschichte_, XX Bd, 1980.

81. _Ibid._, SS. 168-70.

82. Gerhard Bry, _Wages in Germany 1871-1945_ Princeton: 1960, Table 11, p. 32.

83. A.Faust "State and Unemployment in Germany" in _Emergence of the Welfare State in Britain and Germany_, p. 157.

84. _Hannoverschen Courier_, 9. Oktober 1913, Morgenausgabe No. 3069 "Arbeitslosenfluersorge" Dr. Hugo Boettger.

85. Klaus Schoenhoven, _op. cit._, SS. 157-158.

86. Hansjoachim Henning, "Arbeitslosenversicherung vor 1913. Das Genter System und Seine uebernahme in Deutschland", SS. 286 87. Wirtschaftspolitik und Arbeitsmarkt. Bericht ueber die 4. Arbeitstagung der Gesellschaft fuer Sozial- und Wirtschaftsgeschichte in Wien am 14, und 15. 4.1971. Munich: 1974.

87. As we noted with regard to the 1895 census, various occupations experienced widely divergent levels of unemployment. This was true of organized as well as non-union labor. _Soziale Praxis_ reported in 1897 that tobacco workers had a mere 0.875% unemployment and ten unions reported idleness of one to two percent. At the same time, 16 unions reported unemployment of two to three percent; of these, only four unions--hat makers, brewers, printers and glaziers--provided unemployment coverage. Nine unions experienced three to five percent rates; of these only the coppersmiths provided unemployment subsidies. Fifteen unions reported unemployment in excess of five percent including many seasonal trades such as shipping with 19% idle and no unemployment coverage. See _Soziale Praxis_ V.7, 1897-98, SS. 121-22.

88. _Soziale Praxis_, V.11 1901-02, Nr. 38, S.1004.

89. Klaus Schoenhoven, _op. cit._, SS. 177-85.

90. In this context it is also worth noting that union recruiting devices worked far better in urban than rural settings. Physical proximity both on and off the job plus better educational means and less dependence on employers all contributed to greater union organizing success among urban industrial workers.

91. _Soziale Praxis_, V.11 1901-02, Nr. 22, S.559.

92. On this point see Martin Kitchen, _op. cit._

93. _Ibid._

94. Theoretically, with rapid expansion of the working population, it should be possible to direct those entering the labor market toward jobs that compensate for fluctuations in demand and thus minimize unemployment. When industries or entire sectors experience contractions in demand, measures which induce labor to transfer will diminish unemployment. When slack demand due either to technologically obsolete skills or reduced consumption produces work shortages solutions are available in various combinations of wage reductions and mobility. Wage rates are likely to be most responsive to unemployment in markets where the potential for mobility is least. The harder it is for the unemployed to relocate, the larger the incentive for all workers in that area to tolerate lower pay. Greater mobility tends to lessen unemployment directly when the movement of wage rates is fixed. And mobility tends to increase unemployment indirectly by diminishing the elasticity of wage rates. Any movement between jobs automatically entails a certain amount of unemployment because of the time lag inherent in transferring from one position to another. Loss of work time equal to the number of persons moving multiplied by the average number of days involved in the transition will occur.

95. In rapidly expanding sectors such as the Ruhr coal industry, job mobility was used as a means of negotiating working conditions and pay-scales. Employment itself became a pawn in the negotiations over piece rates, with managers threatening dismissals and employees threatening walk-outs. The efficacy of such threats was of course contingent upon prospects for alternate employment, the pool of surplus labor and the current demand for coal. On this point, see Evans, _op. cit._, p. 224.

96. See Schanz, _op. cit._, S.7. Figures from Duisburg between April 1912 and March 1913 show a 10:1 ratio between single persons and household heads in Osnabruck Dep 3bV Fach 45/46 No. 33 Deutscher Staedtetag Zentralstelle, S.5.

97. Schanz, _op. cit._, S.7.

98. _Ibid._

99. _Ibid._, S.203.

100. Gerhard Bry, _Wages in Germany_, p. 15.

101. _Soziale Praxis_ VII, 1897-8, S.331 gives an excellent discussion of demographic change during the 1890's with some attention to earlier years.

102. See W.G. Hoffmann, _Das Wachstum deutschen Wirtschaft seit der Mitte des 19. Jahrhunderts_. Berlin: 1965, S.15.

103. _Ibid._, SS. 172-94.

104. _Ibid._, S.177.

105. _Ibid._, S.18.

106. Garraty, _op. cit._, p. 29.

107. Schanz, _op. cit._, S.10.

108. _Statistisches Jahrbuch fuer das Deutsche Reich_ (1904), S.22.

109. _Handbuch der deutschen Wirtschafts- und Sozialgeschichte_ Bd. 2, Stuttgart: 1976, S.30. "To be sure you obtain less acute distress (push-effect), particularly through the expansion of the labor supply in the accelerated industrialization process which has largely reduced the relative overpopulation, but agrarian population surpluses occurred earlier than the prospect of peasant settlement overseas (pull-effect) or the supply of industrial labor in Germany."

110. _Ibid._, S.20.

111. See Frank B.Tipton, Jr., _Regional Variations in the Economic Development of Germany During the Nineteenth Century_. Middletown, Connecticut: 1976, P.97.

112. _Handbuch_, S.20.

113. _Ibid._, SS. 21-22.

114. Tipton, _op. cit._, pp.90-92.

115. _Handbuch_, S.22.

116. Vernon L.Lidtke, _The Outlawed Party: Social Democracy in Germany 1878-1890_. Princeton: 1966. P.12.

117. "Das Problem der Arbeitslosenversicherung," _Zeitschrift fuer Versicherungswesen_, Nr. 36 Mittwoch den 16. September 1908.

118. "Deutschlands Soziale Gefahren II. Die industrielle Verhaeltnisse", _Der Beobachter_ Ein Volksblatt aus Schwaben 1884 Samstag 24. Mai.

119. Berndt, _op. cit._, SS. 18-19.

120. Soziale Praxis, V.4 1894-95, No. 29, S.394.

121. Ibid. "Looking around, wandering and direct inquiries about work as well as a series of newspaper inserts or public posters"

122. Soziale Praxis, V.18 1908-09, S.130.

123. Reichsarbeitsblatt, Juni 1913, SS. 12-13.

124. Niedersaechsischen Staatsarchiv Osnabruck Dep 3bV Fach 45/46 No. 33 Deutscher Staedtetag Zentralstelle. Beitritt die Arbeitslosenfrage. Rundschreiben an die Mitglieder des Deutschen Staedtetags, SS. 1-3.

125. Volker Hentschel, "Prosperitaet und Krise in der Wuerttembergischen Wirtschaft 1871-1879. Methodische Ueberlegungen und deskriptive Untersuchung" Vierteljahrschrift fuer Sozial und Wirtschaftsgeschichte, 63. Band, Heft 3 (1976) Wiesbaden, S.380.

126. See Berufs- und Gewerbezaehlung vom 14. Juni 1895, SdDR N.F.Bd. 111, Berlin: 1899, S.49 and Tipton, "Regional Variations", P.158.

127. Gottfried Haberler, Prosperity and Depression A Theoretical Analysis of Cyclical Movements. Cambridge, Mass.: 1960, pp. 260-61.

128. Hentschel, op. cit., S.375.

129. Otto Most, The Problem of Unemployment in Germany, London: 1910, P.23.

130. Ibid., pp. 22-23.

131. Haberler, op. cit. This was not a uniquely German phenomenon but was generally applicable to countries in the process of industrialization.

132. Karl Jantke, Der Vierte Stand, SS. 174-75 and Handbuch, SS. 270-71.

133. Herbst, Methoden der deutschen Arbeitslosenstatistik, S. 119. "Beyond that winter frequently resulted in a homeward migration of workers employed in large cities during the summertime; in order to participate in support through the home community, in consideration of cheaper means of subsistence, they could survive the time of unemployment more easily there."

134. Rickling, op. cit., S.93.

135. _Ibid._, S.107.

136. See Ausdruck aus dem Handworterbuch der Staatswissenschaft. Herausgeben von Conrad, Elster, Lexis, Leonig. Jahrbucher fuer Nationaloekonomie und Statistik. Supplementband Jena: 1895. "Arbeitslosigkeit" Georg Adler, SS. 117-39. Soziale Praxis, V.5 1894-95, No. 9, SS. 238-39. Hirschberg, Massnahmen...Arbeitslosigkeit, S.19.

137. On this point see, Wuerttembergische Kammer der Abgeordneten 166. Sitzung 31. Maerz 1903, speech by Hildebrand. E150-1760 Stuttgart.

138. Staatsarchiv Koblenz, Abt. 403, Nr. 8322. Die Lage der Industrie, Arbeiterentlassungen, Arbeitereinstellungen 1886-Juli 1887, S.37. Report from Regierungs-President, Aachen 12. April 1886. "The greater part of home weavers in the silk and velvet industries are still without employment. The weaver must again and again seek work as an agricultural laborer. It turns out not to be undesirable that there in the same weaving district the farmers had to complain about a scarcity in the labor force."

139. There the rapid transformation from handicraft to factory organization was evident along with a pool of relatively inexpensive female labor. Urban girls and wives of unskilled workers were especially active in the production of ready-to-wear clothing.

139a. Statistik des Deutschen Reichs, N.F. Bd. 111 (Berlin: 1899) S. 204, SS. 97-101, 201-202, 215-216.

140. Niedersaechsischen Staatsarchiv Osnabruck Rep. 335 No. 8764 Melle 19. Oktober 1875, S. 26 + Rs.

141. Handbuch, S.618.

142. Hoffman, op. cit.

143. For an excellent discussion of the fate of small, independent craftsman, see Schulamit Angel-Volkov, op. cit., pages 180-81.

144. Kitchen, op. cit., p. 179.

145. See citation in note 138 above.

146. K.Oldenburg, Schmollers Jahrbuch 1895, S.258. "One would bring up, for example, a large employer, who insured his personnel lasting employment, and as this already occurs now, with work stoppage he still pays a portion of the wage; perhaps in the use of labor exchanges he offers more open places, on the other side the individual employer

contributes to the unemployment fund according to the number of those annually laid off by him. Such further mentioned anonymous persons are rightly emphasized below. With very large employers and namely with cartelized branches of industry there would occur by itself out of private relief of the designated kind a sort of insurance (self-insurance) against unemployment. An urgent need remains on the other hand for real insurance in small industries."

147. Evans, op. cit., p. 26.

148. Bry, op. cit., p. 27.

149. Handbuch, S.537.

150. Ibid., S.549-51.

151. Ashok V.Desai, Real Wages in Germany 1871-1913. Oxford: 1968, p. 101.

151a. Berufs- und Gewerbezaehlung vom 14. Juni 1895 (SdDR N.F. Bd. 111) Berlin: 1899, S.113.

152. Ibid., S. 116.

153. Soziale Praxis, V.5 1895-6 No. 1, S.18.

154. Hans-Ulrich Wehler, Das Deutsche Kaiserreich 1871-1918, Goettingen: 1973, S.43.

155. Georg Adler, "Arbeitslosigkeit", Conrads Jahrbuch 1895, S. 124.

156. W.Fischer, Wirtschaft und Gesellschaft, S.190.

157. Bry, op. cit., p. 6.

158. Ibid.

159. Desai, op. cit., p. 98.

160. Ibid.

161. Bry, op. cit., p. 62.

162. The former includes capital and consumer goods, the latter only consumer products.

163. During periods of high unemployment and falling prices such as occurred after 1873, union pressure for higher wages and better working conditions typically abated.

164. See Haberler, op. cit., p. 405.

165. Bry, op. cit., p. 71.

166. Ibid., p. 78.

167. Ibid., p. 83.

168. Handbuch, S.619.

169. Bry, op. cit., p. 472.

170. Handbuch, s.620.

171. Desai, op. cit., p. 35.

172. Hans Mottek, "Die Grunderkrise Produktionsbewegung, Wirkungen, theoretische Problematik" Jahrbuch fuer Wirtschaftsgeschichte 1966. Teil II. Berlin: 1966, SS. 96-117.

173. Kuczynski, Studien zur Geschichte der zyklischen Uberproduktions Krisen in Deutschland 1873 bis 1914. Berlin: 1961, S.30.

174. Mottek, "Grunderkrise", S.101.

175. Handbuch, S.540.

176. Hoffmann, Wachstum, S.84.

177. Bry, op. cit., p. 78.

178. Hentschel, op. cit., pp. 341-42.

179. Handbuch, S.561.

180. Ibid., SS. 252-53.

181. In the well-known case of the handloom weavers, higher productivity meant obsolescence and unemployment.

182. See the discussion by Carl Hirsch in Soziale Praxis, V. 4 1894-95, No. 16, S.185.

183. Garraty, op. cit., p. 9.

184. Hentschel, op. cit., S.355.

185. Kuczynski, Studien..Uberproduktionskrisen, S.87.

186. Ibid., S.86.

187. Ibid., SS. 135 u. 127.

188. Soziale Praxis, V.11 1901-02, Nr. 15. S.370. "In many trades one tries, through forced sales abroad, through reduction of the work time, through preservation of holiday shifts to prevent the worst, the lay-off of workers. In other industries tariff associations persist which assure the workers some protection in times of business depressions."

189. Hauptstaatsarchiv Duesseldorf: Regierung Duesseldorf Nr. 38245, S.85.

190. Hoffmann, op. cit., S.26.

191. Niedersaechsischen Staatsarchiv Osnabrueck, Rep. 335, No. 8764, SS. 224+ Rs.

192. Staatsarchiv Koblenz, Abt. 403, Nr. 8323. Die Lage der Industrie, Arbeiterentlassungen, Arbeitseinstellungen August 1887--Juli 1891, S.504.

193. Kuczynski, Studien...Ueberproduktionskrisen, S.130.

194. Niedersaechsischen Staatsarchiv Osnabrueck Rep 335, No. 8764. Osnabrueck 20. Oktober 1875, SS. 31-32.

195. Hentschel, op. cit., SS. 380-81.

196. The fact that contemporaries recognized this is reflected in Staatsarchiv Koblenz, Abt. 403 Nr. 8322, S.424.

197. Ibid, S.37. Also Niedersaechsischen Staatsarchiv Osbabrueck Dep 29bI Stadt Lingen No. 3935 No. 3936 S.94 + Rs. also Osnabrueck Rep. 335 No. 8764, S. 158.

198. Niedersaechsischen Staatsarchiv Osnabrueck Rep. 335 No. 8764 11. Juli 1876 S.89.

199. See also the record of workers dismissed by a Cologne sugar manufacturer in September of 1888. Staatsarchiv Koblenz Abt. 403 Nr. 8323. Die Lage der Industrie, Arbeiterentlassungen, Arbeitseinstellungen. August 1887-Juli 1897. SS. 121-22.

200. Staatsarchiv Koblenz, Abt. 403 Nr. 8322, SS. 177-78. Acta des rheinischen Ober-Prasidiums betreffend: Die Lage der Industrie, Arbeiterentlassungen, Arbeitseinstellungen 1886-Juli 1887, SS. 177-78. "Here many of the supposed work reductions first occur during the early part of the year, the greaterst part of the unemployed workers very soon again get temporary field work, construction jobs, stone crushing, and work in other factories. Fortunately, previously dismissed workers might return to their home and as a result

of this fewer hours need more generally stand out as
infrequently as disorder and disturbance."

201. Lidtke, op. cit., p. 211.

202. Deutsches Zentralarchiv I, Potsdam Reichsamt des
Innern. Acta betreffend: die Versicherung gegen Arbeitslosigkeit (Ausserungen der Presse) vom 20. Sept. 1882 bis 4.
Oktober 1904. Vol. 1. 1004 Arbeiterversicherung No. 7.
"[I]f the gentlemen always insist on the eight hour workday,
I perceive no preventive measure therein to work against
unemployment, but I see in the general stereotypical eight
hour workday the certain way to more general unemployment;
it will either decrease the wages--which the gentlemen
themselves certainly do not want--or, the wages can remain
at the loss of foreign markets accompanied by greater
unemployment."

203. Soziale Praxis, V.11 1901-02, Nr. 31, S.812.

204. Bry, op. cit., p. 45.

205. Soziale Praxis, V.9 1899-1900, SS. 1169-1170.

206. Bry, op. cit., p. 46.

207. Hoffmann, op. cit., S.19.

208. Regelung der Notstandsarbeiten in deutschen Staedten,
S.109.

209. Hirschberg, op. cit., S.10.

210. Kuczynski, Studien...Ueberproduktionskrise, S.94.

211. Niedersaechsischen Staatsarchiv Osnabrueck Dep 3bV
Fach 45/46 No. 32 "Zur Frage der Arbeitslosenversicherung"
13. Nov. Elberfeld. "The Elberfeld industries have in
general previously a dearth of qualified skilled workers.
This can also be explained by the fact that they prefer the
necessary cutbacks of production through shortening of the
work time along with preservation of the existing labor
force over the lay-off of workers during periods of bad
business conditions."

212. Soziale Praxis, V.21 1911-12, SS. 695-96.

213. Richard Calwer, "Handel und Wandel", 1901, SS. 68-69.

214. Kaiserliche Statistisches Amt. Abschrift II 3135. 6.
Juli 1905.

215. Herbst, op. cit., SS. 90-92.

216. Garraty, op. cit., p. 190.

217. Pigou, op. cit., p. 254.

218. See Bry, op. cit., p. 6. The time lag of German wages in responding to changes in general business conditions should be recalled here.

219. Soziale Praxis, V.4, 1895-96, No. 15, S.174.

220. Kuczynski, Studien...Ueberproduktionskrise, S.26.

221. Ibid., 94.

222. Ibid., S.126.

223. Ibid., SS. 44-45.

224. Wehler, Deutsche Kaiserreich, S.148.

225. Ibid.

226. Garraty, op. cit., p. 260.

227. Hauptstaatsarchiv Stuttgart E150-1768 Deutscher Arbeitgeberbund fuer das Baugewerbe, Berlin 1. Nov. 1894. Vorstellung betreffend die Versicherung gegen Arbeitslosigkeit.

228. Garraty, op. cit., p. 260.

229. Soziale Praxis, V.21 1911-19, S.693.

230. Soziale Praxis, V.5 1895-96, No. 39, S.1039.

NOTES: PART FOUR

1. For an acceptable definition of this problematic term, see C. E.Black, The Dynamics of Modernization A Study in Comparative History, New York: 1967. P. 7.

2. Die bestehenden Einrichtungen zur Versicherung gegen die Folgen der Arbeitslosigkeit im Ausland und im Deutschen Reich. Teil I: Die Versicherung gegen die Folgen der Arbeitslosigkeit. Kaiserlichen Amt Abteilung fuer Arbeiterstatistik. Berlin: 1906. S.543. (Hereafter abbreviated as in Note 10 below).

3. Niedersaechsischen Staatsarchiv Osnabrueck Dep 3b V Fach 45/46 No. 32 ss. 193-195 rs. Deutscher Arbeitgeberbund fuer das Baugewerbe E.D. Berlin 20 Nov 1913 Eingabe gegen die Einfuehrung der offentlichen Arbeitslosenunterstuetzung.

4. Cooperative societies or Konsumvereins were rarely used during the nineteenth century to deal with unemployment--the only significant instance of this kind was the Konsum- Bau- und Sparvereins Produktion founded in Hamburg during 1899.

5. Reichsarbeitsblatt (hereafter abbreviated RAB) IV, Nr. 11 (1906) ss. 1006-1013 "Arbeitsvermittelung und Arbeitslosigkeit" s. 1013.

6. Suddeutsche Industrie Organ des Verbandes Suddeutscher Industrieller. Mannheim 20. September 1909 "Rundschreiben betr. Arbeitslosenvericherung". "With the increasing industrialization of the economy this unemployment assumed a size which was previously unknown. Longer lasting unemployment produces along with difficult economic and moral disadvantages for those affected also dangers for the public welfare and order. Therefore the question of how to oppose this evil condition enters more and more into the forefront of public interest."

7. See Otto Most, The Problem of Unemployment in Germany London: 1910.

8. Hauptstaatsarchiv Stuttgart E150-1768 "Arbeitslosenver-sicherung in Suddeutschland" 1909.

9. RAB IV, Nr. 11 (1906), s. 1013. "The objection that the reference to self-help subjects the worker to injustice will also be raised against compulsory savings, which in contrast to the principle of insurance 'all for one' is based on the foundation of the individualistic axiom 'each for himself alone'; it has been proposed as a substitute for unemployment insurance and as a guarantee against the results of unemployment.

"All proposals are in agreement and all practical knowledge demonstrates that of more significant meaning for each form of unemployment support or insurance is the existence and the improvement of procuring work."

10. <u>Versicherung gegen die Folgen der Arbeitslosigkeit</u>, S.561.

11. Hauptstaatsarchiv Stuttgart E150-1768 Mit Gott fuer Kaiser und Reich. Ein Appell an das deutsche Volk im Sinne der Sedanrede Sr. Majestaet des Kaisers von G.Kosub. Breslau: 1895. S.5. "It must seem in large degree hopeless, that the winter rather than placing increased demands on the creative power of the head of the family has already brought unemployment with more vigorous force and an inability with the best will to alter the fact that his wife and children are subjected to hunger, cold and penury.

"One cannot object that such cases occur only sporadically; they are not isolated but are the rule for hundreds of thousands in Germany--especially for the building trades in the winter."

12. <u>Zur Frage der Arbeitslosen-Verisicherung</u>. Untersuchungen von Dr. Georg Schanz. Bamberg: 1895. Ss. 1-2. "Unemployment is a terrible scourge for the working population, it brings them the danger of material and moral ruin. The majority of men are held on the path of righteousness through the regular flow of employment and income, as soon as this flow is interrupted and necessity knocks at the door, they stumble. The best characters show themselves to be weak against this force. On many this already has a very deadening effect, if as a result of more prolonged unemployment, they become dependent on charity. Self-confidence and modesty often suffer damage. The unmarried unemployed easily turn into transients, living through idleness and begging, become neglectful in their clothing, fall into alcohol abuse and uncleanliness and sink so completely into the class of tramps and vagabonds, as to frequently end as criminals. The unmarried female unemployed are exposed to the abuse of the registry office and prostitution. This also happens to the married unemployed and with them their families. The man, who all week long has nothing to do, becomes a loafer and public-house patron. Often in such situations, it is only the wife through her work who preserves the family including the husband and this also has a demoralizing effect on the man. If the wife's earnings are not sufficient, if any existing small savings are used up, then come debts for the most essential necessities of life and rent and finally, when the credit is exhausted, the bitterest need. With unemployment is soon associated homelessness and once the family is in the street, then their complete disintegration

is scarcely to be further prevented. One might not wonder if then the courage of those in question sinks if they totally let themselves go and if on the final road of gradual decay they wind up as a persistent burden on the community. But not unfrequently it ends before it comes this far, through unemployment and need, families through violent scenes are brought to ruin in mass death."

13. See also, for example, Ephrem Rickling, Die deutsche Wanderarbeitsstaetten. Muenchen-Gladbach: 1912.

14. Ibid.

15. RAB, IV, Nr. 6 (1906) 22. 518-21. "Arbeitsvermittelung und Arbeitslosigkeit. Die Versicherung gegen die Folgen der Arbeitslosigkeit I" s. 519. "The deterioration into reliance on poor relief should already be hindered. The basic difference is that poor relief has as a prerequisite total destitution and need. Unemployment support does not have destitution as a prerequisite, on the contrary, it seeks to avert the onset of this most extreme condition, which already signifies the economic negation of an existence. But the worker also does not want to become dependent on charity. Charity gives alms. If only private or public charity were able to cope with greater unemployment, the worker who through no fault of his own became unemployed wished, not to receive alms, but was not able to help himself, might advance a claim for help."

16. Hauptstaatsarchiv Stuttgart E150-1768 Drittes Morgenblatt der Frankfurter Zeitung 14. November 1909 "Die badische Konferenz Ueber die Arbeitslosen Versicherung" Dr. Alfons Fischer. "Furthermore, it would be said that unemployment insurance would be demoralizing because men are not born with a preclivity for work; through the expectation of unemployment support their own feeling of responsibility would be diminished."

17. Hauptstaatsarchiv Stuttgart E150-1768 "Arbeitslosenversicherung in Suddeutschland" 1909. "The paid support should also not be so high that it would by chance encroach upon the unemployment. It should only enable the most makeshift sustenance."

18. Hauptstaatsarchiv Stuttgart E150-1768 Mit Gott fuer Kaiser und Reich s. 5. "The right to work is to be sure at the time only an imaginary idea; it will be legally acknowledged only insofar as, grossly mistaken, it has guaranteed a penalty against the duty to work; However, will not seem less deplorable, that someone inspired by the wish to earn the daily bread for himself and his family through honest work will be hindered in the application of this duty simply through the influence of Providence."

19. Ibid, s. 6. [T]oday the workers' pub is the place where it is still easiest to hear about work opportunities and therefore the unemployed man roams from building to building, on the streets--from pub to pub--for days, often weeks and even months and was nowhere to be found and at home wife and child need bread. Is it any wonder that the worker is unhappy with such circumstances and gives expression to his displeasure, that he goes astray as a socialist?

The resigned, not the sick, worker must be brought to participate as a result of greater state welfare, if indeed change should occur, for unemployment is the grave of every family fortune, the true foster-mother of Social Democracy.

20. Suddeutsche Industrie Mannheim 20. September 1909 "Rundschreiben betr. Arbeitslosenversicherung". "There unemployment as is well known occurs in expanded quantities primarily in times of economic decline, but the employer under the onus of the business cycles suffers at least as much as the worker himself; already in times of economic depression numerous existences of employers are ruined, therefore it might far exceed the boundaries of the possible if one were to impose still further social burdens in this area on the employers."

21. Hauptstaatsarchiv Stuttgart E150-1768 Drittes Morgenblatt der Frankfurther Zeitung 14. November 1909 "Die badische Konferenz ueber die Arbeitslosenversicherung".

22. Ibid. "The representative of the agricultural board has stressed that the rural areas have no interest in unemployment insurance; in the countryside there is no unemployment in winter. The land can assume no burden for those workers living in the city especially since they already suffer from a shortage of hands. Also the city might not subsidize the unemployment fund; this is much more a problem for the cities which have an interest in the expansion of industry. But the urban representatives expressed the gravest reservations against the unemployment insurance."

23. Niedersaechsischen Staatsarchiv Osnabrueck Dep 36V Fach 45/46 No. 32 194 Rs.

24. RAB, IV Nr. 10 ss. 902-26. "Arbeitsvermittelung und Arbeitslosigkeit. Die Versicherung gegen die Folgen der Arbeitslosigkeit. V.Die Projekte einer Arbeitslosenversicherrung fuer das Deutsche Reich". s. 903. "The Elm range of ideas is based on the assumption that it is basically and primarily the duty of the state and society to care for the unemployed, 'to protect them against the results of the capitalist economic system.' The basic idea of the ruling economic order is on the contrary that the single individual, be it alone or through cooperative

federation, first of all has to help himself, and that the state, apart from its police duties, should intervene only insofar as the public interest, be it the national health, the fitness for military service or something else that requires it and as self-help with normal requirements is not able by itself to take these interests into account. Only where self-help fails does the state aid come into question as a supplement."

25. Most, op cit., p. 4.

26. Hauptstaatsarchiv Stuttgart E150-1768 Ausschnitt aus der Zeitschrift fuer Versicherungswesen Nr. 36 Mittwoch den 16. September 1908 "Das Problem der Arbeitslosigkeitsversicherung". "In the winter of each year the factory workers constitute by far the largest contingent of unemployed, with 35.66 percent, and next the construction workers with 15.61 percent, while the unemployed agricultural workers constitute only 3.62 percent."

27. See, for example, Rickling, op. cit., s. 121 and Hauptstaatsarchiv Duesseldorf: Regierung "Duesseldorf Nr. 38245 ss. 74 und 94. 4. April 1894 Cleve; Neuss 29. Januar 1894.

28. Most, op. cit., s. 5.

29. Ibid.

30. RAB, IV (1906) Nr. 6 ss 518-21.

31. Ibid, s. 519. "The fight against unemployment through preventive and repressive measures does not form the real opposition of the statement given here. There is a series of such measures. Here above all are to be named the regulation of apprentices etc. as well as the adjustment of available work and the labor supply (relief works)."

32. Vernon L. Lidtke, The Outlawed Party: Social Democracy in Germany, 1878-1890. Princeton: 1966. p. 211.

33. Ibid, p. 81. Lidtke indicates that by 1879 all unions with overt Social Democratic sympathies had disappeared but those with liberal connections, like the Hirsch-Dunker Associations, survived.

34. On this relationship, see RAB II Nr. 2 ss. 109-121 "Arbeitslosikeit...Arbeitslosenzahlungen in deutschen Stadten" s. 118 or RAB IV Nr. 7 ss. 622-24 "Arbeitslosigkeit in deutschen Fachverbaenden im 2. Quartal 1906" s. 623.

35. RAB VIII Nr. 6 (1910) ss. 424-25 "Arbeitsvermittelung und Arbeitslosigkeit. Zur neuesten Entwickelung der Arbeitslosenversicherung VI Nachtrag. On the unemployment policies of the

relatively small but highly vocal Hirsch-Dunker Trade Associations, see Die Arbeitslosigkeit Ihre Bekaempfung und Statistik Inaugural-Dissertation der hohen philosophischen Fakultaet der Vereinigten Friedrichs-Universitaet Halle-Wittenberg zur Erlangen der Doktorwuerde vorgelegt von Paul Berndt aus Koeln. Halle a.S. 1899. S.40.

36. See Hajo Holborn, A History of Modern Germany 1840-1945. New York: 1969. P.359.

37. Berndt, op. cit., s. 41. "The unions are lacking a more secure base. They could be disbanded by every police office and hindered in their development. The leaders of the organization have permanent fears of protecting their wealth from confiscation. Under such circumstances the unions could collect greater wealth only with the greatest precaution, as they are necessary for such protective arrangements. First one grants the workers the right to unite freely and to participate in the communal and state administration, then the way for unemployment insurance will be free and from that unions will also become secure."

38. Ibid., s. 42.

39. Hauptsaatsarchiv Stuttgart E150-1768 Fuersorge fuer die Stellenlose 1910, ss. 16-17.

40. Hauptsaatsarchiv Stuttgart Beilage zur Soziale Praxis Materialien zur Frage der Arbeitslosenversicherung Dr. jur. Richard Freund Berlin: 1903, s. 7.

41. Hauptsaatsarchiv Stuttgart E150-1768 Der Beobachter Nr. 298, 19. Dezember 1907 Wuerttemberg. Die Arbeitslosigkeit, Vortrag von Dr. Fr. Rosenfeld.

42. There were a few instances in which efforts were made to establish unemployment funds supported jointly by employers and employees but few of them ever amounted to much.

43. Versicherung gegen die Folgen der Arbeitslosigkeit ss. 458-461.

44. Hauptsaatsarchiv Stuttgart E150-1768 Soziale Praxis 21. Maerz 1901. "The employee is culpable for the unemployment particularly in the following instances a) groundless abandonment of the work b) loss of work opportunity as a result of notice of the workers c) loss of work opportunities in cases of trade regulations."

45. Versicherung gegen die Folgen der Arbeitslosigkeit, ss. 458-461.

46. Ibid.

47. <u>RAB</u> IV Nr. 9 ss. 803-808 "Versicherung gegen...Arbeits-
losigkeit" s. 806.

48. Niedersaechsischen Staatsarchiv Osnabrueck Dep 3b V Fach
45/46 No. 32, S. 195. "They see their main problem in the
improvement of the wage and working conditions of their
members. The unemployment support is no obstacle for them
in this struggle, but an excellent means to more rapid
advancement. The unemployment support binds the members to
the organization, which at best has shown that in spite of
all efforts, numerous construction workers have not been
moved to transfer out of the associations with unemployment
support into our organizations. The unemployment support
contributes to the preservation of the workers' ability to
fight."

49. See <u>Versicherung gegen die Folgen der Arbeitslosigkeit</u>,
s. 543.

50. Niedersaechsischen Staatsarchiv Osnabrueck Dep 3b V Fach
45/46 No. 32 s. 193 Ruckseite. Deutscher Arbeitgeberbund
fuer das Baugewerbe.

51. Hauptstaatsarchiv Stuttgart E150-1768 Drittes Morgenblatt der <u>Frankfurter</u> <u>Zeitung</u> 14 November 1909. "Die
badische Konferenz ueber die Arbeitslosenversicherung".
"Industrialists point out that the time is now unfavorable,
one suffers under the tariff policy and also through the new
imperial insurance regulation, the employers are threatened
with further great expenditures. It would further be
stressed that the industrial conditions in Baden, which
prossesses neither iron nor coal and is situated far from
fens, are in no way particularly favorable and on the other
side already here the unemployment in comparison to other
areas has assumed no great size."

52. <u>RAB</u> VIII (1910) Nr. 2 s. 106 "Arbeitsvermittelung und
Arbeitslosigkeit. Zur neuesten Entwickelung der Arbeitslosenversicherung". "As reasons against the planned
insurance, the petition urged among other things the
following: In Germany and Baden a positive unemployment
could not be discussed, as long as a shortage of workers
prevails in agriculture and also in individual trades and
places. From the insurance is to be feared a diminution of
the workers' feeling of self responsibility, an increasing
pampering of the unskilled labor force, abandoning hard
working foreigners, a check on the return of workers to the
country in times of bad business conditions in industry, a
cessation of the currently successful further employment of
workers in times of depression through numerous industrialists, a further financial burden on the employer and a
decrease of the export potential of Baden industry. The
Ghent system in particular means participation of the state

and the community in the economic struggle in favor of the organized laborer. As a step toward opposing unemployment and its results, one recommends the application of furthering savings, especially also support of the plans of the insurance bank for Germany (national insurance), enabling the institution of the compulsory savings for youth, which had previously existed in other Baden operations but was given up on grounds of trade regulations, finally cession of arable land on the part of communities to the industrial worker and general land acquisition through this."

53. Die Regelung der Notstandsarbeiten in deutschen Staedten, S. 67. Beitraege zur Arbeiterstatistik Nr. 2 Berlin: 1905.

54. Rickling, op. cit., s. 124.

55. Reinhold August Dorwart, The Prussian Welfare State before 1740, Cambridge, Mass.: 1971.

56. Gerhard A.Ritter (ed.) Von Wohlfahrtsausschuss zum Wohlfahrtsstaat. Der Staat in der modernen Industiregesell-schaft Koeln: 1972. Ss. 29-68. Hans-Juergen Puhle "Vom Wohlfahrtsausschuss zum Wohlfahrtsstaat" s. 31.

57. See Puhle article cited in previous note for discussion of these developments.

58. Most, op. cit., pp. 6-7.

59. See Dorwart, op. cit.

60. Ibid.

61. Niedersaechsischen Staatsarchiv Osnabrueck Dep 3b V Fach 45/46 No. 32 s. 198 Hannoverscher Courier Freitag, 5. September 1913, No. 30711 morgens. "Die Staedte im Kampf gegen die Arbeitslosigkeit".

62. Hauptstaatsarchiv Stuttgart E150-1768 Der Beobachter Nr. 294, 14. Dezember 1907. Dr. Rosenfeld.

63. Hauptstaatsarchiv Stuttgart E150-1768 Denkschrift betreffend die Einfuehrung der Arbeitslosenversicherung (Stuttgart 20. Januar 1909) Zentralverband der Handlungs-gehilfen und Gehilfinnen Deutschlands (Sitz. Hamburg).

64. Hauptstaatarchiv Duesseldorf. Regierung Duesseldorf 38245 Teil I.Liegnitz 25. Februar 1893 s. 6 + rs. "If an obligation of the community to the unemployed, especially to assist those drawn from elsewhere to the necessary subsistence through employment with communal labor does not persist, we consider it nevertheless one of the most

pressing problems of the urban authorities to offer the persons, who are able and willing to carry out assigned work the opportunity to support themselves and their family members without resorting to poor relief. This goal can be reached in appropriate ways only if one or more labor exchanges are organized on the part of the community."

65. Niedersaechsischen Staatsarchiv Osnabrueck Dep 3b Stadt Osnabrueck V Fach 45/46 No. 33 Arbeitslosigkeit 1913 "Zur Frage der Arbeitslosen Versicherung in der Gemeinde" Otto Landschreiber, Pankow.

66. Darmstadt Anzeige-Blatt fuer den Kreis Schotten No. 93 Freitag, den 21. November 1884 32. Jahrgang "Massregeln gegen das Vagantenthum" Dr. Wolf 19. November 1884. "In order to differentiate the professional vagrant from the genuinely needy and perhaps innocent unemployed traveler, the assignment of support is recommended only after allotting appropriate work for the community, like street cleaning, snow shoveling, wood chopping."

67. Hauptstaatsarchiv Stuttgart E150-1768 Mit Gott fuer Kaiser und Reich, ss. 7-8.

68. Versicherung gegen die Folgen der Arbeitslosigkeit, s. 87.

69. Ibid, s. 630. "The establishment of unemployment insurance with the most intimate connection to the organization of the labor exchange is not only possible but absolutely necessary. . . . Unemployment is generally not present where for those workers engaged in a particular employment, a different suitable place stands vacant; the worker who without cause refuses to accept such a place, has no claim on the payment of the unemployment insurance."

70. Ibid, s. 644.

71. Dr. E.Hirschberg, Die Massnahmen gegenueber der Arbeitslosigkeit. Berlin: 1894.

72. Hauptstaatsarchiv Duesseldorf (Bestand: Regierung Duesseldorf) Nr. 38245 Central-Verein fuer Arbeits-Nachweis zu Berlin: Geschafts-Bericht fuer das Jahr 1894 nebst Referat betr. die Errichtung eines staedtischen Arbeitsnachweises..." von Dr. jur. Richard Freund, s. 33.

73. Beitrage zur Arbeiterstatistik Nr. 2 Gebiete und Methoden der amtlichen Arbeitsstatistik in den wichtigsten Industriestaaten. Bearbeitet im Kaiserlichen Statistischen Amte Abteilung fuer Arbeiterstatistik. Berlin: 1913. I.Statistik des Arbeitsmarkts des Arbeitsnachweises, der Arbeitslosigkeit und der Arbeiterwanderung ss. 44-45.

74. Hauptstaatsarchiv Duesseldorf (Bestand: Regierung Duesseldorf) Nr. 38245 Central-Arbeitsnachweisestelle fuer Rheinland und Westfalen, Januar 1894.

75. Hauptstaatarchiv Duesseldorf (Bestand: Regierung Duesseldorf) Nr. 38245 Volkswohl No. 44 XVII. Jahrgang Dresden 2. November 1893 "Arbeitslosigkeit und Arbeitsnachweis" ss. 127-28.

76. Die Regelung der Notstandsarbeiten in deutschen Staedten, s. 3.

77. Hauptstaatsarchiv Stuttgart E150-1768 Der Beobachter Nr. 297 18. Dezember 1907. "Under relief works we understand the extraordinary work which from the public collective economy (community, district, province, state) is undertaken for the specific purpose of employing the jobless in times of unemployment.

"Under relief work, one understands such works, which the community or the state organizes in times of unemployment in order to enable their citizens not to devolve upon poor relief but to produce economic and moral value through their work in a time of sinking business activity."

78. Die Regelung der Notstandsarbeiten in deutschen Staedten, ss. 4-5 und 8.

79. Niedersaechsischen Staatsarchiv Osnabrueck Dep 3b V Fach 45/46 No. 33 Koelnische Zeitung Nr. 1195 (12.11.09) "Arbeitslosigkeit im Kommenden Winter" s. 23. "The remark of the administration is especially important that the unemployment question will not be solved with the relief works; that this on the contrary is an international matter which requires an international solution."

80. Niedersaechsischen Staatsarchiv Osnabrueck Dep 29b I Stadt Lingen No. 3935 s. 32 Rusckseite. "Province of Osnabrueck. Berlin. February 3, 1877: With regard to my ordinance of the twenty-third of the month, dealing with the employment of the working population in the districts of Waldenburg, Neurode, Reichenbach and Glatz through the railroad administration, I urge the royal government to a quick exhibition moreover, up to and insofar as steps are taken, to guarantee the unemployed population of the designated districts the opportunity for employment in road repairs and highway construction about which the report from the tenth of this month contains nothing. Osnabrueck, February 16, 1877: while we allow the government of our administrative district to heed the preceding copy of a decree of the Minister of Trade from the third of the month in addition to the lost report and notice, we will at the

same time look forward to a rapid report about 1. whether
already now enough employment is available there for the
working population, perhaps whether unemployment for those
in the near future is expected, 2. how high the current
daily wage stands on average, 3. whether in the case of a
positive response to our inquiry under 1 perhaps the prospect of greater works from private associations or communities will offer the workers enough employment or perhaps
additional reinforcements from outside might be necessary."

81. Niedersaechsischen Staatsarchiv Osnabrueck Dep 3b V Fach
45/46 No. 32, ss. 193-94. 20. November 1913 Eingabe gegen
die Einfuehrung der offentlichen Arbeitslosenunterstuetzung.

82. Regelung der Notstandsarbeiten in deutschen Staedten, s.
76. "As instances of the variety mentioned, Cologne names:
drunkenness as well as excessive conduct against the over-
grown officials; with the latter Offenbach also names
refractory conduct of the worker. Frankfurt a.M. and Mainz
mention in almost verbatim harmony: refusal to accept other
offered work, neglect of the related provisions and unexcused absence, disobedience, disturbance of the peace and
order of the workplace, with the situation that in such
cases a rehiring of the dismissed by those in the present
winter engaged in organized relief works is prohibited.
From Frankfurt a.M., where, as in Strassburg, persons
excluded in this way at most still can find employment with
the poor administration, unexcused absences also will be
mentioned as cause for immediate lay-off from cultivation to
snow-removal work."

83. Ibid., s. 83. "As something further for the compensation of relief work, characteristic motives already follow
from the previous pronouncements that the height of wages
paid to the unemployed do not always vary exclusively
according to the quantity of actual work performed, but
perhaps will also be regulated according to the momentary
degree of the need for support."

84. Ibid., s. 120.

85. RAB IV Nr. 11 (1906) s. 1006 "Arbeitsvermittelung und
Arbeitslosigkeit Die Versicherung gegen die Folgen der
Arbeitslosigkeit. Die Projekte fuer das Deutsche Reich.
Die Stellung der Regierungen VI (Schluss).

86. RAB I Nr. 10 (1903) ss. 806-819 "Arbeitslosigkeit in
deutschen Fachverbaenden", s. 819.

87. Regelung der Notstandsarbeiten in deutschen Staedten, s.
27. "As regards the kind of work, A. the following were
considered as relief work in the narrow sense: 1) gravel
breaking and perhaps street cleaning work 2) the laying out

of tree holes in the eastern city expansion 3. modification
of the playing field in the Luise park 4. transformation of
the Neckarau Woods into a park 5. cleaning of the palace
yard and laying a street through the palace garden.

B. Extraordinary work for the employment of the jobless: 6. restoration of the Luise park 7. new planting of
large trees in the eastern city extension 8. breaking up of
the park surface in the Augusta park 9. leaf moulding in the
Luise park 10. widening of the Stephanie promenade."

88. The following cities are grouped according to the kinds
of work which they adopted to engage their unemployed
residents during the first five years of the new century.
The first and largest category "Erdarbeiten" subsumed a
variety of jobs including "Anschuettungsarbeiten, Wege-,
Strassenbau- Regulierungsarbeiten, Legon von Kanal- und
Wasserleitungen, Ausschachtungen, Gewinnung von Kies und
Sand und dergl., auch Handarbeiten". Forty cities were
included among those offering this type of employment.

Aachen	Darmstadt	Giessen	Mainz
Augsburg	Dresden	Goerlitz	Mannheim
Barmen	Duesseldorf	Halle a.S.	Muenchen
Bielefeld	Duisburg	Hamburg	Nuernberg
Bochum	Elberfeld	Hannover	Offenbach
Breslau	Erfurt	Kassel	Pforzheim
Chemnitz	Essen	Leipzig	Strassburg
Coeln	Frankfurt a.M.	Ludwigshafen	Stuttgart
Crefeld	Freiburg	Luebeck	Ulm
Danzig	Fuerth	Magdeburg	Worms

Twenty-five cities hired unemployed workers to macadamize
roads.

Aachen	Dresden	Karlsruhe	Mainz	Nuernberg
Augsburg	Frankfurt a.M.	Kassel	Mannheim	Strassburg
Charlottenburg	Freiburg	Koenigsberg	Muehlhausen	Stuttgart
Coeln	Fuerth	Leipzig	Muenchen	Ulm
Darmstadt	Halle a.S.	Ludwigshafen	M.-Gladbach	Worms

Projects were undertaken at Bielefeld, Bremen, Magdeburg,
Strassburg and Ulm. Street cleaning consisting primarily of
ice and snow removal was performed by the unemployed in
Barmen, Darmstadt, Duesseldorf, Elberfeld, Frankfurt a.M.,
Freiburg, Kassel, Ludwigshafen, Mainz, Mannheim, and Strassburg. Strassburg and Mannheim also provided work through
forestry and planting projects. Wood chopping was sponsored
by the communities of Aachen, Braunschweig and Kassel while

Krefeld supported straw-plaiting or matmaking projects and Stuttgart offered copy work to the unemployed. As the above lists showed, some twenty cities had only one kind of public works project during the early twentieth century; fourteen cities offered two; ten cities supported three; Mannheim undertook four and Strassburg, five different types of municipal employment for resident jobless laborers.

89. R.Herbst, <u>Die Methoden der deutschen Arbeitslosenstatistik</u> Leipzig und Berlin: 1914. S.119. "Moreover a migration back home often ensued in the winter of those workers employed in the large cities during the summer, in order to participate in support through the home community and in consideration of the cheaper cost of living in the provinces it was easier to spend the time of unemployment there."

90. Pastor F.von Bodelschwingh, "Ratschlaege fuer den ernstlich Arbeit suchenden oder Kranken mittellosen Wanderer", Bielefeld. "The home support law, which 28 of you have approved guaranteed a legal right to shelter, food, necessary clothing, requisite hospital care through the local poor association of your place of residence; it is valid in the entire German empire with the exception of Bavaria and Alsace-Lorraine.

"1. Ask about the town hall, lord mayor's office, ministry hall, village mayor's office, village magistrate, local doctor, charitable doctor, hospital.

"2. Appear moderate but determined. Ask about the civil service, refuse admittance to the poor administration. Ask about its representative. You want neither to beg nor to steal, but you find no work, have no shelter and no food, and are forced to ask for charitable support.

"3. If you are nevertheless repelled and sent away then ask the authority who he is (name and official position). You must trouble yourself about it with the appointed authorities; who is the nearest appointed authority?

"4. If you cannot reach this one, then seek one of those persons named in the ministerial decree, a minister or a director of the inn; show your travel pass with the proof of protection and ask that they care for you. Otherwise you must beg or commit a punishable act and they must pass judgment as a witness that you have tried in vain to exercise your rights with the local authorities.

"5. If you can write or find someone who is prepared to write for you, then write a letter to the undersigned, wherein is stated the actual course of events briefly and strictly truthfully, with your name, occupation, birth place

and date and name and position of those to whom you turned
for help in vain, with more exact statement of the place, of
the date and of the time of day and declare how you have
then helped yourself.

"6. If you have no paper and no postage stamp, then
ask the house father of the nearest inn of the home or
otherwise anyone around; I will refund the postage to him if
he asks me for it.

"7. Always stay informed and strictly comply with the
truth. Otherwise you will run a risk of being punished
because of fraud and be a disgrace to our fiery speech."

91. Rickling, op. cit., s. 17. "The number taken into
police custody in Berlin because of begging and homelessness
amounted to in the year 1875: 8688, 1876: 13,192, 1877:
21,407; in Breslau in the year 1875: 4748, 1876: 6166.
The arrests due to begging, vagrancy and the like supplied
the police directorate in Dresden in the year 1875 2,683,
1876 3,967, 1877 5,298, 1878 6,634.

"According to a further calculation of the Saxon
statistical bureau, during the year 1879/80 the occupational
classes which had already suffered most from the economic
standstill supplied the largest contingent for each punishment: 26,547 were arrested in the Kingdom of Saxony from
April 1, 1879 until March 31, 1880, due to begging and
vagrancy; these persons belonged to the following categories:

machinery assistants or workers without more precise designation	5665
the textile industry	3385
the food and household goods industry	3268
the trade of clothing and cleaning	2241
the building trades	2159

"That is a total of 19,684 or 74 percent of all offenders."

92. Hirschberg, op. cit., s. 6.

93. Rickling, op. cit., ss. 22-23. "[V]ery many resort to
wandering due to lack of a job. Their position in many
cases thereby becomes even worse. If you are left to your
own resources and you temporarily find no new work opportunity, then the bitterest need soon sets in. This neces-
sitates finally pawning or selling of one's better clothing
etc. so that the external appearance becomes more and more
similar to a tramp. The prospect of permanent work becomes
increasingly diminished because an employer cannot easily
hire a 'vagabond'. No wonder, if in misfortune, gradually
deep embitterment takes root and he seeks to deaden his

sorrow through alcohol. Still the last and most secure bulwark, his feeling of honor, holds before the abyss. But need has already led him into the society of the lowest human classes. Soon he will himself belong there. If he has once put out his hand for the gains of begging and brought the disdain of the public on himself, then a gap between him and human society begins to open which always deepens itself more. He begins to become insensible to his position. He goes down hill at a rapid pace. Very soon he lives off of begged or stolen bread, which enables him to live quite easily without work, and the work which he previously had sought in vain, is now a matter of indifference and hatred for him. He disappears into the mass of the lost.

"The indigence itself, as soon as it lives off of strange, free support, very soon kills the love and willingness for regular work in men, however lasting, if the slow wandering and hostel life leads to poverty. This works tends to directly relax and enervate the inner and outer man and leads straightway to an aversion for work. In many cases, drink, theft and the like join in whereby his retreat will be blocked permanently."

94. Hessischen Staatsarchiv Darmstadt. Pastor F.von Bodelschwingh Herrenhaus 26. Februar 1908 Ist Arbeitsangebot an Stelle von Almosen fuer alle ortsfremden Wanderer im ganzen Deutschen Reich und allezeit moeglich? s. 8. "On one of the greatest travel routes of the world, namely from Berlin to Cologne, on which in past times of need up to 50 unemployed knocked at each door where they hoped to get a piece of bread for their hunger (because work is lacking far and wide) I have laid out close by the door of my parsonage, on a slope of the Teutoburg forest, a small quarry, supplied with the necessary tools and placed under the supervision of a hardworking foreman. This quarry offers above all the certain distinction between all of those wandering poor of the highway who are willing to work and those who are work-shy. Only after an hour of hard work in the quarry will a midday repast be offered. This gave the place a wonderful trade: from 20 of the different cooks of our institution at most only 2 ever remain knocking; the rest could eat without work with sympathetic peasants. No begger can now be seen at my door and all workshy rabble have disappeared. On the contrary, the news that one could receive bread for work here was quickly spread in the district and now those unemployed who prefer to work rather than beg their bread present themselves."

95. Niedersaechsischen Staatsarchiv Osnabrueck Dep 3b V Fach 45/46 No. 33, s. 37 Verein fuer soziale innere Kolonisation Deutschlands E.V. 18. August 1913. "The unemployed of the great cities should be engaged in the tilling of the German

moor and waste lands. Not the already ruined but those able to work, those who became unemployed through seasonal work and crises should be offered a sound support through paid employment opportunities. The important means which administrative authorities, communities, unions, welfare associations and private persons have previously distributed unproductively for the support of the unemployed and their dependents should be productively applied. Industry and trade should preserve the necessary reserve army able to work, agriculture will open up new areas."

96. Alternate employment was an unacceptable solution because workers permanently deflected from the industrial sector would not be available to man extant jobs during boom periods.

97. Arbeiter Kolonie Correspondenzblatt fuer die Interessen der deutschen Arbeiter Kolonien und Natural-Verpflegungs-Stationen zugleich Organ des Deutschen Herbergvereins. Herausgeben von den Central-Vorstand deutscher Arbeiter-Kolonien. Fuenfter Jahrgang Nr. 1 Januar 1888 s. 2. "In the first place these institutions are certainly in no way established in order to obtain the greatest possible agricultural or other pecuniary profit: to furnish unemployed but willing to work poor some, if also temporary, employment; to make those separated from work again confident in the proceeds of regular work, to again inculcate faith in those of your rejected colleagues despairing of themselves and the world, forever to help ready love and self-trust--that is the first duty of the labor colonies."

98. Ibid, 5. Jahrgang, Nr. 2, Februar 1888, s. 42. "But now--and that is one of our mean reasons--the greatest part of the wanderers needing help belong to the class of the land-poor. The majority of those who have given themselves over to an itinerant life stem from the original relations, which have no duration and their restlessness hinders them if they find secure and good work from remaining permanently in one place. They are either children of the land-poor or they soon become land-poor and with few exceptions they remain land-poor if they once become so."

99. Ibid, 5. Jahrgang, Nr. 1, Januar 1888, ss. 31-32.

100. Ibid, s. 4.

101. Rickling, op. cit., s. 134.

102. Arbeiter Kolonie Correspondenzblatt, 5. Jahrgang, Nr. 1, Januar 1888, s. 5. "These protests come from areas where a need for a labor force makes itself felt; the idea that everyone who wants to work can find work and that consequently the labor colony has no practical value for the

affected area, will rightly be opposed; the colony is intended primarily for the absorption of elements which have been weaned from regular and strenuous work for a longer time and mostly also in their expressions have been taken down so far that scarcely anyone will agree to hire them in this situation; and they consequently through a longer stay in the colony should again become educated to organized activity and become useful members of human society, insofar as this is still generally possible."

103. Ibid, s. 11.

104. Ibid, 5. Jahrgang, Nr. 2, Februar 1888, s. 33.

105. Ibid, 5. Jahrgang, Nr. 1, Januar 1888, s. 1.

106. Ibid, s. 12.

107. Ibid, 5. Jahrgang, Nr. 5, Mai 1888, ss 151-52. "The provinces I according to the number of districts with stations and II according to the decline of offenders classified by percentages, yield the following result:"

108. Rickling, op. cit., s. 144.

109. Ibid, ss 65-66.

110. Ibid, ss. 22-23.

111. Arbeiter Kolonie Correspondenzblatt, 5. Jahrgang, Nr. 1, Januar 1888, s. 21.

112. Ibid, 5. Jahrgang, Nr. 2, Februar 1888, s. 60. "Inns of the home may not be equated with boarding stations for the destitute; the former are for ordinary itinerants, the latter for tramps."

113. Ibid, 5. Jahrgang, Nr. 5, Mai 1888, s. 147.

114. Ibid, 5. Jahrgang, Nr. 3, Maerz 1888, s. 81.

115. Rickling, op. cit., s. 98. "The connection between labor exchanges and homes for itinerant workers is a very intimate one. In the cities where there are public labor exchanges the itinerants meet only with a good reception in the work places if they have sought jobs in vain through the labor office. Where no labor exchange is available, one should be established in the facilities for itinerant workers."

116. Ibid, s. 115.

117. RAB V Nr. 8 (1907) s. 783 Wanderarbeitsstaettengesetz vom 29. June 1907.

118. RAB IV Nr. 6 (1906) ss. 518-21 "Arbeitsvermittelung und Arbeitslosigkeit. Die Versicherung gegen die Folgen der Arbeitslosigkeit I" s. 519. "The unemployment support starts with the fact of unemployment, without regard to whether or not its beginning can be foreseen, without regard to the probability of its occurrence and its duration. Under insurance one understands on the contrary basic economic arrangements for the purpose of protecting against random assessable need. If one takes this definition also as the basis for the insurance against the results of unemployment, it follows that the insurance situation (unemployment) must be an accidental one, that its voluntary inducement should be excluded as much as possible, that further need must not occur with all participants and in equal degree. But it also appertains to the unemployment insurance that each participant has a right to the coverage of his assets. Where no right exists but only the hope for granting free access, there insurance is not under consideration."

119. RAB IV Nr. 10 ss 902-26 "Arbeitsvermittelung und Arbeitslosigkeit. Die Versicherung gegen die Folgen der Arbeitslosigkeit. V.Die Projekte einer Arbeitslosenversicherung fuer das Deutsche Reich. s. 902.

120. Niedersaechsischen Staatsarchiv Osnabrueck Dep 3b V Fach 45/46 No. 32 Die ArbeitslosenVersicherung der Stadt Strassburg im Jahre 1909.

121. Niedersaechsischen Staatsarchiv Osnabrueck Dep 3b Stadt Osnabrueck V Fach 45/46 No. 33 Arbeitslosigkeit 1913/15 "Zur Frage der Arbeitslosen Versicherung in der Gemeinde" Otto Landschreiber, Pankow.

122. Hauptstaatsarchiv Stuttgart E150-1768 Denkschrift, betreffend die Einfuhrung der Arbeitslosenversicherung (Stuttgart 20. Januar 1909) Zentralverband der Handlungsgehilfen und Gehilfinnen Deutschlands (Sitz Hamburg). "[T]hat it is a duty of the empire, state and community, to protect employees and workers with unemployment support, and certainly in the form of a subsidy to every union which pays legal unemployment insurance."

123. RAB IV Nr. 6 s. 521 "Die Stadtkoelnische Versicherungskasse gegen Arbeitslosigkeit im Winter im Jahre 1905/06".

124. Hauptstaatsarchiv Stuttgart E150-1768 Soziale Praxis No. 18, s. 441.

125. RAB VIII Nr. 1 (1910) ss. 35-44 "Die Stellenlosigkeit im kaufmaennischen und technischen Verbaenden im 4. Vierteljahr 1909" s. 39.

126. Versicherung gegen die Folgen der Arbeitslosigkeit, s. 593.

127. The Deutsche Volkspartei was the first political party to take an active interest in communal unemployment insurance. See, for example, Parteitage zu Ulm 1896 and Mainz 1899.

128. Versicherung gegen die Folgen der Arbeitslosigkeit, s. 630.

129. RAB IV Nr. 11 (1906) ss. 1006-1013 "Arbeitsvermittelung und Arbeitslosigkeit"

130. Ibid. "As a result of production, it is above all emphasized that the struggle against unemployment succeeds not in the direction of insurance, but that the struggle takes place partially through preventive measures of a general nature (regulation of production, general economic policy, increasing popular education, regulation of apprentices, etc.) partially through supplying available work and through work procurement (relief works), while insurance only offers a guarantee against the consequences resulting from unemployment itself."

131. RAB VIII Nr. 2 (1910) ss 99-107 "Arbeitsvermittelung und Arbeitslosigkeit, s. 107. "[T]he cession of acreage from the community to the industrial worker and general land acquisition through this."

132. Osnabrueck Dep 3b V Fach 45/46 No. 32 Dr. jur. Moldenhauer's remarks to September 25 conference in Koeln to discuss unemployment insurance. "Until now only the unions have shown a special interest in unemployment insurance, which is perceived by them as an important means for the execution of their wage struggle. Certainly the more the state and community take over the costs of unemployment insurance, the more the unions are in a position to make their resources available for strike support. A state unemployment insurance therefore supports the legal struggle of the unions against the employer. But this will have the added consequence of more strongly encouraging the influx into the great cities and the countryside will be deprived of still more of the labor force. The employment of foreign workers, which is especially necessary as a result of the rural exodus, signifies a danger which might be still further increased through the introduction of unemployment insurance. For all these reasons, provision for the unemployed cannot follow the path of insurance, but the direct

struggle against unemployment must be pursued through appropriate measures of supplying, distributing, and pro-curing work."

NOTES: EPILOG

1. See Garraty, _op_. _cit_., pp. 198-99.

BIBLIOGRAPHY

ARCHIVAL SOURCES

Bayerischen Hauptstaatsarchiv
    Abteilung II-Geheimes Staatsarchiv Muenchen
    MA 1921 Auswaertige Verhaeltnisse
        Nr. 59884-59902 Arbeiterfrage, Arbeitsschutzge-
        setzgebung, Lohnbewegungen, Bemuehungen um inter-
        nationale Arbeitsschutzgesetzgebungen. Arbeits-
        losenfuersorge. 1865-1904.
        Nr. 321-77 516 Arbeiterversicherungen im Reich
        Berufsgenossenschaften 1874-1910.

Deutsches Zentralarchiv I, Potsdam
    Reichsministerium des Innern
        Arbeiterversicherung No. 7
            Adh. 3, Vol. 3; Adh. 5, Vol. 1, Vol. 3, Vol.
            4; Adh 7, Vols. 1-3; Adh. 9, Vol. 1.
        Armenwesen No. 2 Adh. 2 Vols. 1-3.
    Reichskanzleramt, Handel
        gen. 7, adh. 13, 440/1, adh. 16, 438, Bd. 4

Deutsches Zentralarchiv II, Merseburg
    Geheimnis Zivilkabinett 2.2.1.,
        Rep. 89 H Nr. 27869 Abt. XIII No. 1, Vol. 2,
            Nr. 29962 Abt. XIII No. 49
    Ministerium fuer Handel und Gewerbe
        Rep. 120A
            Abt. I, fach 1, No. 141B, Vol. 1
            Abt. II, fach 5, No. 10, Vol. 2.
                fach 5e, No. 10, Vol. 1.
            Abt. V, fach 1, No. 6, Vols. 1-5.
            Abt. VIII, fach 1, No. 13, Vols. 1 and 2.
            Abt. XII, fach 2, No. 62, Vol. 1.
        Rep. 120BB
            Abt. I, fach 1
                No. 1, Vol. 5
                No. II, Vol. 3, Adh. 10
            Abt. VII, fach 1
                No. 1, Vols. 2-5
                No. 1a
                No. 1b, Vols. 2-17, 20, 22
                No. 3, Vol. 13
                No. 3a, Vol. 1
                No. 3c, Vol. 1
                No. 4, Vol. II cfr. Vol. 12
                No. 8, Vol. 2, cfr. Vol. 3
                No. 11, Vol. 5
                No. 15, Vol. 1, cfr. Vol. 2
                No. 17, Vol. 3, cfr. Vol. 4
                    Adh. 38, Vols. 1-3
                    Adh. 40, Vols. 1-3

No. 17a, Vol. 1 cfr. Vol. 2
No. 38, Vol. 4
No. 124, Vol. 6, cfr. Vol. 7
No. 125, Vol. 2 cfr. Vol. 3
No. 125, Vol. 2 cfr. Vol. 4
Vol. 3 cfr. Vol. 4
Abt. VII, fach 3 No. 32
Abt. IX, fach 1 No., 9 Vol. 1

Hauptstaatsarchiv Duesseldorf
1062 Praesidialbuero: Lage der Arbeitsverhaeltnisse und Bekaempfung der Arbeitslosigkeit. Heimarbeit im Tabakgewerbe, Bd. 1, 1901-1913.
13655 Gewerbl. Unterstuetzungskassen zum Zwecke der Unterstuetzung von Arbeitern im Falle der Arbeitslosigkeit, namentl. im Falle der Arbeitseinstellungen, sog. Streikkassen, Bd. 1, 1872-1899
24685 Arbeiterentlassungen, Bd. 3, 1892-1916
38245-38247 Erwerbslosenfuersorge. Arbeitsaemter, Bd. 1-3, 1893-1899.
38249-38255 Desgl., Bd. 5-11, 1900-1915

Regierung Koeln
2233-4 Arbeitseinstellung und sonstige Erscheinungen auf sozialem Gebiet, Gen. 1859-1923
2235 Wohlfahrtseinrichtungen fuer Arbeiter, Arbeiterstatistik, Gen. 1899-1914
2236 Schutz der Arbeiter gegen Gefahren, Arbeitsordnungen, Arbeiterausschuesse, Gen. 1892-1904
2237 Schutz der Arbeiter bei Bauten, Gen. 1897-1904

Landratsaemter
1. Landratsamt Bonn
   308 Arbeitslosenfuersorge 1902-1921
   1563 Arbeiterlohnbewegung, Arbeiterausstaende und Aussperrungen 1890-1930
2. Landratsamt Gummersbach
   487 Lage der Arbeiter 1888-1929
3. Landratsamt Euskirchen
   139, 270 Arbeiterverhaeltnisse 1875-1913
5. Landratsamt Essen
   75 Arbeitslage. Entlassungen 1877
7. Landratsamt Siegburg
   295 Beschaeftigung jungendlicher Arbeiter in den Fabriken und Lage auf dem Arbeitsmarkt 1839-1913
13. Landkreis Moenchen-Gladbach
   455 Verhaeltnis von Arbeitgebern und Arbeitern 1848-1880

Regierung Aachen
7754

13888
13942-44
1632
4896

Praesidialbuero
559-560 Die Zuweisung von Arbeit an unbeschaeft-
igte fabrikarbeiter, die Lage der Arbeitsverhaeltnisse in den Hauptindustriezweigen des Regierungs-
bezirks Aachen und die Gefahren des Ausbruchs
einer Arbeiternot 1830-1913

Hauptstaatsarchiv Stuttgart
E14-16 Kabinettsakten IV
1205-1210 Armenwesen, Wohltaetigkeit, 1817-
1899
1211   Verein fuer das Wohl der arbeitenden Klassen 1866-1899
1269   Schiedsgericht fuer Arbeiterversicherung 1900-1911
E46-48   Ministerium der Auswaertigen Angelegen-
heiten III
275   Kommission fuer Arbeiterstatistik,
1892-1905, 1913
301-05   Unfall-, Kranken-, Arbeiterversicherung 1874-1886
931-32   Fabrik-, Arbeitswesen, Arbeiter-
fuersorge, 1855-1912
E150 Ministerium des Innern IV
1768   Versicherung gegen Arbeitslosigkeit
1895-1909

Hessischen Hauptstaatsarchiv Wiesbaden
405 Reichsstadt Frankfurt a.M.
J2 Arbeiterfrage
1260-62, 2625-6, 2808-9, 3358, 3596, 3728,
3730, 3748, 8509
1109-1120
407 Polizeipraesidium Frankfurt
44 Arbeiter-Ausstaende und Aussperrungen
412 Obertaunuskreis (Bad Homburg v.d.H.)
123, 203, 238 Die Fabrikarbeiter, 1871-1922
415 Rheingaukreis (Ruedesheim)
130 Arbeitseinstellungen; Arbeiterunruhen, 1870-
1913
417 Unterlahnkreis (Diez)
5,197 Arbeitereinstellungen, 1870-1924
423 Wetzlar
402-403, 1098 Arbeitrentlassungen in groesseren
industriellen Betrieben, 1896-1917
425 Main-Taunus-Kreis (Frankfurt-Hoechst)
798 Arbeitslosigkeit 1908-1909

Hessischen Staatsarchiv Darmstadt
Der Reichsarbeiterminister IV 16105/26 Nr. 2885
III. Wahlperiode 1924/27 Reichstag
VIII. Arbeitslosigkeit in den Arbeiterfachverbanden
Deutschlands und Grossbritanniens

B19   Innenministerium
Abt., XVI, 2 Armen- und Wohltaetigkeitspolizei
B20   Justizministerium Ablieferung 1
2013-2   Arbeitslosigkeit, Erwerbslosenfuersorge,
Mitgliederung der Arbeitslosigkeit,
Arbeitslosenfuersorge, -versicherung,
Arbeitsvermittlung 1901-1926
2014   Arbeitslosigkeit, Arbeitsnachweise,
Erwerbslosenfuersorge 1900-36
2016   Arbeitsbeschaffung; 1. Vergebung oef-
fentlicher Arbeiten zur Milderung der
Arbeitslosigkeit 1901-35
B42   Hessisches Landesstatistisches Amt
3560/2   Arbeiterstatistik 1892-1905
B39 und B61   Kreise (Kreisaemter, Landratsaemter)
XXIV Soziale Fuersorge I. Arbeiterversicherung
II. Arbeitsnachweis III Wohnungsfuersorge
Kreis Alsfeld (insgesamt 3m), Ablieferung 2
55 (XVIII, 1) Naturalverpflegung (Generalia),
Verein fuer Beschaeftigung Arbeitsloser
1885-1921
Kreis Bergstrasse (Heppenheim mit Bensheim)
Ablieferung 2
1048-1059 (XXIV) Arbeitsbeschaffung, Arbeits-
losenfuersorge, Arbeitsnachweise 1910-44

Historischen Archiv der Stadt Koeln
Abt. III Kommunalpolit. Vereinigung der deutschen
Zentrumspartei
694 Arbeitslosenfuersorge, 4 Bde., 1909-1933

Niedersaechsischen Staatsarchiv Osnabrueck
Dep 3 b V Stadtarchiv Osnabrueck
Fach 45/46 Nr. 28 Der Nachweis von Arbeit fuer
heimatberechtigte Arbeiter infolge allge-
meinen Notstandes, Generalia 1877-1909
Fach 45/46 Nr. 29 desgl., Spezialia 1877-1908
Fach 45/46 Nr. 32 Arbeitslosenfuersorge 1913-14
Fach 45/46 Nr. 33 Arbeitslosigkeit 1913-15
Dep 29 b I Stadtarchiv Lingen-Bestand I
Nr. 3935 Lage der Industrie und Arbeitseinstel-
lungen, Textilarbeiter Generalia 1870-1896
Nr. 3936 desgl., Spezialia 1875-1906
Rep. 335 Landdrostei/Regierung
Nr. 8764 Bd. I Reg. Osnabrueck (1875/81)

Nr. 8938 Das Gesuch der Maurergesellen zu Meppen um Feststellung der Arbeitszeit und Arbeitslohnes

Nr. 5793, 5794, 5856 Die Beschaeftigung jugendlichen Arbeiter und Frauenzimmer in Fabriken Bd. I-III 1865-1879

Nr. 5857 Bestimmungen wegen Beschaeftigung von Frauen und Minderjaehrigen in Fabriken 1867-1877

Nr. 13858 Gewerbliche Arbeiterinnen und jugendliche Arbeiter, auch Arbeitsbuecher und Ueberarbeit, Generalia 1880-1898

Rep. 350 Bers II Amt Bersenbrueck II
Nr. 1088 Arbeiterentlassungen und Arbeitseinschraenkungen 1875-1878

Rep. 350 Osn I - Amt Osnabrueck I
Nr. 2335 Wohlfahrtseinrichtungen fuer Arbeiter, Arbeiterentlassungen, Arbeitseinschraenkungen, Lage der Industrie 1875-1895

Rep. 450 Mel-Landratsamt Melle
Nr. 477 Industrieverhaeltnisse, namentlich Arbeiterbeschaeftigung 1875-1899

Nr. 478 Uebersicht ueber die Zu- und Abnahme der Fabrikarbeiter 1881-1919

Nr. 479 Lage der Industrie und gewerbliche Arbeitseinstellungen 1882-1929

Rheinisch-Westfaelisches Wirtschaftsarchiv zu Koeln e.V.
Industrie- und Handelskammer zu Koeln Abt. 1 No. 57

Staatsarchiv Bremen
Bestandsgruppe 3-S3. Statistik Arbeiterstatistik (1892-1914) Erhebungen Ueber die Lage des Arbeiterstandes und der Industrie (1893-1903)
Bestandsgruppe 6, 12 Gewerbekammer. Arbeitseinstellungen und Streiks, Arbeitslosigkeit (1873-1930)

Staatsarchiv Koblenz
Abt. 403 Oberpraesident der Rheinprovinz
Nr. 912 Die in der Rheinprovinz bestehenden Vereine gegen die verderblichen Wirkungen des Pauperismus und der sittlichen Roheit der niederen Volksklassen (2 Bde.) 1844-1882

Nr. 8293-8302 Die Eroerterung der gewerblichen- und Arbeitsverhaeltnisse (10 Bde.) 1848-1911

Nr. 8319-8327 Die Lage der Industrie, Arbeiterentlassungen, Arbeitseinstellungen usw. (9 Bde.) 1875-1901

Abt. 441 Regierung zu Koblenz
Nr. 12796-19801 Die Arbeiterstatistik 1901-11

Nr. 17585-17595 Erscheinungen und Bewegungen auf sozialem Gebiete, auf dem Gebiete der Lohnar-

beiter- und Gesellenfrage, sowie Arbeitseinstell-
ungen (11 Bde.) 1890-1909
Nr. 5540 f. Armen- und Unterstuetzungssachen, Wohl-
fahrtseinrichtungen, Arbeitsanstalten usw. (etwa
200 Aktenbaende) 1816-1920
Abt. 442 Regierung zu Trier
Nr. 3842 Bekaempfung der Arbeitslosigkeit
Nr. 4211 Die Verbesserung der Erwerbsverhaeltnisse im
Handwerkerstande und die in gewerblicher Beziehung
getroffen Massregeln zur Abhuelfe der Pauperismus
Nr. 4251 Arbeitsnachweisstellen, Arbeitsverhaeltnisse,
Arbeitslosigkeit 1891-1901
Nr. 4115 Desgl. 1901-1904
Nr. 4390, 10272, 10271 Arbeitseinstellungen 1872-1938

Staatsarchiv Muenster
Oberpraesidium 824, 825, 826, 1205, 2791
Regierung Muenster 719, 720
Regierung Arnsberg I 1485
Landesratsamt
Kreis Beckum 244
Kreis Hagen 207
Kreis Borken 60, 145
Kreis Schwelm 311, 312
Kreis Hoerde 12
Kreis Meschede 774
Kreis Siegen 1723
Kreis Tecklenberg 390

Stadtarchiv Braunschweig
Akten DIV
478 Arbeiterkolonie Kaestorf 1881
296 Beschaeftigung staedt. Arbeiter 1884

Stadtarchiv Nuernberg
Titel V C9: Gemeindewesen, Arbeitsgesetzgebung
8681
8682
8740
Nr. 19
Nr. 118

PUBLISHED SOURCES

Abel, Wilhelm, Massenarmut und Hungerkrisen im vorindustriellen Deutschland (Goettingen: 1972)

Adler, George, "Arbeitslosigkeit", Abdruck aus dem Hand-
woerterbuch der Staatswissenschaften. Herausgeben von
Conrad, Elster, Lexis, Loening. Jahrbuecher fuer
Nationaloekonomie and Statistik, Supplementband. (Jena:
1895) ss 117-139.

------, Die Versicherung der Arbeiter gegen Arbeitslosigkeit
im Kanton Basel-Stadt (1895).

Angel-Volkov, Shulamit, The "Decline of the German Handicrafts - Another Reappraisal", VSWG 61/2.

Arbeiter-Kolonie, Correspondenzblatt fuer die Interessen der
deutschen Arbeiter-Kolonien und Natural-Verpflegungs-
Stationen zugleich Organ des Deutschen Herbergsvereins.
Herausgeben von den Central-Vorstand deutscher Arbeiter-Kolonien.

Barkin, Kenneth, The Controversy Over German Industrialization (Chicago: 1970).

Berndt, Paul, Die Arbeitslosigkeit ihre Bekaempfung und
Statistik; Inaugural-Dissertation der hohen philosophischen Fakultaet der vereinigten Freidrichs-Univer-
sitaet Halle-Wittenberg (Halle a.S: 1899).

von Bodelschwingh, Pastor, Herrenhaus, 26 Februar 1908. 1.
Arbeitsangebot an Stelle von Almosen fuer alle ortsfremden Wanderer in ganzen Deutschen Reich und allezeit
moeglich?

Boehme, Helmut, Deutschlands Weg zur Grossmacht, Sutdien zum
Verhaeltnis von Wirtschaft und Staat waehrend der
Reichsgruendungszeit 1848-1881. (Cologne: 1966).

Boehmert, Victor, "Zur Statistik der Arbeitslosigkeit, der
Arbeitsvermittlung und der Arbeitslosenversicherung" in
Zeitschrift des Koeniglichen Statistischen Bureaus
1894, Heft 3 und 4.

Borchardt, Knut, "Trend, Zyklus, Strukturbrueche, Zufaelle;
Was bestimmt die deutsche Wirtschaftsgeschichte des 20.
Jahrhunderts?" VSWG, 64. Bd., Heft 2 (1977), ss.
145-178.

Brentano, Lujo, Mein Leben im Kampf um Die Soziale Entwicklung Deutschands. (Jena: 1931).

Bromme, M., Lebensgeschichte eines modernen Fabrikarbeiters, ein besonders erschuetterndes Zeugnis fuer Arbeitslosigkeit (1905).

Bry, Gerhard, Wages in Germany 1871-1945, (Princeton: 1960).

Cherin, W. B., "The German Historical School of Economics: A Study In the Methodology of the Social Sciences." (unpublished dissertation, Berkeley: 1933).

Clapham, J. H., Economic Development of France and Germany 1815-1914 (Cambridge: 1966).

Conrad, Johannes, "Agrarstatistische Untersuchungen," Jahrbuecher fuer Nationaloekonomie und Statistik, XVII, ss. 225-297; XVIII, ss. 12-63, 377-416; L, ss. 121-170; LVII, ss. 817-844; LVIII, ss. 481-495; LXI, ss. 27-59, 516-542; LXV, ss. 706-739; LXX, ss. 705-729.

------, "Die Laendliche Arbeiteverhaeltnisse und die Enquette," Verein fuer Sozialpolitik - Schriften, LVIII, ss. 106-111.

------, "Die Statistik Der Landwirtschaftlichen Produktion," Jahrbuecher fuer Nationaloekonomie und Statistik, X, ss. 81-140.

Craig, Gordon A., The Politics of the Prussian Army 1640-1945 (New York: 1964).

Dahrendorf, Ralf, Class and Class Conflict in Industrial Society (Stanford: 1959).

Dawson, William Harbutt, The Vagrancy Problem. The Case for Measures of Restraint for Tramps, Loafers and Unemployables; With a Study of Continental Detention Colonies and Labor Houses (London: 1910).

Desai, Ashok V., Real Wages in Germany. 1871-1913 (Oxford: 1968).

Die Arbeitslosenunterstuetzung im Reich, Staat und Gemeinde, Denkschrift der General Kommission der Gewerkschaften Deutschlands fuer die gesetzgebenden Koerperschaften des Reiches und der Bundesstaaten und fuer die Gemeindevertretungen. (Berlin: 1914).

Die bestehenden Einrichtungen zur Versicherung gegen die Folgen der Arbeitslosigkeit im Ausland und im Deutschen Reich. Teil I: Die Versicherung gegen die Folgen der Arbeitslosigkeit. Teil II: Der Stand der gemeinnuetzigen Arbeitsvermittlung offentlicher und privater Verbaende im Deutschen Reich. (Berlin: 1906).

Die Regelung der Notstandsarbeiten in deutschen Staedten. Beitraege zur Arbeiterstatistik Nr.2 (Berlin: 1905).

Dorwart, R. A., The Prussian Welfare State before 1740 (Cambridge, Mass.: 1971).

Ehrenberg, Richard, "Anfaenge und Ziele Industrieller Normalisierung," Archiv fuer Exakte Wirtschaftsforschung, VII (1916), ss. 119-171.

------, "Landwirtschaft, Gewerbe und Handel," Archiv fuer Exakte Wirtschaftsforschung, IX (1919).

------, "'Selbstinteresse' und Geschaeftsinteresse," Archiv fuer Exakte Wirtschaftsforschung, I (1906).

------, "Das Wesen der Neuzeitlichen Unternehmungen," Archiv fuer exakte Wirtschaftsforschung I, ss. 34-97 (1906).

Evans, Richard J., ed., Society and Politics in Wilhelmine Germany (New York: 1978).

Fischer, Wolfram, Wirtschaft und Gesellschaft in Zeitalter der Industrialisierung. Kritische Studien zur Geschichtswissenschaft 1. (Goettingen: 1972).

Fishman, Betty G. and Leo, Employment, Unemployment and Economic Growth (1969).

Gahlen, B. Die Uerberpruefung produktionstheoretischen Hypothesen fuer Deutschland 1850-1913 (1968).

Garraty, John A., Unemployment in History. Economic Thought and Public Policy. (New York: 1978).

Gebiete und Methoden der amtlichen Arbeitsstatistik in den wichtigsten Industriestaaten. Beitraege zur Arbeiterstatistik Nr. 2. Bearbeitet im Kaiserlichen Statistischen Amte Abteilung fuer Arbeitsnachweises, der Arbeitslosigkeit und der Arbeiterwanderungen. (Berlin: 1913).

Gerschenkron, Alexander, Bread and Democracy in Germany (Berkeley: 1943).

------, Continuity in History and Other Essays (Cambridge, Mass.: 1968).

------, Economic Backwardness in Historical Perspective, (Cambridge, Mass.: 1962).

von der Goltz, Theodor, Lage der laendlichen Arbeiter im deutschen Reich (Berlin: 1875).

------, Die laendliche Arbeiterfrace und ihre Loesung. (Danzig: 1874).

Gollwitzer, Heinz, Die Standesherren: Die Politische und Gesellschaftliche Stellung der Mediatisierten 1815-1918 (Goettingen: 1964).

Guertler, Alfred, Das Problem des Rhythmus des Arbeitsmarktes und die Methode seiner Erfassung und Darstellung. (Graz: 1906).

Haberler, Gottfried, Prosperity and Depression. A Theoretical Analysis of Cyclical Movements (Cambridge, Mass.: 1960).

Hamerow, Theodore S., Restoration, Revolution, Reaction. Economics and Politics in Germany 1815-1871. (Princeton: 1958).

------ The Social Foundations of German Unification 1858-1871 Ideas and Institutions (Princeton: 1969).

Handbuch der deutschen Wirtschafts- und Sozialgeschichte Bd.2 Das 19. und 20. Jahrhundert. Herausgeben von Wolfgang Zorn (Stuttgart: 1976).

Hardach, Karl W., Die Bedeutung Wirtschaftlicher Faktoren bei der Wiedereinfuehrung der Eisen- und Getreidezoelle in Deutschland, 1879. (Berlin: 1967).

Henning, Hansjoachim, "Arbeitslosenversicherung vor 1914: Das Genter System und seine Uebernahme in Deutschland in Wirtschaftspolitik und Arbeitsmarkt." Bericht ueber die 4. Arbeitstagung der Gesellschaft fuer Sozial- und Wirtschaftsgeschichte in Wien am 14. and 15. 4. 1971. Hrsg. Hermann Kellenbenz (Muenchen: 1974)., ss. 271-87.

Hentschel, Volker, "Prosperitaet und Krise in der wuerttembergischen Wirtschaft 1871-1879. Methodische Ueberlegungen und deskriptive Untersuchung" VSWG, 63. Bd., Heft 3 (1976), ss. 339-389.

Herbst, Richard, Die Methoden der deutschen Arbeitslosenstatistik. Erganzungshefte zum deutschen statistischen Zentralblatt. Heft 6. (Leipzig und Berlin: 1914).

Hirschberg, Dr. E., Die Massnahmen gegnueber der Arbeitslosigkeit (Berlin: 1894).

Hoffmann, W. G., F. Grumbach und H. Hesse, Das Wachstum der deutschen Wirtschaft seit der Mitte des 19. Jahrhunderts. (Berlin: 1965).

Holtfrerich, Carl-Ludwig, Quantitative Wirtschaftsgeschichte des Ruhrkohlenbergbaus im 19. Jahrhundert (Dortmund: 1973).

Hughes, H. Stuart, Consciousness and Society The Reorientation of European Social Thought 1890-1930 (New York: 1958.

Ipsen, Gunther, "Die preussische Bauernbefreiung als Landesausbau," in Zeitschrift fuer Agrargeschichte und Agrarsoziologie., Bd.2 (1954).

Jansen C. R. and E. K. Johansen, "The Study of Unemployment. Remarks Based on Unemployment Research in Nineteenth-Century Denmark," XIV International Congress of Historical Sciences, San Francisco, August 22-29, 1975.

Jantke, Carl, Der Vierte Stand, Die Gestaltenden Kraefte der deutschen Arbeiterbewegung im XIX. Jahrhundert. (Freiburg: 1955).

Kaiserliches Statistisches Amt. Abteilung fuer Arbeiterstatistik. Abschrift II 3135. Berlin, 6. Juli 1905.

Kehr, Eckart, Der Primat der Innenpolitik. (Berlin: 1965).

Kerr, Dunlop, Harbison and Myers, Industrialism and Industrial Man (New York: 1969).

Kitchen, Martin, The Political Economy of Germany 1815-1914. (London and Montreal: 1978).

Knapp, G. F., Die Bauernbefreiung und der Ursprung der Landarbeiter in den aelteren Theilen Preussens, Bd.2 (Leipzig: 1887).

Kohn-Bramstedt, E., Aristrocracy and the Middle Classes in Germany. Social Types in German Literature 1830-1900 (London: 1937).

Koellmann, W., Sozialgeschichte der Stadt Barmen im 19. Jahrhundert (Tubingen: 1960).

Kondratieff, N.D., "Die langen Wellen der Konjunktur", Archiv fuer Sozialwissenchaft und Socialpolitik, Bd. 56 (December 1926) SS 573-609.

Kuczynski, Juergen, Darstellung der Lage der Arbeiter in Deutschkand von 1871 bis 1900 Bd. 3 Die Geschichte der Lage der Arbeiter unter dem Kapitalismus.

------, Darstellung der Lage der Arbeiter in Deutschland von 1900 bis 1917/18 Bd. 4 Die Geschichte der Lage der Arbeiter unter dem Kapitalismus.

------, Studien zur Geschichte der Zyklischen Ueberproduktionskrisen in Deutschland 1873 bis 1914. Bd. 12, Die Geschichte der Lage der Arbeiter unter dem Kapitalismus (Berlin: 1961).

Kuznets, Simon, Economic Change: Selected Essays in Business Cycles, National Income and Economic Growth (New York: 1953).

------, "Schumpeter's Business Cycles", American Economic Review XXX, No. 2, pp. 250-71 (June 1940).

Lambi, Ivo, Free Trade and Protection in Germany, VSWG, Beiheft 44 (Wiesbaden: 1963).

Landes, David S., The Unbound Prometheus: Technological Change and Industrial Development in Western Europe from 1750 to the Present (Cambridge: 1969).

Lebovics, Herman, "'Agrarians' Versus 'Industrializers'; Social Conservative Resistance to Industrialism and Capitalism in Late Nineteenth-Century Germany", International Review of Social History, XII, SS 31-65. (1967).

Lidtke, Vernon L., The Outlawed Party: Social Democracy in Germany 1878-1890 (Princeton: 1966).

Lipset, Seymour Martin and Bendix, Reinhard, Social Mobility in Industrial Society (Berkeley and Los Angeles: 1967).

McConnell, Campbell R., (ed.), Economic Issues: Readings and Cases (New York: 1963).

Michels, Robert, Political Parties, A Socialogical Study of the Oligarchical Tendencies of Modern Democracy (New York: 1962).

Monatshefte zur Statistik des deutschen Reichs fuer das Jahr 1883 v. 59:2 ss. 82-4. Die Berufsstellung innerhalb der Berufsgruppen der Bevolkerung des Deutschen Reichs nach den vorlaeufigen Ergebnissen der Aufnahme vom 5. Juni 1882.

Moore, Wilbert E., The Impact of Industry, Modernization of Traditional Societies Series (Englewood Cliffs, N.J.; 1965).

Most, Otto, "Arbeitslosenstatistik (Kritische Bemerkungen)." Conrads Jahrbuch, III. Folge, Bd. XL, 1. Heft, Juli 1910.

------, The Problem of Unemployment in Germany (London: 1910).

Mottek, Hans, "Die Gruenderkrise, Produktionsbewegung, Wirkungen, Theoretische Problematik" Jahrbuch fuer Wirtschaftsgeschichte 1966: Teil I (Berlin: 1966), SS. 51-128.

Mottek, Hans, Walter Becker, Alfred Schroeter, Wirtschafts-geschichte Deutschlands Ein Grundriss, Band III Von der Zeit der Bismarckschen Reichsgruendung 1871 bis Zur Niederlage des faschistischen deutschen Imperialismus 1945. 2. Auflage (Berlin: 1975).

Mottek, Blumberg, Wutzmer, Becker, Studien zur Geschichte der Industriellen Revolution in Deutschland (Berlin: 1960).

Muncy, Lysbeth Walker, The Junker in the Prussian Adminis-tration Under William II 1888-1914 (Providence, R.I.: 1944).

Nichols, J.A., Germany After Bismarck (Cambridge: 1958).

Nipperdey, Thomas, Gesellschaft, Kultur, Theorie Gesammelte Aufsaetze zur neuen Geschichte (Goettingen: 1976).

Nisbet, Robert A., Social Change and History: Aspects of the Western Theory of Development (New York: 1969).

Parsons, Talcott and Smelser, Neil J., Econony and Society (New York: 1965).

Oldenburg, Karl, "Arbeitslosen Statistik, Arbeitsvermit-telung und Arbeitslosenversicherung" in Schmollers Jahrbuch XIX, 2.

Pigou, A.C., The Theory of Unemployment (London: 1933).

Pollard, Sidney, The Genesis of Modern Management. A Study of the Industrial Revolution in Great Britian (Baltimore: 1968).

Post, H., Untersuchungen ueber den Umfang der Erwerbslosig-keit innerhalb der Einzelnen Berufe und Berufsgruppen (Jena: 1914).

Puhle, Hans-Juergen, Agrarische Interessenpolitik und Preussischer Konservatismus im Wilhelminischen Reich 1893-1914 (Hannover: 1967).

Pulzer, Peter G.J., The Rise of Political Anti-Semitism in Germany and Austria (New York: 1964).

Reischsarbeitsblatt, 1903-1913.

Ephrem Rickling, Die deutschen Wanderarbeitsstaetten (Muen-chen-Gladbach 1912).

Ritter, Gerhard A., ed., Vom Wohlfahrtsausschuss zum Wohl-fahrtsstaat. Der Staat in den Modernen Industriege-sellschaft (Koeln: 1973).

Rohr, Donald G., The Origins of Social Liberalism in Germany (Chicago: 1963).

Rosenberg, Arthur, Imperial Germany The Birth of the German Republic 1871-1918 (Boston: 1966).

Rosenberg, Hans, "The Economic Impact of Imperial Germany, Agricultural Policy," Journal of Economic History (Supp. 3:1943) pp. 101-107.

------, Grosse Depression und Bismarckzeit, Wirtchaftsab-lauf, Gesellschaft, und Politik in Mitteleuropa (Berlin: 1967).

------, Machteliten und Wirtschafts-Konjunkturen Studien zur neueren deutschen Sozial und Wirtschaftsgeschichte (Goettingen: 1978).

------, "Political and Social Consequences of the Great Depression of 1873-1896 in Central Europe", Economic History Review (1943).

------, Probleme Der Deutschen Sozialgeschichte (Frankfurt: 1969).

Rostow, W.W., The Process of Economic Growth (New York: 1962).

------, The Stages of Economic Growth. A Non-Communist Manifesto (Cambridge: 1971).

Saul, S.B., The Myth of the Great Depression, 1973-1896 (London: 1969).

Schanz, Georg, Zur Frage der Arbeitslosen-Versicherung. (Bamberg: 1895).

Schikowski, John, Ueber Arbeitslosigkeit und Arbeitslosenstatistik (Leipzig: 1894).

Schorske, Carl E., German Social Democracy 1905-1917. The Development of the Great Schism (Canbridge, Mass.: 1955).

Schumpeter, Joseph A., "The Analysis of Economic Change", Review of Economic Statistics XVII, No. 4, pp. 2-10 (May; 1935).

------, Business Cycles. A Theoretical, Historical and Statistical Analysis of the Capitalist Process. 2 Vols. (New York: 1939).

Sering, Max, "Die Agrarfrage und der Socialismus", Jahrbuch fuer Gesetzgebung, Verwaltung und Rechtspflege, N.F. XXIII, ss. 1493-1556 (1899).

------, "Die Innere Kolonisation in Oestlichen Deutschland", Verein fuer Sozialpolitik-Schriften, LVI, ss. 1-330 (Leipzig: 1893).

Smelser, Neil J., Theory of Collective Behavior (New York: 1962).

Soziale Praxis, 1892-1914.

Statistik des Deutschen Reichs, Neue Folge, Band III (Berlin: 1899).

Stuermer, Michael, ed., Das Kaiserliche Deutschland: Politik und Gesellschaft 1870-1918 (Duesseldorf: 1970).

Supple, Barry E., The Experience of Economic Growth. Case Studies in Economic History (New York: 1963).

Tipton, Frank B., Jr., Regional Variations in the Economic Development of Germany During the Nineteenth Century. (Middletown, Connecticut: 1976).

Veblen, Thorstein, Imperial Germany and the Industrial Revolution (New York: 1939).

Wehler, Hans-Ulrich, Bismarck und der Imperialismus. (Cologne: 1969).

------, ed., Moderne deutsche Sozialgeschichte (Cologne: 1966).

------, Das deutsche Kaiserreich 1871-1918 (Goettingen: 1973).

Wolf, Dr., "Massregeln gegen das Vagantenthum", Anzeige-Blatt fuer den Kreis Schotten, No. 93 Freitag, den 21. November 1884, 32. Jahrgang.